Lecture Notes in Artificial Intelligence 2366

Subseries of Lecture Notes in Computer Science
Edited by J. G. Carbonell and J. Siekmann

Lecture Notes in Computer Science
Edited by G. Goos, J. Hartmanis, and J. van Leeuwen

T0134646

Lecture Notes in Artificial Intelligence   2360

Subseries of Lecture Notes in Computer Science

Edited by J. G. Carbonell and J. Siekmann

Lecture Notes in Computer Science

Springer
Berlin
Heidelberg
New York
Barcelona
Hong Kong
London
Milan
Paris
Tokyo

Mohand-Saïd Hacid   Zbigniew W. Raś
Djamel A. Zighed   Yves Kodratoff (Eds.)

Foundations of Intelligent Systems

13th International Symposium, ISMIS 2002
Lyon, France, June 27-29, 2002
Proceedings

 Springer

Volume Editors

Mohand-Saïd Hacid
Université Claude Bernard Lyon I, UFR d'Informatique
8, boulevard Niels Bohr, 69622 Villeurbanne Cedex, France
E-mail: mshacid@bat710.univ-lyon1.fr

Zbigniew W. Raś
University of North Carolina, Dept. of Computer Science
College of IT, Charlotte, NC 28223, USA
E-mail:ras@uncc.edu

Djamel A. Zighed
Université Lumière Lyon 2, Bât. L.
Equipe de Recherche en Ingénierie des Connaissances
5, avenue Pierre Mendes-France, 69676 Bron Cedex, France
E-mail: zighed@univ-lyon2.fr

Yves Kodratoff
Université Paris Sud, LRI, Bât. 490
91405 Orsay Cedex, France
E-mail: yk@lri.fr

Cataloging-in-Publication Data applied for

Die Deutsche Bibliothek - CIP-Einheitsaufnahme

Foundations of intelligent systems : 13th international symposium ;
proceedings / ISMIS 2002, Lyon, France, June 27 - 29, 2002. Mohand-Saïd
Hacid ... (ed.). - Berlin ; Heidelberg ; New York ; Barcelona ; Hong Kong ;
London ; Milan ; Paris ; Tokyo : Springer, 2002
    (Lecture notes in computer science ; Vol. 2366 : Lecture notes in
    artificial intelligence)
    ISBN 3-540-43785-1

CR Subject Classification (1998): I.2, H.3, H.2.8, H.4, H.5.2, K.4.4

ISSN 0302-9743
ISBN 3-540-43785-1 Springer-Verlag Berlin Heidelberg New York

Springer-Verlag Berlin Heidelberg New York
a member of BertelsmannSpringer Science+Business Media GmbH

http://www.springer.de

© Springer-Verlag Berlin Heidelberg 2002

Typesetting: Camera-ready by author, data conversion by PTP-Berlin, Stefan Sossna e.K.
Printed on acid-free paper   SPIN 10870326   06/3142   5 4 3 2 1 0

Preface

This volume contains the papers selected for presentation at the 13th International Symposium on Methodologies for Intelligent Systems – ISMIS 2002, held in Lyon, France, 27-29 June, 2002. The symposium was organized by the Université Claude Bernard Lyon 1, the Université Lumière Lyon 2, l'Institut National des Sciences Appliquées de Lyon, and hosted by the Université Claude Bernard Lyon 1.

The ISMIS conference series was started in 1986 in Knoxville, Tennessee. Since then it has been held in Charlotte (North Carolina), Knoxville (Tennessee), Turin (Italy), Trondheim (Norway), Warsaw (Poland), and Zakopane (Poland).

The program committee selected the following major areas for ISMIS 2002: Intelligent Multimedia, Intelligent Information Retrieval, Intelligent Information Systems, Knowledge Representation and Integration, Learning and Knowledge Discovery, Logic for Artificial Intelligence, Methodologies (modeling, design, validation, performance evaluation), and Soft Computing.

The contributed papers were selected from approximately 160 full draft papers by the following program committee: L. Carlucci Aiello, N. Belkhiter, P. Berka, E. Bertino, P. Bosc, H. Briand, J. Calmet, S. Carberry, L. Carbonara, B. Catania, T. Catarci, N.J. Cercone, J. Chen, W. Chu, L. De Raedt, J. Debenham, R. Demolombe, B.C. Desai, E. El-Kwae, T. Elomaa, P. Emmerman, F. Esposito, J. Fan, P.A. Flach, P. Gallinari, A. Giordana, M.-S. Hacid, M. Hadzikadic, H.J. Hamilton, D. Hislop, C.A. Johnson, W. Kloesgen, Y. Kodratoff, L. Lakhal, T.Y. Lin, D. Malerba, D. Maluf, S. Matwin, R. Meersman, R.S. Michalski, S. Miguet, M. Mukaidono, N. Nicoloyannis, S. Ohsuga, L. Padgham, J.-M. Petit, V. Raghavan, Z.W. Ras, J. Rauch, G. Ritschard, M.-C. Rousset, L. Saitta, M. Sebag, A. Skowron, R. Slowinski, N. Spyratos, V.S. Subrahmanian, E. Suzuki, F. Toumani, S. Tsumoto, M. Vazirgiannis, G. Venturini, L. Wehenkel, G.P. Zarri, M. Zemankova, N. Zhong, D.A. Zighed.

Additionally, we acknowledge the help in reviewing papers from: A. Appice, M.-A. Aufaure, Y. Batistakis, M. Bernadet, S. Camu, M. Ceci, S. Cerrito, Y. Chevaleyre, R. Cicchetti, F. de Marchi, M. del Pilar Pozos Parra, C. Djeraba, R. Esposito, S. Ferilli, C. Froidevaux, A. Gabillon, A. Giacommetti, F. Goasdoue, F. Guillet, E. Gyftodimos, M. Halkidi, M. Kääriäinen, K. Kersting, M. Komosinski, K. Krawiec, P. Lamarre, A. Laurent, D. Laurent, M. Leclere, S. D. Lee, L. Liétard, A. Lin, F. A. Lisi, D. Mezaour, M. Nykänen, O. Pivert, L. Popelinsky, G. Ramstein, D. Rocacher, M. Roche, J. Rousu, D. Sacharidis, S. Simoff, D. Slezak, R. Susmaga, P. Synak, A. Termier, F. Trichet, T. Tweed, Y. Tzitzikas, I. Varlamis, J. Wroblewski, D. Xue

We wish to express our thanks to Stan Matwin, Marie-Christine Rousset, and Katia Sycara who presented invited talks at the symposium. We express our appreciation to the sponsors of the symposium and to all who submitted papers for presentation and publication in the proceedings. Our sincere thanks go to the Organizing Committee of ISMIS 2002. Also, our thanks are due to Alfred Hofmann of Springer-Verlag for his continuous support.

April 2002

Mohand-Saïd Hacid
Zbigniew W. Raś
Djamel A. Zighed
Yves Kodratoff

Table of Contents

Invited Papers

Intelligent User Interface and Ontologies

Learning and Knowledge Discovery

Logic for Artificial Intelligence

Knowledge Representation, Reasoning, Integration

Intelligent Information Retrieval

Learning and Knowledge Discovery

Logic for Artificial Intelligence

Methodologies and Soft Computing

Learning and Knowledge Discovery

Intelligent Information Retrieval

Methodologies

Intelligent User Interfaces

Intelligent Information Systems

Learning and Knowledge Discovery

Knowledge Representation for Information Integration

Marie-Christine Rousset

University of Paris Sud - CNRS (L.R.I) & INRIA (Futurs)
L.R.I, Building 490,
91405, Orsay Cedex, France
mcr@lri.fr, http://www.lri.fr/people/mcr.html

The emergence of the World-Wide Web has made available a multitude of autonomous data sources which can as a whole satisfy most of users information needs. However, it remains a tedious and long task for users to find the data sources that are relevant to their request, to interact with each of those sources in order to extract the useful pieces of information which then have to be combined for building the expected answer to the initial request.

Information integration systems are *mediation systems* between users and multiple data sources which can be syntactically or semantically heterogeneous while being related to a same domain (e.g., tourism, culture). An information integration system provides a *uniform* interface for querying collections of pre-existing data sources that were created independently. They are based on a *single mediated schema* in terms of which users pose queries, and the data sources to integrate are described. The source descriptions specify semantic relationships between the contents of data sources and the mediated schema. They are exploited by the query processor of the information integration system which must reformulate the original query into queries against the source schemas. Information integration systems must deal with large and constantly changing collections of data sources. This requires powerful languages and flexible mechanisms for describing and handling data sources which may have overlapping or contradictory contents, semantic mismatches, limited capabilities, etc ...

In this invited talk, I will discuss the advantages and the challenges of using rich knowledge representation formalisms for modeling the semantic relationships between source schemas through a mediated schema. I will outline the impact of the choice of the knowledge representation formalism on the query reformulation problem, which is the core algorithmic problem for answering queries in an information integration system. Clearly, as the languages for describing data sources, the mediated schema, or the users' queries become more expressive, the query reformulation problem becomes harder. The key challenge is then to identify formalisms offering a reasonable tradeoff between expressive power and good computational properties for the accompanying reformulation algorithm. I will survey different tradeoffs made in several existing information integration systems (e.g., TSIMMIS[3], Information Manifold[7], Infomaster[4], SIMS[1], OBSERVER[8],MOMIS[2]). I will mention in more details the approaches chosen in two projects I have been involved in: PICSEL[5,9] and Xyleme[11,10].

Finally, I will present the central role of knowledge representation techniques that I see for making the promising vision of *Semantic Web* a reality. The

M.-S. Hacid et al. (Eds.): ISMIS 2002, LNAI 2366, pp. 1–3, 2002.

Semantic Web envisions a world-wide distributed architecture where data and computational resources will easily interoperate to coordinate complex tasks such as answering queries or global computing. Semantic marking up of web resources using *ontologies* is expected to provide the necessary glue for making this vision work. I think that the de-centralized nature of the Web makes inevitable that communities of users or software developers will use their own ontologies to describe their data or services. In this vision of the Semantic Web based on distributed ontologies, the key point is the mediation between data, services and users, using mappings between ontologies.

Complex mappings and reasoning about those mappings are necessary for comparing and combining ontologies, and for integrating data or services described using different ontologies. Existing information integration systems are centralized systems of mediation between users and distributed data, which exploit mappings between a single mediated schema and schemas of data sources. Those mappings are modeled as views (over the mediated schema in the *local-as-view* approach, or over the source schemas in the *global-as-view* approach) which are expressed using knowledge representation formalisms that vary from a system to another.

For scaling up to the Web, this centralized approach of mediation is probably not flexible enough, and *distributed systems of mediation* are more appropriate. For an easy deployment of distributed data management systems [6] at the scale of the Web, it will be essential to use expressive and declarative languages for describing semantic relationships between ontologies serving as schemas of distributed data or services.

References

1. Yigal Arens and Craig A. Knoblock. SIMS: Retrieving and integrating information from multiple sources. In Peter Buneman and Sushil Jajodia, editors, *Proceedings of the 1993 ACM SIGMOD International Conference on Management of Data*, pages 562–563, Washington, D.C., 26–28 May 1993.
2. Domenico Beneventano, Sonia Bergamaschi, Silvana Castano, Alberto Corni, R. Guidetti, G. Malvezzi, Michele Melchiori, and Maurizio Vincini. Information integration: The MOMIS project demonstration. In Amr El Abbadi, Michael L. Brodie, Sharma Chakravarthy, Umeshwar Dayal, Nabil Kamel, Gunter Schlageter, and Kyu-Young Whang, editors, *VLDB 2000, Proceedings of 26th International Conference on Very Large Data Bases, September 10–14, 2000, Cairo, Egypt*, pages 611–614, Los Altos, CA 94022, USA, 2000. Morgan Kaufmann Publishers.
3. Sudarshan Chawathe, Hector Garcia-Molina, Joachim Hammer, Kelly Ireland, Yannis Papakonstantinou, Jeffrey D. Ullman, and Jennifer Widom. The TSIMMIS project: Integration of heterogeneous information sources. In *16th Meeting of the Information Processing Society of Japan*, pages 7–18, Tokyo, Japan, 1994.
4. Michael R. Genesereth, Arthur M. Keller, and Oliver M. Duschka. Infomaster: an information integration system. In Joan M. Peckman, editor, *Proceedings, ACM SIGMOD International Conference on Management of Data: SIGMOD 1997: May 13–15, 1997, Tucson, Arizona, USA*, volume 26(2) of *SIGMOD Record (ACM Special Interest Group on Management of Data)*, pages 539–542, New York, NY 10036, USA, 1997. ACM Press.

5. François Goasdoué, Véronique Lattes, and Marie-Christine Rousset. The Use of CARIN Language and Algorithms for Information Integration: The PICSEL System. *International Journal of Cooperative Information Systems*, 9(4):383–401, décembre 2000.

6. A. Halevy, Z. Ives, D. Suciu, I. Tatarinov. Schema Mediation in Peer Data Management Systems. *Technical Report, University of Washington*, 2002.

7. T. Kirk, A. Y. Levy, Y. Sagiv, and D. Srivastava. The Information Manifold. In C. Knoblock and A. Levy, editors, *Information Gathering from Heterogeneous, Distributed Environments*, AAAI Spring Symposium Series, Stanford University, Stanford, California, March 1995.

8. E. Mena, Vipul Kashyap, Amit Sheth, and A. Illarramendi. OBSERVER: An approach for query processing in global information systems based on interoperation across pre-existing ontologies. In *4th Int. Conf. on Cooperative Information Systems*, pages 14–25, Bruessels, Belgium, 1996.

9. PICSEL project.
http://www.lri.fr/~picsel/.

10. Xyleme.
http://www.xyleme.com.

11. Lucie Xyleme. A dynamic warehouse for xml data of the web. *IEEE Data Engineering Bulletin*, 2001.

Infrastructure and Interoperability for Agent-Mediated Services

Katia Sycara

The Robotics Institute
School of Computer Science
Carnegie Mellon University
Pittsburgh, PA. 15213
katia@cs.cmu.edu
http://www.cs.cmu.edu/~softagents/

Abstract. An increasing number of services are appearing both within agent communities and as Web Services on the World Wide Web. As these services proliferate, humans and agents need to be able to find, select, understand and invoke these services. Today, services (e.g. travel services, book selling services, stock reporting services etc) are discovered and invoked manually by human users. In the near future, such service discovery and use will be mediated by agents acting on behalf of their human users. Such use of agent technology will be the next Web revolution. Instead of populated with human-readable documents, the Web will be populated with Agent-Mediated Services. For this to be accomplished, the Web must become agent-understandable, i.e. allow for *semantic annotation* of content.

Up to now, this vision has been conceived and pursued mainly in academia and research labs. However, recent industrial interest in such services, and the availability of tools to enable service automation (e.g. UDDI, WSDL, X-lang, WSFL, e-speak, .NET etc) holds the promise of fast progress in the automation in the Web Services area. Agent Mediated discovery, selection, execution and monitoring of Web Services will be a crucial test of Agent Technology. Agent Mediated Web Services is a confluence of Agent Technology and the Semantic Web.

In order to enable stable and scalable Agent Mediated Services, a widely used, widely accessible and extensible Multiagent (MAS) infrastructure is crucial. Part of this infrastructure should be languages for semantic annotation of content as well as for describing services, so that they can be discovered, invoked and composed. DAML-S is such a language for semantic descriptions of services. Another part of the MAS infrastructure should define communication and interoperability of agents. Various standards bodies (e.g. FIPA) are attempting to define standards for various aspects of MAS infrastructure, such as Agent Communications Languages.. However, there is no coherent account of what constitutes a MAS infrastructure, what functionality it supports, what characteristics it should have in order to enable various value-added abilities, such as Agent Based Mediation of Services, and what its possible relation with and requirements it may impose on the design and structure of single agents.

In this talk, we will present a model of MAS infrastructure, and our implemented RETSINA system that is an example of the general infrastructure model. In addition, we will show how RETSINA implements Agent Mediated Web Services through a variety of tools and mechanisms. Moreover, we will present DAML-S and illustrate its utility in the area of Agent Mediated Services.

M.-S. Hacid et al. (Eds.): ISMIS 2002, LNAI 2366, p. 4, 2002

Improving Classification by Removing or Relabeling Mislabeled Instances

Stéphane Lallich, Fabrice Muhlenbach, and Djamel A. Zighed

ERIC Laboratory – University of Lyon 2
5, av. Pierre Mendès-France
F-69676 BRON Cedex – FRANCE
{lallich, fabrice.muhlenbach, zighed}@univ-lyon2.fr

Abstract. It is common that a database contains noisy data. An important source of noise consists in mislabeled training instances. We present a new approach that deals with improving classification accuracies in such a case by using a preliminary filtering procedure. An example is suspect when in its neighborhood defined by a geometrical graph the proportion of examples of the same class is not significantly greater than in the whole database. Such suspect examples in the training data can be removed or relabeled. The filtered training set is then provided as input to learning algorithm. Our experiments on ten benchmarks of UCI Machine Learning Repository using 1-NN as the final algorithm show that removing give better results than relabeling. Removing allows maintaining the generalization error rate when we introduce from 0 to 20% of noise on the class, especially when classes are well separable.

1 Introduction – Outliers Issue

In this paper, we address the learning process of a categorical variable Y, on the basis of an example database described by p numerical attributes, denoted by X_1, X_2, ... X_p. Our focus is on mislabeled examples that constitute a specific category of outliers. We suggest a filtering strategy which identifies suspect examples in order to improve the generalization performance of the learning algorithm. We consider two options: removal or relabeling. This strategy is based on the *cut weighted edges statistic* [16] defined by geometrical neighborhood [17] and associated with 1-NN prediction.

Identifying outliers is an important step in any instance-based knowledge discovery process [2]. By outliers, we mean examples whose exceptional nature disturbs generalization. Barnett and Lewis [1] define an outlier as "an observation (or subset of observations) which appears to be inconsistent with the remainder of that set of data".

Outliers can have different origins, and we will now handle the most common. We will first mention inclusion errors, that happen when an example is wrongly included in the learning set. Either the reference population was wrongly defined or the error happened at the time of sampling, as can be seen in medicine or marketing. Then, we consider appreciation, coding or data-input errors, be it on

M.-S. Hacid et al. (Eds.): ISMIS 2002, LNAI 2366, pp. 5–15, 2002.

the predictors or on the class. One should also talk about observations regarding rare examples, which are often associated with variable asymmetry and are an important cause for leverage points. Lastly, the model error can be strongly affected if a relevant attribute has been forgotten and this may wrongly show some examples as outliers.

Outliers disturb the learning process, mainly when the latter includes the variable's statistical moments; the mean and even more so the variance are usually very sensitive to exceptional values. Estimations and especially confidence intervals and the associated p-values may then be distorted. This can lead to faulty conclusions, particularly in a regression.

We distinguish between works which aim at identifying outliers for themselves (e.g., in the cases of fraud detection or records [7]) and those which look into limiting their noisy effects [6,4,5]). Our study belongs to this latter category. In order to remedy to the outliers issue in this second case, we can either remove the suspect examples from the learning set [6,5], or relabel them (cf. relaxation models [8]).

In the learning process, we often prefer to talk about noise, distinguishing the noise on the class from the noise on the attributes [10]. In this last case, Quinlan has shown that when the noise level increases, the fact of removing the noise from the attributes decreases the generalization performance of the classifier if the data to be classified presents the same attribute noise. As regards the class noise, the problem can be seen in different terms, because noise only concerns the learning set. Thus, Brodley and Friedl [4,5] have demonstrated that whatever the base or the filtering strategy experimented, identifying and removing those examples improves substantially the predictive accuracy in generalization as long as the level of noise does not exceed 20%, or even 30 to 40% in some cases.

2   Works Related to Mislabeled Examples

We will now get into the details of the works that deal with class noise. Because our aim is not to reduce the size of the learning set but to filter it, we will mainly discuss the work of Wilson [14], John [6] as well as Brodley and Friedl [4,5].

Wilson [14] has suggested the E-k-NN rule (Edited k Nearest Neighbor rule) which consists in using the k-NN classifier ($k = 3$) to filter the whole of the learning set before proceeding to the prediction by 1-NN. Only instances that the k-NN classifies properly are retained for the 1-NN. This rule edits out mislabeled instances, as well as the ones which are close border cases, leaving smoother decision boundaries while retaining all internal instances. Therefore this algorithm clearly is a filtering one rather than a reducing one. One may apply the E-k-NN rule repeatedly, until all remaining instances have a majority of same class neighbors. An alternative use was introduced by Tomek [12], who applies repeatedly the E-k-NN rule for growing values of k. This process was included by Wilson and Martinez [15] in different techniques of instances selection (DROP 3 for filtering) for instance-based learning algorithms.

As regards decision trees methods, and more particularly C4.5, John [6] suggests to build robust trees. After the complete tree is built, through successive splits of nodes, C4.5 prunes it to make it simpler and avoid overfitting on noisy examples (cf. Quinlan [11]). John defines confusing instances as those incorrectly classified by the final decision tree, obtained after pruning. He removes them from the learning set before rebuilding the tree using the reduced learning set. On the basis of his experiments, John shows a slight but meaningful decrease in the mean error and in the variability of the error rate while reducing the number of nodes by up to 70%.

Brodley and Friedl [4,5] introduce a two-step procedure to improve classification accuracies in case of mislabeled training data. The first step consists in identifying mislabeled examples and removing them from the training set. The authors use m ($m = 3$) learning algorithms to create classifiers that serve to filter training data using a 10-fold cross-validation. An example may be qualified as mislabeled either at the majority (2 out of 3) or by consensus (all 3) of filtering algorithms. The three filtering algorithms are decision trees (C4.5), k-NN and Linear Machine (LM). The LM classifier associates discriminant linear functions related to each class to assign an instance to one of the classes. For the second step, a classification algorithm, 1-NN or decision tree, is applied to the final training set. Experiments have been carried on five databases. Brodley and Friedl introduce from 0 to 40% of random noise on the labels into the training data in order to simulate the most plausible labeling errors. Results show that filtering allows to maintain accuracy near to the baseline accuracy (when 0% of noise) for noise levels up to 20% on all databases, and for noise levels up to 30% on two of the databases. As Brodley and Friedl point it out [5], in order to improve classification accuracy, one needs to proceed in two steps: a filtering step to identify and handle mislabeled examples followed by a prediction step on the reduced training set. The uniqueness of our approach lies on the filtering procedure which calls up *neighborhood graphs* and *cut weighted edges* notions. We will first go into the details of those notions and then introduce our method.

3 Neighborhood Graphs and Cut Weighted Edges

A neighborhood graph [17] can explain that two examples are close or not in the representation space. Such graphs are the Relative Neighborhood Graph (RNG), the Gabriel Graph (GG), the Delaunay Triangulation(DT) or the Minimum Spanning Tree (MST). For our work we have used the Relative Neighborhood Graph of Toussaint [13].

Definition: Let V be a set of points in a real space R^p (with p the number of attributes). The Relative Neighborhood Graph (RNG) of V is a graph with vertices set V and the set of edges of the RNG graph of V which are exactly those pairs (a, b) of points for which $d(a, b) \leq Max\,(d\,(a, c)\,, d\,(b, c))\,\forall c, c \neq a, b$, where $d(u, v)$ denotes the distance between two points u and v in R^p.

This definition means that *lune* $L_{(u,v)}$ –constituted by the intersections of hypercircles centered on u and v with range the edge (u, v)– is empty. For example, on **Fig. 1** (a), vertices 13 and 15 are connected because there is no vertex on the *lune* $L_{(13,15)}$.

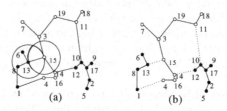

(a)

(b)

Fig. 1. Relative Neighborhood Graph and clusters with two classes: the black and the white points

Following Zighed et Sebban [17] we introduce the concept of "cluster" to express that a set of close points have the same class. We call *cluster* a connected sub-graph of the neighborhood graph where all vertices have the same class. To construct all clusters required for characterizing the structures of the scattered data points, we proceed in two steps:

1. we generate the geometrical neighborhood graph on the learning set (DT, GG, RNG or MST);
2. we suppress the edges connecting two vertices belonging to different classes, obtaining connected sub-graphs where all vertices have the same class.

The number of clusters generated gives a partial information on the class separability. If a number of clusters is low –at least the number of classes–, the classes are well separable and we can find a learning method capable of exhibit the underlying model. For example on **Fig. 1** (b), after having cut the four edges connecting vertices of different colors (in dotted line), we have three clusters for the two classes. But if this number tends to increase, close to the number of clusters that we could have in a random situation, the classes can not be learned.

Actually, this number of clusters cannot ever characterize some little situations that seems intuitively different. For the same number of clusters, the situation can be very different depending on wether the clusters are easily isolated in the neighborhood graph or not. As soon as $p > 1$, rather than study the number of clusters, we will prefer to take an interest in the edges cut for building the clusters and we will calculate the relative weight of these edges in the edges set. In our example on **Fig. 1** (b), we have cut four edges for isolating three clusters. To take into account the distances between the considered example i and its neighbors (i.e., j), it is possible to weight the edges. The weight, denoted $w_{i,j}$, can be based on the distances or ranks. When $w_{i,j} = 1$ the weight matrix W is equivalent to the connection matrix. If W is not symmetrical we can make it symmetrical by computing its transposed matrix and making the average between the components of the two matrices. Since the term *cut weighted edges statistic* is introduced [16].

4   New Method

Dealing with mislabeled points raises three types of problems:

- identification of suspect examples;
- handling of suspect examples;
- prediction based on the filtered training set.

The uniqueness of our method lies on both the identification of mislabeled points which exploits locally *cut weighted edges statistic* and in the handling of such examples. In a previous work we chose to remove them [9]. As suggested by Brodley and Friedl [5] another option may be contemplated which consists in relabeling *spurious* examples. The contribution of our article is to propose a method that associates both options *remove* and *relabel* while letting the user the possibility to adjust the definition of both options.

4.1   Identification of Suspect Examples

An example label is subject to caution when its class is different to the one of the examples belonging to its geometrical neighborhood. And this even more as classes are well discernible in the representation space. In order to identify such an example, we offer to calculate the sum of the cut edges weights that run from this example (i.e., edges which link this example to other examples in its geometrical neighborhood that do not have the same label).

Let i be an example whose class is $y_{r(i)}$. We denote by $\pi_{r(i)}$ the global proportion of the class $y_{r(i)}$ in the learning set. An example i is considered as a *good* example if in its geometrical neighborhood the proportion of examples that do not have the same label $y_{r(i)}$ is significantly smaller than $1 - \pi_{r(i)}$.

We denote H_0 the matching null hypothesis. Thus, for a good example the weight of cut edges is significantly smaller than its expected value under H_0.

Under H_0, the probability for an example in the neighborhood of i not to be of the same class than i is $1 - \pi_{r(i)}$. We note n_i the number of examples belonging to the neighborhood of i, w_{ij} is the weight of the edge connecting the vertices i and j, and J_i is the absolute weight of cut edges running from i.

$$J_i = \sum_{j=1}^{n_i} w_{ij} I_i(j)$$

where $I_i(j)$ are independent and identically distributed random variables, according to the Bernouilli law of parameter $1 - \pi_{r(i)}$, under H_0. The mean E and the variance Var of J_i under H_0 are given by:

$$E(J_i/H_0) = \left(1 - \pi_{r(i)}\right) \sum_{j=1}^{n_i} w_{ij}$$

$$Var(J_i/H_0) = \pi_{r(i)} \left(1 - \pi_{r(i)}\right) \sum_{j=1}^{n_i} w_{ij}^2$$

We propose to rank examples i, $i = 1, 2, ..., n$, according to the level of the normal repartition function to which the realization of J_i corresponds under H_0 (left unilateral p-value). In doing so, we define ideally three categories of examples: *good* examples located in the left rejection region (significantly less cut edges than expected under H_0, and consequently more neighbors of same label), *doubtful* examples that do not contradict H_0 and *spurious* examples located in the right rejection region (significantly more cut edges than expected under H_0, and consequently less neighbors of same label).

If n_i is great enough and the weights not too unbalanced, one can use the normal approximation of J_i^s (J_i standardized). Otherwise, we can proceed to a simulation in order to calculate the associated p-values to each J_i. In order to efficiently characterize those three types of examples, we have chosen to control two parameters that are fixed by the user:

- θ_1, the left risk, poses the frontier between *good* and *doubtful* examples;
- θ_2, the complement of the right risk, poses the frontier between *doubtful* and *spurious* examples.

An example will be considered as *good, doubtful* or *spurious*, depending on J_i^s left unilateral p-value being smaller than θ_1, between θ_1 and θ_2 or greater than θ_2. By playing with θ_1 and θ_2, we can modulate the definition of each type of example. The closer θ_1 is to 0, the more we are severe for the definition of *good* examples. The closer θ_2 is to 1, the more we are severe for the *spurious* examples. The closer θ_2 is to θ_1, the less is the place for *doubtful* examples.

4.2   Suspect Examples Processing: Remove or Relabel

To process *suspect* examples (respectively *doubtful* or *spurious*), we can either remove these examples [6,5] or relabel them [8]. Our formalization allows to associate in a general way *doubtful* example removing and *spurious* examples relabeling when playing on θ_1 and θ_2 parameters (option "*Remove and Relabel* (θ_1, θ_2)").

Another possibility consists in considering only two categories of examples, by gathering the *doubtful* and *spurious* types in one *suspect* type ($\theta = \theta_1 = \theta_2$), and using only one of the two processing. We then have the choice between removing (option "*Remove* (θ)" used in a preceding work [9]) and relabeling (option "*Relabel* (θ)") as suggested by Brodley and Friedl in the conclusion of their work [5].

In practice, considering the bad results of relabeling, whatever the chosen option and the value of control parameters, we introduce and experiment a further option (option "*Relabel else Remove* (θ)"). This one consists in relabeling a *suspect* example according to the majority label amongst the neighbors of the very example which are *good* examples. If the *suspect* example does not have neighbors that are *good* examples, the very example is removed (**Fig. 2**).

4.3   Prediction from Filtered Training Set

Once *spurious* or *doubtful* exemples are identified, one can apply a prediction algorithm to the final training set stemming from the filtering procedure. For our experiments, we used 1-NN algorithm. Other prediction algorithms can be preferred in order to extract more comprehensible knowledge like decision trees.

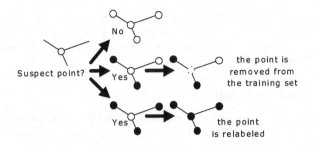

Fig. 2. How to deal with the *suspect* points

4.4 Complexity of the Method

The method needs different steps. Computing the matrix distance is in $O(k \times n^2)$, with n the number of examples and k the classes. Building the neighborhood graph in R^p is in $O(n^3)$ (with p the number of attributes). Removing or relabeling the suspect points is in $O(n^2)$. The method is then in $O(n^3)$ due to the neighborhood graph computation.

5 Experimental Validation

5.1 Organization of the Experiments

We have performed experiments on a collection of ten domains from the UCI Repository of Machine Learning Databases [3]. The domains have been chosen for having only numerical attributes –continuous or discrete or boolean (transformed in 0/1 form) data– with a qualitative class attribute. Because the geometrical neighborhood are sensitive to the scale measure, we have standardized all attributes of the domains. The noise is introduced on the training set only otherwise we couldn't see if we have correctly removed or relabeled the data when we generalize the model.

   For each domain, we have repeated the following process:

- first, we have split the base in two sets of the same size: the training set and the testing set of data;
- on the training set, we have introduced some noise by relabeling the class of the data by another one for 0 to 20% of the total of instances;
- we have used the Relative Neighborhood Graph of Toussaint [13] for generating a geometrical neighborhood graph;
- with this graph, we have used our statistical test based on the *cut weighted edges* for detecting the suspect points;
- we then composed our learning model (1) without filtering, (2) by *removing* only the suspect instances or (3) by *relabeling else removing* the suspect instances, with $\theta = 0.1$;
- we have tested our three models on the testing set using 1-NN;
- we have repeated this 25 times.

We have tried different values of θ_1 and θ_2 for the option "Remove and Relabel" and different values of θ for the option "Relabel" but the results were not fruitful, thus we present the results obtained for the option "Relabel else Relabel" with one value of $\theta = 0.1$.

5.2 Experimental Results

On **Fig. 3** we show the number of removed and relabeled instances (related to the total size of the learning set of the domain) when varying the noise from 0 to 10% on the learning set for the ten domains.

Dataset	Total points	Removing only						Relabeling else Removing											
		Removed points						Removed points						Relabeled points					
	Noise	0%	2%	4%	6%	8%	10%	0%	2%	4%	6%	8%	10%	0%	2%	4%	6%	8%	10%
Breast cancer	341	19%	20%	25%	29%	31%	34%	13%	12%	15%	17%	18%	21%	4%	4%	4%	4%	4%	4%
House votes 84	217	28%	33%	38%	41%	43%	48%	13%	17%	20%	22%	24%	27%	10%	10%	8%	8%	6%	7%
Image segmentation	105	16%	18%	22%	24%	26%	29%	8%	10%	13%	15%	16%	19%	6%	6%	6%	6%	5%	5%
Ionosphere	175	67%	70%	73%	76%	76%	78%	61%	64%	67%	71%	71%	74%	2%	2%	2%	1%	2%	1%
Iris plants	75	19%	25%	27%	28%	34%	39%	12%	18%	19%	21%	26%	31%	6%	6%	6%	6%	5%	5%
Iris (Bezdek)	75	19%	25%	27%	28%	34%	39%	13%	18%	20%	21%	26%	31%	6%	7%	6%	5%	5%	5%
Musk clean 1	238	60%	62%	66%	67%	70%	70%	45%	49%	53%	54%	58%	59%	10%	10%	9%	8%	7%	6%
Pima Indians diabetes	384	71%	72%	75%	75%	76%	78%	58%	60%	63%	64%	65%	68%	8%	6%	6%	6%	5%	5%
Waveform (Breiman)	500	32%	36%	39%	42%	44%	46%	14%	16%	18%	19%	22%	24%	13%	13%	13%	12%	12%	12%
Wine recognition	89	23%	23%	29%	31%	35%	39%	14%	13%	18%	20%	23%	27%	2%	2%	2%	2%	2%	2%

Fig. 3. Percentage of removed or relabeled instances for a noise rate from 0 to 10%

The results on **Fig. 4** and **Fig. 5** show the error rate and standard deviation on generalization when varying the noise rate from 0 to 20%. On these figures, we present the results obtained when we test **All** instances (no filtering) when we remove all suspect instances (**Removed** points) or when we do the relabeling else removing process to the suspect instances (**R else R**).

For our experiments, we have chosen only databases that have a reduced error rate in generalization (less than 30%) because our filtering method can only deal with databases that have a sufficient class separability. At 0% of noise, our filtering method –with the "Removing" or "Relabeling else Removing" option– is better than using all the database on 6 bases out of 10. From 4% of noise, filtering is better on 9 bases out of 10.

Except for the *Breast cancer* database, the results are surprisingly better when we remove all suspect points instead of relabeling else removing. The *Breast cancer* database is the easiest to learn, the class values are well separable, the results after filtering are better for *Relabel else Remove* than for *Remove*, and this even without noise in the database.

As one can see on **Fig. 3**, for each domain the number of removed examples is much higher than the number of relabeled examples. This can be explained by the fact that we only relabel examples whom neighbors are considered as well labeled. When the neighbors of the example considered are from heterogeneous classes, the relabeling cannot be performed and the very example is removed.

The rate of examples removed or relabeled varies from a domain to another but the number of removed points grows linearly as a fonction of the noise

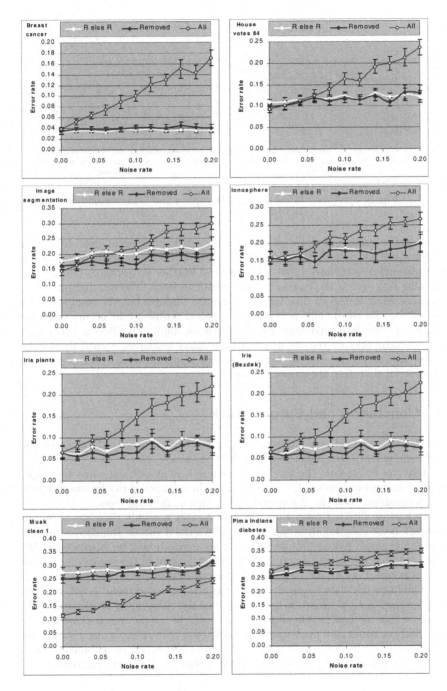

Fig. 4. Error rate on the domains *Breast cancer, House vote 84, Image segmentation, Ionosphere, Iris plants, Iris Bezdek, Musk "clean 1"* and *Pima Indians diabetes*

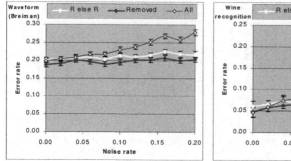 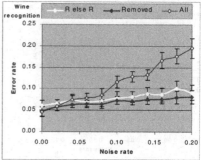

Fig. 5. Error rate on the domains *Waveform* and *Wine recognition*

whereas the number of relabeled points is the same or decreases just a little. Our filtering method is not adapted to *Musk "clean 1"* database probably because it contains many attributes (166) for a reduced number of instances (238 for the learning set) even if the base is not so difficult to learn. The filtering procedure removes many instances (like for *Pima Indians diabetes* but the results are not so bad for this base). This is actually a classical problem that occurs when the classes are not well separable. Finally when we apply our filtering process on some benchmarks we remove or relabel too many instances, even if there is no noise. We can correct this by taking a higher value for our θ criterium used in the test for detecting the suspect points.

6   Conclusion and Future Work

The results obtained seem quite promising, especially when the database can be successfully learn by geometrical neighborhood.

One can notice that the filtering procedure is more efficient when we simply remove suspect examples. The filtering procedure proposed can be associated to other classifiers than the nearest neighbor, such as decision trees.

Otherwise filtering procedure allows to correct not only the class noise but also the noise on attributes, particularly if we use a robust standardization. In fact, an example having a noisy value for an attribute will be misplaced in R^p. This example will be suspected if its neighbors are not of the same class. In this case it seems more logical to remove it than to relabel it.

The more the class values are separable, the more successful is our method. Our method is all the more so successful since the class values are separable. To improve this method we intend to link the value of the parameter θ used in the test and the result of a prior test of classificability, for example our *cut weighted edges test* [16]. In that way, the user applying the method to real-life data can adjust the θ parameter, which controls the definition of suspect examples.

References

1. V. Barnett and T. Lewis. *Outliers in statistical data.* Wiley, Norwich, 1984.
2. R. J. Beckman and R. D. Cooks. Oulier...s. *Technometrics*, 25:119–149, 1983.
3. C. L. Blake and C. J. Merz. UCI repository of machine learning databases. Irvine, CA: University of California, Department of Information and Computer Science [http://www.ics.uci.edu/~mlearn/MLRepository.html], 1998.
4. C. E. Brodley and M. A. Friedl. Identifying and eliminating mislabeled training instances. In *Proceedings of the Thirteenth National Conference on Artificial Intelligence*, pages 799–805, Portland OR, 1996. AAI Press.
5. C. E. Brodley and M. A. Friedl. Identifying mislabeled training data. *Journal of Artificial Intelligence Research*, 11:131–167, 1999.
6. G. H. John. Robust decision trees: removing outliers from data. In *Proceedings of the First International Conference on Knowledge Discovery and Data Mining*, pages 174–179, Montréal, Québec, 1995. AAI Press.
7. E. M. Knorr, R. T. Ng, and V. Tucakov. Distance-based outliers: Algorithms and applications. *The VLDB Journal*, 8(3):237–253, February 2000.
8. C. Largeron. *Reconnaissance des formes par relaxation : un modèle d'aide à la décision.* PhD thesis, Université Lyon 1, 1991.
9. F. Muhlenbach, S. Lallich, and D. A. Zighed. Amélioration d'une classification par filtrage des exemples mal étiquetés. *ECA*, 1(4):155–166, 2001.
10. J. R. Quinlan. Induction of decisions trees. *Machine Learning*, 1:81–106, 1986.
11. J. R. Quinlan. *C4.5: Programs for Machine Learning.* Morgan Kaufmann, San Mateo, CA, 1993.
12. I. Tomek. An experiment with the edited nearest neighbor rule. *IEEE Transactions on Systems, Man and Cybernetics*, 6(6):448–452, 1976.
13. G. Toussaint. The relative neighborhood graph of a finite planar set. *Pattern recognition*, 12:261–268, 1980.
14. D. Wilson. Asymptotic properties of nearest neighbors rules using edited data. *In IEEE Transactions on systems, Man and Cybernetics*, 2:408–421, 1972.
15. D. R. Wilson and T. R. Martinez. Reduction techniques for exemplar-based learning algorithms. *Machine Learning*, 38:257–268, 2000.
16. D. A. Zighed, S. Lallich, and F. Muhlenbach. Séparabilité des classes dans R^P. In *Actes des 8èmes Rencontres de la SFC*, pages 356–363, 2001.
17. D. A. Zighed and M. Sebban. Sélection et validation statistique de variables et de prototypes. In M. Sebban and G. Venturini, editors, *Apprentissage automatique.* Hermès Science, 1999.

Incremental Learning with Partial Instance Memory

Marcus A. Maloof[1] and Ryszard S. Michalski[2]

[1] Department of Computer Science, Georgetown University,
Washington, DC 20057, USA,
`maloof@cs.georgetown.edu`
[2] Machine Learning and Inference Laboratory, School of Computational Sciences,
George Mason University, Fairfax, VA 22030, USA,
`michalski@mli.gmu.edu`
Also, Institute of Computer Science, Polish Academy of Sciences, Warsaw

Abstract. Agents that learn on-line with partial instance memory reserve some of the previously encountered examples for use in future training episodes. We extend our previous work by combining our method for selecting extreme examples with two incremental learning algorithms, AQ11 and GEM. Using these new systems, AQ11-PM and GEM-PM, and the task computer intrusion detection, we conducted a lesion study to analyze trade-offs in performance. Results showed that, although our partial-memory model decreased predictive accuracy by 2%, it also decreased memory requirements by 75%, learning time by 75%, and in some cases, concept complexity by 10%, an outcome consistent with earlier results using our partial-memory method and batch learning.

1 Introduction

On-line learning systems with *partial instance memory* select and maintain a portion of the training examples from an input stream, using them for future training episodes. Depending on the task at hand and the goals of the learner, certain examples may be of higher utility than others, and in previous work [1], we selected *extreme examples* from the boundaries of induced concept descriptions under the assumption that such examples enforce, map, and strengthen these boundaries. To evaluate our method, we built an experimental system called AQ-PM that operates in a *temporal-batch* fashion: It processes training examples over time, combines them with the current set of extreme examples, induces a new set of concept descriptions, and selects a new set of extreme examples.

In this paper, we extend this work by combining our method for selecting extreme examples with two incremental learning algorithms: AQ11 [2] and GEM [3]. Although both are incremental, AQ11 discards its training examples, whereas GEM keeps all of its. Using these methods, we built two experimental systems, AQ11-PM and GEM-PM, and applied them to a variety of problems. Here, we present results for the problem of computer intrusion detection, one task from our earlier investigation of AQ-PM [1].

M.-S. Hacid et al. (Eds.): ISMIS 2002, LNAI 2366, pp. 16–27, 2002.

By conducting a lesion study, we examined the trade-offs between predictive accuracy, examples held in memory during learning, concept complexity, and learning time. Results mirror those of our previous inquiry [1]: By selecting and using examples from the boundaries of concept descriptions, learners can decrease memory requirements, concept complexity, and learning time at the expense of predictive accuracy.

In the following sections, we describe more fully the notion of partial instance memory and briefly examine past, related work. In the third section, we present the learning algorithms and the experimental systems that we developed. In Section 4, we discuss the data set used for evaluation, which we follow with descriptions of our experimental design and the experimental results. After analyzing these empirical findings, we conclude with a discussion of future directions.

2   Partial-Memory Learning

Agents that learn on-line will have potentially two types of memory—two types of concern to us—memory for storing concept descriptions and memory for storing instances. Not surprisingly, on-line learners vary widely in their use of these two types of memory.

Focusing on instance memory, IB1 [4], for example, is an instance-based method that stores all previously encountered training cases; thus, we call it a learner with *full instance memory* [3]. A related system, IB2 [4], stores only those instances that it misclassifies. It is an example of a system with partial instance memory. Finally, some on-line systems learn from and then discard new instances [29]. STAGGER [5] and WINNOW [6] are examples of such learners, ones with *no instance memory*.

Of concern here are systems with partial instance memory, which we will henceforth refer to as simply "partial-memory systems." An important issue is how such learners select examples from the input stream. One scheme is to select and store *prototypical examples* or *representative examples* [7]. Another approach is to remember a consecutive sequence of examples over a fixed [8] or changing window of time [9]. Yet another is to keep those examples that lie on or near the boundaries of concept descriptions [1].

In Figure 1, we present an general algorithm for incremental learning with partial instance memory. Input to the algorithm (line 1) is some number of data sets, one for each time step. While we are assuming that time is discrete, we place no restrictions of the number of examples present in each set: There could be none, there could be one, there could be several. This issue is important because it lets the learner track the passage of time. It also lets the learner operate at different time scales.

We assume that the learner begins with no concepts in concept memory and no instances in partial memory (lines 2 and 3). During the first time step (line 4, $t = 1$), assuming there are data (line 5), the learner operates in batch mode, and since there are no concepts, all of the examples in the data set are treated as if misclassified (line 6). Since partial memory is empty, the training set contains

1. **Incrementally-Learn-Partial-Memory(Data_t**, *for* $t = 1 \ldots n$)
2.   **Concepts$_0$** = $\emptyset$;
3.   **PartialMemory$_0$** = $\emptyset$;
4.   *for* $t = 1$ *to* n *do*
5.   *if* ($\text{Data}_t \neq \emptyset$) *then*
6.   **Missed$_t$** = **Find-Missed-Examples(Concepts$_{t-1}$, Data$_t$)**;
7.   **TrainingSet$_t$** = **PartialMemory$_{t-1}$** $\cup$ **Missed$_t$**;
8.   **Concepts$_t$** = **Learn(TrainingSet$_t$, Concepts$_{t-1}$)**;
9.   **PartialMemory$'_t$** = **Select-Examples(TrainingSet$_t$, Concepts$_t$)**;
10.   **PartialMemory$_t$** = **Maintain-Examples(PartialMemory$'_t$, Concepts$_t$)**;
11.   *end*; /* if */
12. *end*; /* for */
13. *end*. /* Incrementally-Learn-Partial-Memory */

Fig. 1. Algorithm for incremental learning with partial memory, after [1]

those examples present in the first data set (line 7). Using these, the learning element generates concept descriptions (line 8).

The next step (line 9) is to select the examples for partial memory, and we select those examples in the current training set from the boundaries of the current concept descriptions. We will describe the algorithm for selecting extreme examples in the next section.

After selecting examples to store in partial memory, depending on the learning task, it may be necessary to maintain these examples (line 10). If concept drift is detected, then the learner may need to forget old examples. Alternatively, if an example appears frequently in the input stream, then perhaps the learner should weight it more heavily than others.

For the subsequent time steps (line 4, $t > 1$), provided that the data set is not empty (line 5), the learner uses its concept descriptions to identify any misclassified examples and combines these with the instances held in partial memory (lines 6 and 7). An incremental learner uses these examples and its current concept descriptions to form new concept descriptions, whereas a temporal-batch learner uses only the extreme examples and any new training instances (line 8).

With these new descriptions and new training examples, the learner identifies new instances to store in partial memory (line 9). In doing so, it may be necessary to reevaluate all of the examples in the training set, both new examples and those previously held in partial memory, to determine which are on boundaries. Alternatively, circumstances may warrant identifying extreme examples only among the new examples from the input stream and then accumulating these with those already stored in partial memory.

We have investigated both policies of reevaluation and accumulation for learning static and changing concepts [1,10]. How a learner selects examples for partial memory depends on its goals, task, concept description language, and other such factors. Therefore, before providing the details of how we select examples for partial memory, in the next section, we ground discussion by explaining the particulars of our experimental learning systems.

3   Description of the Experimental Systems

Inducing rules from training examples is an instance of the set-covering problem. Computing covers, which is NP-hard, is necessary but not sufficient for machine learning, for any covering algorithm must take into account negative training examples. AQ [11] is a quasioptimal algorithm for computing minimal rule sets under this constraint. Although we cannot provide full details of this algorithm and its many implementations, these have been studied and documented extensively. Other rule induction methods include CN2 [12] and RIPPER [13].

Systems based on AQ represent examples and concepts using a variable-valued system of logic called VL_1 [14]. We encode both rules and examples as implications, in which the antecedent is a conjunction of conditions and the consequent assigns the class label to the decision variable.

The performance element finds a rule that is true for a given instance. However, rules carve out decision regions in the representation space, leaving some of it uncovered, so it is possible that no rule will match the instance. In these situations, flexible matching may be more appropriate, in which the system finds the rule that best matches. Researchers have developed several schemes for flexible matching [15], but for the problem investigated here, the best was the proportion of conditions an instance matches.

The learning element begins by randomly selecting a positive training example called the *seed*, which it then generalizes maximally without covering any negative example. With this rule, the algorithm removes from the training set those positive examples the rule covers, and repeats until covering all positive examples. AQ forms rules for the negative class in a similar manner, and it generates rules for multiple classes by selecting one class, using all of its examples as if they were positive, using the examples from all other classes as if negative, applying the AQ algorithm, and then by repeating this process for each class present in the training set.

The AQ11 learning system [2] works similarly, but rather than operating in batch mode, it generates new rules incrementally using its existing rules and new training examples. AQ11 discards its instances after learning new concepts, so it has no instance memory, and its learning element consists of three main steps.

Focusing on a rule of the positive class, the first step determines which of the new training examples its rules misclassify. If the positive rule covers a new negative example, then in the second step, AQ11 uses its covering algorithm to specialize the rule so it no longer covers the example. The third step combines the specialized positive rule and the new positive training examples, and generalizes these as much as possible without intersecting any of the negative rules and without covering any of the new negative examples. AQ11 uses the same procedure described previously to learn rules for the negative class and for multiple classes.

Generalization of Examples by Machine (GEM) [3] is also an incremental learning program based on the AQ algorithm, but unlike AQ11, GEM learns concepts incrementally using full instance memory. GEM's learning element begins by identifying which of the new training examples its rules misclassify. If, say, a positive rule covers any new negative examples, then the rule requires specialization. GEM uses the AQ algorithm to specialize the positive rule using the misclassified negative examples and all of the *covered* positive training examples—both old and new.

As a result of specialization using only covered positive examples, the positive rule may now misclassify some of the positive examples. Therefore, GEM again uses the AQ algorithm to generalize the rule to cover these positive examples. At this point, the rule covers both old and new examples of the positive class.

GEM uses the same process to learn rules for the negative class and for multiple classes, as we described previously. As we will see in the next section, using our method for identifying extreme examples, we can use both AQ11 and GEM as the basis for new systems that learn incrementally with partial memory.

3.1   Partial-Memory Learning with AQ11-PM and GEM-PM

In earlier work [1], we studied an experimental batch learning system called AQ-PM that, after each learning episode, selects and maintains examples from the boundaries of the current concept descriptions. Although we explored these ideas using batch learning, there is no reason why we could not use the same method for selecting extreme examples for AQ11 and GEM: We can use our method as a post-processing step to learning and then include the selected examples in the next training set.

The AQ systems generate rules from training examples, and these can be either *discriminant rules* or *characteristic rules* [16]. Discriminant rules consist only of the attributes and their values necessary to discriminate among the classes. For example, the number of sails is sufficient to discriminate between sloops and yawls. Sloops have two, yawls have three. Characteristic rules, however, are much more specific and consist of all attributes and their values for all class objects represented in the training set.

We represent problems by mapping them into a discrete space, and induced rules form hyper-rectangles about the training examples in this space. Geometrically, a characteristic rule forms the tightest hyper-rectangle about the examples from which it was derived. For a problem with n attributes, using these characteristic descriptions (i.e., n-dimensional hyper-rectangles), we can identify the extreme examples as those on the corners, the edges, or the surfaces.

The algorithm for locating extreme examples manipulates the conditions of a set of characteristic rules so they match the desired cases. For instance, removing intermediate values from conditions causes a rule to match cases on the corners of the description. Now, adding all values within a range of a single condition causes the rule to match with cases on an edge of the description. Further modification to the conditions yields a version that selects examples from surfaces of the concept description.

As an illustration, we applied this procedure to two classes of a discrete version of the Iris data set [17], originally obtained from the UCI Repository [18]. The left diagram of Figure 2 shows a visualization of the training examples for the setosa and versicolor classes. Each example of an iris has four attributes: petal length (pl), petal width (pw), sepal length (sl), and sepal width (sw).

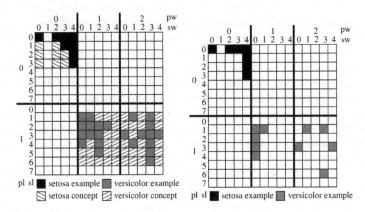

Fig. 2. Visualization of the setosa and versicolor classes from the Iris data set [1]. Left: Training examples and characteristic rules. Right: Extreme examples. © 2000 Kluwer Academic Publishers. Used with permission

Applying the AQ algorithm to the examples pictured in the left diagram of Figure 2 results in the following two characteristic rules:

```
[CLASS = setosa] if [pl=0] & [pw=0] & [sl=0..3] & [sw=0, 2..4]
[CLASS = versicolor] if [pl=1] & [pw=1..2] & [sl=1..6] & [sw=0..4]
```

With these characteristic rules and the training examples pictured in the left diagram, when we apply the algorithm for finding extreme examples, it returns those pictured in the right diagram.

If we have a concept description with r characteristic rules, then for an n-dimensional problem, each rule will have n conditions. Furthermore, each condition of each rule will have a list of attribute values of size s. As we have proven previously [1], in the worst case, a full-memory learner stores $O(rs^n)$ examples, whereas a partial-memory learner that selects examples from the edges of its concept descriptions stores $O(rn2^{n-1}s)$.

Rarely would we confront these worst-case bounds with real-world applications; however, they do capture the relative number of examples that full- and partial-memory methods select, as we will see in the section describing our experimental results. Before presenting these results, we provide the details of the data set we used in the empirical evaluation.

4   Computer Intrusion Detection

Researchers have applied machine-learning methods to a variety of data sources for intrusion detection and misuse detection. These sources include key strokes

[19], command sequences [20], and logs of network traffic [21]. Our work [1,22] has concentrated on audit logs from the UNIX acctcom command.

We derived our data set from over 11,200 audit records for 32 users collected over a period of 3 weeks. Each record contained a variety of information, such as the user's name, their teletype device, the command executed, and its start and end times. However, we focused on seven numeric measures that characterized the execution time of the command (system, real, and user times), its load on the processor (CPU and hog factors), and the amount of data manipulated (characters transferred and total blocks read and written).

Since these attributes are numeric and vary with each command over time, the measures for a given user's sequence of commands are a multivariate time series. We characterized each by computing the minimum, average, and maximum over continuous periods of activity [23], which we defined as those separated by either logouts or twenty minutes of idle time. After selecting the nine users with the most activity, transforming the data in this manner resulted in 238 training examples, each with 21 continuous attributes.

In earlier work [1], we used the SCALE implementation [24] of the ChiMerge algorithm [25] to discretize attribute values and the PROMISE measure [26] to select the most relevant, a process resulting in thirteen attributes. However, the current implementations of AQ11 and GEM are in Pascal and have an upper limit of 58 attribute values. Three attributes (average real time, average CPU time, and maximum hog factor) had more than 58, so we removed them, leaving ten: maximum real time (7 levels), average and maximum system time (23 and 28 levels), average and maximum user time (3 and 31), average and maximum characters transferred (27 and 3), average blocks read and written (24), maximum CPU factor (8), and average hog factor (30).

5   Experimental Method and Results

To evaluate AQ11-PM and GEM-PM, we applied the algorithm **Incrementally-Learn-Partial-Memory**, presented in Figure 1, using the AQ11 and GEM algorithms as the **Learn** function (line 8), to the problem of computer intrusion detection. For this experiment, we selected examples from the edges of concept descriptions for partial memory. To assess the effect of learning incrementally with partial instance memory, we conducted a lesion study by comparing to the unmodified, original systems, AQ11 and GEM.

To create the training and testing sets, we randomly partitioned the original data into ten sets. For a given run, we selected the tenth set for testing and processed the others in order as the training sets Data_t, for $t = 1, 2, \ldots, 9$. We conducted thirty such runs.

For each run, we applied the four experimental systems: AQ11, GEM, AQ11-PM, and GEM-PM. At each time step, for each of these systems, we measured percent correct on the cases in the test set, the number of examples held in partial memory, the complexity of the induced rules in terms of number of conditions

and number of rules, and time spent learning.[1] After computing the average
of each of these measures over the thirty runs, we calculated 95% confidence
intervals. We also included IB2 [4] for the sake of comparison. In the following
section, we present performance curves for predictive accuracy and show the
average measures for the final time step. To estimate statistical significance, we
conducted an analysis of variance [27].

5.1 Experimental Results for Computer Intrusion Detection

After applying our experimental method, we plotted the results as performance
curves. Unfortunately, due to space restrictions, we cannot present all of these
curves, so we summarized these measures for the last time step in tabular
form. Regarding predictive accuracy, measured as percent correct, AQ11-PM and
GEM-PM performed worse than their lesioned counterparts (i.e., those systems
with partial-memory extensions disabled), as depicted in Figure 3. However, on
this task, the degradation of performance was slight: only one or two percent.
The first column of Table 1 shows this clearly, and these results were significant
at $p < 0.1$. IB2's predictive accuracy for the last time step was 88.95±1.29%.

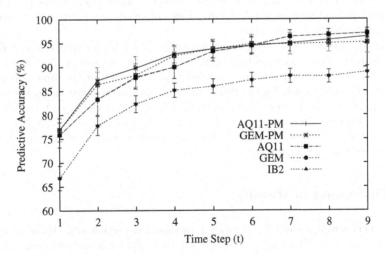

Fig. 3. Predictive accuracy for intrusion detection

Turning to the number of examples that each maintained during learning,
GEM, being a full memory learner, accumulated examples throughout the run.

---

[1] We wanted to compare testing time, but the current executables do not measure this.
We attempted to modify AQ11 and GEM, but we have not been able to re-compile
the source with available Pascal compilers. However, since testing time depends on
concept complexity, which was similar for these systems, we suspect there will be
little difference. Empirical results from an earlier study support this claim [10].

Table 1. Performance measures for the last time step of the intrusion-detection problem. Results are averages computed over thirty runs and are accompanied by 95% confidence intervals. Measures of percent correct are significant at $p < 0.1$

System	Percent Correct*	Examples Maintained	Number of Rules	Number of Conditions	Learning Time (s)
AQ11-PM	96.38±1.28	55.97±1.25	13.21±0.48	23.79±1.85	0.23±0.01
AQ11	97.07±1.04	0.00±0.00	13.79±1.08	29.45±4.78	0.91±0.05
GEM-PM	95.17±2.27	55.97±1.25	11.79±0.45	20.72±1.65	0.10±0.01
GEM	97.07±1.04	218.00±0.00	13.00±0.37	25.17±1.50	0.61±0.05

$^*F(3, 84) = 2.198, p < 0.1$

AQ11, of course, maintained no examples in memory. The learners with partial memory kept fewer examples than GEM, with IB2 storing slightly fewer than AQ11-PM and GEM-PM. By the end of the experiment, GEM had accumulated 218 examples, while AQ11-PM and GEM-PM had stored only about 56. IB2 at this point maintained 49.48±0.81 examples.

As for concept complexity, the fourth and fifth column of Table 1 list the average number of rules and conditions after the ninth and final time step. There appears to be a slight reduction in concept complexity, but not one that we would characterize as notable. (IB2 does not produce concept descriptions that generalize the training data.)

Finally, turning to the time spent learning, all methods required about five seconds in the first time step to acquire an initial set of concepts, but then, as rules became more accurate and classified more examples in the input stream, learning time decreased. By the final time step, as shown in the last column of Table 1, the partial-memory learners were notably faster than AQ11 and GEM. (Since it is an instance-based method, learning times for IB2 were negligible.) In the next section, where we analyze our experimental results, we will speculate on the cause for this and other phenomena.

6   Discussion of Results

The experimental results for computer intrusion detection echo those of our other studies (e.g., [1,10,28]). They suggest that AQ11-PM and GEM-PM, when compared to lesioned versions (i.e., systems with partial-memory mechanisms disabled), decreased predictive accuracy on unseen cases and significantly decreased learning time. Furthermore, the partial-memory systems maintained notably fewer examples than full-memory methods, like GEM. We cannot make such a claim about improvement over AQ11 since it maintains no examples.

Regarding learning time, it may seem counterintuitive that, for instance, AQ11-PM could learn more quickly than AQ11. After all, the former system learns from more examples than the latter. While true, we anticipate that the quality of the additional examples (i.e., the extreme examples) positively impacts learning time. Indeed, the utility of so-called *near misses* is well known [29].

However, with the current problem domains, the number of extreme examples in a training set is about 25% of the total used for learning. It is quite possible that, as the percentage of extreme examples decreases, learning time will increase and perhaps exceed that of the unmodified learner. On the other hand, as we increase the number of training examples, the learner may also select more extreme examples, and so this percentage may stay within a range that results in improved learning time, a hypothesis for future work, which we consider in the next section.

7 Future Work

The results of this study and the issues raised in the previous section suggest several opportunities for future work. We have yet to identify the concepts for which our partial-memory systems work well. We envision conducting such an investigation using a variety of synthetic concepts, such as the Monk's problems [30], and analyzing trade-offs in performance, as we did in this study.

We have examined the use of AQ-PM—the temporal batch system with partial memory—for learning changing concepts [1]. Using the STAGGER concepts [5], we made direct comparisons to IB2 [4] and to a lesioned version of AQ-PM, and made indirect comparisons to STAGGER [5] and to FLORA2 [9]. Results were comparable, and AQ-PM maintained fewer examples than FLORA2. We are presently repeating this study with AQ11-PM and GEM-PM. Results appear to be equally promising, but we need to investigate adaptive forgetting mechanisms so our method will generalize to other types of nonstationary concepts.

Finally, we recently acquired about 10 gigabytes of computer audit data, so we can test how our systems scale to larger data sets. In doing so, we hope to better understand how the number of examples held in partial memory increases and how this affects predictive accuracy and learning time.

8 Concluding Remarks

In this paper, we have described two new experimental systems, AQ11-PM and GEM-PM, which are incremental learners with partial instance memory. Such learners store and maintain a portion of the training examples in the input stream for use in future training episodes. Our method selects those examples that lie on the boundaries of induced concept descriptions, and we empirically evaluated both systems using the real-world application of computer intrusion detection. Results from a lesion study echo the outcome of our earlier work with batch learning: Partial-memory learners tend to reduce predictive accuracy but notably decrease memory requirements and learning times.

Acknowledgements. We would like to thank the Department of Computer Science at Georgetown University for their support of this work. We also appreciate the helpful comments of the anonymous reviewers.

This research was conducted in the Machine Learning and Inference Laboratory at George Mason University. Currently, the laboratory's research is supported in part by the National Science Foundation under grants IIS-9906858 and IIS-0097476, and in part by the University of Maryland, Baltimore County, under LUCITE Task #32.

References

1. Maloof, M., Michalski, R.: Selecting examples for partial memory learning. Machine Learning **41** (2000) 27–52
2. Michalski, R., Larson, J.: Incremental generation of VL$_1$ hypotheses: The underlying methodology and the description of program AQ11. Technical Report UIUCDCS-F-83-905, Department of Computer Science, University of Illinois, Urbana (1983)
3. Reinke, R., Michalski, R.: Incremental learning of concept descriptions: A method and experimental results. In Hayes, J., Michie, D., Richards, J., eds.: Machine Intelligence 11. Clarendon Press, Oxford (1988) 263–288
4. Aha, D., Kibler, D., Albert, M.: Instance-based learning algorithms. Machine Learning **6** (1991) 37–66
5. Schlimmer, J., Granger, R.: Beyond incremental processing: Tracking concept drift. In: Proceedings of the Fifth National Conference on Artificial Intelligence, Menlo Park, CA, AAAI Press (1986) 502–507
6. Littlestone, N.: Redundant noisy attributes, attribute errors, and linear-threshold learning using Winnow. In: Proceedings of the Fourth Annual Workshop on Computational Learning Theory, San Francisco, CA, Morgan Kaufmann (1991) 147–156
7. Kibler, D., Aha, D.: Learning representative exemplars of concepts: An initial case study. In: Proceedings of the Fourth International Conference on Machine Learning, San Francisco, CA, Morgan Kaufmann (1987) 24–30
8. Widmer, G.: Tracking context changes through meta-learning. Machine Learning **27** (1997) 259–286
9. Widmer, G., Kubat, M.: Learning in the presence of concept drift and hidden contexts. Machine Learning **23** (1996) 69–101
10. Maloof, M.: Progressive partial memory learning. PhD thesis, School of Information Technology and Engineering, George Mason University, Fairfax, VA (1996)
11. Michalski, R.: On the quasi-minimal solution of the general covering problem. In: Proceedings of the Fifth International Symposium on Information Processing. Volume A3. (1969) 125–128
12. Clark, P., Niblett, T.: The CN2 induction algorithm. Machine Learning **3** (1989) 261–284
13. Cohen, W.: Fast effective rule induction. In: Proceedings of the Twelfth International Conference on Machine Learning, San Francisco, CA, Morgan Kaufmann (1995) 115–123
14. Michalski, R.: Pattern recognition as rule-guided inductive inference. IEEE Transactions on Pattern Analysis and Machine Intelligence **2** (1980) 349–361
15. Michalski, R., Kaufman, K.: The AQ-19 system for machine learning and pattern discovery: A general description and user's guide. Reports of the Machine Learning and Inference Laboratory MLI 01-4, Machine Learning and Inference Laboratory, George Mason University, Fairfax, VA (2001)

16. Michalski, R.: A theory and methodology of inductive learning. In Michalski, R., Carbonell, J., Mitchell, T., eds.: Machine Learning: An Artificial Intelligence Approach. Volume 1. Morgan Kaufmann, San Francisco, CA (1983) 83–134
17. Fisher, R.: The use of multiple measurements in taxonomic problems. Annals of Eugenics **7** (1936) 179–188
18. Blake, C., Merz, C.: UCI Repository of machine learning databases. [http://www.ics.uci.edu/~mlearn/mlrepository.html], Department of Information and Computer Sciences, University of California, Irvine (1998)
19. Bleha, S., Slivinsky, C., Hussien, B.: Computer-access security systems using keystroke dynamics. IEEE Transactions on Pattern Analysis and Machine Intelligence **12** (1990) 1217–1222
20. Lane, T., Brodley, C.: Temporal sequence learning and data reduction for anomaly detection. ACM Transactions on Information and System Security **2** (1999) 295–331
21. Lee, W., Stolfo, S., Mok, K.: Adaptive intrusion detection: A data mining approach. Artificial Intelligence Review **14** (2000) 533–567
22. Maloof, M., Michalski, R.: A method for partial-memory incremental learning and its application to computer intrusion detection. In: Proceedings of the Seventh IEEE International Conference on Tools with Artificial Intelligence, Los Alamitos, CA, IEEE Press (1995) 392–397
23. Davis, J.: CONVART: A program for constructive induction on time dependent data. Master's thesis, Department of Computer Science, University of Illinois, Urbana (1981)
24. Bloedorn, E., Wnek, J., Michalski, R., Kaufman, K.: AQ17 — A multistrategy learning system: The method and user's guide. Reports of the Machine Learning and Inference Laboratory MLI 93-12, Machine Learning and Inference Laboratory, George Mason University, Fairfax, VA (1993)
25. Kerber, R.: ChiMerge: Discretization of numeric attributes. In: Proceedings of the Tenth National Conference on Artificial Intelligence, Menlo Park, CA, AAAI Press (1992) 123–128
26. Baim, P.: A method for attribute selection in inductive learning systems. IEEE Transactions on Pattern Analysis and Machine Intelligence **10** (1988) 888–896
27. Keppel, G., Saufley, W., Tokunaga, H.: Introduction to design and analysis. 2nd edn. W.H. Freeman, New York, NY (1992)
28. Maloof, M., Michalski, R.: AQ-PM: A system for partial memory learning. In: Proceedings of the Eighth Workshop on Intelligent Information Systems, Warsaw, Poland, Polish Academy of Sciences (1999) 70–79
29. Winston, P.: Learning structural descriptions from examples. In Winston, P., ed.: Psychology of Computer Vision. MIT Press, Cambridge, MA (1975)
30. Thrun, S., et al.: The MONK's problems: A performance comparison of different learning algorithms. Technical Report CMU-CS-91-197, School of Computer Science, Carnegie Mellon University, Pittsburg, PA (1991)

KDD-Based Approach to Musical Instrument Sound Recognition

Dominik Ślęzak, Piotr Synak, Alicja Wieczorkowska, and Jakub Wróblewski

Polish-Japanese Institute of Information Technology
Koszykowa 86, 02-008 Warsaw, Poland

Abstract. Automatic content extraction from multimedia files is a hot topic nowadays. Moving Picture Experts Group develops MPEG-7 standard, which aims to define a unified interface for multimedia content description, including audio data. Audio description in MPEG-7 comprises features that can be useful for any content-based search of sound files. In this paper, we investigate how to optimize sound representation in terms of musical instrument recognition purposes. We propose to trace trends in evolution of values of MPEG-7 descriptors in time, as well as their combinations. Described process is a typical example of KDD application, consisting of data preparation, feature extraction and decision model construction. Discussion of efficiency of applied classifiers illustrates capabilities of further progress in optimization of sound representation. We believe that further research in this area would provide background for automatic multimedia content description.

1 Introduction

Automatic extraction of multimedia information from files is recently of great interest. Usually multimedia data available for end users are labeled with some information (title, time, author, etc.), but in most cases it is insufficient for content-based searching. For instance, the user cannot find automatically all segments with his favorite tune played by the flute in the audio CD. To address the task of automatic content-based searching, descriptors need to be assigned at various levels to segments of multimedia files. Moving Picture Experts Group has recently elaborated MPEG-7 standard, named "Multimedia Content Description Interface" [8], that defines a universal mechanism for exchanging the descriptors. However, neither feature (descriptor) extraction nor searching algorithms are encompassed in MPEG-7. Therefore, automatic extraction of multimedia content, including musical information, should be a subject of study.

All descriptors used so far reflect specific features of sound, describing spectrum, time envelope, etc. In our paper, we propose a different approach: we suggest observation of feature changes in time and taking as new descriptors patterns in trends observed for particular features. We discuss how to achieve it by applying data preprocessing and mining tools developed within the theory of rough sets introduced in [13].

M.-S. Hacid et al. (Eds.): ISMIS 2002, LNAI 2366, pp. 28–36, 2002.
© Springer-Verlag Berlin Heidelberg 2002

The analyzed database origins from audio CD's MUMS [12]. It consists of 667 samples of recordings, divided onto 18 classes, corresponding to musical instruments (flute, oboe, clarinet, violin, viola, cello, double bass, trumpet, trombone, French horn, tuba) and their articulation (vibrato, pizzicato, muted).

2 Sound Descriptors

Descriptors of musical instruments should allow to recognize instruments independently on pitch and articulation. Sound features included in MPEG-7 Audio are based on research performed so far in this area and they comprise technologies for musical instrument timbre description, sound recognition, and melody description. Audio description framework in MPEG-7 includes 17 temporal and spectral descriptors divided into the following groups (cf. [8]):

- basic: instantaneous waveform, power values
- basic spectral: log-frequency power spectrum, spectral centroid, spectral spread, spectral flatness
- signal parameters: fundamental frequency, harmonicity of signals
- timbral temporal: log attack time and temporal centroid
- timbral spectral: spectral centroid, harmonic spectral centroid, spectral deviation, spectral spread, spectral variation
- spectral basis representations: spectrum basis, spectrum projection

Apart from the features included in MPEG-7, the following descriptors have been used in the research ([6], [10], [17], [18]):

- duration of the attack, quasi-steady state and ending transient of the sound in proportion to the total time
- pitch of the sound
- contents of the selected groups of harmonics in spectrum, like even/odd harmonics Ev/Od

$$Ev = \frac{\sqrt{\sum_{k=1}^{M} A_{2k}^2}}{\sqrt{\sum_{n=1}^{N} A_n^2}} \qquad Od = \frac{\sqrt{\sum_{k=2}^{L} A_{2k-1}^2}}{\sqrt{\sum_{n=1}^{N} A_n^2}} \qquad (1)$$

and lower/middle/higher harmonics $Tr_1/Tr_2/Tr_3$ (Tristimulus parameters [14], used in various versions)

$$Tr_1 = \frac{A_1^2}{\sum_{n=1}^{N} A_n^2} \qquad Tr_2 = \frac{\sum_{n=2,3,4} A_n^2}{\sum_{n=1}^{N} A_n^2} \qquad Tr_3 = \frac{\sum_{n=5}^{N} A_n^2}{\sum_{n=1}^{N} A_n^2} \qquad (2)$$

where A_n denotes the amplitude of the nth harmonic, N – the number of harmonics available in spectrum, $M = \lfloor N/2 \rfloor$ and $L = \lfloor N/2 + 1 \rfloor$
- vibrato amplitude
- statistical properties of sound spectrum, including average amplitude and frequency deviations, average spectrum, standard deviations, autocorrelation and cross-correlation functions ([2])
- descriptors based on wavelet analysis and numerous other features

3 KDD Process

One of the main goals of data analysis is to properly classify objects (described by some attributes) to some classes. Reasoning with data can be stated as a classification problem, concerning prediction of decision class basing on information provided by attributes. For this purpose, one stores data in so called decision tables, where each training case drops into one of predefined decision classes.

A decision table takes the form of $\mathbf{A} = (U, A \cup \{d\})$, where each attribute $a \in A$ is identified with a function $a : U \to V_a$ from the universe of objects U into the set V_a of all possible values on a. Values $v_d \in V_d$ correspond to mutually disjoint decision classes of objects. In case of the analysis of the musical instrument sound data [12], one deals with a decision table consisting of 667 records corresponding to samples of musical recordings. We have 18 decision classes corresponding to various kinds of musical instruments – flute, oboe, clarinet, violin, viola, cello, double bass, trumpet, trombone, French horn, tuba – and their articulation – vibrato, pizzicato, muted ([17]). These classes define decision attribute d.

Methods for construction of classifiers can be regarded as tools for data generalization. These methods include rule-based classifiers, decision trees, k-NN classifiers, neural nets, etc. However, the process of analyzing data cannot be restricted just to the classifier construction. In the particular case of the musical instrument analysis, one has to extract a decision table itself – to choose the most appropriate set of attributes-descriptors A, as well as to calculate values $a(u) \in V_a$, $a \in A$, for particular objects-samples $u \in U$. Thus, it is better to write about this task in terms of a broader methodology.

Knowledge Discovery in Databases (KDD) is a process which, according to widely accepted scheme, consists of several steps (see e.g. [5]), such as understanding application domain, determining a goal, creating/selecting a target data set, preprocessing, data reduction and transformation, selection of data mining method, algorithms and parameters, model construction (data mining), and interpretation of results. In case of musical instruments classification, the first two steps comprises of the musical domain analysis. Next, proper selection ([9]) and reduction ([13]) of the set of features is crucial for efficiency of classification algorithm. In some cases a set of attributes is worth transforming into more suitable form before it is used to model the data. For instance, when the data set is described by decision rules, one may transform attribute values to gain higher support of rules, keeping their accuracy, and increasing generality of a model. The need of such a transformation is shown for various kinds of feature domains: numeric, symbolic, as well as, e.g., for time series (see e.g. [11], [15], [16], [19]).

4 Preprocessing of Musical Sound Data

The goal of this research is to be able to construct classifiers for the musical instrument sound recognition. Thus, we need to prepare the training data in the form of decision table $\mathbf{A} = (U, A \cup \{d\})$, where each element $u \in U$ corresponds to a sound sample, each element $a \in A$ is a numeric feature corresponding to one of sound descriptors and decision attribute $d \notin A$ labels particular object-sound with integer codes adequate to instrument. For such a preparation we need a framework for preprocessing original data, in particular, for extracting features most relevant to the task of the sound recognition.

The main difficulty of sound analysis is that many useful attributes of sound are not concerned with the whole sample. E.g. spectrum-based attributes (tristimulus parameters, pitch, etc.) describe rather a selected time frame on which the spectrum was calculated than the whole sound (moreover, these attributes may change from one segment of time to another). One can take a frame from quasi-steady part of a sample and treat it as a representative of the whole sound but in this case we may loose too much information about the sample. Our approach is to take into account both sample based attributes (e.g. envelope-dependent as steady state or transient duration) and window based ones. Because the latter vary in time, they should be treated as time series and gathered within an additional table. Further preprocessing is then needed to transform such a family of time series into a set of attributes.

There are numerous mathematical approaches for approximation of fundamental signal frequency and thus – estimation of the length of periods in case of instrument sounds. We have used the following function (see e.g. [17]):

$$AMDF(i) = \frac{1}{N} \sum_{k=0}^{N} |A_k - A_{i+k}| \tag{3}$$

where N is the length of interval taken for estimation and A_k is the amplitude of the signal. Values of $AMDF(i)$ within the interval of admissible period lengths approximate the period for a given sound. In our experiments, we used a mixed approach to approximate periods – based both on searching for stable minima of $AMDF$ and maxima of spectrum obtained using DFT.

We propose to analyze the following descriptors:

1. Envelope descriptors: Each sample was split onto 6 intervals of equal length. Average values of amplitudes within these intervals are referred, respectively, as $Envelope1, \ldots, 6$.
2. Temporal descriptors:
   - Signal length, denoted as $Length$
   - Relative length of the attack (till reaching 75% of maximal amplitude), quasi-steady (after the end of attack, till the final fall under 75% of maximal amplitude) and decay time (the rest of the signal), denoted, respectively, by $Attack$, $Steady$ and $Decay$
   - The moment of reaching maximal amplitude, denoted by $Maximum$
   - Area under the curve of envelope (approximated by means of values $Envelope1, \ldots, 6$), denoted by $EnvFill$
   - Numbers of envelope based clusters of two types (see Section 5), denoted by $Cluster6$ (number of the closest of 6 representative envelope curves, shown at Fig. 1) and $Cluster9$ (similarly, but for 9 representatives)

3. Spectral descriptors:
   - Harmonics defined by (1), denoted by *EvenHarm* and *OddHarm*
   - Brightness and Irregularity (see e.g. [17])
   - Tristimulus parameters defined by (2), denoted by $Tristimulus1, 2, 3$
   - Fundamental frequency, denoted by *Frequency*

We consider the following structure of database: Table INSTRUMENTS (667 records, 18 columns) gathers temporal and spectral descriptors. It is linked in 1:1 manner with Table ENVELOPES (667 records, 7 columns). It has additional column *Instrument* which states the code of musical instrument, together with its articulation (18 values). We also define table WINDOWS (190800 records, 10 columns), where each record corresponds to a small interval of the sound sample. We decided to set up the length of those intervals as 4 times the fundamental period of the sound. We decompose each musical sound sample onto such intervals and calculate value sequences and final features for each of them. For each sample we thus obtain (Length∗Frequency/4) records. Each record is labeled with spectral descriptors defined in the same way as for INSTRUMENTS but calculated locally. As a result, we obtain the relational database, where INSTRUMENTS and WINDOWS are linked in 1:n manner, by the code of the instrument sample (primary key for INSTRUMENTS and foreign key for WINDOWS).

5   Time Domain Features

The basis of musical sound recognition process is a properly chosen set of descriptors that potentially contains relevant features distinguishing one instrument from another. It seems to be very important to choose not only descriptors characterizing the whole sample at once, but also those describing how parameters change in time. Features described in Section 2 can be used to describe a segment with a summary value or with a series of sampled values. Descriptors can be stored as a sequence corresponding to the dynamic behavior of a given feature over the sound sample. Analysis of regularities and trends occurring within such a temporary sequence can provide the values of conditional features labeling objects-sounds in the final decision table. Especially interesting trends are supposed to be observed during the attack part of signal.

We propose to search for temporal patterns that can potentially be specific for one instrument or a group of instruments. Such patterns can be further used as new descriptors, like Cluster6 and Cluster9 in table INSTRUMENTS (see Section 4). Values of those columns were calculated in the following way:

1. The most representative sound envelopes occurring in data were extracted. For column Cluster6 we found 6 representatives shown in Fig. 1. (Similarly, we derived 9 representatives for Cluster9).
2. For each object (sound sample) we calculated the Euclidean distance (calculated with respect to 6 envelope values, for both Cluster6 and Cluster9) to the closest representative.

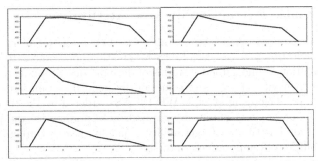

Fig. 1. Centroids (the most typical shapes) of sound envelopes, used in clustering.

The above attributes describe general trends of the amplitude values in time. Results presented in Section 7 show potential importance of such features. Similar analysis can be performed over spectral features stored in table WINDOWS (see Section 4), by searching for, e.g., *temporal patterns* (cf. [16]).

Generation of temporal patterns requires the choice of descriptors that would be used to characterize sound samples and a method to measure values of those descriptors in time. For the latter we propose to use time window based technique. We browse a sample with time windows of certain size. For a given time window we compute values of all descriptors within it, and this way generate one object of a new temporal information system $\mathbf{A} = (\{x_1, x_2, ..., x_n\}, A)$, where x_i is a measurement from the i-th window using descriptors from A (Actually, we constructed table WINDOWS by repeating this procedure for all samples of sounds). Next, we use it to determine optimal *temporal templates* that respond to temporal patterns.

Temporal templates can be of numeric or symbolic type. In the former case, one can compare them with temporal clustering methods. In the latter case they are built by using expressions $(a \in V)$, where $a \in A$ and $V \subseteq V_a$. Formally, *template* is then a set of expressions involving any subset $B \subseteq A$:

$$T = \{(a \in V) : a \in B, V \subseteq V_a\} \tag{4}$$

By *temporal template* we understand

$$\mathbf{T} = (T, t_s, t_e), \quad 1 \le t_s \le t_e \le n \tag{5}$$

Templates and temporal templates are intensively studied in literature ([1], [11], [16]). To outline the intuition, which is behind these notions, let us understand template as a strong regularity in data, whereas temporal template as strong regularity occurring in time.

In one musical sound sample we can find several temporal templates. They can be time dependent, i.e. one can occur before or after another. Though, we can treat them as sequence of events. From such a sequence we can discover frequent *episodes* – collections of templates occurring together (see e.g. [7], [16]). We expect some of such episodes to be specific only for particular instrument or group of instruments.

6   Automatic Extraction of New Attributes

Extraction of temporal templates or temporal clusters is an exemplary method of using 1:n connection between data tables for creating new, aggregated columns. Here, aggregation is understood in terms of deriving descriptors corresponding to trends in behavior of values of some locally defined columns (in our case: spectral columns belonging to table WINDOWS), ordered by the time column. One of the main goals of our future research is to automatize the process of defining temporal attributes, to get ability of massive search through the space of all possibilities of temporal descriptors.

Such a process has been already implemented for SQL-like aggregations in [19]. Exemplary features, found automatically as SQL-like aggregations from table WINDOWS, are the following: *average LocOdd from WINDOWS* and *sum LocTri3 from WINDOWS where LocTri3 < LocTri2*. The goal of the searching algorithm is here to extract aggregations of potential importance while distinguishing instrument decision classes. Such attributes can be added as new columns to table INSTRUMENTS. In some situations adding such new features improves and simplifies the laws of reasoning about new cases.

Automatic extraction of significantly new features is possible also for single data tables, not embedded into any relational structure. In case of numerical features, such techniques as discretization, hyperplanes, clustering, and principle component analysis (see e.g. [11]), are used to transform the original domains into more general or more descriptive ones. One can treat the analysis process over transformed data either as a modeling of a new data table (extended by new attributes given as a function of original ones) or, equivalently, as an extension of model language. The latter means, e.g., change of metric definition in k-NN algorithm or extension of language of rules or templates.

In our approach the original data set is extended by a number of new attributes defined as a linear combination of existing ones. Let $B = b_1, ..., b_m \subseteq A$ be a subset of attributes, $|B| = m$, and let $\alpha = (\alpha_1, ..., \alpha_m) \in \mathbf{R}^m$ will be a vector of coefficients. Let $h : U \to \mathbf{R}$ be a function defined as:

$$h(u) = \alpha_1 b_1(u) + ... + \alpha_m b_m(u) \qquad (6)$$

Usefulness of new attribute defined as $\bar{a}(u) = h(u)$ depends on proper selection of parameters B and α. The new attribute $\bar{a}$ is useful, when the model of data (e.g. decision rules) based on discretized values of $\bar{a}$ becomes more general (without loss of accuracy). Evolution strategy algorithm optimizes $\bar{a}$ using quality function based on intuition that a model with lower number of (consistent) decision rules is better than the others (cf. [3], [13]). For further details refer to [15].

7   Results of Experiments

Fig. 2 presents the results of classification of sounds with respect to the kinds of instruments and their usage. We consider 18 decision classes and 667 records. We use standard CV-5 method for evaluation of resulting decision models. Presented results correspond to two approaches to constructing classifiers:

- Best k-NN: Standard implementation with tuning parameter k
- RS-decision rules: Algorithm implemented in [3] for finding optimal ensembles of decision rules, based on the theory of rough sets [13]

Attributes	Best k-NN	RS-decision rules
Envelope	36,3%	17,6%
Envelope with linear combinations	42,1%	11,1%
Temporal	54,3%	39,4%
Spectral	34,2%	14,6%
Temporal + Spectral	68,4%	46,9%

Fig. 2. Experimental results

Particular rows of the table in Fig. 2 correspond to performance of the above algorithms over decision tables consisting of various sets of conditional attributes. Groups of features correspond to notation introduced in Section 4:

- Envelope: 36% of correct classification of new cases into 18 possible decision classes – a good result in case of k-NN over 6 quite naive conditional features.
- Envelope with linear combinations: Improvement of correct classification in case of k-NN after adding linear combinations over original Envelope of dimensions, found by the approach discussed in Section 6. This confirms the thesis about importance of searching for optimal linear combinations over semantically consistent original features, stated in [15].
- Temporal: Incredible result for just a few, very simple descriptors, ignoring almost the whole knowledge concerning the analysis of music instrument sounds. Still k-NN (54,3%) better than RS-decision rules (39,4%).
- Spectral: Classical descriptors related to spectrum analysis seem to be not sufficient to this type of task. From this perspective, the results obtained for Temporal features are even more surprising.
- Temporal + Spectral: Our best result, 68,4% for k-NN, still needing further improvement. Again, performance of RS-decision rules is worse (46,9%), although other rough set based methods provide better results – e.g., application of the algorithm for the RSES library (see [4]) gives 50,3%.

8   Conclusions

We focus on methodology of musical instrument sound recognition, related to KDD process of the training data analysis. We propose a novel approach, being a step towards automatic extraction of musical information within multimedia contents. We suggest to build classifiers by basing on appropriately extracted features calculated for particular sound samples – objects in a relational database. We use features similar to descriptors from MPEG-7, but also consider the time series framework, by taking as new descriptors temporal clusters and patterns observed for particular features. Experience from both signal analysis and other data mining applications suggests us to use additional techniques for automatic new feature extraction as well.

Acknowledgements. Supported by Polish National Committee for Scientific Research (KBN) in the form of PJIIT Project No. 1/2001 and KBN grant No. 8T11C02417.

References

1. Agrawal, R., Mannila, H., Srikant, R., Toivonen, H., Verkamo, I.: Fast Discovery of Association Rules. In: Proc. of the Advances in Knowledge Discovery and Data Mining. AAAI Press / The MIT Press, CA (1996) pp. 307–328.
2. Ando, S., Yamaguchi, K.: Statistical Study of Spectral Parameters in Musical Instrument Tones. J. Acoust. Soc. of America, 94, 1, (1993) pp. 37–45.
3. Bazan, J.G., Nguyen, H.S., Nguyen, S.H, Synak, P., Wróblewski, J.: Rough Set Algorithms in Classification Problem. In: Polkowski, L., Tsumoto, S., Lin, T.Y. (eds), Rough Set Methods and Applications: New Developments in Knowledge Discovery in Information Systems. Physica-Verlag (2000) pp. 49–88.
4. Bazan, J.G., Szczuka, M.: RSES and RSESlib – A collection of tools for rough set computations. In: Ziarko, W. , Yao, Y.Y. (eds), Proc. of RSCTC'00, Banff, Canada (2000). See also: http://alfa.mimuw.edu.pl/~rses/.
5. Düntsch I., Gediga G., Nguyen H.S.: Rough set data analysis in the KDD process. In: Proc. of IPMU 2000, Madrid, Spain (2000) vol. 1, pp. 220–226.
6. Herrera, P., Amatriain, X., Batlle, E., Serra X.: Towards instrument segmentation for music content description: a critical review of instrument classification techniques. In: Proc. of ISMIR 2000, Plymouth, MA (2000).
7. Mannila, H., Toivonen, H.,Verkamo, A.I.: Discovery of frequent episodes in event sequences. Report C-1997-15, University of Helsinki, Finland (1997).
8. ISO/IEC JTC1/SC29/WG11: Overview of the MPEG-7 Standard. Doc. N4031.
9. Liu, H., Motoda, H. (eds): Feature extraction, construction and selection – a data mining perspective. Kluwer Academic Publishers, Dordrecht (1998).
10. Martin, K.D., Kim, Y.E.: 2pMU9. Musical instrument identification: A pattern-recognition approach. 136-th meeting of the Acoustical Soc. of America (1998).
11. Nguyen S.H.: Regularity Analysis And Its Applications In Data Mining. Ph.D. Dissertation, Warsaw University, Poland (2000).
12. Opolko, F., Wapnick, J.: MUMS – McGill University Master Samples. CD's (1987).
13. Pawlak, Z.: Rough sets – Theoretical aspects of reasoning about data. Kluwer Academic Publishers, Dordrecht (1991).
14. Pollard, H.F., Jansson, E.V.: A Tristimulus Method for the Specification of Musical Timbre. Acustica, Vol. 51 (1982) pp. 162–171.
15. Ślęzak, D., Wróblewski, J.: Classification algorithms based on linear combinations of features. In: Proc. of PKDD'99. Praga, Czech Republik, LNAI 1704, Springer, Heidelberg (1999) pp. 548–553.
16. Synak, P.: Temporal templates and analysis of time related data. In: Ziarko, W. , Yao, Y.Y. (eds), Proc. of RSCTC'00, Banff, Canada (2000).
17. Wieczorkowska, A.A.: The recognition efficiency of musical instrument sounds depending on parameterization and type of a classifier (in Polish), Ph.D. Dissertation, Technical University of Gdańsk, Poland (1999).
18. Wieczorkowska, A.A., Raś, Z.W.: Audio Content Description in Sound Databases. In: Zhong, N., Yao, Y., Liu, J., Ohsuga, S. (eds), Proc. of WI'01, Maebashi City, Japan, LNCS/LNAI 2198, Springer-Verlag (2001) pp. 175–183.
19. Wróblewski, J.: Analyzing relational databases using rough set based methods. In: Proc. of IPMU'00. Madrid, Spain (2000) 1, pp. 256–262.

Learning Significant Alignments: An Alternative to Normalized Local Alignment

Eric Breimer and Mark Goldberg*

Computer Science Department, Rensselaer Polytechnic Institute, 110 Eight Street,
Troy NY 12180, USA, breime@cs.rpi.edu

Abstract. We describe a supervised learning approach to resolve difficulties in finding biologically significant local alignments. It was noticed that the $O(n^2)$ algorithm by Smith-Waterman, the prevalent tool for computing local sequence alignment, often outputs long, meaningless alignments while ignoring shorter, biologically significant ones. Arslan *et. al.* proposed an $O(n^2 \log n)$ algorithm which outputs a *normalized local alignment* that maximizes the degree of similarity rather than the total similarity score. Given a properly selected normalization parameter, the algorithm can discover significant alignments that would be missed by the Smith-Waterman algorithm. Unfortunately, determining a proper normalization parameter requires repeated executions with different parameter values and expert feedback to determine the usefulness of the alignments. We propose a learning approach that uses existing biologically significant alignments to learn parameters for intelligently processing sub-optimal Smith-Waterman alignments. Our algorithm runs in $O(n^2)$ time and can discover biologically significant alignments without requiring expert feedback to produce meaningful results.

1 Background

Local sequence alignment is an essential technique for identifying similarity between biological sequences [6,8,10]. The Smith-Waterman algorithm [15] is considered the standard tool for computing local sequence alignment. However, it was noticed (see, [2,4]) that the algorithm has two essential flaws. It often combines two or more segments of high similarity and aligns internal segments that are not related; the *mosaic effect*, see Fig. 1 (ii). Occasionally, it finds long alignments with a high score and misses shorter ones with a higher degree of similarity; the *shadow effect*, see Fig. 1 (i).

A number of attempts have been made to correct the flaws of the Smith-Waterman algorithm, including unsuccessful approaches that were abandoned [11,14], approaches that are computationally expensive [12,17], and approaches that require sensitive heuristics [18,3]. Further attempts were made to consider length in the computation of alignments [5,13,16]. The most recent and successful

---

* Supported by a grant from Rensselaer Polytechnic Institute.

M.-S. Hacid et al. (Eds.): ISMIS 2002, LNAI 2366, pp. 37–45, 2002.

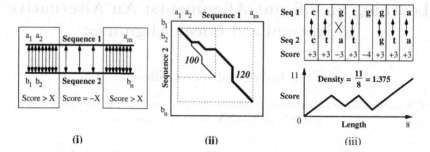

Fig. 1. (i) Mosaic effect: Two high scoring segments are joined into a single alignment that is not biologically significant. (ii) Shadow effect: Sub-optimal alignments with high degree of similarity are ignored in favor of longer alignments. (iii) Alignment Density: Alignment score divided by the length of the alignment.

approach was proposed by Arslan et. al. [4]. This approach seeks to maximize the *normalized score* S_N defined by

$$S_N = \frac{S}{l+N},$$

where S is the conventional alignment score, l is the sum of the lengths of the two aligned segments, and N is the *normalization parameter* used to control the degree of normalization. Arslan et. al. [4] designed an $O(n^2 \log n)$ algorithm for computing normalized local alignment (*nla*) that uses the fractional programming technique developed in [9]. Unfortunately, the algorithm is very sensitive to the value of N. If N is too small, the algorithm is indistinguishable from an exact matching algorithm, whereas if N is too large, the algorithm suffers from the same negative side effects of the Smith-Waterman algorithm. The useful range for N is input-dependent and the relationship between the input and the appropriate value of N is generally unclear [4]. Thus, applying the algorithm requires *guessing* a preliminary value for N, and obtaining meaningful alignments may require repeated execution of the algorithm with a varying value of N. Repeatedly executing the *nla*-algorithm and manually evaluating the results is tedious and time consuming. For large scale applications, a more automated and efficient process is still needed.

For the remainder of this paper, an alignment that captures biologically significant similarity is called a *motif*. In practice, motifs are identified by expert biologists. Coincidental alignments without biological significance are called *padding*. The training data consists of pairs of sequence segments where all motifs are known. Thus, given any alignment, we can identify the specific segments that are motifs and those that are padding. Degree of similarity, also called *density*, refers to the alignment's score divided by the alignment's length (see Fig. 1 (iii)). Alignment density, although similar to normalized score, does not include a normalization parameter and defines length to be the number of aligned symbol pairs.

```
while i < m_A and j < m_B
    if (A_i^x == B_j^x)
        if (A_i^y == B_j^y) Mark that A_i and B_j overlap
        i = i + 1
        j = j + 1
    else if (A_i^x > B_j^x) j = j + 1
    else i = i + 1
```

Fig. 2. Algorithm for computing the overlap between two alignments A and B of lengths m_A and m_B respectively. Each alignment is represented as a sequence of index pairs $\{(x_1, y_1), (x_2, y_2), \ldots, (x_m, y_m)\}$ where (x_i, y_i) indicates that the symbols a_{x_i} and b_{y_i} from input sequences $a = a_1 \ldots a_n$ and $b = b_1 \ldots b_n$ are aligned.

2   Learning Approach

Our learning approach uses input sequences with known motifs to train an algorithm to align and extract these motifs with high probability. It is expected that the motifs possess certain generalizable characteristics that the trained algorithm can use to perform well on similar inputs. This expectation is not unreasonable for biological sequences given that the motifs arise from underlying processes of mutation and conservation that are common among all inputs. We describe a system that learns a strategy for exploring sub-optimal Smith-Waterman alignments and learns parameters for processing these alignments to identify motifs and ignore padding. The main goals are to train an algorithm that is superior to the Smith-Waterman algorithm in its ability to align biologically similar regions and to improve upon the $O(n^2 \log n)$ runtime of the *nla* algorithm.

2.1   Sub-optimal Alignments

It is well known (see [2]) that the alignment's degree of similarity is an important measure in identifying biologically significant similarity. Alignments with the highest degree of similarity may not be captured by the maximum scoring Smith-Waterman alignment, but are often captured by sub-optimal alignments [19]. Given a training input, we use a modification of the Smith-Waterman algorithm similar to that proposed in [7] to efficiently output the non-overlapping maximal scoring alignments to see if a motif is discovered, *i.e.*, contained within a sub-optimal alignment. The precise locations of overlap between any two alignments can be computed in linear time using the algorithm in Fig. 2.

In practice, alignments that arise from coincidence rarely score higher than motifs. A Smith-Waterman alignment that contains a motif will naturally score higher than the motif alone, otherwise the algorithm would have returned the motif and ignored the lower scoring alignment. If a motif is embedded in a sub-optimal alignment, it will typically be among the top k scoring alignments, where k is the number motifs in the input. If the number of expected motifs is known, we can limit the number of computed alignments to improve the efficiency of training or the efficiency of the learned algorithm.

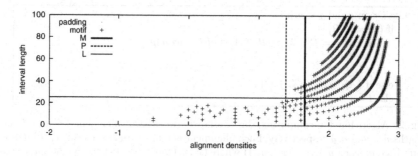

Fig. 3. Alignment densities: Given a training sample, we examine the top k Smith-Waterman alignments using different sampling interval lengths. The left and right clusters represent intervals contained within padding and motif respectively.

2.2 Alignment Density

Due to the mosaic effect, high scoring alignments often contain two or more motifs separated by padding. A single motif may also be embedded in a large alignment with padding to the left and right of the motif. In practical input, the motifs have significantly higher alignment density compared to the padding. To sample density, we choose two alignment indices i and j ($i < j$) and compute density d defined by

$$d = \frac{s(j) - s(i)}{j - i + 1}$$

where $s(i)$ and $s(j)$ are the alignment scores at position i and j, and $j - i + 1$ is defined at the *sampling interval length*. Given an alignment with known motifs, we can sample the density of the motifs and the padding to determine thresholds for discriminating the two. However, this density difference is not evident if the sampling interval length is very small. Small segments of the padding may have high density; similarly, small segments of the motif may possess low density. A large sampling interval may cover two or more motifs, which hinders the ability to identify the start and end of individual motifs. To use density thresholds effectively, one must carefully choose the sampling interval length.

By sampling and plotting segment densities using different interval lengths we can simultaneously detect the minimum interval length and density thresholds that adequately discriminates motif from padding. Figure 3 shows alignment density plotted over interval length. The right cluster represents intervals entirely contained within a motif, while the left cluster represents intervals entirely contained within the padding. Intervals that overlap motifs and padding are omitted from the plot. As the interval length increases the disparity between motif density and padding density increases. Our goal is to find the minimal interval length L that adequately discriminates motif from padding. Since very long intervals are undesirable, we can limit the length of the sampling intervals so that this process is efficient.

```
length = 1
Sort m in ascending order according to density
Sort p in descending order according to density
while (m_j^d < p_k^d)
    length = length + 1
    For all m_i, if m_i^l < length then remove m_i
    For all p_i, if p_i^l < length then remove p_i
    j = |m| * (1 − r)
    k = |p| * (1 − r)
L = length
M = m_j^d
P = p_k^d
```

Fig. 4. Algorithm for computing L, M, and P where r is the percentage of points that must achieve the thresholds, m_l^i and m_d^i are the length and density of the ith motif data point, and p_l^i and p_d^i are the length and density of the ith padding data point.

Minimum interval length (L)
    The minimum length L such that all motif points above L fall to the right of some density threshold and all padding points fall to the left of that threshold.

Maximum motif threshold (M)
    The maximum density M such that all motif points above L fall to the right of M.

Minimum padding threshold (P)
    The minimum density P such that all padding points above L fall to the left of P.

These thresholds are relaxed so that a small percentage of outlying points can be ignored. Figure 4 shows the algorithm for computing L, P, and M. Preliminary experiments indicate that the thresholds accurately identify the start and end of the motifs. Moreover, these thresholds do not significantly change as the motif lengths and padding lengths of the training data are varied, or if the number of motifs or their relative positioning in the input sequences vary.

2.3   Learning

Our learning system uses the observations above to generate a local alignment algorithm. To generate an algorithm, the system requires at least one training sample and implements the following steps.

Learning Stage
    1. **Find the motifs:** Given an input pair with k known motifs, output k maximal scoring Smith-Waterman alignments in order of total alignment score. Search each alignment for the known motifs and label each alignment accordingly.

```
j = 0; i = 1
while (i < mₐ)
    while (Aᵢˢ < Aⱼ²)
        Mark Aᵢ as padding; j = j + 1; i = i + 1
    m = 0; dₘ = 0.0; w = min(i + L, mₐ - 1)
    d_f = (A_wˢ - Aᵢˢ)/(w - i); d_b = (Aᵢˢ - Aⱼˢ)/(i - j)
    if (d_f > M)
    while (d_f > M or (d_f > P and d_b > M))
        Mark Aᵢ as motif
        if (Aᵢˢ > dₘ)
            dₘ = Aᵢˢ; m = i
        i = i + 1; w = min(i + L, mₐ - 1)
        d_f = (A_wˢ - Aᵢˢ)/(w - i); d_b = (Aᵢˢ - Aⱼˢ)/(i - j)
    z = i - 1
    while (z > m)
        Mark Aᵢ as padding; z = z - 1
    j = i; i = j + 1
```

Fig. 5. Algorithm for processing sub-optimal alignments where m_A is the length of alignment A and A_i^s is the alignment score at position i.

2. **Obtain density statistics:** From the labeled alignments, scan each motif segment with varying intervals and obtain the motif density statistics. Likewise, scan each padding segment and obtain the padding density statistics.

3. **Compute thresholds:** Repeat steps one and two until the training data is exhausted or until some time or computation limit has exceeded. After training is complete compute L, M, and P accordingly.

Our algorithm requires $O(n^2)$ time and $O(n + k)$ space to output the score and the endpoints of k alignments. Each alignment can be generated using $O(n_i^2)$ time and $O(n_i)$ space, where n_i is the individual length of each alignment. If k is reasonably small, i.e., $k < 200$, the total time to compute and sort all k alignments is only 2 or 3 times longer than the basic Smith-Waterman algorithm. Computing the overlap locations between the top k alignments and the known motifs is linear with respect to the sum of the lengths of the alignments. After labeling the sub-optimal alignments, the system samples the scoring densities of all the contiguously labeled segments and computes the thresholds. Once obtained, the thresholds define a customized algorithm for processing sub-optimal alignments. Assuming that the learned thresholds generalize well over a broad set of input, the new algorithm is expected to discover alignments that exhibit the same characteristics as the motifs used for training.

Figure 5 shows the post-processing algorithm for labeling alignments. The algorithm scans the alignment until the score begins increasing. From the start position of the increase j, the algorithm marks each successive position i as a motif if one of two conditions is satisfied: (i) the alignment density from i to

$i + L$ exceeds the motif threshold M, or (ii) the alignment density from i to $i + L$ exceeds the padding threshold P and the alignment density from j to i exceeds the motif threshold M. The first condition indicates that i is the beginning of a significantly long alignment that satisfies the motif threshold. The second condition indicates that i is towards the end of a motif but is not yet at the beginning of a significantly long alignment that satisfies the padding threshold. We mark the position m where the maximum score occurs so that when the two conditions are violated we can mark every position from m to i as padding, since this segment decreases the score. Other post-processing algorithms were tested but were not as effective or efficient.

3 Experiments

We experimented on specific regions of the human[1] and mouse [2] genome where there exist highly conserved segments that have been identified as significant by biologists. We extracted a pair of sub-regions, one from the human and one from the mouse, which shared k motifs ranging in length from n_1 to n_2. We train on several samples, compute the thresholds, and cross-test to verify that the post-processing algorithm accurately identifies the known motifs of the training data. We then apply the learned thresholds to unseen samples with known motifs.

To discover a motif the algorithm must compute a contiguous alignment that contains 90% of a particular motif (called the *accuracy requirement*). To extract a motif the post-processing algorithm must identify a contiguous segment such that the length of overlap between the segment and the true motif is greater than 90% of the length of the segment (called the *precision requirement*).

We compare the output of our algorithm before and after post-processing. Before post-processing, our algorithm outputs the top k scoring alignments and computes how many motifs were discovered according to the accuracy requirement. After post-processing, zero or more segments may be identified as potential motifs. For each of these segments, we test to see if they satisfy both the accuracy requirement and the precision requirement. Our expectation is that every motif discovered before post-processing is precisely extracted by the post-processing algorithm. Table 1 summarizes the results of these experiments. In both training and testing combined, the post-processing algorithm extracted 54 out of 55 motifs that were discovered by the Smith-Waterman algorithm. It is important to note that the majority of these motifs (30 out of 55) were embedded into very long alignments that contained more than one motif.

4 Discussion

When the normalization parameter N is carefully selected, the *nla* algorithm can potentially output significant alignments that would not be contained in

---

[1] Homo sapiens ATP-binding cassette, sub-family B (MDR/TAP), member 11

[2] Mus musculus ATP-binding cassette, sub-family B (MDR/TAP), member 11

Table 1. Training and Testing

Training					Testing				
Trial	k	n_1-n_2	Discovered	Extracted	Trial	k	n_1-n_2	Discovered	Extracted
1	3	112–218	3/3	3/3	1	3	118–204	3/3	3/3
2	4	103–147	4/4	4/4	2	4	114–185	4/4	4/4
3	5	99–123	5/5	5/5	3	6	103–157	6/6	6/6
4	7	64–111	6/7	6/6	4	8	66–128	7/8	7/7
5	10	52–106	8/10	8/8	5	10	64–105	9/10	8/9
		Summary	26/29	26/26			Summary	29/31	28/29

any of the sub-optimal alignments produced by the Smith-Waterman algorithm. This occurs when significant alignments partially overlap the padding of two adjoined motifs (a result of the mosaic effect) or when significant alignments partially overlap a very long, insignificant alignment (a result of the shadow effect). By isolating padding and recomputing the alignment, it may be possible to discover alignments hidden in the padding between adjoined motifs. Adding another stage that identifies and isolates padding for further motif discovery may prove to be useful. It is important to note that such a stage would be impossible without an approach for discriminating motifs and padding.

While it is unclear how to discover significant alignments hidden by the shadow effect, it is important to consider the likelihood of such alignments in practical data. Although the *nla* algorithm appears promising, determine the proper range and granularity of N-values to compute these alignments is also unclear. One approach might be to apply supervised learning to automatically determine an appropriate range for N. Unfortunately, training on one sample requires the repeated execution of the $O(n^2 \log n)$ *nla* algorithm. In our approach, training on one sample requires only a single execution of our algorithm followed by post-processing, which together requires $O(n^2)$ time in practice.

While our algorithm does not eliminate all the flaws of the Smith-Waterman algorithm, it improves its discovery capabilities without adding severe computational costs. Our approach uses supervised learning to automatically generate thresholds for post-processing. We provide a system where existing knowledge of biological similarities can be used to automatically generate effective heuristics.

References

1. Alexandrov, N., Solovyev, V.: Statistical significance of ungapped alignments. Pacific Symp. on Biocomputing (1998) 463–472
2. Altschul, S., Erickson, B.: Significance levels for biological sequence comparison using nonlinear similarity functions. Bulletin of Mathematical Biology **50** (1988) 77–92

3. Altschul, S., Madden, T., Schaffer, A., Zhang, J., Zhang, Z., Miller, W., Lipman, D.: Gapped Blast and Psi-Blast: a new generation of protein database search programs. Nucleic Acids Research **25** (1997) 3389–3402

4. Arslan, A., Eğecioğlu, Ö., Pevzner, P.: A new approach to sequence comparison: normalized sequence alignment. Proceeding of the Fifth Annual International Conference on Molecular Biology (2001) 2–11

5. Arslan, A., Eğecioğlu, Ö.: An efficient uniform-cost normalized edit distance algorithm. 6th Symp. on String Processing and Info. Retrieval (1999) 8–15

6. Bafna, V., Huson, D.: The conserved exon method of gene finding. Proc. of the 8th Int. Conf. on Intelligent Systems for Molecular Bio. (2000) 3–12

7. Barton, G.: An efficient algorithm to locate all locally optimal alignments between two sequences allowing for gaps. Computer Applications in the Biosciences **9** (1993) 729–734

8. Batzoglou, S., Pachter, L., Mesirov, J., Berger, B., Lander, E.: Comparative analysis of mouse and human DNA and application to exon prediction. Proc. of the 4th Annual Int. Conf. on Computational Molecular Biology (2000) 46–53

9. Dinkelbach, W.: On nonlinear fractional programming. Management Science **13** (1967) 492–498

10. Gelfand, M., Mironov, A., Pevzner P.: Gene recognition via spliced sequence alignment. Proc. Natl. Acad. Sci. USA **93** (1996) 9061–9066

11. Goad, W., Kanehisa, M.: Pattern recognition in nucleic acid sequences: a general method for finding local homologies and symmetries. Nucleic Acids Research **10** (1982) 247–263

12. Huang, X., Pevzner, P., Miller, W.: Parametric recomputing in alignment graph. Proc. of the 5th Annual Symp. on Comb. Pat. Matching (1994) 87–101

13. Oommen, B., Zhang, K.: The normalized string editing problem revisited. IEEE Trans. on PAMI **18** (1996) 669–672

14. Seller, P.: Pattern recognition in genetic sequences by mismatch density. Bull. of Math. Bio. **46** (1984) 501–504

15. Smith, T., Waterman, M.: Identification of common molecular subsequences. Journal of Molecular Biology **147** (1981) 195–197

16. Vidal, E., Marzal, A., Aibar, P.: Fast computation of normalized edit distances. IEEE Trans. on PAMI **17** (1995) 899–902

17. Zhang, Z., Berman, P., Miller, W.: Alignments without low-scoring regions. J. Comput. Biol. **5** (1998) 197–200

18. Zhang, Z., Berman, P., Wiehe, T., Miller, W.: Post-processing long pairwise alignments. Bioinformatics **15** (1999) 1012–1019

19. Zuker, M.: Suboptimal sequence alignment in molecular biology: alignment with error analysis. Journal of Molecular Biology **221** (1991) 403–420

A Plausibility Description Logics for Reasoning with Information Sources Having Different Formats and Structures

Luigi Palopoli, Giorgio Terracina, and Domenico Ursino

Dipartimento di Informatica, Matematica, Elettronica e Trasporti
Università degli Studi "Mediterranea" di Reggio Calabria
Via Graziella, Località Feo di Vito, 89060 Reggio Calabria, Italy
{palopoli,terracina,ursino}@ing.unirc.it

Abstract. The aim of this paper is to illustrate how a probabilistic Description Logics, called DL_P, can be exploited for reasoning about information sources characterized by heterogeneous formats and structures. The paper first introduces DL_P syntax and semantics. Then, a DL_P-based approach is illustrated for inferring complex knowledge assertions from information sources characterized by heterogeneities in formats and representational structures. The thus obtained complex knowledge assertions can be exploited for constructing a user profile and for improving the quality of present Web search tools.

1   Introduction

In the last years Description Logics have been adopted as the reference formalism for inferring, representing and handling knowledge about heterogeneous databases. As an example, in [5], a Description Logic is introduced for representing databases as well as structural properties holding among database objects. In [10], the Description Logic of [5] is extended by introducing plausibility factors by which a probabilistic Description Logic, called DL_P, is obtained. DL_P is exploited in [10] for inferring complex knowledge assertions, i.e. terminological and structural relationships involving several objects belonging to heterogeneous databases. [4] shows how Description Logics can be exploited for integrating databases in the context of Data Warehousing.

Recently, the enormous diffusion of the Internet led massive amounts of data to be stored not only in traditional databases but also in semi-structured information sources, such as HTML and XML documents, and this trend seems to be confirmed for the future with the generalized adoption of the XML as the standard for data exchange, thus causing obvious and increasing problems in information access and delivery. One of the most difficult problems typically found over the Internet can be summarized in the difficulty for the user to efficiently access the information she/he needs or, in the system perspective, to deliver the right information to the right user in the right format at the right time. Such difficulties basically arise from the unavailability of formalisms and associated

M.-S. Hacid et al. (Eds.): ISMIS 2002, LNAI 2366, pp. 46–54, 2002.

inference techniques capable to allow for reasoning about source content and relationships. Description Logics, however, seem to feature sufficient semantical richness to allow designers to reason about those heterogeneous information sources.

An interesting attempt in this direction is the exploitation of a particular Description Logic coupled with Datalog-like rules in the context of Information Manifold [6], a fully implemented system that provides uniform access to an heterogeneous collection of information sources on the Web. Another interesting attempt is described in [3], where a particular Description Logic is given for representing and reasoning with Document Type Definitions of XML documents. Given a DTD, the paper shows how this can be translated in a DL knowledge base. Then, given several DTDs, by reasoning with their associated knowledge bases, the paper shows how to state several interesting relationships thereof, namely, strong and structural equivalence, inclusion, disjointness of XML document sets conformant to the given DTDs and conformance of an XML document to a given DTD. Finally, it is worthwhile to mention the application of the Description Logics in MOMIS [2], a system for the integration and query of multiple, heterogeneous information sources, containing structured and semi-structured data. Here, a particular Description Logic, called OLCD (Object Language with Complements allowing Descriptive cycles), derived from the KL-ONE family [13], is the core of the module ODB-Tools [1] which exploits OLCD along with suitable Description Logic inference techniques for *(i)* building a consistent Common Thesaurus of involved information sources, which has the role of a shared ontology for them and *(ii)* providing support for semantic optimization of queries at the global level, based on defined mapping rules and integrity constraints. Other and different exploitations of DL within the database context regard the definition of hybrid languages, notably, the CARIN language family [7]. CARIN languages are defined by merging DATALOG with DL. Concepts, as well as role predicates, are allowed in rule bodies. Recursion is also allowed. It is notable that these languages have been applied in database integration scenarios.

In this paper our aim is to continue in this attempt of verifying the possibility of exploiting Description Logics for inferring, representing and handling knowledge about information sources of different nature. In particular, we show that DL_P, with the support of a particular conceptual model called SDR-Network [12], can be used to: *(i)* represent information sources having different formats and structures; *(ii)* infer complex knowledge assertions from these sources; *(iii)* handle and exploit these inferred assertions.

In the following, we therefore first introduce the syntax and the semantics of the DL_P. Then, we illustrate the SDR-Network, a conceptual model these authors recently proposed for describing both structured and semi-structured information sources, as well as for deriving simple properties holding for them (Section 2). A set of rules is also provided that produce a DL_P representation of an SDR-Network (Section 3). Then, the paper describes the DL_P-based inference mechanism for reasoning about information structures by extracting complex knowledge patterns from them. Intuitively, these patterns are DL_P assertions between class expressions (equivalences, subsumptions) involving concepts belonging to distinct sources (Section 4).

Complex knowledge assertions can be exploited in various application contexts. Some of them, such as the integration of heterogeneous information tools, are typical of the traditional research area of information systems. Other ones are newer and characterize some Web-based development of information systems. As an example, the more and more frequent exploitation of the Web for handling data access and distribution, along with the enormous growth of the data present over the Web, requires the definition of new paradigms and approaches for allowing a *user-based* interaction with available data sources. This kind of interaction is presently very poor. Indeed, today's users of Web data sources are basically bound to exploit such information in those forms providers supply for it. A substantial improvement in the quality of information exploitation would be attained if the information could be automatically mediated through a "personal" user profile. In this respect, user-profiled interaction with data source should become one of the main ways to solve important problems such as the customized search of information through the Web. As illustrated into detail in [9], DL_P complex assertions we derive in this paper can be used in this context for both defining and handling user profiles and exploiting them for improving the quality of present Web search tools.

2   Preliminaries

2.1   The Language DL_P: Syntax and Semantics

DL_P [10] is a specialized logics developed to model complex data domains. The language is based on an alphabet B of symbols including class names, the special symbols $\top, \bot, \sqcap, \sqcup, \exists, \forall$ and usual parentheses. A class expression is either an entity expression or a relationship expression. An entity expression over B is constructed according to the following rules:

$$C, F \longrightarrow E|C \sqcup F|C \sqcap F|\neg C|\forall R[U].T_1 : C_1, ..., T_n : C_n|$$
$$\exists R[U].T_1 : C_1, ..., T_n : C_n|\forall A.D|\exists A.D$$

where C, F and E are entity expressions, R is a relationship symbol from B, and $T_1, ..., T_n, U$ are role symbols. A relationship expression is an expression of the form $R[U_1, U_2, ..., U_n]$ where R is a relationship symbol over the alphabet B and $\{U_1, U_2, ..., U_n\} = rol(R)$ are the roles associated with R. Knowledge about scheme properties is expressed in such a logic in the form of assertions. An *assertion* can be either a statement of the form $L_1 \doteq L_2$, where L_1 and L_2 are class expressions of the same type, or a statement of the form $L_1 \leq_{W_{\langle L_1, L_2 \rangle}} L_2$, where, again, L_1 and L_2 are class expressions of the same type and $W_{\langle L_1, L_2 \rangle}$ is a coefficient in the real interval $[0, 1]$.

Language semantics is based on interpretations. An interpretation $I = (\Delta^I, .^I)$ consists of: *(i)* a non empty set Δ^I, called *universe of I*; *(ii)* a mapping $.^I$, called *interpretation function of I*. For each I, the interpretation function of I assigns a subset of Δ^I to each entity expression, according to the following rules:

$$\top^I = \Delta^I \qquad \bot^I = \emptyset \qquad (C \sqcap F)^I = C^I \cap F^I$$

$$(C \sqcup F)^I = C^I \cup F^I \qquad (\neg C)^I = \{a \in \Delta^I \mid a \notin C^I\}$$

$$(\forall R[U].T_1 : C_1, ..., T_n : C_n)^I = \{a \mid (\forall r \in R^I)((r[U] = a) \Rightarrow (r[T_1] \in C_1^I \wedge ... \wedge$$
$$r[T_n] \in C_n^I))\}$$

$$(\exists R[U].T_1 : C_1, ..., T_n : C_n)^I = \{a \mid (\exists r \in R^I)((r[U] = a) \wedge (r[T_1] \in C_1^I \wedge ... \wedge$$
$$r[T_n] \in C_n^I))\}$$

$$(\forall A.D)^I = \{a \mid (\forall(a,b)) \, ((a,b) \in A^I \Rightarrow (b \in D^I))\}$$

$$(\exists A.D)^I = \{a \mid (\exists(a,b)) \, ((a,b) \in A^I \Rightarrow (b \in D^I))\}$$

The interpretation function of I assigns a set of labeled tuples to each relationship expression as: $(R[U_1, U_2, ..., U_n])^I = R^I$, where, if R is a relationship with roles $\{U_1, U_2, ..., U_m\}$, R^I is a set of labeled tuples of the form $\langle U_1 : u_1, ..., U_m : u_m \rangle$ and $u_1, ..., u_m \in \Delta^I$. In the following, if r is an instance of R we shall use $r[U_i]$ to denote the object which R associates with U_i.

The semantics of *assertions* $L_1 \lesssim_{W_{\langle L_1, L_2 \rangle}} L_2$ and $L_1 \doteq L_2$ is as follows: *(i)* $L_1 \lesssim_{W_{\langle L_1, L_2 \rangle}} L_2$ is satisfied if all instances of L_1 are also instances of L_2 and $W_{\langle L_1, L_2 \rangle}$ is the fraction of instances of L_2 which are also instances of L_1; *(ii)* $L_1 \doteq L_2$ is satisfied in I if $L_1 \lesssim_1 L_2$ (i.e., all instance of L_1 are also instances of L_2 and vice versa).

Example 1. Referring to a source concerning information about a university, the assertion $\exists \texttt{Attend}[\texttt{Participant}].\texttt{C} : \texttt{Specialistic\_Course} \lesssim_{0.2} \texttt{Student}$ denotes that all *participants to some specialistic courses* are *students* and that 20% of *students* attend at least one *specialistic course*.

2.2   The SDR-Network

The SDR-Network (Semantic Distance and Relevance Network) is a conceptual model that can be used to describe, in a uniform fashion, heterogeneous information sources so as to derive and represent both their intra-source and their inter-source semantics [11,12]. An SDR-Network $Net(IS)$, representing an information source IS, is a rooted labeled graph $Net(IS) = \langle NS(IS), AS(IS) \rangle$ where $NS(IS)$ is a set of nodes, each characterized by a name and representing a concept of IS. Nodes in $NS(IS)$ are called *atomic nodes* if they do not have outgoing arcs, *complex nodes* otherwise. Since an SDR-Network node represents a concept, from now on, we use the terms "SDR-Network node" and "concept" interchangeably. Note that a node N represents all the instances of the associated concept present in IS.

$AS(IS)$ denotes a set of arcs; an arc represents a relationship between two concepts. Specifically, an arc from S to T, labeled $[d_{ST}, r_{ST}]$ and denoted by $\langle S, T, [d_{ST}, r_{ST}] \rangle$, indicates that the concept represented by S is semantically related to the concept denoted by T. S is called the "source node", whereas T is called the "target node". d_{ST} is called the *semantic distance coefficient* and indicates the capability of the concept associated with T to characterize the concept denoted by S. r_{ST} is called the *semantic relevance coefficient* and expresses the "participation degree" of the concept represented by T in the

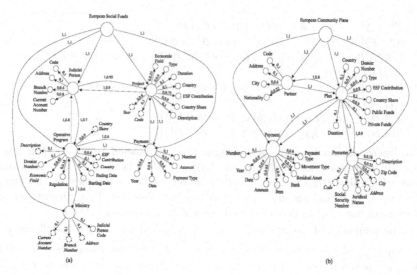

Fig. 1. The SDR-Networks of the European Social Funds (a) and the European Community Plans (b) information sources

definition of the concept denoted by S. Intuitively, this participation degree indicates the fraction of instances of the concept denoted by S whose complete definition requires at least one instance of the concept denoted by T.

Two examples of SDR-Networks are shown in Figure 1. They are derived from the set of Italian Central Government Office Information Sources and represent the information sources relative to European Social Funds (hereafter ESF) and European Community Plans (hereafter ECP). In the figure, in order to simplify its layout, a dotted node with name N indicates that the arc incident onto it must be considered incident onto the solid node having the same name N.

SDR-Network nodes such as *Judicial Person, Project, Payment*, etc. in ESF represent the involved concepts. The arc $\langle$*Judicial Person, Project*, $[1, 0.95]\rangle$ indicates that 95% of judicial persons are involved in some project. The other arcs have an analogous semantics.

Semantic preserving translations have been provided from some interesting source formats, such as XML, OEM and E/R to SDR-Network [11,12].

In the sequel of this paper, we use the SDR-Network and the DL_P for deriving complex structural properties holding among concepts of different information sources. Since the SDR-Network is capable to uniformly handle heterogeneous source formats, the techniques we are going to illustrate immediately apply to all of them.

3   Translations from SDR-Networks to DL_P

Let IS be an information source and let $Net(IS) = \langle NS(IS), AS(IS) \rangle$ be the associated SDR-Network. In order to obtain a set of DL_P entities, relationships and assertions describing $Net(IS)$, we are defining some transformation rules, which are illustrated next.

Rules for obtaining entities and relationships. *(i)* A DL_P entity E_i is introduced for each node $N_i \in NS(IS)$. *(ii)* Let N_C be a complex node of $Net(IS)$ and let $N_{A_1}, \ldots, N_{A_n}$ be the set of atomic nodes connected to N_C; a DL_P relationship $R_C[U_C, U_{A_1}, \ldots, U_{A_n}]$ is introduced for representing arcs connecting N_C to N_{A_i}, $1 \leq i \leq n$. In R_C, the filler for role U_C is N_C whereas the filler for role U_{A_i} is N_{A_i}, $1 \leq i \leq n$. However, suppose that there exists an instance of N_C that is not connected to any instance of N_{A_j}, for some j. Let r be the corresponding tuple of R_C. Then $r[U_j] = null$. Note that this situation is quite common in semi-structured information sources. *(iii)* Let N_{C_1} and N_{C_2} be two complex nodes of $Net(IS)$ connected by an arc $\langle N_{C_1}, N_{C_2}, L_{12} \rangle$; a DL_P relationship $R_C[U_1, U_2]$ is introduced whose filler for role U_1 (resp., U_2) is N_{C_1} (resp., N_{C_2}).

As an example consider the SDR-Network ESF shown in Figure 1(a). From it, the following entities, among others, are obtained: *Judicial Person, Code, Address, Branch Number* and *Current Account Number*. In addition we obtain, among others, the n-ary relationship $R_1[JP, C, A, BN, CAN]$, whose fillers for roles JP, C, A, BN, CAN are *Judicial Person, Code, Address, Branch Number* and *Current Account Number*, resp. Also we obtain the binary relationship $R_2[JP, P]$, whose fillers for roles JP and P are *Judicial Person* and *Project*, resp.

Rules for obtaining intra-source assertions. Let $\langle C_1, C_2, [d_{12}, r_{12}] \rangle$ be an arc in $Net(IS)$. We associate with it a DL_P assertion $\exists R[U_1].U_2 : C_2 \preceq_{r_{12}} C_1$, where *(i)* R is a DL_P relationship associated with the arc according to the rules described above; *(ii)* U_1 and U_2 are two roles of R and C_1 and C_2 are the corresponding fillers; *(iii)* r_{12} represents the proportion of instances of C_1 that are fillers of role U_1 in at least one tuple t in R such that, for t, one filler of U_2 is in C_2. This assertion directly derives from the definition of the semantic relevance coefficient r_{12} as the participation degree of the concept represented by C_2 in the definition of the concept associated with C_1.

As an example consider, again, the SDR-Network shown in Figure 1(a). From the arc $\langle Judicial\ Person, Project, [1, 0.95] \rangle$ we derive: $\exists R[JP].P : Project \preceq_{0.95}$ *Judicial Person*.

Rules for obtaining inter-source assertions. Inter-source assertions relate concepts belonging to different information sources. Let $Net(IS_1)$ and $Net(IS_2)$ be the SDR-Networks associated with information sources IS_1 and IS_2. In order to obtain some basic inter-source assertions we must consider synonymies between concepts of IS_1 and IS_2. A synonymy between two concepts C_1 and C_2 indicates that they have the same meaning (see [2,8,11,12] for approaches aiming at extracting synonymies).

Basic inter-source assertions are derived as follows. Suppose that $Net(IS_1)$ contains an arc from N_{11} to N_{12} and that $Net(IS_2)$ contains a node N_{22} which is synonym with N_{12}. If the assertion $\exists R_{[S_1]}[U_1].U_2 : N_{12} \dot{\leq}_\alpha N_{11}$ holds, then we derive the assertion $\exists R_{[S_1]}[U_1].U_2 : N_{22} \dot{\leq}_\alpha N_{11}$. Furthermore, consider an arc $\langle C_1, C_2, [d_{12}, r_{12}] \rangle$ in $Net(IS)$ and the corresponding assertion $\exists R[U_1].U_2 : C_2 \dot{\leq}_{r_{12}} C_1$, indicating the percentage of instances of C_1 that are fillers of the role U_1 in at least one tuple t in R such that, for t, one filler of U_2 is in C_2. Observe that, if an instance O of C_1 exists with this property, due to the particular structure of SDR-Networks, all tuples of R having O as the filler for role U_1 have an instance of C_2 as the filler for role U_2; as a consequence if $\exists R[U_1].U_2 : C_2 \dot{\leq}_{r_{12}} C_1$ holds then $\forall R[U_1].U_2 : C_2 \dot{\leq}_{r_{12}} C_1$ holds as well.

Rules for obtaining other assertions. Rules presented above allow to automatically obtain assertions from the structure of the involved SDR-Networks. However, it is possible for the domain expert to provide other assertions which cannot be derived automatically from the structure of SDR-Networks and which encode knowledge the expert claims to hold for the given application domain.

4   Exploiting DL_P for Deriving Complex Knowledge Assertions

As already pointed out, a main problem to be faced in the analyzed context is that of deriving complex assertions holding for data sources. In this section we present inference techniques by which complex assertions, relative to information sources possibly having different formats, can be obtained from simpler ones. These apply to both intra- and inter- source assertions obtained directly from the SDR-Network, and produce both intra- and inter- source complex assertions. Inference techniques we present here extend those illustrated in [10], developed for databases, in order to operate on information sources of different nature. In particular, they work by case analysis; we illustrate each of such cases in the following subsections.

4.1   Expressions Containing $\sqcap$ and $\sqcup$

Assume the properties $A \dot{\leq}_{W_{\langle A,C \rangle}} C$ and $B \dot{\leq}_{W_{\langle B,C \rangle}} C$ have been already extracted; the inference process derives the assertions $(A \sqcap B) \dot{\leq}_{W_{\langle A \sqcap B,C \rangle}} C$ and $(A \sqcup B) \dot{\leq}_{W_{\langle A \sqcup B,C \rangle}} C$, where the coefficients are as follows:

$$W_{\langle A \sqcap B,C \rangle} = \frac{min(W_{\langle A,C \rangle}, W_{\langle B,C \rangle}) + max(0, W_{\langle A,C \rangle} + W_{\langle B,C \rangle} - 1)}{2}$$
$$W_{\langle A \sqcup B,C \rangle} = \frac{max(W_{\langle A,C \rangle}, W_{\langle B,C \rangle}) + min(1, W_{\langle A,C \rangle} + W_{\langle B,C \rangle})}{2}$$

Due to space limitations we cannot illustrate here the reasoning underlying the definition of these formulas, as well as of the other ones we derive in the following. However, it is analogous, even if not identical, to the reasoning presented in [10]; the interested reader is referred to that paper for all details about it.

4.2 Expressions Containing ∃

Suppose that the assertion $\exists R[U].T_1 : C_1 \stackrel{.}{\leq}_{W_{\langle C_1 \exists E \rangle}} E$ has been already obtained; then, our inference process derives some further assertions; in particular the following cases are to be considered:

Case 1: A subset property holds between an expression E' and the entity C_1. Assume the assertion $E' \stackrel{.}{\leq}_{W_{\langle E',C_1 \rangle}} C_1$ has been already derived, where E' is a generic DL_P expression. Then $\exists R[U].T_1 : E' \stackrel{.}{\leq}_{W_{\langle E' \exists E \rangle}} E$ can be inferred, where $W_{\langle E' \exists E \rangle} = 1 - min\left(1, \left[\left(1 - W_{\langle C_1 \exists E \rangle}\right) \times \left(1 + \alpha \times W_{\langle E',C_1 \rangle}\right)\right]\right)$ and α is a coefficient which is used to normalize $W_{\langle E',C_1 \rangle}$ in the formula; we have experimentally set α to 1.5.

Case 2: An entity F includes the entity E. Suppose that the assertion $E \stackrel{.}{\leq}_{W_{\langle E,F \rangle}} F$ holds. Then, our inference process derives $\exists R[U].T_1 : C_1 \stackrel{.}{\leq}_{W_{\langle C_1 \exists F \rangle}} F$ where $W_{\langle C_1 \exists F \rangle} = W_{\langle C_1 \exists E \rangle} \times W_{\langle E,F \rangle}$.

Case 3: Entity C_1 is included in an entity C_2. Assume that $C_1 \stackrel{.}{\leq}_{W_{\langle C_1,C_2 \rangle}} C_2$ has been derived. Then it is possible to infer $\exists R[U].T_1 : C_2 \stackrel{.}{\leq}_{W_{\langle C_2 \exists E \rangle}} E$, where $W_{\langle C_2 \exists E \rangle} = 1 - \left[\left(1 - W_{\langle C_1 \exists E \rangle}\right) \times \frac{1}{1 + \alpha \times W_{\langle C_1,C_2 \rangle}}\right]$.

Case 4: R has more than one role. Assume the assertions $\exists R[U].T_1 : C_1 \stackrel{.}{\leq}_{W_{\langle C_1 \exists E \rangle}} E$ and $\exists R[U].T_2 : C_2 \stackrel{.}{\leq}_{W_{\langle C_2 \exists E \rangle}} E$ have been already derived. Then we can derive $\exists R[U].T_1 : C_1, T_2 : C_2 \stackrel{.}{\leq}_{W_{\langle Expr \rangle}} E$. Since DL_P expressions where two roles occur in the selection part are equivalent to intersection expressions, we can use the same line of reasoning as in Section 4.1 to set $W_{\langle Expr \rangle} = \frac{min\left(W_{\langle C_1 \exists E \rangle}, W_{\langle C_2 \exists E \rangle}\right) + max\left(0, W_{\langle C_1 \exists E \rangle} + W_{\langle C_2 \exists E \rangle} - 1\right)}{2}$.

4.3 Combination of Complex Expressions

Assume that the assertions $A \stackrel{.}{\leq}_{W_{\langle A,C \rangle}} C$ and $E \stackrel{.}{\leq}_{W_{\langle E,C \rangle}} C$ have been derived, where E is a complex expression (i.e., not simply an entity symbol) and A and C can be either simple or complex expressions. Now, if $W_{\langle A,C \rangle} < W_{\langle E,C \rangle}$, we can derive $A \stackrel{.}{\leq}_{W_{\langle A,E \rangle}} E$, where $W_{\langle A,E \rangle} = \frac{max\left(0, W_{\langle A,C \rangle} + W_{\langle E,C \rangle} - 1\right) + W_{\langle A,C \rangle}}{2 \times W_{\langle E,C \rangle}}$.

4.4 Expressions Containing Negations

Generally, in Description Logics, the negation of a class represents all instances of the domain which are not instances of that class. For preserving evaluation safety, we must avoid computing complements w.r.t. the entire domain; as a consequence, we must evaluate negation by intersection with some superset class. Thus, properties for negation of a class can be inferred only if that class appears in an inclusion property. Therefore, assume that $B \stackrel{.}{\leq}_{W_{\langle B,A \rangle}} A$ has been already derived; then, we can infer $\neg B \stackrel{.}{\leq}_{W_{\langle \neg B,A \rangle}} A$, where $W_{\langle \neg B,A \rangle} = 1 - W_{\langle B,A \rangle}$. Once $\neg B \stackrel{.}{\leq}_{W_{\langle \neg B,A \rangle}} A$ has been obtained, $\neg B$ can be handled as any other subset of A for inferring further complex properties.

54   L. Palopoli, G. Terracina, and D. Ursino

References

1. D. Beneventano, S. Bergamaschi, C. Sartori, and M. Vincini. ODB-Tools: A description logics based tool for schema validation and semantic query optimization in object oriented databases. In *Proc. of Advances in Artificial Intelligence, 5th Congress of the Italian Association for Artificial Intelligence (AI*IA'97)*, pages 435–438, Roma, Italy, 1997. Lecture Notes in Computer Science, Springer Verlag.
2. S. Bergamaschi, S. Castano, and M. Vincini. Semantic integration of semistructured and structured data sources. *SIGMOD Record*, 28(1):54–59, 1999.
3. D. Calvanese, G. De Giacomo, and M. Lenzerini. Representing and reasoning on XML documents: a description logic approach. *Journal of Logic and Computation*, 9(3):295–318, 1999.
4. D. Calvanese, G. De Giacomo, M. Lenzerini, D. Nardi, and R. Rosati. Source integration in data warehousing. In *Proc. of Workshop on Data Warehouse Design and OLAP Technology*, pages 192–197, Wien, Austria, 1998. IEEE Computer Society.
5. T. Catarci and M. Lenzerini. Representing and using interschema knowledge in cooperative information systems. *Journal of Intelligent and Cooperative Information Systems*, 2(4):375–398, 1993.
6. A. Levy, A. Rajaraman, and J. Ordille. Querying heterogeneous information sources using source descriptions. In *Proc. of International Conference on Very Large Data Bases (VLDB'96)*, pages 251–262, Bombay, India, 1996. Morgan Kaufmann.
7. A. Levy and M.C. Rousset. Combining horn rules and description logics in CARIN. *Artificial Intelligence*, 104(1–2):165–209, 1998.
8. J. Madhavan, P.A. Bernstein, and E. Rahm. Generic schema matching with cupid. In *Proc. of International Conference on Very Large Data Bases (VLDB 2001)*, pages 49–58, Roma, Italy, 2001. Morgan Kaufmann.
9. L. Palopoli, D. Rosaci, G. Terracina, and D. Ursino. Supporting user-profiled semantic web-oriented search. In *Proc. of International Conference on Cooperative Information Agents (CIA 2001)*, pages 26–31, Modena, Italy, 2001. Lecture Notes in Artificial Intelligence, Springer Verlag.
10. L. Palopoli, D. Saccà, and D. Ursino. DL_P: a description logic for extracting and managing complex terminological and structural properties from database schemes. *Information Systems*, 24(5):403–425, 1999.
11. L. Palopoli, G. Terracina, and D. Ursino. A graph-based approach for extracting terminological properties of elements of XML documents. In *Proc. of International Conference on Data Engineering (ICDE 2001)*, pages 330–340, Heidelberg, Germany, 2001. IEEE Computer Society.
12. G. Terracina and D. Ursino. Deriving synonymies and homonymies of object classes in semi-structured information sources. In *Proc. of International Conference on Management of Data (COMAD 2000)*, pages 21–32, Pune, India, 2000. McGraw Hill.
13. W.A. Woods and J.G. Schmolze. The KL-ONE family. *Computer & Mathematics with Applications*, 23(2–5):133–177, 1991.

Roles of Ontologies for Web Intelligence

Ning Zhong and Norichika Hayazaki

Department of Information Engineering
Maebashi Institute of Technology
460-1, Kamisadori-Cho, Maebashi-City, 371, Japan
zhong@maebashi-it.ac.jp

Abstract. The paper investigates the roles of ontologies for Web intelligence, including issues on presentation, categories, languages, and automatic construction of ontologies. Three ontology categories are suggested, some of the research and development with respect to the three categories is presented, the major ontology languages are surveyed, and a multi-phase process of automatic construction of the *domain-specific* ontologies is discussed.

1 Introduction

With the rapid growth of Internet and World Wide Web (WWW), we have now entered into a new information age. The Web has significant impacts on academic research, business, and ordinary everyday life. It revolutionizes the way in which information is gathered, stored, processed, and used. The Web offers new opportunities and challenges for many areas, such as business, commerce, marketing, finance, publishing, education, research and development.

The concept of Web Intelligence (WI for short) was first introduced in our papers and book [23,21,24]. Web Intelligence (WI) exploits Artificial Intelligence (AI) and advanced Information Technology (IT) on the Web and Internet. It is the key and the most urgent research field of IT for business intelligence. Ontologies and agent technology can play a crucial role in Web intelligence by enabling Web-based knowledge processing, sharing, and reuse between applications. Generally defined as shared formal conceptualizations of particular domains, ontologies provide a common understanding of topics that can be communicated between people and agent-based systems.

The paper investigates the roles of ontologies for Web intelligence, including issues on presentation, categories, languages, and automatic construction of ontologies. In Section 2, representation of ontologies is discussed, three ontology categories are suggested, and some of the research and development with respect to the three categories is situated. In Section 3, the roles of ontologies for Web Intelligence are described, and the major ontology languages for Web intelligence are surveyed. In Section 4, a multi-phase process of automatic construction of the *domain-specific* ontology is discussed. Finally, Section 5 gives concluding remarks.

M.-S. Hacid et al. (Eds.): ISMIS 2002, LNAI 2366, pp. 55–65, 2002.

2   Representation and Categories of Ontologies

Although many definitions of ontologies have been given in the last decade, the best one that characterizes the essence of an ontology is that *an ontology is a formal, explicit specification of a shared conceptualization* [10,19]. Here, *conceptualization* means modelling some phenomenon in real world to form an abstract model that identifies the relevant concepts of that phenomenon; *formal* refers to the fact that the ontology should be machine readable, that is, an ontology provides a machine-processable semantics of information sources that can be communicated between different agents; *explicit* means that the type of concepts used and the constraints on their use are explicitly defined. In other words, ontologies are content theories about the sorts of objects, properties of objects, and relations between objects that are possible in a specified domain of knowledge [3]. It provides a vocabulary of terms and relations to model the domain and specifies how you view the target world.

An ontology typically contains a network of concepts within a domain and describes each concept's crucial properties through an attribute-value mechanism. Such network is either directed or undirected one. It might also be a special type of network, that is, a concept hierarchy (tree). Further relations between concepts might be described through additional logical sentences.

An ontology can be very high-level, consisting of concepts that organize the upper parts of a knowledge base, or it can be domain-specific such as a chemical ontology. We here suggest three categories of ontologies: *domain-specific, task,* and *universal* ones.

A *domain-specific* ontology describes a well-defined technical or business domain.

A *task* ontology might be either a quite domain-specific one, or a set of ontologies with respect to several domains (or their reconstruction for that task), in which relations between ontologies are described for meeting the requirement of that task.

A *universal* ontology describes knowledge at higher levels of generality. It is a more general-purpose ontology (or called a common ontology) that is generated from several domain-specific ontologies. It can serve as a bridge for communication among several domains or tasks.

3   Ontologies for Web Intelligence

This section discusses the roles of ontologies and ontology languages for Web intelligence.

3.1   The Roles of Ontologies

Generally speaking, a domain-specific (or task) ontology forms the heart of any knowledge information system for that domain (or task). Ontologies will play a major role in supporting information exchange processes in various areas. The roles of ontologies for Web intelligence include:

- communication between Web communities,
- agents communication based on semantics,
- knowledge-based Web retrieval,
- understanding Web contents in a semantic way,
- and Web community discovery.

More specifically, new requirements for any exchange format on the Web are:

- Universal expressive power.
  A Web based exchange format must be able to express any form of data.
- Syntactic interoperability.
  Applications must be able to read the data and get a representation that can be exploited.
- Semantic interoperability.
  One of the most important requirements for an exchange format is that data must be understandable. It is about defining mappings between terms within the data, which requires content analysis.

One of the fundamental issues of WI is to study the *semantics* in the Web, called the "semantic Web", that is, modeling *semantics* of Web information. Advantages of the semantic Web include:

- Allowing more of the Web content (not just form) to become machine read-able and processible,
- Allowing for recognition of the semantic context in which Web materials are used,
- Allowing for the reconciliation of terminological differences between diverse user communities.

Thus, information will be machine-processible in ways that support intelligent network services such as information brokers and search agents [2,8].

The semantic Web requires interoperability standards that address not only the syntactic form of documents but also the semantic content. Ontologies serve as metadata schemas for the semantic Web, providing a controlled vocabulary of concepts, each with explicitly defined and machine-processable semantics.

A semantic Web also lets agents utilize all the (meta) data on all Web pages, allowing it to gain knowledge from one site and apply it to logical mappings on other sites for ontology-based Web retrieval and e-business intelligence [18]. For instance, ontologies can be used in e-commerce to enable machine-based communication between buyers and sellers, vertical integration of markets, description reuse between different marketplaces. Web-search agents use ontologies to find pages with words that are syntactically different but semantically similar.

In summary, ontologies and agent technology can play a crucial role in enabling such Web-based knowledge processing, sharing, and reuse between applications.

3.2   Ontology Languages

Ontologies provide a way of capturing a shared understanding of terms that can be used by human and programs to aid in information exchange. Ontologies have been gaining popularity as a method of providing a specification of a controlled vocabulary. Although simple knowledge representation such as Yahoo's taxonomy provides notions of generality and term relations, classical ontologies attempt to capture precise meanings of terms. In order to specify meanings, an ontology language must be used. So far, several ontology languages such as OIL, SHOE, and DAML have been proposed.

OIL (Ontology Inference Layer) is an Ontology Interchange Language for the Web [9,8]. It is an effort to produce a layered architecture for specifying ontologies. The major functions of OIL include:

- It provides the modelling primitives commonly used in frame-based ontologies.
- It has a simple, clean, and well defined semantics based on description logics.
- Automated reasoning support may be specified and provided in a computationally efficient manner.

SHOE (Simple HTML Ontology Extensions) is an extension to HTML which provides a way to incorporate machine-readable semantic knowledge in HTML or other World-Wide Web documents such as XML [13,16]. It provides:

- A hierarchical classification mechanism for HTML documents (and optionally non-HTML documents) or subsections of HTML documents.
- A mechanism for specifying relationships between classified elements and other classified elements or specific kinds of data (numbers, dates, etc.)
- A simple way to specify ontologies containing rules that define valid classifications, relationships, and inferred rules.

DAML (DARPA Agent Markup Languages) is a new DARPA research program. One of main tasks of this program is to create an Agent Mark-Up Language (DAML) built upon XML. It is a *semantic* language that ties the information on a page to machine readable semantics (ontology). It is a step toward a "semantic Web" where agents, search engines and other programs can read DAML mark-up to decipher meaning rather than just content on a Web site [14].

4   Automatic Construction of Ontologies

Automatic construction of ontologies is a challenge task in both ontology engineering and WI. This section describes a process of construction of task (or domain-specific) ontologies.

4.1   An Overview

Although ontology engineering has been studied over the last decade, few of (semi) automatic methods for comprehensive ontology construction have been developed. Manual ontology construction remains a tedious, cumbersome task that can easily result in a bottleneck for Web intelligence.

Maedche et al proposed an ontology learning framework as semi-automatic with human intervention, adopting the paradigm of balanced cooperative modeling for constructing ontologies for the semantic Web [17]. Their framework extends typical ontology engineering enviroments by using semi-automatic ontology construction tools.

Zhong et al proposed a process of construction of task (or domain-specific) ontologies [22]. It is a multi-phase process in which various text mining techniques and natural-language understanding methods are used.

Much of data is now in textual form. This could be data on the Web, e-mails, e-library, or electronic papers and books, among others, namely *text databases* in this paper. Text mining is to mine knowledge (regularities) from semi-structured or unstructured text. Text mining is a multidisciplinary field, involving various techniques such as data mining, information retrieval, natural-language understanding, case-based reasoning, statistics, and intelligent agent technology.

Figure 1 shows a sample process of construction of a task ontology on software marketing. The major steps in the process include morphological analysis, text classification, generation of classification rules, conceptual relationship analysis, generation of ontology, as well as refinement and management of ontology. A thesaurus is necessary to be used as a background knowledge base in the process. We emphasize that the process is iterative, and may repeat at different intervals when new/updated data come. At the rest of the section, we discuss the major techniques used in the process and show some preliminary results.

4.2   Text Classification

In order to discover a task (or domain-specific) ontology from text databases, we first need to annotate the texts with class labels. This annotation task is that of text classification. However, it is expensive that the large amounts of texts are manually labeled. This section introduces a semi-automatic approach to classify text databases, which is based on uncertainty sampling and probabilistic classifier. The main contribution of ours is to extend the method proposed by Lewis et al. [15] for multiple classes classification.

We use a variant of the Bayes' rule below:

$$P(C|w) = \frac{\exp(\log \frac{P(C)}{1-P(C)} + \sum_{i=1}^{d} \log(P(w_i|C)/P(w_i|\overline{C})))}{1 + \exp(\log \frac{P(C)}{1-P(C)} + \sum_{i=1}^{d} \log(P(w_i|C)/P(w_i|\overline{C})))} \quad (1)$$

where $w = \{w_1, \ldots, w_d\}$ is a set of the terms in a text, and C is a class. Although we treat, in this equation, only two classes $C_1 = C$ and $C_2 = \overline{C}$ with $P(\overline{C}) =$

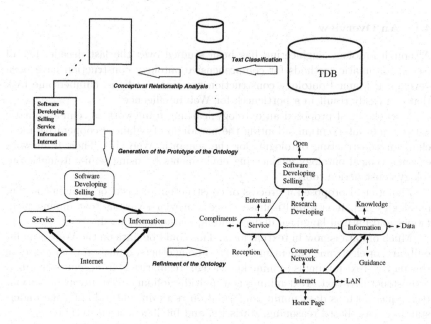

Fig. 1. A sample process of construction of the ontology

$1 - P(C)$, it can be extended to deal with multiple classes classification by using the method to be stated in the end of this section.

However, Eq. (1) is rarely used directly in text classification, probably because its estimates of $P(C|w)$ are systematically inaccurate. Hence we use Logistic regression, which is a general technique for combining multiple predictor values to estimate a posterior probability, in Eq. (1). Thus, we obtain the following equation:

$$P(C|w) = \frac{\exp(a + b \sum_{i=1}^{d} \log(P(w_i|C)/P(w_i|\overline{C})))}{1 + \exp(a + b \sum_{i=1}^{d} \log(P(w_i|C)/P(w_i|\overline{C})))}. \tag{2}$$

Intuitively, we could hope that the logistic parameter a would substitute for the hard-to-estimate prior log odds in Eq. (1), while b would serve to dampen extreme log likelihood ratios resulting from independence violations.

Furthermore, we use the following equation to estimate the values $P(w_i|C)/P(w_i|\overline{C})$ as the first step in using Eq. (2),

$$\frac{P(w_i|C)}{P(w_i|\overline{C})} = \frac{\frac{c_{pi}+(N_p+0.5)/(N_p+N_n+1)}{N_p+d(N_p+0.5)/(N_p+N_n+1)}}{\frac{c_{ni}+(N_n+0.5)/(N_p+N_n+1)}{N_n+d(N_n+0.5)/(N_p+N_n+1)}} \tag{3}$$

where N_p and N_n are the numbers of terms in the positive and negative training sets, respectively, c_{pi} and c_{ni} are correspondingly the numbers of examples of w_i

in the positive and negative training sets, respectively, and d is the number of different terms in a text.

Based on the preparation stated above, we briefly describe the main steps of text classification below:

Step 1. Select examples (terms) as an initial classifier for N classes by a user and all the N classes are regarded as a set of the negative classes.

Step 2. Select a class from the set of the negative classes as a positive class, and the remaining ones are regarded as a set of the negative classes.

Step 3. While a user is willing to label texts.

Step 3.1 Apply the current classifier to each unlabeled text.

Step 3.2 Find the k texts for which the classifier is least certain of class membership by computing their posterior probabilities in Eq (2).

Step 3.3 Have the user label the subsample of k texts.

Step 3.4 Train a new classifier on all labeled texts.

Step 4. Repeat *Step 2* to *Step 3* until all classes were selected as a positive class.

Selecting examples (terms) as an initial classifier by a user is an important step because of the need for personalization applications. The requirements and biases of a user are represented in the classifier.

For example, we have a text database in which there are a lot of mixed texts on soccer teams, software marketing, hot-spring, etc. And this database has been pre-processed by using morphological analysis. Thus we may use the text classification method stated above to obtain the classified sub-databases on soccer teams, software marketing, hot-spring, respectively.

4.3   Generation of Ontology

Based on the result of text classification, the process of generation of ontology can be divided into the following two major stages.

The first stage is *conceptual relationship analysis* [20,4]. We first compute the combined weights of terms in texts by Eqs. (4) and (5), respectively,

$$D_i = \log d_i \times tf_i \tag{4}$$

$$D_{ij} = \log d_{ij} \times tf_{ij} \tag{5}$$

where d_i and d_{ij} are the text frequency, which represent the numbers of texts in a collection of n texts in which term i occurs, and both term i and term j occur, respectively, tf_i and tf_{ij} are the term frequencies, which represent the numbers of occurrences of term i, and both term i and term j, in a text, respectively.

Then a network-like concept space is generated by using the following equations to compute their similarity relationships.

$$Rel(i,j) = \frac{D_{ij}}{D_i} \tag{6}$$

$$Rel(j, i) = \frac{D_{ij}}{D_j} \qquad (7)$$

where Eqs. (6) and (7) compute the relationships from term i to term j, and from term j to term i, respectively. We also use a threshold value to ensure that only the most relevant terms are remained. Table 1 shows a portion of the similarity relationships of the terms on soccer teams.

Table 1. The similarity relationships of the terms

Term i	Term j	$Rel(i, j)$
team	soccer	0.7385
league	soccer	0.7326
university	soccer	0.5409
player	soccer	0.4929
Japan	soccer	0.4033
region	soccer	0.4636
game	soccer	0.1903
sports	soccer	0.1803
gymkhana	soccer	0.1786
soccer	team	0.7438
league	team	0.8643
university	team	0.5039
player	team	0.1891
Japan	team	0.1854
region	team	0.1973
...	...	...

The second stage is to generate the prototype of the ontology by using a variant of the Hopfield network. Each remaining term is used as a neuron (unit), the similarity relationship between term i and term j is taken as the unidirectional, weighted connection between neurons. At time 0,

$$\mu_i(0) = x_i : 0 \leq i \leq n - 1$$

where $\mu_i(t)$ is the output of unit i at time t, and x_i indicates the input pattern with a value between 0 and 1. At time 0, only one term receive the value 1 and all other terms receive 0. We repeat to use the following equation n times (i.e. for n terms):

$$\mu_j(t + 1) = f_s[\sum_{i=0}^{n-1} w_{ij}\mu_i(t)], \quad 0 \leq j \leq n - 1 \qquad (8)$$

where w_{ij} represents the similarity relationship $Rel(i, j)$ as shown in Eq.(6) (or Eq.(7) for w_{ji}), f_s is the sigmoid function as shown below:

$$f_s(net_j) = \frac{1}{1 + exp[(\theta_j - net_j)/\theta_0]} \tag{9}$$

where $net_j = \sum_{i=0}^{n-1} w_{ij}\mu_i(t)$, θ_j serves as a threshold or bias, and θ_0 is used to modify the shape of the sigmoid function.

This process is repeated until there is no change between two iterations in terms of output, that is, it converged by checking the following equation:

$$\sum_{j=0}^{n-1}[\mu_j(t+1) - \mu_j(t)]^2 \le \varepsilon \tag{10}$$

where ε is the maximal allowable error.

The final output represents the set of terms relevant to the starting term, which can be regarded as the prototype of a task (or domain-specific) ontology. Figure 2 shows an example of the prototype of a task ontology on soccer teams. It is generated by using each term shown in Table 1 as a starting input pattern for learning on the Hopfield network.

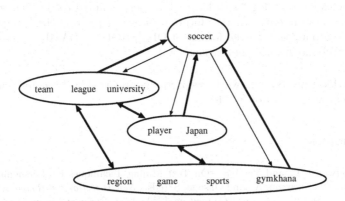

Fig. 2. The prototype of a task ontology on soccer teams

4.4 Refinement of Ontology

There is often a limit to the construction of ontology from text databases, whatever the technique employed. Incorporating any associated knowledge significantly increases the efficiency of the process and the quality of the ontology generated from the text data. A thesaurus is a useful source to be used as a background knowledge base for refinement of ontology. By using the thesaurus, the terms are extended by including their synonym, wider and narrow sense of the terms.

5   Concluding Remarks

The paper presented the roles of ontologies for Web intelligence, including issues on presentation, categories, languages, and automatic construction of ontologies. A task (or domain-specific) ontology forms the heart of any knowledge information system for that task (or domain). Ontologies will play a major role in supporting information exchange processes in various areas. On the other hand, agent technology is required since information on the Web is distributed. The integration of ontologies and agent technology increases the autonomy of Web-based information systems.

We emphasize that the process of automatic construction of ontologies is iterative, and may repeat at different intervals when new/updated data come. Hence how to handle change is an important issue related to refinement of ontology. In particular, during the (long) lifetime of an application session, there may be many kinds of changes such as changes in the text data, the purpose of using both the text data and the ontology, etc. Hence we need to develop a method to reuse the exiting ontology with local adjustment adapted to the changes. This is a future work of ours. Another future work is to transform the automatically constructed ontologies to the format of OIL, SHOE, or DAML representation for real Web intelligence applications.

Acknowledgments. This work was partially supported by Telecommunications Advancement Foundation (TAF).

References

1. Aggarwal, C.C. and Yu, P.S. "On Text Mining Techniques for Personalization", Zhong, N., Skowron, A., and Ohsuga, S. (eds.) *New Directions in Rough Sets, Data Mining, and Granular-Soft Computing*, LNAI 1711, Springer-Verlag (1999) 12-18.
2. Berners-Lee, T., Hendler, J., and Lassila, O. "The Semantic Web", *Scientific American* (2001) 29-37.
3. Chandrasekaran, B., Josephson, J.R., and Benjamins, V.R. "What Are Ontologies, and Why Do We Need Them?", *IEEE Intelligent Systems*, Vol.14, No.1 (1999) 20-26.
4. Chen, H. and Lynch, K.J. "Automatic Construction of Networks of Concepts Characterizing Document Databases", *IEEE Tran. on Sys. Man and Cybernetics*, Vol.22, No.5 (1992) 885-902.
5. Chen, H. "Collaborative Systems: Solving the Vocabulary Problem", *IEEE Computer*, Vol. 27, No. 5 (1994) 58-66.
6. Cooper, W.S., Gey, F.C., and Dabney. D.P. "Probabilistic Retrieval Based on Staged Logistic Regression", *Proc. ACM SIGIR'92* (1992) 198-210.

7. Cooley, R., Mobasher, B., and Srivastavva, J. "Data Preparation for Mining Would Wide Web Browsing Patterns", *Knowledge and Information Systems, An International Journal*, Vol.1, No.1, Springer-Verlag (1999) 5-32.
8. Decker, S., Melnik, S. et al. "The Semantic Web: The Roles of XML and RDF", *IEEE Internet Computing*, Vol. 4, No. 5 (2000) 63-74.
9. Fensel, D. et al. "OIL in a Nutshell", R. Dieng and O. Corby (eds.) *Knowledge Engineering and Knowledge Management: Methods, Models, and Tools*, LNAI 1937, Springer-Verlag (2000) 1-16.
10. Fensel, D. *Ontologies: A Silver Bullet for Knowledge Management and Electronic Commerce*, Springer-Verlag (2001).
11. Frank, G., Farquhar, A., and Fikes, R. "Building a Large Knowledge Base from a Structured Source", *IEEE Intelligent Systems*, Vol.14, No.1 (1999) 47-54.
12. Guarino, N. (ed.) *Formal Ontology in Information Systems*, IOS Press (1998).
13. Heflin, J. and Hendler, J. "Dynamic Ontologies on the Web", *Proc. AAAI-2000*, (2000) 443-449.
14. Hendler, J.A. "Agents and the Semantic Web", *IEEE Intelligent Systems*, Vol.16, No.2 (2001) 30-37.
15. Lewis, D.D. and Catlett, J. "Heterogeneous Uncertainty Sampling for Supervised Learning", *Proc. Eleventh Inter. Conf. on Machine Learning* (1994) 148-156.
16. Luke, S. et al. "Ontology-based Web Agents", *Proc. First International Conference on Autonomous Agents*, ACM Press (1997) 59-66.
17. Maedche, A. and Staab, S. "Ontology Learning for the Semantic Web" *IEEE Intelligent Systems*, Vol.16, No.2 (2001) 72-79.
18. Martin, P. and Eklund, P.W. "Knowledge Retrieval and the World Wide Web", *IEEE Intelligent Systems*, Vol. 15, No. 3 (2000) 18-25.
19. Mizoguchi, R. "Ontological Engineering: Foundation of the Next Generation Knowledge Processing", Zhong, N., Yao, Y.Y., Liu, J., and Ohsuga, S. (eds.) Web Intelligence: Research and Development, LNAI 2198, Springer-Verlag (2001) 44-57.
20. Salton, G. *Automatic Text Processing*, Addison-Wesley Publishing (1989).
21. Yao, Y.Y., Zhong, N., Liu, J., and Ohsuga, S. "Web Intelligence (WI): Research Challenges and Trends in the New Information Age", Zhong, N., Yao, Y.Y., Liu, J., and Ohsuga, S. (eds.) Web Intelligence: Research and Development, LNAI 2198, Springer-Verlag (2001) 1-17.
22. Zhong, N., Yao, Y.Y., and Kakemoto, Y. "Automatic Construction of Ontology from Text Databases", N. Ebecken and C.A. Brebbia (eds.) *Data Mining*, Volume 2, WIT Press (2000) 173-180.
23. Zhong, N., Liu, J., Yao, Y.Y. and Ohsuga, S. "Web Intelligence (WI)", Proc. the 24th IEEE Computer Society International Computer Software and Applications Conference (COMPSAC 2000), a position paper for a panel on Data Mining and Web Information Systems (2000) 469-470.
24. Zhong, N., Yao, Y.Y., Liu, J., and Ohsuga, S. (eds.) *Web Intelligence: Research and Development*, LNAI 2198, Springer-Verlag (2001).

Handling Semantic Inconsistencies in Distributed Knowledge Systems Using Ontologies

Zbigniew W. Raś[1,2] and Agnieszka Dardzińska[3]

[1] University of North Carolina, Department of Computer Science
Charlotte, N.C. 28223, USA
ras@uncc.edu
[2] Polish Academy of Sciences, Institute of Computer Science
Ordona 21, 01-237 Warsaw, Poland
[3] Bialystok University of Technology, Department of Mathematics
15-351 Bialystok, Poland
agnadar@wp.pl

Abstract. Traditional query processing provides exact answers to queries. It usually requires that users fully understand the database structure and content to issue a query. Due to the complexity of the database applications, the so called global queries can be posed which traditional query answering systems can not handle. In this paper a query answering system based on distributed data mining is presented to rectify these problems. Task ontologies are used as a tool to handle semantic inconsistencies between sites.

1 Introduction

In many fields, such as medical, banking and educational, similar databases are kept at many sites. An attribute may be missing in one database, while it occurs in many others. Missing attributes lead to problems. A user may issue a query to a local database S_1 in search for objects in S_1 that match a desired description, only to realize that one component a_1 of that description is missing in S_1 so that the query cannot be answered. The definition of a_1 may be extracted from databases at other sites and used to identify objects in S_1 having property a_1. The simplicity of this approach is no longer in place when the semantics of terms used to describe objects in a client and remote sites differ. Sometime, such a difference in semantics can be repaired quite easily. For instance if "Temperature in Celsius" is used at one site and "Temperature in Fahrenheit" at the other, a simple mapping will fix the problem. If databases are complete and two attributes have the same name and differ only in their granularity level, a new hierarchical attribute can be formed to fix the problem. If databases are incomplete, the problem is more complex because of the number of options available to interpret incomplete values (including null vales). The problem is especially difficult when rule-based chase techniques are used to replace null values by values which are less incomplete.

M.-S. Hacid et al. (Eds.): ISMIS 2002, LNAI 2366, pp. 66–74, 2002.

The notion of an intermediate model, proposed by [Maluf and Wiederhold] [1], is very useful to deal with heterogeneity problem, because it describes the database content at a relatively high abstract level, sufficient to guarantee homogeneous representation of all databases. Knowledge bases built jointly with task ontologies proposed in this paper, can be used for a similar purpose. Knowledge bases contain rules extracted from databases at remote sites.

In this paper, the heterogeneity problem is introduced from the query answering point of view. Query answering system linked with a client site transforms, so called, global queries using definitions extracted at remote sites. These definitions may have so many different interpretations as the number of remote sites used to extract them. Task ontologies are used to find new interpretations representing consensus of all these sites.

2   Distributed Information Systems

In this section, we recall the notion of a distributed information system and a knowledge base for a client site formed from rules extracted at remote sites. We introduce the notion of local queries and give their standard semantics.

By an *information system* we mean $S = (X, A, V)$, where X is a finite set of objects, A is a finite set of attributes, and $V = \bigcup\{V_a : a \in A\}$ is a set of their values. We assume that:

- V_a, V_b are disjoint for any $a, b \in A$ such that $a \neq b$,
- $a : X \longrightarrow 2^{V_a} - \{\emptyset\}$ is a function for every $a \in A$.

Instead of a, we may write $a_{[S]}$ to denote that a is an attribute in S.

By *distributed information system* we mean $DS = (\{S_i\}_{i \in I}, L)$ where:

- I is a set of sites.
- $S_i = (X_i, A_i, V_i)$ is an information system for any $i \in I$,
- L is a symmetric, binary relation on the set I.

A distributed information system $DS = (\{S_i\}_{i \in I}, L)$ is consistent if the following condition holds:

$$(\forall i)(\forall j)(\forall x \in X_i \cap X_j)(\forall a \in A_i \cap A_j)$$
$$[(a_{[S_i]}(x) \subseteq a_{[S_j]}(x)) \text{ or } (a_{[S_j]}(x) \subseteq a_{[S_i]}(x))].$$

Let $S_j = (X_j, A_j, V_j)$ for any $j \in I$. In the remainder of this paper we assume that $V_j = \bigcup\{V_{ja} : a \in A_j\}$.

From now on, in this section, we use A to denote the set of all attributes in DS, $A = \bigcup\{A_j : j \in I\}$. Also, by V we mean $\bigcup\{V_j : j \in I\}$.

Before introducing the notion of a knowledge base, we begin with a definition of $s(i)$-terms and their standard interpretation M_i in $DS = (\{S_j\}_{j \in I}, L)$, where $S_j = (X_j, A_j, V_j)$ and $V_j = \bigcup\{V_{ja} : a \in A_j\}$, for any $j \in I$.

By a set of $s(i)$-terms (also called a set of local queries for site i) we mean a least set T_i such that:

- $\mathbf{0}, \mathbf{1} \in T_i$,
- $w \in T_i$ for any $w \in V_i$,
- if $t_1, t_2 \in T_i$, then $(t_1 + t_2), (t_1 * t_2), \sim t_1 \in T_i$.

By a set of $s(i)$-formulas we mean a least set F_i such that:

- if $t_1, t_2 \in T_i$, then $(t_1 = t_2) \in F_i$.

Definition of DS-terms (also called a set of global queries) and DS-formulas is quite similar (we only replace T_i by $\bigcup \{T_i : i \in I\}$ and F_i by F in two definitions above).

We say that:

- $s(i)$-term t is *primitive* if it is of the form $\prod \{w : w \in U_i\}$ for any $U_i \subseteq V_i$,
- $s(i)$-term is in *disjunctive normal form* (DNF) if $t = \sum \{t_j : j \in J\}$ where each t_j is primitive.

Similar definitions can be given for DS-terms.

Clearly, it is easy to give an example of a local query. The expression:

select * from *Flights*
where *airline* = "*Delta*"
and *departure_time* = "*morning*"
and *departure_airport* = "*Charlotte*"
and *aircraft* = "*Boeing*"

is an example of a non-local query (DS-term) in a database

$Flights(airline, departure\_time, arrival\_time,$
$departure\_airport, arrival\_airport).$

Semantics of $s(i)$-terms is defined by the standard interpretation M_i in a distributed information system $DS = (\{S_j\}_{j \in I}, L)$ as follows:

- $M_i(\mathbf{0}) = \emptyset$, $M_i(\mathbf{1}) = X_i$
- $M_i(w) = \{x \in X_i : w \in a(x)\}$ for any $w \in V_{ia}$,
- if t_1, t_2 are s(i)-terms, then
    $M_i(t_1 + t_2) = M_i(t_1) \cup M_i(t_2),$
    $M_i(t_1 * t_2) = M_i(t_1) \cap M_i(t_2),$
    $M_i(\sim t_1) = X_i - M_i(t_1).$
    $M_i(t_1 = t_2) =$
    (if $M_i(t_1) = M_i(t_2)$ then T else F)
    where T stands for $True$ and F for $False$

The sound and complete axiomatization of the above semantics for a complete distributed information system is given, for instance, in paper by [Ras][5]. This semantics is slightly modified for distributed incomplete information systems (see paper by [Ras and Joshi][7]).

Now, we are ready to introduce the notion of (k, i)-rules, for any $i \in I$. We use them to build a knowledge base at site $i \in I$.

By (k, i)-rule in $DS = (\{S_j\}_{j \in I}, L)$, $k, i \in I$, we mean a triple (c, t, s) such that:

- $c \in V_k - V_i$,
- t, s are $s(k)$-terms in DNF and they both belong to $T_k \cap T_i$,
- $M_k(t) \subseteq M_k(c) \subseteq M_k(t + s)$.

Any (k, i)-rule (c, t, s) in DS can be seen as a definition of c which is extracted from S_k and can be used in S_i.

For any (k, i)-rule (c, t, s) in $DS = (\{S_j\}_{j \in I}, L)$, we say that:

- $(t \rightarrow c)$ is a k-certain rule in DS,
- $(t + s \rightarrow c)$ is a k-possible rule in DS.

Let us assume that $r_1 = (c_1, t_1, s_1)$, $r_2 = (c_2, t_2, s_2)$ are (k, i)-rules. We say that: r_1, r_2 are strongly consistent, if either c_1, c_2 are values of two different attributes in S_k or a DNF form equivalent to $t_1 * t_2$ does not contain simple conjuncts.

Now, we are ready to define a knowledge base D_{ki}. Its elements are called definitions of values of attributes from $V_k - V_i$ in terms of values of attributes from $V_k \cap V_i$.

Namely, D_{ki} is defined as a set of (k, i)-rules such that:
if $(c, t, s) \in D_{ki}$ and the equation $t_1 =\sim (t + s)$ is true in M_k, then $(\sim c, t1, s) \in D_{ki}$.
The idea here is to have definition of $\sim c$ in D_{ki} if already definition of c is in D_{ki}. It will allow us to approximate (learn) concept c from both sites, if needed.

By a knowledge base for site i, denoted by D_i, we mean any subset of $\bigcup \{D_{ki} : (k, i) \in L\}$. If definitions are not extracted at a remote site, partial definitions (c, t) corresponding to $(t \rightarrow c)$, if available, can be stored in a knowledge base at a client site.

3 Semantic Inconsistencies and Distributed Knowledge Systems

In this section, we introduce the notion of a distributed knowledge system (DKS) and next we present problems related to its query answering system QAS. We discuss the process of handling semantic inconsistencies in knowledge extracted at different DKS sites and next we outline query transformation steps based on distributed knowledge mining.

By Distributed Knowledge System (DKS) we mean $DS = (\{(S_i, D_i)\}_{i \in I}, L)$ where $(\{S_i\}_{i \in I}, L)$ is a distributed information system, $D_i = \bigcup \{D_{ki} : (k, i) \in L\}$ is a knowledge base for $i \in I$.

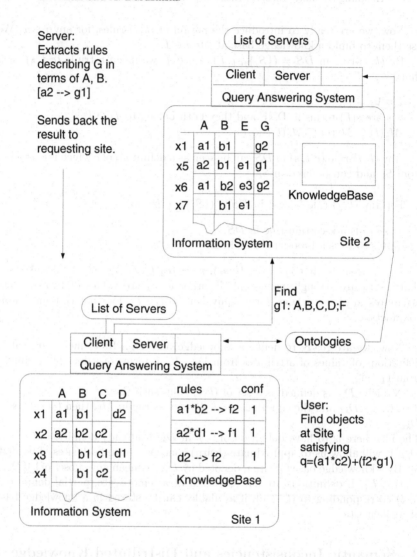

Fig. 1. Sample Model of DKS

Figure 1 shows an example of DKS and its query answering system QAS that handles global queries.

For simplicity reason only two sites of DKS are considered in our example. A user queries site 1 asking for all its objects satisfying $q = (a_1 * c_2) + (f_2 * g_1)$. The user is interested only in objects at site 1. The first part of the query, which is $(a_1 * c_2)$, can be handled by local QAS because both its attribute values are within the domain of the information system at site 1. For instance, taking optimistic interpretation of all attribute values at site 1 (null values are treated as supporting values), objects x_1 and x_2 will satisfy query $(a_1 * c_2)$. Let us consider the second part of the query q, which is $(f_2 * g_1)$. Attribute value f_2 is not in the domain V_1 of the information system S_1 at site 1 but its definition is in knowledge base D_1 at site 1. This definition can be used to replace the value f_2 in q by a term which defines f_2. In our example, either a partial definition $(f_2, a_1 * b_2 + d_2)$ or a definition $(f_2, a_1 * b_2 + d_2, \sim (a_1 * b_2 + d_2) * \sim d_2)$ of f_2 can be generated from D_1. The attribute value g_1 used in a query q is neither in the domain D_1 nor its definition is in D_1. In this case we have to search for a remote site, where definition of g_1 can be extracted from its information system. In our example site 2 satisfies this requirement. Expression (g_1, a_2) can be seen as a partial definition of g_1 which can be extracted from S_2. Alternatively, expression $(g_1, a_2, \sim a_1 * \sim a_2)$ can be used as a definition of g_1 found at site 2. To simplify the problem further, assume that partial definitions of f_2 and g_1 are used to replace query q by a new query which can be handled locally by QAS at site 1. This new query approximating q, described by a term $(a_1 + c_2) + (a_1 * b_2 + d_2) * a_2$, can be seen as a lower approximation of q in rough sets terminology. If we use definition of f_2 and definition of g_1 instead of partial definitions, query q can be replaced by a rough query. Rough queries are especially useful when the boundary area in a rough query representation is small. In a distributed scenario, similar to the one presented in this paper, this boundery area is getting smaller and smaller when more and more sites are used to search for definitions of non-local attributes (f_2 and g_1 in our example). Now, let's go back to term $(a_1 * c_2) + (a_1 * b_2 + d_2) * a_2$. If the distribution law can be applied then our term would be transformed to $(a_1 * c_2) + (a_1 * b_2 * a_2 + d_2 * a_2)$ and next assuming that properties $a_1 * a_2 = 0$ and $0 * t = 0$ hold we would get its final equivalent form which is $a_1 * c_2 + d_2 * a_2$. However if each of our three terms $a_1 * b_2$, d_2, a_2 is computed under three different semantics, then there is a problem with the above tranformation process and with a final meaning of $(a_1 * b_2 * a_2 + d_2 * a_2)$.

For instance, let us assume a scenario where partial definition $(f_2, a_1 * b_2)$ was extracted under semantics M_1, partial definition (f_2, d_2) under semantics M_2, and (g_1, a_2) under semantics M_3. Null value is interpreted below as a set of all possible values for a given attribute. Also, x has the same meaning as the pair $(x, 1)$.

Semantics M_1 (see [Ras and Joshi][7]) is defined as:

- $M_1(v) = \{(x, k) : v \in a(x)$ & $k = card(a(x))\}$ if $v \in V_a$,
- $M_1(t_1 * t_2) = M_1(t_1) \otimes M_1(t_2)$, $M_1(t_1 + t_2) = M_1(t_1) \oplus M_1(t_2)$.

To define $\otimes$, $\oplus$, let us assume that $P_i = \{(x, p_{<x,i>}) : p_{<x,i>} \in [0, 1]$ & $x \in X\}$ where X is a set of objects. Then, we have:

- $P_i \otimes P_j = \{(x, p_{<x,i>} \cdot p_{<x,j>}): x \in X\}$,
- $P_i \oplus P_j = \{(x, max(p_{<x,i>}, p_{<x,j>})): x \in X\}$.

Semantics M_2 is defined as:

- $M_2(v) = \{x : v \in a(x) \ \& \ card(a(x)) = 1\}$ if $v \in V_a$,
- $M_2(t_1 * t_2) = M_2(t_1) \cap M_2(t_2)$, $M_2(t_1 + t_2) = M_2(t_1) \cup M_2(t_2)$.

Finally, semantics M_3 is defined as:

- $M_3(v) = \{x : v \in a(x)\}$ if $v \in V_a$,
- $M_3(t_1 * t_2) = M_3(t_1) \cap M_3(t_2)$, $M_3(t_1 + t_2) = M_3(t_1) \cup M_3(t_2)$.

Assume now, the following relationship between semantics M_i and M_j:
$M_i \preceq M_j$ iff $[\ (x, k) \in M_i(a) \longrightarrow (\exists k_1 \geq k)[(x, k_1) \in M_j(a)] \ ]$.
It can be easily proved that $\preceq$ is a partial order relation.
In our example, for any $v \in V_a$, we have: $M_2(v) \preceq M_1(v) \preceq M_3(v)$.
We say that functors $+$ and $*$ preserve monotonicity property for semantics
N_1, N_2 if the following two conditions hold:

- $[N_1(t_1) \preceq N_2(t_1) \ \& \ N_1(t_2) \preceq N_2(t_2)]$ implies $N_1(t_1 + t_2) \preceq N_2(t_1 + t_2)$,
- $[N_1(t_1) \preceq N_2(t_1) \ \& \ N_1(t_2) \preceq N_2(t_2)]$ implies $N_1(t_1 * t_2) \preceq N_2(t_1 * t_2)$.

Let $(\Omega, \preceq)$ be a partially ordered set of semantics. We say that it preserves
monotonicity property for $+$ and $*$, if $+$ and $*$ preserve monotonicity property
for any N_1, N_2 in Ω. It can be easily checked that $(\{M_1, M_2, M_3\}, \preceq)$ preserves
monotonicity property for $+$ and $*$.

We adopt the definition of ontology proposed by Mizoguchi [2]. He claims that
ontology should consist of *task* ontology which characterizes the computational
architecture of a (distributed) knowledge system which performs a task and
domain ontology which characterizes the domain knowledge where the task is
performed.

In the scenario presented in our paper, a number of remote sites for a given
client site has to be accessed. The same terms, used in knowledge extraction
or local query processing, can have different interpretations at each of these
sites. In a query transformation process, many subterms forming any of these
intermidiate queries may come from definitions extracted not necessarily from
the same site of DKS. Clearly, in this situation our query can not be processed
unless a common, possibly optimal, semantics for all these subterms is found.

We claim that one way to solve this problem is to assume that partially
ordered set of semantics $(\Omega, \preceq)$, preserving monotonicity property for $+$ and $*$,
is a part of global ontology (or task ontology in Mizoguchi's [2] definition).

In our example, we evaluate query q taking first M_2 and next M_3 as two
common semantics for all subterms obtained during the transformation process
of q because $M_2(v) \preceq M_1(v) \preceq M_3(v)$. In general, if $(\Omega, \preceq)$ is a lattice and
$\{M_i\}_{i \in I}$ is a set of semantics involved in transforming query q, then we should
take $M_{min} = \bigcap\{M_i\}_{i \in I}$ (the greatest lower bound) and $M_{max} = \bigcup\{M_i\}_{i \in I}$ (the
least upper bound) as two common semantics for processing query q.

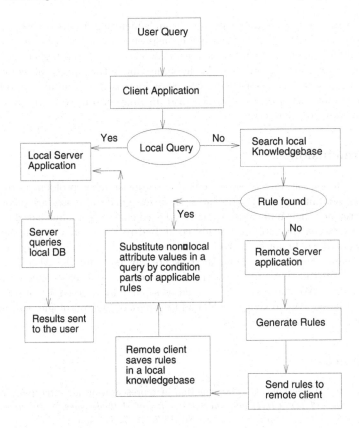

Fig. 2. Query and Rough Query Processing by DKS

Common semantics is also needed because of the necessity to prove soundness and possibly completeness of axioms to be used in a query tranformation process.

Figure 2 gives a flowchart of a query transformation process in QAS assuming that local query semantics at all contacted sites is the same and DKS is consistent (granularity levels of the same attributes at remote sistes and the client site are the same). This flowchart will be replaced by two similar flowcharts (corresponding to M_{min} and M_{max}) if semantics at contacted remote sites and a client site differ. Semantics M_{min} and M_{max} can be seen jointly as a rough semantics.

The word *rough* is used here in the sense of rough sets theory (see [Pawlak][3]). Saying another words, the semantics used during query transformation process can be seen only as one which is between two semantics M_{min} and M_{max}.

If we increase the number of sites from which definitions of non-local attributes are collected and then resolve inconsistencies among them (see [Ras][4]), the local confidence in resulting definitions is expected to be higher since they represent consensus of more sites. At the same time, if the number of remote sites involved in a query transformation process is increased, the number of different semantics may increase as well which in result may also increase the roughness of the answer to the query.

4   Conclusion

Clearly, the easiest way to solve semantic inconsistencies problem is to apply the same semantics at all remote sites. However when databases are incomplete and we replace their null values using rule-based chase algorithms based on rules locally extracted then we are already commited to the semantics used by these algorithms. If we do not keep track what and how null values have been replaced by rule-based chase algorithms, there is no way back for us. Also, it sounds rather unrealistic that one semantics for incomplete databases can be chosen as a standard. We claim that in such cases a partially ordered set of semantics $(\Omega, \preceq)$ or its equivalent structure should be a part of *task* ontologies to solve the problem.

References

1. Maluf, D., Wiederhold, G., "Abstraction of representation for interoperation", in *Proceedings of Tenth International Symposium on Methodologies for Intelligent Systems*, LNCS/LNAI, Springer-Verlag, No. 1325, 1997, 441-455
2. Mizoguchi, R., "Ontological engineering: foundation of the next generation knowledge processing", in *Proceedings of Web Intelligence: Research and Development*, LNCS/LNAI, Springer-Verlag, No. 2198, 2001, 44-57
3. Pawlak, Z., "Rough classification", in *International Journal of Man-Machine Studies*, Vol. 20, 1984, 469-483
4. Ras, Z., "Dictionaries in a distributed knowledge-based system", in *Concurrent Engineering: Research and Applications, Conference Proceedings*, Pittsburgh, Penn., Concurrent Technologies Corporation, 1994, 383-390
5. Ras, Z., "Resolving queries through cooperation in multi-agent systems", in *Rough Sets and Data Mining* (Eds. T.Y. Lin, N. Cercone), Kluwer Academic Publishers, 1997, 239-258
6. Ras, Z., "Query answering based on distributed knowledge mining", in *Intelligent Agent Technology, Research and Development*, Proceedings of IAT'01 (Eds. N. Zhong, J. Lin, S. Ohsuga, J. Bradshaw), World Scientific, 2001, 17-27
7. Ras, Z., Joshi, S.,"Query approximate answering system for an incomplete DKBS", in *Fundamenta Informaticae*, IOS Press, Vol. 30, No. 3/4, 1997, 313-324

Structured Ontology and Information Retrieval for Email Search and Discovery

Peter Eklund and Richard Cole

School of Information Technology and Electrical Engineering
The University of Queensland
St. Lucia, QLD 4072
`peklund@itee.uq.edu.au, rcole@itee.uq.edu.au`

Abstract. This paper discusses an document discovery tool based on formal concept analysis. The program allows users to navigate email using a visual lattice metaphor rather than a tree. It implements a virtual file structure over email where files and entire directories can appear in multiple positions. The content and shape of the lattice formed by the conceptual ontology can assist in email discovery. The system described provides more flexibility in retrieving stored emails than what is normally available in email clients. The paper discusses how conceptual ontologies can leverage traditional document retrieval systems.

1 Introduction

Client-side email management systems are document management systems that store email as a tree structure in analog to the physical directory/file structure. This has the advantage that trees are simply explained as a direct mapping from the structure of the file system to the email. The disadvantage is that at the moment of storing an email the user must anticipate the way she will later retrieve the email. How then should email be organized? Should we store it as a specialization or a generalization hierarchy? Are we trying to give every email a unique key based on its content or cluster emails broadly on their content?

This problem generalizes to other document types, organization is both context and query dependent (after the fact). One such organization of an *associative store* is a virtual file structure that maps the physical file structure to a view based on content. Information retrieval gives us the ability to index every meaningful word in a text by generating an the inverted file index. The index can then be reduced by stemming, compression and frequency analysis. These scalable techniques from information retrieval can be extended by re-using conceptual ontologies as a virtual file structure.

In this paper, we profile *HierMail*[1] (previously referred to in various stages as CEM, ECA or WARP9) that follows from earlier work in medical document retrieval reported in [3]. HIERMAIL is a lattice-based email retrieval and storage program that aids in knowledge discovery by a conceptual and virtual view over

---

[1] see *http://www.hiermail.com*

M.-S. Hacid et al. (Eds.): ISMIS 2002, LNAI 2366, pp. 75–84, 2002.

email. It uses a conceptual ontology as a data structure for storing emails rather than a tree. In turn, formal concept analysis can be used to generate a concept lattice of the file structure. This permits clients to retrieve emails along different paths and discover interesting associations between email content.

In HIERMAIL, email retrieval is independent of the physical organization of the file system. This idea is not new, for instance, the concept of a *virtual folder* was introduced in a program called VIEW MAIL (VM)[5]. A virtual folder is a collection of email documents retrieved in response to a query. The virtual folder concept has more recently been popularized by a number of open-source projects[2]. Other commercial discovery tools for email are also available, see *http://80-20.com* for example. HIERMAIL differs from those systems in the understanding of the underlying structure – via formal concept analysis – as well as in the details of implementation. It therefore extends the virtual file system idea into document discovery.

Concept lattices are defined in the mathematical theory of *Formal Concept Analysis* [4]. A concept lattice is derived from a binary relation which assigns attributes to objects. In our application, the objects are all emails stored by the system, and the attributes *classifiers* like 'conferences', 'administration' or 'teaching'. We call the string matching regular expressions *classifiers* since HIERMAIL is designed to accommodate any form of pattern matching algorithm against text, images or multimedia content. The idea of automatically learning classifiers from documents has been the focus of the machine learning and text classification communities[1] but is not specifically considered in this treatment.

2   Background

Formal Concept Analysis (FCA) [4] is a long standing data analysis technique. Two software tools, TOSCANA [7] and ANACONDA embody a methodology for data-analysis based on FCA. A Java-based open-source variant of these programs, called TOSCANAJ, has also been developed[3]. Following the FCA methodology, data is organized as a table in a RDBMS and modeled mathematically as a multi-valued context, (G, M, W, I) where G is a set of objects, M is a set of attributes, W is a set of attribute values and I is a relation between G, M, and W such that if (g, m, w_1) and (g, m, w_2) then $w_1 = w_2$. In the RDBMS there is one row for each object, one column for each attribute, and each cell can contain an attribute value. Organization over the data is achieved via conceptual scales that map attribute values to new attributes and are represented by a mathematical entity called a *formal context*.

A *conceptual scale* is defined for a particular attribute of the multi-valued context: if $\mathbb{S}_m = (G_m, M_m, I_m)$ is a conceptual scale of $m \in M$ then we require $W_m \subseteq G_m$. The conceptual scale can be used to produce a summary of data in the multi-valued context as a *derived context*. The context derived by $\mathbb{S}_m = (G_m, M_m, I_m)$ w.r.t. to plain scaling from data stored in the multi-valued context

---

[2] see *http://gmail.linuxpower.org/*
[3] see *http://toscanaj.sourceforge.net*

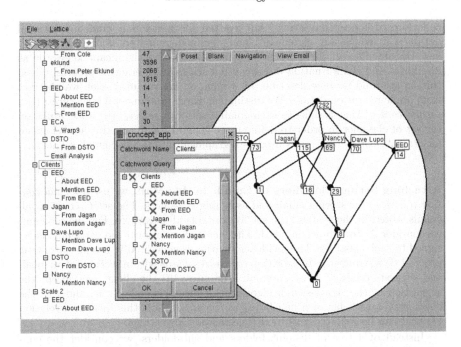

Fig. 1. Scale, classifier and concept lattice. The central dialogue box shows how the scale function (α) can be edited.

(G, M, W, I) is the context (G, M_m, J_m) where for $g \in G$ and $n \in M_m$

$$g J_m n \Leftrightarrow: \exists w \in W : (g, m, w) \in I \quad \text{and} \quad (w, n) \in I_m$$

Scales for two or more attributes can be combined together into a derived context. Consider a set of scales, S_m, where each $m \in M$ gives rise to a different scale. The new attributes supplied by each scale can be combined using a union:

$$N := \bigcup_{m \in M} \{m\} \times M_m$$

Then the formal context derived from combining these scales is (G, N, J) with $g J(m, n) \Leftrightarrow: \exists w \in W : (g, m, w) \in I$ and $(w, n) \in I_m$. The derived context is then displayed to the user as a lattice of concepts (see Fig. 1 (right)).

In practice, it is easier to define a conceptual scale by attaching expressions to objects rather than attribute values. The expressions denote a range of attribute values all having the same scale attributes. To represent these expressions in conceptual scaling we introduce a function called the *composition operator* for attribute m, $\alpha_m : W_m \to G_m$ where $W_m = \{w \in W \mid \exists g \in G : (g, m, w) \in I\}$. This maps attribute values to scale objects. The derived scale then becomes (G, N, J) with: $g J(m, n) \Leftrightarrow: \exists w \in W : (g, m, w) \in I$ and $(\alpha_m(w), n) \in I_m$.

The purpose of this summary is to reinforce that in practice FCA works with structured object-attribute data in RDBMS form, in conjunction with a collection of conceptual scales. An inverted file index is a kind of relational database in which any significant, non-stemmed, non-stop word is a primary key. Documents can therefore be seen as objects and significant keywords as attributes and the formation of conceptual scales an interactive process. Given this background we now describe the system on a structural level: we abstract from implementation details. We distinguish three fundamental structures: (i) a *formal context* that assigns to each email a set of classifiers; (ii) a *hierarchy* on the set of classifier in order to define more general classifiers; (iii) a mechanism for creating *conceptual scales* used as a graphical interface for email retrieval.

Attaching String Classifiers to Email. In HIERMAIL, we use a *formal context* (G, M, I) for storing email and assigning classifiers. The set G contains all emails stored in the system, the set M contains all classifiers. For the moment, we consider M to be unstructured. The incidence relation I indicates emails assigned to each classifier. The incidence relation is generated in a semi-automatic process: (i) a string-search algorithm recognizes words within sections of an email and suggests relations between email attributes; (ii) the client may accept the suggestion of the string-search algorithm or otherwise modify it; and (iii) the client may attach his own attributes to the email. It is this incidence relation (I) that can be replaced with text classification algorithms.

Instead of a tree of disjoint folders and sub-folders, we consider the concept lattice $\mathfrak{B}(G, M, I)$ as the navigation space. The formal concepts replace the folders. In particular, this means that the same emails may appear in different concepts and therefore in different folders. The most general concept contains all email in the collection and the deeper the user moves into the multiple inheritance hierarchy, the more specific the concepts, and subsequently the fewer emails they contain.

Organizing Hierarchies of String Classifiers. To support the semi-automatic assignment of classifiers to email, we provide the set M of classifiers with a partial order $\leq$. For this *subsumption hierarchy*, we assume that the following *compatibility condition* holds: $\forall g \in G$, $m, n \in M$: $(g, m) \in I$, $m \leq n \Rightarrow (g, n) \in I$ (‡), i.e., the assignment of classifiers respects the transitivity of the partial order. Hence, when assigning classifiers to emails, it is sufficient to assign the most specific classifiers only. More general classifiers are automatically added. For instance, the user may want to say that *ismis* is a more specific classifier than *conferences*, and that *ismis2002* is more specific than *ismis* (i.e., *ismis2002* $\leq$ *ismis* $\leq$ *conferences*). Emails concerning the creation of a paper for the ismis'02 conference are assigned by the email client to the *ismis2002* label only (and possibly also to additional classifiers like *cole* and *eklund*). When the client wants to retrieve this email, she is not required to recall the complete pathname. Instead, the emails also appear under the more general label *conferences*. If *conferences* provides too large a list of email, the client can refine the search by choosing a sub-term like *ismis*, or adding a new classifier, for instance *cole*.

Navigating Email. *Conceptual scaling* deals with many-valued attributes. Often attributes are not one-valued as the string classifiers given above, but allow a range of values. This is modeled by a *many-valued context*. A many-valued context is roughly equivalent to a relation in a relational database with one field being a primary key. As one-valued contexts are special cases of many-valued contexts, conceptual scaling can also be applied to one-valued contexts to reduce the complexity of the visualization. In this paper, we only deal with one-valued formal contexts. Readers interested in the exact definition of many-valued contexts are referred to Ganter & Wille [4]. Applied to one-valued contexts, conceptual scales are used to determine the concept lattice that arises from one vertical slice of a large context: a conceptual scale for a subset $B \subseteq M$ of attributes is a (one-valued) formal context $\mathbb{S}_B := (G_B, B, \ni)$ with $G_B \subseteq \mathfrak{P}(B)$. The scale is called consistent w.r.t. $\mathbb{K} := (G, M, I)$ if $\{g\}' \cap B \in G_B$ for each $g \in G$. For a consistent scale $\mathbb{S}_B$, the context $\mathbb{S}_B(\mathbb{K}) := (G, B, I \cap (G \times B))$ is called its *realized scale*.

Conceptual scales are used to group together related attributes. They are determined as required by the user, and the realized scales derived from them when a diagram is requested by the user. HIERMAIL stores all scales that the client has defined in previous sessions. To each scale, the client can assign a unique name. This is modeled by a function ($\mathcal{S}$). Let $\mathcal{S}$ be a set, whose elements are called *scale names*. The mapping $\alpha \colon \mathcal{S} \to \mathfrak{P}(\mathcal{M})$ defines for each scale name $s \in \mathcal{S}$ a scale $\mathbb{S}_s := \mathbb{S}_{\alpha(s)}$. For instance, the user may introduce a new scale which classifies emails according to being related to a conference by adding a new element 'Conferences' to $\mathcal{S}$ and by defining $\alpha(\text{Conference}) := \{\text{ISMIS02, K-CAP '01, ADCS '01, PKDD 2000}\}$.

Observe that $\mathcal{S}$ and M need not be disjoint. This allows the following construction, deducing conceptual scales directly from the subsumption hierarchy: Let $\mathcal{S} := \{m \in M | \exists n \in M \colon n < m\}$, and define, for $s \in \mathcal{S}$, $\alpha(s) := \{m \in M | m \prec s\}$ (with $x \prec y$ if and only if $x < y$ and there is no z s.t. $x < z < y$). This means all classifiers $m \in M$, neither minimal nor maximal in the hierarchy, are considered as the name of scale $\mathbb{S}_m$ and as a classifier of another scale $\mathbb{S}_n$ (where $m \prec n$). This last construction defines a hierarchy of conceptual scales [6].

3   Requirements of HIERMAIL

Requirements are divided along the same lines as the underlying algebraic structures given previously: (i) assist the user in editing and browsing a classifier hierarchy; (ii) help the client visualize and modify the scale function α; (iii) allow the client to manage the assignment of classifiers to emails; (iv) assist the client search the conceptual space of emails for both individual and conceptual groupings of emails. In addition to the requirements stated above, a good email client needs to be able send, receive and display emails: processing the various email formats and interact with popular protocols. Since these requirements are already well understood and implemented by existing email programs they are not discussed further. This does not mean they are not important, rather implicit in the realization of HIERMAIL.

Modifying a String Classifier. The classifier hierarchy is a partially ordered set $(M, \leq)$ where each element of M is a classifier. The requirements for editing and browsing the classifier hierarchy are: (i) to graphically display the structure of the $(M, \leq)$. The ordering relation must be evident; (ii) to make accessible a series of direct manipulations to alter the order relation.

The Scale Function α. The user must be able to visualize the scale function, α. The program must allow an overlap between the set of scale labels S, and the set of classifiers M, this is shown is Fig. 1.

Managing Classifier Assignment. The formal context associates email with classifiers via the incidence relation I. Also introduced earlier was the notion of the *compatibility condition*,($\ddagger$). The program should store the formal context (G, M, I) and ensure that the compatibility condition is always satisfied. It is inevitable that the program will have to modify the formal context in order to satisfy the compatibility condition after a change is made to the classifier hierarchy. The program must support two mechanisms associating classifiers to emails. Firstly, a mechanism in which emails are automatically associated with classifiers based on the email content. Secondly, the user the should be able to view and modify email classifiers.

The Conceptual Space. The program must allow the navigation of the conceptual space of the emails by drawing line diagrams of concept lattices derived from conceptual scales [4] as shown in Fig. 1. These line diagrams should extend to locally scaled nested-line diagrams shown in Fig. 2. The program must allow retrieval and display of emails forming the extension of concepts displayed in the line diagrams.

4   Implementation of HierMail

This section divides the description of the implementation of the HierMail into a similar structure to that presented earlier.

Browsing the Hierarchy. The user is presented with a view of the hierarchy $(M, \leq)$ as a tree widget shown in Fig. 1 (left). The tree widget has the advantage that most users are familiar with its behavior and it provides a compact representation of a tree structure. The classifier hierarchy, being a partially ordered set, is a more general structure than a tree. The following is a definition of a tree derived from the classifier hierarchy for the purpose of defining the contents and structure of the tree widget. Let $(M, \leq)$ be a partially ordered set and denote the set of all sequences of elements from M by $< M >$. Then the tree derived from the classifier hierarchy is comprised of $(T, parent, label)$, where $T \subseteq < M >$ is a set of tree nodes, $<>$ (the empty sequence) is the root of the

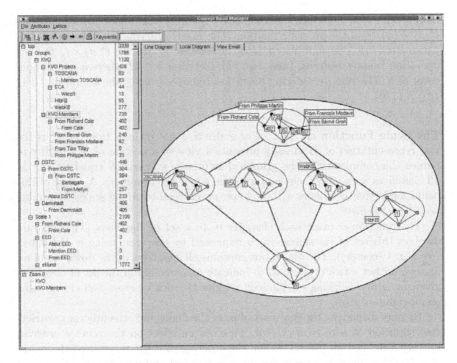

Fig. 2. Scales and the nested-line diagram.

tree, parent : $T/<>\rightarrow T$ is a function giving the parent node of each node (except the root node), and label : $T \rightarrow M$ assigns a classifier to each tree node.
$$T = \{< m_1, \ldots, m_n >\in< M > \mid m_i \preceq m_{i+1} \text{ and } m_n \in \text{top}(M)\}$$

$$\text{parent}(< m_1, \ldots, m_n >) := < m_1, \ldots, m_{n-1} >$$
$$\text{parent}(< m_1 >) \qquad := <>$$
$$\text{label}(< m_1, \ldots, m_n >) \quad := m_1$$

Each tree node is identified by a path from a classifier to the top of the classifier hierarchy.

Modifying the Hierarchy $((M, \leq))$. The program provides four operations for modifying the hierarchy: the insert & remove classifier and the insert & remove ordering. More complex operations provided to the client, moving an item in the hierarchy, are resolved to a sequence of these basic operations. In this section we denote the order filter of m as $\uparrow m := \{x \in M \mid m \leq x\}$, the order ideal of m as $\downarrow m := \{x \in M \mid x \leq m\}$, and the upper cover of m as $\succ_m := \{x \in M \mid x \succ m\}$.

The operation of *inserting a classifier* simply adds a new classifier to M and leaves the $\leq$ relation unchanged. The *remove classifier* operation takes a single parameter $a \in M$ for which the lower cover is empty, and removes a from M and $(\uparrow a) \times \{a\}$ from the ordering relation. The *insert ordering* operation takes two parameters $a, b \in M$ and inserts into the relation $\leq$, the set $(\uparrow a) \times (\downarrow b)$. The operation *remove ordering* takes two parameters $a, b \in M$ where a is an upper cover of b. The remove ordering operation removes from $\leq$ the set $((\uparrow a/ \uparrow (\succ_b /a)) \times (\downarrow b))$.

The Scale Function α. The set of scales S is not disjoint from M, thus the tree representation of M already presents a view of a portion of S. In order to reduce the complexity of the graphical interface, we make S equal to M, i.e. all classifiers are scale labels, and all scale labels are classifiers. A result of this definition is that classifiers with no lower covers lead to trivial scales containing no other classifiers.

The function α maps each classifier m to a set of classifiers. The program displays this set of classifiers, when requested by the user, using a dialog box (see Fig. 1 (center)). The dialog box contains all classifiers in the down-set of m, an icon (either a tick or a cross) to indicate membership in the set of classifiers given by $\alpha(m)$. Clicking on the icon toggles the tick or cross and changes the membership of $\alpha(m)$.

By only displaying the down-set of m in the dialog box, the program restricts the definition of α to $\alpha(m) \subseteq \downarrow m$. This has an effect on the *remove ordering* operation defined on $(M, \leq)$. When the ordering of $a \leq b$ is removed the image of α function for attributes in $\uparrow a$ must be checked and possibly modified.

Associating Emails to Classifiers. Each member of $(M, \leq)$ is associated with a query term: in this application is a set of *section/word pairs*. That is: Let H be the set of sections found in the email documents, W the set of words found in email documents, then a function $\texttt{query}: M \to \mathfrak{P}(H \times W)$ attaches to each attribute a set of section/word pairs.

Let G be a set of emails. An inverted file index stores a relation $R_1 \subseteq G \times (H \times W)$ between documents and section/word pairs. $(g, (h, w)) \in R_1$ indicates that document g has word w in section h. A relation $R_2 \subseteq G \times M$ is derived from the relation R_1 and the function query via: $(g, m) \in R_2$ iff $(g, (h, w)) \in R_1$ for some $(h, w) \in \text{query}(m)$. A relation R_3 stores user judgments saying that an email should have an attribute m. A relation R_4 respecting the compatibility condition ($\ddagger$) is then derived from the relations R_2 and R_3 via: $(g, m) \in R_4$ iff there exists $m_1 \leq m$ with $(g, m_1) \in R_2 \cup R_3$.

Compatibility Condition. Inserting the ordering $b \leq a$ into $\leq$ requires the insertion of set $(\uparrow a/ \uparrow b) \times \{g \in G \mid (g, b) \in R_4\}$ into R_4. Such an insertion into an inverted file index is $O(nm)$ where n is the average number of entries in the inverted index in the shaded region, and m is the number of elements in the shaded region. The real complexity of this operation is best determined via experimentation with a large document sets and a large user defined hierarchy [2].

Similarly the removal of the ordering $b \leq a$ from $\leq$ will require a re-computation of the inverted file entries for elements in $\uparrow a$.

New Email and User Judgments. When new emails arrive, G_b, are presented to HIERMAIL, the relation R_1 is updated by inserting new pairs, R_{1b}, into the relation. The modification of R_1 into $R_1 \cup R_{1b}$ causes an insertion of pairs R_{2b} into R_2 according to query(m) and then subsequently an insertion of new pairs R_{4b} into R_4. $R_{1b} \subseteq G_b \times (H \times W)$ $R_{2b} = \{(g,m) \mid \exists\, (h,w) \in$ query(m) and $(g,(h,w)) \in R_{1b}\}$, $R_{4b} = \{(g,m) \mid \exists\, m_1 \leq m \text{ with } (g,m_1) \in R_{2b}\}$.

For new emails presented to the system for automated indexing the modification to the inverted file index inserts new entries which is a very efficient operation. Each pair inserted is $O(1)$. When the user makes a judgment that an indexed email should be associated with an attribute m, then an update must be made to R_3, which will in turn cause updates to all attributes in the order filter of m to be updated in R_4. The expense of such an update depends on the implementation of the inverted file index and could be as bad as $O(n)$ where n is the average number of documents per attribute. In the case that a client retracts a judgment, saying that an email is no longer associated with an attribute m, requires a possible update to each attribute, n, in the order filter of m.

Conceptual Space Navigation. When the user requests that the concept lattice derived from the scale with name $s \in S$ be drawn, the program computes $\mathbb{S}_{\alpha(S)}$ via the algorithm reported in Cole and Eklund[2]. In the case that the user requests a diagram combining two scales with names labels s and t, then the scale $\mathbb{S}_{B \cup C}$ with $B = \alpha(s)$ and $C = \alpha(t)$ is calculated by the program and its concept lattice $\underline{\mathfrak{B}}(\mathbb{S}_{B \cup C})$ is drawn as a projection into the lattice product $\underline{\mathfrak{B}}(\mathbb{S}_B) \times \underline{\mathfrak{B}}(\mathbb{S}_C)$.

5   Conclusion

This paper provides a description of the algebraic structures used to create a lattice-based view of email. The structure, its implementation and operation, aid the process of knowledge discovery in large collections of email. By using such a conceptual multi-hierarchy, the content and shape of the lattice view is varied. An efficient implementation of the index promotes client iteration. The work shows that the principles of formal concept analysis can be supported by an inverted file index and that a useful and scalable document browsing system results. The program we have realized, HIERMAIL, is available from *http://hiermail.com*.

References

1. J. Brutlag and J. Meek: Challenges of the Email Domain for Text Classification, in *Proceedings of the 17th International Conference on Machine Learning* ICML00, p.103-110, 2000.

2. R. Cole, P. Eklund: Scalability in Formal Concept Analysis: A Case Study using Medical Texts. *Computational Intelligence*, Vol. 15, No. 1, pp. 11-27, 1999.
3. R. Cole, P. Eklund: Analyzing Email using Formal Concept Analysis. *Proc. of the European Conf. on Knowledge and Data Discovery*, pp. 309-315, LNAI 1704, Springer-Verlag, Prague, 1999.
4. B. Ganter, R. Wille: *Formal Concept Analysis: Mathematical Foundations*. Springer-Verlag, Heidelberg 1999.
5. K. Jones: View Mail Users Manual. *http://www.wonderworks.com/vm*. 1999
6. G. Stumme: Hierarchies of Conceptual Scales. *Proc. Workshop on Knowledge Acquisition, Modeling and Management*. Banff, 16.–22. October 1999
7. Vogt, F. and R. Wille, TOSCANA: A Graphical Tool for Analyzing and Exploring Data In: R. Tamassia, I.G. Tollis (Eds) *Graph Drawing '94*, LNCS 894 pp. 226-233, 1995.

Conceptual Clustering of Heterogeneous Sequences via Schema Mapping

Sally McClean, Bryan Scotney, and Fiona Palmer

School of Information and Software Engineering,
University of Ulster, Coleraine BT52 1SA, Northern Ireland
{SI.McClean, BW.Scotney, F.Palmer}@ulst.ac.uk

Abstract. We are concerned with clustering sequences that have been classified according to heterogeneous schema. We adopt a model-based approach that uses a Hidden Markov model (HMM) that has as states the stages of the underlying process that generates the sequences, thus allowing us to handle complex and heterogeneous data. Each cluster is described in terms of a HMM where we seek to find schema mappings between the states of the original sequences and the states of the HMM. The general solution that we propose involves several distinct tasks. Firstly, there is a clustering problem where we seek to group similar sequences; for this we use mutual entropy to identify associations between sequence states. Secondly, because we are concerned with clustering heterogeneous sequences, we must determine the mappings between the states of each sequence in a cluster and the states of an underlying hidden process; for this we compute the most probable mapping. Thirdly, on the basis of these mappings we use maximum likelihood techniques to learn the probabilistic description of the hidden Markov process for each cluster. Finally, we use these descriptions to characterise the clusters by using Dynamic Programming to determine the most probable pathway for each cluster. Such an approach provides an intuitive way of describing the underlying shape of the process by explicitly modelling the temporal aspects of the data; non time-homogeneous HMMs are also considered. The approach is illustrated using gene expression sequences.

1. Background

The model which we adopt, in common with [1], is a Hidden Markov Model (HMM) which has as states the stages of the underlying process. Each cluster is described in terms of a HMM, and we seek to find schema mappings between the states of the original sequences (the data) and the states of the HMM (the model). The states of the HMM here represent stages in the underlying process concept. The general solution that we propose involves several distinct tasks. Firstly there is a clustering problem where we seek to group similar sequences on the basis of similar temporal patterns; for this we use mutual entropy to identify associations between the states of different sequences. Secondly, because we are concerned with clustering heterogeneous sequences, we must determine the mappings between the states of each sequence in a cluster and the states of an underlying hidden process; for this we compute the most probable mapping. Thirdly, on the basis of these mappings we use maximum

M.-S. Hacid et al. (Eds.): ISMIS 2002, LNAI 2366, pp. 85-93, 2002.

likelihood techniques to learn the probabilistic description of the hidden Markov process for each cluster. Finally, we use these descriptions to characterise the clusters by using Dynamic Programming to determine the most probable pathway for each cluster. Such an approach has a number of advantages:

- it provides an intuitive way of describing the underlying shape of the process, in terms of stages, by explicitly modelling the temporal aspects of the data; such segmental models have considerable potential for sequence data, e.g. [2];
- it provides a way of matching heterogeneous sequences via the hidden process model;
- it allows us to take account of natural variability in the process, via probabilistic semantics inherent in the model;
- it allows us to characterise the clusters in terms of a hidden underlying process concept; this concept may then be matched with known processes in the data environment.

We build on our previous work on integration [3, 4, 5] and clustering [6] of multinomial data that are heterogeneous with respect to schema, by extending our approach to the integration and clustering of heterogeneous Markov chains. A similar method is described in [1, 7], but for data that are homogeneous in this regard. In our previous papers we have assumed that the schema mappings are made available by the data providers. In this paper the novelty resides mainly in the fact that we must now learn the schema mappings as well as the cluster memberships and profiles. Our use of non time-homogeneous HMMs in this context is also novel; they allow us to better describe the temporal semantics of a dynamic process evolving in a stochastic environment. Such schema mapping problems are becoming increasingly important with more databases becoming available on the Internet and accompanying opportunities for knowledge discovery from open data sources.

2. The Problem

We are concerned with a conceptual clustering problem where we require to cluster heterogeneous sequences of symbolic data. The sequences are heterogeneous in the sense that they represent either different attributes, or the same attributes held at possibly different granularities. However, the sequences have in common the fact that they are related to a common underlying hidden concept which determines the temporal patterns of related sequences. We conceptualise the underlying concept via a hidden Markov model (HMM). We note that the sequences may also be heterogeneous in terms of length. In Table 1 we present four such sequences, where {Sequence 1, Sequence 2} and {Sequence 3, Sequence 4} form two separate clusters when we perform the mappings presented in Table 2. The data presented are gene expression sequences adapted from [8].

The sequences (U, U/V, W, W, W, W, W, W, W) and (X, X, X, Y, Y, Y, Y, Z, Z) therefore characterise the behaviour of the HMMs for the latent variable underpinning clusters 1 and 2 respectively. Here U/V means that this term may be either U or V. Although, in some circumstances, such schema mappings may be known to the domain expert, typically they are unknown and must be discovered by the algorithm.

Table 1. Gene expression data

Sequence 1	A	A	B	B	B	B	B	B	B
Sequence 2	C	D	E	E	E	E	E	E	E
Sequence 3	F	F	F	G	G	G	G	H	H
Sequence 4	I	I	I	K	K	K	K	J	J

Table 2. Schema mappings for Table 1

A	U
B	W

C	U
D	V
E	W

F	X
G	Y
H	Z

I	X
K	Y
J	Z

Definition 2.1: We define a sequence $S = \{s_1,...,s_L\}$, where L is the (variable) length of the sequence and s_i, i=1,...,L, are members of a set A comprising the letters of a finite alphabet. In what follows we refer to such letters as the states of the sequence.

We define a *correspondence graph* for a set of sequences to be a multipartite graph $G = (X_1 \cup X_2 \cup ... \cup X_n \cup Y, E)$; X_i is the set of nodes corresponding to the classification scheme of the ith sequence; Y is the set of nodes corresponding to the classification scheme of the underlying hidden variable; E is the set of edges which join the nodes in X_i to the nodes in Y. We may regard each sub-graph $G = (X_i \cup Y, E)$ to be bipartite for i = 1, ..., n. Thus each node in Y which represents a value contained in X_i provides an edge. Essentially the graph describes the schema mappings between the sequence and hidden variable ontologies. The correspondence graph for cluster 1 (sequences 1 and 2) of Table 2 is presented in Figure 1, and the associated correspondence table is shown in Table 3; the symbolic values in each sequence are numbered alphabetically.

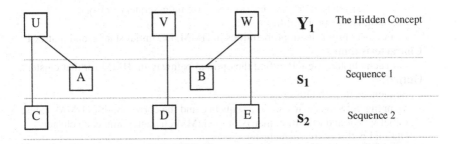

Fig. 1. The correspondence graph for cluster 1 in Table 1

The correspondence graph can be stored using a correspondence table; it is this which we must learn to determine the mappings between heterogeneous sequences.

Table 3. The correspondence table for cluster 1 in Table 1

Hidden Concept 1	Sequence 1	Sequence 2
1	1	1
2	-	2
3	2	3

3. Clustering Heterogeneous Sequence Data

3.1 The General Process

While, in general terms, the tasks in our process may be carried out in an integrated manner, or with feedback between tasks, we have decided, for the sake of simplicity as an initial strategy, to approach these tasks independently. It is important to realise that, in any case, there are two distinct sub-problems. The first sub-problem involves a re-labelling (mapping) of the respective sequence alphabets; in the first task clustering recognises where re-labelling is appropriate, while the second task learns the optimal labelling. The second sub-problem involves learning a HMM based on the mapped sequences, which are now homogeneous (the third task), and using this HMM to characterise the clusters (the final task).

Input:
  A set of heterogeneous sequences S^r for r=1,...,k
Clustering
  Learn clusters (using Mutual Entropy)
Mapping:
  For each cluster:
  For each sequence in that cluster:
        Learn transformations (to minimise inter-sequence error)
  Learning HMM probabilities:
    For each cluster: learn probabilities in HMM, i.e. initial state s_0 and matrix **P**
Characterisation
  For each cluster: use DP to find the optimal pathway in HMM for that cluster
Output:
  Sequences in each cluster;
  Mapping between each state in a sequence and the corresponding HMM states;
  Initial vector and transition matrix of the HMM characterising each cluster;
  Optimal pathway for each cluster.

Fig. 2. Clustering heterogeneous sequences

Mutual entropy identifies where the symbols in the respective (sequence) alphabets co-occur. Finding these schema mappings involves searching over the possible set of mappings. Such a search may be carried out using a heuristic approach, for example, a genetic algorithm, to minimise the divergence between the mapped sequences. In order to restrict the search space we may limit the types of mapping that are permissible, e.g. we may allow only order-preserving mappings; the fitness function may also be penalised to prohibit trivial mappings, e.g. where every symbol in the sequence is mapped onto the same symbol of the HMM. Once we have learned the mappings and the clusters, the next stage is to characterise the sequences in terms of the initial distribution and transition matrix of the HMM; these are learned using maximum likelihood (ML). Finally we characterise the HMMs by finding the optimal pathway; this can be determined using Dynamic Programming. We can therefore define our solution to the problem in terms of the process summarised in Figure 2.

3.2 The Model

3.2.1 Clustering

Clustering may be model-based or distance-based; model-based methods have the advantage of being grounded on well-established principles; they are also better suited to problems involving heterogeneous data [1]. Our approach is intermediate between these two methodologies in that we cluster using a distance metric based on mutual information. A full model-based approach, such as that described in [1], for (in our terminology) homogeneous schema could also be utilised here. The advantage of our strategy is that we decouple clustering from schema learning, thus allowing simpler ad hoc methods to be substituted for either or both of these tasks in the interests of simplicity and computational efficiency.

Definition 3.1: The *distance* between two heterogeneous sequences $\mathbf{S}^1$ and $\mathbf{S}^2$ is defined as the gain in information (mutual information) if we merge the two sequences; i.e. distance = $\mathcal{H}_1 + \mathcal{H}_2 - \mathcal{H}_{12}$ where $\mathcal{H}$ is the entropy, and the subscript denotes the sequence; subscript 12 means sequence 1 and sequence 2 combined.

When testing whether to combine two clusters, we calculate the mutual information for the two clusters separately and then the two clusters combined. If the value of $\mathcal{H}_{12}$ is inside a threshold of $\mathcal{H}_1 + \mathcal{H}_2$, then clusters 1 and 2 are sufficiently close together to be combined. This metric is chosen because it tends to cluster together sequences whose values are associated, i.e. they tend to co-occur. This means that within a cluster we can find a transformation such that mapping associated values onto a common ontology leads to sequences that are similar.

3.2.2 Learning the Mapping

Since the search space for optimal mappings is potentially very large, we propose an ad hoc approach that can be used to initialise a heuristic hill-climbing method such as a genetic algorithm. Our objective is to minimise the distance between sequences and the HMM once the mapping has been carried out. However, since the HMM is a priori unknown, we propose to approximate this function by the distance between mapped sequences. In order to rule out over-simplistic mappings, e.g. where all symbols in a sequence are mapped to the same state of the HMM, we also need to penalise the distance function. Our initialisation method then finds a mapping.

Choose one of the sequences whose number of symbols is maximal ($\mathbf{S}^*$ say); these symbols act as a proxy for the states of the HMM.

For each remaining sequence $\mathbf{S}^i$, calculate prob$\{ s_j^* = r \mid s_j^i = w \} \forall i, r, w$. Here s_j^* is the jth symbol in the alphabet of $\mathbf{S}^i$

The most likely mapping is then from u to r

where prob$\{ s_j^* = r \mid s_j^i = u \} \geq$ prob$\{ s_j^* = w \mid s_j^i = u \} \forall w$.

If we wish to provide a number of solutions, say to form the initial mating pool for a genetic algorithm, we can choose a number of different sequences to act as proxies for the HMM in step 1.

3.2.3 Learning the HMMs

Definition 3.1: We define a *discrete Hidden Markov Model* (HMM) with state space $\mathbf{H}=(h_1,...,h_k)$ and *transition matrix* $\mathbf{P} =\{p_{ij}\}$, where

p_{ij} = Prob {HMM is in state h_j at n+1 | HMM is in state h_i at n} $\forall$ n

are the *transition probabilities*, and $h_i \in \mathbf{A}$, where $\mathbf{A}$ is a finite alphabet.
Here $s_0 = \{s_{0j}\}$ is the *initial state* vector.

We now develop an algorithm for learning the transition matrix of the HMM for a set of heterogeneous sequences, given that the mappings between the respective sequence schema is a priori known. This matrix then characterises the underlying process described by the HMM. Ultimately we want to cluster the sequences, where for each cluster we must learn the schema mappings, i.e. they are a priori unknown, as well as the transition matrix. Thus, our final goal is to determine a clustering of the sequences, where each cluster is characterised by a HMM transition matrix and the elements of each sequence in the cluster can be mapped onto states of the HMM.

Notation 3.1: The data sequences are assumed to be given by $\mathbf{S}^r = \{s_0,... \; s_{L_r} \}$ for $r = 1,...,m$. For sequence $\mathbf{S}^r$ the state space is $\{ v_1^r,..., v_{g_r}^r \}$ for $r = 1,...,m$.

$\mathcal{J}$ is a (schema) mapping from the state spaces of sequences $\mathbf{S}^r$, r=1,...m, to the state space $\mathbf{H}$.

Then, $n_{ij}^r = $ {number of transitions from state s_i of sequence $\mathbf{S}^r$ to state s_j of $\mathbf{S}^r$ }, and

$$\delta_{0j}^r = \begin{cases} 1 & \text{if the initial state of } \mathbf{S}^r \text{ is j} \\ 0 & \text{otherwise} \end{cases}, \text{ and let } q_{ui}^r = \begin{cases} 1 & \text{if } \mathbf{T}(v_u^r) = h_i \\ 0 & \text{otherwise} \end{cases}.$$

We note that the matrix $\mathbf{Q}=\{q_{ij}\}$ is equivalent to the correspondence table defined in the previous section.

Then we want to maximise the log-likelihood of the model given the data and the transformation, which is given by:

$$\mathcal{L} = \sum_{r=1}^{m}\sum_{j=1}^{g_r} n_{0j}^{r}\log(p_{0j}) + \sum_{r=1}^{m}\sum_{u=1}^{g_r}\sum_{v=1}^{g_r} n_{uv}^{r} \log(\sum_{i=1}^{k}\sum_{j=1}^{k}q_{ui}^{r}q_{vj}^{r}p_{ij}) . \tag{1}$$

The solution is then given by the formula:

$$p_{ij} = (\sum_{r=1}^{m}\sum_{u=1}^{g_r}\sum_{v=1}^{g_r} n_{uv}^{r}q_{ui}^{r}q_{vj}^{r})/(\sum_{r=1}^{m}\sum_{u=1}^{g_r}\sum_{v=1}^{g_r} n_{uv}^{r}q_{ui}^{r}) \text{ for } i,j=1,...,m.$$

and $p_{0j} = \sum_{j=1}^{m}\delta_{0j}q_{vj}^{r} / \sum_{j=1}^{m}\delta_{0j}$ for $j=1....m$ \hfill (2)

3.2.4 Characterising the Clusters

Once we have learned the HMM probabilities using equations (1) and (2), the next task is to use these probabilities to characterise the clusters in terms of the optimal pathway for each cluster. We now describe how Dynamic Programming (DP) may be used to compute the optimal pathway for each HMM. This is a special case of a standard technique in the theory of HMM, where such a DP approach is known as the Viterbi Algorithm [9]. For a transition matrix $\mathbf{P}=\{p_{ij}\}$, and HMM states $\{h_i\}$ we define:

$f_n(i)$ = max (probability of going from h_i to any other state in n steps)

and $\quad s_n(i)$ = first state after h_i in this pathway.

Then, $\quad f_n(i) = \max (p_{ij}f_{n-1}(j))$

and $\quad s_n(i) = \{r: p_{ir}f_{n-1}(r) \geq p_{ij}f_{n-1}(j) \; \forall \, j \}$

To start, $f_1(i) = \max (p_{ij})$

and $\quad s_1(i) = \{r: p_{ir} \geq p_{ij} \forall j \}$.

Thus the probability of the most likely pathway of length n can be found by forward recursion using these equations, and the corresponding pathway is then given by backward recursion, where we let

$s^* = \max p_{0i}$.

Here, $s_0 = \{p_{0i}\}$ is the destination for the first transition in the optimal pathway, and this pathway is given by:

$s^* \rightarrow s_n(s^*) \rightarrow s_{n-1}(s_n(s^*) \rightarrow \ldots\ldots\ldots s_1(.. \; s_n(s^*))$.

3.2.5 The Non Time-Homogeneous HMM

While an underlying HMM has been used successfully to model many processes including sequences, our concept here has been of the HMM model providing a means of associating a cluster with an underlying process concept that moves through a series of stages such as developmental stages. In such cases it is possible that the underlying HMM is non time-homogeneous, i.e. the transition matrix of the HMM is a function of time, either changing at random or in response to external stimuli; this process has been termed a Markov model operating in a stochastic environment.

Here we adopt the previous approach of [6] that uses Likelihood ratio tests in a sequential manner to cluster Markov chains at contiguous time points, if appropriate. The log-likelihood function is similar to that presented in Equation (1) evaluated

92   S. McClean, B. Scotney, and F. Palmer

using the solution in equation (2), where we compare likelihood terms for separate values of r. The algorithm is described in Figure 3.

Input:
   A set of sequences for a cluster, homogenised using the mappings

Clustering contiguous time periods:
   Beginning at the first time point, test for similarly of contiguous HMMs
   If HMMs are similar then combine,
   else, compare with previous clusters and combine if similar
   If HMM is not similar to any previous cluster, then start a new cluster

Characterisation of temporal clusters:
   For each cluster: use DP to find the optimal sub-pathway
   Combine optimal sub-pathways to find the overall optimal pathway
Output:
   A set of temporal clusters of contiguous time periods;
   For each temporal cluster: the associated transition matrices;
   The overall optimal pathway

Fig. 3. Temporal clustering for non time-homogeneous HMMs

The similarity metric is given by $\mathcal{L}_{12} - \mathcal{L}_1 - \mathcal{L}_2$, where $\mathcal{L}$ is the log-likelihood function for the elements of the transition matrix given the observed transitions. We are now carrying out dynamic clustering, by comparing transition matrices at the respective time points.

We must now modify the previous algorithm for determining the optimal pathway: for a transition matrix $\mathbf{P}^t = \{ p_{ij}^t \}$, and HMM states $\{h_i\}$ we define:

$f_n^t(i) = \max($ prob. of going from h_i to any other state in n steps, starting at time t)

and $s_n^t(i) =$ first state after h_i in this pathway.

Then, $f_n^t(i) = \max_j (p_{ij}^t \, f_{n-1}^{t+1}(j))$

and $s_n^t(i) = \{r: p_{ir}^t \, f_{n-1}^{t+1}(r) \geq p_{ij}^t \, f_{n-1}^{t+1}(j) \;\; \forall j \}$.

Initially, $f_1^t(i) = \max_j (p_{ij}^t \}$ and $s_1^t(i) = \{r: p_{ir}^t \geq p_{ij}^t \;\; \forall j \}$.

4. Further Work

For the moment we have not considered performance issues since the problem we have identified is both novel and complex. Our focus, therefore, has been on identifying a process and providing a preliminary methodology. In addition to addressing such performance issues, future work will also investigate the related problem of associating clusters with explanatory data; for example our gene expression sequences could be related to the growth process. In conclusion, we believe that this paper has identified, and provided a framework for solving, an important problem for large, possibly distributed, heterogeneous sequences.

Acknowledgement. This work was partially supported by the MISSION (Multi-agent Integration of Shared Statistical Information over the (inter)Net) project, IST project number 1999-10655, which is part of *Eurostat*'s EPROS initiative.

References

1. Cadez, I., Gaffney, S., Smyth, P.: A General Probabilistic Framework for Clustering Individuals. Proceedings of ACM SIGKDD (2000) 140-149
2. Ge, X., Smyth, P.: Deformable Markov Model Templates for Time-series Pattern Matching. Proceedings of ACM SIGKDD (2000) 81-90
3. Scotney, B.W., McClean, S.I.: Efficient Knowledge Discovery through the Integration of Heterogeneous Data. Information and Software Technology (Special Issue on Knowledge Discovery and Data Mining) **41** (1999) 569-578
4. Scotney, B.W., McClean, S.I., Rodgers, M.C.: Optimal and Efficient Integration of Heterogeneous Summary Tables in a Distributed Database. Data and Knowledge Engineering **29** (1999) 337-350
5. McClean, S.I., Scotney, B.W., Shapcott, C.M.: Aggregation of Imprecise and Uncertain Information in Databases. IEEE Trans. Knowledge and Data Engineering **13**(6) (2001) 902-912
6. McClean, S.I., Scotney, B.W., Greer, K.R.C.: Clustering Heterogenous Distributed Databases. Proceedings of KDD Workshop on Knowledge Discovery from Parallel and Distributed Databases. Kargupta, H., Ghosh, J., Kumar, V., Obradovic, Z. (eds.) (2000) 20-29
7. Smyth, P.: Clustering Sequences with Hidden Markov Models. In Mozer, M. C., Jordan, M. I., Petsche, T. (eds.): Advances in Neural Information Processing **9** MIT Press (1997)
8. D'haeseleer, P., Wen, X., Fuhrman, S., Somogyi, R.: Mining the Gene Expression Matrix: Inferring Gene Relationships from large scale Gene Expression Data. In: Paton, R.C., Holcombe, M. (eds.): Information Processing in Cells and Tissues, Plenum Publishing (1998) 203-323
9. Smyth, P., Heckerman, D., Jordan, M.: Probabilistic Independence Networks for Hidden Markov Models. Neural Computation **9**(2) (1997) 227-269

Is a Greedy Covering Strategy an Extreme Boosting?

Roberto Esposito[1] and Lorenza Saitta[2]

[1] Universitá degli Studi di Torino, Italy
esposito@di.unito.it
[2] Universitá del Piemonte Orientale, Alessandria, Italy
saitta@mfn.unipmn.it

Abstract. A new view of majority voting as a Monte Carlo stochastic algorithm is presented in this paper. Relation between the two approaches allows Adaboost's example weighting strategy to be compared with the greedy covering strategy used for a long time in Machine Learning. The greedy covering strategy does not clearly show overfitting, it runs in at least one order of magnitude less time, it reaches zero error on the training set in few trials, and the error on the test set is most of the time comparable to that exhibited by AdaBoost.

1   Introduction

Majority voting classification algorithms, such as boosting [10,6] or bagging [3] are very popular nowadays because of the superior performances shown experimentally on a number of data sets (see, for example, [1,8]). Majority voting methods increase the accuracy of classifiers acquired by weak learners combining their predictions.

An intriguing property of these algorithms is their robustness with respect to overfitting. In fact, their generalization error does not appear to increase, even when the number of voting classifiers ranges in the thousands. A rather convincing argument to explain this behavior is that boosting increases the number of learning examples that have a large classification margin [9].

In this paper we concentrate, for the sake of simplicity, on the case of binary classification.

In the effort to understand why and when boosting works, links with other approaches, such as logistic regression [7] and game theory [5], have been established. In this paper we offer a new perspective, relating majority voting with Monte Carlo stochastic algorithms [2]. In fact, the Monte Carlo approach offers a technique to increase the performance of a simple algorithm by repeatedly running it on the same problem instance. Monte Carlo algorithms have been studied for a long time, and they offer several results that can possibly be transferred to the majority voting framework. For instance, realistic bounds on the number of iterations necessary to reach a given level of performances were already available [2, p.265].

M.-S. Hacid et al. (Eds.): ISMIS 2002, LNAI 2366, pp. 94–102, 2002.

In addition, a subclass of Monte Carlo algorithms (i.e., biased, consistent ones [2]) shows particularly interesting properties with respect to the link between performance increase and number of iterations. Then, a natural question is whether they correspond to some class of machine learning algorithms, which these properties could be transferred to. As it turns out, these special Monte Carlo algorithms correspond to the well known greedy covering strategy, where covered examples are removed at each run, and majority voting becomes an "at least one" combination rule. Then, while Monte Carlo theory suggests that these algorithms are particularly good, past machine learning experience does not confirm this statement. Understanding where the relationship breaks down may help in deepening our knowledge of both majority voting and greedy covering. In order to clarify the above issue, we have taken an experimental approach, using several artificially generated learning problems.

2 Monte Carlo Algorithms

Given a class Π of problems, a Monte Carlo algorithm is a stochastic algorithm that, applied to any instance $x \in \Pi$, always outputs an answer, but, occasionally, this answer is incorrect [2]. In order for an algorithm to be Monte Carlo, any problem instance must have the same probability of being incorrect. More precisely, let p be a real number such that $\frac{1}{2} < p < 1$. A Monte Carlo algorithm is p-correct if the probability that it returns a correct answer is at least p on any problem instance[1]. The difference $(p - \frac{1}{2})$ is the advantage of the algorithm. Moreover, a Monte Carlo algorithm is said to be *consistent* if it never outputs two different correct solutions to the same instance.

Given a p-correct, consistent Monte Carlo algorithm $\mathsf{MC}(x)$, its probability of success can be increased by running it several time on the same instance, and choosing the most frequent answer[2].

More precisely, let ϵ and η be two positive real numbers, such that $\epsilon + \eta < 1/2$. Let $\mathsf{MC}(x)$ be a consistent and $(\frac{1}{2}+\epsilon)$-correct Monte Carlo algorithm. If we define:

$$n(\epsilon) = -\frac{2}{\log_2(1 - 4\epsilon^2)} \tag{1}$$

it is sufficient to call $\mathsf{MC}(x)$ at least

$$T = \left\lceil n(\epsilon) \cdot \log_2 \frac{1}{\eta} \right\rceil \tag{2}$$

times on x, and to return the most frequent answer, to obtain an algorithm that is still consistent and also $(1 - \eta)$-correct ([2, p.263]). We have "amplified" the advantage of $\mathsf{MC}(x)$.

---

[1] This statement is different from saying that the algorithm is correct on most problem instances, being only incorrect on a small subset of them.

[2] The consistency of the algorithm is fundamental for the amplification. For instance, running three times a consistent 0.75-correct Monte Carlo algorithm $\mathsf{MC}(x)$ and taking the most frequent answer leads to a 0.84-correct algorithm, whereas the resulting algorithm is only 0.71-correct, should $\mathsf{MC}(x)$ be not consistent.

2.1 Biased Monte Carlo Algorithms

Let us consider now a Monte Carlo algorithm solving a decision problem, with only two answers: *true* and *false*. Suppose moreover that the algorithm is always correct when it outputs true, errors being only possible on the answer "false". Such an algorithm is said to be a *true-biased* Monte Carlo. With a true-biased Monte Carlo algorithm, majority voting on a sequence of runs is superfluous, because it is sufficient that the answer true be output a single time. More importantly, amplification occurs also for biased p-correct algorithms with $p < \frac{1}{2}$, provided that $p > 0$. More formally [2, p. 265]:

Definition 1. *Let Π be a class of problems and let s_0 be a possible output of a Monte Carlo algorithm $MC(x)$. $MC(x)$ is s_0-biased if there exists a subset X of Π such that:*

1. *$MC(x)$ is always correct on instance x whenever $x \notin X$;*
2. *The correct solution to any $x \in X$ is s_0, but $MC(x)$ may not always return the correct answer on these instances.*

Theorem 1 (Brassard and Bratley). *Running k times a consistent, s_0-biased, p-correct Monte Carlo algorithm (with $0 < p < 1$) yields a consistent, s_0-biased, $[1 - (1 - p)^k]$-correct algorithm.*

Then, in order to achieve a correctness level of $(1 - \eta)$, it is sufficient to run the algorithm at least a number of times:

$$T = \left\lceil \frac{\log_2 \eta}{\log_2 (1 - p)} \right\rceil \tag{3}$$

2.2 Relations between Ensemble Learning and Monte Carlo Algorithms

Let us consider now a learning context in which a weak learner A acquires decision rules $h(x) : X \to Y$, belonging to a set H. X is a set of instances and $Y = \{+1, -1\}$ is a binary set of classes. We will consider positive and negative instances labelled respectively $+1$ and -1.

If we would like to build a Monte Carlo algorithm out of a learning algorithm we would have to find a way to force the weak learner to behave in a stochastic way. Furthermore we shall want to let two calls to the learner be as independent as possible. We have at least two ways to face the problem: we can rewrite the weak learner from the scratch, or we can manipulate the learner input as a way to randomize the algorithm. The only input we can randomize in a learning context is the training set, then a reasonable choice is to iterate the weak learner providing it with different randomly chosen subsamples of the original training set. As long as this technique is successful, i.e. as long as independence between different calls is achieved, and provided that the weak algorithm outperforms random guessing, we will be able to improve its performances in the way we explained in Sect. 2. Bagging does exactly what we have just explained. It iterates the weak algorithm several times providing it with different, randomly chosen, subsamples of the original training set and then it combines the hypotheses with a majority vote.

Since our goal is to increase the difference between two iterations of the same algorithm, we could think of better ways of perturbing the input. In particular it is very likely that the greatest difference between the hypotheses could be obtained by providing the algorithm with the examples that it has misclassified in previous iterations. In fact, since the goal of the weak algorithm is to classify as much examples as possible, it is very likely that a very different hypothesis would be built. AdaBoost reweighting scheme exploits this idea as a way to force the weak learner to induce very different hypotheses.

If we now consider biased Monte Carlo algorithms, we may wonder about what kind of combined classifiers they might correspond to. If a correspondence can be established, it would be reasonable to expect that the learning counterpart shows at least two advantages over more generic boosting methods: first of all, comparable error rates with a much smaller numbers of individual classifiers, and, second, the possibility of using very rough weak learners, because their error rate only needs to be greater than zero. Actually, it turns out that the learning counterpart of a consistent, true-biased and p-correct Monte Carlo algorithm is a greedy covering algorithm (GCA), with the set of positive examples as the X set in Definition 1. In fact, let us consider as weak learner A an algorithm that covers some positive examples and no negative ones. Then, at each repetition of A, we eliminate the already covered positive examples. At the end, when no positive example is left, the majority voting rule becomes an "at least one" rule. In fact, it is sufficient that one among the $h_t(x)$'s says $+1$ to classify the example as positive, due to the bias.

If we now try to make AdaBoost to fit into the Monte Carlo framework, it turns out that AdaBoost seems to lie between GCA and Bagging. In fact both its example weighting scheme and its weighted majority voting scheme are a compromise between the two algorithms. The elimination process performed by the biased Monte Carlo algorithm is a limit process of AdaBoost weighting scheme; besides, the at-least-one vote can be thought of as a hard way of weighting the hypotheses.

Given that the GCA is a biased Monte Carlo algorithm, we expect to obtain much smaller classifiers. This idea is appealing, as one of the drawback of boosting is the generation of incomprehensible classification rules. However, the machine learning field has dealt a long time with greedy covering algorithms, which did not prove to be very robust with respect to generalization error. Then, a pertinent question would be: why? The previous observation suggested us to test the following hypotheses:

1. a GCA allows very simple learners to be boosted in few runs, without bothering about their accuracy (provided that it is greater than zero);
2. GCA's should be prone to overfitting, whereas (most of the times) AdaBoost is not. Then, increasing the number of basic classifiers should let the test error of a GCA increase, contrarily to what happens to AdaBoost;
3. the simple politics adopted by GCA should perform poorly in difficult situations such as noisy datasets.

In order to test the previous hypotheses, we performed experiments on a set of artificial datasets, reported in the following section.

3 Experiments

In this section a description of the experiments we carried out to test the performances of AdaBoost, Bagging, and GCA under different conditions is reported. In particular we were interested in exploring under which conditions the former two algorithms could outperform the latter. Since we planned to use really weak hypotheses, we allowed the algorithms to run for a huge number of iterations (namely five thousands)[3] on twelve different artificial datasets.

The datasets were built on purpose and differ from each other in many aspects. There are three main datasets: *asia*, *triangles* and *fiveD*, which differ in shape of the target concept and in dimensionality. In particular, *asia* contains two fairly large clusters of points, *triangles* contains five small disjunctions, while *fiveD* contains five large balls in a five dimensional space.

The remaining nine datasets have been generated by adding three types of noise in the three main ones (see Subsection 3.1 for further details).

For each dataset the following parameters have been computed:

- η_t, i.e. the training error at step t;
- ω_t, i.e the test error at step t;
- ϵ_t, i.e. the error committed by the weak learner on the set used for its training

These values have been computed at each iteration for $1 \le t \le 100$, and every fifty iterations for $101 \le t \le 5000$. Five-fold cross-validation has been used to increase the confidence in the output.

3.1 Random Noises

In addition, we created nine noisy datasets by introducing three kinds of random noise in the three original noise-free datasets.

The first noise scheme (labels) randomly perturbs the labels given in the original dataset, no matter where the perturbed instance lies. Ten percent of the labels have been changed in this way.

The other two noise schemes take into account the place where the instances lie; in fact, only the instances that are near the borders of the concept have been changed with a probability that depends upon the dataset itself. The difference between these last two noise schemes is that in one of them (marginNoBayes) the label of the perturbed instance is changed, while in the other (marginBayes) the whole instance is reinserted in the dataset, once its label has been changed. This corresponds to deal with a target concept that may return two different labels if called twice (in other words its Bayes error is greater than zero)[4].

---

[3] We forced GCA to run for such a long time even if, as expected, this has lowered its performances.

[4] Noisy datasets have been named joining the name of the original dataset and the name given to the particular kind of noise used for perturbing it, for instance in the following we will denote with *asia.labels* the dataset obtained perturbing *asia* with the kind of noise we explained first in this section.

3.2 Weak Learners

The three algorithms have been tested using two different kinds of weak learners.

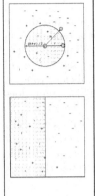

Fig. 1. The sphere and the stump inducers

Both algorithms search a very small hypothesis space and only slightly outperform random guess when used alone with a complex data set. Once again the algorithms have been chosen to be very different, in order to test the three ensemble learners in very different situations.

The first of the two algorithms is a stochastic, positively biased learner[5]. It induces a sphere in the example space, whose center is chosen at random among the positive examples. The radius of the sphere is optimized so that it maximize the coverage of positive examples while preserving its positive bias. A simple example of a hypothesis induced by this learner is reported in the top-most of the figures on the left. The radius is chosen in such a way as to lie half the way between the nearest negative example and the farthest positive one. The second learner is a decision stump inducer, i.e., it induces axis-parallel half planes in the example space. The induced half plane is optimal, as the best attribute and the best value are chosen for the testing attribute (see Fig. 1).

Three main differences exist between the two algorithms:

1. the sphere inducer contains a stochastic step, while the decision stump inducer is totally deterministic;
2. the sphere inducer is positively biased, while the other one is not;
3. the region labelled as positive by the first learner is bounded, the other one extends to infinity (we say that the first hypothesis is "local" whereas the other one is "non-local").

4 Results

Due to space constraints not all the results will be presented: the whole set of tables and pictures can be found in [4]. In the following we will use subscripts to denote which weak learner a given algorithm is coupled with. Furthermore we will use the following abbreviations: **Boost** for Boosting, **GCA** for the greedy covering strategy, **Bag** for Bagging, **SP** for the sphere inducer and **DS** for the decision stump inducer.

As already stated in Sect. 2, Bagging is exactly a non-biased Monte Carlo algorithm. Actually the performances shown by bagging when used along with the sphere inducer matches exactly the ones of the hypothesis that labels each point as negative (we will refer to it as **False**(x) or as the default hypothesis). At first this appears to be a bit counter-intuitive, since one may expect that such an algorithm should amplify the advantage of the weak learner as predicted by the theory. The key point is that Bagging is not suited at all to be used with local biased hypotheses, since this kind of hypotheses violates the independence

---

[5] Here biased is used with the meaning explained in section 2.1

assumption over the weak algorithm. The learned hypotheses will agree over all the negative instances, but for any dataset in which it is unlikely to learn very large spheres, very few of them will agree over positive examples. Therefore the default hypothesis will be learned or, in other words, nothing will be learned at all.

When coupled with decision stumps something similar happens but due to different reasons. The deterministic nature of decision stumps violates once again Monte Carlo assumption of independence between hypotheses. While this is not catastrophic in AdaBoost, which heavily reweights the training set, the small differences in the training sets introduced by Bagging are not sufficient to force the deterministic learner to induce very different hypotheses. This, again, does not allow Bagging to amplify the advantage of the weak learner.

The above considerations derive from Fig. 2 and 3; as we can see, Bag_{SP} quickly converges to the default hypothesis; indeed, the training and test error increase from the initial error made by the weak learner to the error made by $False(x)$. On the other hand, Bag_{DS} does nothing but returning the weak hypothesis.

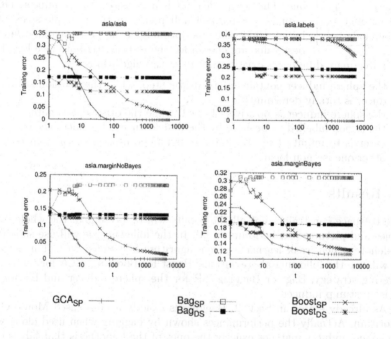

Fig. 2. Training error of all the classifiers over *asia* dataset family

$Boost_{SP}$ seems to work quite well; it monotonically amplifies the performances of the weak learner and there is no sign of overfitting in any of the experiments. The error rate drops exponentially fast on most datasets (note the log scale on

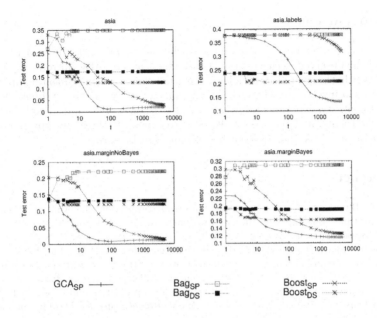

Fig. 3. Test error of all the classifiers over *asia* dataset family

the x-axis). It seems interesting that this does not hold for datasets with noise on labels. The experiments with the other datasets seem to confirm this behavior.

Boost$_{DS}$ learns quite bad hypotheses. It seems that even if the hypothesis spaces searched by the decision stumps inducer and by the sphere inducer share the same VC-dimension (namely VCdim(DS) = VCdim(SP) = 3), the space of their linear combinations is quite different. In particular, it seems that combining spheres leads to much more expressive hypotheses than combining decision stumps. The graphs show that Boost$_{DS}$ slightly improves the performances of the weak learner, converging quickly to a final hypothesis. Plots of ϵ_t (not included here due to space constraints) clearly shows that AdaBoost takes few rounds to drive the error of the stump inducer to 0.5: after this point no further learning occurs.

Most astonishing is that, against our initial guess, GCA outperforms AdaBoost (and all the other algorithms) on almost all datasets. It reaches zero error on the training data in few rounds, and even when it is forced to learn for a long period (while its stopping criterion says that it should stop as soon as the training data are covered), it shows a really small overfitting.

Interestingly enough, even though AdaBoost does not overfit at all, it never reaches GCA's performances.

As a last observation we may note that even if performances of Boost$_{DS}$ are worse than the others, it seems to be quite invariant with respect to different kind of noises. However, definite conclusions cannot be drawn without further investigations.

5   Conclusion

Relating Ensemble Learning to Monte Carlo theory can shed light over the reasons of the observed performances of ensemble learners. After introducing basic Monte Carlo theory and terminology, the article takes an experimental approach as a way to investigate where the predictions given by the theory break down. On the contrary, experimental results seems to suggest what immediately follows from the theory, and the theory allows us to explain both the unexpected good results of the GCA and the poor performances of Bagging.

References

1. Eric Bauer and Ron Kohavi. An empirical comparison of voting classification algorithms: Bagging, boosting, and variants. *Machine Learning*, 36:105, 1999.
2. G. Brassard and P. Bratley. Algorithmics: theory and practice, 1988.
3. Leo Breiman. Bagging predictors. *Machine Learning*, 24(2):123–140, 1996.
4. R. Esposito and L. Saitta. "Is a Greedy Covering Strategy an Extreme Boosting?": table of experiments. http://www.di.unito.it/~esposito/mcandboost.
5. Y. Freund and R. Schapire. Game theory, on-line prediction and boosting. In *Proceedings, 9th Annual Conference on Computational Learning Theory*, pages 325–332, 1996.
6. Yoav Freund and Robert E. Schapire. Experiments with a new boosting algorithm. In *Proc. 13th International Conference on Machine Learning*, pages 148–146. Morgan Kaufmann, 1996.
7. J. Friedman, J. Stochastic, T. Hastie, and R. Tibshirani. Additive logistic regression: a statistical view of boosting. Technical report, Department of Statistics, Stanford University, 1999.
8. J. R. Quinlan. Bagging, boosting and c4.5. In *Proc. AAAI'96 National Conference on Artificial Intelligence*, 1996.
9. R. Schapire, Y. Freund, P. Bartlett, and W. Lee. Boosting the margin: A new explanation for the effectiveness of voting methods. *Annals of Statistic*, 26(5):1651–1686, 1998.
10. Robert E. Schapire. The strength of weak learnability. *Machine Learning*, 5:197, 1990.

Acquisition of a Knowledge Dictionary from Training Examples Including Multiple Values

Shigeaki Sakurai, Yumi Ichimura, Akihiro Suyama, and Ryohei Orihara

Corporate Research & Development Center, Toshiba Corporation

Abstract. A text mining system uses two kinds of background knowledge: a concept relation dictionary and a key concept dictionary. The concept relation dictionary consists of a set of rules. We can automatically acquire it by using an inductive learning algorithm. The algorithm uses training examples including concepts that are generated by using both lexical analysis and the key concept dictionary. The algorithm cannot deal with a training example with more than one concept in the same attribute. Such a training example is apt to generate from a report, when the concept dictionary is not well defined. It is necessary to extend an inductive learning algorithm, because the dictionary is usually not completed. This paper proposes an inductive learning method that deals with the report. Also, the paper shows the efficiency of the method through some numerical experiments using business reports about retailing.

1 Introduction

Although large amounts of reports are stored on computers, the ability to process them is limited and it is not always possible to process them efficiently. This is the context in which text mining techniques have been studied with a view to using reports efficiently [Feldman et al., 1998][Ichimura et al., 2001][Tan et al., 2000] . [Ichimura et al., 2001] proposed a text mining technique that analyzes many reports and classifies them using two kinds of knowledge dictionaries: a key concept dictionary and a concept relational dictionary. If this technique is applied, only the reports included in a class of interest are read, not all the reports.

On the other hand, [Sakurai et al., 2001] proposed a method whereby a concept relation dictionary is acquired automatically. The method learns the dictionary inductively from training examples, each of which is composed of some concepts extracted from a report using a key concept dictionary and a text class given by a reader. Here, the key concept dictionary describes important words concerning a target problem by using three layers: a concept class, a key concept, and an expression. The method regards a report that has concepts included in the same concept class as a report with contradiction and excludes it from the training examples, because the method assumes that a well-defined key concept dictionary is given and some key concepts included in the same concept class are not extracted. However, a well-defined key concept dictionary is not always used and some concepts included in the same concept class often are extracted. So,

M.-S. Hacid et al. (Eds.): ISMIS 2002, LNAI 2366, pp. 103–113, 2002.

the exclusion of the report leads to generation of a concept relation dictionary that lacks an important relation.

This paper proposes a method that processes reports with some concepts included in the same class and acquires a concept relation dictionary from reports including them. Also, this paper shows that the proposed method acquires a more appropriate concept relation dictionary with precision of inference by numerical experiments using daily business reports about retailing.

2   A Concept Relation Dictionary

2.1   Text Mining System

The text mining system classifies daily business reports by using two kinds of knowledge dictionaries. A key concept dictionary is composed of three layers: a concept class, a key concept, and an expression. Each concept class shows a set of concepts that have the common feature, each key concept shows a set of expressions that have the same meaning, and each expression shows important words for a target problem. On the other hand, a concept relation dictionary is composed of relations, which have a condition part with some key concepts and a result part with a text class. Each relation describes a meaning created by combination of concepts.

The system decomposes a daily business report into words by lexical analysis. Each word is checked as to whether the word is registered in a key concept dictionary. If a word is registered in the dictionary, a key concept corresponding to the word is assigned to the report. The report is also checked as to whether there is a key concept set described in a concept relation dictionary. If the report has the set, a text class corresponding to the set is assigned to the report. The method puts reports that have the same text class into a group. Therefore, it is sufficient for readers to read only those reports classified into classes which represent their interests. At the same time, the system allows the readers to follow the trend of the key concepts for all reports.

2.2   Learning Method

[Sakurai et al., 2001] have proposed a method that acquires a concept relation dictionary. The method extracts concepts from a report by using lexical analysis and a key concept dictionary. It regards a concept class as an attribute, a key concept as an attribute value, and a text class given by a reader as a class of a training example, and generates training examples from given reports. It applies the examples to a fuzzy inductive learning algorithm IDTF [Sakurai and Araki, 1996] shown in Table 1, and acquires a concept relation dictionary described by the format of a fuzzy decision tree. In Table 1, fuzzy sets which represent an attribute are called fuzzy class items and their membership functions are defined by formula (1). The formula shows that an unknown attribute value has equal relationship with all attribute values given in learning phase.

$$\begin{aligned} &\text{If } \quad l_{ikr} = a_i, \quad \text{then} \quad grade_{ikr} = 1 \\ &\text{If } \quad \forall r, l_{ikr} \neq a_i, \text{then} \quad grade_{ikr} = \frac{1}{|L_{ik}|} \\ &\text{Otherwise,} \qquad grade_{ikr} = 0 \end{aligned} \qquad (1)$$

Here, a_i is a key concept in the i-th attribute of an example to be evaluated, L_{ik} is a key concept subset in the i-th attribute corresponding to the k-th interior node, l_{ikr} is the r-th element of L_{ik}, and $|\cdot|$ is an operation that calculates the number of elements included in a set.

Also, each degree of certainty for an example in a node is calculated according to normalized grade. That is, the degree is defined by formula (2).

$$q_{ikrs} = \frac{grade_{ikr}}{\sum\limits_{t} grade_{ikt}} \cdot p_{ks} \qquad (2)$$

Here, p_{ks} is degree of certainty which the s-th example in the k-th node has.

Table 1. IDTF algorithm

1. Allocate a training example set to a new node and stack up the node.
2. Pick out a node(N_k) from the stack. This algorithm is over when there is not a node.
3. If the ratio of the maximum class in the node is larger than a threshold or the density of examples in the node is smaller than other threshold, let the node be a terminal node assigned classes with degree of certainty and return to step 2. Otherwise, go to next step.
4. a) Create fuzzy class items from a training subset included in the node. Then, the items are generated for each attribute.
   b) Calculate a *gain_ratio* [Quinlan, 1992] of each attribute, but the value is calculated based on sum of degree of certainty instead of number of training examples.
   c) Select an attribute with the best *gain_ratio* and allocate the attribute to the node.
   d) Regard training examples corresponding to each item as a new subset and allocate each subset to a new node.
   e) Create branches that connect the original node to each new node and allocate each item to its corresponding branch.
   f) Stack up the new nodes and return to step 2.

2.3   Inference Method

When a new report is given, an inference method extracts some concepts from the report and generates an example that does not have a text class. Also, the method decides a text class by applying the example to an acquired fuzzy decision tree. The decision based on the tree takes into consideration imprecision included in an example. That is, in an interior node, the inference method transfers an example to its lower nodes if the interior node does not have a fuzzy class item that is equal to an attribute value of the example. In a terminal node, the degree of certainty corresponding to the transferred example is multiplied by the degree of certainty corresponding to each class of the node. The degree is summed up for each class. Lastly, the inference method normally selects a class that has the maximum degree of certainty and regards it as the class of the example. So, it is possible for the inference method to decide a text class even if an example to be evaluated has an attribute value that does not occur in the learning phase

For example, an example and a fuzzy decision tree shown in Figure 1 are given. At first, the inference method evaluates the example with initial degree of certainty ($= 1$) in an interior node N_1. The example has a key concept "Normal sales", which is not equal to two key concepts of fuzzy class items in the attribute "Sales". So, the method transfers the example with $\frac{1}{2}$ degree of certainty to both a terminal node N_2 and an interior node N_3, respectively. Next, the method evaluates the example with $\frac{1}{2}$ degree of certainty in the node N_3 and transfers it to a terminal node N_4. Lastly, the method gets both a class "Missed opportunity" with 0.6 degree of certainty and a class "Best practice" with 0.4 degree of certainty based on the total of degree of certainty. The method also selects the class "Missed opportunity". Figure 1 shows an outline of the inference.

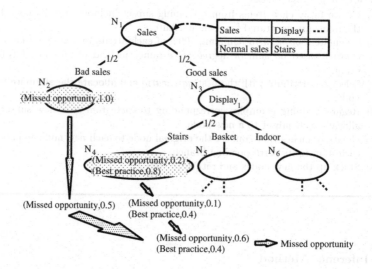

Fig. 1. Inference based on a fuzzy decision tree

3   Multiple Values

3.1   Reports with Contradiction and an Ill-Defined Key Concept Dictionary

The learning method and inference method assume that there is a well-defined key concept dictionary. The well-defined dictionary gives at most a key concept of each concept class to a report, because each key concept with the same concept class is exclusive and does not occur in a text simultaneously. If a report is against the premise, the report is regarded as a report with contradiction. The report is excluded from training examples in the learning phase. Also, a class of the report is not inferred using an acquired concept relation in the inference phase. However, a key concept dictionary is not always well defined and the evaluation that the report has contradiction is not always right. In the experiments reported in [Sakurai et al., 2001], a key concept dictionary given by a human expert was revised by decomposing some concept classes with a view to extract only a key concept from the same concept class. By this revision, the number of reports with contradiction decreased.

In many cases, it is not easy to generate a well-defined key concept dictionary. Also, it takes a lot of time to generate one. On the other hand, the information included in reports with contradiction will be missed if they are excluded. It is necessary to process such reports too. Thus, we propose a method that processes a report with multiple key concepts included in the same concept class in the following section.

3.2   Process of Multiple Values

The learning method generates training examples, applies them to a fuzzy inductive learning algorithm IDTF, and generates a concept relation dictionary. Fortunately, it is possible for the IDTF to process multiple values included in an attribute, if appropriate fuzzy class items are defined for the attribute. So, the learning method processes a report that has multiple key concepts included in a concept class by regarding a set of the concepts as an attribute value. In the following, we consider how the items, which express the set, should be defined.

We can regard such a case that a key concept is given in an attribute as a specialized case. It is necessary for each membership function of fuzzy class items to include formula (1). Also, we normally do not have such information that measures the importance of each key concept in the attribute. Each function should process each key concept equally. Moreover, we have to process an example to be evaluated with a key concept that does not occur in training examples in the inference phase. Then, it is impossible to evaluate the key concept in an interior node with corresponding concept class. Each function should transfer the example to all lower nodes of the interior node with equal degree of certainty and evaluate the example with the lower nodes.

Thus, this paper defines a membership function for a key concept of an example to be evaluated in an interior node as the formula (3) shows. The membership function expresses that a fuzzy class item gets weight $\frac{1}{v_i}$ if a key concept of the fuzzy class item is equal to the key concept of the example, and all fuzzy class items corresponding to the interior node get equally decomposed weight $\frac{1-\alpha}{|L_{ik}|}$ if their key concepts are not equal to the key concept. Then, $\frac{1}{v_i}$ shows weight corresponding to a key concept of an example included in the fuzzy class items and $1 - \alpha$ shows weight corresponding to the rest concepts excluded from them. Also, each degree of certainty for each lower node is calculated by the formula (2).

$$\text{If} \quad l_{ikr} \in v_i, \text{ then} \quad grade_{ikr} = \frac{1}{|v_i|} + \frac{1-\alpha}{|L_{ik}|}$$
$$\text{If} \quad l_{ikr} \notin v_i, \text{ then} \quad grade_{ikr} = \frac{1-\alpha}{|L_{ik}|} \tag{3}$$
$$\alpha = \frac{|v_i \cap L_{ik}|}{|v_i|}$$

Here, v_i is a key concept subset in the i-th attribute of an example to be evaluated, L_{ik} is a key concept subset in the i-th attribute corresponding to the k-th interior node, l_{ikr} is the r-th element of L_{ik}, and $|\cdot|$ is an operation that calculates the number of elements included in a set. The formula shows that interior nodes with the same attribute do not always have equal key concept subsets.

Figure 2 shows that an example with multiple values is evaluated using membership functions defined by this section. In Figure 2, an interior node N_3 is the first interior node in interior nodes with second concept class "Display". Also, the node has three fuzzy class items, where each item has a key concept "Stairs", "Basket", and "Indoor", respectively. That is, $L_{21} = \{$"Stairs", "Basket", "Indoor"$\}$. We consider the case of a report with 1 degree of certainty and two key concepts "Stairs" and "Outdoor" of the concept class "Display" in the node N_3. That is, $v_i = \{$"Stairs", "Outdoor"$\}$. Each key concept has $\frac{1}{2}$ degree of certainty. A key concept "Stairs" in v_i is equal to a key concept "Stairs" in L_{21}. The method gives $\frac{1}{2}$ degree of certainty to a lower node N_4. On the other hand, the other concept "Outdoor" is not equal to any key concepts in L_{21}. The method gives $\frac{1}{6}(=\frac{\frac{1}{2}}{3})$ degree of certainty to each lower node N_4, N_5, and N_6. So, the report with $\frac{2}{3}$ $(=\frac{1}{2}+\frac{1}{6})$ degree of certainty transfers to the node N_4 and the report with $\frac{1}{6}$ degree of certainty transfers to the node N_5 and the node N_6, respectively. The evaluation process is continued in all lower nodes.

4   Numerical Experiments

4.1   Experimentation

Training examples. The text mining system proposed by [Ichimura et al., 2001] classifies daily business reports concerning retailing into three text classes: "Best practice", "Missed opportunity", and "Other". In this system, a key concept dictionary made by a human expert is composed of 13 concept classes and the concept classes have 312 key concepts. Each attribute of a training example has either key concepts included in a concept class or "nothing" as an attribute value,

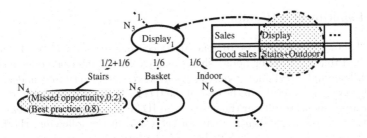

Fig. 2. Inference for multiple values

where "nothing" shows a report does not have a key concept in the concept class. Also, a class of a training example is decided by a concept relation dictionary. The dictionary is given by a human expert and has 349 concept relations.

In the experiments, we use 1,029 daily business reports and generate 1,029 training examples. However, 232 reports do not have a key concept extracted by the key concept dictionary and generate training examples in which all attribute values are "nothing". We exclude the examples from 1,029 training examples and use 797 examples in the experiments, because we consider important information is not described in the excluded examples. In fact, only a few of the 232 reports describe meaningful contents. The key concept dictionary has to be improved in order to extract the information from the reports with the meaningful contents. In the future, we are going to consider a method for improving a key concept dictionary by using the excluded reports that do not have a key concept.

Evaluation. The proposed method is evaluated using 10-fold cross-validation in order to avoid the bias of the training examples. That is, the training example set is decomposed into 10 training example subsets. In the learning phase, a concept relation dictionary described by a fuzzy decision tree is acquired from training examples included in 9 subsets. In the inference phase, a text class is inferred for each training example included in the remaining subset. The inferred text class is compared with the text class pre-assigned to the training example. The learning phase and the inference phase are repeated 10 times by replacing the subset used in the inference phase with a different subset. Lastly, the error ratio is calculated by dividing number of misclassified examples by number of evaluated example and multiplying by 100.

Also, we perform experiments that use the C4.5 [Quinlan, 1992] and the IDTF that does not process multiple values [Sakurai et al., 2001]. But, the experiments exclude training examples with multiple values and use training examples with only single value.

4.2   Experimental Results

Table 2 shows average size of 10 generated decision trees for the IDTF and the C4.5. In Table 2, "Interior node" shows average size of interior nodes included in each tree and "Terminal node" shows average size of terminal nodes. Also, "IDTF_new" shows results in the case of the IDTF that processes multiple values. "IDTF_old" shows results in the case of the IDTF that does not process them, and "C4.5" shows results in the case of the C4.5. In the following, the former IDTF is referred to as the old IDTF and the latter is referred to as the new IDTF.

Table 2. Decision tree size

	IDTF_new	IDTF_old	C4.5
Interior node	21.0	10.9	10.9
Terminal node	90.5	45.7	362.3

Table 3 shows error ratio for the IDTF and the C4.5. In Table 3, "Single" shows error ratios in the case of evaluating training examples with only single value, "Multiple" shows error ratios in training examples with multiple values, and "Average" shows error ratios in all training examples. Also, "All" shows the whole trend which does not consider the influence of the classes, "Best" shows the trend in the class "Best practice", "Missed" shows the trend in the class "Missed opportunity", and "Other" shows the trend in the class "Other". But, in the case of both the old IDTF and the C4.5, it is assumed that the most frequent class "Other" is inferred for a training example with multiple values.

Table 3. Error ratio

	IDTF_new(%)				IDTF_old(%)				C4.5(%)			
	All	Best	Missed	Other	All	Best	Missed	Other	All	Best	Missed	Other
Single	0.594	0.00	0.00	0.664	0.149	3.03	0.00	0.00	4.16	42.4	36.8	0.00
Multiple	8.06	26.7	33.3	2.06	(21.8)	(100.0)	(100.0)	(0.00)	(21.8)	(100.0)	(100.0)	(0.00)
Average	1.76	8.33	8.00	0.858	(3.51)	(33.3)	(24.0)	(0.00)	(6.90)	(60.4)	(52.0)	(0.00)

Lastly, Figure 3 shows parts of a learned fuzzy decision tree using the new IDTF. In Figure 3, each interior node stores a concept class and each terminal node stores text classes with degree of certainty. Also, each label on a line shows a key concept corresponding to the concept class described at its left side.

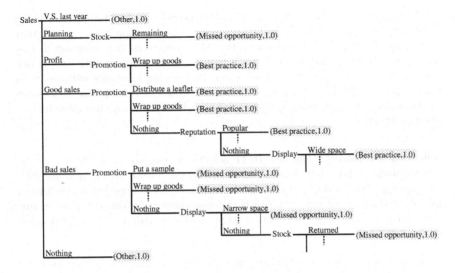

Fig. 3. Parts of a learned fuzzy decision tree

4.3   Discussion

Error ratios. In the case of "Single", the old IDTF gives a lower error ratio than the new IDTF. The old IDTF is apt to acquire a fuzzy decision tree dependent on examples with only single value, because the old IDTF does not use examples with multiple values. So, fuzzy decision trees based on the old IDTF infer the examples with single value with lower error ratio.

In the case of "Multiple", error ratios in the old IDTF and the C4.5 are not too high, because the number of examples with the class "Other" is much larger than the number of examples with the class "Best practice" or "Missed opportunity". The new IDTF gives a lower error ratio for the examples. In the case of "Average", the new IDTF also gives the lowest error ratio among the ratios. We consider that fuzzy decision trees based on the new IDTF infer all examples with low error ratio.

Table 3 shows that the new IDTF more correctly infers examples with the class "Best practice" and the class "Missed opportunity". In this task, it is appropriate that the examples are classified more correctly than examples with the class "Other", because almost all readers are interested in the class "Best practice" or the class "Missed opportunity". The new IDTF gives more appropriate results.

So, we consider the new IDTF acquires a concept relation dictionary with low error ratio from training examples.

Size. The C4.5 generates interior nodes corresponding to all attribute values, even if an attribute value is not given in the learning phase. On the other hand, the IDTF generates only interior nodes corresponding to attribute values given in the learning phase. So, the IDTF generates a more compact concept relation dictionary than the C4.5 does. In fact, the IDTF generates more compact dictionaries as Table 2 shows. The old IDTF uses training examples with only single value and does not acquire relations given by training examples with multiple values. The old IDTF may generate a concept relation dictionary that lacks some relations. So, we consider that the size of the old IDTF is smaller than that of the new IDTF.

Selected attributes. The new IDTF selects the concept class "Sales" as the top attribute in all cases. That is, the text classes have a strong relation with the concept class "Sales". This result corresponds to the knowledge of a human expert as the concept class "Sales" is the most important concept class in this task. Thus, we conclude that the new IDTF precisely acquires a concept relation dictionary.

In summary, the new IDTF acquires a correct relation dictionary by using training examples with multiple values. Also, the new IDTF acquires a comparatively compact concept relation dictionary by generating only branches corresponding to key concepts given in the learning phase.

5   Summary and Future Work

The paper proposed a method that processes an example with multiple values and revised the method that acquired a concept relation dictionary for a text mining system. Also, the paper showed that the revised method generated a compact and correct concept relation dictionary through numerical experiments based on 10-fold cross-validation and using daily business reports about retailing.

In future work, we intend to acquire a key concept dictionary automatically or semi-automatically, because it takes a lot of time for a human expert to generate the dictionary. We are developing a tool that generates the dictionary through GUI and are planning to incorporate the function into the tool. Also, we intend to consider a method that revises a key concept dictionary. Only a few of the 232 reports, which do not extract a key concept, have meaningful contents. It is necessary to revise the dictionary in order to extract information from the reports. Moreover, we intend to develop a system that classifies an email by using the proposed method.

References

[Feldman et al., 1998] R. Feldman and H. Hirsh, "Mining text using keyword distributions," Journal of Intelligent Information Systems, 10:281-300, 1998.
[Ichimura et al., 2001] Y. Ichimura, Y. Nakayama, M. Miyoshi, T. Akahane, T. Sekiguchi, Y. Fujiwara, "Text mining system for analysis of a salesperson's daily reports," Proceedings of the PACLING 2001, 127-135, 2001.

[Quinlan, 1992] J.R. Quinlan, "C4.5: Programs for machine learning," Morgan Kaufmann, 1992.

[Sakurai and Araki, 1996] S. Sakurai and D. Araki, "The improvement of a fuzzy inductive learning algorithm," T. IEE Japan, 116(9):1057-1063, 1996 (*in Japanese*).

[Sakurai et al., 2001] S. Sakurai, Y. Ichimura, A. Suyama, and R. Orihara: "Acquisition of a knowledge dictionary for a text mining system using an inductive learning method," IJCAI 2001 workshop on Text Learning: Beyond Supervision, 45-52, 2001.

[Tan et al., 2000] P.-N. Tan, H. Blau, S. Harp, and R. Goldman, "Textual data mining of service center call records," Proceedings of the 6th International Conference on Knowledge Discovery and Data Mining, 417-423, 2000.

Mining Bayesian Network Structure for Large Sets of Variables

Mieczysław A. Kłopotek

Institute of Computer Science, Polish Academy of Sciences, Warsaw, Poland also
Institute of Computer Science, University of Podlasie, Siedlce, Poland,
klopotek@ipipan.waw.pl

Abstract. A well-known problem with Bayesian networks (BN) is the practical limitation for the number of variables for which a Bayesian network can be learned in reasonable time. Even the complexity of simplest tree-like BN learning algorithms is prohibitive for large sets of variables. The paper presents a novel algorithm overcoming this limitation for the tree-like class of Bayesian networks. The new algorithm space consumption grows linearly with the number of variables n while the execution time is proportional to $n \ln(n)$, outperforming any known algorithm. This opens new perspectives in construction of Bayesian networks from data containing tens of thousands and more variables, e.g. in automatic text categorization.

1 Introduction

Bayesian networks (BN) [11] encode efficiently properties of probability distributions. Their usage is spread among many disciplines. A Bayesian network is an acyclic directed graph (dag) nodes of which are labeled with variables and conditional probability tables of the node variable given its parents in the graph. The joint probability distribution is then expressed by the formula:

$$P(x_1, \dots\dots\dots, x_n) = \prod_{i=1\dots n} P(x_i | \pi(x_i)) \tag{1}$$

where $\pi(X_i)$ is the set of parents of the variable (node) X_i. On the one hand, BNs allow for efficient reasoning, and on the other many algorithms for learning BNs from empirical data have been developed [9].

A well-known problem with Bayesian networks is the practical limitation for the number of variables for which a Bayesian network can be learned in reasonable time. In a comparative experiment using BNLEARN system [9], for a network with 8 nodes and 8 edges and sample size 15,000, several known algorithms had the following computational speed: Chow/Liu: 2s, Pearl: 2s, PC: 12s, K2: 7s, SGS: 107s. For a network of 210 nodes and 301 edges (7 times replicated ALARM network) and sample size 60,000, same algorithms had execution times: Chow/Liu: 40 min., Pearl: 40 min, PC: 12 hours, K2: 11 hours, SGS: could not be determined. The Chow/Liu [4,5] algorithm learning tree-like Bayesian networks

M.-S. Hacid et al. (Eds.): ISMIS 2002, LNAI 2366, pp. 114–122, 2002.

(and its derivative Pearl algorithm learning poly-trees) performed consistently better than the othe ones. However, also this algorithm has an important limitation, related to the time and space consumption. The time and space required are both quadratic in the number of variables. This may prove also prohibitive for high dimensional data.

The paper presents a novel algorithm overcoming this limitation for the tree-like class of Bayesian networks. The new algorithm space consumption grows linearly with the number of variables n while the execution time is proportional to $n \ln(n)$, hence both are better than those of Chow/Liu algorithm. This opens new perspectives in construction of Bayesian networks from data containing tens of thousands and more variables, e.g. in automatic text categorization. Section 2 presents a brief introduction to the Chow/Liu algorithm. Section 3 introduces the concept of edge trees, upon which the new algorithm, introduced in section 4, is based. The properties of the new algorithm are investigated in section 5. Section 6 summarizes experiments with the Chow/Liu and the new algorithm. Section 7 contains some concluding remarks.

2   The Chow/Liu Algorithm

A tree-like Bayesian network is a quadruple $(\mathbf{X}, \mathbf{E}, P_{\mathbf{X}}, P_{\mathbf{E}})$ where $\mathbf{E}$ is a set of edges constituting a tree over the set of nodes $\mathbf{X}$, $P_{\mathbf{X}}$ is a set of marginal probability distributions for elements of $\mathbf{X}$, and $P_{\mathbf{E}}$ is a set of probability distributions for edges from $\mathbf{E}$ such that for each edge $XY = \{X, Y\}$ $P_{\mathbf{E}}(XY)$ is marginally consistent with $P_{\mathbf{X}}(X)$ and $P_{\mathbf{X}}(Y)$. Then, for any partial order $\prec$ of nodes such that for each edge $\{X, Y\}$ either $X \prec Y$ or $Y \prec X$ and for no two edges $\{X, Y\}$, $\{X, Z\}$ both $Z \prec X$ and $Y \prec X$ hold, and there exists $X0$ being a node such that for no $Y \in \mathbf{X}$ $Y \prec X0$ holds, the joint probability distribution represented by the Bayesian network, is given by:

$$P(\mathbf{X}) = P_{\mathbf{X}}(X0) \cdot \prod_{\{X,Y\} \in \mathbf{E}, X \prec Y} P_{\mathbf{E}}(\{X, Y\})/P_{\mathbf{X}}(X) \qquad (2)$$

Learning tree-like Bayesian networks from data is of special interest because the discovered tree structure may be a starting point for other Bayesian network learning algorithms [3,12]. Reasioning in tree-like structures is of orders of magnitude simpler than in general-type BNs. The best known tree-learning Chow/Liu algorithm is of significantly lower order of complexity than general BN learning algorithms. For these two reasons tree-like BNs are applied, whenever the number of variables is expected to be high (hundreds or thousands) like in tasks of text classification (TAN - type classifiers [6,1,?]), in intelligent genetic algorithms for feature selection [7]. The best known algorithm for construction of tree-like Bayesian networks from data seems to be the Chow/Liu algorithm [4,5]. For probability distributions described by tree-like Bayesian networks it recovers robustly the underlying tree structure and for general type probability distributions it recovers the closest tree-like Bayesian network [13]. It is based on the idea of maximum weight spanning tree, spanned between variables with dependence measure $DEP(X,Y)$ between variables X,Y equal to:

$$DEP(X,Y) = \sum_{x,y} P(x,y) \log \frac{P(x,y)}{P(x) \cdot P(y)} \tag{3}$$

where x,y run through the domains of X and Y respectively. $P(x,y)$ is the probability of co-occurrence of the events $X = x$ and $Y = y$, in practice it is calculated as relative frequency from some database.

It should be mentioned that the algorithm of Chow/Liu relies on the following property of the $DEP()$: If in the true underlying Bayesian network the node Z lies on the path from node X to node Y, then $DEP(X,Z) > DEP(X,Y) < DEP(Y,Z)$.[1] The basic outline of the algorithm is as follows:

Algorithm CL(D,X)

(D is a probability distribution over a set of variables including the set of variables **X**)

1. Let **X** be the set of (discrete) variables. Find $X_1, X_2 \in$ **X** such that $DEP(X_1, X_2) \geq DEP(Y_1, Y_2)$ for any $Y_1, Y_2 \in$ **X**
2. Form two sets of nodes **T**, **N**, and the set of edges **E**, and initialize **T**= $\{X_1, X_2\}$, **N**=**X-T**, **E**= $\{(X_1, X_2)\}$
3. If **N** is empty, **STOP**.
4. Otherwise find $X_1 \in$ **T**, $X_2 \in$ **N** such that $DEP(X_1, X_2) \geq DEP(Y_1, Y_2)$ for any $Y_1 \in$ **T**, $Y_2 \in$ **N**.
5. Update **E** := $E \cup \{(X_1, X_2)\}$, **T** = **T** $\cup \{X_2\}$, **N** = **N** $- \{X_2\}$
6. Go to step 3.

End of Algorithm

As a result **Tr**=(**X,E**) is the tree being the backbone (the direct acyclic graph) of the resulting tree-like Bayesian network. The most time-consuming step of the algorithm is the calculation of $DEP(X,Y)$, because it is connected to calculations involving all records from the database. In step 1 $DEP(X,Y)$ is accessed $(card(X) - 1) \cdot card(X)/2$ times and upon each execution of step 4 it is accessed $(card(\mathbf{T}) - 1) \cdot card(\mathbf{N})$ times. If $card(\mathbf{X}) = n$, then the total amounts to $(n \cdot (n-1)/2) + n \cdot n \cdot (n-1)/2 - (2n-1) \cdot (n-1) \cdot n/6$ which grows with n^3 for large n. It is easily seen that for a given pair of variables X, Y, $DEP(X,Y)$ is accessed many (up to n) times. For purposes of time saving the practical implementations create a table $TDEP[X,Y]$ for storing the values of

---

[1] Usage of the DEP measure in this context as defined after Chow/Liu is justified only for variables with the same range of values. This is the case in the application domain in the background of this research: in text processing variables are binary and indicate presence or absense of a word in text.

$DEP(X, Y)$ so that we need only to calculate the $DEP()$ function only $(n \cdot (n - 1)/2)$ times. For large n the number of times the whole database is searched through is proportional to n^2 only. The algorithm changes then to Algorithm CL1(D,X), in which the DEP is calculated only once and later read from the table $TDEP$. [2] Though in $TDEP[]$ we do not need the diagonal elements and the table is symmetric $(DEP(X, Y) = DEP(Y, X))$, it requires still $n(n-1)$ cells and as many $DEP()$ calculations, which may be prohibitive even for moderate size $n = 10,000$ which may be required in free text applications. The goal of this paper is to propose a new algorithm for building the tree-like Bayesian networks with memory consumption proportional to n and with time complexity significantly below the CL1 algorithm. Notice that for execution time, also the space consumption of main memory may be a critical factor (disk access would slow down the process beyond any acceptable limits).

3   The Concept of an Edge Tree

The new algorithm relies on the paradigm of tree representation of subsets of edges. Consider a typical tree **Tr**=(**X,E**) like that in Fig.1a.

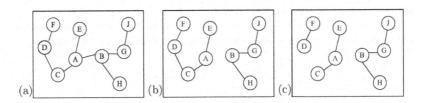

Fig. 1. (a)A tree **Tr**, (b) Trees **Tra** and **Trb** ,(c) Trees **Trac**, **Trad**, and **Trb**.

Here $X=\{A, B, C, D, E, F, G, H, J\}$, $E=\{AB, AF, AC, CD, DF, AE, BH, BG, GJ\}$. Removal of any edge, for example AB, will split this tree into two parts, two trees, e.g.: **Tra** and **Trb**, each containing one end of the removed edge, e.g. **Tra** containing A, and **Trb** containing B, as in Fig.1b.

Each of the sub-trees could be split further by removal of edges. For example, removing edge DC splits **Tra** into **Trac** and **Trad** containing C and D resp. (Fig.1c).

We can continue this process until no more edges will be there. Now imagine the construction of the following oriented tree that we shall call "edge tree". Let **Tr** be a tree. If it contains no edges then its edge tree is empty. Otherwise if **Tr** is not empty, then let AB be an edge in it, A be called the left and B the right element of $A = B$, **Tra** containing A, and **Trb** containing B be two sub-trees obtained from **Tr** by removing AB from it. Then the edge tree of **Tr** consists of

---

[2] Further reductions in time consumption are possible for sparse data (see e.g. [10]).

the node denoted by the oriented pair $A = B$ (A be called the left and B the right element of $A = B$) as its root and of edge trees of **Tra** and **Trb** with an additional oriented so-called "left edge" leading from node $A = B$ to the root of edge tree of **Tra** if it is not empty, and with an additional oriented so-called "right edge" leading from node $A = B$ to the root of edge tree of **Trb** if it is not empty. Clearly, there may be several different edge trees for the same tree. Example edge trees for the tree in Fig.1a are shown in Fig.2.

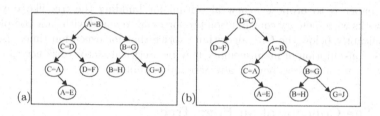

(a)   (b)

Fig. 2. Possible edge trees for the tree from Fig.1

It does not surprise that the number of nodes in an edge tree is equal to the number of edges in the original tree.

Obviously, in an edge node, for each tree node X there exists an oriented path such that it contains all the edge nodes containing X (see Fig.3).

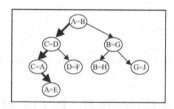

Fig. 3. Oriented path containing all occurrences of A.

Tree-structured representation is usually used to achieve a quick access to data. The quickest access is guarantied by "balanced trees". The edge-tree has a very special way of balancing due to the above-mentioned oriented path requirement. Imagine in an edge-tree (or in a sub-tree) you want to shift the root node of the left sub-tree ($C = D$ in Fig.3) of the current edge tree root node ($A = B$ in Fig.3). Then you have to identify the oriented path with all occurrences of the left element of the current root node (A in Fig.3, see the thick arrows). Below the left sub-tree root node you have to distinguish the sub-tree containing the marked subpath (sub-tree of A in Fig.4) and the other, not containing it (non-A sub-tree in Fig.4a). Then you put the root of the left sub-tree as a new root together with the sub-tree not containing the marked path, the sub-tree containing the marked path will become the new left sub-tree of the current root node, and the current root node will become the root node of other sub-tree (see Fig.4b) An analogous procedure is applicable, if one wants to balance the other way: when the root of the right subtrree is to become the root.

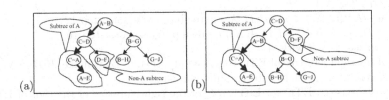

Fig. 4. Tree balancing: (a) sub-tree identification, (b) sub-tree to the top.

From this exposition it is obvious that a balanced edge tree does not need to be identical with traditional balanced tree because of the marked path condition. It is obvious that the new edge tree represents the same underlying tree as that before balancing operation. It means only that the edge removal represented by edge tree root of the left (right) sub-tree has been put before the edge removal represented by the edge tree root.

4   The Description of the New Algorithm

Imagine that for the set $\mathbf{X}$ you define a series of sets $\mathbf{X}_2 \subset \mathbf{X}_3 \subset \ldots \subset \mathbf{X}_{n-1} \subset \mathbf{X}_n = \mathbf{X}$ with $card(\mathbf{X}_i) = i$. Let $\mathbf{Tr}_i = (\mathbf{X}_i, \mathbf{E}_i)$ be a tree constructed by the algorithm CL1 for a given set of nodes $\mathbf{X}_i$ and the background database. $\mathbf{E}_i$ be the set of triples $(X, Y, DEP(X, Y))$ with $X, Y \in \mathbf{X}_i$. By the way, we can consider the problem of building $\mathbf{Tr}_i$ as a problem of building a Bayesian network from data with hidden (or latent) variables $\mathbf{X} - \mathbf{X}_i$. We claim now that we can construct $\mathbf{Tr}_i$ from $\mathbf{Tr}_{i-1}$ and the set of dependences $DEP(X, X_i)$ with $X \in \mathbf{X}_{i-1}$ and X_i being the only element from $\mathbf{X}_i - \mathbf{X}_{i-1}$.

Below we present the new algorithm, called here "Edge Tree Construction" (ETC) Algorithm. We shall use an extended edge tree node representation, denoted as $[C]A = B[D]$ with $A = B$ being the proper edge tree node, and C and D being the left and right region focal points.

Algorithm ETC(D,X)

(D is a probability distribution over a set of variables including the set of variables $\mathbf{X}$)

1 Define the sequence of sets $\mathbf{X}_2 \subset \mathbf{X}_3 \subset \ldots \subset \mathbf{X}_{n-1} \subset \mathbf{X}_n = \mathbf{X}$ with $\mathbf{X}_i = \{X_1, X_2, \ldots, X_i\}$ for $i = 2, \ldots, n$.

120   M.A. Kłopotek

2 Initialize **ETr** as **ETr** := $(\mathbf{T} = ([X_1]X_1 = X_2, [X_2], DEP(X_1, X_2)), \mathbf{E} = \{\}$
  and $i := 2$
3 **ETr'** := &**ETr** (reference assignment)[3]
4 $i := i + 1$
5 if $i > n$ STOP otherwise balance **ETr'**
6 Let $[C]A = B[D]$ be the root node of **ETr'**. Calculate $DEP(C, X_i)$ and
  $DEP(D, X_i)$.
7 if $DEP(C, X_i) < DEP(D, X_i)$ goto step 8 else goto step 12
8 if $DEP(A, B) < DEP(A, X_i)$ goto step 9, else goto step 10
9 replace $A = B$ with $A = X_i$
10 if the right sub-tree of **ETr'** root is empty, then in **ETr'** make $[B]B = X_i[X_i]$
   the root of the right sub-tree, and goto step 3
11 Otherwise in **ETr'** set **ETr'** to & of the right sub-tree of the root of **ETr'**,
   and goto step 6.
12 if $DEP(A, B) < DEP(B, X_i)$ goto step 13, else goto step 14
13 replace $A = B$ with $X_i = B$
14 if the left sub-tree of **ETr'** root is empty, then in **ETr'** make $[X_i]X_i = A[A]$
   the root of the left sub-tree. Then goto step 3
15 Otherwise in **ETr'** set **ETr'** to & of the left sub-tree of the root of **ETr'**,
   and goto step 6.

End of Algorithm

Obviously the result of ETC is a tree-like Baysian network. Let us stress here
that this algorithm is time and space-saving. Instead of about $n^2/2$ cells required
by CL1, it needs at most $(n-1)+2$ cells for storing DEP: $(n-1)$ cells for storing
distances between nodes in the current tree and 2 cells for storing distances of the
ingoing node to the nodes currently in the root of the currently considered tree.
Thanks to the balancing step, we save also time. If the tree can be well balanced,
in each iteration, when including the jth node we need about $4 \cdot \log_2 j$ calculations
of $DEP()$ function. This amounts to about $((n-1) \cdot \ln(n-1) - (n-1)) \cdot 4/\ln(2)$.
Recall that for CL1 requires $(n \cdot (n-1)/2)$ $DEP()$ calculations.

5   Claims about the ETC Algorithm

Given that the ETC algorithm is applied to data stemming from a tree-like
distribution, rationality of the new algorithm can be demonstrated. The ETC
algorithm is based essentially on the *tree- common-sense-assumption:*

Assumption for a tree like distribution, if X is on the path from Z to A and
  X is on the path from Z to B, then $DEP(A, Z) > DEP(B, Z)$ if and only
  if $DEP(A, X) > DEP(B, X)$.

In [8] numerous interesting properties of ETC have been proven. the most
important ones are given below.

---

[3] & marks the fact that we work here with "shadow" variables instead of creating of
  any copies of the tree or its parts.

Theorem 1. *In the ETC, the tree obtained after inclusion of all the nodes is identical with the intrinsic underlying tree.*

Theorem 2. *In the ETC, the tree obtained after inclusion of any number of nodes is identical with the tree that would be obtained by CL for these nodes.*

Theorem 3. *The algorithm ETC1 obtained from ETC by inclusion of the following activity after each niode inclusion: "replace $[C]A = B[D]$ with $[A]A = B[B]$" will yield identical results to the original ETC algorithm.*

6   Experiments

To verify the lemmas raised in this paper, experimental implementations of CL1 and ETC (with ETC1 version) were tested on identical artificial data sets generated from tree-like Bayesian networks with binary variables. Networks with 50 up to 5,000 nodes were considered. Conditional probabilities of success on success and failure on failure of the variables were varied from 0.6 to 0.9. Branching factors of the underlying trees were chosen in the range from 2 to 8. Sample sizes ranged from the number of variables to the tenfold of the number of variables. The sequence of variable inclusions was randomized. Apparently the branching factor did not influence the number of $DEP()$ calculations needed in ETC. The time needed for single DEP calculation was linearly dependent on the sample size. Therefore, in Fig.5 only the dependence of the number of DEP calculations on the number of variables was presented.Notice that both axes are logarithmically scaled. The advantage of ETC over Chow/Liu algorithm is visible. In separate runs (for ETC and ETC1 alone, because the runtime of CL1 exceeded 1 hour for 2,000 variables on a PC Pentium) it has been verified that networks with 20,000 nodes can be reconstructed from data in reasonable time. The hypothesis of the tree-commen-sense assumption was confirmed for a wide range of conditional probabilities.

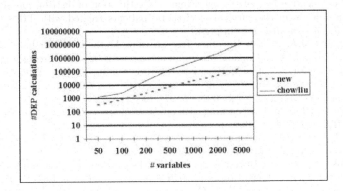

Fig. 5. Comparison of the new algorithm with Chow/Liu algorithm

7 Conclusions

This study demonstrated the possibility of reducing space and time consumption when constructing tree like Bayesian network from data from quadratic in the number of variables by the Chow/Liu algorithm to a linear one and to a proportional to n ln n respectively. A new algorithm achieving this goal has been proposed and it has been demonstrated that the resulting tree will have no worse properties than the one delivered by the Chow/Liu algorithm. Thus, new application possibilities are open. Bayesian network construction for applications with 100,000 nodes and more as needed in free text classifications will be possible. The new approach is independent of other approaches to improvements of efficiency of the Chow/Liu algorithm. For example the sparse data time saving algorithms proposed in [7,8,9] may still be applied in the context of the new algorithm. The experiments carried out so far were concerned with artificial data for a restricted set of tree-like distributions. Both theoretical and experimental should be pursued for other than tree-like distributions of variables.

References

1. Cerquides, J.: Applying General Bayesian Techniques to Improve TAN Induction, *Knowledge Discovery and Data Mining*, 1999, pp 292-296.
2. Cheng, J., Bell, D.A., Liu, W.: An algorithm for Bayesian belief network construction from data, *Proceedings of AI & STAT'97*, Ft. Lauderdale, Florida, 1997.
3. Cheng, J., Bell, D.A., Liu, W.: Learning belief networks from data: an information theory based approach. *Proceedings of the Sixth ACM International Conference on Information and Knowledge Management*, 1997.
4. Chow, C. K., Liu, C. N.: Approximating discrete probability distributions with dependence trees, *IEEE Trans. on IT*, IT-14, No.3, 1968, pp. 462-467
5. Chou, C. K., Wagner, T. J.: Consistency of an estimate of tree-dependent probability distribution, *IEEE Transactions on Information Theory*, IT-19, 1973, 369-371
6. Friedman, N., Geiger, D., Goldszmidt, M.: Bayesian Network Classifiers, *Machine Learning* vol. 29, 1997, pp.131.
7. Inza, N., Merino, M., Larranaga, P., Quiroga, J., Sierra, B., Girala, M.: Feature Subset selection by genetic algorithms and estimation of distribution algorithms. A case study in the survival of cirrhotic patients treated with TIPS. *Artificial Intelligence in Medicine* (in press)
8. Kłopotek M.A.: A New Bayesian Tree Learning Method with Reduced Time and Space Complexity. *Fundamenta Informaticae*, 49(2002), IOS Press, in press
9. Kłopotek, M. A., et al. : Bayesian Network Mining System. *Proc. X International Symposium on Intelligent Information Systems*, Zakopane, 18-22 June, 2001, Springer-Verlag, New York 2001. pp. 97-110
10. Meila, M., Jordan, M.: Learning with mixtures of trees. *Journal of Machine Learning Research*, Vol. 1, 2000,
11. Pearl, J.: *Probabilistic Reasoning in Intelligent Systems: Networks of Plausible Inference*, Morgan Kaufmann, San Mateo CA, 1988.
12. Suzuki, J.: Learning Bayesian Belief Networks based on the Minimum Descripion Length Principle: Basic Properties,*IEICE Trans.Found.*, Vol. E82-A, Oct. 1999
13. Valiveti, R. S., Oommen, B. J.: On using the chi-squared statistics for determining statistic dependence, *Pattern Recognition* Vol. 25 No. 11, 1992, pp. 1389-1400.

Automatic Generation of Trivia Questions

Matthew Merzbacher

University of California, Berkeley CA, USA
Mills College, Oakland CA, USA

Abstract. We present a (nearly) domain-independent approach to mining trivia questions from a database. Generated questions are ranked and are more "interesting" if they have a modest number of solutions and may reasonably be solved (but are not too easy). Our functional model and genetic approach have several advantages: they are tractable and scalable, the hypothesis space size is limited, and the user may tune question difficulty. This makes our approach suitable for application to other data mining problems. We include a discussion of implementation on disparate data sets.

Keywords: data mining, knowledge discovery, functional programming, relational algebra, automated systems, genetic algorithms

1 Introduction

Data mining techniques are mostly used for two purposes – to find general patterns of behavior (e.g. association rules) or to find outliers and exceptions [3]. However, it is not enough to locate all possible exceptions; rather, the exceptions must be shown to be useful. That is, the system must have a way of discriminating information that is both relevant and interesting to the end user.

The same problems arise when devising trivia questions. A good trivia question skirts the edge of relevance while remaining interesting and fun. Questions must neither be too simple nor too outlandish.

We describe an approach to mining good trivia questions from a relational database using a functional approach. The general idea is to construct questions by composing several functions from a general library. In this regard, our technique is similar to the AM mathematical discovery system [6]. Our approach is nearly domain–independent and automatic, requiring only modest human expertise and guidance. We have implemented a prototype of this system that generates and ranks questions in terms of perceived difficulty.

1.1 Making Good Trivia

According to professional trivia setters, good trivia questions have several properties[7]:

M.-S. Hacid et al. (Eds.): ISMIS 2002, LNAI 2366, pp. 123–130, 2002.

- Interesting and fun – One way to make questions more interesting (and less subject to dispute) is "Doubling up". This means having two questions wrapped into one. For example, "This American President was the first to move into the White House and also had a son who became President" can be reasoned by knowing one of two relevant facts.
- Challenging (but not too challenging) – Similarly, knowing the audience's expertise can lead to questions that are appropriately difficult.
- Modest number of answers – limit questions to a single answer, ideally. At the most, only have a short list of answers (in some cases, the difficulty of the question can be tuned by requiring only a portion of the list, such as "Name three of the five Great Lakes.").
- Multiple Choice – questions can also be turned into multiple choice. This limits the setter's liability for wrong answers, as one can't be surprised by unusual responses.
- Up-to-date – facts become stale. Questions either need to be independent of time or have a time stamp, such as "This was the world's tallest building in 1950."
- Solid sources and careful wording – By its nature, trivia is on the extrema of knowledge and therefore requires accuracy in source material and explicit phrasing.
- Unopinionated – good questions are limited to facts, not opinions.

Our system fulfills these properties. It has no opinion, relying on a specific set of data; the data can be updated to remain timely; the system can be tuned to generate harder (or easier) questions; and it can even generate reasonable candidate wrong answers for use in multiple choice questions.

1.2   Example Database

To illustrate our approach, consider a relational database that includes data about the Academy Awards[1], also known as the Oscars. For each of twenty-three main categories, there are several nominated films and the people responsible. One, occasionally more, of the films is a winner. Acting categories, ostensibly awarded to people, are always associated with specific films, so this representation works for them as well. For the sake of discussion, we have added "cost" and "take" fields that indicate the film's cost and box–office gross[2] revenue. We ignore several other fields to avoid complexity in our presentation.

Figure 1 shows an non-normalized version of the relation.[3] We finesse issues of normalization at this point, as using a universal relation simplifies our system. Ultimately, we can decompose the relation appropriately and reconstruct it carefully using joins in our queries. For now, using the universal relation keeps

---

[1] "Academy Award(s)" and "Oscar(s)" are registered trademarks of the Academy of Motion Picture Arts and Sciences

[2] Hollywood is notorious for fabricating these numbers. In this case, we use the US theater revenue, but it's only an example.

[3] Dates for Oscars are a year after the film release date

our generated queries clearer. We allow categories to be lists of values, less than even second normal form.

Year (date)	Category (string)	Title (string)	People (list of strings)	Win? (bool)	Cost (int)	Take (int)
2001	Best Picture	Gladiator	Wick, Frangoni, Lustig	T	$103M	$187M
2001	Best Picture	Chocolat	Brown, Golden, Holleran	F	$23M	$71M
			etc.			

Fig. 1. The Oscar Relation

2   The Functional Approach

Our approach constructs a query as a series of functions on the relation. These functions include, but are not limited to, the standard relational algebra operators. For example, the question, "Which film won the Best Picture Oscar in 2001" is written:

$$\pi_{Film}(\sigma_{win=T}(\sigma_{year=2001}(\sigma_{category=Best\ Picture}(Oscar))))$$

Each selection operation, σ, contains a simple condition, either between two attributes or between an attribute and a specific value (in this case, the comparisons are for equality, but the usual operators are available). Boolean connectives are not allowed, but can be synthesized through composition, as in this example where the three selections form a logical conjunction.

The available functions include:

select   based on a single selection criterion
project   a subset of the attributes
union   merges two relations (not eliminating duplicates)
intersect   tuples appearing in two relations
difference   tuples in one of two relations
cross   cross product of two relations
join   a cross product with a selection and projection
distinct   eliminates duplicate tuples (different from standard relational algebra)
sort   a useful general sorting function, based on a sort criterion
first   returns first tuple
last   returns last tuple
median   returns median tuple

In addition to these general relational functions, there are functions that operate on specific domains, such as **mean**, which takes a list of numbers. We intend to add grouping functions, similar to SQL's **group by** function, but until that happens, we use a series of **select** functions to achieve the same ends.

Although not strictly necessary, it proves useful to combine certain functions, such as **sort** with **first/last** to derive **minimum/maximum** functions. Ultimately, certain patterns of functions will improve the range of the system (see Future Work).

Most functions return a new relation (perhaps only a single tuple or empty) which can be saved and named for further use. A trivia question is then just a sequence of functions composed together and applied to one or more relations.

2.1 Finding Trivia Questions

The system searches for trivia questions using a modified genetic approach [5]; good questions are constructed out of promising pieces. The pieces are scored along the way and only the highest scoring pieces are retained. A random factor allows some non-optimal pieces to be retained across generations so that new territory may sometimes be explored. The algorithm:

```
add all base relations to permanent query set
set temporary query set to empty

repeat {
  select random function
  select random relation(s) from permanent & temporary query sets
  apply function to relation(s), yielding new query
  score resulting relation and query
  if (score > trivia-threshold)
    print query and result
  if (score > piece-threshold)
    add query to temporary set (with relation)
  drop excess members of temporary set
}
```

The permanent set contains queries and relations that will frequently be reused, while the temporary set contains promising queries that might end up in bigger trivia questions.

There are several controls over the random selections in algorithm. The first is the selection of the function. Certain functions are *a priori* more promising than others. For example, **cross product** is almost worthless, as it is extremely unlikely to yield interesting trivia, while **select** is often a very good step toward our goal of finding a good trivia question. Each function is assigned a weight in advance that is its relative likelihood of being chosen. We assigned weight assignments by deconstructing several "real" trivia questions and seeing which functions appeared most frequently. However, these weights are preliminary at this time.

Once the function is chosen, it must be applied to one or more relations, depending on the function's arity. For unary functions, a single relation from is drawn from the permanent and temporary query sets. For binary relations, two relations are drawn from the sets, subject to certain obvious constraints based on the function and schema (e.g., intersection only works between two relations that share a schema). At any time the function may be applied to the original relation (which is in the permanent set) or to a partially developed query. Again, certain combinations of functions and relations prove more useful than others. Eventually, we plan to add common popular groups of functions as single functions to our list.

After the function and relations are selected, the function is applied to the relation. For some functions (e.g. **union, difference**) this is straightforward. Other functions require additional parameter(s). For example, **project** requires a list of attributes and **select** requires a condition (attribute, operation, and value or second attributes).

As an example, consider the sample query of the previous section. First, the function picker chooses **select**. The relation picker chooses the only available relation ($Oscar$), which is in the permanent set. Next, the **select** subsystem identifies $Category$ as the attribute (see below) and, using some domain knowledge, chooses $Best\ Picture$ for the value, yielding $\sigma_{category=\text{"}BestPicture\text{"}}(Oscar)$. The query and its result are then added to the temporary set for the next iteration.

For **select**, the attribute is chosen from the available attributes, again randomly with certain attributes weighted more heavily. This is the primary piece of domain-specific control in the system. For example, in the $Oscar$ relation, $Cost$ and $Take$ are the least interesting attributes. In practice, it turned out to be useful to decompose $Oscar$ by category, because for acting categories the name of the winner is important, while for most others it isn't. In general, another way to achieve this is to pre-define certain relations in the permanent set, such as $Best\ Picture$ winners.

Once the attribute has been selected, the comparison operation and a value or second attribute must be chosen. For value selection, this is done by considering the distribution of values from the relation and selecting one randomly (again in a weighted manner). For comparing using equality, the maximum and minimum possible values are heavily weighted, while the median is also a "good" value. In this way, the function $\sigma_{year=2001}$ is chosen.

Other good values, especially for non-numeric data, are the values that appear either very frequently or only once. For example, suppose we have already isolated the $Actor$ category into a single relation containing all nominees for Best Actor. Further, the system has already chosen to apply the function, $\sigma_{name=?}(Actor)$. The only question is which value to choose for the name. Based on the "very frequent" heuristic, the system could choose an actor who was nominated many times. The next iteration of the algorithm could then take that result and find the one time when that actor won the award, yielding the trivia question, "For which film did oft-nominated actor X finally win a Best Actor award?"

After building the entire query, we apply the function and score the result. Scores depend on the functions, the relations, the parameters, and, most importantly, the outcome size (see next section). If the score is high enough, then the query is printed as a candidate trivia question. At this point, a natural-language back-end could turn the relational query into pseudo-English, but we currently generate only the functional representation and leave it up to the human to decode it. Even if the result isn't trivia worthy, it may be useful as a piece, so if it scores high enough, it is retained for future use. Again, there is some randomness at this stage, so that non-promising pieces may be retained sometimes.

Lastly, we throw away excess members of the temporary set. This step isn't strictly necessary (and we don't bother in our prototype), but ultimately the temporary set will grow too large and have to be pruned. In this way, the hypothesis space for likely good questions can be arbitrarily limited in size, making our solution scalable.

2.2   Scoring Questions

How do we score questions for trivia worthiness and retention? Our evaluation approach matches the criteria list in the introduction [7]. The score for a question is calculated based on a combination of the size of the result, which functions were used (and how many), which attributes were returned, and which values were used in the queries. The same weights used for the random selection processes are used in this stage.

For functions, selection is typically a "good" function and scores highly. For example, **difference** and **intersection** only score well as the last (or next-to-last) function to be applied ("Name the most recent film to win Best Director but no other awards").

For attributes, the score again reflects the weights assigned by the domain-specific user. For attribute values, the maximum and minimum are scored much more heavily than arbitrary intermediate values. It is possible that "round" values are also more meaningful ("Name the first film to gross more than $100M"), though this isn't currently done.

3   Results, Problems, and Future Work

We have built a prototype implementation (in Java) and are currently testing and it extensively. The system maintains the relations in memory, instead of using a true relational database, which will ultimately lead to frustrations when scaling our approach. The prototype generates very simple trivia questions that are not bad, but tends to get wild after that. Further, there are still far too many stupid avenues that are explored by the system. For example, it will try to run selection on the same attribute repeatedly (which may be necessary to get a range of values, but is otherwise pointless).

Unless they are very simple, the generated questions are almost unreadable. Most are a sequence of functions that may be a good question or may not, but it is very hard for even an expert human to tell. We expect to spend more time on the back-end presentation so that a human can follow the results.

There is a relationship between the concepts of recall and precision of information retrieval [4] and measuring the results of our system. Specifically, we would like to know how many of the generated questions are "good" (precision) and how many of the "good" questions get generated (recall). The latter is very difficult to determine, as even an expert would have trouble generating all good trivia questions. Precision can be estimated by looking at the results and depends on the threshold values. The higher those values, the better the precision, but certain good queries are weeded out, lowering recall.

One goal of our approach is to have as much domain-independence as possible. To test this, we are using three separate database domains. In addition to the *Oscar* relation, we are testing the system on data about the countries of the world, population, land area, languages, religions, and so on. This data is from the online CIA World Fact Book [2] and is extremely dirty with lots of errors (such as listing some populations in millions and others in exact values, so that India originally appeared to have only a thousand people). As a result, the system tends to generate queries centered on the dirtiest data (the dirty values tend to be outliers, naturally). Thus, we have some hope that the system may be extended to identify potentially dirty data in a larger database system.

We are also trying to apply the system on data to baseball statistics. Sports is a rich area for trivia and provides challenges that are not found in the other domains. In particular, the data covers individual games, seasons, and careers. The season can be viewed as an aggregation of the individual games, but this will surely lead to unbearable inefficiencies. One advantage of the baseball domain is that we can reverse engineer existing trivia questions to try to force new capabilities on our system. We also used this approach to get some of our domain-dependent values for the Oscars and it seems to work.

Our system is intended to be open enough so that domain-specific functions might be added by hand. It might be reasonable to keep the *Oscar* relation as a single universal relation but add a few permanent queries that apply reasonable decompositions. Similarly, in the baseball domain, we could pre-encode the aggregations for season and career statistics from the game data.

Along these lines, we plan to add other domain-independent pre-canned patterns to the list of functions. For example, if there are two relations R and S with the same schema, then:

$$(\sigma_X R) \cap (\sigma_X S)$$

is an interesting function, where X is the same condition (but determined at runtime). That is, tell me all things that fulfill X in both R and S.

3.1   Conclusion

We have presented a new system for automatically generating trivia questions with limited domain knowledge. This application, while seemingly lighthearted, is leading to the development of new techniques based on our functional approach. These techniques are suitable for data mining, data cleansing, and intelligent information retrieval. The next steps are to attach the system on a real relational database, add a presentation module to make the results readable, and determine a good method for estimating appropriate values for the control weights in our algorithm.

References

1. Binstead, K. and Ritchie, G. "An implemented model of punning riddles." *Proceedings of the Twelfth National Conference on Artificial Intelligence (AAAI-94)*, Seattle, 1994.
2. Central Intelligence Agency "CIA World Factbook." [online]. Available through: www.cia.gov/cia/publications/factbook, November 2001.
3. U. Fayyad, G. Piatetsky-Shapiro, P. Smyth, R. Uthurusamy (Eds.). *Advances in Knowledge Discovery and Data Mining*. AAAI Press, Melo Park, CA, 1996.
4. Gordon, M. and Kochen, M. "Recall-Precision Trade-Off: A Derivation." *Journal of the American Society for Information Science*, 40(3), pp. 145–151, 1989.
5. Koza, J. R. *Genetic Programming*. MIT Press, 1992.
6. Lenat, D. and Brown, J. S. "Why AM and EURISKO apear to work." *Artificial Intelligence*, 23, pp. 269–294, 1984.
7. Paquet, P. (2001). "Cornerstone Question Clinic: Writing Good Trivia Questions." [online]. Available through: www.triviahalloffame.com/writeq.htm, November 2001.

Answering Queries Addressed to Several Databases: A Query Evaluator which Implements a Majority Merging Approach

Laurence Cholvy and Christophe Garion

ONERA-Toulouse, BP 4035
31055 Toulouse Cedex 4, France

Abstract. The general context of this work is the problem of merging data provided by several sources which can be contradictory. Focusing on the case when the information sources do not contain any disjunction, this paper first defines a propositional modal logic for reasoning with data obtained by merging several information sources according to a majority approach. Then it defines a theorem prover to automatically deduce these merged data. Finally, it shows how to use this prover to implement a query evaluator which answers queries addressed to several databases. This evaluator is such that the answer to a query is the one that could be computed by a classical evaluator if the query was addressed to the merged databases. The databases we consider are made of an extensional part, i.e. a set of positive or negative ground literals and an intensional part i.e. a set of first order function-free clauses. A restriction is imposed to these databases in order to avoid disjunctive data.

Keywords: Database merging, majority merging, logic.

1 Introduction

The problem of merging information sources has been intensively studied for some years [BKMS91], [BKMS92], [Cho93], [Sub94], [Lin96], [Cho98a], [LM98], [SDL+98], [KPP98], [KPP99], [Lia00]. This is due to the growing number of applications in which accessing several information sources to make a decision is needed. The main problem in dealing with multiple information sources is the possible inconsistency between sources. The many works which address this problem show that there is not an unique method for merging information. Obviously, the adequate merging process depends on the type of the information to be merged. This information can be beliefs the sources have about the real world and in this case, the aim of the merging process is to refine our perception of the real world. But this information can also be a description of a world that is considered to be more or less ideal. This is the case for instance when merging requirements expressed by several agents about an artifact to be built or a software to be designed. In that case, the aim of the merging process is to find a consensus between the agents in order to define a description of that ideal

M.-S. Hacid et al. (Eds.): ISMIS 2002, LNAI 2366, pp. 131–139, 2002.

world on which the agents agree. But the merging process also depends on the meta-information about the sources. For instance, in the case of merging beliefs provided by several sources, if the respective reliability of the sources is known, it obviously must be used in the merging process: the more reliable a source is, the more we trust it. In the case of requirement merging, if the respective importance of the agents that provide the requirements is known, it also must be used in the merging process: the more important an agent is, the more the result of the merging must agree it. But, if this meta-information is not known, some other types of merging processes must be defined. Konieczny and Pino-Pérez's [KPP98], [KPP99] address this last case since they do not assume a priority order between the sources to be merged. They define two kinds of merging operators respectively called majority merging operators and arbitration merging operators. The first ones aim at implementing a kind of majority vote between the sources, and the second ones aim at reaching a consensus between the sources by trying to satisfy as much as possible all of them. Konieczny and Pino-Pérez define these two families of merging operators from a semantical point of view. Our work takes as a starting point one of the majority merging operator that have been semantically characterized in the previous work. Our first aim is to define a logic (language, model theory and proof theory) that allows one to reason with data provided by several sources according to that majority operator. Our second aim is to apply these results in the database context and to specify a query evaluator which answers queries addressed to several databases according to a majority approach. This present paper partially presents these results. It is organized as follows. In section 2, we focus on the case when the information sources do not contain disjunctions and we present a propositional modal logic, called MF (Majority Fusion). In [CG01], we have presented a Hilbert-type proof-theory of that logic and we have proved that this logic effectively axiomatizes a majority merging operator but it is not recalled here. Section 3 presents a theorem-prover, defined as a meta-program of a PROLOG-type interpreter, which allows one to automatically deduce the data contained in the merged information sources. Section 4 presents the application of this prover in the context of first-order databases. We specify a query evaluator which answers queries addressed to several databases. Databases we consider are made of an extensional part (i.e. a set of positive or negative facts) and an intensional part (i.e. a set of function-free clauses). A restriction is imposed to these databases in order to avoid disjunctive data. Extensions to this work are discussed in section 5.

2   The Propositional Logic MF

2.1   Preliminaries

Definition 1. A multi-set is a set where redundant occurrences are accepted. Let $MS_1 = [S_1, ..., S_n]$ and $MS_2 = [S_{n+1}, ..., S_m]$ be two multi-sets. The union of two multi-sets is defined by: $MS_1 \bigsqcup MS_2 = [S_1, ..., S_m]$. The membership relation is defined by: $S \in^i MS$ iff there are exactly i occurrences of S in the multi-set MS. Notice that, in the limit case, $S \in^0 MS$ iff there is no occurrence of S in MS, i.e. $S \notin MS$.

Notation. If db and db' denote two information sources, then $db * db'$ will denote the information source obtained by merging db and db'. By information source we mean any information source to be merged (in that case, we call it primitive) and also any information source obtained after merging some information sources.

Example. For instance, if we face three (primitive) information sources db_1, db_2 and db_3 then $db_1 * db_2$, and $(db_1 * db_2) * db_3$ are information sources but they are not primitive. The first one denotes the one obtained by merging db_1 and db_2. The second one denotes the one obtained by merging $db_1 * db_2$ and db_3.

2.2 MF Language and Its Semantics

Let us call L the propositional language used to describe the contents of the information sources to be merged. The language L' of logic MF is obtained from L by adding several modal operators of the following form: B_{db}^i and B_{db}, where i is an integer and db denotes an information source (primitive or not). The formula $B_{db}^i l$ will mean that there are exactly i occurrences of the literal l in db. And the formula $B_{db}F$ will mean that the information source db believes F. Informally speaking, we introduce the modalities B_{db}^i for being able to count the occurrences of a literal in an information source. The idea is that, when merging two information sources, the number of occurrences of a literal is the sum of the numbers of its occurrences in the two information sources respectively. Then we want that a literal is believed by an information source if the number of occurrences of that literal is strictly greater than the number of occurrences of its negation. The formal definition of L' is the following:

Definition 2. If F is a formula of L and if B_{db}^i and B_{db} are modal operators, then $B_{db}^i F$ and $B_{db}F$ are formulas of L'. If F_1 and F_2 are formulas of L' then, $\neg F_1$, $F_1 \wedge F_2$ are formulas of L'. $F_1 \vee F_2$ and $F_1 \rightarrow F_2$ are defined from the previous ones as usually.

One can notice that modal operators only govern formulas without modal operators.

The semantics of MF is a Kripke-type one [Che80]. Models are defined by:

Definition 3. Models of MF. A model of MF is a tuple $< W, val, R, B >$ such that: W is a set of worlds; val is a valuation function[1] which associates any proposition of L with a set of worlds of W; R is a set of functions denoted f_{db}, where db is an information source (primitive or not). Each function f_{db} associates any world of W with a multi-set of sets of worlds of W; B is a set of functions denoted g_{db}, where db is an information source (primitive or not). Each function g_{db} associates any world of W with a set of worlds of W.

This tuple is constrained by two constraints given below, but before, we need to give the following definition:

---

[1] It satisfies: $val(P) \neq \emptyset$ iff P is a satisfiable propositional formula, $val(\neg P) = W \setminus val(P)$, $val(P \wedge Q) = val(P) \cap val(Q)$.

Definition 4. Let w and w' be two W worlds. The distance $d(w, w')$ between w and w' is defined by the number of propositional letters p such that $w \in val(p)$ and $w' \notin val(p)$ (that distance is usually called Hamming distance). Let $MS = [S_1...S_n]$ be a multi-set of sets of worlds. Then the distance $dsum(w, MS)$ between a world w and MS is defined by : $dsum(w, MS) = \sum_{i=1}^{n} Min_{w' \in S_i} d(w, w')$. Finally, any multi-set of sets of worlds MS is associated with a pre-order $\leq_{MS}$ or W defined by: $w \leq_{MS} w'$ iff $dsum(w, MS) \leq dsum(w', MS)$.

Definition 3 (continued). Models of MF.
The previous tuple $< W, val, R, B >$ is constrained by the two following constraints:

(C1) If db and db' denote two information sources, then:
$\forall w \in W \ f_{db*db'}(w) = f_{db}(w) \bigsqcup f_{db'}(w)$

(C2) If db is an information source, then $\forall w \in W \ g_{db}(w) = Min_{\leq_{f_{db}}(w)} W$

The constraint **(C1)** reflects the fact that the occurrences of a literal in the merged information source $db * db'$ are the union of its occurrences in db and of its occurrences in db'. So it will be the case that the number of its occurrences in $db * db'$ is the sum of the number of its occurrences in db and the number of its occurrences in db'. The constraint **(C2)** corresponds, as it is proved in [CG01] to one majority merging operator defined in [KPP98]. The models of the information source which is obtained by this majority merging operator are the minimal W worlds according to the pre-order $\leq_{f_{db}}(w)$.

Definition 5. Satisfaction of formulas.
Let $M =< W, val, R, B >$ be a model of MF and let $w \in W$. Let p be a propositional letter of L. Let F, F_1 and F_2 be formulas of L'.
$M, w \models_{MF} p$ iff $w \in val(p)$
$M, w \models_{MF} \neg F_1$ iff $M, w \not\models_{MF} F_1$
$M, w \models_{MF} F_1 \wedge F_2$ iff $M, w \models_{MF} F_1$ and $M, w \models_{MF} F_2$
$M, w \models_{MF} B_{db}^i F$ iff $val(F) \in^i f_{db}(w)$
$M, w \models_{MF} B_{db} F$ iff $g_{db}(w) \subseteq val(F)$

Definition 6. Valid formulas in MF.
Let F be a formula of L'. F is a valid formula in MF iff $\forall M$ model of MF, $\forall w \in W, \ M, w \models_{MF} F$. We note $\models_{MF} F$.

Definition 7. Let $db_1...db_n$ be n finite sets of literals to be merged, each of them being consistent. We define the formula ψ by:

$$\psi = \bigwedge_{i=1}^{n} (\bigwedge_{l \in db_i} B_{db_i}^1 l \wedge \bigwedge_{l \notin db_i} B_{db_i}^0 l)$$

ψ lists the information we have about the content of the given sources to be merged.

3   Automated Deduction in MF

In this section, we deal with implementation aspects. We present a theorem prover logic MF. It allows one to answer questions of the form: "given the description of the information source contents, is the atomic formula F deducible after merging them?" i.e. it allows one to prove theorems of the form: $\psi \to B_{db}F$. Extension to non-atomic formulas will be discussed in section 5. One will notice that in this prover, the formula ψ introduced previously will not be used. Indeed, ψ was introduced for theoretical reasons. Its aim was to describe in extension what is believed and what is not believed in the primitive information sources. But in the prover, we will only need to list the explicit beliefs of the sources. Propositions which are not believed will be derived by negation as failure.

Let us consider a meta-language ML, based on language L, defined by:

- Constants symbols of ML are propositional letters of L, names of informations sources plus a constant symbol denoted nil and constants denoting integers: 1, 2, etc.

- A binary function noted $*$. By convention, $(db_{i_1} * ... * db_{i_k})$ represents the term: $db_{i_1} * (db_{i_2} ... * (db_{i_k} * nil)...)$. This function will be used to denote the information sources obtained by merging information sources $db_{i_1}...db_{i_k}$.

- A binary function denoted $+$ which is the sum of integers.

- A unary function symbol $\neg$. By convention, $\neg l$ represents the term $\neg(l)$. This function will be used to describe the object-level negation.

- The binary meta-predicate symbols are: $B_{exp}, B, =$ and $>$

- A ternary meta-predicate symbol is R.

- A unary meta-predicate symbol is NIL.

$B_{exp}(db, l)$ is true if literal l is explicitly stored in the primitive information source db; $R(db, l, i)$ is true if l appears i times in the information source db; $B(db, l)$ is true if the information source db believes l; $NIL(db)$ is true if db is nil; $i = j$ (resp., $(i > j)$) is true if integers i and j are equal (resp., if integer i is strictly greater than integer j). These two predicates will be defined in extension, in the meta-program, by a finite number of facts.

If the information sources to be merged are $db_1...db_n$, then let META be the following set of the ML formulas:

(1) $B_{exp}(db, l)$ if the literal l belongs to the primitive information source db

(2) $\neg NIL(db_2) \wedge R(db_1, l, i) \wedge R(db_2, l, j) \wedge (k = i + j) \to R(db_1 * db_2, l, k)$

(3) $NIL(db_2) \wedge B_{exp}(db_1, l) \to R(db_1 * db_2, l, 1)$[2]

(4) $NIL(db_2) \wedge \neg B_{exp}(db_1, l) \to R(db_1 * db_2, l, 0)$

(5) $R(db, l, i) \wedge R(db, \neg l, j) \wedge (i > j) \to B(db, l)$

(6) $NIL(nil)$

(7) $k = (r + l)$ and $(r + l) = k$ for any k in $\{1...n\}$ for any r in $\{1...k\}$ and for any l such that $l = k - r$

(8) $k > r$ for any k in $\{1...n\}$ and for any r in $\{1...k\}$ such that $k > r$.

The following result ensures the correctness of this meta program.

Proposition 1. Let l be a literal, let db denoting an information source (primitive or not). Then, using negation-as-failure on the meta-program META,

(1) PROLOG succeeds in proving $B(db, l)$ iff $\models_{MF} (\psi \to B_{db}l)$

(2) PROLOG fails in proving $B(db, l)$ iff $\models_{MF} (\psi \to \neg B_{db} l)$

---

[2] Recall that primitive sources are sets of literals so each literal which belongs to a source has exactly one occurrence in it

4 Application to Multi-databases: Specification of a Query Evaluator

In this section we apply the previous results for specifying a query evaluator which answers queries addressed to several databases. But in order to export these results to first order databases, we consider only databases which are "equivalent to sets of ground literals". Such databases are defined below.

Definition 8 . Let LO be a first order language. A database is a pair $DB =<EDB, IDB >$ such that EDB is a non empty and finite set of ground literals[3] of LO and IDB is a finite set of clauses of LO written without function symbol such that $EDB \cup IDB$ is consistent.

Definition 9. Let $DB =< EDB, IDB >$ a database. Let $a_1...a_n$ (resp. $P_1 \ldots P_k$) be the constant (resp. predicate) symbols which appear in the formulas of $EDB \cup IDB$. The Herbrand base is the set of positive literals written with the P_i and the a_j. A Herbrand interpretation of DB is an interpretation whose domain is $\{a_1, ..., a_n\}$. A Herbrand model of DB is a Herbrand interpretation which satisfies $EDB \cup IDB$.

Definition 10. Let $HM_1...HM_n$ be the Herbrand models of $EDB \cup IDB$.
Let $L = \{l : l$ is a literal of the Herbrand base such that $\exists \; HM_i \; \exists \; HM_j \; HM_i \models l$ and $HM_j \models \neg l\}$ The database $DB =< EDB, IDB >$ is equivalent to a set of ground literals iff for any satisfiable conjunction $l_1 \wedge ... \wedge l_m$ where $\forall i \in \{1...m\}$ such that $l_i \in L$ or $\neg l_i \in L$, there exists HM_{i_0} such that $HM_{i_0} \models l_1 \wedge ... \wedge l_m$.

Example. Consider $DB_1 =< EDB_1, IDB_1 >$ with $EDB_1 = \{p(a)\}$ and $IDB_1 = \{\neg p(x) \vee \neg q(x), p(x) \vee r(x)\}$. The Herbrand models of DB_1 are[4]: $\{p(a)\}$ and $\{p(a), r(a)\}$. We have: $L = \{r(a)\}$ We can check that $\neg r(a)$ is satisfied in the first Herbrand model and that $r(a)$ is satisfied in the second. So DB_1 is equivalent to a set of ground literals. Consider now $DB_2 =< EDB_2, IDB_2 >$ with $EDB_2 = \{p(a)\}$ and $IDB_2 = \{\neg p(x) \vee q(x) \vee r(x)\}$. The Herbrand models of DB_2 are $\{p(a), q(a)\}$, $\{p(a), r(a)\}$ and $\{p(a), q(a), r(a)\}$. We have $L = \{r(a), q(a)\}$. We can check that none of the Herbrand models satisfy $\neg q(a) \wedge \neg r(a)$. Thus DB_2 is not equivalent to a set of ground literals.

Proposition 2. Let $DB =< EDB, IDB >$ a database which is equivalent to a set of ground literals. Let $l_1...l_n$ be some ground literals of LO such that $l_1 \vee ... \vee l_n$ is not a tautology. Then,

$$EDB \cup IDB \models l_1 \vee ... \vee l_n \quad \text{iff} \quad \exists i_0 \in \{1...n\} \;\; EDB \cup IDB \models l_{i_0}$$

This result ensures that, in a database equivalent to a set of ground literals, a disjunction of ground literals which is not a tautology is deducible from the database iff one of these literals is deducible from the database. This implies that there is no real disjunctive data deducible from these databases.

In the following, we use the meta-program defined in section 3 in order to specify a query evaluator which answers queries addressed to several databases. The answers computed by the evaluator are the same that could be computed

---

[3] Notice that literals in EDB can be positive or negative.
[4] A model is denoted here by the set of its positive facts

by a classical evaluator when the query is addressed to the database obtained by merging several databases according to a majority attitude. However, it must be noticed that the database merging is never computed.

The meta-program defined in section 3 assumes that the information sources are sets of positive or negative propositional literals. Considering only databases which are equivalent to sets of ground literals will allow us to re-use that meta-program: each ground literal will be consider as a propositional one. However, we must extend the meta-program in order to take the clauses of IDB into account.

Extension of the meta-program to take IDB into account:

Let us denote by h the function which associates any clause of IDB with a set of formulas in the following way:

$h(l_1 \vee ... \vee l_n) = \{(\neg l_1 \wedge ... \neg l_{i-1} \wedge \neg l_{i+1} ... \wedge \neg l_n) \rightarrow l_i, \quad i \in \{1, ...n\}\}$

Then, the axiom (1) of the meta-program is replaced by the following ones:

(1.1) $EDB(db, l)$ if the ground literal l is in the EDB part of the database db.

(1.2) $IDB(db, f)$ if the formula f is in h(c), where c is a clause in the IDB part of db.

(1.3) $EDB(db, l) \rightarrow B_{exp}(db, l)$

(1.4) $IDB(db, (r \rightarrow l)) \wedge Bconj(db, r) \rightarrow B_{exp}(db, l)$

(1.5) $Bconj(db, nil)$

(1.6) $B_{exp}(db, l_1) \wedge Bconj(db, r_1) \rightarrow Bconj(db, l_1 \wedge r_1)$

Proposition 3. Let $db = <EDB, IDB>$ such that IDB is not recursive. Let l be a ground literal. Then PROLOG proves $B_{exp}(db, l)$ iff $EDB \cup IDB \models l$.

This result ensures that, if IDB is not recursive, axiom (1) can be replaced by axioms (1.1)...(1.6). Thus, using proposition 1, if IDB is not recursive, the meta-program defined for informations sources which are sets of propositional literals can be used in the case of first order databases which are equivalent to sets of ground literals.

Closed queries. Let $db_1...db_n$ be n databases, each of them being equivalent to a set of literals. Let F be a ground literal. The answer to the closed query "Is F true in the database obtained by merging $db_1...db_n$?" is defined by:

$answer((db_1 * ... * db_n), F) = YES$ iff PROLOG proves $B((db_1... * db_n), F)$

$answer((db_1 * ... * db_n), F) = NO$ iff PROLOG proves $B((db_1... * db_n), \neg F)$

$answer((db_1 * ... * db_n), F) = ?$ else

Open queries. Let $db_1...db_n$ be n databases, each of them being equivalent to a set of literals. Let $F(X)$ be an open literal. The answer to the open query "What are the X which satisfy F in the database obtained by merging $db_1...db_n$", is defined by: $answer((db_1 * ... * db_n), F(X)) = \{A :$ tuple of constant symbols such that PROLOG proves $B((db_1 * ... * db_n), F(A))\}$

Example. Let us consider the three following databases: $db_1 = <EDB_1, IDB>$, $db_2 = <EDB_2, IDB>$, $db_3 = <EDB_3, IDB>$ with:

$EDB_1 = \{student(John), employee(Louis), self(Philip), self(Donald),$
$restaurant(Louis)\}$
$EDB_2 = \{employee(Philip), employee(Louis), restaurant(John),$
$restaurant(Henry)\}$
$EDB_3 = \{student(John), employee(Philip)\}$
$IDB = \{\forall x \ student(x) \rightarrow self(x), \forall x \ employee(x) \rightarrow restaurant(x),$
$\forall x \ \neg self(x) \lor \neg restaurant(x)\}$

One can notice that each database is equivalent to a set of ground literals and that IDB is not recursive. Here are some queries and the answers generated by the query evaluator:

$answer((db_1 * db_2 * db_3), student(John)) = YES$
$answer((db_1 * db_2 * db_3), \neg employee(John)) = YES$
$answer((db_1 * db_2 * db_3), student(Donald)) = ?$
$answer((db_1 * db_2), student(x)) = \emptyset$
$answer((db_1 * db_2 * db_3), student(x)) = \{John\}$
$answer((db_1 * db_2 * db_3), employee(x)) = \{Philip, Louis\}$
$answer((db_1 * db_2 * db_3), self(x)) = \{John, Donald\}$
$answer((db_1 * db_2 * db_3), restaurant(x)) = \{Louis, Philip, Henry\}$
$answer((db_1 * db_2), student(John)) = ?$

5   Concluding Remarks

Several remarks can be done concerning the previous query evaluator.

First of all, let us say that this query evaluator has been implemented in a PROLOG interpreter written in LISP.

Secondly, we insist on the fact that the merging of the databases is only virtual i.e. the merging of the databases is never computed for answering questions. This implies, for instance, that the user may address a query to db_1, db_2 and db_3 and latter on address a query to db_2 and db_3.

Thirdly, even if we have restricted our presentation to atomic queries, it must be noticed that this query evaluator can easily be extended for answering queries which are not atomic. The solution for extending the evaluator to non-atomic queries is the same that has been described in [Cho98b]. This extension allows one to ask (closed or open) queries which are conjunctions of disjunctions (where any disjunction which is a tautology is removed). The meta-language is extended by two meta-functions $\wedge$ and $\vee$ and the evaluator is extended by adding the following meta-axioms:

$C(db, nil)$
$D(db, s) \wedge C(db, c) \rightarrow C(db, d \wedge c)$
$B(db, l) \rightarrow D(db, l \vee d)$
$B(db, d) \rightarrow D(db, l \vee d)$

Finally, let us say that extending this evaluator in the case when databases contain disjunctive data is still an open question. The model theory of the logic

MF can easily be extended when information sources contain disjunctions. However, we must admit that we have not yet found a complete proof-theory corresponding to this model theory nor a correct prover.

References

[BKMS91] C. Baral, S. Kraus, J. Minker, and V.S. Subrahmanian. Combining multiple knowledge bases. *IEEE Trans. on Knowledge and Data Engineering*, 3(2), 1991.

[BKMS92] C. Baral, S. Kraus, J. Minker, and V.S. Subrahmanian. Combining knowledge bases consisting of first order theories. *Computational Intelligence*, 8(1), 1992.

[CG01]   L. Cholvy and Ch. Garion. A logic to reason an contradictory beliefs with a majority approach. In *Proceedings of the IJCAI'01 Workshop: Inconsistencies in Data and Knowledge*, Seattle, august 2001.

[Che80]   B. F. Chellas. *Modal logic, an introduction*. Cambridge University Press, 1980.

[Cho93]   L. Cholvy. Proving theorems in a multi-sources environment. In *Proceedings of IJCAI*, pages 66–71, 1993.

[Cho98a] L. Cholvy. Reasoning about merged information. In *Handbook of defeasible reasoning and uncertainty management*, volume 1. Kluwer Academic Publishers, 1998.

[Cho98b] L. Cholvy. Reasoning with data provided by federated databases. *Journal of Intelligent Information Systems*, 10(1), 1998.

[KPP98]   S. Konieczny and R. Pino-Pérez. On the logic of merging. In *Proc. of KR'98*, Trento, 1998.

[KPP99]   S. Konieczny and R. Pino-Perez. Merging with integrity constraints. In *Proc. of ESCQARU'99*, 1999.

[Lia00]   C. Liau. A conservative approach to distributed belief fusion. In *Proceedings of 3rd International Conference on Information Fusion (FUSION)*, 2000.

[Lin96]   J.. Lin. Integration of weighted knowldege bases. *Artificial Intelligence*, 83:363–378, 1996.

[LM98]   J. Lin and A.O. Mendelzon. Merging databases under constraints. *International Journal of Cooperative Information Systems*, 7(1), 1998.

[SDL+98] S.Benferhat, D. Dubois, J. Lang, H. Prade, A. Saffiotti, and P. Smets. A general approach for inconsistency handling and merging information in prioritized knowledge bases. In *Proc. of KR'98*, Trento, 1998.

[Sub94]   V.S. Subrahmanian. Amalgamating knowledge bases. *ACM Transactions on Database Systems*, 19(2):291–331, 1994.

Minimal Generalizations under OI-Implication

Nicola Fanizzi and Stefano Ferilli

Dipartimento di Informatica, Università degli Studi di Bari
Via E. Orabona 4, I-70125 Bari, Italy
{fanizzi,ferilli}@di.uniba.it

Abstract. The adoption of the *object identity* bias for weakening implication has lead to the definition of OI-implication, a generalization model for clausal spaces. In this paper, we investigate on the generalization hierarchy in the space ordered by OI-implication. The decidability of this relationship and the existence of minimal generalizations in the related search space is demonstrated. These results can be exploited for constructing refinement operators for incremental relational learning.

1   Generalization Models

The choice of the generalization model for a clausal space affects both its algebraic structure and, as a consequence, the definition of refinement operators for the ordered set. An optimal choice should be a tradeoff between the expressiveness of the representation and the efficiency of the definable learning operators.

Logical implication, as an ordering relationship on clausal spaces, has proven particularly hard to handle due to many negative results descending from its intrinsic complexity and non-decidability [10]. Thus θ-*subsumption* is the relationship universally employed in relational learning for being more tractable. Still it is not fully satisfactory because of the complexity issues that anyhow the resulting search space presents, although subspaces and methods have been found where this generalization model is more manageable [4,8].

Solutions have been proposed to weaken these strong ordering relationships so to derive more tractable orders. Consider, for instance, relationships derived from implication, e.g. *T-implication* [6], or from θ-subsumption, such as *weak subsumption* [1]. *Reduction* is a bias over the clausal space often adopted in conjunction to θ-subsumption [9]. It focuses on the minimal representatives for each equivalence class with respect to the underlying order. Yet, besides the high computational cost of the operation [5], it was proven that ideal refinement operators cannot be defined in reduced spaces, unless further restrictions are imposed on the size measures of the clauses of the space [9].

Weakening implication by assuming the *object identity* bias has led to the definition of *OI-implication* [2,3], a relationship which makes the search space more manageable. Moreover, we proved the existence of *ideal* refinement operators [9, 1] in this generalization model [2], while they do not exist in spaces ordered by implication [9]. Ideality has been recognized as suitable for theory refinement in spaces with *dense solutions*. Nevertheless, *non-redundant* operators, that are

M.-S. Hacid et al. (Eds.): ISMIS 2002, LNAI 2366, pp. 140–148, 2002.

more appropriate for spaces with *rare* solutions, can be derived from ideal ones
[1].

In this work, we investigate on the algebraic structure of the search space
when ordered by OI-implication. Based on the decidability of the relationship,
the main result demonstrated is the existence of minimal generalizations in a
search space ordered by the generalization model based on OI-implication. This
problem has not yet found a solution for logical implication, probably due to its
non-decidability. However, when a more restricted language is assumed, e.g. the
space of the function-free clauses or the one of *self-saturated* clauses [9], a proof
of the existence of least generalizations has been found.

This paper is organized as follows. In Section 2, we present the semantics and
proof-theory of OI-implication and prove its decidability. Then, in Section 3, the
algebraic structure of the clausal space is studied, with the proof of existence
of minimal generalizations with respect to this order. Lastly, Section 4 briefly
summarizes the achievements of this research outlining possible developments.

2   OI-Implication

In our framework, we adopt a representation language $\mathcal{C}$ expressing theories as
logic programs made up of *clauses*.

The framework we propose relies essentially on the following bias [2,3]:
Assumption (Object Identity). *In a clause, terms denoted with different*
symbols must be distinct, i.e. they represent different entities of the domain.

The intuition for this bias is the following: let us take into account two
clauses $C = p(X, X)$ and $D = p(X, X), p(X, Y), p(Y, Z), p(Z, X)$; in a clausal
space where θ-subsumption is adopted as the generalization model, C and D are
equivalent (in fact C is the *reduced* clause of D). This is not so natural as it
might appear, since more elements of the domain may be involved in D than in
C (indeed in our framework C is more general than D).

The expressive power is not diminished by this bias, since it is always possible
to convey the same meaning of a clause, yet it might be necessary to employ
more clauses. For instance $C = p(X, Y)$ is equivalent to the couple of clauses
$\{C_1 = p(X, X); C_2 = p(X, Y)\}$ when object identity is assumed.

Example 2.1. Suppose that we are refining the concept *car* currently defined:
$car(X) \leftarrow wheel(Y_1, X), wheel(Y_2, X).$
Suppose, also, the following new (counter-)examples are available:
$E_1 = \{bicycle(b), wheel(w_1, b), wheel(w_2, b)\}$ and
$E_2 = \{motorbike(m), wheel(w_3, m), wheel(w_4, m), engine(e, m)\}$
While it is easy to specialize the concept with respect to the E_1 (adding the
literal $engine(Z, X)$ to the clause), for E_2 it is necessary to add information that
a *car* contains four distinct objects that are to be recognized as *wheels*:
$car(X) \leftarrow wheel(Y_1, X), wheel(Y_2, X), wheel(Y_3, X), wheel(Y_4, X), engine(Z, X).$

From a syntactic viewpoint, our setting is similar to weak subsumption [1],
where only substitutions which do not identify literals are taken into account.
Yet, our approach to fulfill the bias is based on semantics and it is more similar

to *unique substitution semantics* [7]. The following definitions specify how the object identity assumption can be captured in the syntax and in the semantics of a clausal representation. We start off discussing substitutions regarded as mappings from the variables to terms of a language. We require these functions to satisfy additional properties to avoid the identification of terms[1]:

Definition 2.1. *Given a set of terms T, a substitution σ is an* OI-substitution w.r.t. T iff $\forall t_1, t_2 \in T$: $t_1 \neq t_2$ implies $t_1\sigma \neq t_2\sigma$.

Based on OI-substitutions, it is possible to define related notions [3]. In particular, taking into account OI-substitutions and interpretations, the resulting semantics can be defined as follows:

Definition 2.2. *Given a non-empty domain $\mathcal{D}$, a pre-interpretation J of the language $\mathcal{C}$ assigns each constant to an element of $\mathcal{D}$ and each n-ary function symbol f to a mapping from $\mathcal{D}^n$ to $\mathcal{D}$. An OI-interpretation I based on J is a set of ground instances of atoms with arguments mapped in $\mathcal{D}$ through J.*
Given a ground OI-substitution γ mapping vars$(\mathcal{C})$ to $\mathcal{D}$, an instance $A\gamma$ of an atom A is true *in I iff $A\gamma \in I$ otherwise it is* false *in I. A negative literal $\neg A\gamma$ is* true *in I iff $A\gamma$ is not, otherwise it is* false *in I.*
I is an OI-model for the clause C iff for all ground OI-substitutions γ there exists at least a literal in $C\gamma$ that is true in I, otherwise the clause is false in I.

The standard notions of *tautology, contradiction, satisfiability* and *consistency* can be straightforwardly transposed to this semantics. Hence, we have defined the form of implication that is compliant with this semantics [3]:

Definition 2.3. *Given a set of clauses Σ and a clause C, Σ* OI-implies *C or C is a logical consequence under object identity of Σ (denoted with $\Sigma \models_{OI} C$) iff all OI-models I for Σ are also OI-models for C.*

Now we briefly recall the definition of the related proof-theory:

Definition 2.4. *Given a finite set of clauses S, θ is an* OI-unifier *iff $\exists E$ such that $\forall E_i \in S$: $E_i\theta = E$ and θ is an OI-substitution w.r.t. terms(E_i). An OI-unifier θ for S is a* most general OI-unifier *for S, denoted $mgu_{OI}(S)$, iff for each OI-unifier σ of S there exists an OI-substitution τ such that $\sigma = \theta\tau$.*

Definition 2.5. *Let C and D be clauses that are supposed standardized apart. A clause R is an* OI-resolvent *of C and D iff there exist $M \subseteq C$ and $N \subseteq D$ such that $\{M, \overline{N}\}$ is unifiable through the mgu_{OI} θ and $R = ((C\setminus M)\cup(D\setminus N))\theta$.*

An OI-derivation, denoted with $\vdash_{OI}$, is obtained by chaining OI-resolution steps.

This proof-procedure was proven sound in [3]. Moreover, an important property of the clausal spaces in the standard semantics states that it is possible to focus on Herbrand models only. It can be extended also to our setting [3]:

Proposition 2.1. *Let Σ be a set of clauses in a first order language $\mathcal{C}$. Then Σ has an OI-model iff Σ has an Herbrand OI-model.*

---

[1] We omit the set of terms T when it is obvious.

In order to cope with the object identity assumption, a relationship was derived from the classic θ-subsumption:

Definition 2.6. *Given two clauses C and D, C θ_{OI}-subsumes D iff there exists an OI-substitution σ w.r.t. terms(C) such that $C\sigma \subseteq D$.*

Since OI-substitutions do not identify literals, equivalent clauses under θ_{OI}-subsumption have the same number of literals. Thus, a space ordered by θ_{OI}-subsumption is made up of non-redundant clauses:

Proposition 2.2. *Let C and D be clauses. If C θ_{OI}-subsumes D then $|C| \leq |D|$. Moreover, $C \sim_{OI} D$ iff they are alphabetic variants.*

In order to prove the Subsumption Theorem for OI-implication, we needed two theorems that are valid for the notion of unsatisfiability for standard interpretations but can be proven also when the object identity is assumed [3]:

Theorem 2.1. *A set of clauses Σ has no OI-model iff there exists a finite set Γ of ground instances of clauses from Σ that has no OI-model.*

Theorem 2.2. *Let Σ be a non-empty set of clauses and C be a ground clause. $\Sigma \models_{OI} C$ iff there exists a finite set Γ of ground instances of clauses from Σ such that $\Gamma \models_{OI} C$.*

As a consequence, the following Subsumption Theorem holds [3], bridging the gap from model-theory to proof-theory in our framework:

Theorem 2.3. *Let Σ be a finite set of clauses and C be a clause. Then $\Sigma \models_{OI} C$ iff there exists a clause D such that $\Sigma \vdash_{OI} D$ and D θ_{OI}-subsumes C.*

Similarly to the standard case, it is nearly straightforward to demonstrate some corollaries of the Subsumption Theorem originally due to Gottlob [3]:

Definition 2.7. *Given a clause C, we denote with C^+ and C^-, respectively, the sets of its positive and negative literals. A clause C is ambivalent when there are two literals $L_1 \in C^+$, $L_2 \in C^-$ with the same predicate symbol. Besides, if they can be unified then C is also recursive.*

Of course only unification through OI-substitutions is taken into account.

Proposition 2.3. *Let C and D be clauses. If C is not recursive and D is not tautological, then $C \models_{OI} D$ iff C θ_{OI}-subsumes D.*

Proposition 2.4. *Let C and D be clauses. If $C \models_{OI} D$ then C^+ θ_{OI}-subsumes D^+ and C^- θ_{OI}-subsumes D^-.*

Then, it is possible to prove the following results on the depth and cardinality:

Definition 2.8. *The depth of a term t is 1 when t is a variable or a constant. If $t = f(t_1, \ldots, t_n)$, then $depth(t) = 1 + max_{i=1}^{n}(depth(t_i))$. The depth of a clause C, denoted $depth(C)$, is the maximum depth among its terms.*

Proposition 2.5. *Given the clauses C and D, if $C \models_{OI} D$ then it follows that: $depth(C) \leq depth(D)$ and $|C| \leq |D|$.*

Proof. Note that OI-substitutions do not decrease depth or cardinality of the clauses they are applied to. The result holds as a consequence of Proposition 2.4.

In order to prove the decidability of OI-implication, some properties related to Skolem substitutions will be exploited. Notice that such substitutions are indeed OI-substitutions. Then, as a further consequence of the Subsumption Theorem (and Proposition 2.1), also the following result holds [3]:

Proposition 2.6. *Let Σ be a set of clauses and C be a clause. Let σ be a Skolem substitution for C w.r.t. Σ. Then $\Sigma \models_{OI} C$ iff $\Sigma \models_{OI} C\sigma$.*

Now some notions originally presented in [6] are adapted to our framework:

Definition 2.9. *Let C be a clause, $vars(C) = \{X_1, \ldots, X_n\}$, and T be a set of terms. The* instance set *of C w.r.t. T is: $\mathcal{I}(C, T) = \{C\theta \mid \theta = \{X_i/t_i \mid t_i \in T, \forall i = 1, \ldots, n\}, \theta$ is an OI-substitution$\}$. If $\Sigma = \{C_1, \ldots, C_m\}$ is a set of clauses, then the* instance set *of Σ w.r.t. T is: $\mathcal{I}(\Sigma, T) = \mathcal{I}(C_1, T) \cup \cdots \cup \mathcal{I}(C_m, T)$. Let σ be a Skolem substitution for Σ. Then the* term set *of Σ by σ is the set of all terms (and subterms) occurring in $\Sigma\sigma$.*

Now let us notice that, during successive steps of resolution, some terms are resolved away and, thus, they do not appear in the conclusions. This has suggested that such terms can be substituted in the premises, yielding a new valid derivation [6]. The next example, adapted from [9], shows how OI-implication can be reduced to a relationship between ground clauses.

Example 2.2. Consider the clause $D = p(f^2(X), Y, Z) \leftarrow p(Y, Z, f^2(X))$ and the Skolem substitution $\sigma = \{X/a, Y/b, Z/c\}$ with term set $T = \{a, f(a), f^2(a), b, c\}$. Considered $C = p(X, Y, Z) \leftarrow p(Z, X, Y)$ and $C' = p(X, Y, Z) \leftarrow p(Y, Z, X)$, note that C' can be derived from C by self-resolution (i.e., $C \vdash_{OI} C'$). Besides, $C' \geq_{OI} D$. Thus, by Theorem 2.3, it follows that $C \models_{OI} D$. Now, examine $D\sigma = p(f^2(a), b, c) \leftarrow p(b, c, f^2(a))$ and the instances of C, $C_1 = p(f^2(a), b, c) \leftarrow p(c, f^2(a), b)$ and $C_2 = p(c, f^2(a), b) \leftarrow p(b, c, f^2(a))$
Observe that $C_1, C_2 \in \mathcal{I}(C, T)$ and $(C_1, C_2) \vdash_{OI} D\sigma$.
For the soundness of the OI-resolution, we can conclude that: $\mathcal{I}(C, T) \models_{OI} D\sigma$.

This reduction can be proven true in general. In fact, in this setting it is possible to prove the following result, holding for standard logical implication only in special cases such as for function-free clauses [9]:

Proposition 2.7. *Let C and D be two clauses, σ a Skolem substitution for D w.r.t. $\{C\}$ and T be the related term set. Then $C \models_{OI} D$ iff $\mathcal{I}(C, T) \models_{OI} D\sigma$.*

Proof. ($\Rightarrow$) *If D were a tautology, then $D\sigma$ would be a tautology too. Suppose $D\sigma$ is not a tautology. By Theorem 2.2 and Proposition 2.6 it follows that, being $D\sigma$ ground, there exists a set S of ground instances of C such that $S \models_{OI} D\sigma$. By Theorem 2.3, $\exists E \in C$ such that $S \vdash_{OI} E$ and $E \geq_{OI} D\sigma$. Thus, $E \subseteq D\sigma$ and $terms(E) \subseteq T$, since E and $D\sigma$ are ground. Now let S' be obtained by replacing each term of the clauses in S that is not in T with one[2] in T. Then S' is made up of ground instances of C also. An*

---

[2] T is bound to contain enough distinct terms for $C \models_{OI} D$ to hold.

OI-derivation of E from S can be turned into an OI-derivation from S': each term in an OI-resolution from S can be replaced by a corresponding one from S' because of the replacement defined above; terms that are in S but not in T have been replaced in S' and cannot occur in E because $E \subseteq D\sigma$.

Then, $S' \vdash_{OI} E$ and $E \geq_{OI} D\sigma$, which implies $S' \models_{OI} D\sigma$, by Theorem 2.3. Since $terms(S') \subseteq T$, it follows that $S' \subseteq \mathcal{I}(C, T)$; thus $\mathcal{I}(C, T) \models_{OI} D\sigma$.

($\Leftarrow$) Let us observe that $C \models_{OI} \mathcal{I}(C, T)$ and $\mathcal{I}(C, T) \models_{OI} D\sigma$. Then the thesis holds for Proposition 2.6 and transitivity of $\models_{OI}$.

Corollary 2.1. *Let Σ be a set of clauses, C be a clause, σ be a Skolem substitution for C w.r.t. Σ and T be the related term set. $\Sigma \models_{OI} C$ iff $\mathcal{I}(\Sigma, T) \models_{OI} C\sigma$.*

We have shown that $\Sigma \models_{OI} C$ can be reduced to $\mathcal{I}(\Sigma, T) \models_{OI} C\sigma$ which is a relationship between ground clauses. Besides, the following holds:

Lemma 2.1. *Let Σ be a set of ground clauses and C be a ground clause. Then the problem whether $\Sigma \models_{OI} C$ is decidable.*

Proof. Let I be the set of all ground atoms occurring in Σ and C.

Then $\Sigma \models_{OI} C$ iff $\Sigma \cup \neg C$ has no OI-model (by the Deduction Theorem, proven in [3]) iff $\Sigma \cup \neg C$ has no Herband OI-model (by Proposition 2.1) iff no $I' \subseteq I$ is a Herband OI-model of $\Sigma \cup \neg C$. Since I is finite, this is decidable.

Finally, given that $\mathcal{I}(\Sigma, T)$ and $C\sigma$ are both ground, the decidability of OI-implication descends from Lemma 2.1 and Corollary 2.1:

Theorem 2.4. *Let Σ be a set of clauses and C be a clause. The problem whether $\Sigma \models_{OI} C$ is decidable.*

3   The Structure of the Search Space

In this section we discuss the properties of the clausal space provided with the order induced from OI-implication; in particular, we focus on the existence of minimal generalizations in such a space and algorithms for their computation.

Preliminarily, the definitions on minimal generalizations is briefly recalled:

Definition 3.1. *Let S be a set of clauses and $\succeq$ a quasi-order, with $\sim$ as the induced equivalence relation. G is a minimal generalization of S w.r.t. $\succeq$ iff $\forall C \in S: G \succeq C$, and for each G' such that $\forall C \in S, G' \succeq C$ it follows that $G \succeq G'$ implies $G \sim G'$. If G is unique, it is a least generalization of S w.r.t. $\succeq$.*

θ_{OI}-subsumption induces the quasi-order denoted with $\geq_{OI}$ upon a clausal space. Besides, a notion of equivalence $\sim_{OI}$ for this order can be defined. Similarly, also OI-implication induces a quasi-ordering ($\models_{OI}$) and an equivalence relationship. Then, given a set of clauses S, we will employ the notions of *minimal generalizations w.r.t. OI-implication* (respectively *w.r.t. θ_{OI}-subsumption*), denoted with $MG_{OI}(S)$ (resp. with $MGS_{OI}(S)$).

The computation of least general generalizations under θ-subsumption can be performed by means of Plotkin's algorithm [9], though the resulting clauses may turn out to be quite redundant and therefore require reduction, which is a very expensive operation from a computational point of view [5]. In spaces ordered by logical implication the problem has been proven decidable only for restricted cases (e.g. function-free clausal spaces) [9]. As a consequence of the Subsumption Theorem, we proved some limitations as concerns depth and cardinality for a clause that implies another clause under object identity. This yields a bound to the proliferation of possible generalizations:

Proposition 3.1. *Let C and D be two clauses. The set of generalizations of C and D w.r.t. OI-implication is finite.*

The proof is straightforward since the depths and cardinalities of the generalizations are limited, by Proposition 2.5.

Given two clauses C and D, let us denote with G the set of generalizations of $\{C, D\}$ w.r.t. OI-implication. Observe that $G \neq \emptyset$ since $\square \in G$. Proposition 3.1 yields that G is finite. Thus, since the test of OI-implication between clauses is decidable, it is possible to determine the minimal elements of G by comparing the clauses in G and eliminating those that are overly general. The remaining incomparable clauses constitute $MG_{OI}(\{C, D\})$.

As mentioned above, the existence of a minimal generalization is guaranteed for standard implication only in case the language is function-free [9], while results (based on Proposition 2.7) do not make any restriction. Now, we turn to show a result that shows a more operational way to compute generalizations under OI-implication. First, we need to prove some lemmas:

Lemma 3.1. *Let C and D be two clauses such that $C \models_{OI} D$ and σ be a Skolem substitution for D w.r.t. $\{C\}$, with T as its related term set. Then, it follows that $\forall E \in MGS_{OI}(\mathcal{I}(C, T))$: $E \models_{OI} D$.*

Proof. Considered any $E \in MGS_{OI}(\mathcal{I}(C, T))$, we have that $E \geq_{OI} H, \forall H \in \mathcal{I}(C, T)$ and hence $E \models_{OI} \mathcal{I}(C, T)$. From $C \models_{OI} D$, using Proposition 2.7, we have $\mathcal{I}(C, T) \models_{OI} D\sigma$. Combining the previous results, it follows that: $E \models_{OI} D\sigma$.

Notice that $E \in MGS_{OI}(\mathcal{I}(C, T))$ implies that $consts(E) \subseteq consts(C)$, hence $consts(E) \subseteq consts(D)$. We conclude that σ is a Skolem substitution also for D w.r.t. $\{E\}$. Then, by Proposition 2.6, $E \models_{OI} D$.

Lemma 3.2. *Let C be a clause and σ be a Skolem substitution for C. Then, it follows that $C\sigma \models_{OI} C$.*

Proof. Since $C\sigma$ is ground we can define a pre-interpretation J with a mapping δ from the constants in $C\sigma$ to the domain $\mathcal{D}$. An OI-model I of $C\sigma$ is such that $C\sigma\delta \cap I \neq \emptyset$. A ground OI-substitution $\gamma = \sigma\delta$ from $vars(C)$ to $\mathcal{D}$ can be defined for each δ. Given that $\forall L \in C : L\sigma \in C\sigma$, we can conclude that $\forall\gamma \exists L \in C : L\gamma \in I$, that is I is an OI-model for C.

In the standard setting, $C \cup D$ is a clause that preserves the models of either clause. In our setting, as expected, we need more than a single clause:

Definition 3.2. *Let C_1 and C_2 be two clauses such that C_1 and C_2 are standardized apart and K a set of new constants such that: $|K| \geq |vars(C_1 \cup C_2)|$. We define $C_1 \sqcup C_2 = \{C | C = (C_1\sigma_1 \cup C_2\sigma_2)\sigma_1^{-1}\sigma_2^{-1}\}$ where σ_1 and σ_2 are Skolem substitutions for, respectively, C_1 and C_2 with K as their term set.*

Example 3.1. Let $C_1 = p(X, Y), q(X)$ and $C_2 = p(X', Y'), r(X')$ be two clauses. The OI-substitutions $\sigma_1 = \{X/a, Y/b\}$ and $\sigma_2 = \{X'/a, Y'/b\}$ yield the following clause: $F_1 = p(X, Y), q(X), r(X)$. Similarly $\sigma_3 = \{X/a, Y/b\}$ and $\sigma_4 = \{X'/b, Y'/a\}$ yield the clause: $F_2 = p(X, Y), p(Y, X), q(X), r(X)$ and so on.

The clauses in $C \sqcup D$ preserve the OI-models of C and D:

Proposition 3.2. *Let C, D and E be clauses such that C and D are standardized apart. If $C \models_{OI} E$ and $D \models_{OI} E$ then $\forall F \in (C \sqcup D): F \models_{OI} E$.*

Proof. Let $F \in C \sqcup D$. Then there exist a term set T and two Skolem substitutions σ_1 and σ_2 such that: $F = (C\sigma_1 \cup D\sigma_2)\sigma_1^{-1}\sigma_2^{-1}$. Let us consider an OI-model I for F. By Proposition 2.6, I is an OI-model for $F\sigma_2$ and $F\sigma_2\sigma_1$. Now, $F\sigma_2\sigma_1 = C\sigma_1 \cup D\sigma_2$. Then I is an OI-model for $C\sigma_1$ or I is an OI-model for $D\sigma_2$, hence, by Lemma 3.2, I is an OI-model for C or for D. In both cases, since $C \models_{OI} E$ and $D \models_{OI} E$, we conclude that I is an OI-model for E. Thus, $F \models_{OI} E$.

Note that this result implies that $C \sqcup D$ contains maximal specializations w.r.t. OI-implication. This proposition is exploited here for proving the existence of maximal specializations w.r.t. OI-implication in this search space:

Theorem 3.1. *Let S be a set of non-tautological clauses. Then, $\exists F \in MG_{OI}(S)$.*

Proof. Let us denote with $G = \{C_1, C_2, \ldots\}$ the set of generalizations of S w.r.t. OI-implication. Observe that $G \neq \emptyset$ since $\square \in G$. Proposition 3.1 yields that G is finite. Thus, there exists a certain k such that $|G| = k$. Now, let us consider $E_i \in MGS_{OI}(\mathcal{I}(C_i, T)), \forall i \in [1, k]$ and suppose that the E_i's are standardized apart. Let $F \in \bigsqcup_{i=1}^{k} E_i$. Observe that $\forall i \in [1, k]$ $E_i \models_{OI} C_i$. But the C_i's are generalizations w.r.t. OI-implication of S. Then we can conclude that $F \models_{OI} S$.

If $\exists h \in [1, k]: F \models_{OI} C_h$, since $E_h \geq_{OI} F$ by construction, then we have: $E_h \models_{OI} C_h$. Now, C_h is a generalization w.r.t. θ_{OI}-subsumption for $\mathcal{I}(C_h, T)$, we can infer: $C_h \geq_{OI} E_h \geq_{OI} F$. We conclude that, C_h is equivalent to F, then F is a minimal generalization w.r.t. OI-implication.

The proof given above relies on the computation of minimal generalizations w.r.t. θ_{OI}-subsumption. Also in this case, the number of generalizations is finite then MGS_{OI} could be computed by successive eliminations.

4   Conclusions

We showed that, by assuming a bias over a clausal search space, it is possible to define a weaker form of implication which induces a decidable ordering relationship. In the search space ordered by this relationship, we proved the existence of minimal generalizations. Although, this proof outlines an algorithm, we plan to investigating restricted spaces where this problem is tractable. The results found on the algebraic structure make this clausal space particularly appealing for being adopted as an approach to relational learning in structured domains.

We mentioned that ideal refinement operators can be defined in this search space. Yet when solutions to search problems are rare, *non-redundant* operators [1] are better suited. We intend to investigate more on this problem in our framework. Moreover, the specialization hierarchy under OI-implication needs a deeper insight, for the specification of downward refinement operators. The multiplicity of minimal generalizations (and maximal specializations) calculated through the operators leads us to think that ensemble methods for relational learning might be developed in this framework.

References

[1] L Badea and M. Stanciu. Refinement operators can be (weakly) perfect. In S. Džeroski and P. Flach, editors, *Proceedings of the 9th International Workshop on Inductive Logic Programming*, volume 1634 of *LNAI*, pages 21–32. Springer, 1999.

[2] F. Esposito, N. Fanizzi, S. Ferilli, and G. Semeraro. A generalization model based on OI-implication for ideal theory refinement. *Fundamenta Informaticae*, 47:15–33, 2001.

[3] F. Esposito, N. Fanizzi, S. Ferilli, and G. Semeraro. OI-implication: Soundness and refutation completeness. In B. Nebel, editor, *Proceedings of the 17th International Joint Conference on Artificial Intelligence*, pages 847–852, Seattle, WA, 2001.

[4] G. Gottlob. Subsumption and implication. *Information Processing Letters*, 24(2):109–111, 1987.

[5] G. Gottlob and C.G. Fermüller. Removing redundancy from a clause. *Artificial Intelligence*, 61:263–289, 1993.

[6] P. Idestam-Almquist. Generalization of clauses under implication. *Journal of Artificial Intelligence Research*, 3:467–489, 1995.

[7] R. Khardon. Learning function-free Horn expressions. *Machine Learning*, 37(3):241–275, December 1999.

[8] Jörg-Uwe Kietz. A comparative study of structural most specific generalisations used in machine learning. In *Proceedings of the Third International Workshop on Inductive Logic Programming*, pages 149–164, Ljubljana, Slovenia, 1993. J. Stefan Institute Technical Report IJS-DP-6707.

[9] S.-H. Nienhuys-Cheng and R. de Wolf. *Foundations of Inductive Logic Programming*, volume 1228 of *LNAI*. Springer, 1997.

[10] M. Schmidt-Schauss. Implication of clauses is undecidable. *Theoretical Computer Science*, 59:287–296, 1988.

I-Search: A System for Intelligent Information Search on the Web

E. Di Sciascio, F.M. Donini, and M. Mongiello

Dipartimento di Elettrotecnica ed Elettronica
Politecnico di Bari
Via Re David, 200 – 70125 BARI, Italy
{disciascio,donini,mongiello}@poliba.it

Abstract. Current Web search engines find new documents basically crawling the hyperlinks with the aid of spider agents. Nevertheless, when indexing newly discovered documents they revert to conventional information retrieval models and single-document indexing, thus neglecting the inherently hypertextual structure of Web documents. Therefore, it can happen that a query string, partially present in a document, with the remaining part available in a linked document on the same site, does not correspond to a hit. This considerably reduces retrieval effectiveness. To overcome this and other limits we propose an approach based on temporal logic that, starting with the modeling of a web site as a finite state graph, allows one to define complex queries over hyperlinks with the aid of Computation Tree Logic (CTL) operators. Query formulation is composed by two steps: the first one is user-oriented and provides a user with a friendly interface to pose queries. The second step is the query translation in CTL formulas. The formulation of the query is not visible to the user that simply expresses his/her requirements in natural language. We implemented the proposed approach in a prototype system. Results of experiments show an improvement in retrieval effectiveness.

1 Introduction

Web search engines find new documents basically crawling the hyperlinks with the aid of spider agents. Typical retrieval models and ranking algorithms derive from classical textual Information Retrieval (IR) and are based on single documents indexing. Instead, the hypertextual structure of web documents could provide further information on the context of the web document and the content of the linked pages and could be used for improving the retrieval effectiveness. See the example of knowledge representation on the web in [3]: "the last name of the person is Cook, she works for a company in your client list and has a son attending your alma mater, Avondale University". This is a meaningful example clarifying the importance of a structural approach in combining information contained in different web pages. The search engine should be able to put together pieces of information belonging to different pages of different web sites and to carry out a process for correctly locating *e.g.*, a person, using partially remembered knowledge.

M.-S. Hacid et al. (Eds.): ISMIS 2002, LNAI 2366, pp. 149–157, 2002.
© Springer-Verlag Berlin Heidelberg 2002

In this paper we propose the use of a logical language within a temporal framework for expressing structural queries in a web environment, using Computation Tree Logic (CTL). The temporal framework assumes the meaning of sequence of states in the graph of a web site. The web is hence modelled as a graph in which pages represent states and links represent transitions between states. Navigation through the links is performed as reachability between states in the graph.

With respect to an approach based on a single document, an approach that considers the structural links between pages has many advantages. First, a structural approach could improve the quality of search results. For example, the home page in a web site provides summary information on the site content; therefore, vertical links conduct to pages and documents with more detailed information with respect to the home page; horizontal links to related pages could probably contain information that meet user expectations. Consider an example: the home-page of a university web-site is an index to more detailed information contained in linked pages. The user might be interested in finding information about the research activities in the department of computer science, and particularly in people working on Artificial Intelligence. Therefore he/she wishes to find a path linking the home page to the Artificial Intelligence research activity page and to the page of people involved in that research activity. Following horizontal or vertical links the user would find further useful information. The approach we propose provides, as result of the search process, a set of paths, instead of a set of single documents belonging to distinct web sites with different contents. The paths involve relevant information found parsing the web site link structure. As a second advantage, the proposed method provides a set of results that are more refined with respect to the set of results of a search engine. Generally, the search results of current search engines provide a list of documents sorted on relevance. The user has to consult each document or page to state its relevance for his/her current search and, if applicable, use relevance feedback to refine the set of results. Using the powerful operators of temporal logic more expressive predicates with respect to simple boolean connectives can be formulated, thus reducing the cardinality of the set of retrieved documents while maintaining a query structure simple enough for the average user. Finally, the search is automatic and precise.

With reference to previous work on the subject, our approach follows that proposed in [2] where a language based on a modal logic was introduced to process queries involving the structure of hypermedia systems. In the Web environment such an approach has not been widely explored, and commercial search engines still use simple methods based on single-documents indexing. On the other hand, in database environments query languages are used to select and transform information from large source of structured data. Other approaches consider languages not specifically developed for the web but usefully applied to the web environment since based on hyperlinks over a graph structure [8]. Logical languages deriving from first order logic are used for querying relational databases, e.g., the relational calculus adopted in defining SQL or Datalog.

The use of query languages in web-based IR could allow the use of complex predicates on the data to be retrieved also in a web environment thus processing complex queries as in a database management system. To this purpose, several languages based on a logical framework have been proposed considering the web as a huge database. A survey of first and second generation of SQL or Datalog like web query languages is in [8]. In [10] a hypertext is modeled as a set of facts, and queries as negation-free Datalog programs. The language is incomparable with CTL, since, on one hand, Datalog is a function-free first-order language, while on the other hand, Datalog cannot express negation, nor quantifications on all paths like $AF\varphi$. A second method of indexing the web is based on semistructured data; therefore query languages for semistructured data might be useful in retrieving information on the web, as LOREL and XML-QL that combines XML syntax with query language techniques for semistructured data, both defined in [1]. Notice that, though the Semantic Web approach promises, with the aid of XML, the structuring of the Web content, still for years to come there will be millions of HTML based web pages. In [5], a very expressive query language for retrieving XML documents is proposed. The language includes Propositional Dynamic Logic, hence the admissible queries are a strict superset of the queries we propose here, based on CTL [7]. However, that proposal has not been implemented so far, hence no experiment on the effectiveness of the language with reference to precision, recall, and usability can be pursued. Our choice of using CTL, instead, allowed us to immediately use off-the-shelf implementations for CTL model checking, hence developing a working prototype, which allows concentrating on experiments about the effectiveness of the approach.

The remaining of the paper is organized as follows. In Section 2 we describe the semantics of the formulas we use to express queries with different degree of selectiveness. Section 3 defines the logical scheme of the search engine. The retrieval effectiveness of the proposed approach can not be evaluated using the classical recall and precision measure for IR retrieval, therefore in Section 4 we describe the evaluation method we adopt. Section 5 draws the conclusions.

2   Formal Model of Web Queries

For lack of space, we refer to [6], [7] for the definition of CTL.

The logical formulas are interpreted on a finite state model, which represents the web site. The model we adopt is a graph whose nodes represent the web pages, and whose transitions represent hyperlinks. Nodes in the graph, *e.g.*, a web page or a document, are identified by their Uniform Resource Locator (URL). Obviously formulation of queries regards paths within a given web site. Every keyword w is a propositional predicate which is true exactly for those nodes representing documents containing w.

CTL operators are useful for our purpose. To explain their use consider a query example concerning the marketing issue: *The market is the food and drinks one, particularly, I am interested in drinks trade, and in the marketing area of beer. Guinness is the brand I am interested in.*

We consider the following CTL formula resulted from the translation from natural language:

$$(EF foodanddrink \land (EF drink \land (EF beer \land (EF Guinness)))) \quad (1)$$

The previous formula finds a path in a graph in which the specified properties are present in states linked to each other. Considering the formula as a query it can retrieve the paths in the web sites containing the text strings that the user specified in his/her query, *e.g.*, *drink, beer, Guinness* and so on. Intuitively, the formula asserts the existence of a sequence of particular states in the graph of the web site. In details, there exist documents d_1, d_2, d_3, d_4 such that d_1 is reachable and the text string *food and drink* appears in it, then from d_1 one can reach document d_2 where *drink* appears, then d_3 with *beer*, then d_4 with *Guinness*. Some of d_1, d_2, d_3, d_4 may coincide.

Such kind of search ensures that documents with non-relevant issues containing some , but not all, of the required keywords are not retrieved as results of the search. Observe that the EF operator may be nested differently. Formula (1) is more restrictive than the following:

$$(EF foodanddrink) \land (EF drink) \land (EF beer) \land (EF Guinness) \quad (2)$$

since (1) specifies the order in which the text strings must be found in documents in the path, while (2) specifies no particular order in the links.

Following the semantics, the EF operator admits the presence of some pages so-called dummy, *e.g.*, documents belonging to the retrieved path but not containing relevant text strings. In fact, EF is less restrictive than the operator EX that requires the validity of the specified properties in a directly linked document.

More complex operators of CTL might refine the query depending on the user requirements. For example if the user would exclude dummy pages from the retrieved path, the EU operator might be used, as explained below. Other operators of CTL can be used to express properties concerning the structure of the links and are more restrictive than EF.

Consider the U operator (*Until*) combined with the connective E or A. It searches for a sequence of pages along a path excluding dummy pages, therefore it is more selective then the EF operator. The choice of the operator depends on the specific query. $E(\phi U \psi)$ means that there exists a path in which ψ is true in a state and in all the preceding states ϕ is true. Different meanings derive from nesting the U operator.

The above example query might be changed by nesting the EU operator as follows:

$$E((drink \lor beer) U Guinness) \quad (3)$$

the string *Guinness* may appear in the first document and the path is empty; otherwise the path reaches a document in which appears the text *Guinness* but in the previous nodes the text *beer* or *drink* appear. Such a query has the advantage to exclude dummy pages in its search. The query might be further refined through the U operator.

3   Experimental Environment

Query formulation is composed by two steps: the first one is user-oriented in order to provide a non-expert user with a friendly interface to pose queries. The second step is the query translation in CTL formulas. The formula is not visible to the user that simply expresses his/her requirements. The CTL formulas corresponding to the query is built straight from its semantic formulation in natural language.

Terms in the query are given increasing weights depending on the order inside the query. The use of levels in structuring the query is a powerful means to refine the query without using relevance feedback techniques. In fact, search engines provide only simple boolean operator such as *and, or*. For complex queries, the user can reach the desired resulting after having analyzed many results documents and refining the set of retrieved documents. The use of weighted levels ensures a deep search in the structure of the site and the possibility to retrieve documents in the lower nodes of the corresponding graph that a query based on boolean connectives could not retrieve. In this way results can be obtained in a single retrieval step.

Our system can independently process four different kinds of query, increasingly selective. The simplest kind of query selects paths containing some of the terms in the query even if not available in the same order see *e.g.*, 2. Such kind of query selects all the paths except those composed only by dummy pages. The second kind of query selects paths in which many strings of the query appear in the same order in which they are specified in the query. Both kind of queries can be obtained using formula $E(l_1 \vee l_2 U page)$ where l_1 and l_2 represents terms in the query. The third kind of query selects the paths in which all terms of the query appear and are in the same order of the query but does not care for dummy pages; queries are translated using formula $EF(l_1 \wedge EF page)$. The fourth kind of query selects only the paths having all terms in the same order of the query without dummy pages; queries of this kind are obtained using formula $E(E(l_1 U l_2) U page)$.

A prototype system has been implemented in a Java2 environment to test the proposed approach. A standard search engine provides the initial set of results. The Web site analyzer builds the graph structure of the site using the results of the first search obtained through the search agent. The analyzer parses the HTML source page of the web site starting with the URL of the documents retrieved by the spider. The module searches inside the page for the terms of the query. Our search engine is a full text indexer, this means that a document will match any query that uses any word contained in it excluded stop words.

The translator parses the query expressed in natural language and extracts the meaningful keywords for the search through the spider. The query is translated in a formal model using CTL formulas.

The query and the structure of the site defined in the previous module are given as input to the model verifier SMV [7].

SMV is an external module based on model checking algorithms of verification of CTL formulas on a finite states model of a system. The model verifier has been developed at CMU and is freely distributed through the Internet.

The main drawback we had to face in using SMV was its nature of verifier and not of analyzer. So we had to force the behavior of the verifier towards our needs. Given a specification to verify, SMV response states whether it is verified, otherwise it provides a counterexample, *i.e.*, a sequence of states that does not verify the required specification. Therefore, we used negation of the main formulas in order to obtain the desired paths: *e.g.*, the execution sequence returned as a counterexample the path verifying the formula.

A second drawback was due to the limit of SMV that stops at the first counterexample: this would prevent us from finding all the paths verifying the given specification. To overcome this limit, we had to replicate each query for each leaf node of the site graph by introducing a further atom in each query that depends on the leaf node.

A scoreboard module receives the results of the exhaustive verification performed by SMV. The module sorts the results based on the following ranking measure:

$$score = \frac{N_r}{N_t} \sum_{k=1}^{N_p} N_o(k,i) w(k,i) N_w 100 \tag{4}$$

where N_t is the number of pages in the path and N_r the number of relevant pages in the path. $N_o(k,i)$ is the number of occurrences of strings belonging to the level i in each page k. N_w is the total number of terms in a path. $w(k,i)$ is a weighting factor whose value depends on the query level of each term in the query and on the number of terms in the query. In computing the score, each page is assigned the query level of the higher term appearing in the page.

4   Evaluation of the Proposed Method

Experiments were conducted to test the system performances by measuring retrieval effectiveness [13]. We adopted the same criteria commonly used in studies for comparison of search engine and compared the performances of I-Search with two commercial search engine: Google and Altavista and considered some qualitative features commonly adopted in evaluation studies for search engines comparison.

The search experiments were motivated by genuine information needs of searchers. An information need is an explanation of the information the individual would like to obtain from the search. From the information need appropriate terms have to be extracted and processed by the search engine.

Relevance judgements for the search results were made by the individual who needed the information. Otherwise if the experimenters decide on results relevance, numerous mis-evaluation due both to the experimenter's lack of familiarity with the subject being searched and to the impossibility for him/her to know the user's needs and motivation may result.

The comparison with other search engines was not based on a statistical test since the study is in an embryonal stage, in which we are interested in evaluating the validity of the proposed approach rather than providing an accurate measure of the differences in performances.

A quantitative measure was obtained conforming, as much as possible, to IR accepted measurements [13]. Traditional measures of retrieval effectiveness in IR are recall and precision: recall measures the ability of the system to present all relevant items, precision measures the ability to present only the relevant items. Unfortunately, such measures cannot be applied in a straightforward way in the Web environment, since it is not possible to know in advance for *every page n the Web* relevance of an item to a given information need [12]. Therefore a measure generally adopted is a modification of precision and refers to the measure of *precision* the user is interested in at a given cut-off value, *e.g.*, the precision of the results displayed in the first 10 results. For recall measure, following the approach in [9] we computed what is called in IR literature *relative recall* as a percentage of the retrieved documents that the evaluator judged to be relevant.

In the first experiment, an expert in the field of marketing filled out a form describing his information needs. We experimented with 20 queries. The information needs varied widely in the areas of commercial goods and services. The information needs were translated in queries for I-Search and for the other two search engines. The query to process with I-Search was translated in the four different selections allowed by the system.

After processing the query, the expert assessed his relevance judgements both on the results obtained by I-Search and on the results obtained by Google and Altavista. Table 1 summarizes the precision and recall for the set of experiments. For each kind of query results are described considering an initial set of 10 or 20 web sites, filtered by the agent.

Table 1. Retrieval effectiveness

Search engine	Precision top 5		Precision top 10		Relative Recall	
I-Search	#10	#20	#10	#20	#10	#20
1st	0.83	0.81	0.81	0.8	0.3	0.29
2nd	0.84	0.81	0.82	0.8	0.35	0.32
3th	0.88	0.82	0.87	0.86	0.4	0.39
4th	0.9	0.86	0.88	0.87	0.46	0.4
Altavista	0.75		0.7		0.12	
Google	0.79		0.75		0.23	

The second set of experiments was "non-commercial" and oriented to information seeking in the context of scientific articles.

The Web may be considered as a digital library and the experiments carried out aimed to retrieve documents, articles, publications in a specific field. Even though the search was conducted on the Web in which the number of pages and documents is not restricted as in digital library, the results were selective enough.

In this experiment two students and two researchers experimented with the system. Each subject submitted his query to I-Search using only the selective type of queries, third and fourth ones.

After query processing, the experts assessed their relevance judgements on the results obtained by I-Search expressing their evaluation in terms of retrieved path. In fact, the power of the language relies on its capability to search the text strings that the user required not only in a single document but on the whole structure of the site.

Generally, web sites might contain all the words even though in distinct pages. The keywords specified in the query might belong to a single page (of course this is a positive circumstance, but not a probable one). Exploiting the link structure, our approach finds such pages and extracts the link structure like in a hypertext. This means that the keywords expressed in the query might belong to distinct documents linked by a path along the same site. Besides, such kind of search ensures the exclusion of sites not interesting for the search even though containing strings belonging to the user query but in a different context. In this way the user would be able to retrieve only very valuable pages.

In this set of experiments a measure of retrieval effectiveness should take into account an evaluation of the quality of the retrieved paths compared with the query. In this aspect the performances of the system were referred to criteria generally adopted in the field of citation analysis and of the bibliometric systems.

Previous studies of connectivity analysis algorithms have been conducted in the field of topic distillation by Kleinberg and refined by Henzinger in [11], [4] and are based on considering pages as *authoritative* sources or *hub* depending on the number of links referred to or conducting to the considered page.

The measure of system performances was conducted in terms of relative recall and precision after 5 documents, see Table 2. Measures were referred to the path retrieved after the search and are not comparable with performance of commercial search engines since the evaluation is based on the quality of the retrieved paths.

Table 2. Retrieval effectiveness for paths

I-Search	Precision top 5	Relative Recall
3th	0.91	0.64
4th	0.93	0.65

5   Conclusion and Future Work

We proposed a logical approach to information retrieval on the web. We used a temporal logic to define the syntax of a structural query to be processed on the graph model of a web site. We implemented a prototype system to validate the proposed approach. The system behaves as a search engine that provides the possibility to pose query of increasing level of complexity. Note that, apart form the previously described functionalities, the system may be used as a web site analyzer since the analyzer module parses the structure of links and pages then it is able to evaluate the structure of a web site, finding dead links and performing reachability evaluation. We are currently working on an extension of the language and the integration of the site analyzer with the retrieval module.

Acknowledgements. This work has been partially supported by MIUR project CLUSTER22 workpackage: "Sistema informativo per il collocamento dei prodotti ortofrutticoli pugliesi" and by a research contract with SudSistemi s.r.l..

References

1. S. Abiteboul, P. Buneman, and D. Suciu. *Data on the web*. Morgan Kaufmann, Los Altos, 2000.
2. 2. C. Beeri and Y. Kornatzky. A logical query language for hypermedia systems. *Information Sciences* 77:1–37, 1994.
3. T. Berners-Lee, J. Hendler, and O. Lassila. The semantic web. *Scientific American* 501(5):1–3, 2001.
4. K. Bharat and M.R. Henzinger. Improved algorithms for topic distillation in a hyperlinked environment. In *ACM SIGIR-98* pages 104–111, 1998.
5. D. Calvanese, G. De Giacomo, and M. Lenzerini. Representing and reasoning on xml documents: A description logic approach. *Journal of Logic and Computation* 9(3): 295–318, 1999.
6. E.M. Clarke, O.M. Grumberg, and D.A. Peled. *Model Checking* The MIT Press, 1999.
7. E. A. Emerson. Automated temporal reasoning about reactive systems. In *Logics for Concurrency* number 1043 in Lecture Notesin Computer Science. Springer-Verlag, 1996.
8. D. Florescu, A.Y. Levy, and A. Mendelzon. Database techniques for the world-wide-web: a survey. *SIGMOD Record* 27(33):59–74, 1998.
9. 9. M. Gordon and P. Pathak.Finding information on the World Wide Web: the retrieval evectiveness of search engines. *Information Processing and Management* 35:141–180, 1999.
10. M. Hacid and F. Toumani. Logic-based approach to semistructured data retrieval. In *ISMIS 2000* number 1932 in Lecture Notesin Artificial Intelligence, pages 77–85. Springer-Verlag, 2000.
11. J. Kleinberg. Authoritative sources in a hyperlinked environment. In *SODA-98* pages 668–677,1998.
12. M. Kobayashi and K. Takeda. Information retrieva on the web. *ACM Computing Surveys* 32(2): 145–173, 2000.
13. G. Salton and M.J. McGill. *Introduction to modern Information Retrieval* McGraw-Hill, New York, 1989.

Four-Valued Knowledge Augmentation for Representing Structured Documents

Mounia Lalmas and Thomas Roelleke

Department of Computer Science, Queen Mary University of London
London, E1 4NS, England
{mounia,thor}@dcs.qmul.ac.uk
http://qmir.dcs.qmul.ac.uk

Abstract. Structured documents are composed of objects with a content and a logical structure. The effective retrieval of structured documents requires models that provide for a content-based retrieval of objects that takes into account their logical structure, so that the relevance of an object is not solely based on its content, but also on the logical structure among objects. This paper proposes a formal model for representing structured documents where the content of an object is viewed as the knowledge contained in that object, and the logical structure among objects is captured by a process of knowledge augmentation: the knowledge contained in an object is augmented with that of its structurally related objects. The knowledge augmentation process takes into account the fact that knowledge can be incomplete and become inconsistent.

1 Introduction

We view a structured document as being composed of *objects* with a content and a logical structure [1,9]. These objects correspond to the document components. The content refers to the content of objects. The logical structure refers to the way structured documents are organised. The *root* object, which is unique, embodies the whole document. *Atomic* objects are document components that are not composed of other components. All other objects are referred to as *inner* objects.

With the widespread development of structured document repositories (e.g. CD-ROM, the Internet and digital libraries), there is a need to develop retrieval models that dynamically return objects of varying granularity (e.g. [4, 6,7,8]). A retrieval result may then consist of entry points to a same document: an entry to the root object when the entire document is relevant to a query, an entry to an atomic object when only that object is relevant to the query, or an entry to an inner object when that object and its structurally related objects are relevant to the query. Returning objects of varying granularity requires sophisticated models that go beyond the purely term-based models of classical information retrieval, so that the relevance of an object is not solely based on its content, but also takes into account the logical structure among objects.

M.-S. Hacid et al. (Eds.): ISMIS 2002, LNAI 2366, pp. 158–166, 2002.

This paper proposes a formal model for representing structured documents that allows the retrieval of objects of varying granularity[1]. The model exploits the content and the logical structure among objects to arrive at a representation of the structured document. The content of an object is viewed as the *knowledge* contained in that object, and the structure among objects is captured by a process of *knowledge augmentation*: the knowledge contained in an object is *augmented* with the knowledge contained in its structurally related objects. The knowledge augmentation process is a combination of knowledge specifically defined to provide for a representation of the object that is based on its own content and that of its structurally related objects. It is this representation that can then be used to estimate the relevance of the object to a query. This paper is concerned with the definition of the knowledge augmentation process, which takes into account the fact that knowledge can be incomplete and become inconsistent. Incompleteness is due to the fact that knowledge that is not explicit in an object should not be considered false. Inconsistent arises when two objects upon which the augmentation process is based contain knowledge that is contradictory.

The outline of this paper is as follows. Section 2 describes the model for representing content and structural knowledge of objects. Section 3 and 4 present two approaches for describing the knowledge augmentation process. Section 5 shows that the two approaches are equivalent. Section 6 concludes and discusses future work.

2   Representing Content and Structural Knowledge

The syntax used to characterise the content and structural knowledge of a structured document is given in Figure 1. A structured document is described by a *program*, which is a set of *clauses*, which are either *facts* or *contexts*. A *context* consists of an object identified by an object name, called the *context name*, in which a program is nested. We use "this" to refer to the context name associated with the global program (i.e. representing the structured document). The set of object names is called C. A *fact* is a *proposition* preceded by *truth-list*. We call Φ the set of propositions. *truth-list* represents the four truth values: "1" means *true*, "0/1" means *false*, "0/0/1" means *inconsistent*, and "0/0/0/1" means *unknown*. In this paper, we use "proposition" for "1 proposition".

Let d and s be context names and "sailing" be a proposition. A context clause is called an *atomic context* clause when it contains only facts, but no context clauses; e.g., "d[sailing]" is an atomic context clause expressing that the content of the object modelled by the context name d is described by the proposition "sailing". Otherwise, a context clause is called a *structured context* clause; e.g., "d[s[sailing]]" is a structured context clause expressing that the object represented by d is composed of the object represented by s, which content is described by the proposition "sailing". We refer to s as *a subcontext* of d, and d as *the supercontext* of s. A supercontext can have several subcontexts, whereas

---

[1] A full version of this paper, which includes examples and proofs, can be found at http://www.dcs.qmul.ac.uk/~mounia/CV/pubconf.html/KA.pdf.

```
program      ::= clause | clause program
clause       ::= fact | context
fact         ::= truth-list proposition
proposition  := NAME
truth-list   ::= '1' | '0/1' | '0/0/1' | '0/0/0/1'
context      ::= NAME '[' program ']'
NAME         ::= [a-z][a-zA-Z0-9_]*
```

Fig. 1. Syntax of programs

a subcontext has exactly one supercontext. Atomic context clauses characterise atomic objects, whereas structured context clauses characterise non-atomic objects (i.e. inner and root objects). A function $sub : C \rightarrow \wp(C)$ yields the set of subcontexts of a supercontext for a given program.

The semantics of programs is defined upon an *interpretation structure M* and an *interpretation function* $\models$. We consider contexts as "agents" that possess *knowledge* concerning their content and their structure and use a Kripke structure (see [3,5]) to define the semantics of programs. Different from [5], we use the terminology "context" instead of "agent" and we consider four truth values [2]. We first define an interpretation structure with respect to a set of propositions Φ and a set of context names C.

Definition 1. (Interpretation structure M): *An* interpretation structure *M for a set Φ of propositions and a set C of context names is a tuple $M = (W, \pi, \mathcal{R})$ where*

- $W := \{w_d : d \in C\} \cup \{w_{slot}\}$ *is a finite set of possible worlds. For each context name, a possible world is defined. W includes the possible worlds w_{this} for the global context "this" and w_{slot} to model the access to "this".*
- $\pi : W \rightarrow (\Phi \rightarrow \{\text{true}, \text{false}, \text{inconsistent}, \text{unknown}\})$ *is a function that yields a truth value assignment for all world w in W, which is a function that assigns a truth value to each proposition in Φ, where the four truth values are defined as* true:=$\{t\}$*,* false:=$\{f\}$*,* inconsistent:=$\{t,f\}$*, and* unknown:=$\{\}$*.*
- $\mathcal{R} := \{R_d : d \in C\}$ *is a finite set of binary relations on W, called accessibility relations, one for each context name. For any supercontext d and subcontext s, i.e. s $\in$ sub(d), $\{(w_d, w_s)\} \in R_s$ where R_s is the accessibility relation associated to s, and w_d and w_s are the possible worlds associated with d and s, respectively. We say that context s accesses or reaches world w_s from world w_d. The accessibility relation for the global context "this" is defined as $R_{this} := \{(w_{slot}, w_{this})\}$.*
- *The function $R_d(w) := \{w'|(w, w') \in R_d\}$ for $w \in W$ and $R_d \in \mathcal{R}$ yields the set of worlds that can be reached from world w by the context d.*

The semantics of the content and structural knowledge of objects is based upon considering context names as modal operators, referred to as *knowledge modal operators*. The atomic context clause "d[sailing]" becomes interpreted as "d knows sailing" and captures the content knowledge of the corresponding object. The structured context clause "d[s[sailing]]" becomes interpreted as "d knows that s knows sailing" and captures the structural knowledge of the object represented by d. With this interpretation in mind, we define the interpretation function $\models$ that assigns truth values to propositions, facts, atomic and structured context clauses, and programs with respect to the interpretation structure defined above. The following and all definitions in this paper are based on an interpretation structure $M = (W, \pi, \mathcal{R})$ as defined above.

Definition 2. (Interpretation function $\models$): *Let $\varphi \in \Phi$ and $w \in W$. Let d, s $\in \mathcal{C}$. Let $R_d \in \mathcal{R}$ be the accessibility relation corresponding to d. The interpretation of facts is defined as follows:*

$$(M, w) \models 1 \; \varphi : \Longleftrightarrow \pi(w)(\varphi) = \text{true}$$
$$(M, w) \models 0/1 \; \varphi : \Longleftrightarrow \pi(w)(\varphi) = \text{false}$$
$$(M, w) \models 0/0/1 \; \varphi : \Longleftrightarrow \pi(w)(\varphi) = \text{inconsistent}$$
$$(M, w) \models 0/0/0/1 \; \varphi : \Longleftrightarrow \pi(w)(\varphi) = \text{unknown}$$

The interpretation of atomic context clauses is defined as follows:

$$(M, w) \models \text{d}[1 \; \varphi] : \Longleftrightarrow \forall w' \in R_d(w) : (M, w') \models 1 \; \varphi$$
$$(M, w) \models \text{d}[0/1 \; \varphi] : \Longleftrightarrow \forall w' \in R_d(w) : (M, w') \models 0/1 \; \varphi$$
$$(M, w) \models \text{d}[0/0/1 \; \varphi] : \Longleftrightarrow \forall w' \in R_d(w) : (M, w') \models 0/0/1 \; \varphi$$
$$(M, w) \models \text{d}[0/0/0/1 \; \varphi] : \Longleftrightarrow \forall w' \in R_d(w) : (M, w') \models 0/0/0/1 \; \varphi$$

The interpretation of structured context clauses is defined as follows:

$$(M, w) \models \text{d}[\text{s}[\text{fact}]] : \Longleftrightarrow \forall w' \in R_d(w) : (M, w') \models \text{s}[\text{fact}]$$

The interpretation of a program within a context d is defined as follows, where program* is the set of clauses given in the program:

$$(M, w) \models \text{d}[\text{program}] \Longleftrightarrow \forall \text{clause} \in \text{program}^* : (M, w) \models \text{d}[\text{clause}]$$

An interpretation structure M is called a model *of a program P iff this[P] is true in all worlds with respect to M. We use "valid" for "true in all worlds". The notation $M \models$ this[P] reads "this[P] is valid".*

The formalism is next extended so that the knowledge of an object is augmented with that of its structurally related objects, necessary to allow for the retrieval of objects at varying granularity.

3   Knowledge Augmentation Using Modal Operators

Consider the program "d[s1[sailing] s2[boats]]". A model for the program is based on an interpretation structure M defined upon a set of possible worlds $W = \{w_{slot}, w_{this}, w_d, w_{s1}, w_{s2}\}$, the accessibility relations $R_{this} = \{(w_{slot}, w_{this})\}$, $R_d = \{(w_{this}, w_d)\}$, $R_{s1} = \{(w_d, w_{s1})\}$ and $R_{s2} = \{(w_d, w_{s2})\}$, and the truth value assignments $\pi(w_{s1})(sailing) = \pi(w_{s2})(boats) = true$, and *unknown* in all other cases. Definition 2 yields $(M, w_{w_d}) \models$ s1[sailing] and $(M, w_d) \models$ s2[boats] characterising the knowledge content of s1 and s2 (s1 knows sailing and s2 knows

boats), and $(M, w_{this}) \models$ d[s1[sailing]] and $(M, w_{this}) \models$ d[s2[boats]] characterising the structural knowledge of d (d knows that s1 knows sailing and s2
knows boats). Contexts s1 and s2 would be relevant to queries about "sailing"
and "boats", respectively, but none of the contexts s1 and s2 would be relevant
to a query about "sailing and boats". The supercontext d should be relevant to
such a query because it knows that one of its subcontext contains sailing and the
other contains boats. This could be inferred if the knowledge content of d is augmented with that of its subcontexts. However, a knowledge augmentation process
can lead to inconsistent knowledge. Consider the program "d[s1[sailing] s2[0/1
sailing boats]]". Subcontext s1 knows sailing; subcontext s2 knows the opposite.
The example makes evident that augmenting the content knowledge of d by that
of s1 and s2 leads to inconsistent knowledge regarding the proposition "sailing",
since we have evidence for true from s1 and false from s2. In the augmented
context d(s1,s2), "sailing" is therefore inconsistent.

To distinguish between the content knowledge of a context and its *augmented
content knowledge*, we introduce the terminology of *augmented context* as opposed to *basic context*. Basic contexts are context names (e.g. d, s1 and s2),
whereas *augmented contexts* consist of a supercontext name and a list (group)
composed of augmented contexts or basic contexts (e.g. d(s1(s11),s2)). A context
clause with only basic contexts is called a *basic context clause* (e.g. "d[sailing]"
is a basic atomic context clause and "d[s[sailing]]" is a basic structured context clause). A context clause with augmented contexts is called an *augmented
context clause* (e.g. "d(s1,s2)[sailing]").

The knowledge augmentation process *combines* knowledge of a supercontext
with that of its subcontexts. Modal operators have been defined to formalise specific combination of knowledge (e.g. common knowledge and distributed knowledge [5]). However, as discussed in [9], these operators are not appropriate for a
combination of knowledge that arises from a knowledge augmentation process.
We therefore define other modal operators.

The first operator is the *united knowledge modal operator* denoted U_G, which
is used to represent the combined knowledge of a group of context $G = (s1,\ldots,sn)$
referred to as a *united context*. Here, we are aiming at capturing the combined
knowledge of a group of context, not the knowledge of an augmented context.

Definition 3. (United knowledge operator U_G): *Let w be a world in W,
φ a proposition in Φ, and G a united context from C.*

$$(M, w) \models U_G[1 \; \varphi] : \iff \exists s \in G : (M, w) \models s[1 \; \varphi] \; and$$
$$\forall s \in G : ((M, w) \models s [1 \; \varphi] \; or \; (M, w) \models s [0/0/0/1\varphi])$$
$$(M, w) \models U_G[0/1 \; \varphi] : \iff \exists s \in G : (M, w) \models s[0/1 \; \varphi] \; and$$
$$\forall s \in G : ((M, w) \models s [0/1 \; \varphi] \; or \; (M, w) \models s[0/0/0/1\varphi])$$
$$(M, w) \models U_G[0/0/1 \; \varphi] : \iff (\exists s \in G : (M, w) \models s[1 \; \varphi] \; and$$
$$\exists s \in G : (M, w) \models s[\; 0/1 \; \varphi]) \; or$$
$$\exists s \in G : (M, w) \models s[0/0/1 \; \varphi]$$
$$(M, w) \models U_G[0/0/0/1 \; \varphi] : \iff \forall s \in G : (M, w) \models s[0/0/0/1 \; \varphi]$$

We define now the knowledge of augmented contexts through the introduction of an *augmented knowledge modal operator* A_{dG} where dG is an augmented context (d is the supercontext and G is the united context formed with the subcontexts of d, i.e. $G =$ (si : si $\in$ sub(d))). The knowledge of the united context is combined with the knowledge of the supercontext. The augmented knowledge modal operator is therefore defined upon the united knowledge modal operator.

Definition 4. (Augmented knowledge operator A_{dG}): *Let w be a world in W, φ a proposition in Φ, d, s1, ..., sn contexts in C such that sub(d) = {s1,...,sn}, and R_d the accessibility relation in $\mathcal{R}$ associated with the supercontext d.*

$(M, w) \models A_{d(s1,...,sn)}[1 \; \varphi] : \Longleftrightarrow$

$((M, w) \models d[1 \; \varphi]$ *and*

$\quad \forall w' \in R_d(w) : ((M, w') \models U_{(s1,...,sn)}[1 \; \varphi]$ *or* $(M, w') \models U_{(s1,...,sn)}[0/0/0/1 \; \varphi]))$ *or*

$((M, w) \models d[0/0/0/1 \; \varphi])$ *and* $\forall w' \in R_d(w) : (M, w') \models U_{(s1,...,sn)}[1 \; \varphi])$

$(M, w) \models A_{d(s1,...,sn)}[0/1 \; \varphi] : \Longleftrightarrow$

$((M, w) \models d[0/1 \; \varphi]$ *and*

$\quad \forall w' \in R_d(w) : ((M, w') \models U_{(s1,...,sn)}[0/1 \; \varphi]$ *or* $(M, w') \models U_{(s1,...,sn)}[0/0/0/1 \; \varphi]))$ *or*

$((M, w) \models d[0/0/0/1 \; \varphi])$ *and* $\forall w' \in R_d(w) : (M, w') \models U_{(s1,...,sn)}[0/1 \; \varphi])$

$(M, w) \models A_{d(s1,...,sn)}[0/0/1 \; \varphi] : \Longleftrightarrow$

$((M, w) \models d[0/0/1 \; \varphi]$ *or* $\forall w' \in R_d(w) : (M, w') \models U_{(s1,...,sn)}[0/0/1 \; \varphi])$ *or*

$((M, w) \models d[1 \; \varphi]$ *and* $\forall w' \in R_d(w) : (M, w') \models U_{(s1,...,sn)}[0/1 \; \varphi])$ *or*

$((M, w) \models d[0/1 \; \varphi]$ *and* $\forall w' \in R_d(w) : (M, w') \models U_{(s1,...,sn)}[1 \; \varphi])$

$(M, w) \models A_{d(s1,...,sn)}[0/0/0/1 \; \varphi] : \Longleftrightarrow$

$(M, w) \models d[0/0/0/1 \; \varphi]$ *and* $\forall w' \in R_d(w) : (M, w') \models U_{(s1,...,sn)}[0/0/0/1 \; \varphi]$

4 Knowledge Augmentation Using Truth Value Assignment Functions

In this section, we define the knowledge augmentation process based on a graphical representation of worlds and accessibility relations formalised through the notions of G-world-trees. This follows the approach adopted in [5], where combination of knowledge was defined upon the notion of "G-reachability". Two truth value assignment functions are defined upon G-world trees to characterise united knowledge and augmented knowledge. The logical structure of a non-atomic object is described as trees, referred to as *G-world-trees*. These tree structures are also reflected in the way possible worlds and accessibility relations are defined with respect to contexts. An empty united context is denoted "()", and for a context name s in C, s is treated as augmented context with an empty united context (e.g. s is the same as s()).

Definition 5. (G-world-trees): *Let* d *be a context in* C *with accessibility relation* R_d *in* R. *Let* w *and* w_0 *be worlds in* W. *Let* G_n *be the united context* (s1,...,sn) *and let* G_{n+1} *be the united context* (s1,...,sn+1), *for* s1, ..., sn+1 *in* C. *The set of G-world-trees associated with a united context is defined inductively as follows:*

$$trees(w, G_{n+1}) := \{(w, S) | \exists S_n, t : (w, S_n) \in trees(w, G_n) \land$$
$$t \in trees(w, s_{n+1}) \land S = S_n \cup \{t\}\}$$

A tuple (w, S) *is a G-world-tree of a world* w *and a united context* G_{n+1} *if there exists a set* S_n *such that* (w, S_n) *is a G-world-tree of the world* w *and the united context* G_n, *there exists a G-world-tree* t *of the world* w *and the context* sn+1, *and* $S = S_n \cup \{t\}$.

The G world-tree of a world w *and an empty united context* () *is* $(w, \{\})$.

The set of trees associated with an augmented context is defined inductively as:

$$trees(w_0, dG) := \{(w, S) | w \in R_d(w_0) \land (w, S) \in trees(w, G)\}$$

A tuple (w, S) *is a G-world-tree of a world* w_0 *and an augmented context* dG *if* $w \in R_d(w_0)$ *and* (w, S) *is a G-world-tree of the world* w *and the united context* G.

The G-world tree of an augmented context d(s1,...,sn) formalises the accessibility of possible worlds associated with the subcontexts si from the possible world associated with the context d, and for each si, the accessibility of the possible worlds associated with the subcontexts of the si from the possible world associated with the context si, etc. This reflects the logical structure among d, its subcontexts si, the subcontexts of si, etc. We call T the set of G-world trees associated with an interpretation structure M.

The next step is to define truth value assignment functions with respect to G-world trees to capture the logical structure among the contexts. First we define the truth value value assignment function, referred to as *united truth value assignment function* associated with a united context to model the united knowledge of the united context. Here, the definition of the four truth values as sets (see Definition 1) is exploited to arrive at the *united truth value.*

Definition 6. (United truth value assignment function π_U**):** *Let* (w, S) *be a G-world-tree in* T *of world* $w \in W$ *and a united context* G *from* C. *The united truth value function* $\pi_U : T \to (\Phi \to \{\text{true, false, inconsistent, unknown}\})$ *of a G-world-tree* (w, S) *is defined as the union of the truth value functions* $\pi(w')$ *where the worlds* w' *are the roots of the subtrees* $(w', \{\})$ *in the set* S. *Formally, for all proposition* φ *in* Φ:

$$\pi_U((w, S))(\varphi) := \bigcup_{(w', \{\}) \in S} \pi(w')(\varphi)$$

For an empty set S, *the united truth value* $\pi_U((w, \{\}))(\varphi) := \text{unknown}$.

We define now the truth value assignment function, referred to as *augmented truth value assignment function*, associated with an augmented context to model its augmented knowledge.

Definition 7. (Augmented truth value assignment function π_A): *Let d be a context in $\mathcal{C}$ and G a united context in $\mathcal{C}$. Let (w, S) be a G-world-tree in $\mathcal{T}$ of world w_0 in W and the augmented context dG. The augmented truth value function $\pi_A : \mathcal{T} \rightarrow (\Phi \rightarrow \{\text{true}, \text{false}, \text{inconsistent}, \text{unknown}\})$ of a G-world-tree (w, S) is defined as the union of the truth value function $\pi(w)$ of world w and the united truth value function $\pi_U((w, S))$ of the G-world-tree (w, S). Formally, for all φ in Φ:*

$$\pi_A((w, S))(\varphi) := \pi(w)(\varphi) \cup \pi_U((w, S))(\varphi)$$

5   Equivalence of the Two Approaches

Sections 3 and 4 present two approaches that formalise the knowledge augmentation process. The two approaches are based on different formalisations of united knowledge and augmented knowledge. This section presents two theorems that show that the two approaches are equivalent, that is, they lead to the same knowledge augmentation process (the detailed proofs can be found at http://www.dcs.qmul.ac.uk/~mounia/CV/pubconf.html/KA.pdf). Theorem 1 states that the definitions of united truth value assignment function (Definition 6) and united knowledge modal operator (Definition 3) lead to the same truth value assignment to a proposition in a united context. The same applies for Theorem 2, with respect to the definitions of the augmented truth value assignment (Definition 7) and the augmented knowledge modal operator (Definition 4).

Theorem 1. (United knowledge): *In a world $w \in W$, a proposition $\varphi \in \Phi$ is true in a united context G iff for each tree (w, S) of world w and united context G, the united truth value equals* true. *Formally $\forall s$ in $G : R_s(w) \neq \{\}$:*

$$(M, w) \models U_G[\varphi] \iff \forall (w, S) \in trees(w, G) : \pi_U((w, S))(\varphi) = \text{true}$$

Theorem 2. (Augmented knowledge): *In a world w_0 in W, a proposition φ in Φ is true in an augmented context dG iff for each tree (w, S) of world w_0 and an augmented context dG, the augmented truth value equals* true.

$$(M, w_0) \models dG[\varphi] \iff \forall (w, S) \in trees(w_0, dG) : \pi_A((w, S))(\varphi) = \text{true}$$

Our first formalism (Section 3) is, therefore, compatible with the well-known framework defined in [5] for modelling the combination of knowledge (Section 4).

6 Conclusion and Future Work

This paper describes a formal model for representing the content and logical structure of structured documents for the purpose of their retrieval. To obtain a representation that allows for the retrieval of objects of varying granularity, the content of an object is viewed as the knowledge contained in that object, and the structure among objects is captured by a process of knowledge augmentation, which leads to a representation of the object that is based on its own content and that of its structurally related objects. The knowledge augmentation process takes into account the fact that knowledge can be incomplete and become inconsistent. The model is based on the definitions of four truth values, modal operators, possible worlds, accessibility relations and truth value assignments used to characterise content knowledge, structural knowledge, augmented knowledge, incompleteness and inconsistency.

The formalism described in this paper is the basis of the development of a model for structured document retrievals that allows for the retrieval of objects of varying granularity. Future work will present the representation of the uncertainty inherent to the information retrieval process, which will be used to estimate the degree to which an object is relevant to a query.

References

1. ABITEBOUL, S., CLUET, S., CHRISTOPHIDES, V., MILO, T., MOERKOTTE, G., AND SIMEON, J. Querying documents in object databases. *International Journal on Digital Libraries 1* (1997), 1–9.
2. BELNAP, N. A useful four-valued logic. In *Modern Uses of Multiple-valued Logic*, J. Dunn and G. Epstein, Eds. Reidel, Dordrecht, 1977.
3. CHELLAS, B. *Modal Logic.* Cambridge University Press, 1980.
4. CHIARAMELLA, Y., MULHEM, P., AND FOUREL, F. A model for multimedia information retrieval. Tech. Rep. Fermi ESPRIT BRA 8134, University of Glasgow, 1996.
5. FALGIN, R., HARPEN, J., MOSES, J., AND VARDI, M. *Reasoning about Knowledge.* MIT Press, Cambridge, Massachusetts, 1995.
6. FRISSE, M. Searching for information in a hypertext medical handbook. *Communications of the ACM 31*, 7 (1988), 880–886.
7. FUHR, N., AND GROSSJOHANN, K. XIRQL: A query language for information retrieval in XML documents. In *Proceedings of ACM-SIGIR Conference on Research and Development in Information Retrieval* (New Orleans, USA, 2001), pp. 172–180.
8. MYAENG, S., JANG, D. H., KIM, M. S., AND ZHOO, Z. C. A flexible model for retrieval of SGML documents. In *Proceedings of ACM-SIGIR Conference on Research and Development in Information Retrieval* (Melbourne, Australia, 1998), pp. 138–145.
9. ROELLEKE, T. *POOL: Probabilistic Object-Oriented Logical Representation and Retrieval of Complex Objects - A Model for Hypermedia Retrieva.* PhD thesis, University of Dortmund, Germany, 1999.

WISECON – An Intelligent Assistant for Buying Computers on the Internet

Tomas Kroupa, Petr Berka, and Tomas Kocka

Laboratory for Intelligent Systems, University of Economics
W. Churchill Sq. 4, 130 67 Prague, Czech Republic
{kroupa,berka,kocka}@vse.cz

Abstract. Internet shopping using some on-line catalogue of products is one of the fastest growing businesses now. An intelligent support for selecting a product in such a catalogue should work as an assistant (on request), not forcing the user to perform any unnecessary steps. As many Internet portals which support browsing and search, the proposed solution should support browsing (the catalogue) and recommending. Our paper describes some ongoing work on intelligent shopping assistant of an on-line catalogue of a hardware vendor who sells a relatively restricted scale of products (PC's) manufactured by a single company. We propose a solution that will make browsing the catalogue easier, will recommend products, and will adapt its behavior to different types of users. Grouping the products into easily interpretable clusters can enhance browsing. To recommend a product and to adapt the system to different users, we propose to use a Bayesian network. We believe that our solution will be able to automatically follow the changes in the notions of computer characteristics (as the performance of new products increases), will be able to easy incorporate new products and will be able to understand requests from different types of users.

1 Introduction

Internet shopping using some on-line catalogue of products is one of the fastest growing businesses now. In contrast to the classical selling channels, Internet shopping dramatically reduces the cost per transaction. Intelligent systems for support of Internet shopping help the user to decide what products to buy, find specifications and reviews of the products, make recommendations, find the best price for the desired product (comparison shopping), monitor new products on the product list or watch for special offers or discounts [1].

This paper deals with an intelligent shopping assistant for browsing/recommending suitable products from an on-line catalogue of a hardware vendor who sells a relatively restricted scale of products (PC's) manufactured by a single company. Our focus will be on the recommendation part of the system – we describe the basic concept and a small prototype version for the category of desktop computers.

M.-S. Hacid et al. (Eds.): ISMIS 2002, LNAI 2366, pp. 167–175, 2002.

The paper is organized as follows: Section 2 discuses the usual on-line shopping possibilities, Section 3 describes the proposed intelligent shopping assistant WISECON, Section 4 gives some plans of our future work.

2   Internet Shopping: Browsing or Recommending

Internet shopping is usually based on work with some on-line catalogue of the products. The simplest way is to let the potential customer browse through the list of products. In case of non-technical products (e.g. books or CD's) this is a convenient way. This mode of access can be further extended by some search facilities (usual in a form of search for a substring in a textual description), or by collaborative filtering (people interested in this book are also buying these books – see e.g. amazon.com). Nevertheless, in case of technical products (e.g. handies or computers), where the description gives a number of technical details this way is less comfortable for unskilled customer. So some assistant recommending suitable product will be of great help. A recommending system should ask the user some simple questions ant then will point him to a group of products that fulfill given requirements. The assignment of products to requirements can be done using querying a database of products ("hard match") or using some adaptive techniques that reflect imprecise and vague requests of the customer ("soft match"). In our paper we are focusing on the later case.

3   Intelligent Shopping Assistant WISECON

The WISECON (**Wise Con**figurator) system is being built to improve the access to an on-line catalogue of a hardware vendor who sells PC's. The current way of interacting with the catalogue seems to be quite problematic. The interested customer has to browse through this partial catalogue to find a desired configuration. Only limited search (search for a substring in the textual description of a model) is available to support this browsing.The main drawback of this approach is that the customer is expected to be at least an experienced user of computers. He must understand the technical parameters of the models, some of them being irrelevant for the choice since they have the same value for all models on the stock. Since the vendor wants to attract broader range of customers, there is an effort to make the communication with the system substantially more intuitive and user-friendly.

3.1   Overall Architecture

An intelligent shopping assistant should not force the user to perform any unnecessary steps. As many Internet portals supporting browsing and search, the proposed solution should support browsing (the catalogue) and recommending. Further on, we want to make our solution adaptive to different types of users (customers). Therefore, the proposed improvement of the on-line catalogue system is focused on *three goals:*

- Improve browsing the catalogue
- Recommend products
- Control the communication with the user

It is quite easy to fulfill the first goal. The products can be grouped (according to few basic technical parameters) into some smaller „natural" categories. The categories of products should have some reasonable interpretation (e.g. cheap low-end models, fast computers with relatively small external memory etc.) This grouping can be formulated by an expert or can be done automatically using cluster analysis.

The goal of recommending is to narrow the choice of products as much as possible on the basis of users' requests. When the user is browsing the catalogue, the intelligent component of the system should recommend the products. This module should be able to find products that mostly comply with the user's criteria. Clearly, there is a certain controversy between the requirement to recommend only a very limited scale of products (few computers which match the criteria) and to maintain the friendly communication with the user (ask only few questions). When interacting with an user during recommendation, the system has to consider various types of users. Each type of the user is expected to be able to answer only a limited set of questions and each user can have different optimal time period of the interaction with the system until the automatic offer and some other characteristics. The type of the user could be deduced by an introductory question or inferred by the system from the behavior of the user (i.e., questions answered by the user). This will help the system to estimate the applicable questions.

Any approach should reflect the fact that the technology of manufacturing computers is evolving in time. Thus the notion „fast computer" or „small harddisk" evolves in time as well. Design of clusters and especially assignment of the specific configurations to the clusters should follow these changes. New products in the offer of the vendor will also influence the discriminating power of the product characteristics (some parameters can become irrelevant for discriminating between models or groups if they become the same for the whole offer).

Additional information that is relevant to the customer's decision can be the number of sold computers of a specific model. Both this piece of information and the price of the model will be used as a sorting criterion of products within a group or even in the complete offer.

3.2   Clustering the Products

The building of WISECON started with clustering the products. We believe that having the computers divided into smaller, "natural" groups can be useful for both browsing and recommending. We used the data about technical parameters (type and frequency of processor, amount of RAM and VRAM, size of HDD, speed of CD drive, operating system, sound card) and price to cluster the computers in the category "desktop".

We have found some easily interpretable clusters - computers with different performance (Fig. 1). So e.g. cluster **A** is a cluster of low-end computers, cluster **F** is a cluster of high-end computers, or cluster **C** is a cluster of fast computers with small HDD and without CD[1]. Far from surprising is the fact that the price of the models corresponds to the performance. Our experiments have proven that different subsets of the technical parameters are sufficient to assign a computer to a cluster. Therefore, in recommending mode, different sets of questions can result in the same list of products.

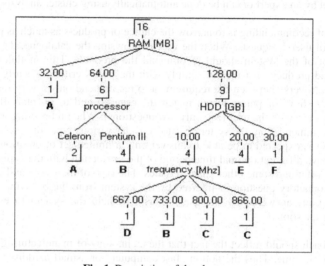

Fig. 1. Description of the clusters

3.3   Bayesian Network WISECON

As already mentioned, the smart component of the system is represented by the Bayesian network WISECON . The structure of this probabilistic model is depicted in Figure 2. The network has rather regular structure. There are four kinds of variables in the model:

- Goal variable (**Computer**),
- Configuration variables (**Frequency, Processor, RAM, HDD, CD, Price**),
- Information variables (**Frequency_Q, Processor_Q, RAM_Q, HDD_Q, CD_Q, Price_Q, Applications**),
- Other variables (**Cluster** – i.e. cluster (A-F) assigned to the computer, **Customer** – i.e. type of customer).

---

[1] If we think about these clusters in a way similar to categories of cars, then cluster C will be a cluster of "cabrio" computers.

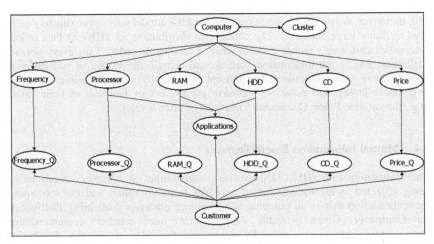

Fig. 2. The structure of WISECON

The variable **Computer** takes values from a set of 16 desktop computers sold by the hardware vendor. Category A-F is assigned to each computer in the variable **Cluster**. The configuration variables specify a configuration of each computer on the stock. For example, **HDD** determines the capacity of harddisk in GB and it can take value 10, 20 or 30 (according to current vendor's offer); the value of each computer (in Czech crowns) is stored in the variable **Price** etc. Realize that there is a deterministic link (a table that defines conditional probability distributions contains only zeros and ones) between the variable **Computer** and all configuration variables and there is one between **Computer** and **Cluster** as well. Variable **Applications** specifies the prevailing use of the computer (office/ multimedia/ games). For the sake of simplicity, we suppose that the selection of the application field is influenced by only 3 hardware components – **Processor**, **RAM** and **HDD**. Appropriate assessment of customer's competence can be performed by setting the variable **Customer** to one of the values expert/ medium experienced/ not experienced. Only the information variables and **Customer** can be answered directly by the customer. All conditional probabilities were subjectively assessed. WISECON was built in the software package *MSBNx*[2].

The crucial concept of WISECON is that of conditioning the information variables (except **Applications**) on both **Customer** and the respective configuration variable (without suffix **_Q**). This conditioning allows to assess the ability of each user to specify correctly his requirements with respect to his profile (variable **Customer**) and it can be justified by the reasonable assumption stating that only a computer expert knows exactly what he wants whereas the one being an inexperienced customer needs to be guided through the catalogue. For example, consider parental variables **HDD** and **Customer** of the variable **HDD_Q**. A set of possible values of **HDD** is a list of all hard discs on the stock. Variable **HDD_Q** can then take the same values as **HDD**

---

[2] See the website http://www.research.microsoft.com/adapt/MSBNx/ for further details.

and, moreover, *vague values* specifying the harddisk model only approximately (e.g., low/ medium/ large harddisk). The conditional distribution for **HDD_Q** then indeed determines customer's competence to make a reasonable order. Thus every domain (definition set) of the information variable can contain the values of two different nature: *vague values* describing the concept in generally comprehensible adjectives (e.g. small, large), and *values of technical parameters or intervals* of their values (e.g., the variable **Price_Q** contains 5 intervals of price levels).

3.4   Mutual Information Based Diagnosis

The consultation with WISECON involves iterative input of customer's requirements being reflected as an instantiation of variables to given values and the subsequent recommendation that is an outcome of computing posterior probability distribution for **Computer**. Given available evidence, the most reliable recommendation (computer configuration) is naturally maximizing the value of posterior distribution for **Computer**. In the next paragraph, we describe a technique for accelerating the consultation by an apt selection of the information variable to be answered by the customer. This method is aiming at attaining the highest 'lift' in value of posterior for **Computer** among all possible information variables and it can therefore speed up the diagnostic procedure of finding the most reliable recommendation

We employ the technique based on information-theoretical quantity called *mutual information* (see [2] for a thorough theoretical exposition) that represents *value of information* for an information variable in our network. Mutual information is computed as follows. Suppose that $P(X,Y)$ is a joint probability distribution of two discrete random variables with a finite set of possible values. Mutual information $I(P(X,Y))$ equals

$$I(P(X,Y)) = \sum_{x,y} P(x,y) \log \frac{P(x,y)}{P(x)P(y)},$$

where the summation is taken over all pairs x, y such that $P(x,y) > 0$ and the logarithm is natural. In a way, mutual information characterizes dependence of variables X and Y. The key idea is that the user must be always asked the question with the highest value of mutual information between this question and the goal variable **Computer.** This can narrow the choice as much as possible asking only a minimal number of questions. A certain care must be nonetheless taken because the value of mutual information depends also on the cardinality of the domain which is the summation taken over. The last point that we want to make in connection with the mutual information based diagnostic is to stress that it is merely a *heuristics* – it can't guarantee achievement of the highest lift for a selected information variable in any stage of the consultation.

The recommendation procedure not only must be able to advise the most reliable computer configuration but it should also order the most probable computers according to their posterior probabilities. Afterwards, the resulting list of products can utilize the predefined grouping (**Cluster**).

3.5   Example

We will show the use of WISECON on a simple example. Assume that John wants a cheap computer to run office applications (writing documents, mails etc.). The values of mutual information (score) for all prior distributions are detailed in Table 1.

Table 1. Mutual information for priors (**Computer** - information variable)

Information variable	Score
Price_Q	3.97
CD_Q	1.80
Frequency_Q	1.61
RAM_Q	1.32
HDD_Q	1.00
Processor_Q	0.86
Applications	0.28
Customer	3×10^{-3}

John enters his requirements as the evidence **Applications**=office and **Price_Q**=20 000-30 000 (this price category represents cheap low-end computers). Given this answer, conditional probability distribution for **Computer** acquires its maximal value 0.2028 for the two computers denoted as comp4 and comp5. Two more computers (comp3, comp6) have the posterior probability[3] higher than 0.2. The computer comp3 is assigned to cluster A, comp4-comp8 are members of cluster B – all of them have the price within specified range.

Node Name	State 0	State 1	State 2	State 3	State 4	State 5	State 6	State 7
Computer	comp1	comp2	comp3	comp4	comp5	comp6	comp7	comp8
	0,0678	0,0527	0,2027	0,2028	0,2028	0,2027	0,0226	0,0151

Fig. 3. Posterior probabilities (**Appplications**=office, **Price_Q**=20 000-30 000) for computers comp1-comp8

Since the values of conditional probabilities for comp3-comp6 are almost identical, John must be asked to provide another piece of information in order to discriminate among the four and hence make more reliable recommendation. We may assume that the highest value of the conditional probability distribution must be higher than a given threshold to recommend any computer; let the threshold equals 0.7 in our case. What question should be asked in the present stage of the consultation? In other words, what is the variable with the maximal value of information? The one with the highest value of mutual information. As shown in Table 2, it is the variable **Frequency_Q** with the score 1.87.

---

[3] The Figure 5 depicts the table for computers comp1-comp8. The remaining computers comp9-comp16 have the conditional probability lower than 0.02.

Table 2. Mutual information for posteriors (**Computer** - information variable)

Information variable	Score
Frequency_Q	1.87
CD_Q	1.23
Processor_Q	1.23
RAM_Q	0.71
Customer	0.31
HDD_Q	0.02

Afterwards, John is asked to enter the required frequency of processor. Having some preliminary idea about the performance of processors, John demands the processor with the frequency in the range 600-700 MHz. His selection results in the new posterior distribution for **Computer** in Figure 4.

Note that the posterior probability of comp3 is now higher than the specified threshold and it is thus reasonable to recommend comp3 as a suitable computer model for John. Indeed, comp3 is a desktop with Celeron 633 MHz, 10GB HDD. It costs 20 400 CZK and seems to be suitable for ordinary office applications.

Node Name	State 0	State 1	State 2	State 3	State 4	State 5	State 6	State 7
Computer	comp1	comp2	comp3	comp4	comp5	comp6	comp7	comp8
	0,0173	0,1525	0,7510	0,0095	0,0095	0,0530	0,0012	0,0039

Fig. 4. Posterior probabilities (**Appplications**=office, **Price_Q**=20 000-30 000, **Frequency_Q**=600-700) for computers comp1-comp8

4   Conclusions and Further Work

We believe that a very simple yet fruitful idea has been presented to cope with a task of recommending suitable computer configurations. Employing a Bayesian network has two advantages. First it can easily reflect the changes of the market by adapting to new customers behavior (updating with sold products data) or by expert setting. Second, on the other hand, if the graphical structure of the model is specified in advance, we are likely claim that any further modification of the structure is not necessary. Therefore, the qualitative structure (directed acyclic graph) represents the *stable* part of the model whereas the quantitative parameters (probabilities) can be simply *adapted*. To add new computer to the network, one has to add (deterministic) tables that relate the computer to the configuration variables and to the cluster.

Diagnostic procedure based on mutual information provides a convenient way of controlling question-answering mode enabling simple assessment of potential information gains that determines the question to be asked.

In our further work we want to make an effort to develop a technique for *estimating the type of the customer*. Now we propose that the type of the customer is specified in the beginning of each session. Later we expect that the customer-type modeling would become sophisticated. The number of customer types and their description could be discovered from the data about customers and their behavior. The set of potential questions should always contain the most informative one that can answer any customer. Then the system will deduce from already answered questions the type of the user and concentrate the choice of questions to the right group of users only.

Another improvement can involve the application of a problem-solving method called *troubleshooting* [6]. Not only it is more sophisticated approach to analyze value of the information, it can also handle various kinds of variables (actions, causes, questions) and makes it possible to specify the utilities resulting from knowing an exact value of a variable. This could help, prior to any decision-making process, to distinguish that some pieces of information are more relevant to the final decision than the other. For example, price of the computer is more valuable information than the specification of a graphical controller since e.g., a low performance graphical controller can appear in a cheap desktop as well as in an expensive network server.

Schafer et al [5] give a nice taxonomy of recommending systems. According to this taxonomy, our approach is an example of broad recommendation list model. WISECON uses attributes as customer input, no community input (this will be extended to purchase history), prediction (posterior probabilities) as output, and attribute based recommendation method. The level of personalization, which is no will be extended to ephemeral. The results are delivered in an ordered list.

References

1. Berka, P.,: Intelligent Systems on the Internet. Tech. Rep. LISp-98-01, University of Economics, Prague (1998)
2. Hájek, P., Havránek, T., Jiroušek, R.: Uncertain Information Processing in Expert Systems. CRC Press, Boca Raton (1992)
3. Cowell, R., Dawid, A., Lauritzen, S., Spiegelhalter, D.: Probabilistic Networks and Expert Systems. Springer (1999).
4. Kocka, T., Berka, P., Kroupa, T.: Smart adaptive support for selling computers on the Internet. In: Proc. EUNITE symposium (2001)
5. Schafer J.B., Konstan J.A., Riedl,J.: E-Commerce Recommendation Applications. Data Mining and Knowledge Discovery 5 (2001) 115-153
6. Skaaning C., Jensen F., Kjaerulff U.: Printer troubleshooting using Bayesian networks. 13th International Conference on Industrial and Engineering Applications of AI and Expert Systems (2000)

Basic Semantics of the Logic of Plausible Reasoning

Bartłomiej Śnieżyński

Institute of Computer Science, AGH Technical University, Kraków, Poland
sniezyn@agh.edu.pl

Abstract. Logic of plausible reasoning (LPR) is a formalism which is based on human inference patterns. In the paper the LPR is defined as a labeled deductive system. Knowledge base consists of labeled formulas representing object-attribute-value triples, implications, hierarchies, dependencies and similarities between objects. Labels are used to represent plausible parameters. In the paper LPR basic semantics is defined and the proof system is proved to be correct. Finally, several examples of inference pattern application are presented.

Keywords: logic of plausible reasoning, uncertain knowledge representation, semantics of the logic of plausible reasoning.

1 Introduction

In this paper the logic of plausible reasoning (LPR) is considered. It was developed by Collins and Michalski in 1989 [2]. This formalism is a knowledge representation and inference technique, which is based on human reasoning [1]. In LPR several inference patterns are defined (not only Modus Ponens) and many parameters estimate certainty. Therefore LPR differs from others theories such as fuzzy logic [13], multiple-valued logic [5], certainty factors [11], Dempster-Shafer theory [10], rough sets [8] and belief networks [9] used in AI to represent uncertain knowledge.

LPR can be defined as a labeled deductive system introduced by Gabbay [3]. The knowledge is represented using labeled formulas, where labels are estimates of certainty. The formalism is similar to a semantic network [4] with 4 types of links: hierarchy links, which represent the is-a and the part-of relations; similarity links representing similarity of objects; dependency links used to represent dependencies between objects and relational links representing values of attributes of objects. Additionally there is possibility to represent implications. These 5 types of information allows to perform broad range of inference patterns:

- generalization and specialization of properties (e.g. we know that duck has good flying capabilities, hence mallard has it too);
- abstraction and concretion of statements (e.g. if we know that somewhere live mallards we can say at less detailed level, that there live ducks);

M.-S. Hacid et al. (Eds.): ISMIS 2002, LNAI 2366, pp. 176–184, 2002.

- reasoning by analogy (e.g. if swan is similar to ducks in foot build and we know that swimming capabilities depend on it, given that duck can swim we can conclude that swan can swim too);
- deduction – applying modus ponens rule;

These inference patterns were proposed by Collins and Michalski in [2] using variable-valued logic notation (see [6]). Proof system and semantics were not explicitly defined. Below we present LPR from more formal point of view. Using semantics proposed, it is possible to show that LPR is correct: if a given formula is a syntactic consequence of a given set of formulas, it is a semantic consequence of this set too.

LPR has an interesting property. Contexts give an alternative way to represent exceptions in inheritance. In a semantic network preclusion is used [12] and this theory is nonmonotonic. In LPR we can use context to restrict inheritance: only these attributes are inherited which depend on a given context. As a result LPR is monotonic and its semantics is simpler.

2 Language

In this section we define basic LPR language. It consists of a set of constant symbols C, four relational symbols (V, H, S, E representing respectively: statements, hierarchy, similarity and dependency) and logical connectives: $\rightarrow, \wedge$.

Statements are represented as object-attribute-value triples: $V(o, a, v)$, where $o, a, v \in C$. It is a representation of a fact that object o has an attribute a equal v. Value should be a sub-type of an attribute: if $V(o, a, v)$ is in a knowledge base, there should be also $H(v, a, c)$. If object o has several values of a, there should be several statements in a knowledge base. We write $o.a = v$ as an abbreviation of $V(o, a, v)$ and $o.a$ as an abbreviation of "attribute a of object o".

Relation H represents hierarchy between constant symbols. $H(o', o, c)$, where $o', o, c \in C$, means that o' is o in a context c. Context is used for specification of the range of inheritance. o' and o have the same value for all attributes which depend on $o.c$.

S is a similarity relation. $S(o_1, o_2, o, a)$ represents a fact, that o_1 is similar to o_2 ($o_1, o_2, o, a \in C$). Context, as above, specifies the range of similarity. Only these attributes of o_1 and o_2 have the same value which depends on $o.a$. We use a notation $S(o_1, o_2, o.a)$ to emphasize that a is an attribute of o.

To express dependency relation E is used. $E(o_1, a_1, o_2, a_2)$, where $o_1, a_1, o_2, a_2 \in C$, means that values of $o_1.a_1$ depend on $o_2.a_2$. Similarly as above, we use the notation $E(o_1.a_1, o_2.a_2)$.

Using relational symbols we are able to define well formed formulas of LPR.

Definition 1. *If* $o, o', o_1, ..., o_n, a, a_1, ..., a_n, v, v_1, ..., v_n, c \in C$ *then* $V(o, a, v)$, $H(o', o, c)$, $S(o_1, o_2, o, a)$, $E(o_1, a_1, o_2, a_2)$, $o_1.a_1 = v_1 \wedge ... \wedge o_n.a_n = v_n \rightarrow$ $o.a = v$ *are well formed formulas of LPR.*

As we can see, only positive statements are considered. There were two more formulas defined in [2]: dissimilarity between objects (one object is dissimilar to another in a given context) and negative statement (is not true that $o.a = v$). They are omitted here. They would be introduced in the future together with a negation.

To deal with uncertainty we use labels (see [3]). Hence we need a label algebra $\mathcal{A} = (A, \{f_{r_i}\})$. A is a set of labels which estimate uncertainty. $\{f_r\}$ is a set of functions which are used in proof rules to generate a label of a conclusion: for every proof rule r_i an appropriate function f_{r_i} should be defined. For rule r_i with premises $p_1 : l_1, ..., p_n : l_n$ the plausible label of its conclusion is equal $f_{r_i}(l_1, ..., l_n)$.

Label algebra depends on a problem where LPR is used. An example is presented in the section 6. Formulas with labels are basic knowledge components. A set of labeled formulas can be considered as a knowledge base.

Definition 2. *Labeled formula is a pair $f : l$ where f is a formula and l is a label.*

3   Proof System

In this section we introduce LPR proof system. Inference patterns presented in [2] can be formalized as a proof rules. They are slightly modified to assure correctness.

There are 5 types of rules: *GEN, SPEC, SIM, TRAN* and *MP*. They correspond to the following inference patterns: generalization, specialization, similarity transformation, transitivity transformation and modus ponens. Every transformation can be applied to different types of formulas, therefore indexes are used to distinguish different versions of rules. Rules can be divided into several groups according to type of formulas on which rules operate and types of inference patterns.

First group is *statement proof rules*. It consists of 6 rules presented in table 1. They are used to perform reasoning on statements, hence first premises and the conclusions are object-attribute-value triples. Rules indexed by o transform object argument, what correspond to generalization and specialization of the statement. Rules indexed by v operate on values, which changes the detail level of a description and corresponds to abstraction and concretion.

Second group consist of 6 *implication proof rules* presented in table 2. They are used to transform implication formulas in a similar way as previous group.

Third group is *dependency proof rules*, which is shown in table 3. They operate on dependency formulas and allow to use generalization, specialization and analogy inference patterns to change objects in dependency relations.

Next group, *transitivity proof rules* represent a transitivity transformation of dependencies and implications. It is presented in 4.

Last group, shown in table 5, consist of only one rule, modus ponens. It is well known inference rule.

Having inference rules, proof can be defined in a standard way.

Table 1. Statement proof rules.

$$
GEN_o \ \frac{\begin{array}{c} o'.a = v \\ H(o',o,c) \\ E(o.a,o.c) \end{array}}{o'.a = v}
\qquad
SPEC_o \ \frac{\begin{array}{c} o.a = v \\ H(o',o,c) \\ E(o.a,o.c) \end{array}}{o'.a = v}
\qquad
SIM_o \ \frac{\begin{array}{c} o'.a = v \\ S(o',o'',o.c) \\ E(o.a,o.c) \end{array}}{o''.a = v}
$$

$$
GEN_v \ \frac{\begin{array}{c} o'.a = v' \\ H(v',v,c) \\ H(v,a,o) \\ E(a.o,a.c) \\ H(o',o,c_1) \end{array}}{o'.a = v}
\qquad
SPEC_v \ \frac{\begin{array}{c} o'.a = v \\ H(v',v,c) \\ H(v,a,o) \\ E(a.o,a.c) \\ H(o',o,c_1) \\ H(v',a,c_2) \end{array}}{o'.a = v'}
\qquad
SIM_v \ \frac{\begin{array}{c} o'.a = v_1 \\ S(v_1,v_2,a.c) \\ E(a.o,a.c) \\ H(o',o,c_1) \\ H(v_1,a,o) \\ H(v_2,a,o) \end{array}}{o'.a = v_2}
$$

Table 2. Proof rules based on implications.

$$
GEN_{o\rightarrow} \ \frac{\begin{array}{c} o'.a_1 = v_1 \wedge \ldots \wedge o'.a_n = v_n \rightarrow \\ o'.a = v \\ H(o',o,c_1) \\ \vdots \\ H(o',o,c_n) \\ H(o',o,c) \\ E(o.a_1,o.c_1) \\ \vdots \\ E(o.a_n,o.c_n) \\ E(o.a,o.c) \end{array}}{\begin{array}{c} o.a_1 = v_1 \wedge \ldots \wedge o.a_n = v_n \rightarrow \\ o.a = v \end{array}}
\qquad
SPEC_{o\rightarrow} \ \frac{\begin{array}{c} o.a_1 = v_1 \wedge \ldots \wedge o.a_n = v_n \rightarrow \\ o.a = v \\ H(o',o,c_1) \\ \vdots \\ H(o',o,c_n) \\ H(o',o,c) \\ E(o.a_1,o.c_1) \\ \vdots \\ E(o.a_n,o.c_n) \\ E(o.a,o.c) \end{array}}{\begin{array}{c} o'.a_1 = v_1 \wedge \ldots \wedge o'.a_n = v_n \rightarrow \\ o'.a = v \end{array}}
$$

$$
SIM_{o\rightarrow} \ \frac{\begin{array}{c} o_1.a_1 = v_1 \wedge \ldots \wedge o_1.a_n = v_n \rightarrow \\ o_1.a = v \\ S(o_1,o_2,o.c_1) \\ \vdots \\ S(o_1,o_2,o.c_n) \\ S(o_1,o_2,o.c) \\ E(o.a_1,o.c_1) \\ \vdots \\ E(o.a_n,o.c_n) \\ E(o.a,o.c) \end{array}}{\begin{array}{c} o_2.a_1 = v_1 \wedge \ldots \wedge o_2.a_n = v_n \rightarrow \\ o_2.a = v \end{array}}
\qquad
GEN_{v\rightarrow} \ \frac{\begin{array}{c} o'.a_1 = v_1 \wedge \ldots \wedge o'.a_n = v_n \rightarrow \\ o'.a = v' \\ H(v',v,c) \\ H(v,a,o) \\ E(a.o,o.c) \\ H(o',o,c_1) \end{array}}{\begin{array}{c} o'.a_1 = v_1 \wedge \ldots \wedge o'.a_n = v_n \rightarrow \\ o'.a = v \end{array}}
$$

$$
SPEC_{v\rightarrow} \ \frac{\begin{array}{c} o'.a_1 = v_1 \wedge \ldots \wedge o'.a_n = v_n \rightarrow \\ o'.a = v \\ H(v',v,c) \\ H(v,a,o) \\ E(a.o,a.c) \\ H(o',o,c_1) \\ H(v',a,c_2) \end{array}}{\begin{array}{c} o'.a_1 = v_1 \wedge \ldots \wedge o'.a_n = v_n \rightarrow \\ o'.a = v' \end{array}}
\qquad
SIM_{v\rightarrow} \ \frac{\begin{array}{c} o'.a_1 = v_1 \wedge \ldots \wedge o'.a_n = v_n \rightarrow \\ o'.a = v' \\ S(v',v'',a.c) \\ E(a.o,a.c) \\ H(o',o,c_1) \\ H(v',a,o) \\ H(v'',a,o) \end{array}}{\begin{array}{c} o'.a_1 = v_1 \wedge \ldots \wedge o'.a_n = v_n \rightarrow \\ o'.a = v'' \end{array}}
$$

Table 3. Proof rules based on dependencies.

$$GEN_E \; \frac{\begin{array}{l} E(o'.a_1, o'.a_2) \\ H(o', o, c) \\ E(o.a_1, o.c) \end{array}}{E(o.a_1, o.a_2)} \qquad SPEC_E \; \frac{\begin{array}{l} E(o.a_1, o.a_2) \\ H(o', o, c) \\ E(o.a_1, o.c) \end{array}}{E(o'.a_1, o'.a_2)} \qquad SIM_E \; \frac{\begin{array}{l} E(o_1.a_1, o_1.a_2) \\ S(o_1, o_2, o.c) \\ E(o.a_1, o.c) \end{array}}{E(o_2.a_1, o_2.a_2)}$$

Table 4. Transitivity proof rules.

$$TRAN_E \; \frac{\begin{array}{l} E(o.a_1, o.a_2) \\ E(o.a_2, o.a_3) \end{array}}{E(o.a_1, o.a_3)} \qquad TRAN_\rightarrow \; \frac{\begin{array}{l} o.a_1 = v_1 \wedge ... \wedge o.a_n = v_n \rightarrow o.a_0 = v_0 \\ o.a_0 = v_0 \rightarrow o.a = v \end{array}}{o.a_1 = v_1 \wedge ... \wedge o.a_n = v_n \rightarrow o.a = v}$$

Table 5. Modus ponens rule.

$$MP \; : \; \frac{\begin{array}{l} o_1.a_1 = v_1 \wedge ... \wedge o_n.a_n = v_n \rightarrow o.a = v \\ o'_1.a_1 = v_1 \\ \vdots \\ o'_n.a_n = v_n \end{array}}{o'.a = v}$$

Definition 3. Proof *of a labeled formula φ from a set of labeled formulas F is a finite sequence of labeled formulas $\alpha_1, ..., \alpha_n$, where $\alpha_n = \varphi$, and for every $i \in \{1, 2, ..., n\}$ we have:*

1. *$\alpha_i \in F$ or*
2. *α_i is a consequence of a proof rule applied to formulas $\alpha_{j_1}, \alpha_{j_2}, ..., \alpha_{j_k}$, where $j_m \in \{1, 2, ..., i-1\}$ for every $1 \le m \le k$.*

Using proof definition we can introduce syntactic consequence relation, which is defined below.

Definition 4. *We say that a labeled formula φ is a* syntactic consequence *of a set of labeled formulas F (we write $F \vdash \varphi$) iff there exist a proof of φ from F.*

4   Semantics of LPR

In the following section we introduce semantics of LPR. We define model, $\models$ relation and we make some assumptions to limit the space of models. Because plausible algebra depends on the application of a system, labels are omitted here.

Definition 5. LRP model *consists of a three relations: $M = (<, \mathcal{E}, \mathcal{V})$. $< \subset C^2, \mathcal{E} \subseteq C^4, \mathcal{V} \subseteq C^3$. $<$ is a hierarchy relation between objects, $\mathcal{E}$ is an interpretation of dependency relation, $\mathcal{V}$ is an interpretation of statements.*

In this section we use an abbreviation to represent a fact, that two objects have the same values of a given attribute. If M is a model, $o_1, o_2, x \in C$, $M \models o_1.x = o_2.x$ is an abbreviation for $\forall v \in C : M \models o_1.x = v \leftrightarrow M \models o_2.x = v$.

Now we are able to define semantic consequence ($\models$), the fundamental semantical relation. If $M \models \varphi$ we say, that M is a model for a formula φ.

Definition 6. *Let* $M = (<, \mathcal{E}, \mathcal{V})$*;*

$$M \models E(o_1.a_1, o_2.a_2) \quad \textit{iff} \quad (o_1, a_1, o_2, a_2) \in \mathcal{E}$$
$$M \models o.a = v \quad \textit{iff} \quad (o, a, v) \in \mathcal{V}$$
$$M \models H(o', o, c) \quad \textit{iff} \quad o' < o \wedge \forall x \in C : M \models E(o.x, o.c) \rightarrow$$
$$M \models o'.x = o.x$$
$$M \models S(o_1, o_2, o.c) \quad \textit{iff} \quad \forall x \in C : M \models E(o.x, o.c) \rightarrow o_1.x = o_2.x$$
$$M \models o_1.a_1 = v_1 \wedge \ldots \quad \textit{iff} \quad \exists 1 \leq i \leq n : \neg M \models o_i.a_i = v_i \vee$$
$$\wedge o_n.a_n = v_n \rightarrow o.a = v \quad M \models o.a = v$$

To prove the correctness of inference rules we need 3 assumptions which limit the space of models. First assumption is transitivity of dependency relation. E is not binary, so we have to define what we mean by transitivity.

Definition 7. *We say that model* M *has* transitive dependency relation *iff for all* $o, a_1, a_2, a_3 \in C$*:*

$$M \models E(o.a_1, o.a_2) \text{ and } M \models E(o.a_2, o.a_3) \text{ then } M \models E(o.a_1, o.a_3).$$

Second assumption is a symmetry of model. It represents the following reasoning pattern. If we know, that cat has green eyes and cat is a mammal, we can derive, that a mammal with green eyes is a cat. It is formalized below.

Definition 8. *We say that model* M *is* symmetric *iff for all* $o', o, a, c, v \in C$*:*

$$M \models o'.a = v \text{ and } M \models H(o', o, c) \text{ then } M \models v.o = o'.$$

Third assumption shows how dependency is related to hierarchy and similarity. We want to preserve dependencies between attributes if we change objects using hierarchy or similarity links.

Definition 9. *We say that model* M preserves dependencies *iff for all* $o, o', a_1, a_2, c \in C$*:*

$$\text{if } M \models E(o'.a_1, o'.a_2) \text{ and } M \models H(o', o, a_1) \text{ then } M \models E(o.a_1, o.a_2),$$
$$\text{if } M \models E(o.a_1, o.a_2) \text{ and } M \models H(o', o, a_1) \text{ then } M \models E(o'.a_1, o'.a_2),$$
$$\text{if } M \models E(o_1.a_1, o_1.a_2) \text{ and } M \models S(o_1, o_2, o.a_1) \text{ then } M \models E(o_2.a_1, o_2.a_2).$$

To prove the correctness of a system, we need two properties of $\models$ relation. Proofs of these properties are straightforward, therefore they are omitted. First property is symmetry of similarity relation.

Property 1. *Relation* S *is symmetric, which means that for all* $o, o_1, o_2, c, \in C$*:*

$$\text{if } M \models S(o_1, o_2, o.c) \text{ then } M \models S(o_2, o_1, o.c).$$

Second property allows to change the context in hierarchy and similarity relations. For example, if we know that object o_1 is similar to o_2 in context c_1 and c_2 depends on c_1, it is reasonable to conclude that o_1 is similar to o_2 in the context c_2.

Property 2. *Every transitive model M allows for dependent context changes, which means that for all $o, o', o_1, o_2, c, c_1 \in C$:*

> *if $M \models H(o', o, c)$ and $M \models E(o.c_1, o.c)$ then $M \models H(o', o, c_1)$,*
> *if $M \models S(o_1, o_2, o.c)$ and $M \models E(o.c_1, o.c)$ then $M \models S(o_1, o_2, o.c_1)$.*

Definition 10. Semantics *of the logic of plausible reasoning is a triple $LPR = (\mathcal{F}, \mathcal{M}, \models)$, where $\mathcal{F}$ is a set of well formed formulas, $\mathcal{M}$ is a set of symmetric models with transitive dependency relation, preserving dependencies and $\models$ is defined as above.*

We say that a formula φ is a semantic consequence of a set of formulas F (we write $F \models \varphi$) iff every model $M \in \mathcal{M}$ such that $M \models F$ is a model for φ: $M \models \varphi$.

As we can see LPR can be translated into predicate calculus. If we add appropriate formulas representing LPR proof rules we get a system which is at least as strong as LPR. However proof constructed using LPR rules is much more clear and easy to interpret by human.

5   Correctness of the Proof Rules

It is possible to show, that the following theorem is true, which means that LPR proof system is correct: if a given formula is a syntactic consequence of a given set of formulas, it is a semantic consequence of this set too.

Theorem 1. *For every set of formulas F and every formula φ: if $F \vdash \varphi$ then $F \models \varphi$.*

Proof: It is easy to show, that every rule is correct: if its premises are semantic consequences of a given model, its conclusion is a semantic consequence of this model too. Using this result it is possible to prove the theorem by induction.

6   Example

In this section example of using LPR proof rules is presented. First we define plausible labels, next we show chosen rules applications. Each label is a tuple of certainty parameters, see table 6. For each type of formula specific set of plausible parameters is appropriate. Hence specific label for each type of formulas are defined, see table 7.

We assume, that a domain of all parameters is $(0, 1]$. Higher values means, that the strength of dependency or similarity (or other property) is high. If value is closer to 0, the strength of the property is lower. Parameter γ is used in all types of formulas. It is used to represent a degree of certainty that a formula is true, it is analogy to certainty factor of a fact used in Mycin [11]. E.g. γ can estimate the confidence in the source of the information represented by formula. Parameter ϕ is used in the statements $o.a = v$ to specify how common

Table 6. Certainty parameters

Parameter	Description
α	Strength of implication and dependency
γ	Degree of certainty that a formula is true
τ	Degree of typicality in a hierarchy
σ	Degree of similarity
ϕ	Frequency of the value in object domain
δ	Dominance of a subset in a set

Table 7. Plausible labels

Formula	Plausible label
$o.a = v$	(γ, ϕ)
$H(o_1, o_2, c)$	(γ, δ, τ)
$S(o_1, o_2, a)$	(γ, σ)
$E(o_1.a_1, o_2.a_2)$	(γ, α)
$\psi_1 \wedge ... \wedge \psi_n \rightarrow \varphi$	(γ, α)

is the value v in the object (or objects) o. $\phi = 0.5$ means that half of o has such value. Hierarchy formulas are described by two additional parameters. In a formula $H(o, o', c) : (\gamma, \delta, \tau)$ parameter δ shows how big part of object o' is its descendant o. Parameter τ represents typicality of o: how common are the values of appropriate attributes of o in o'. In similarity formula σ estimates how similar are two objects in a given context. It is used in SIM-based proof rules to derive a certainty of the conclusion. Parameter α is used in implication and dependency formulas. It represents a strength of a rule or dependency. It is similar to certainty factor assigned to rules in Mycin [11].

Because of the limited space only two rules application are demonstrated. First example is GEN_o. Its plausible function is presented below. Plausible parameters appearing in the definition are indexed. Indexes refer to the position of the premise described by the parameter in the rule definition:
$f_{GEN_o}((\gamma_1, \phi_1), (\gamma_2, \delta_2, \tau_2), (\gamma_3, \alpha_3)) = (\gamma = \min(\gamma_1, \gamma_2, \gamma_3, \alpha_3), \phi = \tau_2)$.

If we know, that mallard has good flying capabilities, mallard is a typical duck in build context and we believe that flying capabilities depend on build, we can derive that probably duck fly well too. This reasoning pattern is presented below.

$mallard.flyingCapab = goodFC : (\gamma = 1, \phi = 0.95)$
$H(mallard, duck, build) : (\gamma = 1, \delta = 0.1, \tau = 0.8)$
$E(duck.flyingCapab, duck.build) : (\gamma = 0.9, \alpha = 0.9)$
$duck.flyingCapab = goodFC : (\gamma = 0.9, \phi = 0.8)$

Next we show $TRAN_E$ rule application. Its plausible function is defined as follows: $f_{TRAN_E}((\gamma_1, \alpha_1), (\gamma_2, \alpha_2)) = (\gamma = \min(\gamma_1, \gamma_2), \alpha = \min(\alpha_1, \alpha_2))$.

If we know that for a bird its flying distance depends on the flying capabilities and flying capabilities depend on its build, we can conclude that flying distance depends on the build:

$$E(bird.flyingDistance, bird.flyingCapabilities) : (\gamma_1 = 1, \alpha_1 = 0.9)$$
$$\underline{E(bird.flyingCapabilities, bird.built) : (\gamma_2 = 0.9, \alpha_2 = 0.8)}$$
$$E(bird.flyingDistance, bird.built) : (\gamma = 0.9, \alpha = 0.8)$$

7 Conclusions

We have demonstrated that LPR can be defined as a labeled deductive system. Next, we have defined a semantics for this formalism and we have showed that proof system is correct.

Further research will concern formalism extensions such as adding negation symbol or new proof rules. Important extension would be aggregation of proofs. The same conclusion inferred from several different sources should be more certain then formula inferred from one source.

Improving plausible algebra by making plausible labels and functions more sophisticated is the second problem.

Different applications of LPR formalism will be also considered. Using it in intelligent information systems for retrieving information is one field. Second, is using it in machine learning algorithms, where using abstraction/concretion, generalization/specialization and analogy seems to be very helpful [7].

References

1. D. Boehm-Davis, K. Dontas, and R. S. Michalski. Plausible reasoning: An outline of theory and the validation of its structural properties. In *Intelligent Systems: State of the Art and Future Directions*. North Holland, 1990.
2. A. Collins and R. S. Michalski. The logic of plausible reasoning: A core theory. *Cognitive Science*, 13:1–49, 1989.
3. D. M. Gabbay. *LDS – Labeled Deductive Systems*. Oxford University Press, 1991.
4. F. Lehmann. Semantic networks. In F. Lehmann, editor, *Semantic Networks in Artificial Intelligence*. Pergamon Press, 1992.
5. J. Lukasiewicz. Many-valued systems of propositional logic. In S. McCall, editor, *Polish logic*. Oxford University Press, 1967.
6. R. S. Michalski. A theory and methodology of inductive learning. *Artificial Intelligence*, 20:111–161, 1983.
7. R. S. Michalski. Inferential theory of learning: Developing foundations for multistrategy learning. In R. S. Michalski, editor, *Machine Learning: A Multistrategy Approach, Volume IV*. Morgan Kaufmann Publishers, 1994.
8. Z. Pawlak. Rough sets. *Int. J. Comp. Inf. Sci.*, 11:344–356, 1982.
9. J. Pearl. Fusion, propagation, and structuring in bayesian networks. *Artificial Intelligence*, 29:241–288, 1986.
10. G. Shafer. *A Mathematical Theory of Evidence*. Princeton University Press, 1976.
11. H. Shortliffe and B. G. Buchanan. A model of inexact reasoning in medicine. *Mathematical Biosciences*, 23:351–379, 1975.
12. R. H. Thomason. Netl and subsequent path-based inheritance theories. In F. Lehmann, editor, *Semantic Networks in Artificial Intelligence*. Pergamon Press, 1992.
13. L. A. Zadeh. Fuzzy sets. *Information and Control*, 8:338–353, 1965.

Logic-Based Reasoning on Delegatable Authorizations

Chun Ruan, Vijay Varadharajan, and Yan Zhang

School of Computing and Information Technology
University of Western Sydney
Penrith South DC, NSW 1797, Australia
{chun,vijay,yan}@cit.uws.edu.au

Abstract. In this paper, we propose a logic program based formulation that supports delegatable authorizations, where negation as failure, classical negation and rules inheritance are allowable. A conflict resolution policy has been developed in our approach that can be used to support the controlled delegation and exception. In our framework, authorization rules are specified in a Delegatable Authorization Program (DAP) which is an extended logic program associated with different types of partial orderings on the domain, and these orderings specify various inheritance relationships among subjects, objects and access rights in the domain. The semantics of a DAP is defined based on the well-known stable model and the conflict resolution is achieved in the process of model generation for the underlying DAP. Our framework provides users a feasible way to express complex security policies.

1 Introduction

Authorization specification and evaluation is a significant issue in any secure computer systems. In our previous paper [5], we developed a labelled graph based approach, which allows both positive and negative authorizations, and supports delegation of access rights between subjects, which is a important feature for a distributed environment. Especially, we have proposed a conflict resolution method for delegatable authorizations that is based on the underlying delegation relations. Intuitively speaking, if s_1 delegates s_2 a right to *grant* others *read* on file F, then when it happens that s_1 and s_2 grant s_3 *read* and *not read* on F respectively, the grant by s_1 will override the grant by s_2 since it is s_1 that delegates s_2 the right to grant. We believe that this controlled delegation can take the advantage of both distributed and centralized administration of access rights. If users want to distribute the administration of rights without further control, they just delegate the rights to others and let them do grant thereafter. Whenever users want to take some control of the rights, their grants will always have higher priorities. In [5], we do not consider relationships between subjects, objects and access rights.

In this paper, we extend our previous work to consider more complex domains where subjects, objects and access rights are hierarchically structured

M.-S. Hacid et al. (Eds.): ISMIS 2002, LNAI 2366, pp. 185–193, 2002.
© Springer-Verlag Berlin Heidelberg 2002

and authorization inheritance along the hierarchies is taken into account. For example, a member of a group usually can inherit all the access rights granted to the group. If someone is granted to write a directory, it is usually implied that he/she should be able to read the directory and all files in that directory. Supporting inheritance of authorizations can often effectively simplify the specification and evaluation of authorizations, especially in some application domains where inheritance is an important feature, such as object-oriented databases. When authorization inheritance is under consideration, the problem of conflict becomes more complex since a lot of implicit conflicts among different types of authorizations may arise. To take advantage of strong expressive and reasoning power of logic programming, we will develop our framework based on extended logic programs [3], which supports both negation as failure and classical negation. The extended logic programs, which is formalised based on nonmonotonic reasoning semantics, has strong expressive power in the sense that it can deal directly with incomplete information in reasoning. Since the incomplete information is a common issue in the security world, many access control policies are easier to specify in extended logic programs. For example, if we want to express negation by default, like s is denied to read the file F if s is not granted to read it, the negation as failure (weak negation) is often the most direct way to express this intention. On the other hand, in many situations, classical negation (strong negation) is useful to explicitly specify that something is forbidden.

In our framework, authorization rules are specified in a delegatable authorization program (DAP) which is an extended logic program associated with different types of partial orderings on the domain, and these orderings specify various inheritance relationships among subjects, objects and access rights in the domain. The semantics of a DAP is defined based on the well-known stable model semantics and the conflict resolution is achieved in the process of model generation of the underlying DAP. The paper is organised as follows. Section 2 describes the syntax of DAP, while Section 3 defines the semantics of the program. Section 4 concludes the paper with some remarks.

2   Syntax of Delegatable Authorization Programs

Our language $\mathcal{L}$ is a many-sorted first order language, with four disjoint *sorts* for subject, object, access right and authorization type respectively. Let $\mathcal{L}$ has the following vocabulary:

1. *Sort subject*: with subject *constant* poset $(S, <_S)$: $\natural, s, s', s'', s_1, s_2, ...$, and subject *variables* $\_s, \_s_1, \_s_2, ...$

2. *Sort object*: with object *constant* poset $(O, <_O)$: $o, o', o'', o_1, o_2, ...$, and object *variables* $\_o_1, \_o_2, \_o_3, ...$

3. *Sort access right*: with access right *constant* poset $(A, <_A)$: *read, write,a, a',* $a'', a_1, a_2, ...$ and access right *variables* $\_a, \_a_1, \_a_2, ...$

4. *Sort authorization type*: with authorization type *constant* set $T = \{-, +, *\}$, and authorization type *variables* $\_t, \_t_1, \_t_2, ...$

We suppose ♯ in S denotes the security administrator, and it is not comparable to any subjects in S w.r.t. $<_S$. In the constant set of authorization types $T = \{-, +, *\}$, $-$ means *negative*, $+$ means *positive*, and $*$ means *delegatable*. A negative authorization specifies the access that must be forbidden, while a positive authorization specifies the access that must be granted. A delegatable authorization specifies the access that must be delegated as well as granted. That is, $*$ means $+$ together with administrative privilege on the access. The partial orders $<_S, <_O, <_A$ represent inheritance hierarchies of subjects, objects and access rights respectively.

5. *Predicate Symbol* set P

P consists of a set of ordinary predicates defined by users, and one built-in predicate symbol for delegatable authorization, *grant*. *grant* is a 5-term predicate symbol with type $S \times O \times T \times A \times S$. The first argument is the *grantee*, the second argument is the *object*, the third argument is the *authorization type*, the fourth argument is the *access right*, and the fifth argument is the *grantor* of this authorization. Intuitively, $grant(s, o, t, a, g)$ means s is granted by g the access right a on object o with authorization type t. *grant* is called *authorization predicate*.

A *term* is either a variable or a constant. Note that we prohibit function symbols in our language. An *atom* is a construct of the form $p(t_1, ..., t_n)$, where p is a predicate of arity n in P and $t_1, ..., t_n$ are terms. A *literal* is either an atom p or the negation of the atom $\neg p$, where the negation sign $\neg$ represents classical negation. Correspondingly, a literal that has an authorization predicate is called an *authorization literal*. Two literals are *complementary* if they are of the form p and $\neg p$, for some atom p. A *rule r* is a statement of the form:

$$b_0 \leftarrow b_1, ..., b_k, not\, b_{k+1}, ..., not\, b_m, m >= 0$$

where $b_0, b_1, ..., b_m$ are literals, and *not* is the negation as failure symbol. The b_0 is the *head* of r, while the conjunction of $b_1, ..., b_k, not\, b_{k+1}, ..., not\, b_m$ is the *body* of r. Obviously, the body of r could be empty. We sometimes use $Head_r$ and $Body_r$ to denote the head and body of r respectively. Correspondingly, when b_0 is an authorization literal, the rule is called *authorization rule*.

A *Delegatable Authorization Program*, DAP, consists of a finite set of rules.

A term, an atom, a literal, a rule or program is *ground* if no variable appears in it.

Example 1. Let $S = \{\sharp, s_1, s_2; s_1 <_S s_2\}, O = \{o_1, o_2; o_1 <_O o_2\}, A = \{write, read; write <_A read\}$, then the following is an example DAP $\varPi$:

$r_1 : dba(s_1) \leftarrow$

$r_2 : \neg dba(s_2) \leftarrow$

$r_3 : \neg secret(o_1) \leftarrow$

$r_4 : secret(o_2) \leftarrow$

$r_5 : grant(s_1, o_2, *, write, \sharp) \leftarrow$

$r_6 : grant(s_2, o_2, -, write, s_1) \leftarrow$

$r_7 : grant(\_s, \_o, -, write, \sharp) \leftarrow secret(\_o), not\, dba(\_s)$

3   Semantics of Delegatable Authorization Programs

Let Π be a DAP, the *Base* B_Π of Π is the set of all possible ground liter-als constructible from the predicates appearing in the rules of Π and the con-stants occurring in S, O, A, and T. Two ground literals are *conflicting* on sub-ject s, object o and access right a if they are of the form $grant(s, o, t, a, g)$ and $grant(s, o, t', a, g')$ and $t \neq t'$. Note that type $*$ and $+$ are considered conflict-ing in the sense that $*$ holds the administrative privilege while $+$ does not. A *ground instance* of r is a rule obtained from r by replacing every variable x in r by $\delta(x)$, where $\delta(x)$ is a mapping from the variables to the constants in the same sorts. Two ground rules r and r' are *conflicting* if $Head_r$ and $Head_{r'}$ are complementary or conflicting literals. Let $G(\Pi)$ denotes all ground instances of the rules occurring in Π.

A subset of the Base of B_Π is *consistent* if no pair of complementary or conflicting literals is in it. An *interpretation* I is any consistent subset of the Base of B_Π.

Given an interpretation $I \subseteq B_\Pi$, a ground literal L is *true* in I if $L \in I$. L is *false* in I if $\neg L \in I$, otherwise L is *unknown* in I. Given a ground rule $r \in G(\Pi)$ of the form

$b_0 \leftarrow b_1, ..., b_k, not\, b_{k+1}, ..., not\, b_m, m \geq 0$

the body of r is *true* in I if every literal $b_i, 1 \leq i \leq k$ is true in I and every literal $b_i, k+1 \leq i \leq m$ is not true in I. Rule r is *satisfied* in I if either the head of r is true in I or the body of r is not true in I.

Let Π be a DAP, its semantics is formally defined by four steps. First, trans-form Π into Π^D according to the requirement of delegation correctness. Sec-ond, for the ground version of Π^D, $G(\Pi^D)$, evaluate its inheritance propagation $G^*(\Pi^D)$ induced by the partial orders on the subjects, objects and access rights. Third, define the conflict resolution rules to solve the possible contradictions. Fourth, extend the classical concept of an answer set to take into account of the presence of possible contradictions.

3.1   Transformation of DAP

We say that an authorization set is *delegation correct* if it satisfies the following two conditions: (a) subject s can grant other subjects an access right a over object o if and only if s is the security administrator $\sharp$ or s has been granted a over o with a delegatable type $*$; (b) if subject s receives a delegatable authorization directly or indirectly from another subject s' on some object o and access right a, then s cannot grant s' any further authorization on the same o and a later on.

We first introduce two new predicates *cangrant* and *delegate*. *cangrant* has a type of $S \times O \times A$, and *cangrant*(s, o, a) means subject s has the right to grant access a on object o to other subjects. *delegate* has a type of $S \times S \times O \times A$, and *delegate*$(g, s, o, a)$ means subject g has directly or indirectly granted subject s access a on object o with type $*$. The two predicates are derived by the system using logical rules of inference.

Let Π be a DAP, we transform Π to Π^D through the following steps.

Step 1

Adding the following four rules into Π^D to derive the delegation relation for any object o and access right a w.r.t. Π.

d_1. $cangrant(\sharp, \_o, \_a) \leftarrow$
d_2. $cangrant(\_s, \_o, \_a) \leftarrow grant(\_s, \_o, *, \_a, \_g)$
d_3. $delegate(\_g, \_s, \_o, \_a) \leftarrow grant(\_s, \_o, *, \_a, \_g)$
d_4. $delegate(\_s, \_s_1, \_o, \_a) \leftarrow delegate(\_s, \_s_2, \_o, \_a), delegate(\_s_2, \_s_1, \_o, \_a)$
We denote $D = \{d_1, d_2, d_3, d_4\}$.

Step 2

For any authorization rule r in Π, it is transformed into $\hat{r}$ by the following, and added to Π^D:

$\hat{r}$: $Head_r \leftarrow Body_r, cangrant(Head_r.g, Head_r.o, Head_r.a),$
$\qquad Head_r.g \neq Head_r.s,$
$\qquad not\ delegate(Head_r.s, Head_r.g, Head_r.o, Head_r.a)$
where $Head_r.s, Head_r.g, Head_r.o, Head_r.a$ denote the grantee, grantor, object and access right argument of the predicate $grant$ of $Head_r$ respectively.

Step 3

Copy the remaining rules of Π to Π^D.

Example 2. (Example 1 continued) For the DAP Π in Example 1, the Π^D is $\{r_1, r_2, r_3, r_4, \hat{r}_5, \hat{r}_6, \hat{r}_7\} \cup D$, where $\hat{r}_5, \hat{r}_6$ and $\hat{r}_7$ are :
$\hat{r}_5$: $grant(s_1, o_2, *, write, \sharp) \leftarrow cangrant(\sharp, o_2, write), \sharp \neq s_1,$
$\qquad\qquad\qquad not\ delegate(s_1, \sharp, o_2, write)$
$\hat{r}_6$: $grant(s_2, o_2, -, write, s_1) \leftarrow cangrant(s_1, o_2, write), s_1 \neq s_2,$
$\qquad\qquad\qquad not\ delegate(s_2, s_1, o_2, write)$
$\hat{r}_7$: $grant(\_s, \_o, -, write, \sharp) \leftarrow secret(\_o), not\ dba(\_s), cangrant(\sharp, \_o, write),$
$\qquad\qquad\qquad \sharp \neq \_s, not\ delegate(\_s, \sharp, \_o, write)$

3.2   Authorization Propagation

Now we consider the authorization propagations along hierarchies of subjects, objects and access rights represented by the corresponding partial orders. We consider the ground version of Π^D, $G(\Pi^D)$. The basic idea is to give every rule in $G(\Pi^D)$ a three-ary identifier which indicates what this rule is about in terms of subject, object and access right. Then, the propagations of a rule along the underlying hierarchies can be evaluated by replacing each occurrence of the proper coordinate of its identifier in the rule by any greater subject, object or access right w.r.t. the corresponding partial order. The identifiers of rules will also be used for solving conflict, which will be illustrated later.

We say a constant c is *minimal* in a rule r w.r.t. some partial order $<$ if c is in r and there is no constant c' in r such that $c' < c$. Add $\perp$ to the constant sets S, O and A, and suppose $\perp$ is not comparable to any element in the sets w.r.t $<_S, <_O$ and $<_A$ respectively. Then, we have

Definition 1. *Function rid: $G(\Pi^D) \to S \times O \times A$, is defined by the following:*

$$rid(r) = \begin{cases} (\perp, \perp, \perp) & \text{if } r \in G(D) \\ (Head_r.s, Head_r.o, Head_r.a) & \text{if } r \text{ is an authorization rule} \\ (s, o, a) & \text{otherwise, where} \end{cases}$$

s is minimal in r w.r.t $<_S$ or $\perp$ if $\neg \exists \_s(\_s \in S \wedge \_s$ is in $r)$,
o is minimal in r w.r.t $<_O$ or $\perp$ if $\neg \exists \_o(\_o \in O \wedge \_o$ is in $r)$,
a is minimal in r w.r.t $<_A$ or $\perp$ if $\neg \exists \_a(\_a \in A \wedge \_a$ is in $r)$.

There may exist more than one minimal subjects, objects or access rights in a rule, simply select any one in this situation.

Example 3. (Example 2 continued) $G(\Pi^D) = \{r_1, ..., \hat{r}_6, \hat{r}_{71}, \hat{r}_{72}, \hat{r}_{73}, \hat{r}_{74}, \hat{r}_{75}, \hat{r}_{76}\} \cup G(D)$, where $\hat{r}_{71}, \hat{r}_{72}, ..., \hat{r}_{76}$ are ground instances of rule $\hat{r}_7$ obtained by replacing $\_s$ and $\_o$ with s_1 and o_1, s_1 and o_2, s_2 and o_1, s_2 and o_2, $\sharp$ and o_1, or $\sharp$ and o_2 respectively.
$\hat{r}_{71} : grant(s_1, o_1, -, write, \sharp) \leftarrow secret(o_1),$not $dba(s_1),$not $delegate(s_1, \sharp, o_1, write),$

$$cangrant(\sharp, x, write), \sharp \neq s_1$$

...
The following rules are in $G(D)$:
$d_{11} : cangrant(\sharp, o_2, write) \leftarrow$
$d_{21} : cangrant(s_1, o_2, write) \leftarrow grant(s_1, o_2, *, write, \sharp)$
$d_{31} : delegate(\sharp, s_1, o_2, write) \leftarrow grant(s_1, o_2, *, write, \sharp)$
...
The rid values for rules in $G(\Pi^D) - G(D)$ are:
$rid(r_1) = (s_1, \perp, \perp)$, $rid(r_2) = (s_2, \perp, \perp)$, $rid(r_3) = (\perp, o_1, \perp)$, $rid(r_4) = (\perp, o_2, \perp)$, $rid(\hat{r}_5) = (s_1, o_2, write)$, $rid(\hat{r}_6) = (s_2, o_2, write)$, $rid(\hat{r}_{71}) = (s_1, o_1, write)$, $rid(\hat{r}_{72}) = (s_1, o_2, write)$, $rid(\hat{r}_{73}) = (s_2, o_1, write)$, $rid(\hat{r}_{74}) = (s_2, o_2, write)$, $rid(\hat{r}_{75}) = (\sharp, o_1, write)$, $rid(\hat{r}_{76}) = (\sharp, o_2, write)$

Let R_{rid} be a relation on $G(\Pi^D)$ such that $rR_{rid}r'$ iff $rid(r) = rid(r')$. It is easy to see that R_{rid} is an equivalence relation (reflexive, symmetric, and transitive) on $G(\Pi^D)$. Hence the equivalence classes of R_{rid} form a partition of $G(\Pi^D)$. Let $x = rid(r)$ for some r, we use $G_x(\Pi^D)$ to denote the equivalence class of R_{rid} that contains all the rules with the same rid value x. That is: $G_x(\Pi^D) = \{r | r \in G(\Pi^D) \wedge rid(r) = x\}$.

Let $r_{c/c'}$ means to replace every occurrence of c in r by c', then we have the following definition.

Definition 2. *Let Π be a DAP, $G_{(s,o,a)}(\Pi^D)$ be any equivalence class of $G(\Pi^D)$ w.r.t. R_{rid}, then we define:*

$$G^*_{(s,o,a)}(\Pi^D) = G_{(s,o,a)}(\Pi^D) \cup$$
$$\{r_{s/s',o/o',a/a'} | r \in G_{(s,o,a)}(\Pi^D) \text{ and } (s \leq_S s') \text{ and } (o \leq_O o')$$
$$\text{and } ((Head_r \text{ is not an authorization literal and } a \leq_A a')$$
$$\text{or } (Head_r \text{ is an authorization literal and } Head_r.t \neq - \text{ and } a \leq_A a')$$
$$\text{or } (Head_r \text{ is an authorization literal and } Head_r.t = - \text{ and } a' \leq_A a))\}$$
$$G^*(\Pi^D) = \cup G^*_x(\Pi^D) \text{ where } G_x(\Pi^D) \text{ is an equivalence class of } R_{rid}.$$

The denotion $c \leq c'$ denotes $c < c'$ or $c = c'$. Note that $G^*(\Pi^D)$ contains all the rules that implied by the hierarchies of subjects, objects and access rights, as well as the rules to guarantee the authorization set derived by Π to be delegation correct. It is worth to mention that a rule may be derived by propagation from several equivalence classes. We treat the respective one as distinct. Thus all the $G^*_x(\Pi^D)$, where $G_x(\Pi^D)$ is an equivalence class of R_{rid}, also form a partition of $G^*(\Pi^D)$.

Example 4. (Example 3 continued) The partition of $G(\Pi^D)$ w.r.t. R_{rid} is:
$$G_{(s_1,\perp,\perp)} = \{r_1\}, G_{(s_2,\perp,\perp)} = \{r_2\}, G_{(\perp,o_1,\perp)} = \{r_3\}, G_{(\perp,o_2,\perp)} = \{r_4\},$$
$$G_{(s_1,o_1,write)} = \{\hat{r}_{71}\}, G_{(s_1,o_2,write)} = \{\hat{r}_5, \hat{r}_{72}\}, G_{(s_2,o_1,write)} = \{\hat{r}_{73}\},$$
$$G_{(s_2,o_2,write)}$$
$$= \{\hat{r}_6, \hat{r}_{74}\}, G_{(\sharp,o_1,write)} = \{\hat{r}_{75}\}, G_{(\sharp,o_2,write)} = \{\hat{r}_{76}\}, G_{(\perp,\perp,\perp)} = G(D)$$
Then $G^*(\Pi^D)$ is the union of the following sets:
$$G^*_{(s_1,\perp,\perp)} = \{r_1, r_1^1\}, G^*_{(s_2,\perp,\perp)} = \{r_2\}, G^*_{(\perp,o_1,\perp)} = \{r_3, r_3^1\}, G^*_{(\perp,o_2,\perp)} = \{r_4\},$$
$$G^*_{(s_1,o_1,write)} = \{\hat{r}_{71}, \hat{r}_{72}, \hat{r}_{73}, \hat{r}_{74}\}, G^*_{(s_1,o_2,write)} = \{\hat{r}_5^1, \hat{r}_5^2, \hat{r}_5^3, \hat{r}_{72}, \hat{r}_{74}''\},$$
$$G^*_{(s_2,o_1,write)} = \{\hat{r}_{73}, \hat{r}_{74}'''\}, G^*_{(s_2,o_2,write)} = \{\hat{r}_6, \hat{r}_{74}\}, G^*_{(\sharp,o_1,write)} = \{\hat{r}_{75}, \hat{r}_{76}'\},$$
$$G^*_{(\sharp,o_2,write)} = \{\hat{r}_{76}\}, G^*_{(\perp,\perp,\perp)} = G(D), \text{ where}$$
$$r_1^1 : dba(s_2) \leftarrow$$
$$r_3^1 : \neg secret(o_2) \leftarrow$$
$$\hat{r}_5^1 : grant(s_1, o_2, *, read, \sharp) \leftarrow \text{ not } delegate(s_1, \sharp, o_2, read),$$
$$\qquad\qquad\qquad\qquad\qquad cangrant(\sharp, o_2, read), \sharp \neq s_1$$
$$\hat{r}_5^2 : grant(s_2, o_2, *, write, \sharp) \leftarrow \text{ not } delegate(s_2, \sharp, o_2, write),$$
$$\qquad\qquad\qquad\qquad\qquad cangrant(\sharp, o_2, write), \sharp \neq s_2$$
$$\hat{r}_5^3 : grant(s_2, o_2, *, read, \sharp) \leftarrow \text{ not } delegate(s_2, \sharp, o_2, read),$$
$$\qquad\qquad\qquad\qquad\qquad cangrant(\sharp, o_2, read), \sharp \neq s_2$$
Note that $\hat{r}_{72}'$ means an occurrence of $\hat{r}_{72}$ in another equivalence class, and so on.

3.3 Conflict Resolution

The partial orders on S, O and A are extended to $S \times O \times A$ by using lexicographical ordering.

Definition 3. *A relation* $<_{S,O,A}$ *on* $S \times O \times A$ *is defined by:* $(s, o, a) <_{S,O,A} (s', o', a')$ *if* $s <_S s' \vee (s = s' \wedge o <_O o') \vee (s = s' \wedge o' = o \wedge a <_O a')$.

From the definition, we know that $<_S$ dominates, except for equality, in which case we consider $<_O$. If equality holds again, we pass to $<_A$. It is easy to see that $<_{S,O,A}$ is a partial order on $S \times O \times A$.

To achieve our purpose of solving conflict, we now define a relation $<_r$ on $G^*(\Pi^D)$ in terms of the classes the rules belong to. Basically, the class that a rule belongs to tell us where this rule comes from. For example, if $r \in G_x^*(\Pi^D)$, then we can infer that r is either in $G_x(\Pi^D)$ or derived from $G_x(\Pi^D)$ through inheritance of subjects, objects or access rights.

Definition 4. *Let Π be a DAP, a relation $<_r$ on $G^*(\Pi^D)$ is defined by: $r <_r r'$ if $r \in G_x^*(\Pi^D) \wedge r' \in G_y^*(\Pi^D) \wedge x <_{S,O,A} y$. $<_r^*$ is the transtive clousure of $<_r$.*

Obviously $<_r$ is a partial order. Intuitively speaking, $r <_r r'$ means that r' is more specific than r. Now we are ready to define the conflict resolution rules.

Example 5. (Example 4 continued) According to the definition of $<_{S,O,A}$, the following holds: $(s_1, \bot, \bot) < (s_2, \bot, \bot), (s_2, o_1, write), (s_2, o_2, write); (\bot, o_1, \bot) < (\bot, o_2, \bot); (s_1, o_2, write) < (s_2, o_1, write), (s_2, o_2, write); (s_1, o_1, write) < (s_1, o_2, write), (s_2, o_1, write), (s_2, o_2, write); (s_2, o_1, write) < (s_2, o_2, write)$.
Therefore, we have: $r_1, r_1^1 < r_2, \hat{r}_{73}, \hat{r}_{74}''', \hat{r}_6, \hat{r}_{74}; r_3, r_3^1 < r_4; \hat{r}_5^1, \hat{r}_5^2, \hat{r}_5^3, \hat{r}_{72}, \hat{r}_{74}'' < \hat{r}_6, \hat{r}_{74}''', \hat{r}_{73}, \hat{r}_{74}; ...$
Note that we omit the subscript for $<$, which is easy to see from the context.

Definition 5. *Suppose I is an interpretation for $G^*(\Pi^D)$, r and r' are conflicting ground rules, we say that r overrides r' in I if: (1). $body_r$ is true in I, and (2). at least one of the following conditions holds: (a). $Head_r$ and $Head_{r'}$ are conflicting literals on object o and access right a, and $delegate(Head_r.g, Head_{r'}.g, o, a)$ is true in I; (b). $Head_r$ and $Head_{r'}$ are conflicting literals on object o and access right a, $Head_r.g = Head_{r'}.g$ and $r' <_r^* r$; (c). $Head_r$ and $Head_{r'}$ are complementary literals and $r' <_r^* r$.*

Note that $Head_r.g$ denotes the *grantor* in predicate *grant* of $Head_r$, and so does $Head_{r'}.g$. When there are multiple occurrences of a rule r, r override r' if one occurrence of r overrides r'. r is overridden by r' if all the occurrences of r are overridden by r'.

According to our conflict resolution method, the authorizations granted by ♯ can never be overridden by authorizations granted by other grantors, since all the access rights must be first delegated from the administrator ♯. In other words, ♯ has the highest priority, while the subjects that directly receive delegatable access rights from ♯ have the second highest priorities, and so on. In this way we can realise the controlled delegation of authorizations. When grantors are the same, the more specific rule will dominate, which can support exception.

3.4   The Stable Model Semantics

The concept of answer set is based on the so-called stable model semantics. We need to extend the traditional definition of answer set by considering the explicit contradictions.

Definition 6. *Let I be an interpretation for a DAP Π, the reduction of Π w.r.t I, denoted by Π^I, is defined as the reduction of $G^*(\Pi^D)$ w.r.t I. That is the set of rules obtained from $G^*(\Pi^D)$ by deleting (1) every rule overridden in I, and (2) every rule that has a formula not L in its body with $L \in I$, and (3) all formulas of the form not L in the bodies of the remaining rules.*

Given a set R of ground rules, we denote by $pos(R)$ the positive version of R, obtained from R by considering each negative literal $\neg p(t_1, ..., t_n)$ as a positive one with predicate symbol $\neg p$.

Definition 7. *Let M be an interpretation for Π. We say that M is an answer set for Π if M is a minimal model of the positive version $pos(\Pi^M)$. If M is an answer set for Π, then its subset of all the authorization literals $\mathcal{A}$ is called authorization answer set for Π.*

4 Conclusions

In this paper, we have proposed a logic program based formulation that supports delegatable authorizations, where negation as failure, classical negation and rules inheritance are allowable. Since the administration of access rights can be delegated, our model suits for large-scale distributed systems where distributed administration of access rights are needed. The expressive power and nonmonotonic reasoning of extended logic programs provide users a feasible way to express complex security policy. We have also presented a conflict resolution method which support the controlled delegation and exception. Exception is supported by using the more specific-take-precedence rule, while controlled delegation is supported by giving higher priorities to the predecessors w.r.t the delegation relation path.

References

1. E. Bertino, F.buccafurri, E.Ferrari, P.Rullo, A logical framework for reasoning on data access control policies. *proceedings of the 12th IEEE Computer Society Foundations Workshop*, pp.175-189,1999.
2. J.Crampton, G.Loizou, G.O'Shea A logic of access control. *The Computer Journal*, vol.44, pp.54-66, 2001.
3. M.Gelfond and V.Lifschitz, Classical negation in logic programs and disjunctive databases. *New Generation Computing*, 9:pp365-385, 1991.
4. S. Jajodia, P. Samarati, and V.S. Subrahmanian, A logical language for expressing authorizations. *Proc. of the 1997 IEEE Symposium on Security and Privacy*, pp 31-42, 1997.
5. C. Ruan and V. Varadharajan, Resolving conflicts in authorization delegations. Submitted, 2002.

Mixing Selections and Foreign Key Joins in Queries against Possibilistic Databases

Patrick Bosc and Olivier Pivert

IRISA/ENSSAT
Technopole Anticipa BP 447
22305 Lannion Cedex – France

Abstract. This paper deals with the querying of databases containing ill-known attribute values represented by possibility distributions. It investigates a query language with two operators: selection and a foreign key join operator which allows to express queries involving several relations at a time. The key idea is to impose a strong connection between the relations resulting from the operators and their interpretation in terms of more or less possible worlds. From a computational point of view, an interesting property of the queries considered is that they can be evaluated in a "compact" way, i.e., they do not require explicit handling of the possible worlds attached to the possibilistic database.

1 Introduction

In various application domains, there is a growing need for information systems capable to deal with ill-known data. This is also the case in data warehouses where the gathering of information coming from various sources generally induces imprecision in the data. Possibility theory [7] provides a unified framework for representing precise values, as well as imprecise ones (regular sets) or vague ones (fuzzy sets), and various null value situations (see [4] for more details). From a manipulation point of view, some works in the mid-80s have laid down the bases for the selection and projection operations [6], but, although mandatory in practice (from an expression power point of view), no composition of such (possibilistic) relations is permitted [3]. This is indeed the objective of this paper to overcome this limitation and it constitutes an original concern since no research works (to our knowledge) have dealt with it yet.

In presence of imperfect information represented as disjunctive sets of candidates, the design of a join operation raises a number of questions among which, that of the semantics of the resulting relation, since this framework does not provide a representation system in the sense of [5]. Indeed, when both join attributes (A in r(R) and B in s(S)) take ill-known values, evaluating a (possibilistic) join cannot consist in computing, for each pair (t, u) of tuples from r and s respectively, the possibility and the necessity that $\theta(t.A, u.B)$ holds – where θ denotes a comparator –, because some of the tuples appearing in the result are indeed mutually exclusive (see [1]).

As a consequence, one objective is to provide a specific (although useful) join operation in order to overcome both the lack for composing relations and the problem mentioned before. Moreover, it is of great importance to have a thorough semantic

M.-S. Hacid et al. (Eds.): ISMIS 2002, LNAI 2366, pp. 194-202, 2002.
© Springer-Verlag Berlin Heidelberg 2002

basis for the operators of the query language and we focus on the interpretation of the relations resulting from these operators in terms of more or less possible worlds. We will point out that equivalences between expressions valid in the usual case (with precise information) do not always hold in this framework. From a computational point of view, an interesting property of the queries considered is that they can be evaluated in a "compact" way, i.e., they do not require explicit handling of the possible worlds attached to the possibilistic database. This is obviously a very important point inasmuch as it guarantees that the complexity of the evaluation process will remain reasonable.

The structure of the paper is the following. In section 2, the interpretation of possibilistic relations in terms of worlds is recalled and the definition of the selection proposed by Prade & Testemale in the mid 80's is revised in order to cope with our interpretation requirement. A specific join operation (foreign key join) is proposed in section 3. It will be shown that the relation resulting from this join can be interpreted in a satisfactory way in terms of more or less possible worlds. In section 4, some queries calling on combinations of selections and fk-joins are investigated. Syntactic rules that queries must obey in order to get a valid result are defined. Finally, section 5 is devoted to some conclusions and perspectives for future works.

2 Possibilistic Relations, Worlds and a Revised Selection

A possibilistic relation [4] is a relation where some attributes may take imprecise values represented as possibility distributions. The choice of one of the candidate values for each such distribution in any tuple leads to a "more or less" possible world whose possibility degree is the minimum of the grades tied to each choice.

Example 1. Let us consider the relation schema PUR(ss#, date, car-t, city) in the context of cars purchased by persons at a certain date in a given city. In the following extension of the (possibilistic) relation p(PUR), the values of the attribute city (resp. car-t) take imprecise values in the second (resp. third) tuple and six worlds can be drawn from this extension.

p	ss#	date	car-t	city
	1	d1	Avensis	Marseille
	1	d2	Taurus	{1/Lille + 0.3/Rennes}
	2	d3	{1/Camry + 0.7/Taurus + 0.4/Avensis}	Rennes

For instance, the following extension corresponds to a world that is 0.3 possible (i.e., to a weakly preferred instance).

ss#	date	car-t	city
1	d1	Avensis	Marseille
1	d2	Taurus	Rennes
2	d3	Taurus	Rennes

♦

In order to have a coherent framework for their manipulation, initial possibilistic relations are provided with two grades (possibility and necessity) whose value is 1 in each tuple (thus meaning that each tuple belongs for sure to the relation).

According to [6], when a selection applies to a possibilistic relation, any initial tuple gives birth to a tuple of the result additionally provided with a grade of possibility and a grade of necessity telling the extent to which it is a possible / necessary (certain) answer. Considering a relation schema $R(A_1,..., A_n)$ and a tuple t of r(R) where $A_i(t)$ is the possibility distribution representing the value of attribute A_i in t, $\pi_{A_i(t)}(u)$ stands for the extent to which u is an acceptable value for $A_i(t)$ and the predicate P represents a condition applicable to A_i, these degrees for tuple t are respectively given by:

$$\Pi P(t) = \min(poss(P; A_i(t)), \Pi_r(t)) = \min(\sup_{u \in dom(A_i)} \min(\pi_{A_i(t)}(u), P(u)), \Pi_r(t))$$
$$NP(t) = \min(nec(P; A_i(t)), N_r(t)) = \min(\inf_{u \in dom(A_i)} \max(1 - \pi_{A_i(t)}(u), P(u)), N_r(t)).$$

So doing, it is obvious that some worlds can be drawn from the output relation that are indeed quite impossible (in the sense that they are not compatible with the selection condition).

Example 2. Let us consider the initial extension of example 1 and the query searching for those people who have bought a Taurus or a Camry in Rennes. Formally, it is expressed in an algebraic setting as:

select(p, car-t $\in$ {"Taurus", "Camry"} **and** city = "Rennes").

This query returns the following result:

ss#	date	car-t	city	Π	N
1	d2	Taurus	{1/Lille + 0.3/Rennes}	0.3	0
2	d3	{1/Camry + 0.7/Taurus + 0.4/Avensis}	Rennes	1	0.6

The "derived" extension containing the two tuples <1, d2, Taurus, Lille> and <2, d3, Avensis, Rennes> corresponds to a world whose possibility is min(min(1, 1, 0.3), min(0.4, 1, 1)) = 0.3, whereas none of its tuples satisfy the selection criterion ♦

In order to avoid this behavior, we suggest a definition of the selection such that any interpretation (world) of the resulting relation complies with the selection. In the case of a selection over a relation r whose schema is $R(A_1, ... , A_n)$, if the condition P bears on attribute A_i, we propose to reduce the distribution associated with A_i to those values in accordance with P (other values remain unchanged as well as Π and N).

Example 3. Coming back to example 2, the result of the query, given hereafter, has the desired property. It can be remarked that it would even be possible to drop the degree Π which can be derived from the grades attached to each attribute value.

ss#	date	car-t	city	Π	N	
1	d2	Taurus	{0.3/Rennes}	0.3	0	
2	d3	{1/Camry + 0.7/Taurus}	Rennes	1	0.6	♦

The counterpart of this choice is the possible non normalization of the obtained possibility distributions, but we think that this point is not crucial as far as they are carefully manipulated further. Finally, let us point out that this operator maintains the equivalence between the expressions: select(r, P_1 **and** P_2) and select(select(r, P_1), P_2), which is not valid in general with the initial definition suggested in [6].

Remark. The conditions allowed are of the form "attribute θ constant" (where θ denotes any comparator) or "attribute$_1$ = attribute$_2$", or a conjunctive combination of those. For other types of conditions, the result cannot be in general represented as a possibilistic relation, i.e., with independent sets of candidates for the attributes.

3 A Proposal for a Foreign Key Join Operator: The f-Join

3.1 Definition

As mentioned previously, the design of a general join operator able to work at the "compact" level of possibilistic relations is not feasible. To overcome this limitation, we consider the situation where queries call on the composition of a (possibilistic) relation r(X, Z) where X (and Z) may take imprecise values on the one hand and a (regular) relation s(X, Y) describing a precise function between the sets of attributes X and Y on the other hand. As discussed in [2], such a case is connected with the notion of a functional dependency extended to fuzzy databases. Indeed, relations r and s come from the decomposition of an initial relation (gathering X, Y and Z) aiming at the limitation of redundancy (tied to the presence of a function connecting X and Y).

Example 4. Let us consider the set of attributes {ss#, date, car-t, car-m, city, region} describing the type (car-t) and manufacturer (car-m) of cars purchased by persons (ss#) at a certain date in a city located in a given region. The associated database schema will be made of three relation schemas: CAR(car-t, car-m) where car-t is the key, LOC(city, region) where city is the key, PUR(ss#, date, car-t, city) where the pair {ss#, date} is the key. It is assumed that each of the first two relations describes the graph of a (precisely known) function. However, it may happen that the values of the attributes city and/or type (car-t) take imprecise values in the relation p(PUR)♦

Queries such as "find the persons who own a car whose brand is toyota" or "find the persons who have purchased a car in Brittany" call on a (foreign key) join operation which must be defined even in presence of imperfect values. Let us notice that, in a context of regular (precise) databases, join queries very often involve foreign-key joins. The foreign-key join operator considered in the following has the same basic semantics as the usual one, but it allows to deal with the case where the values of the joining attribute are ill-known in one of the relations. In this framework, the resulting relation is by nature uncertain and each tuple resulting from a join is provided with a possibility and a necessity degree.

We suggest an operator, called f-join, able to compute the image of a joining attribute value (through the function). If r is a relation defined on the schema (X, Z) where X may contain imprecise values and s is a regular relation describing a function between X and Y, this operation is defined as follows:

f-join(r, s, =(X, X)) =
  $\{<[\Pi, N] / t> \mid t = xyz$ where $\exists\, t' = <[\Pi', N'] / x', z> \in r$ such that
  supp(x) = supp(x') $\cap$ proj(s, X)$\}$ and
  supp(y) = $\{y_j \mid \exists\, x_i \in$ supp(x) such that $(x_i, y_j) \in s\}$ and
  $\forall x_i \in$ supp(x), $\pi_x(x_i) = \pi_x(x_i)$ and $\forall y_j \in$ supp(y), $\pi_y(y_j) = \max_{i \mid <x_i, y_j> \in s} \pi_x(x_i)$ and
  $\Pi = \min(\Pi', \max_{x_i \in supp(x)} \pi_x(x_i)$ and $N = \min(N', 1 - \max_{x_i \in (supp(x') - supp(x))} \pi_x(x_i))\}$

where supp(x) denotes the support of the possibility distribution x, $\pi_x(x_i)$ denotes the possibility degree associated with the candidate value x_i in x, and proj(s, X) denotes the projection of relation s onto attribute X.

The schema of the resulting relation is (X, Y, Z) and each tuple of the result can be seen as a kind of completion of a tuple of r (via its X-component) thanks to the knowledge of the function connecting X and Y-values materialized in s. It is worth mentioning that: i) the values appearing in the distribution for X in a resulting tuple correspond only to the candidates that have an image in s and ii) the problem raised in the general case by the appearance in the result of a join of disjunctive tuples is avoided here since a tuple of relation r gives birth to at most one tuple in the result.

Example 5. Let us consider the relations p and c whose respective schemas are PUR(ss#, date, car-t) and CAR(car-t, car-m) with the following extensions:

p

ss#	date	car-t	Π	N
1	d1	Avensis	1	1
1	d2	Taurus	1	1
2	d3	{1/Camry + 0.7/Taurus + 0.4/Astra}	1	1

c

car-t	car-m
Camry	Toyota
Avensis	Toyota
Taurus	Ford

An f-join based on the equality of the attribute car-t can be performed and the result is:

ss#	date	car-t	car-m	Π	N
1	d1	Avensis	Toyota	1	1
1	d2	Taurus	Ford	1	1
2	d3	{1/Camry + 0.7/Taurus}	{1/Toyota + 0.7/Ford}	1	0.6

Such an f-join can be invoked in a query such as: find the people (ss#) who have bought a "Toyota" or a "Ford", and then relation c is issued from a selection. It can be observed that the resulting (possibilistic) relation is a compact representation of the possible worlds stemming from the query and complying with the function between car-t and car-m. The only valid worlds are drawn with either <Camry, Toyota> or <Taurus, Ford> (due to the function tying car-t and car-m values)♦

The proof that this operator produces a result that has a valid interpretation in terms of worlds is not given here for the sake of brevity, but let us say that its basis lies in the removal of X candidates which have no image through the function.

Remark. The case where X (the considered foreign key) is a set of attributes: $X = \{X_1, ..., X_n\}$ cannot be dealt with. The problem resides in the removal of the X-candidates which have no image through the function, because in general, proj(s, X) cannot be expressed as: $subset(X_1) \times ... \times subset(X_n)$.

3.2   Characteristics of the Foreign Key Join

It turns out that f-join is significantly different from the usual join for several reasons and its major characteristics are now outlined. First of all, this operator is an extension of the usual natural join where an equi-join is understood. Other comparison operators (e.g., $>$, $\leq$) would not really make sense for f-join.

An important point lies in the fact that such an operator cannot be expressed as the projection of the selection of a Cartesian product, as it is feasible in the regular case. This difference has some consequences on query equivalences (see Section 4).

Example 6. Let us consider relations p and c of example 5. Evaluating the join as a projection of the selection of the Cartesian product, the result would be:

ss#	date	car-t	car-m	Π	N
1	d1	avensis	toyota	1	1
1	d2	taurus	ford	1	1
2	d3	camry	toyota	1	0.3
2	d3	taurus	ford	1	0

which is obviously not the correct result (cf. example 5)♦

Moreover, f-join is a nonsymmetric operator contrary to the usual join where relations are interchangeable. This is due to the fact that the objective is to "complete" a possibilistic relation thanks to the knowledge of a function represented by the other table that is a "regular" one. It is then clear that the operands are typed, the first one is any possibilistic relation whose joining attribute may take ill-known values and the other one indeed describes a function where the joining attribute cannot be imprecise.

4 About the Combination of Selections and f-Joins

In the usual relational setting, if r (resp. s) is defined over the schema R(X, Z) (resp. S(X, Y)), the following equality holds:

$$\text{select(join(r, s, } \theta(X, X)), \text{cond}_r \text{ and cond}_s) =$$
$$\text{join(select(r, cond}_r), \text{select(s, cond}_s), \theta(X, X)) \tag{1}$$

where θ is a comparison operator and cond_r (resp. cond_s) is a condition over relation r (resp. s).

We now point out two situations (by means of examples) in order to understand what happens as to the validity of formula 1 with imprecise values. Let us first consider the query "find all information about purchases made between January 1, 1998 and September 30, 1999" which can usually be expressed indifferently:

$$\text{select(f-join(p, c, =(car-t, car-t)), date } \in [01/01/98, 09/30/99]) \tag{E1}$$
or $\text{f-join(select(p, date } \in [01/01/98, 09/30/99]), c, =(car-t, car-t)) \tag{E2}$.

If we take the extensions of example 5 where dates d1 and d3 are assumed to satisfy the selection criterion, the result of E1 is:

ss#	date	car-t	car-m	Π	N
1	d1	Avensis	Toyota	1	1
2	d3	{1/Camry + 0.7/Taurus}	{1/Toyota + 0.7/Ford}	1	0.6

and identical to that of E2. The validity of the equivalence (1) lies in the fact that the selection predicate applies only to r (cond_s is void) and is independent from the joining attribute. Let us now take the following extensions of relations p (purchases) and c (car):

p	ss#	date	car-t	Π	N
	1	d1	Camry	1	1
	1	d2	Taurus	1	1
	2	d3	{1/Camry + 0.7/Taurus + 0.4/Avensis}	1	1

c	car-t	car-m
	Camry	Toyota
	Avensis	Toyota
	Taurus	Ford

The query "find all the information about the people who have bought a Toyota" has two possible expressions:

$$\text{f-join(p, select(c, car-m = "Toyota"), =(car-t, car-t))} \tag{E3}$$
and $\text{select(f-join(p, c, =(car-t, car-t)), car-m = "Toyota")} \tag{E4}$.

The result res3 of E3 and res4 of E4 are given hereafter and it turns out that they differ in the value of the attribute car-t. More precisely, the second result is not correct since there exists a candidate for the car-t value in the second tuple of res4 (namely Taurus) that does not correspond to any valid world (i.e., that can indeed not be chosen since it does not comply with the selection criterion and has no image in car-m).

res3	ss#	date	car-t	car-m	Π	N
	1	d1	Camry	Toyota	1	1
	2	d3	{1/Camry + 0.4/Avensis}	Toyota	1	0.3

res4	ss#	date	car-t	car-m	Π	N
	1	d1	Camry	Toyota	1	1
	2	d3	{1/Camry + 0.7/Taurus + 0.4/Avensis}	Toyota	1	0.3

This example shows that formula (1) may no longer hold. Beyond this particular example, it is possible to prove the validity of the following results.

Case 1: $cond_s$ is void and $cond_r$ relates to Z. We have the equivalence:

$$select(f\text{-}join(r, s, =(X, X)), cond_r) = f\text{-}join(select(r, cond_r), s, =(X, X)).$$

Case 2: $cond_r$ is void and $cond_s$ relates to Y. The following expressions:

$$select(f\text{-}join(r, s, =(X, X)), cond_s) \qquad (E5)$$
$$f\text{-}join(r, select(s, cond_s), =(X, X)) \qquad (E6)$$

are not equivalent in general. It is straightforward to prove that the correct result is obtained using (E6).

Case 3: Let us consider a condition $cond_X$ over attribute X. The expressions:

$$select(f\text{-}join(r, s, =(X, X)), cond_X) \qquad (E7)$$
$$f\text{-}join(select(r, cond_X), s, =(X, X)) \qquad (E8)$$
$$f\text{-}join(r, select(s, cond_X), =(X, X)) \qquad (E9)$$

are not equivalent in general. It is possible to prove that expressions (E8) and (E9) always produce the correct result.

Case 4: Let us consider a conjunctive selection condition "$cond_X$ and $cond_Y$" over attributes X and Y. The following expressions:

$$select(f\text{-}join(r, s, =(X, X)), cond_X \text{ and } cond_Y) \qquad (E10)$$
$$f\text{-}join(r, select(s, cond_X \text{ and } cond_Y), =(X, X)) \qquad (E11)$$
$$f\text{-}join(select(r, cond_X), select(s, cond_Y), =(X, X)) \qquad (E12)$$

are not equivalent in general. It is possible to prove that the expressions (E11) and (E12) always produce the correct result.

To sum up, one can say that it is necessary to perform the selections first, in order to comply with the requirement over the interpretations in terms of worlds. These results mean that some transformations (rewritings) undertaken for performance purposes, that are valid in presence of precise attribute values, must be forbidden in general (i.e., when we are not in case 1) with imprecise values. Consequently, the formulation of user queries has to obey strict rules, and queries must be evaluated as they are expressed.

5 Conclusion

This paper is concerned with databases where some pieces of information are ill-known and represented as possibility distributions. In this context, an operator able to combine two relations has been proposed. This operator, which is an extended foreign key join, works only in the context where one of the relations describes a regular function, which is likely to appear frequently in practice. It is defined so as to produce a "compact" resulting relation whose interpretations are all valid (i.e., correspond to a "more or less" possible world). In order to be coherent with this view, the definition of the selection operation applying to possibilistic relations initially proposed by Prade and Testemale has also been revised. From a computational point of view, an interesting property of the queries considered is that they can be evaluated in a "compact" way, i.e., they do not require explicit handling of the possible worlds attached to the possibilistic database (this would not be true with a "general" join operator, whose result cannot be represented in a compact way anyhow).

The initial work presented here should be continued along two major directions. The first one aims at a more exhaustive study of the properties of the operator and the way it can be used in complex queries, in particular when several joins are needed. The other line for future research concerns the integration of this operator in an SQL querying environment able to deal with databases that contain imperfect data.

References

1. Bosc, P., Liétard, L., Pivert, O.: About ill-known data and equi-join operations. Proc. 4th Conference on Flexible Query-Answering Systems (FQAS'2000), Warsaw, Poland (2000) 65-74
2. Bosc P., Liétard L., Pivert O.: An approach to functional dependencies in fuzzy databases. Proc. 9th International Conference on Fuzzy Systems (Fuzz-IEEE'2000), San Antonio, USA (2000) 917-922
3. Bosc P., Pivert O.: At the crossroads of database systems and fuzzy sets. Proc. of the Joint 9th IFSA World Congress and 20th NAFIPS International Conference, Vancouver, Canada (2001), 2114-2119
4. Bosc, P., Prade, H.: An introduction to fuzzy set and possibility theory-based approaches to the treatment of uncertainty and imprecision in data base management systems. In: Motro, A., Smets, P. (eds.): Uncertainty Management in Information Systems – From Needs to Solutions. Kluwer Academic Publishers (1997) 285-324
5. Imielinski, T., Lipski, W.: Incomplete information in relational databases. Journal of the ACM **31** (1984) 761-791
6. Prade, H., Testemale, C.: Generalizing database relational algebra for the treatment of incomplete/uncertain information and vague queries. Information Sciences **34** (1984) 115-143
7. Zadeh, L.A.: Fuzzy sets as a basis for a theory of possibility. Fuzzy Sets and Systems **1** (1978) 3-28

Aggregates as Meta Functions

Shingo Kashikawa[1], Shogo Ogura[1], Isamu Shioya[2], and Takao Miura[1]

[1] Dept. of Elect. and Elect. Engr, Hosei University,
Kajinocho 3-7-2, Koganei, Tokyo, Japan
miurat@k.hosei.ac.jp
[2] Dept. of Informatics, SANNO University,
Kamikasuya 1573, Isehara, Kanagawa, Japan
shioya@mi.sanno.ac.jp

Abstract. OLAP operations have been widely accepted as a suitable method for decision support by data analysis. Among others, roll-up and drill-down are practically implemented by using database operations. However, we cannot define them as inverses of each other since they assume how to manage materialized views. In this work, we model these operators in the framework of meta objects, and extend relational algebra by introducing meta operators group and apply. Then we show two OLAP operations can be managed within the framework of (new) database operations.

Keywords: Data Warehousing Foundation, Metadata Management

1 Motivation

Operations for decision support on data warehouse are called OLAP (Online Analytical Processing) operations[Chaudhuri97]. Among others, roll-up and drill-down have been paid much attention, by which we can climb up or go down along with abstract levels of *interests*. *climbing up* abstract levels mean *make grouping* by aggregate functions. roll-up operation can be described by SQL database language[Gray97]. On the other hand, there exists no way to implement drill-down in SQL since we don't have any *inverse* operations against aggregate functions. Practically, this operation could be seen as *selection* of materialized views. Putting it into other words, in OLAP we utilize basic information and *one-way* abstraction to them. To obtain inverse operation, many view information should be managed in a systematic and integrated manner.

To improve such situation, we introduce a new paradigm based on *meta objects* to keep the warehouse information consistent and to *move* around abstraction hierarchy. We have already proposed HOME (Harmonized Objects and Meta-objects Environment) system [Miura99] where meta objects are managed as first class citizens. In this system, there is a group operator to generate meta objects dynamically, by which we define stage-up operation for aggregate processing. We will describe OLAP operations (such as roll-up and drill-down) within this framework.

M.-S. Hacid et al. (Eds.): ISMIS 2002, LNAI 2366, pp. 203–212, 2002.

In the next section, we introduce meta objects and the relevant queries. In section 3 we describe characteristic aspects of OLAP operations, while section 4 contains some definitions of **group** and aggregate operations based on them. In section 5, we describe new framework of OLAP based on meta objects. After summarizing relevant works, we conclude our work.

2   Meta Objects and Databases

Objects are information of interests that are captured into databases. They carry individual semantics where the common knowledge among them are described as *meta objects* into a *database scheme*. We can evaluate meta objects and obtain a collection of objects corresponded to them. For example, *relations* or *tuples* are a collection of objects, *relational schemes* and *attributes* are meta-objects. Relation schemes are evaluated as relations. Since meta objects are kept consistent in databases, there must be meta objects that describe themselves. By this feature, to define new relations, it is enough to add some tuples to database schemes. The results by query expressions are described virtually by means of the resulting scheme (**RESULT**). We assume we manage the scheme within our framework in a temporal manner.

When we give queries to manipulate objects, we describe expressions containing meta objects. The expressions are called *object queries*. *Meta queries* are query expressions that contain *meta conditions*. That is, in a meta query, we give conditions to extract meta objects *and* some conditions to the objects corresponded to the meta objects.

To evaluate both objects and meta objects *seamlessly*, we introduce *deification* mechanism[Miura99], denoted by \$m to a meta object m. Conversely, for objects $\{o_1, .., o_n\}$, we introduce a meta object o, called *reification* of $\{o_1, .., o_n\}$ where $\$o = \{o_1, .., o_n\}$. We denote o by $'\{o_1, .., o_n\}$. Note there might be several reification meta objects for $\{o_1, .., o_n\}$. In the followings, we describe a fresh new reification meta object by **new** $'\{o_1, .., o_n\}$.

We would like to define scheme within own scheme structure. This means, if we define the treatment of special scheme (by some software), we can define *every* scheme structures in terms of *our* scheme structure. To do that, it is enough to show some materialization of the scheme structure which is consistent with our assumption. And this is called *core set* of the scheme structure.

We define 3 relations in our scheme; **RelationCatalog**, **AttributeCatalog** and **DomainCatalog**. Thus we expect that **RelationCatalog** relation contains 3 tuples which correspond to these 3 relation schemes. We assume **name** domain has values of 32 byte long and **numeric**, **count** and **type** domains have 4 byte integer. Since our schemes are also relations, they should be described within our framework. In fact, **RelationCatalog** has 40 byte tuples because of one **name** domain and two **count** domains. In a similar manner, we have the specific **DomName** relation as below:

RelationCatalog		
RelName	Arity	Width
RelationCatalog	3	40
AttributeCatalog	5	104
DomainCatalog	3	40

DomainCatalog		
DomName	ValueType	ValueSize
name	CHARACTER	32
count	INTEGER	4
type	TYPE	4

`AttributeCatalog` relation should contain 11 tuples for the 11 attributes of the 3 relation schemes:

AttributeCatalog				
RelName	AttrName	DomName	Offset	Position
RelationCatalog	RelName	name	0	1
RelationCatalog	Arity	count	32	2
RelationCatalog	Width	count	36	3
AttributeCatalog	RelName	name	0	1
AttributeCatalog	AttrName	name	32	2
AttributeCatalog	DomName	name	64	3
AttributeCatalog	Offset	count	96	4
AttributeCatalog	Position	count	100	5
DomainCatalog	DomName	name	0	1
DomainCatalog	ValueType	type	32	2
DomainCatalog	ValueSize	count	36	3

Note the type values `CHARACTER`, `INTEGER`, `TYPE` are 1,2,3 respectively describing what kind of values on this domain are held. In our prototype system, they are represented as string, integer and integer respectively.

3 Grouping and Aggregates Based on Meta Objects

3.1 Grouping

Since we have meta objects as first class citizens, it is possible to apply algebraic operators to meta objects same as objects, in addition to deification (evaluation of meta objects). Moreover, we extend relational algebra by **group** and **apply** mechanisms for meta objects. A **group** operator generates meta objects dynamically by grouping a collection of tuples in such a way that distinct meta object corresponds to every subset through deification. This operator can be seen as a kind of abstraction, in fact, a kind of *reification*. Note **group** doesn't generate nested relations and algebraic properties are preserved. The operator is described as follows:

   group [$\mathcal{A}$] **RelExpr**

We must have $\mathcal{A} \subseteq \mathcal{S}$ if `RelExpr` has a scheme $\mathcal{S}$. All tuples in `RelExpr` are grouped and projected into $R_1, .., R_k$ over $(\mathcal{S} - \mathcal{A})$ based on $\mathcal{A}$-values $v_1, .., v_k$. For each R_i (and v_i), a new meta object t_i is generated where $\$t_i = R_i$, and $\langle v_i, t_i \rangle$ is output. All values in $\$t_i$ carry common schematic information over $(\mathcal{S} - \mathcal{A})$.

The result relation has the scheme $\mathcal{A}$ and ∇_g where ∇_g is a new meta object generated by reification of $\{t_1, .., t_k\}$. Here we consider ∇_g as **new** $'\{t_1, .., t_k\}$. Also we regard ∇_g as a relation scheme which consists of one attribute ∇_g, thus we have $\$\nabla_g = \{t_1, .., t_k\}$. In the followings, we denote ∇_g by $\nabla_g(\mathcal{S} - \mathcal{A})$.

EXAMPLE 1 Assume we have a relation of CompanyA. Then we do grouping according to *Department* attribute:

group [Department] (CompanyA)

By the query, four meta objects $t_1, .., t_4$ are generated whose deification is defined over Employee, Salary.

CompanyA

Department	Employee	Salary
A	Kawada	300
A	Katakura	300
B	Tanaka	500
B	Takura	600
C	Kawada	300
D	Nakamura	400

(RESULT)

Department	∇_g
A	t1
B	t2
C	t3
D	t4

t1 Employee	Salary
Kawada	300
Katakura	300

t2 Employee	Salary
Tanaka	500
Takura	600

t3 Employee	Salary
Kawada	300

t4 Employee	Salary
Nakamura	400

□

3.2   Aggregate Functions

To obtain aggregate values, we assume *aggregate* functions which take meta objects as input and we define apply operator to evaluate them. By apply operator, we can avoid complicated mechanism for the evaluation while keeping orthogonality between first order functions and aggregate functions.

An apply operator is defined as follows:

apply[Attribute:= FuncExpr] RelExpr

Assume RelExpr has a scheme S. We apply FuncExpr to each tuple in RelExpr, and take the result as a new Attribute value. The scheme of the result relation consists of S and Attribute.

FuncExpr contains two or three parameters (the last parameter can be omitted).

func($\mathcal{F}$, $\mathcal{A}$, $\mathcal{C}$)

A FuncExpr has a function func and three parameters. During the evaluation, it takes a tuple as an input. $\mathcal{F}(\subseteq S)$ means attributes on which each tuple is processed by func. In a case of first order functions, the readers can imagine add, subtract, multiply and so on as a func. In the case of aggregate functions, $\mathcal{F}$ value should contain meta objects which correspond to a collection of tuples (objects) defined over some scheme $\mathcal{T}$. $\mathcal{A} \subseteq \mathcal{T}$ should hold and $\mathcal{A}$-values are processed. Only func knows how to process (evaluate) a tuple through deification. For example, after grouping, the func takes meta objects over ∇_g as input, and it calculates an aggregate value of the corresponding objects. In our approach there are 7 aggregate functions built-in: COUNT, SUM, AVG, MAX, MIN, ANY and ALL. The last parameter $\mathcal{C}$ is discussed later on.

Note there exists no difference of description between first order functions and aggregate functions but the latter has meta objects as input.

EXAMPLE 2 In EXAMPLE 2, we have a relation of CompanyA. Also we illustrated grouping results and, then, we can generate the answer. First, we

want to find average salary to each department in this relation. Our query can
be described as:

```
project [Department,Total]
    apply [Total:= SUM(∇_g,"Salary")]  group[Department] CompanyA
```

Then we have the answer relation:

(RESULT)

Department	Total
A	600
B	1100
C	300
D	400

In order to obtain *total salary* in CompanyA, we can describe the query like:

```
project [Total]
apply [Total:= SUM("CompanyA","Salary") ] ({ })
```

In this query, all the salaries in "CompanyA" are summarized to an empty
relation. There might be duplicate values on Salary attribute but all of them are
summed up. Note the first parameter "CompanyA" is an instance as meta object
thus the aggregate value can be calculated independent of the input relation, and
no value is looked up to the empty relation. The (RESULT) becomes that Total
is 2400. □

3.3 Context in Aggregate Functions

The third parameter C in FuncExpr, called *context*, means how the function
should be applied. As described before, $\nabla_g(T)$ has implicit scheme information
T. If $C \subseteq T$ is given, we project $\$t_i$ onto C, i.e., C can be seen as *scope*. Note,
unless no confusion arises, we give C to ∇_g, denoted by $\nabla_g[C]$. If C is omitted,
T is assumed to be a context. *Context* plays an essential role to obtain answers
correctly as shown in the next example.

EXAMPLE 3 We assume we have a different relation CompanyB where Salary
depends on Employee but an employee many belong to several departments and
several projects.

CompanyB

Department	Employee	Project	Salary
A	Kawada	1	300
A	Katakura	1	300
A	Kawada	2	300
B	Tanaka	2	500

We want to obtain average salary to each department. But we might give several
queries because we can give several scopes in aggregate functions.

```
(1) project [Department,Total]
apply [Total:= SUM(∇_g,"Salary", "Emp,Project,Salary")]
group[Department] CompanyB
(2) project [Department,Total]
apply [Total:= SUM(∇_g,"Salary", "Emp,Salary")]
group[Department] CompanyB
```

(3) project [Department,Total]
apply [Total:= SUM(∇_g,"Salary", "Salary")]
group[Department] CompanyB

The first query is illegal since a same employee (Kawada) appears twice. The last one is also illegal since Kawada and Katakura earn same salary. Only (2) is correct, because SUM ignores Project information by means of "Emp,Salary" context, and we can calculate salary correctly. □

4   OLAP Operations Based on Meta Objects

4.1   Relations and OLAP

Here we define OLAP operations roll-up and drill-down consistently over abstraction hierarchy. Before developing our story, let us define some terminologies for OLAP. A relation R(A1,..,An;B1,..,Bm) over attributes A1,..,An;B1,..., Bm ($n, m > 0$) is called an *OLAP relation* if every Bj has numeric domain and a functional dependency A1,..,An → B1,..,Bm holds. Each Ai is called an *axis* attribute and Bj a *value* attribute. Very often we illustrate an OLAP relation in a form of n dimensional cube as the next example.

EXAMPLE 4 Here is an OLAP relation CompanyC described below. We denote this relation by CompanyC(Prefecture, Date, Product; SalesAmount). We also have an abstraction hierarchy about AreaDomain over Prefecture, Area and State as below.

CompanyC

Prefecture	Date	Product	SalesAmount
Tokyo	10	Socks	40
Chiba	10	Socks	30
Tokyo	11	Pencil	40
Miyazaki	10	Socks	5

AreaDomain

Prefecture	Area
Tokyo	Kanto
Chiba	Kanto
Miyazaki	Kyushu
Hyogo	Kansai

It is illustrated as a 3-cube over Prefecture, Date, Product and SalesAmount.

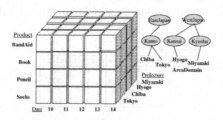

□

Another construct, an *abstraction hierarchy*, is a binary relation to describe a special kind of relationship among objects. That is, we assume H(PQ) where each tuple $(v_1, v_2) \in$ H means v_2 is more abstract than v_1. Naturally P → Q holds. In a context of OLAP relations R(A1,..,An;B1,..,Bm), axis attributes may have abstraction hierarchies such as H1(A1,C1), by which we may rollup the relation.

4.2 Stage-Up Operation

We are ready to introduce stage-up operation to generate meta objects for *roll-up* and to *drill-down*. Informally, by the new operation, we create meta objects by applying group. From the database point of view, this is defined as group after join. Formally we define stage-up($\mathcal{W}$) (R,S) as:

   group[$\mathcal{W}$] join(R,S)

where S describes an abstraction hierarchy over A1, H1 (A1 means an (axis) attribute and H1 an attribute of higher abstraction and we must have A1 $\rightarrow$ H1), while R(A1,A2,..,An;B1,..,Bm) means an OLAP relation to be staged up. Note that A1 appears in both R and S while H1 only in S. And, $\mathcal{W}$ means H1,A2,..,An. We say A1 is staged up.

As a result, we will have an OLAP relation R'(H1,A2,..,An;∇_g) where each set of tuples in ∇_g is defined over A1,B1,..,Bm. Let us note that A1 $\rightarrow$ B1,..,Bm holds in each set since the set is generated by grouping on each H1,A2,..,An value while A1,..,An $\rightarrow$ B1,..,Bm holds in R.

EXAMPLE 5 Using a hierarchy relation AreaDomain described as the previous example, let us stage up CompanyC onto AreaInfo.

   stageup[Area, Product, Date](CompanyC, AreaDomain)
Now the result AreaInfo(Area,Product,Date; ∇_g) contains:

(RESULT)

Area	Product	Date	∇_g
Kanto	Socks	10	t_α
Kanto	Pencil	11	t_β
Kyushu	Socks	10	t_γ

t_α	Prefecture	SalesAmount
	Tokyo	40
	Chiba	30

t_β	Prefecture	SalesAmount
	Tokyo	40

t_γ	Prefecture	SalesAmount
	Miyazaki	5

☐

4.3 Roll-Up Operation

A roll-up operation is introduced to obtain aggregated values from OLAP relations. Informally we stage-up OLAP relations into RelExpr, then we define this operation rollup[$\alpha, \beta, \mathcal{F}$] RelExpr as follows:

   project[α, β] apply[β:= FuncExpr] RelExpr
where FuncExpr means application of an aggregate function $\mathcal{F}$ which is one of COUNT,MAX,MIN,SUM,AVG. $\mathcal{F}$ takes meta-objects over a ∇_g attribute appeared in RelExpr as input, which could be generated by stage-up operation. The function calculates aggregate values from collections of meta objects in $\$\nabla_g$. Also β means an attribute to be aggregated, and finally α a set of attributes in RelExptr except the meta object attribute (like ∇_g). As the result, we have an OLAP relation R'(α ; β).

EXAMPLE 6 From Area attribute, let us obtain SalesAmount-summary over Date and Product. In the previous example, we have already staged up our OLAP relation.

rollup[Area,Product,Date,AreaSales,SUM](AreaInfo) By applying SUM aggregate function, we take $t_\alpha, t_\beta, t_\gamma$ as input and we obtain individual AreaSales information to each Area, Product and Date. □

4.4 Drill-Down Operation

Similar to roll-up operation, we define drill-down operation by means of *deifi-cation* to meta-objects. More formally, the operation drilldown[$\mathcal{P}, \mathcal{Q}$] RelExpr is given by:

project[$\mathcal{P}, \$\mathcal{Q}$] RelExpr

where $\mathcal{Q}$ means a meta-object (axis) attribute and $\mathcal{Q}$ should appear in a scheme of RelExpr. $\mathcal{P}$ means all other axis attributes in RelExpr. As the result, we have an OLAP relation R'($\mathcal{P}$,A; B) where A,B are the common scheme of the deification of meta objects in $\$\mathcal{Q}$ and A means a staged-up attribute. Note that we must have $\mathcal{P}$, A → B because of the stage-up operation.

EXAMPLE 7 Let us discuss our running example. Using an attribute Area, we drill the relation down to Prefecture. Similar to the previous examples, we evaluate the relevant meta objects:

drilldown[Product,Date, ∇_g] (AreaInfo)

Each meta object in AreaInfo is evaluated commonly over an attribute ∇_g. And $\mathcal{P}$ means Product and Date in this case. □

5 Stage-Up and Drill-Down

Let us show drill-down and stage-up are inverse operations with each other.

Let S(A_n,B,C;D) be an OLAP relation to be staged up, and let $t_1, t_2, .., t_n$ be a tuple in S. We put our focus on A_n. By stage-up operation, a new attribute A_{n+1} of higher abstraction is appended to the scheme which captures meta objects over A_n and D. Then we assume all the tuples are $u_1, u_2, .., u_m$ over (A_{n+1},B,C;∇_g[A_n,D]).

Let us drill this relation down. Note that, by drill-down operation, an attribute A_{n+1} is eliminated. Meta objects over ∇_g are evaluated, whose values are along with A_n, D. In short, we have a new scheme B,C, A_n ,D on which $u_1, u_2, .., u_m$ are evaluated as $t_1, t_2, .., t_n$. Then we must have the identical scheme and tuple values.

Conversely, let T(A_n, ∇_g[A_{n-1},D], B, C) be a database scheme to be drill-downed. This scheme turns into T(A_{n-1}, D, B, C) by drill-down operation, which becomes T(A_n,B,C,∇_g[A_{n-1},D]) by stage-up operation. Thus we come back to the original scheme.

Let $v_1, v_2, .., v_m$ be all the tuples to be drilled down. They get to $w_1, w_2, .., w_n$ by means of drill-down operation. Similar to the above discussion, we come back to $v_1, v_2, .., v_m$ by stage-up operation. Note that we must have other set of meta-objects but whose deification of the deification is identical to the original $v_1, v_2, .., v_m$. We say the two relations are identical *up to meta objects*.

As a summary, we can say the two operations are inverse with each other. roll-up.

6   Related Works

There are a lot of researches paid much attention for aggregate function from the viewpoints of relational algebra[Gray89], *multi-set* and defined extended relational algebra[Klug82], sophisticated operations such as *Pack* and *Unpack* [Özsoyoğlu87], characteristics of aggregate functions[Cabibbo99] and formal semantics [Feragas95]. Among them, [Gray89] discusses how to extend relational algebra stressing the equivalence with relational calculus. In fact, two operators **extend** and **group-by** have been introduced and proved to be equivalent to (extended) relational calculus. An operator **extend** means we append new attributes where the attribute values are obtained by applying some procedures to each tuple. An aggregate function takes *nested relation* as input and generates a single value as output, thus we avoid nested relations directly since every subset is converted to a single value. Here COUNT, SUM, AVERAGE, MAX, MIN, ANY and ALL are provided as the built-in functions. The approach seems similar to us, but there exist some important distinctions. First, the operators are applied not to individual tuples but to each collection of tuples. Thus the users have to examine what kinds of functions work since there's no distinction between first order function and aggregate functions. Also *grouping operator* is not separated clearly from *aggregate operators*, we can't distinct with each other. Second, we are forced to imagine scheme structure different from usual operators, because aggregate functions can treat set-valued processing. In fact, grouping and aggregate operators manipulate nested relations in their nature. And it is hard for us to think about special scheme dependent on aggregate functions. And finally, we have to utilize **extend** and **group-by** separately according to first order functions and aggregate functions. In our case, when we give **apply**, we can evaluate function expressions no matter what kinds of functions we have.

7   Conclusion

In this investigation, we have described **group** and **apply** operations based on meta objects, then we have defined **stage-up** operation as well as **roll-up** and **drill-down** by means of these operators. Then we have introduced objects hierarchy corresponds to an abstraction hierarchy over OLAP scheme, and integrated meta object operations for OLAP in a consistent manner. Also we have shown that **stage-up** and **drill-down** are inverse operations with each other, and that we can establish new framework of data warehouse processing within a database framework but not through view management mechanism.

References

[Cabibbo99] Cabibbo, L. and Torlone, R.: A Framework for the Investigation of Aggregate Functions in Database Queries, proc. *ICDT* (1999),pp 383-397

[Chaudhuri97] S. Chaudhuri et al: An Overview of Data Warehousing and OLAP Technology. ACM SIGMOD Record, Vol. 26 No.1 P.65-74, March 1997

[Feragas95] Fegaras, L. and Maier, D.: Towards An Effective Calculus for Object Query Languages, proc.SIGMOD (1995)

[Gray89] Gray, P.M.D.: LOGIC, ALGEBRA AND DATABASES, Sangyou ToSho (1989)

[Gray97] Jim Gray, Surajit Chaudhuri, Adam Bosworth, Andrew Layman, Don Reichart, Murali Venkatrao, Frank Pellow, Hamid Pirahesh: Data Cube: A Relational Aggregation Operator Generalizing Group-by, Cross-Tab,and Sub Totals, Data Mining and Knowledge Discovery 1(1): 29-53 (1997)

[Klug82] Klug,A. : Equivalence of Relational Algebra and Relational Calculus Query Languages Having Aggregate Functions, J. ACM, Vol.29,No. 3, pp. 699-717 (1982)

[Miura99] Miura,T.,Matsumoto,W.: Managing Meta Objects for Design of Warehouse Data, proc.DaWaK (1999), pp.33-40

[Özsoyoğlu87] Özsoyoğlu,G., Özsoyoğlu, Z.M. and Matos, V.: Extending Relational Algebra and Relational Calculus with Set-Valued Attributes and Aggregate Functions, ACM TODS vol 12, No.4, pp. 566-592 (1987)

A Knowledge-Based Approach to Querying Heterogeneous Databases

M. Andrea Rodríguez and Marcela Varas

Department of Information Engineering and Computer Science
University of Concepción,
Edmundo Larenas 215, Concepción, Chile.
`andrea@udec.cl,mvaras@inf.udec.cl`

Abstract. Query processing plays a fundamental role in current information systems that need to access independent and heterogeneous databases. This paper presents a new approach to querying heterogeneous databases that maps the semantics of query objects onto database schemas. The sematics is captured by the definitions of classes in an ontology, and a similarity function identifies not only equivalent but also semantically similar classes associated with a user's request. These similar classes are then mapped onto a database schema, which is compared with schemas of heterogeneous databases to obtain entities in the databases that answer the query.

1 Introduction

New approaches to knowledge-based retrieval have highlighted the use of ontologies and semantic similarity functions as a mechanism for comparing objects that can be retrieved from heterogeneous databases [1,2,3,4]. Ontologies aim to capture the semantics of a domain through concept definitions [5], which are used as primitives of a query specification and as primitives of resource descriptions. In current knowledge-based information systems, accessing information involves a semantic matching between users' requests and stored data. In environments with multiple and heterogeneous databases, this semantic matching is predicated on the assumption that independent databases share the same ontology or agree to adopt an ontology derived from the integration of existing ones [1,2,4]. But, given the need to query heterogeneous databases that use different conceptualizations (i.e., different ontologies), we need to modify the single-ontology paradigm of semantic matching for information access.

We present an approach to querying heterogeneous databases based on ontologies and similarity evaluations. We start at the top-level with users' requests expressed by terms defined in a *user ontology*. In this context, a user ontology provides terms definitions concerning a given domain [6]. By using such an ontology we can capture a richer semantics in the users' requests, and we allow users to express their queries without the need to know the schemas of data representation.

M.-S. Hacid et al. (Eds.): ISMIS 2002, LNAI 2366, pp. 213–222, 2002.
© Springer-Verlag Berlin Heidelberg 2002

The scope of this work is the retrieval of information described by classes of objects. For example, consider the following query to a Geographic Information System (GIS): "retrieve *utilities* in Atlanta, Georgia." This work concentrates on whether or not heterogeneous databases contain such an entity as *utility* or conceptually similar entities, such as *power plant* and *pipeline*. We leave for future work the treatment of query constraints given by, for example, attribute values or spatial constraints.

Unlike other approaches to knowledge-based retrieval that map the local terms of a database onto a shared ontology [4,7,8], we map the user ontology onto a database schema and subsequently compare this schema with each of the schemas of the heterogeneous databases. Our approach does not force heterogeneous databases to commit to a common single ontology, it just retrieves from these databases entities that are most likely similar according to our similarity measurement to the conceptual classes requested by the user. The strategy of this work is to map ontological descriptions of query objects onto database schemas, since extracting semantics from logical representation of data is a much harder process than mapping semantic definitions onto logical structures. Thus, it combines ontologies and database schemas with the goal of leading to intelligent database systems.

The organization of this paper is as follows. Section 2 describes our main approach to querying heterogeneous databases. Section 3 describes components of the ontology specification and the similarity model to compare entity classes in this ontology. Section 4 describes the mapping process to the database schema and the similarity evaluation between heterogeneous database schemas. A study case in the spatial domain is presented in Section 5. Conclusions and future research directions are described in Section 6.

2   Components of the Knowledge-Based Query Process

The general *query process* is described as follows. A user query is pre-processed to extract terms identifying entity classes in a *user ontology*. Using a *semantic similarity model* (Section 3), we compare entity classes in this ontology to determine all classes that are semantically similar to the ones that we extract from the user's request. In this way, even if the databases do not contain exactly what the user is searching for, they may still be able to provide some semantically similar answers.

Once the set of classes associated with concepts requested by the user has been determined, the definitions of these classes are mapped onto a database schema. To do this mapping, a set of transformations tied to the type of database schema (e.g., relational or object-oriented databases) is defined and applied over the classes' definitions to create a *query schema*, i.e., the schema of entity classes that models the user's request. For this paper we have used the traditional relational database schema [9] and we provide a summary of transformations that map entity classes onto this database schema. The generated *query schema* is then compared to each heterogeneous database (See Section 4).

In summary, our main approach includes two types of similarity assessments: (1) a semantic similarity assessment that aims at capturing classes that are semantically similar to the user query and (2) a database similarity measure that compares representations of entities in database schemas. Instead of making all similarity evaluations at the database schema level or at the ontological level, we combine these two similarity assessments for the following reasons:

- by using a user ontology we allow users to express queries in their own terms according to their own ontology without having to know the underlying modeling and representation of data in heterogeneous databases.

- we extract from the specified query and a semantic similarity model entity classes in a user ontology that are semantically associated with the user's request. We compare these classes at the ontological level where we have a more complete description of their semantics and we can obtain a set of possible answers.

- we assume that commonly existing databases have no ontological descriptions of their stored entities so, we are not provided with the full semantic description of entities stored in heterogeneous databases. Therefore, we use available components of the schema representation to compare entities through a database similarity model.

3   Ontology and Semantic Similarity

In a previous work [10, 11], we introduced an ontology defined with retrieval purposes whose basic specification components are described as follows.

3.1 Components of the Entity Classes' Definitions

Components of our ontology are entity class definitions in terms of the classes' semantic interrelations and distinguishing features. We refer to entity classes by words or sets of synonyms, which are interrelated by hyponymy or is-a relations and by meronymy relations or part-whole relations. We use the distinguishing features of classes to capture details among descriptions of classes that otherwise are missed in the classes' semantic interrelations. For example, we can say that a *hospital* and an *apartment building* have a common superclass *building*; however, this information falls short when trying to differentiate a *hospital* from an *apartment building*. We suggest a finer identification of distinguishing features and classify them into functions, parts, and attributes. Function features are intended to represent what is done to or with a class. Parts are structural elements of a class, such as the *roof* and *floor* of a *building*, that may have not be defined as entity classes. Finally, attributes can correspond to additional characteristics of a class that are not considered by either the set of parts or functions. This classification of distinguishing features into parts, functions, and attributes attempts to facilitate the implementation of the entity class representation, as well as it enables the separate manipulation of each type of distinguishing feature [11].

3.2 Semantic Similarity

We define a computational model that assesses similarity by combining a feature-matching process with a semantic-distance measurement [11]. The global similarity function $S_c(c_1,c_2)$ is a weighted sum of the similarity values for parts, functions, and attributes. For each type of distinguishing feature we use a similarity function $S_t(c_1,c_2)$ (Equation 1), which is based on the *ratio model* of a feature-matching process [12]. In $S_t(c_1,c_2)$, c_1 and c_2 are two entity classes, t symbolizes the type of features, and C_1 and C_2 are the respective sets of features of type t for c_1 and c_2. The matching process determines the cardinality ($|\ |$) of the set intersection ($C_1 \cap C_2$) and the set difference ($C_1 - C_2$).

$$S_t(c_1,c_2) = \frac{|C_1 \cap C_2|}{|C_1 \cap C_2| + \alpha(c_1,c_2) \cdot |C_1 - C_2| + (1-\alpha(c_1,c_2)) \cdot |C_2 - C_1|} \tag{1}$$

The function α determines the relative importance of different features between entity classes. This function α is defined in terms of the degree of generalization of entity classes in the hierarchical structure, which is determined by a semantic-distance measurement. This definition assumes that a prototype is generally a superclass for a variant and that the concept used as a reference (i.e., the second argument) should be more relevant in the evaluation [12,13].

Our similarity model has two advantages over semantic similarity models based on semantic distances and their variations [14,15,16]. First, it allows us to discriminate among closely related classes. For example, we could distinguish similarity between pairs of subclasses (between *hospital* and *house* an between *hospital* and *apartment building*, which are all subclasses of *building*) and between classes that are indirectly connected in the hierarchical structural (*stadium* as a subclass of *construction* and *athletic field* as a subclass of *field*). Second, our model does not assume a symmetric evaluation of similarity and allows us to consider context dependencies associated with the relative importance of distinguishing features [10,11].

4   Mapping and Comparison of Database Schemas

Once we have the desired entity classes, the next step in processing the query is to map the entities classes of our ontology onto database schemas, which are then compared with schemas of heterogeneous databases. We describe our approach to mapping with databases that are modeled with the relational database schema [9]; however, we could have used another type of database schema, such as an object-oriented schema, in which case new mapping transformations should be defined.

4.1   From Ontology to Database Schema

We assume that the existing database schemas (target schemas) are represented in the relational model with the following constructors:

- Entities: names, attributes, primary key, and foreign keys.
- Attributes: names.
- Foreign keys (FK): relations that they belong and refer to.

Prior to transforming the entity classes' definitions into a relational schema, we apply preprocessing to these definitions in order to keep only those components that can be mapped onto a relational schema:

- *Semantic relations extraction:* semantic relations are considered while descriptions and distinguishing features are eliminated in the subsequent mapping process. As we will explain in Section 4.2, we do not compare attributes (i.e., distinguishing features) since this would give misleading results due to the strong application dependences of attribute definitions in existing databases.
- *Synonym extraction:* Since synonyms are important to managing the multiple ways that people can refer to the same entity class, and since synonyms are not directly handled in the relation schema, we define an additional structure to deal with synonym sets of entity classes. This structure includes the set of synonym sets and an index as unique key.

Then, we take the simplified entity classes' definitions and we map them onto a relational schema. There is a direct mapping of entity classes onto relational schema; however, we also need to define transformations for mapping is-a, is-part- and whole-of semantic relations. Since there are several alternatives to mapping semantic relations onto relational schemas, we define a subset that considers only relational tables or entities' interrelations mapped through foreign keys (Table1).

Table 1. Mapping transformations from the entity class definition onto a relational schema

Semantic Relation	Transformation
Is-A	• *Isa₁:* Create an entity for each of the *children* entities with a foreign key pointing to the parent entity.
Part-Of	• *Part₁:* Define new structures (relations) that associate *whole* entities with *part* entities.
	• *Part₂:* Create a foreign key in a *part* entity for each of its *whole* entities.
Whole-Of	• *Whole₁:* Define new structures (relations) that associate *whole* entities with *part* entities.
	• *Whole₂* Create a foreign key in a *whole* entity for each its *part* entities.

The combination of the alternative transformations (i.e., 1 alternative for is-a relations, 2 alternatives for whole-of and part-of relations) gives us 4 possible mapping transformations.

4.2   Comparing Database Schemas

Comparing databases schemas is difficult due to the intrinsic differences in the database design and modeling. To deal with this problem in the most general case, we consider all possible mapping transformations over the reduced number of entity classes obtained from the semantic similarity assessment.

At the bottom line, we compare character strings of entities' names, attributes domains, and foreign keys' references (Equation 2). This string matching is over all synonyms that refer to entities in the query schema, which are defined in the complementary structure *synSet*. In Equation 2, e_j^o corresponds to an entity j in the query schema (user ontology), e_i^p corresponds to an entity i in a database schema p, t_i represents a term (e.g. *building*) or composite term (e.g., *building_complex*) that refers to an entity, attribute domain, or foreign key's reference.

$$S_w(e_i^p, e_j^o) = \max_{tj \in synSet_{e_j^o}} \left[\frac{|t_{e_i^p} \cap t_j|}{|t_{e_i^p} \cap t_j| + |t_{e_i^p} - t_j| + |t_j - t_{e_i^p}|} \right] \tag{2}$$

In order to complement the name-matching evaluation, we take the semantic relations (is-a, part-of, and whole-of relations) as the subject of comparison. The idea is to compare whether compared entities are related to the same set of entities. Thus, comparing semantic relations becomes a comparison between the semantic neighborhoods of entities, where the semantic neighborhood of an entity is the set of entities related through the is-a, part-of, and whole-of relations. The general approach to compare semantic neighborhoods is to use name matching over their components in a database schema. In the case of relational schema, entities in semantic neighborhoods are represented by *references* in the description of foreign keys or by values in the domain of an attribute type in an entity. Thus, we define a similarity function based on alternatives of the semantic relation representation assuming that the query schema will always represent entities in a semantic neighborhood by foreign keys in the corresponding relational tables (Equation 3). In Equations 3, n is the number of foreign keys in the ith entity of the database p (e_i^p), m is the number of attributes domain available in entity e_i^p, $FK_{i,e}$ corresponds to the *reference-to* specification of the ith foreign key in entity e, $D_{l,j,e}$ is the lth domain value in attribute j of entity e, and β is the number of domain attributes in e_i^p with similarity greater than zero to any of the foreign keys in e_j^o. The variable β is defined during the similarity process, since we cannot consider all attributes as attribute types that represent a semantic relation.

$$S_n(e_i^p, e_j^o) = \frac{\sum_{ii=1}^{n} Max S_w(FK_{ii,e_i^p}, FK_{jj,e_j^o}) + \sum_{ii=1}^{m} Max S_w(D_{l,ii,e_i^p}, FK_{jj,e_j^o})}{n + \beta} \tag{3}$$

This comparison is asymmetric. Specifically, the base element of the comparison (i.e., the second argument) comes from an ontology definition, and the target entity (i.e., the first element) is an entity of an existing database, which is likely to have a subset of the full semantic description of the concept. In our previous work [10] we showed that in comparing concepts from different ontologies, a good indication of whether or not these entity classes are similar across ontologies is obtained by matching entities' names and matching entities in a semantic neighborhood. Although we explored attribute matching, our previous work showed that attributes are application-dependent components of entities' representations, and so there would be less chance that two databases would have many attributes in common.

In order to integrate the information obtained from the similarity assessments of name matching and semantic neighborhoods, we use a similarity function that is defined by the weighted sum of the similarity of each specification component.

5   Example

We have implemented our approach in a prototype that includes an ontology definition and the similarity models. We applied our approach in the spatial domain and we created a user ontology derived from a subset of two already available information sources: WordNet [17] and The Spatial Data Transfer Standard [18]. We created this ontology with 260 definitions to exploit a more complete definition of entity classes (i.e., semantic relations from WordNet and distinguishing features from SDTS). As an existing spatial database, we consider a relational schema derived from the specification of the Vector Smart Map (VMAP) level 0 of the National Imagery Mapping Agency (NIMA).

As an example, we consider the simple query to spatial databases to retrieve information about "*utilities.*" Then we took the entity *utility* in our user ontology and we applied a semantic similarity evaluation that results in a set of three semantically similar entity classes: *electrical system*, *heating system*, and *plumbing system*. In this example we considered as candidate answers all entities whose similarity to the entity class *utility* is larger than 0.5. We then mapped the definitions of each of these candidate entity classes onto a relational schema (Table 2). In Table 2 we show only the mapping schema that leads to the best results of similarity, using the transformations *is₁* and *whole₁*, and transformations for *part-of* relations being unnecessary for this case.

Table 2. Definitions of entity class *utility* and its semantically similar entity classes

Entity class	Relational Schema

entity_class {
  name: {utility}
  description: A Unit composed of one or more
    pieces of equipment connected to a structure
    and designed to provide service such as heat,
    light, water, or sewage disposal.
  is_a: {facility} part_of: {} whole_of: {}
  parts: {}
  functions: {{transmit,conduct,carry}}
  attributes: {{name},{condition},
    {support_type},{location}}
	Utility(FK$_{facility}$)
	Foreign key: FK$_{facility}$ references to Facility

entity_class {
  name: {electrical_system}
  description: Equipments that provide electricity
    or light.
  is_a: {utility}
  part_of: {}
  whole_of: {{power_plant},
    {cable,wire,line,transmission line}}
  parts: {{power_plant},
    {cable,wire,line,transmission line}}
  functions: {{transmit,conduct,carry}}
  attributes: {{name},{condition},
    {support_type}, {location},
    {signal_type},{single_multiple_wires}}
	Electrical system (FK$_{utility}$, FK$_{power\_plant}$,
	FK$_{cable}$)
	Foreign key: FK$_{utility}$ reference to Utility
	Foreign key: FK$_{power\_plant}$ reference to
	Power_Plant
	Foreign key: FK$_{cable}$ reference to Cable
	Power plant(FK$_{electrical\ system}$)
	Foreign key: FK$_{electrical\ system}$ references to
	Electrical system
	Cable(FK$_{electrical\ system}$,)
	Foreign key: FK$_{electrical\ system}$ references to
	Electrical system

entity_class {
  name: {heating_system}
  description:
  is_a: {utility}
  part_of: {}
  whole_of: {{pipeline,piping,pipage,pipe}}
  parts: {{pipeline,piping,pipage,pipe}}
  functions: {{transmit,conduct,carry},
    {warm,heat}}
  attributes: {{name},{condition},
    {support_type},{location}}
	Heating system (FK$_{utility}$, FK$_{pipeline}$)
	Foreign key: FK$_{utility}$ references to Utility
	Foreign key: FK$_{pipeline}$ reference to Pipeline
	Pipeline (FK$_{Heating\ system}$, FK P$_{lumbing\ system}$)
	Foreign key: FK$_{Heating\ system}$ references to
	Heating system
	Foreign key: FK P$_{lumbing\ system}$ references to
	Plumbing System

entity_class {
  name: { plumbing_system}
  description:
  is_a: {utility}
  part_of: {}
  whole_of: {{pipeline,piping,pipage,pipe}}
  parts: {{pipeline,piping,pipage,pipe}}
  functions: {{transmit,conduct,carry},
    {dispose,throw out,throw away}}
  attributes: {{name},{condition},
    {support_type}, {location}}
	Plumbing system (FK$_{utility}$, FK$_{pipeline}$)
	Foreign key: FK$_{utility}$ references to Utility
	Foreign key: FK$_{pipeline}$ reference to Pipeline

The final similarity values between entities in the database that best match entities in the query schema are shown in Table 3.

Table 3. Results of similarity evaluation between the DB_VMAP and QS

Entity in the DB_VMAP	Entity in the QS	S_w	S_n	Similarity Total
Utility Point Feature	Electrical System	0	0.65	0.31
Pipeline Line Feature	Heating System	0	0.65	0.31
Pipeline Line Feature	Plumbing System	0	0.65	0.31
Utility Line Feature	Electrical System	0	0.45	0.23

As the results in Table 3 show, when we deal with heterogeneous databases, we cannot expect high values of similarity, but at least we are able to offer entities that have a strong chance of being associated with the concepts specified in the query.

6   Conclusions and Future Work

We have defined a new approach to querying heterogeneous databases based on similarity functions at an ontological level corresponding to a user's query and, at the logical level, between database schemas. The main characteristics of our approach are that we do not assume that databases share some level of the same conceptualization and we search for possible common components within the entities' representations.

The results of our experiment indicate that our approach detects correspondences between entities that are most likely similar; however, it may not detect all cases of similarity. In particular, further research needs to be done to recognize in the similarity evaluation when relational tables are just structures that represent semantic relations (e.g., structures created by transformation *part1* and *whole1*), as opposed to structures representing entities. In addition, we have not considered attributes in our comparison, but if we wish to process the whole query, we need to treat query constraints, which are usually described by attributes values.

Acknowledgement. This work has been partially funded by Fundación Andes, Chile. Andrea Rodríguez's research is further funded by Conicyt under grant Fondecyt 1010897. Marcela Varas's research is funded by the Dirección de Investigación of Universidad   the Concepción under grant number 99.093.003-1. We also want to thanks to Max Egenhofer's contribution to the previous work upon which this paper is based, and to Jim Farrugia for his valuable comments.

References

1.   Guarino, N., Masolo, C., Verete, G.: OntoSeek: Content-Based Access to the Web. IEEE Intelligent Systems **14** (1999) 70-80.

2.   Bergamaschi, B., Castano, S., de Vermercati, S., Montanari, S., Vicini, M.: An Intelligent Approach to Information Integration. In: N. Guarino (ed.): First International Conference on Formal Ontology in Information Systems. IOS Press, Trento Italy (1998) 253-268

3.   Voorhees, E.: Using WordNet for Text Retrieval. In: Fellbaum C. (ed.): WordNet: An Electronic Lexical DatabaseCambridge. The MIT Press, MA (1998) 285-303

4.   Mena, E., Illarramendi, A., Kashyap, V., Sheth, A.: OBSERVER: An Approach for Query Processing In Global Information Systems Based on Interoperation across Pre-existing Ontologies. Distributed and Parallel Databases 8 (2000) 223-271

5.   Bertino, E., Catania, B., Zarri, G.: Intelligent Database Systems. ACM Press, London UK (2001)

6.   Guarino, N.: Formal Ontology in Information Systems. In: Guarino, N. (ed.): Formal Ontology in Information Systems. IOS Press, Trento, Italy (1998) 3-15

7.   Bright, M., Hurson, A., Pakzad, S.: Automated Resolution of Semantic Heterogeneity in Multidatabases. ACM Transactions on Database Systems 19 (1994) 212-253

8.   Fankhause, P., Neuhold, E.: Knowledge Based Integration of Heterogeneous Databases. In: Hsiao, H., Neuhold, E., Sacks-Davis, R. (eds.): Database Semantics Conference on Interoperable Database Systems IFIP WG2.6. Elsevier Science Publishers, North-Holland (1992) 155-175

9.   Codd, E.: A Relational Model of Data for Large Shared Data Banks. Communications of the ACM 13 (1970) 377-387

10.   Rodríguez, A., Egenhofer, M.: Determining Semantic Similarity among Entity Classes from Different Ontologies. IEEE Transactions on Knowledge and Data Engineering (in press)

11.   Rodríguez, A. Egenhofer, M.: Putting Similarity Assessment into Context: Matching Functions with the User's Intended Operations. In: Sefarini, L., Brezillon, O., Castellano, F., Bouquet, P. (eds): Modeling and Using Context CONTEXT99. Lecture Notes in Computer Science Vol. 1688. Springer-Verlag, Berlin (1999) 310-323

12.   Tversky, A.: Features of Similarity. Psychological Review 84 (1977) 327-352

13.   Rosch, E.: Cognitive Representations of Semantic Categories. Journal of Experimental Psychology 104 (1975) 192-233

14.   Rada, R., Mili, H., Bicknell, E., Blettner, M.: Development and Application of a Metric on Semantic Nets. IEEE Transactions on System, Man, and Cybernetics 19 (1989) 17-30

15.   Sussna, M.: Word Sense Disambiguation for Free-text Indexing Using a Massive Semantic Network. In: Second International Conference on Information Knowledge Management, CIKM'93 (1993)

16.   Resnik, O.: Semantic Similarity in a Taxonomy: An Information-Based Measure and its Application to Problems of Ambiguity and Natural Language. Journal of Artificial Intelligence Research 11 (1999) 95-130

17.   Miller, G., Beckwith, R., Fellbaum, C., Gross, D., Miller, K.: Introduction to WordNet: An On-Line Lexical Database. International Journal of Lexicography 3 (1990) 235-244.

18.   USGS: View of the Spatial Data Transfer Standard (SDTS) Document (1998)

Using User Profiles in Intelligent Information Retrieval

Czesław Daniłowicz and Huy Cuong Nguyen

Department of Information Systems, Wrocław University of Technology,
Wyb. St. Wyspianskiego 27, 50-370 Wrocław, Poland
{danilowicz, cuong}@zsi.pwr.wroc.pl

Abstract. Personalization has been recently one of the most important features of intelligent information retrieval. An intelligent system should store information about user interests and utilize this information to deliver to the user documents he really needs. In such a system the information needs of a user should be represented by means of so called a user profile. User profiles, in other hand, should be used together with queries to sort retrieved information in such order that is adequate to user preferences. In this paper a vector-based information system model is presented, in which the user information needs and preferences (profiles) are defined and the methods for updating user profiles and automatic learning about user preferences are worked out.

1   Introduction

The advances of Internet technology have recently caused World Wide Web to become the largest universal information source, where users may not only retrieve, but also store their own information. Using existing search engines users can obtain needed information in relatively short time and easy way. However, there are still many problems that should be solved for enabling users to use this resource in more effective way. Some of these problems are the following:

- Users still have troubles in formulating their own information needs in chosen query language and the mechanisms for query modification are still not perfect. In the consequence, using methods based on user feedback requires multiple repetitions of retrieval, which are very time-consuming.
- There is usually large difference between document rankings given by a search engine and the one that a user would like to receive. In other words, it is widely recognized that irrelevant documents are often among top items of the system recommendation.
- The system answer for a given query often contains hundreds items and only several of them are relevant. Checking all items is impossible to realize in practice.

If the above problems may be solved then an end-user can expect such a kind of information retrieval systems, in which:

- during query formulation, he (she) does not have to realize all aspects of his (her) information needs, which should affect the relevance of system answers,
- the effectiveness of system should be independent from the user knowledge about the mechanism of the search engines, the organization of the database etc.,

M.-S. Hacid et al. (Eds.): ISMIS 2002, LNAI 2366, pp. 223-231, 2002.
© Springer-Verlag Berlin Heidelberg 2002

- the is no necessity for query modification by the user in purpose to get better results, and
- the document ranking in the system answer should be consistent with the user information needs, such that the most relevant documents should be in the begin of the ranking. Owing to this, the user does not waste time for downloading and reading irrelevant documents, appearing in the end of the ranking.

The realization of systems satisfying the mentioned above postulates is rather very hard on the basis of conventional approaches in information retrieval. It is then necessary to define new tools within the intelligent information retrieval technology, which should be capable to make decisions on automatic query modification.

The capability of making decisions can be realized by introducing a software agent that determines preferences of an individual user and utilizes them in searching process. In personalized information retrieval systems, an information agent is a computer program, which should save information about user interests in the form of so called *user profiles*. A user profile is used to rank items in the document space not only according to a query formed by the user, but also referring to his preferences. User profiles should be created in an independent way such that the participation of users is minimal. In this paper, we present a model of information retrieval systems with user profiles. Assuming that the user profiles are created we deal with working out retrieval functions that should take into account not only queries of users but also their profiles.

This paper is organized as follows. In section 2 a brief overview of existing methods for user preference representations and using them in information retrieval systems is presented. Section 3 shows a model for information retrieval system with user profiles. Finally, section 4 presents some conclusions and describes the future works.

2   User Profile in Information Retrieval – An Overview

In this section, we present the state-of-art of researches in using user profiles in information retrieval. We show how user profiles are created and modified, and how they can be used in retrieval processes.

2.1. User Profile – Methods for Creation and Modification

A profile of a user is understood as the representation of his (her) information needs, which are assumed to be relatively stable in some period of time [5]. In traditional information retrieval systems, a user expresses his (her) temporary information needs only by means of queries, which often are insufficient to establish the relevance degree of documents in a database. Experiments have proved that different users may expect different answers for the same query, and the same user for the same query may expect different answers in different periods of time. This means that the information preferences (or profile) of a user should be changeable in retrieval processes [9]. It implies that the abilities of creation and modification of user profiles should be the most important feature of an information agent.

The main task of an information agent is to establish profile structures and to learn algorithms that adapt to changes of user interests [12]. The agent usually gathers information about user interests from implicit and explicit feedback. Implicit feedback is based on user behavior and is determined by observing the user's actions in using the system, usually without user's involvement. For examples, if a user selects an article, it can be inferred implicitly that in some degree he (she) is interested in the content of this article [12]. In [17] several factors (*time for reading*, *bookmark*, *following up*) are used with appropriate weights to count the total score of implicit feedback in a Web filtering system called WAIR. Information about the user can be then gathered from an interaction process, during which the user is given some queries, and his profile is built on the basis of his (her) answers [7]. In [5] the author has introduced a method, which enables to construct the user profile from queries given to the system by the user.

The advantage of implicit feedback is that it makes the information agent more user-friendly. However, the ambiguity in the interpretation of user interests may bring about imprecise results in retrieval processes. For examples, an unread document could be treated by a search engine as irrelevant to the user profile. Therefore, accurate interpretation of user interests through implicit feedback is a very difficult task and requires sophisticated tools for observing user behaviors [14].

On the contrary, although explicit feedback methods involve the user's cooperation, they are easier to realize in practice. The advantage of explicit feedback is that information from users is unambiguous and more confident than implicit feedback. Strong positive or negative feedback should result in a significant change of profiles, which makes profile more dynamic. If the feedback indicates that a user really does not like a piece of information from the system's answer, then similar information should not appear in future answers. In contrast, a high-rating document should make similar documents to be presented in top ranking among others documents. After analyzing the system's recommendation, the user indicates documents, which he (she) is interested in, and his (her) profile is constructed as an average of those documents [4] or by consensus methods [11]. Chen [1] developed WebMate, an agent that helps users to effectively browse and search the Web. WebMate keeps tracks of user interests in different domains through multiple weighted vectors. The domains become a subject of information agents' learning automatically as users give positive feedback. In Chen's system, a new domain category is created for user feedback if the number of domains is still below its upper limit. If the number of domains has reached its maximum limit, the document to be learned should be used to modify the vector with the greatest similarity. McElligot and Sorensen in [8] developed a neural network approach employing two-layer connectionist model to filter news article on the Internet. In addition to keywords, their system uses the context in which it occurs to present a user profile. This system operates in two modes. The first mode consists of the learning phase, where sample documents are presented on input. The second mode consists of the comparison phase, where retrieved documents are filtered out to the user. Owing to this the system can enter the learning phase to learn additional interesting documents.

Owing to mentioned above advantages, explicit feedback is usually used in retrieval systems as the main method to gather information about user preferences.

2.2   User Profiles in Retrieval Processes

As the representation of user interests, a user profile may be used in different ways in retrieval processes. In personalized information systems there are four methods for using user profiles, which can be formulated as follows:

- Using user profiles for information filtering: the user does not need to give queries to the system, only system recommendations are regularly delivered to him (her). This approach is usually used in personalized news services or information filtering systems, where information sources are updated regularly.

- Modifying user queries: because a user query is more or less inaccurate and incomplete, it seems desirable to adjust the representation of the query by the representation of the profile. As a result, we have a new modified query that affects the retrieval process.

- Reordering the output: the user profile is treated as a post-filter to the system answer for the user query.

- Modeling with two focal points: a profile and a query can be considered as the same kind of entity directing in the retrieval process.

Widyantoro [14] has developed a model of information filtering system using so called a *personalized news agent*. The user profile is composed of different interest categories, each of them contains a positive descriptor, a negative descriptor and a long-term descriptor. The positive and negative descriptors maintain a feature vector learned from documents with positive and negative feedback respectively, while the long-term descriptor maintains the feature vector of documents obtained from both types of feedback. Each descriptor has also a weight to present the interest level of the corresponding descriptor's interest category. The information filtering process is performed as follows: Given a document feature vector, the system finds out the most relevant category in the user profile, and the document score is determined as the difference between positive similarity (similarity of the positive descriptor and the document vector) and negative similarity (similarity of the negative descriptor and the document vector). The greater a document score is, the better is the document. The set of first n documents with greatest scores will be given to the user as system's recommendation. The disadvantage of this approach is that the user can not use the query as the expression of his (her) temporary information need, which is not the same as user interests.

Myaeng and Korfhage [9] have proposed some methods for modifying queries using user profiles in a vector space model. In their approach, the two original entities (query and profile) are no longer considered, and only the modified query affects the retrieval process. Different linear dependences of queries and profiles were studied for their simplicity and intuitive appeal.

Dani•owicz [4] has introduced a model based on Boolean information retrieval model, a well-known model for its simplicity and intuitive query forming. For given query the system's answer consists of a set of documents. A user profile is created on the basis of queries formed by the user or on the basis of documents marked by the user as relevant. The user profile is used to rank documents according to ascending order of distances from them to the profile.

In order to formulate a more complex and flexible shell in the vector space model, a concept of two focal points is introduced [9], where a user query and a user profile are used at the same time to judge documents. The document score is depended on two variables: the distance from the document to the query and the distance from the document to the user profile.

In all mentioned above approaches, one important thing has not been considered: the non-linear dependence between a query and a user profile, which means the dynamic relation between user stable interests and his (her) temporary information needs, has not been considered.

3   Model of Information Retrieval System

In this section, we present a model of information retrieval system, which is based on conventional vector space model. We show how to introduce a user profile into the system, which affects the retrieval process in the form of a retrieval function. We also propose an algorithm for profiles creation and modification. Some properties of the system are presented and discussed.

3.1   Information Retrieval Based on Vector Space Model

The basic element of classic vector space model is n-dimensional vector space V_n. In a information retrieval system, documents and queries are represented by vectors such that the i-th component of a vector is a real number indicating the weight of i-th index term describing a document or a query. Vectors are usually described by expression $u=(w_{u1},w_{u2},....,w_{un})$ or $u=((u_1,w_{u1}), (u_2,w_{u2}),....., (u_n,w_{un}))$. For each pair $u,v \in V_n$, a distance function $d(u,v)$ or a similarity function $s(u,v)$ should be defined. In addition, in information retrieval system based on vector space model, for given query q and document x, a retrieval function $f(q,x)$ should be established.

The retrieval function in the vector space model is defined on basis of a similarity function or a distance function between vectors [13], [15]. Conventional vector space model then can be presented as a triple $\langle X, Q, d \rangle$, where X is the set of documents, Q – set of queries and d – distance function.

In the purpose to integrate user profiles in retrieval processes, it seems desirable to introduce the extended vector space model, which allows introducing retrieval function $f(q,p,x)$. Assume that function $f(q,p,x)$ belongs to the class of functions:

$$f(q,p,x) = \alpha_1.d(q,x) + \alpha_2.\sqrt[\beta]{(d(q,x))^{\beta_1}.(d(p,x))^{\beta_2}} , \qquad (1)$$

where $\alpha_1 > 0$; α_2, β_1, $\beta_2 \geq 0$; $\beta = \beta_1 + \beta_2$; d is a distance function defined in the classical vector space model. We can present the extended vector space model for information retrieval as a quintuple $\langle X, Q, P, d, f \rangle$, where P is the set of users' profiles and f is the retrieval function.

In this paper, we do not verify proposed retrieval functions, but only present its characteristics. The other aim is introducing a method for user profile creation and modifying.

C. Daniłowicz and H.C. Nguyen

3.2 Retrieval Functions

The mentioned above class of retrieval functions $f(q,p,x)$ can be an interesting subject for further researches on extended vector space models, because each function of this class possesses some characteristic properties expected from an ideal retrieval function, such as:

1. Function f aggregates query and profile, that means, for given a query q and a profile p if two documents x_1 and x_2 have the same retrieval value, i.e. $f(q,p,x_1) = f(q,p,x_2)$, and $d(q,x_1) < d(q,x_2)$ then $d(p,x_1) > d(p,x_2)$. Conversely, if $d(p,x_1) < d(p,x_2)$, then $d(q,x_1) > d(q,x_2)$.
2. For given a query q, a profile p and two documents x_1, x_2, if $d(p,x_2) = d(q,x_1) < d(p,x_1) = d(q,x_2)$, then $f(q,p,x_1) < f(q,p,x_2)$, that is document x_1 is better because it is nearer query q than document x_2, although document x_2 is nearer profile p than x_1. This is an intuitive condition because the query should have larger influence on the retrieval results than the user profile.
3. If profile p is identical to query q, that is $p=q$, then $f(q,p,x) = \gamma.d(q,x)$ where γ is a constant. In this case we should have the classical vector space model for retrieval.
4. In the case when a document x is fully agreeable with a query q, that is $q=x$, then there should be $f = 0$ independently of the profile.

The mentioned above properties of the proposed class of retrieval functions come directly from their definition, therefore we do not present their proofs in this paper.

3.3 User Profiles in Information Retrieval System

In this model, a user profile is created and modified on the basis of explicit feedback, which is a credible information source for a representation of user preferences. A user profile has the same structure as a query or a document in the system and is represented by a vector in the vector space. After the first feedback of a user, his profile is created. After any next feedback, the profile is modified. Because we have assumed that user profile represents user interests, which are relatively stable in time, it seems to be necessary to consider the number of performed modifications before updates of the profile. If we denote by t the current number of profile modifications ($t \in N$), then of course before profile creation, we have $t=0$.

A method for user profile updating was proposed in [4], in which two processes for profile creation and modification were presented separately. In this paper, we synthesize in one integrated process consisting of the following steps:

1. The user sends query q to the information retrieval system.
2. If $t=0$ (user does not have his own profile yet), system ranks documents according to ascending values of distance function $d(q,x_i)$. In other case, while user has his own profile p' already, system ranks documents according to ascending values of function $f(q,p',x_i)$. As a result the order $o' = (x_1', x_2'..., x_n')$ is displayed on the output as the system's answer for query q.
3. On base of the order o' proposed by the system, the user reorders documents according to his own justification gives new order $o'' = (x_1'', x_2''..., x_n'')$ and sends it to the system as the user feedback.

4. The temporary profile p^u is created from ranking o^u on base of the following rule: If we take query q and profile p^u into account in ranking the documents set, we should get in result order o^u. In other words, for any pair of documents x_i^u and x_j^u, if $x_i^u \succ x_j^u$ (i.e. x_i^u precedes x_j^u) in the order o^u where $i<j$, then $f(q, p^u, x_i^u) \le f(q, p^u, x_j^u)$. Generally, profile p^u can be calculated as following:

$$p^u = \frac{\sum_{i=1}^{n} \omega_i . x_i^u}{\sum_{i=1}^{n} \omega_i}, \tag{2}$$

where $\omega_1,...., \omega_n$ – parameters denoting parts of particular documents in profile vector, which are set by system to fulfill the following condition:

$$i>j \implies f(q, p^u, x_i^u) \ge f(q, p^u, x_j^u).$$

We do not present the algorithm for the calculation of $\omega_1,..., \omega_n$ because of the limited size of this paper.

5. Cases of the number t of profile modifications:
   - If $t=0$: Profile is to be created for the first time, let $p^1 = p^u$.
   - If $t \ge 1$: Profile is to be modified for the $(t+1)$ time by the following expression:

$$p^{t+1} = \frac{p^t . t + p^u}{t + 1} \tag{3}$$

According to the presented method, in the feedback process, the user has to reorder whole set of documents, which seems to be impossible in practice. However, in such case, a acceptable ranking strategy can be employed [2],[16]: If a user has no preference of two documents, then he (she) is really not interested in how these documents should be ranked. The user can put a few documents in an order as a feedback portion, then the system should regard that these documents are most interesting for the user and they should be moved to the top of ranking in the reordering process (step 3). All other documents may remain in the same order as the system's recommendation.

Below we present some examples illustrating the method.

Example 1. Suppose that the documents set contains 100 documents $\{x_1, x_2,..., x_{100}\}$. On base of system's order $(x_1, x_2,..., x_{100})$, the user reorders according to his preference $x_4 \succ x_2 \succ x_{90} \succ x_8$. We assume that the following order: $(x_4, x_2, x_{90}, x_8, x_1, x_3, x_5, x_6, x_7, x_9, x_{10},..., x_{89}, x_{91},..., x_{99}, x_{100})$ is an acceptable ranking for this user, which can represent his preferences.

The mechanism for updating the user profile in step 5 is based on linear adding of vectors, which is used in algorithms worked out by Rocchio [3] and other authors [2] for updating retrieval queries.

Example 2. Given three documents represented by the following vectors:
   $x_1=\{0.7;0.5;0.9\}$; $x_2=\{0.9;0.7;0.7\}$; $x_3=\{0.5;0.9;0.5\}$;

Let the retrieval function be the following: $f(q,p,x) = d(q, x) + \sqrt{d(q, x).d(p, x)}$.

Assume that after giving the first query $q^1=\{1.0; 0; 0\}$ a user ranks these items in order (x_1, x_2, x_3), that means the user is asking about the first term, but he (she) is more interested in the third term. The profile then is calculated as $p^1=\{0.700; 0.609; 0.791\}$, which confirms the prediction about user preference.

Suppose that the next query is $q^2=\{0; 0; 1.0\}$, but the user ranks documents in other order (x_2, x_1, x_3), what means his preference has changed to the first term, but he is asking about the third term. After calculation, his modified profile would be $p^2=\{0.780; 0.655; 0.745\}$, which represents his current interests.

The bigger is the number of modification is, the higher is the stability of user preference. Suppose after 8 modifications, the profile is $p^8=\{0.700; 0.609; 0.791\}$, if $q^9=\{0; 0; 1.0\}$ then the modified profile at 9th modification is $p^9=\{0.718; 0.619; 0.780\}$: there is only little change in term weights, while the third term is still the most "important", what indicates that the user is interested in this term for a long time.

Suppose after t where $t\geq1$ modifications, the user profile is p^t, and a query q is given to the system. After studying the system answer o^t, the user corrects it and sends back a new order o^u. On the basis of p^t and o^u, the user profile is modified as p^{t+1}. Now the user does all things once again, that means he gives to the system the same query q, and sets the same order o^u as his feedback, then his profile is modified again as p^{t+2}. It is possible to prove that in the model the following inequality:

$$d(p^{t+2}, p^{t+1}) \leq d(p^{t+1}, p^t) \qquad (4)$$

is always true. This statement shows very important feature of this model, that is user profiles in this model are convergent. The interpretation of this theorem is the following: the more stable the user preference in a topic (represented by a query) is, the more stable the profile is in that topic. This is an important property of user profile, which is a necessary condition for correct representation of user preferences [10].

4   Conclusions

The model we have presented in this paper satisfies postulates for intelligent information retrieval system, which were formulated in Introduction. In particular, a user should be satisfied with search results without necessity of understanding search methods, document indexing or query modification rules etc., which are usually elements of knowledge of an expert in information retrieval domain. The effectiveness of the system is due to introducing users' profiles and exploring the retrieval functions, which aggregate in one formula the distance between queries and documents with the distance between profiles and documents. The future works should concern verification of retrieval functions and profile modifying methods in terms of maximizing the retrieval effectiveness.

References

1.   Chen L., Sycara K.: Webmate - Personal Agent for Browsing and Searching. In: Proceedings of the Second International Conference on Autonomous Agents, St. Paul, MN, May, ACM Press, New York (1998) 132-139.

2.   Chen Z.: Multiplicative adaptive algorithms for user preference retrieval. In Proceedings of the Seventh Annual International Computing and Combinatorics Conference, Springer-Verlag (2001).
3.   Chen Z., Zhu B.: Some Formal Analysis of Rocchio's Similarity-Based Relevance Feedback Algorithm. Lecture Notes in Computer Science **1969** (2000) 108-119.
4.   Daniłowicz C.: Modeling of User Preferences and Needs in Boolean Retrieval Systems. Information Processing & Management, **30** (1994) 363-378.
5.   Daniłowicz C.: Models of Information Retrieval Systems with Special Regard to Users' Preferences. Scientific Papers of the Main Library and Scientific Information Center of the Wrocław University of Technology No.6, Monographs No.3, Wrocław (1992).
6.   Daniłowicz C., Nguyen H.C.: User Profile in Information retrieval Systems. In: Proceedings of the 23rd International Scientific School ISAT 2001, PWr Press (2001) 117-124.
7.   Kok A.J., Botman A.M.: Retrieval Based on User Behavior. In: Proceedings of the 11th ACM Annual International Conference SIGIR, France (1988) 343-357.
8.   McElligot M., Sorensen H.: An Evolutionary Connectionist Approach to Personal Information Filtering. In: Proceeding of the Fourth Irish Neural Network Conference, Dublin, Ireland (1994) 141-146.
9.   Myaeng S.H., Korfhage R.R.: Integration of User Profiles: Models and Experiments in Information Retrieval. Information Processing & Management **26** (1990) 719-738.
10. Nguyen H.C.: Model of Fuzzy Information Retrieval System Using User Profile. In: Proceedings of the First MISSI National Conference, Wrocław University of Technology, 1998, PWr Press (1998) 179-187.
11. Nguyen N.T.: Using Consensus Methods for Solving Conflicts of Data in Distributed Systems. Lecture Notes in Artificial Intelligence **1963** (2000) 409-417.
12. Stadnyk I., Kass R.: Modeling Users' Interests in Information Filters. Communications of the ACM **35** (1992) 49-50.
13. Wang Z.W., Wong S.K.M., Yao Y.Y.: An Analysis of Vector Space Models Based on Computational Geometry. In: Proceedings of the 15th ACM Annual International Conference SIGIR, Denmark (1992) 152-160.
14. Widyantoro D.H.: Dynamic Modeling and Learning User Profile in Personal News Agent. Master Thesis, Dept. of Computer Science, Texas A&M University (1999).
15. Wong S.K.M., Ziarko W.: On Modeling of Information Retrieval Concepts in Vector Spaces. ACM Transactions on Database Systems, **12** (1987) 299-321.
16. Wong S.K.M., Yao Y.Y., Bollmann P. Linear structures in information retrieval. In Proceedings of the 1988 ACM-SIGIR Conference on Information Retrieval (1988) 219-232.
17. Young W.S., Byoung T.Z.: A Reinforcement Learning Agent for Personalized Information Filtering. In: Proceedings of the 2000 ACM International Conference on Intelligent User Interfaces (2000) 248-251.

Partition-Refining Algorithms for Learning Finite State Automata

Tapio Elomaa

Department of Computer Science, P. O. Box 26 (Teollisuuskatu 23)
FIN-00014 University of Helsinki, Finland, `elomaa@cs.helsinki.fi`

Abstract. Regular language learning from positive examples alone is infeasible. Subclasses of regular languages, though, can be inferred from positive examples only. The most common approach for learning such is the specific-to-general technique of merging together either states of an initial finite state automaton or nonterminals in a regular grammar until convergence.

In this paper we seek to unify some language learning approaches under the general-to-specific learning scheme. In automata terms it is implemented by refining the partition of the states of the automaton starting from one block until desired decomposition is obtained; i.e., until all blocks in the partition are uniform according to the predicate determining the properties required from the language.

We develop a series of learning algorithms for well-known classes of regular languages as instantiations of the same master algorithm. Through block decomposition we are able to describe in the same scheme, e.g., the learning by rote approach of minimizing the number of states in the automaton and inference of k-reversible languages.

Under the worst-case analysis partition-refinement is less efficient than alternative approaches. However, for many cases it turns out more efficient in practice. Moreover, it ensures the inference of the canonical automaton, whereas the state-merging approach will leave excessive states to the final automaton without a separate minimization step.

1 Introduction

The main representation formalisms for formal languages are grammars and automata. These formalisms have their well-known connections, which will not be surveyed here. Throughout this paper we assume familiarity with automata and formal languages as given, e.g., in [7]. The class of *regular languages* consists of those formal languages that can be recognized with finite state automata, FSA. Even inference of this most basic class of languages from positive data only is infeasible [5]. It has also been shown that the equivalent problem of learning FSA cannot be approximated efficiently within any polynomial [17]. There are, though, subclasses of regular languages that are learnable. One of the best-known such a subclass are the *k-reversible languages* [2].

Despite the discouraging negative results on learning regular languages from positive data only, the quest to find subclasses of regular languages that are

M.-S. Hacid et al. (Eds.): ISMIS 2002, LNAI 2366, pp. 232–243, 2002.
© Springer-Verlag Berlin Heidelberg 2002

learnable still continues [9,11,12,13,18]. One of the main inspirations for this study is linguistic: the man's ability to acquire language skills from mainly positive data [4,16]. Also inferring regular grammars for expressing the structure of, e.g., SGML documents has received some attention [1].

Those learning algorithms for formal languages which use the automaton representation typically transform the given set of positive examples into a straightforward acceptor for recognizing these strings only. In order to generalize the given examples this initial automaton has to be modified somehow. Most common approach is to take the trivial partition of the states of this automaton — each state as its own partition block — as the starting point and then by some criterion merge together blocks that contain similar states [2,3,8,10,14,15]. Muggleton [15] reviews state-merging algorithms for learning regular languages. A review of algorithms operating on the merging approach, but representing the hypothesis as a grammar is given by Mäkinen [11]. In grammar representation nonterminals rather than states are merged together.

The state-merging approach of generalizing the information contained in the initial automaton corresponds as learning strategy to *generalization*. In this paper we explore the possibilities to learn subclasses of regular languages by the *specialization* approach. We start from the initial automaton as usual, but rather than have all of its states form their own partition blocks, we start with all states in one block. Hence, our approach is iterative refinement of states into equivalence classes. Probably the best-known partition-refining algorithm is the state minimization algorithm for deterministic finite automata [7].

The rest of this paper is organized as follows. Section 2 describes the master algorithm for partition refinement. Subsequent learning algorithms are instantiations of this method. In Section 3 we recapitulate the well-known state minimization algorithm for deterministic finite automata [7]. It can be seen to be the space-efficient learning by rote algorithm. k-tail heuristic [3], which is a straightforward generalization of the state minimization algorithm, is considered in Section 4. Zero- and k-reversible languages [2] are considered separately in Section 5. Finally, Section 6 presents the concluding remarks of this study.

2   The Master Algorithm

The following sections present — as instantiations of the same partition-refining scheme — different algorithms that, given a set of positive examples, construct an automaton. Let us now present the master algorithm and its subprograms that are varied in different instantiations of the method. All following algorithms first convert the given sample into an automaton.

2.1   Prefix-Tree Acceptor

From a given sample of positive examples we, in the first phase, construct a *prefix-tree acceptor* (PTA), in which there is a unique path from the unique initial state to an accepting state for each separate example of the sample. The

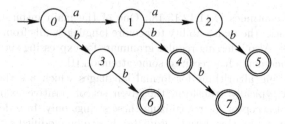

Fig. 1. The prefix-tree acceptor $PT(S^+)$ for the positive sample $S^+ = \{ab, bb, aab, abb\}$.

paths, however, may overlap. We will not elaborate on the straightforward linear-time algorithm for constructing a PTA given a positive sample. The following example illustrates the construction of the PTA.

Example 1. Let us consider the sample $S^+ = \{ab, bb, aab, abb\}$ [15]. The prefix-tree acceptor $PT(S^+)$, with a path to a unique final state for each word in S^+, for this sample is shown in Fig. 1. The size of the PTA, obviously, is linear in the total combined length of the examples.

Thus, a sample is directly transformed into an automaton. However, the PTA is not necessarily the smallest automaton accepting exactly those strings that are part of the positive sample. Next, we present the master algorithm.

2.2   Block Decomposition

In generalizing the information contained in the PTA, there are two directions to proceed to: either start with the trivial partition of its states, in which each state makes up a block on its own, and merge similar states into blocks or start with all the states in one block and refine the partition by dividing blocks (into two) until no more blocks need to be divided. As learning strategy the former corresponds to generalization and the latter to specialization.

The master algorithm for block decomposition is shown in Table 1. As input the algorithm receives a positive sample S^+. The first step is the construction of the initial automaton A_0, which is equal to the prefix-tree acceptor $PT(S^+)$. A *partition* of this automaton's states is searched for. A partition of the states is their mutually exclusive division into blocks. The minimum number of blocks in the partition is one, and the maximum number is that of the states. A block of states has all the transitions of its component states. As our search strategy is partition refinement, the first partition candidate, in principle, consists of a single block containing all the states of the PTA. However, since many algorithms are easier to express starting from, say, two blocks, we choose the initial partition with the function `initialize`. This function will be specified separately for each of the subsequent algorithms.

Table 1. The master algorithm for block-decomposition.

```
Automaton refineBlocks( Sample S⁺ )
{
    int i = 0;
    Automaton A₀ = (Q₀,Σ,δ₀,q₀,F₀) = PT(S⁺);
    Partition Π₀ = initialize( A₀ );
    int threshold = set( A₀ );
    while ( i < threshold )
        if ∃B ∈ Πᵢ : χ(B,i) { Πᵢ₊₁ = Πᵢ \ B ∪ Divide(B); i++; }
    return A₀/Πᵢ;
}
```

Each of the following algorithms has its own criterion for refining a given partition. Refinement predicate $\chi(\mathtt{B}, \mathtt{i})$ computes the criterion for block $\mathtt{B}$ with respect to the partition Π_i. We specify this predicate separately for all the subsequent algorithms.

Some of the algorithms require an explicit stopping condition for the processing of the automaton. Therefore, integer variable `threshold` is initialized using subprogram `set`, which is allowed to inspect the PTA in deciding the return value. The main functioning of the master algorithm consists of refining the partition of the states as long as the threshold has not been reached and as long as a block of states can be found for which the refinement predicate χ is true.

Finally, the initial automaton A_0 partitioned by Π_i is returned.

3   Minimum State Automaton

State minimization algorithm is the learning by rote method for inferring a finite language from the given finite sample. I.e., nothing is really learned in the sense that no generalization happens. Nevertheless, exactly those strings that have been seen are remembered. Furthermore, this happens space-efficiently; i.e., the returned automaton has the smallest possible number of states.

The theoretical basis of the algorithm is the *k-equivalence* of states. Two states p and q are *k-equivalent*, denoted by $p \overset{k}{\equiv} q$, if for all strings $w \in \Sigma^*$, $|w| \leq k$, $\delta^*(p, w) \in F \Leftrightarrow \delta^*(q, w) \in F$, where δ^* denotes the closure of the transition function δ. In other words, two states are *k-equal*, if starting from these states exactly the same strings of length at most k are accepted. If, for all k, p and q are *k-equivalent*, then they are *equivalent*; $p \equiv q$. If two states p and q are not *k-equivalent*, then they are *k-distinguishable*, denoted by $p \overset{k}{\not\equiv} q$.

Example 2. In any given automaton, the final states make up one 0-equivalence class and the non-final states another, since all final states accept the empty word λ of length 0 and the other states reject it. In the PTA of Fig. 1 the non-final states 2 and 3 are 1-equivalent, since starting from both of them only the

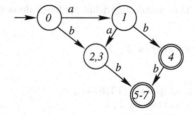

Fig. 2. Minimum state automaton for $S^+ = \{\, ab, bb, aab, abb \,\}$.

string b is accepted. However, for instance the final state 4 is not 1-equivalent with these states, because in addition to string b the empty word is accepted starting from this state. Observe that in general it is true that a final and a non-final state cannot be k-equivalent for any k. The minimum state automaton corresponding to the PTA of Fig. 1 is shown in Fig. 2. The original eight states have reduced to five.

The minimum state automaton for a given sample S is unique up to isomorphism (i.e., a renaming of the states) [7]. Its states correspond to the equivalence classes of the states of the given automaton. Hence, to utilize method `refineBlocks` in automaton minimization, we set $\chi(B) = \{\, \exists p, q \in B : p \not\equiv q \,\}$. The computation of this predicate is infeasible. We use inductive definition of distinguishability instead:

$$p \not\equiv q \Leftrightarrow \exists k \in \mathbb{N} : p \overset{k}{\not\equiv} q.$$

Blocks can be utilized in computing k-distinguishability by checking at each stage 1-distinguishability with respect to the current partition:

$$\chi(B, i) = \{\, \exists p, q \in B : p \overset{1}{\not\equiv}_{\Pi_i} q \,\}.$$

This predicate manifests itself as having block B nondeterministic with respect to the current partition Π_i. I.e.,

$$\chi(B, i) = \{\, \exists p, q \in B, \sigma \in \Sigma : \delta_i(p, \sigma) \neq \delta_i(q, \sigma) \,\}.$$

Observe also that two states can be distinguished from each other only as long as they are in one block. Hence, the number of partition-refining iterations has the upper bound of the number of states in the initial PTA. Thus, we can set the threshold value as the number of states in the initial PTA, even though it is not required in the algorithm.

```
int set ( Automaton A ) { return |A|; }
```

The minimum state automaton algorithm starts from the initial binary partitioning of the states in which the final and non-final states of the PTA make up their own blocks.

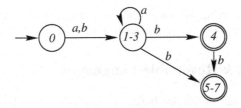

Fig. 3. 1-tail automaton for $S^+ = \{\, ab, bb, aab, abb \,\}$.

```
Partition initialize ( Automaton A₀ = (Q₀, Σ, δ₀, q₀, F₀) )
{ return ⟨F₀, Q₀ \ F₀⟩; }
```

This initial partitioning corresponds to the 0-equivalence of the states: starting from a non-final state using 0 transitions, no string can be accepted, while starting from a final states all strings are accepted, if no transitions are traversed.

The state minimization algorithm operates as long as there are blocks that need to be refined. Because each refinement bisects one block, the maximum number of required iterations is the number of original states in the PTA. Hence, the worst-case time requirement of this algorithm is quadratic in the combined length of the input examples. The most efficient algorithm for minimizing a deterministic finite automaton takes $O(n \log n)$ time [6].

4 k-Tail Heuristic

A natural way to relax the conditions of state equivalence of state minimization algorithm is to require that the states belonging to the same block are k-equivalent only up to some k, instead of being k-equivalent for all k. Thus, we equalize any two states that have an equal "k-tail." This heuristic for learning automata from positive examples was proposed by Bierman and Feldman [3]. Variations to this algorithm are presented by Itoga [8].

Algorithmically there is nothing new in this heuristic, because it is only a simple restriction of the state minimization algorithm. We just set the threshold value as k, instead of letting the algorithm iterate until all possibilities have been checked.

```
int set ( Automaton A ) { return k; }
```

Example 3. Fig. 3 shows the application of this heuristic to our running example with threshold value $k = 1$. The block corresponding to states 1, 2, and 3 in the original PTA has not been refined, since these states have equal 1-tails. Final states are decomposed into two blocks, because the 1-tail of state 4 is $\{\, \lambda, b \,\}$ and the other final states only have the empty string as their 1-tail.

The language accepted by the nondeterministic automaton in Fig. 3 is $(a \mid b)$ $a^*(b \mid bb)$, which includes, e.g., the string $babb$ that would not intuitively seem to belong to the underlying language. Two-tail heuristic for this particular sample would yield the minimum state automaton illustrated in Fig. 2.

5 Zero- and k-Reversible Languages

A well-known family of regular languages learnable from positive data is Angluin's [2] family of k-reversible languages. We review, first, zero-reversible languages separately and then consider the general case.

As shown above, k-tail automata can be nondeterministic. The automata accepting reversible languages are deterministic.

5.1 Zero-Reversible Languages and Automata

To define zero-reversible regular languages, the following basic definitions are needed. The set $\Pr(L)$ of *prefixes* of strings belonging to language L is defined as

$$\Pr(L) = \{\, u \mid uv \in L \text{ for some } v \in \Sigma^* \,\}.$$

The *left-quotient* of L with respect to string w is

$$T_L(w) = \{\, v \mid wv \in L \,\}.$$

The left-quotient of L w.r.t. w is nonempty if and only if w is a prefix of L; i.e., $T_L(w) \neq \emptyset \Leftrightarrow w \in \Pr(L)$. Regular language L is *zero-reversible* if and only if whenever $u_1 v, u_2 v \in L$, $T_L(u_1) = T_L(u_2)$.

The *reverse* of an automaton $A = (Q, \Sigma, \delta, I, F)$ is $A^r = (Q, \Sigma, \delta^r, F, I)$, where δ^r is the reverse of the transition function δ; $\delta^r(q, a) = \{\, q' \mid q \in \delta(q', a) \,\}$ for all $a \in \Sigma$ and $q \in Q$. In other words, in the reverse of an automaton the roles of initial and final states have been interchanged and the directions of the transitions have been reversed. Now, the automaton A is *zero-reversible* if and only if both itself and its reverse are deterministic.

A zero-reversible automaton is a deterministic FSA with at most one final state and such that no two vertices entering a state are labeled with the same symbol. Angluin's [2] algorithm ZR, given a positive sample S^+, constructs a PTA for the sample and merges the states of the automaton as long as the automaton violates zero-reversibility. Observe that the single-state automaton accepting the whole of Σ^* is always zero-reversible and at least it can be finally output. The language accepted by the automaton output by ZR is the smallest zero-reversible language containing S^+. In ZR two blocks of states B_1 and B_2 are merged if:

1. They have a common σ-predecessor block B_3, $\sigma \in \Sigma$; i.e., if there is a nondeterministic block B_3 in the current partition.
2. They have a common σ-follower block B_3, $\sigma \in \Sigma$; i.e., if B_3 is a nondeterministic block in the reverse of the automaton.
3. If they both contain final states.

Fig. 4. Zero-reversible automaton for $S^+ = \{\, ab, bb, aab, abb \,\}$.

In refining a partition one has to pay extra attention, because once a new block has been formed, it cannot be merged together with any other block. Let us first consider the initial refinement performed on the block containing all states of the $PT(S^+)$. By the definition of zero-reversibility all final states will belong to the same block. If there are no transitions between the final states, then no other state can end up in the same block with the final states. In this case, the initial partition will be $\langle F_0, Q_0 \setminus F_0 \rangle$, where Q_0 and F_0 are the states and final states of $PT(S^+)$, respectively. Otherwise—i.e., if there is a transition $\delta(p, \sigma) = q$ between two final states p and q—all other states r having transition $\delta(r, \sigma) = q$, where q is a final state, need to be maintained in the same block with the final states. Iteratively, all states having a σ-transition to a state, which is associated to the same block with the final states, are also taken to the same block. The computation of the initial partition can be done as follows.

```
Partition initialize( Automaton A₀ )
{
    Set B = F₀;
    if ( ∃σ ∈ Σ, p,q ∈ F₀ : δ₀(p,σ) == q )
    {
        while ( ∃q ∈ B, r ∉ B : δ₀(r,σ) == q ) B = B ∪ {r};
        if ( Q₀ \ B ≠ ∅ ) return ⟨B, Q₀ \ B⟩;
    }
    else return ⟨Q₀⟩;
}
```

The initial partition will consist of two blocks if there exists a non-final state such that it does not have a σ-transition leading any state that is associated with the final states, where $\sigma \in \Sigma$ is the label of a transition from one final state to another. Otherwise, a single block partition—which cannot be refined anymore—is returned.

Example 4. In case of our running example all states of the $PT(S^+)$ get gathered into the same set B: Initially all final states (numbers 4, 5, 6, and 7 in the PTA of Fig. 1) are assigned to the set B. There is a transition from state 4 to 7 with the alphabet b. Thus, also states 1, 2, and 3—which have a b-transition to one of the final states—get assigned to B. Finally, state 0 has a b-transition to state 3, which now belongs to B, also gets assigned to B. Hence, the automaton output by **initialize** is the one depicted in Fig. 4, which accepts the universal language $(a \mid b)^*$. Obviously this is not the intuitively correct language inferrable from S^+.

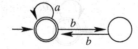

Fig. 5. Zero-reversible automaton for $S^+ = \{\, a, aa, bb, bbaa \,\}$.

After obtaining the initial partition for the states of the PTA, the block containing the final states is not refined anymore. Let us call it a *fixed* block. If there is another block, it may have to be refined further. The refinement predicate χ for zero-reversible languages is as follows. Make a separate block out of those states that have a σ-transition to a fixed block.

$$\chi(B, i) = \{\, \exists p, q \in B : \delta_i(p, \sigma) = C \neq \delta_i(q, \sigma), \; C \in \Pi_i \text{ is fixed} \,\}.$$

The following example shows a sample for which a non-trivial partition is produced by `initialize`.

Example 5. Given the sample $\{\, a, aa, bb, bbaa \,\}$ as input `initialize` gathers all the states of the PTA with an a-transition to the set B, leaving states with only b-transitions out of this set. This initial partition, which is shown in Fig. 5 is also the final partition of the states because both states with b-transitions have their only transition into the same fixed block. The language accepted by this automaton is $(a^*(bb)^*)^*$.

Zero-reversible languages can be identified in nearly linear time using the state merging strategy [2]. Mäkinen [12] has shown that strictly linear time suffices in the grammar formulation. However, the size of the efficiently inferred grammar is larger than the size of the automaton generated by Angluin's algorithm. In fact, in the worst case Mäkinen's approach produces the equivalent of the PTA as its answer.

As shown in the previous examples, the partition refining approach to learning zero-reversible automata can be more efficient than the state-merging approach for some samples. However, in the worst-case the above approach loses efficiency, because it can require a quadratic time.

5.2 k-Reversible Languages and Automata

Let $A = (Q, \Sigma, \delta, I, F)$ be an automaton. The string u is said to be a k-*follower* of the state q in A if and only if $|u| = k$ and $\delta^*(q, u) \neq \emptyset$. The automaton A is *deterministic with lookahead* k if and only if for any pair of distinct states q_1 and q_2, if $q_1, q_2 \in I$ or $q_1, q_2 \in \delta(q_3, \sigma)$ for some $q_3 \in Q$ and $\sigma \in \Sigma$, then there is no string that is a k-follower of both q_1 and q_2. An automaton is k-*reversible* if and only if it is deterministic and its reverse is deterministic with lookahead k.

In terms of the formal languages a regular language L is k-reversible if and only if whenever $u_1 vw, u_2 vw \in L$ and $|v| = k$, $T_L(u_1 v) = T_L(u_2 v)$.

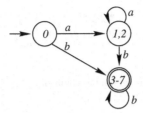

Fig. 6. One-reversible automaton for $S^+ = \{\, ab, bb, aab, abb \,\}$.

Angluin's [2] general inference algorithm for k-reversible languages, k-RI, starts from the trivial partition of the PTA for the given sample and merges together any two blocks that violate the definition of k-reversibility. The possible violations are (i) the automaton itself is not deterministic or (ii) the reverse of the automaton is not deterministic with lookahead k. In case of violation (i) there must exist a block B_3 such that two distinct blocks B_1 and B_2 are its σ-followers for some $\sigma \in \Sigma$. To rectify this violation, blocks B_1 and B_2 are merged together. Violation (ii) is caused when, in the automaton itself, there are two blocks B_1 and B_2 which have a common k-leader and either they both are final states or both blocks have block B_3 as their σ-follower for some $\sigma \in \Sigma$. Again, this is handled by merging blocks B_1 and B_2 together.

Let A_k be the automaton output by k-RI given a nonempty positive sample S^+. The language accepted by A_k, $L(A_k)$, is the smallest k-reversible language containing S^+. Let A_i be the automaton obtained using i-RI for S^+ and, A_j obtained using j-RI, $i < j$, then $L(A_j) \subseteq L(A_i)$.

In this general case Angluin's [2] state-merging algorithm requires $O(kn^3)$ time. Muggleton [15] has improved the time requirement to $O(kn^2)$.

Example 6. Fig. 6 shows the automaton produced by Angluin's state-merging algorithm with $k = 1$ before minimization. The language accepted is a^*b^+, which intuitively seems a reasonable inference for the underlying language.

The automaton of Fig. 6 is not minimal. Applying the minimization algorithm to this automaton gives the result shown in Fig. 7. Next we consider the partition-refining algorithm, which produces the minimal automaton directly. In the following we only review one-reversible languages for clarity.

The computation of the initial partition is done by a generalization of the **initialize** subroutine of zero-reversible languages. We iteratively grow a set B like in case of zero-reversible languages. However, this time we cannot initiate this set to contain all final states, but have to start with those final states that have a common k-leader. (Keep in mind that in the PTA a final state can only have one k-leader). Thus, in fact up to $|\Sigma| + 1$ blocks may be constructed by **initialize**. To keep the method clear, we describe this algorithm verbally rather than in pseudo code.

242   T. Elomaa

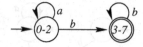

Fig. 7. Minimal one-reversible automaton for $S^+ = \{\,ab, bb, aab, abb\,\}$.

1. **while** (there exists a final state q that is not in a fixed block)
   a) Let $\sigma \in \Sigma$ be the 1-leader of q.
   b) Let B consist of q and all other final states that have σ as their 1-leader.
   c) If there is no transition $\delta(p, \rho) = q$ between any states p and q belonging to B, then B can be marked fixed. Otherwise the set B may still grow.
   d) Iteratively add all the states $r \notin B$ such that $\exists s \in Q$ such that $\delta(s, \sigma) = r$ and $\delta(r, \rho) = q \in B$ to the set B as well. When B stops growing, mark it a fixed block.
2. The states that do not belong to any of the fixed blocks are all non-final states. They are gathered to the same block, which is subject to further refinement.

The general k-reversible method requires inspecting k-leaders of states rather than 1-leaders. Otherwise there is no change to the procedure above.

To partition non-fixed blocks we use a generalization of the predicate χ used in case of zero-reversible languages. A block has to be refined, if it contains two states with an equal 1-leader such that they have different followers with respect to the current partition.

$$\chi(\mathtt{B}, \mathtt{i}) = \{\ \exists p, q, r, s \in B, \rho, \sigma \in \Sigma : \delta_i(s, \rho) = p,\ \delta_i(r, \rho) = q,$$
$$\delta_i(p, \sigma) = C \neq \delta_i(q, \sigma),\ C \in \Pi_i \text{ is fixed}\,\}.$$

Using the implementation techniques of Angluin [2], the partition-refining approach to learning k-reversible languages can be implemented as efficiently as the state-merging approach.

Example 7. Fig. 7 shows the automaton produced by the partition-refining algorithm for our running example with $k = 1$. Observe that the initial state stays in the same block with states 1 and 2. This is the minimum automaton for the language a^*b^+.

6   Conclusion

Instead of using the common state-merging approach to finite state automaton learning, it is possible to unify many diverse language learning algorithms under the general-to-specific learning strategy by taking them to be instantiations of the same partition-refining algorithm. The partition refinement does not always yield the most efficient algorithms. However, using this approach we avoid executing a separate minimization step after the induction phase.

As future work on the partition-refining approach to learning regular languages we submit to extend the approach to other subclasses of regular languages than those that were studied here. It would be interesting to extensively explore the uses of *suffix-tree automata* in this style of inference. Mäkinen [12] has applied them in connection of grammar representation of zero-reversible languages.

References

1. Ahonen, H., Mannila, H., Nikunen, E.: Forming grammars for structured documents: An application of grammatical inference. In: Carrasco, R., Oncina, J. (eds.): *Proc. Second International Colloquium on Grammatical Inference and Applications.* Lecture Notes in Computer Science **862**. Springer-Verlag, (1994) 153–167
2. Angluin, D.: Inference of reversible languages. *J. ACM* **29** (1982) 741–765
3. Bierman, A.W., Feldman, J.A. On the synthesis of finite-state machines from samples of their behavior. *IEEE Trans. Comput.* **21** (1972) 592–597
4. Firoiu, L., Oates, T., Cohen, P.R.: Learning regular languages from positive evidence. In: *Proc. Twentieth Annual Meeting of the Cognitive Science Society.* (1998) 350–355
5. Gold, E.M.: Language identification in the limit. *Inf. Control* **37** (1967) 302–320
6. Hopcroft, J.E.: An $n \log n$ algorithm for minimizing the states in a finite automaton. In: Kohavi, Z. (ed.): *The Theory of Machines and Computations.* Academic Press, New York (1971) 189–196
7. Hopcroft, J.E., Motwani, R., and Ullman, J.D.: *Introduction to Automata Theory, Languages, and Computation.* 2nd Ed. Addison-Wesley, Reading, MA: (2001)
8. Itoga, S.Y.: A new heuristic for inferring regular grammars. *IEEE Trans. Pattern Anal. Mach. Intell.* **3** (1981) 191–197
9. Koshiba, T., Mäkinen, E., Takada, Y.: Learning deterministic even linear languages from positive examples. *Theor. Comput. Sci.* **185** (1997) 63–79
10. Levine, B.: The use of tree derivatives and a sample support parameter for inferring tree systems. *IEEE Trans. Pattern Anal. Mach. Intell.* **4** (1982) 25–34
11. Mäkinen, E.: Inferring regular languages by merging nonterminals. *Int. J. Comput. Math.* **70** (1999) 601–616
12. Mäkinen, E.: On inferring zero-reversible languages. *Acta Cybernetica* **14** (2000) 479–484
13. Mäkinen, E.: On inferring linear single-tree languages. *Inf. Process. Lett.* **73** (2000) 1–3
14. Miclet, L.: Regular inference with a tail clustering method. *IEEE Trans. Syst. Man Cybern.* **10** (1980) 737–743
15. Muggleton, S.: *Inductive Acquisition of Expert Knowledge.* Addison-Wesley, Wokingham, UK (1990)
16. Muggleton, S.: Learning from positive data. *Mach. Learn.*, to appear
17. Pitt, L., Warmuth, M.K.: The minimum consistent DFA problem cannot be approximated within any polynomial. In: *Proceedings of the Twenty First Annual ACM Symposium on Theory of Computing.* New York: ACM Press (1989) 421–432.
18. Sakakibara, Y.: Recent advances of grammatical inference. *Theor. Comput. Sci.* **185** (1997) 15–45

Computing Full and Iceberg Datacubes Using Partitions

(Extented Abstract)

Marc Laporte[1], Noël Novelli[2], Rosine Cicchetti[1,3], and Lotfi Lakhal[1,3]

[1] IUT d'Aix-en-Provence - Département Informatique
Avenue Gaston Berger, F-13625 Aix-en-Provence, Cedex 1, France
`laporte@romarin.univ-aix.fr`

[2] LaBRI, CNRS UMR 5800 - Université de Bordeaux 1, Bât A30
351 Cours de la Libération, F-33405 Talence Cedex, France
`novelli@labri.fr`

[3] LIF Marseille, CNRS FRE-2504 - Université de la Méditerranée, Case 901
163 Avenue de Luminy, F-13288 Marseille Cedex 9, France
`{cicchetti,lakhal}@lif.univ-mrs.fr`

Abstract. In this paper, we propose a sound approach and an algorithm[1] for computing a condensed representation of either full or iceberg datacubes. A novel characterization of datacubes based on dimensional-measurable partitions is introduced. From such partitions, iceberg cuboids are achieved by using constrained product linearly in the number of tuples. Moreover, our datacube characterization provides a loss-less condensed representation specially suitable when considering the storage explosion problem and the I/O cost. We show that our algorithm CCUBE turns out to an operational solution more efficient than competive proposals. It enforces a lecticwise and recursive traverse of the dimension set lattice and takes into account the critical problem of memory limitation. Our experimental results shows that CCUBE is a promising candidate for scalable computation.

1 Motivation

Answering efficiently OLAP queries requires to pre-compute their results, i.e. datacubes [8], and to store them. Computing datacubes is specially costly in execution time [1,15,3] and preserving them is memory consuming because of the disk explosion problem [11].

Althrough intrinsically related, the two issues have been addressed separately. On one hand, various algorithms have been defined to compute datacubes more and more efficiently [1,15]. On the other hand, approaches have been proposed

---

[1] This work is partially supported by the AS CNRS-STIC "Data Mining"

M.-S. Hacid et al. (Eds.): ISMIS 2002, LNAI 2366, pp. 244–254, 2002.
© Springer-Verlag Berlin Heidelberg 2002

to minimize storage requirements. They are based on physical techniques [17], choice of results to be materialized [11], or approximation model [2].

Recently the algorithm BUC was introduced [3]. It addresses the twofold issue of computing and storing cubes by taking into consideration the relevance of results. BUC aims to compute iceberg datacubes which are similar to "multi-feature cubes" proposed in [16]. When computing such cubes, aggregates not satisfying a selection condition specified by user (similar to the clause Having in SQL) are discarded. Let us notice that the algorithm H-Cubing is intended for computing iceberg cubes by enforcing more complex measures [10]. Motivations behind computing iceberg cubes are the following. Firstly, iceberg cubes provide users only with relevant results because scarce or exceptional dimensional combinations of values are discarded. Computation performances can be improved since the lattice to be explored can be pruned (using the selection condition) [3], and storage requirement is decreased. Precomputed iceberg cubes also offer an efficient solution for answering iceberg queries [5]. Another important issue, when computing iceberg cubes, concerns OLAP mining, i.e. the discovery of multidimensional association rules [9], classification rules [13], or multidimensional constrained gradients [4].

In this paper, we propose an approach for achieving full or iceberg datacubes. The originality of our proposal is that it aims to compute a loss-less condensed representation of datacubes which is specially less voluminous than the classical representation of the datacube.

The main contributions of our approach are the following. Firstly, we introduce a novel and sound characterization of datacubes based on the concept of dimensional-measurable partitions, inspired from the partition model [18]. From a dimensional-measurable partition, according to a set of dimensional attributes, computation of the associated cuboid is simple. A cuboid results from a single group-by query according to a certain set of dimensions [9]. This new concept is attractive because dealing with dimensional-measurable partitions means operating linearly set intersections (and thus the use of sorting or hash-based methods is avoided). Secondly, our characterization provides a condensed representation of datacubes in order to minimize disk storage and I/O cost. The third contribution provides a new principle, dictated by the critical problem of main memory limitation, for navigating through the dimensional lattice. It is called lecticwise and recursive traverse of the dimensional lattice, offers a sound basis for our computing strategy, and applies for computing full or iceberg datacubes. Finally, the described ideas are enforced through a new operational algorithm, called Ccube. Ccube has been experimented by using various benchmarks. Our experiments show that Ccube is more efficient than BUC.

The rest of the paper is organized as follows. In section 2, we introduce the novel concepts of our approach and characterize datacubes. Section 3 is devoted to our algorithmic solution and Section 4 to experiments. Finally, we discuss the strengths of our approach and evoke further research work.

2   Condensed Representation of Iceberg Datacubes

In this section, we introduce a novel characterization of datacubes which is based on simple concepts. It offers a condensed representation which can be seen as a logical and loss-less proposal for minimizing the storage explosion.

First of all, we assume that the relation r to be aggregated is defined over a schema R encompassing, apart from the tuple identifier, two kinds of attributes: (i) a set Dim of dimensions which are the criteria for further analysis, and (ii) a measurable attribute M standing for the measure being analyzed[2]. We also make use of the following notations: X stands for a set of dimensions $\{A_1, A_2 \ldots\}$, $X \subseteq Dim$. We assume that an anti-monotonic constraint w.r.t. inclusion $Cond$ is given by the user as well as an additive aggregative function f (e.g. $count$, sum ...).

Inspired from the concept of partition defined in [18], we introduce the concept of Dimensional-Measurable partition according to a set of dimensions.

Definition 1 Dimensional-Measurable Classes
Let r be a relation over the schema $R = (RowId, Dim, M)$, and $X \subseteq Dim$. The Dimensional-Measurable equivalence class of a tuple $t \in r$ according to X is denoted by $[t]_X$, and defined as follows:
$[t]_X = \{ (u[RowId], u[M]) \ / \ u \in r, \ u[X] = t[X] \}.$

Example 1 Let us consider the classical example of studying the sales of a company according to various criteria such as the sold product (Product), the store (Store) and the year (Year). The measure being studied according to the previous criteria is the total amount of sales (Total). An instance of our relation example is illustrated in figure 1.

The DM-equivalence class of the tuple t_1, i.e. having RowId = 1, according to the dimension Product, groups all the tuples (their identifier and measurable value) concerning the product 100:
$[t_1]_{Product} = \{ (1, 70) \ (2, 85) \ (3, 105) \ (4, 120) \ (5, 55) \ (6, 60) \}. \ \square$

A Dimensional-Measurable partition (or DM-partition) of a relation, according to a set of dimensions, is the collection of DM-equivalence classes obtained for the tuples of r and satisfying the anti-monotonic constraint.

Definition 2 DM-Partition
Let r be a relation over the schema R, X a set of dimensions, $X \subseteq Dim$ and $Cond$ an anti-monotonic constraint. The DM-partition of r according to X is denoted by $\Pi_X(r)$, and defined as follows: $\Pi_X(r) = \{ [t]_X \models Cond \ / \ t \in r \}.$

Example 2 Let us resume our relation example given in figure 1. We assume that the condition is: $Sum(Total) > 220$. The DM-partition, according to the attribute Product is given below (the various DM-equivalence classes are

---

[2] All definitions, given in this section, can be easily extended in order to consider a set of measures, like in [16].

Sales				
RowId	Product	Store	Year	Total
1	100	a	1999	70
2	100	a	2000	85
3	100	b	1999	105
4	100	b	2000	120
5	100	c	1999	55
6	100	c	2000	60
7	103	a	1999	36
8	103	a	2000	37
9	103	b	1999	55
10	103	b	2000	60
11	103	c	1999	28
12	103	c	2000	30

Fig. 1. The relation example Sales

delimited by $<>$). $\Pi_{Product}(Sales) = \{< (1,70)(2,85)(3,105)(4,120)(5,55)(6,60) >, < (7,36)(8,37)(9,55)(10,60)(11,28)(12,30) > \}$. □

Let us underline that our implementation of DM-partitions only preserves tuple identifiers which are used for indexing measurable values. In order to efficiently handle DM-partitions, we introduce the concept of constrained product.

Lemma 1 Constrained Product of DM-Partitions
Let r be a relation, and $\Pi_X(r)$, $\Pi_Y(r)$ two DM-partitions computed from r according to X and Y respectively. The product of the two partitions, denoted by $\Pi_X(r) \bullet_c \Pi_Y(r)$, is obtained as follows, and equal to $\Pi_{X \cup Y}$: $\Pi_X(r) \bullet_c \Pi_Y(r) = \{ [t]_X \cap [t]_Y \models Cond \,/\, [t]_X \in \Pi_X(r), [t]_Y \in \Pi_Y(r) \} = \Pi_{X \cup Y}(r)$

Example 3   Let us consider $\Pi_{Product}(Sales)$ and $\Pi_{Store}(Sales)$. Their product, obtained by intersection of the associated DM-equivalence classes, is achieved and classes not respecting the condition are discarded. The result is the following: $\Pi_{Product}(Sales) \bullet_c \Pi_{Store}(Sales) = \{< (3,105)(4,120) > \}$. □

From any DM-partition, an iceberg cuboid can be simply achieved by aggregating the measurable values of its equivalence classes. Moreover the whole relevant information contained in a relation can be represented through the set of DM-partitions computed according to each dimensional attribute of its schema. These partitions are called, in the rest of the paper, the *original DM-partitions*. Provided with such a set of DM-partitions, it is possible to compute iceberg cuboids according to any dimension combination, by making use of constrained product of DM-partitions. Thus the iceberg datacube, derived from r, can be achieved from the original DM-partitions.

In our approach, an iceberg cuboid results from applying an aggregative function f over the measurable attribute M for each class in the DM-partition $\Pi_X(r)$. Each class is symbolized by one of its tuple identifiers.

Definition 3 Condensed Iceberg Cuboids
Let $\Pi_X(r)$ be a DM-partition of r, and f an aggregative function. For each equivalence class in $\Pi_X(r)$, $[t]_X.M$ stands for the set of values of the measurable attribute and $t[RowId]$ a tuple identifier from $[t]_X$. The cuboid aggregating values of M in r according to X is denoted by $Cuboid_X(r)$ and defined as follows:
$$Cuboid_X(r) = \{ (t[RowId], f([t]_X.M)) \ / \ [t]_X \in \Pi_X(r) \}$$

Example 4 Let us consider the cuboid yielded by the following SQL query:
SELECT   Product, Sum(Total) FROM Sales
GROUP BY Product   HAVING Sum(Total) ¿ 220
Since the DM-partition $\Pi_{Product}(Sales)$ encompasses two DM-equivalence classes satisfying the anti-monotonic constraint, our condensed representation of the associated iceberg cuboid groups only two couples (delimited by $<>$):
$Cuboid_{Product}(Sales) = \{< 1, 495 >, < 7, 246 >\}$. The former couple gives the sale amount for the product 100 (for all stores and years) and the latter provides a similar result for the product 103. $\square$

For characterizing cuboids, we state an equivalence between our representation and the result of the aggregate formation defined by A. Klug [12].

Lemma 2 Correctness
Let $Cuboid_X(r)$ be a cuboid according to X, achieved from r by applying the previous definition with $Cond = true$. Then we have:
$$Aggregation < X, f > (r) = \{ \ t[X] \circ y / t \in r, y = f(\{t'/t' \in r, t'[X] = t[X]\}) \ \}^3$$
$$= \{ \ t[X] \circ f([t]_X.M) / \exists \ [u]_X \in \Pi_X(r)$$
$$such \ that \ (t[RowId], t[M]) \in [u]_X \ \}$$

Definition 4 Condensed Iceberg Datacubes
Let r be a relation. The condensed iceberg datacube associated to r, noted $CUBE(r)$, is defined by:
$$CUBE(r) = \{Cuboid_X(r) \neq \emptyset / X \in 2^{Dim}\} \ where \ 2^{Dim} \ is \ the \ power \ set \ of \ Dim.$$

Example 5 Let us consider the following query yielding the iceberg cube according to Product and Store (depicted in figure 2 (left)):
SELECT   Product, Store, Sum(Total) FROM Sales
CUBE BY Product, Store   HAVING Sum(Total) ¿ 220
The single equivalence class in $\Pi_\emptyset(Sales)$ satisfies the given condition (Sum(Total) = 741). When achieving the constrained product of the two DM-partitions given below, the condition is applied and the result is as follows:
$\Pi_{Product}(Sales) \bullet_c \Pi_{Store}(Sales) = \{< (3, 105)(4, 120) > \}$. It is used for building a

---

Sales by Product and Store		
Product	Store	Total
ALL	ALL	741
100	ALL	495
103	ALL	246
ALL	a	228
ALL	b	340
100	b	225

Sales by Product and Store	
$Cuboid_{\emptyset} =$	$\{ <1,741> \}$
$Cuboid_{Product} =$	$\{ <1,495>, <7,246> \}$
$Cuboid_{Store} =$	$\{<1,228>, <3,340> \}$
$Cuboid_{Product,Store} =$	$\{<3,225> \}$

Fig. 2. An iceberg cube example

tuple of the iceberg cuboid ($< 3, 225 >$) which carries the following information: the total amount of sales for the product and the store referred to in tuple t_3 is 225. Figure 2 (right) illustrates the condensed representation of the iceberg datacube example. □

3   Computing Condensed Iceberg Cubes

In this section, we give the foundations of our algorithmic solution. We begin by recalling the definition of the lectic order (or colexicographical order) [7]. Then, we propose a new recursive algorithm schema for enumerating constrained subsets of 2^{Dim} according to the lectic order.

Definition 5 Lectic Order
Let $(R, <)$ be a totally ordered and finite set. We assume for simplicity that R can be defined as follows: $R = \{1, 2, \ldots, n\}$. R is provided with the following operator: $Max : 2^R \rightarrow R$
$$X \rightarrow \text{the last element of } X.$$
The lectic order $<_l$ is defined as follows:
$$\forall X, Y \in 2^R, X <_l Y \Leftrightarrow Max(X - Y) < Max(Y - X).$$

This definition yields a strict linear order on the set of all subsets, called lectic order.
Example 6 Let us consider the following totally ordered set: $R = \{A, B, C, D\}$. Enumerating combinations of 2^R with respect to the lectic order provides the following result: $\emptyset <_l A <_l B <_l AB <_l C <_l AC <_l BC <_l ABC <_l D <_l AD <_l BD <_l ABD <_l CD <_l ACD <_l BCD <_l ABCD$. □

Proposition 1. *[6]*
$$\forall X, Y \in 2^R, X \subset Y \Rightarrow X <_l Y.$$

The previous proposition ensures that minimal subsets not respecting the anti-monotonic constraint (called negative border [14]) are the first ones encountered in the lectic order.

Let us underline that traverses following from lectic or lexicographical orders are both depth-first-search. However the lectic order is compatible with the anti-monotonic constraint whereas lexicographical order is not.

Recursive Algorithm Schema for Constrained Subset Enumeration in Lectic Order

The novel algorithm LCS (*Lectic Constrained Subset*) gives the general algorithmic schema used by CCUBE. It is provided with two dimensional attribute subsets X and Y, and handles a set of attribute combinations: the negative border ($NegBorder$). The latter set encompasses all the minimal attribute subsets not satisfying the anti-monotonic constraint. The algorithm is based on a twofold recursion and the recursive calls form a binary tree in which each execution branch achieves a dimensional subset. The general strategy for enumerating dimensional attribute subsets consists of generating firstly all the constrained subsets (i.e. satisfying $Cond$) not encompassing a dimensional attribute, and then all the subsets which encompass it. More precisely, the maximal attribute, according to the lectic order, is discarded from Y and appended to X in the variable Z. The algorithm is recursively applied with X and the new subset Y. If Z is not a superset of an element in $NegBorder$, then the algorithm assesses whether the condition holds for Z. If it does, the algorithm is recursively called with the parameters Z and Y, else Z is added to $NegBorder$. The first call of LCS is provided with the two parameters $X = \emptyset$ and $Y = Dim$ while $NegBorder$ is initialized to $\{\}$.

Algorithm $LCS(\ X, Y\ )$
1   **if** $Y = \emptyset$ **then**   output X
2   **else**
3       $A := Max(Y)$
4       $Y := Y - \{A\}$
5       $LCS(X, Y)$
6       $Z := X \cup \{A\}$
7   **if** $\nexists\, T \in NegBorder$ such that $T \subseteq Z$
8   **then**
9   **if** $Z \models Cond$
10   **then** $LCS(Z, Y)$
11   **else** $NegBorder := NegBorder \cup Z$

Lemma 3 Algorithm Correctness
The correctness of the algorithm LCS is based on proposition 1 and:

(i)   *due to the anti-monotonic property of Cond, we have:*
      $\forall\, X \subseteq Y,\ Y \models Cond \Rightarrow X \models Cond;$

(ii) *from the distributivity property of the dimensional lattice, we have:* $\forall\, A \in Dim,\ \forall\, X \subset Dim,\ 2^{X \cup \{A\}} \cap 2^{X - \{A\}} = \emptyset.$ *Thus any dimensional subset is enumerated only once.*

Example 7   Let us consider our relation Sales and the condition $Sum(Total) \geq 350$. In this context, the binary tree of recursive calls when running our algorithm is depicted in figure 3. Leaves in this tree correspond to outputs which are, from left to right, ordered in a lectic way. In any left subtree, all subsets not encompassing the maximal attribute (according to the lectic order) of the subtree root are considered while in right subtrees, the maximal attribute is preserved. □

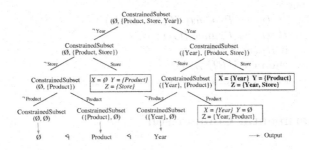

Fig. 3. Execution tree

We propose an algorithm, called CCUBE, for computing full and iceberg datacubes. It fits in the theoretical framework previously presented. A pre-processing step is required in order to build DM-partitions according to each single attribute from the input relation. According to the user need, these DM-partitions can be full or iceberg partitions. While performing this initial step, the computation of the cuboid according to the empty set is operated and its result is yielded.

If the original partitions ($\cup_{A \in Dim} \Pi_A(r)$) cannot fit in main memory, then the fragmentation strategy proposed in [15] and used in [3] is applied. It divides the input relation in fragments according to an attribute until the original associated DM-partitions can be loaded. CCUBE adopts the general algorithm schema described through LCS but it is intended to compute all desired aggregates and thus it yields the condensed representation of all possible cuboids. CCUBE deals with DM-partitions and enforces constrained product of DM-partitions. Like LCS, its input parameters are the subsets X and Y. When Z is not a superset of a negative border element, its DM-partition is computed by applying the constrained product of the in-memory DM-partitions $\Pi_X(r)$ and $\Pi_A(r)$. The constrained product is implemented through two functions called *Product* and *Prune*. The latter discards DM-equivalence classes not satisfying the anti-monotonic constraint and the second recursive call is performed only if the DM-partition according to Z is not empty. The *NegBorder* encompasses the minimal attribute combinaisons Z such that $Cuboid_Z(r) = \emptyset$. The pseudo-code of the algorithm CCUBE is given below.

Algorithm $CCUBE(\ X, Y\ )$
1 **if** $Y = \emptyset$ **then** Write $Cuboid_X(r)$
2 **else**
3    $A := Max(Y)$
4    $Y := Y - \{A\}$
5    $CCUBE(X, Y)$
6    $Z := X \cup \{A\}$
7   **if** $\not\exists\, T \in NegBorder$ such that $T \subseteq Z$
8   **then**
9      $\Pi_Z(r) := Product(\ \Pi_X(r),\ \Pi_A(r)\ )$
10     $\Pi_Z(r) := Prune(\ \Pi_Z(r)\ )$
11   **if** $\Pi_Z(r) <> \emptyset$
12   **then** $CCUBE(Z, Y)$
13   **else** $NegBorder := NegBorder \cup Z$

4   Experimental Comparison

In order to assess performances of CCUBE, the algorithm was implemented using the language C++. An executable file can be generated with Visual C++ 5.0 or GNU g++ compilers. Experiments were performed on a Pentium Pro III/700 MHz with 2 GB, running Linux.

The benchmark relations used for experiments are synthetic data sets automatically generated under the assumption that the data is uniformly and at random distributed. With these benchmarks, optimization techniques (such as attribute ordering used in BUC) do not improve efficiency.

An executable version of BUC is not available from the authors, we have therefore developed a new version of this algorithm under the very same conditions than for CCUBE implementation and with a similar programming style.

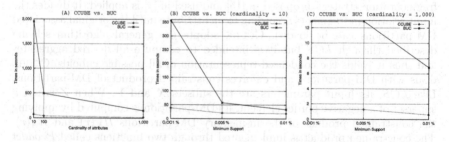

Fig. 4. Execution times in seconds for relations with 100,000 tuples and 10 attributes

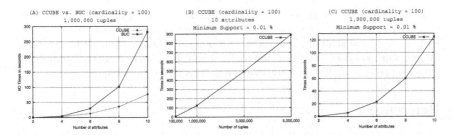

Fig. 5. I/O times in seconds for various numbers of attributes (A) and execution times for various numbers of tuples and attributes with a minimum support (B, C)

Figure 4 (A) gives the execution times of the two algorithms, when computing a fullcube and varying the dimension cardinalities from 10 to 1,000. The input is a relation encompassing 100,000 tuples and 10 attributes. As expected, CCUBE behaves specially well. As mentioned in [3], BUC is penalized when domain cardinalities are small and the gap between execution times of CCUBE and BUC decreases as the domain cardinality increases. Figures 4 (B) and (C) provide execution times of CCUBE and BUC when computing the iceberg cube from the same input relation. The minimum support varies from 0.001 % to 0.01 % and the used function is *Count*. The cardinality of all dimensions is set to 10 or 1,000. In any case, CCUBE is more efficient than BUC.

Figure 5 (A) gives the times required for writing results. The input relation encompasses 1,000,000 tuples and the number of dimensions varies from 2 to 10. Dimension cardinality is set to 100.

The curves, in figure 5 (B, C), illustrate CCUBE scalability according to the tuple number and dimension number when computing an iceberg datacube with a minimum support set to 0.01 %. The tuple number of the input relation varies from 100,000 to 5,000,000. As expected, CCUBE behaves linearly in the number of tuples. The dimension number varies from 2 to 10.

5   Conclusion

The approach presented in this paper addresses the computation of either full or iceberg datacubes. It fits in a formal framework proved to be sound and based on simple concepts. We propose an alternative representation of data sets to be aggregated: the DM-partitions. By selecting relevant DM-partitions, we show that on one hand memory requirement is decreased when compared to BUC one [3], and on the other hand all necessary cuboids can be computed by enforcing in-memory DM-partition products, i.e. by performing set intersections, linearly in the set cardinalities. CCUBE traverses the dimensional lattice by following from the lectic order. Its navigation principles are soundly founded. In addition, we propose a condensed representation of datacubes which significantly reduces the necessary storage space without making use of physical techniques. We show that CCUBE has good scale-up properties and is more efficient than BUC. Intended further work concerns an extension of datacubes that we call decision datacubes which represent small covers for associative classification rules.

References

1. S. Agarwal, R. Agrawal, P. Deshpande, A. Gupta, J.F. Naughton, R. Ramakrishnan, and S. Sarawagi. On the Computation of Multidimensional Aggregates. In *VLDB'96*, pages 506–521, 1996.
2. D. Barbará and M. Sullivan. Quasi-Cubes: Exploiting Approximations in Multidimensional Databases. *SIGMOD Record*, 26(3):12–17, 1997.
3. K.S. Beyer and R. Ramakrishnan. Bottom-Up Computation of Sparse and Iceberg CUBEs. In *ACM SIGMOD, USA*, pages 359–370, 1999.
4. G. Dong, J. Han, J. M. W. Lam, J. Pei, and K. Wang. Multi-Dimensional Constrained Gradients in Data Cubes. In *VLDB'01*, pages 321–330, Italy, 2001.
5. M. Fang, N. Shivakumar, H. Garcia-Molina, R. Motwani, and J.D. Ullman. Computing Iceberg Queries Efficiently. In *VLDB'98, New York City, New York, USA*, pages 299–310. Morgan Kaufmann, 1998.
6. B. Ganter and K. Reuter. Finding all Closed Sets: A General Approach. *Order*, 8:283–290, 1991.
7. B. Ganter and R. Wille. *Formal Concept Analysis: Mathematical Foundations*. Springer-Verlag, 1999.
8. J. Gray, S. Chaudhuri, A. Bosworth, A. Layman, D. Reichart, M. Venkatrao, F. Pellow, and H. Pirahesh. Data Cube: A Relational Aggregation Operator Generalizing Group-by, Cross-Tab, and Sub Totals. *Data Mining and Knowledge Discovery*, 1(1), 1997.
9. J. Han and M. Kamber. *Data Mining: Concepts and Techniques*. Morgan Kaufmann, 2001.
10. J. Han, J. Pei, G. Dong, and K. Wang. Efficient Computation of Iceberg Cubes with Complex Measures. In *ACM SIGMOD'01*, USA, 2001.
11. V. Harinarayan, A. Rajaraman, and J. D. Ullman. Implementing data cubes efficiently. In *ACM SIGMOD'96*, pages 205–216, Montreal, Quebec, Canada, June 1996.
12. A. C. Klug. Equivalence of Relational Algebra and Relational Calculus Query Languages Having Aggregate Functions. *Journal of ACM*, 29(3):699–717, 1982.
13. H. Lu and H. Liu. Decision Tables: Scalable Classification Exploring RDBMS Capabilities. In *VLDB'00*, pages 373–384, Cairo, Egypt, September 2000.
14. H. Mannila and H. Toivonen. Levelwise Search and Borders of Theories in Knowledge Discovery. *Data Mining and Knowledge Discovery*, 10(3):241–258, 1997.
15. K.A. Ross and D. Srivastava. Fast Computation of Sparse Datacubes. In *VLDB'97, Athens, Greece*, pages 116–125, 1997.
16. K.A. Ross, D. Srivastava, and D. Chatziantoniou. Complex Aggregation at Mutiple Granularities. In *EDBT'98*, LNCS vol. 1377, pages 263–277. Springer Verlag, 1998.
17. K.A. Ross and K.A. Zaman. Serving Datacube Tuples from Main Memory. In *SSDM'2000, Berlin, Germany*, pages 182–195, 2000.
18. N. Spyratos. The partition model: A deductive database model. *ACM TODS*, 12(1):1–37, 1987.

A Dynamic Approach to Dimensionality Reduction in Relational Learning

Erick Alphonse and Stan Matwin*

LRI - Bât 490
Université Paris-Sud
91405 ORSAY CEDEX
{alphonse,stan}@lri.fr

Abstract. We propose the first paradigm that brings Feature Subset Selection to the realm of ILP, in a setting where examples are expressed as non-recursive Datalog Horn clauses. The main idea is to approximate the original relational problem by a multi-instance attribute-value problem, and to perform Feature Subset Selection on that modified representation, suitable for the task. The method acts as a filter: it preprocesses the relational data, prior to model building, and produces relational examples with empirically irrelevant literals removed. An implementation of the paradigm is proposed and successfully applied to the biochemical mutagenesis domain.

1 Introduction

Looking back at the many successes of KDD and Data Mining in the last decade, some researchers ask where should the field go next. Many point to limitations of the representations of the data and the derived knowledge in the existing methods. Most of the existing work uses an attribute-value language (AVL), i.e. each data item describes the same single entity. At the logical level, this AVL representation is equivalent to propositional logic. There are compelling reasons to look beyond this representation. An important argument in favor of the use of relational representations is that KDD is best understood invoking the database context. In KDD, even more than in Machine Learning, it is natural to perform inductive discovery working on data derived directly from relational databases. In this context, the presence of foreign keys requires the use of a relatively expressive representation, such as Datalog [1].

In Machine Learning, the idea of inducing general knowledge from examples in First Order Logic (FOL) has been known as Inductive Logic Programming for the last 10 years. Many achievements have been accomplished, but researchers have now realized that there exists a dichotomy between expressiveness of the representation and efficiency of the learner. One of the main difficulties that prevents ILP from tackling large-size problems typical of KDD applications is the dimensionality of the learning space, which is considerably larger than in

---

* On leave from University of Ottawa, Canada.

M.-S. Hacid et al. (Eds.): ISMIS 2002, LNAI 2366, pp. 255–264, 2002.
© Springer-Verlag Berlin Heidelberg 2002

AVL. Even more importantly, the coverage test (or conjunctive query problem in relational database terminology) involves logical matching of FOL formulae representing the hypotheses against the training examples. Since this type of matching is NP-complete, coverage testing, in the worst case, is exponentially more expensive than the same operation in AVL induction. Therefore there is an additional interest in limiting the size of learning spaces to decrease the total cost of coverage tests. In AVL learning, the dimensionality problem has been addressed for years by feature selection techniques. Several successful approaches to feature selection (FS) have been proposed, and are widely used not only in research but also in industrial practice. It is only natural to ask if feature selection could be applied to ILP as well. Following Fürnkranz [2], we argue that the usual static ILP approach to limit the hypothesis space through a restricted hypothesis bias needs to be complemented by a dynamic, data-driven approach similar to the successful FS methods in AVL.

However, the idea of performing FS in an ILP setting runs immediately into a problem. All data-driven FS methods rely on the values of a fixed set of features (attributes) to evaluate their relevance. In ILP, though, due to the level of expressivity, there is no fixed set of features for a given problem: literals change from example to example, and examples have a variable number of literals. If we can agree that filtering a relational problem would output a new relational problem with each example having its irrelevant literals removed, what is the fixed set of features in ILP? The main idea of this paper is to focus on filtering one example at a time. Indeed, using the example as a pattern, we can re-describe the whole relational problem with respect to this pattern. We will obtain a multi-instance problem [3,4] representative of the initial problem, where the fixed set of literals of the pattern is used as the fixed set of features. Extending an FS algorithm to deal with this representation, we will be able to evaluate the relevance of the pattern's literals, that is, of the given example. Finally, considering all examples in turn will filter the whole database.

It has to be noted that Lavrač et al. [5] have proposed a feature selection framework in ILP, using a constrained language named Deductive Hierarchical DataBase (DHDB). This language does not allow non-determinate existential variables and therefore the coverage test is quadratic. Hence, all problems described in DHDB can be compiled into propositional logic in polynomial time. This subset of the first order logic being equivalent to the propositional logic, feature selection techniques can be straightforwardly applied, but this language is too limited to handle current ILP benchmark datasets like mutagenesis (Sect. 4) or multi-relational databases.

2   Logical Setting and the Multi-instance Propositionalization

We address learning in the non-recursive Datalog language of Horn clauses, which is a non recursive Horn clause language without function symbols other than constants. We use the typical learning by implication paradigm [6] which deals with finding a hypothesis that implies or subsumes all positive examples and does not subsume a negative example.

The multi-instance propositionalization (MIP[1]) is a representation shift that reformulates the FOL learning problem as a multi-instance problem, aiming at preserving the expressive power of the original problem. For the lack of space, we just draw here the main lines of the change of representation. The details can be found in [3]. This approach, adapted for different learning systems, is based on the following principle: given an FOL formula P, the propositionalization pattern, each FOL example e is described as a set of attribute-value vectors that have been computed from the set of matching substitutions (partial or complete) between some P's literals and e's literals. In other words, choosing a pattern turns its literals into a fixed set of attributes. All the FOL examples are re-described in terms of these attributes, and each matching substitution is used to provide the values of those attributes (see [7] for details on the different kinds of attributes).

As pointed out in [8], the new instance is no longer a set of positive and negative boolean vectors but is now a *multi-instance problem* [4], where at least one vector of the reformulated positive relational example is positive, and all vectors associated with a negative relational example are negative.

As a first attempt, we do not deal with numerical learning in FOL, even if the multi-instance propositionalization is general enough to address it [8]. We instead focus on structural learning which is typically the non-determinate part of the learning problem, and therefore the part where the dimensionality is most critical. Consequently, in structure learning, the value of each attribute for a particular substitution indicates the matching or not of its corresponding literal: the new instance space is a boolean instance space only.

3   Feature Subset Selection in ILP

Using filtering (feature selection) techniques adapted to work with the reformulated problem, one can select features that correspond to a selection of literals of the propositionalization pattern. If we set a positive[2] example as the propositionalization pattern and select a subset of literals as proposed, we will perform a feature subset selection of this positive example.

However, the space of matchings between two Datalog clauses is exponential in the worst case. Consequently, as [7] pointed out, attribute-value algorithms working on the reformulated problem must deal with data of exponential size wrt the FOL problem. Nevertheless, this set is highly redundant [3] and only few vectors are sufficient to represent the whole instance space. Algorithms can be designed to approximate this set of non-redundant vectors in order to cope with the intractability of the MIP. Indeed, this set is known to be the set of

---

[1] We will refer as MIP to both the change of representation process and the result of this process (a multi-instance problem).

[2] In the learning by implication paradigm, we do not filter negative examples since the more specific they are, the more informative is the training set.

the most specific vectors in the boolean lattice-like instance space (the nearest-misses and nearest-hits of the pattern). An approximation can be achieved by working with a *fixed-size subset* of vectors whose elements are as close as possible to the non-redundant, minimal elements. We refer to this approach as *bounded* multi-instance propositionalization.

Therefore, we propose the following overall scheme for selecting features in ILP:

1. set a not-yet-filtered positive FOL example as the propositionalization pattern and perform a bounded MIP of the relational problem
2. apply a propositional feature selection filter, upgraded for handling MIP (the choice of a relevant filter will be discussed below)
3. output the filtered example, by mapping the selected features onto the relevant literals
4. reiterate with each remaining not-yet-filtered positive examples of the relational database

The result of steps 1-4 represents a reduced FOL representation of the original problem. This reduced representation is then given, as in the AVL FS setting, to an FOL learner to obtain the final solution. In Sect. 4, we empirically evaluate the paradigm with a simple implementation of the above steps. We will discuss its limitations in Sect. 5.

3.1   Bounded Multi-instance Propositionalization

One of the simplest bounded propositionalization schemes has been proposed by Sebag et al. [7]. They apply a stochastic process where k matchings are selected to yield a bounded reformulated problem, with k being a user-supplied parameter. This approach has been successfully used in the learning system STILL.

For the stochastic selection, we use, similarly to STILL, a uniform sampling with replacement. This algorithm works just like the multi-instance proposition-alization described in Sect. 2. Instead of an exhaustive search of all the matchings for a given literal, it picks one of them randomly. Therefore, given k, the number of vectors to be computed, the time complexity is $\mathcal{O}\left(k\,|P|\,|e|\right)$, with P and e being the propositionalization pattern and the example respectively.

3.2   Feature Selection of the Reformulated Problem

In the proposed approach, feature selection is performed by first reformulating the relational problem, and then by applying feature subset selection techniques. Consequently, the filter methods used for feature selection must perform well in the context of a :

– multi-instance representation
– bounded multi-instance propositionalization

More precisely, these two approaches combined will inevitably produce noise, and therefore, the issue of noise resistance has to be addressed while designing a filter algorithm. First of all, it has been pointed out that the underlying multi-instance representation of the reformulated problem could be seen as a class-noisy representation of the positive data [9,10]. According to the definition of a multi-instance problem, each positive FOL example is represented by a set of vectors, such that covering only one of them is sufficient to cover the FOL example. This problem has been studied in the ILP community and relaxing completeness is a typical solution [8,3].

The question of the particular source of noise produced by the bounded MIP, which induces both class and attribute noise, has not been addressed in the literature. We discuss it below.

On the one hand, propositionalization shifts the initial instance space into a boolean one bounded from below by the pattern. Each reformulation of a FOL example is cast onto this new space. For instance, reformulating a negative FOL example will produce a set of negative boolean vectors. The converse does not necessarily hold while reformulating a positive example. Indeed, in the disjunctive learning case, the pattern and the positive example may not belong to the same sub-concept. That is, some literals discriminate between the sub-concept of P and the sub-concept of the example. These literals, used as attributes to describe several reformulations of the example, will not be matched. Therefore the MIP will produce irrelevant vectors which do not have to be taken into account. In this manner, propositionalization introduces class-noise for these particular positive examples which are labelled positive in the training set but which really are negative examples with respect to the pattern.

On the other hand, bounded propositionalization copes with intractability of the change of representation by approximating the set of the most specific vectors. This approximation results in a generalization of the most specific vectors, which can be viewed as obtaining the most specific vectors from a source of noise, in which some attributes' values *true* have been flipped to *false*. Due to our particular learning setting, the attribute-noise impact differs between negative and positive examples. For the former, the so generalized negative examples are still negative. For the latter, flipping *true* to *false* can transform the positive vector into a negative one.

This last property invalidates any pruning scheme able to cope with both class-noise and attribute-noise of positive examples. Moreover, all positive examples other than the pattern are potentially noisy. As far as we know, feature subset selection in a context of a noisy MIP has not been investigated yet. Therefore, as a first attempt to bring feature selection techniques to ILP, we propose here a simple Relief-like algorithm which does not take into account positive examples other than the pattern. The filter uses only the pattern and the attribute-noisy negative examples to assess the relevance of the pattern's attributes.

A Relief-Based Filter for the Reformulated Problem. Relief [11], a fast and reliable algorithm for detecting relevant correlated attributes, has been shown to successfully handle attribute-noise. Relief is inspired by instance-based learning, observing how attributes differ among instances to assess their relevance. It outputs a ranked list of attributes (features), maintaining a weight for each feature, which is increased if the feature seems relevant and decreased if it seems irrelevant. Selection of relevant features is made by setting a threshold, usually set to zero when no prior knowledge is available.

Using Relief in an ILP context has been already discussed in [12] to prune irrelevant branches of refinement graphs. Although we use a Relief-like filter for a completely different task, we share the same weight update procedure.

To assess the relevance of a particular attribute, we can just look at the discrepancy between the attributes' values of the pattern and those of the negative vectors. As the former is the bottommost element of the boolean lattice, i.e. all attributes are set to one, the relevance of an attribute can be assessed based on the negative examples only. So, the gain of an attribute wrt a negative vector depends on whether the attribute is set to one or to zero. In our learning setting[3], if the attribute is one, it can not be used to discriminate the negative vector, hence its gain is negative (-1). In the same way, its gain is positive (+1) if its value is zero. The filtering algorithm is shown figure 1.

filtering(k,E^-,P)
% returns an empirically relevant selection of P's literals
    Set all attributes' weights W[i] to 0.0
    For each FOL negative example e **in** E^- **do**
        Repeat k times
            Compute *one* vector v by propositionalizing e wrt P
            For i := 1 **to** all_attributes **do**
                $W[i] := W[i] + gain(v[i])$
return all attributes whose weight is positive.

Fig. 1. Filtering Algorithm

All FOL negative instances are used. For convenience, we normalize weights between [-1;+1]. If we analyze the two extremal weights, we can see that an attribute with value *true* in every negative example will have a weight equal to -1, as it is not discriminating at all. An attribute not belonging to any negative vectors will get a weight +1, as it is very discriminating.

The time complexity of this algorithm is linear in k, in the number of negative examples and in the complexity of computing one vector by propositionalization. In the case where the sampling scheme described in Sect. 3.1 is used, the total complexity is $\mathcal{O}(k|E^-||P||e|)$. Due to the fact that we do not use the positive

---

[3] When learning by implication, only literals from the bottommost clause's body are used for the discrimination task, and not their negation.

examples, we require neither space in k, nor in the size of the training set, that is to say, the space complexity is constant.

Table 1. The output of the filter algorithm

P	car(T,C1)	short(C1)	h_l(C1,L11)	rect(L11)	car(T,C2)	short(C2)	h_l(C2,L21)	circ(L21)
$\sigma_{NE,1}$	-1	+1	-1	+1	-1	-1	-1	-1
$\sigma_{NE,2}$	-1	+1	-1	+1	-1	+1	-1	+1
$\sigma_{NE,3}$	-1	+1	-1	-1	-1	-1	-1	-1
	-1	+1	-1	+0.33	-1	-0.33	-1	-0.33

The Filter at Work. We illustrate the filtering process on the following relational problem in which E is a positive example and NE a negative one:

E: train(T) :-   car(T,C1),short(C1),has_load(C1,L11),rectangular(L11),
            car(T,C2),short(C2),has_load(C2,L21),circular(L21).
NE: train(T') :- car(T',C1'),long(C1'),has_load(C1',L11'),hexagonal(L11'),
            car(T',C2'),short(C2'),has_load(C2',L21'),circular(L21'),
            car(T',C3'),long(C3'),has_load(C3',L31'),rectangular(L31').

In order to filter E, we use it as the propositionalization pattern. The bounded MIP is computed from sampling $k = 3$ matching substitutions According to Sect. 3.2, for each negative vector computed, each attribute whose value is *true* will have a negative gain, positive otherwise. For instance, given $\sigma_{NE,1} = \{C1/C1', L11/L11', C2/C2', L21/L21'\}$, all literals, *short(C1)* and *rectangular(C1)* excepted, are matched and have a negative gain accordingly. Results are given in Table 1, the last row showing the normalized weight of each feature. The effective selection of attributes is performed by selecting those whose weight is positive, i.e. : *short(C1)* and *rectangular(C1)*.

Therefore, given the relational problem and E as the pattern, the current implementation will produce the following filtered example[4]:

E': train(T) :- short(C1),rectangular(L11).

4   Experiments

We have evaluated the approach by performing experiments with the learning system PROPAL [3] on the two Mutagenesis datasets, well-known ILP problems used as benchmark tests. In these problems, each example consists of a structural description of a molecule as a definite clause. The molecules have to be classified into mutagenic and non-mutagenic ones. The representation language used has

---

[4] This representation of the final example depends of the language of representation used, see Sect. 5.

been defined from background knowledge B_1, which uses only relational literals, tackling nominal and ordinal arguments as constants (see [13] for a detailed explanation). Positive and negative examples of the target concept are molecules described in terms of atoms (between 25 and 40 atoms) and bonds between some of these atoms. To ensure that there is one-to-one mapping between atoms of compounds, we work in the OI-subsumption framework [14]. One of the two datasets contains 188 molecules and is "regression-friendly": regression-based classifier performs well on this data. The other one, "regression-unfriendly", consists of 42 molecules. The experimental protocol is the one provided in [13]. The accuracy of the learned theory for the regression-friendly dataset (RF) is evaluated by a 10-cross-validation (the 10 folds being already given), and the accuracy on the regression-unfriendly (RU) is evaluated by a leave-one-out procedure. Each learning time is calculated by performing learning on the whole dataset.

Table 2. Comparison of the PROPAL's performance on the original datasets and the filtered ones

	RF		RU	
	Accuracy (%)	Time (s.)	Accuracy (%)	Time (s.)
Not filtered	81.80	290	71.4	10
Filtered ($k = 100$)	85.54 ±1.3	69 ±26	80.71 ±1.75	6.34 ±1.61
Filtered ($k = 500$)	85.50 ±1.73	110 ±1	82.61 ±3.73	5.96 ±0.85

Table 2 compares PROPAL's performance on the Mutagenesis datasets filtered and not filtered. The time to filter the two databases is negligible. Due to the stochastic process of the bounded propositionalization used, each accuracy and time have been averaged over 10 runs; the standard deviation is given.

As expected, we can see that the performance of PROPAL has been improved, both in accuracy and time. It is interesting to notice the small standard deviation in accuracy, although in mutagenesis the total number of vectors extracted is really small compared to the size of the matching space. That could be evidence that this space is highly redundant, and the filtering does not suffer from the poor bounded propositionalization scheme, at least for this problem. The deterioration of performance for the $k = 500$ is most likely due to the increased level of noise due to a larger sample of the noisy instance space.

5   Discussion and Conclusion

On the one hand, relational problems typically have to cope with dimensionality challenges harder than those in AVL learning. On the other hand, Machine Learning research has developed effective techniques for dealing with dimensionality by means of feature selection filters. It is not obvious, however, how to perform feature selection in ILP because there is no notion of a fixed set of features for a given ILP task. We have resolved this problem and proposed a general paradigm enabling feature subset selection techniques to be applied in ILP, in languages at least as expressive as non-recursive Datalog language of Horn clauses. Our design criteria focused on the ability to handle FOL problems expressive enough to support KDD applications. As far as we know, it is the first feature selection method which works with subsets of FOL at this level of expressivity. Moreover, our method is applicable to any partial ordering of the learning space (e.g. theta-subsumption).

Several remarks are in order to summarize the implementation of the paradigm used for the validation. Firstly, we use a very simple bounded MIP scheme which does not depend on the application and the structure of the space of matchings being searched. There is need for an informed sampling scheme here, one which would take into account the partial ordering between instances in order to extract vectors as specific as possible and exploit particularities of the application. Secondly, we can observe that the parameter k, specifying the size of the example space sampled from the entire search space, is arbitrary in the approach described here. At this point, we do not have a good grasp of the range of values of k which will allow efficient and yet precise learning from the sample. We can observe that although one could anticipate k to be large, our experiments indicate that even a very small k (wrt the total size of the matching search space) is adequate, at least in the mutagenesis application. Thirdly, with the upgrade of feature selection techniques, there is also an upgrade of the filter algorithm, which has to take into account our particular settings. Tackling a bounded MIP needs to be further investigated. We proposed here a Relief-like algorithm for its ability to cope with attribute-noise and numerical attributes (not yet evaluated). The method described does not use positive examples other that P in the filtering process. Clearly, there is room for improvement here: use of positive examples should allow for a tighter, more focused search space, and consequently a better approximation of the relevant literals. However, the restricted approach proposed here is worth considering further due to its low complexity, and its constant space requirement which could allow to handle arbitrarily large sample size (here, k in Sect. 3.1). Finally, it is clear that the proposed filter may not preserve links between literals in a Datalog clause, and therefore may produce clauses in which determinate variables become free. Let us observe that this problem does not present itself in the mutagenesis domain, where all literals in a clause are linked through the head of the clause. A straightforward solution would be to output the set r of all relevant literals together with the (irrelevant) literals forming the path linking r to the head, but this seems unsatisfactory for top-down learning algorithms. We will investigate this problem further.

In order to evaluate the relevance of the approach, we have proposed a simple implementation. We have experimented with two mutagenesis datasets, a real-word biochemical domain and a benchmark in ILP. The results are encouraging, showing as expected an improvement both in time and accuracy. We plan to further investigate the validity of the approach on problems presented by the KDD community, still considered out of the scope of current ILP techniques.

Acknowledgements. We are very grateful to Michèle Sebag and Céline Rouveirol for fruitful discussions. The support of the Natural Sciences and Engineering Research Council of Canada, Computing and Information Technologies Ontario, the French Ministère de la Recherche and Centre National de la Recherche Scientifique is kindly acknowledged.

References

1. H. Blockeel, L. de Raedt, N. Jacobs, and B. Demoen. Scaling up inductive logic programming by learning from interpretations. *Data Mining and Knowledge Discovery*, 3(1):59–93, 1999.
2. J. Fürnkranz. Dimensionality reduction in ILP: A call to arms. In L. de Raedt and S. Muggleton, editors, *Proceedings of the IJCAI-97 Workshop on Frontiers of Inductive Logic Programming*, pages 81–86, August 1997.
3. E. Alphonse and C. Rouveirol. Lazy propositionalization for relational learning. In W. Horn, editor, *Proc. of the 14th European Conference on Artificial Intelligence (ECAI'2000)*, pages 256–260. IOS Press, 2000.
4. T. G. Dietterich, R. H. Lathrop, and T. Lozano-Pérez. Solving the multiple instance problem with axis-parallel rectangles. *Artificial Intelligence*, 89(1–2):31–71, 1997.
5. N. Lavrač, D. Gamberger, and V. Jovanoski. A study of relevance for learning in deductive databases. *Journal of Logic Programming*, 40(2/3):215–249, 1999.
6. L. de Raedt. Logical settings for concept-learning. *Artificial Intelligence*, 95(1):187–201, 1997.
7. M. Sebag and C. Rouveirol. Tractable induction and classification in first order logic via stochastic matching. In *15th Int. Join Conf. on Artificial Intelligence (IJCAI'97)*, pages 888–893. Morgan Kaufmann, 1997.
8. J.-D. Zucker and J.-G. Ganascia. Changes of representation for efficient learning in structural domains. In *Proc. of 13th International Conference on Machine Learning*. Morgan Kaufmann, 1996.
9. A. Blum and A. Kalai. A note on learning from multiple-instance examples. *Machine Learning*, 30:23–29, 1998.
10. Y. Chevaleyre and J.D. Zucker. Noise-tolerant rule induction for multi-instance data. In *ICML 2000, Workshop on Attribute-Value and Relational Learning*, 2000.
11. K. Kira and L. A. Rendell. A practical approach to feature selection. In *Proc. of the Ninth Int. Conference on Machine Learning.*, pages 249–256. MK, 1992.
12. U. Pompe and I. Kononenko. Linear space induction in first order logic with RELIEFF. In R. Kruse, R. Viertl, and G. Della Ricci, editors, *Mathematical and Statistical Methods in Artificial Intelligence, CISM Course and Lecture Notes 363*, pages 185–220. Springer-Verlag, 1995.
13. A. Srinivasan, S. Muggleton, and R.D. King. Comparing the use of background knowledge by inductive logic programming systems. In L. De Raedt, editor, *Proc, of the 5th ILP*, pages 199–230. Scientific Report, K.U.Leuven, 1995.
14. F. Esposito, N. Fanizzi, S. Ferilli, and G. Semeraro. Ideal theory refinement under object identity. In *Proc. 17th International Conf. on Machine Learning*, pages 263–270. Morgan Kaufmann, San Francisco, CA, 2000.

Incremental and Dynamic Text Mining
Graph Structure Discovery and Visualization

Vincent Dubois and Mohamed Quafafou

IRIN (Université de Nantes)
{dubois;quafafou}@irin.univ-nantes.fr

Abstract. This paper tackles the problem of knowledge discovery in text collections and the dynamic display of the discovered knowledge. We claim that these two problems are deeply interleaved, and should be considered together. The contribution of this paper is fourfold : (1) description of the properties needed for a high level representation of concept relations in text (2) a stochastic measure for a fast evaluation of dependencies between concepts (3) a visualization algorithm to display dynamic structures and (4) a deep integration of discovery and knowledge visualization, i.e. the placement of nodes and edges automatically guides the discovery of knowledge to be displayed. The resulting program has been tested using two specific data sets based on the specific domains of molecular biology and WWW howtos.

1 Introduction

Extracting and displaying graph structures from text collections is usually done in two steps : first, the graph is extracted, then it is displayed. These two steps arise whenever a new document is added to the data collection. Moreover, the end user faces a new graph display, that is not related to the previous one. In this paper, we mixed the extraction step and the visualization step. As a result, the graph display evolves smoothly when new documents are added. Results are displayed continuously during the discovery process. This is of course more user friendly than waiting blindly for the whole process to complete. To achieve this result, we present a semantic based on dependencies between concepts for the graph to be extracted, a relevant metric to evaluate these dependencies, an efficient way of computing this measure, a visualization method, and the integration of all these aspects. In section 2, we present the graph semantic, and our graph display principle. In section 3, we explain our methods and algorithms. Experimental results are given in section 4. Section 5 concludes this paper.

2 Semantic and Principles

2.1 Graph Semantic

We chose to represent relationship between concepts using a graph. Each node in this graph is a concept, and each edge represents a dependency between two

M.-S. Hacid et al. (Eds.): ISMIS 2002, LNAI 2366, pp. 265–273, 2002.

concepts. For the sake of simplicity, we consider each word as a concept, but any other concept definition can be easily applied here. We represent textual data as a list of sets of concepts. Each sentence is represented by a sets of concepts in the list. Because this representation does not rely on the words ordering, it can easily be scaled up. For example, each set of concept may represent keywords of a document, and the list a collection of documents, with the same representation.

Metric. It is quite natural to express the dependence between concepts using the conditional entropy measure, with concepts being boolean random variables (true when present in the set, false otherwise), and textual data a sample of these variable. Given a set of concepts A and a set of concepts B, $H(A|B) = H(A)$ if A does not depends on B, and $H(A|B) = 0$ if A is a function depending of B. An other property of the conditional entropy is that $H(A|B) \leq H(A|B \cup \{b\})$. So we need to complete this measure by adding a size penalty. If we code B using A information, the message length (per instance) is given by the conditional entropy $H(B|A)$. It is logical to add to this length the encoding length of the function used to predict B values based on A values. This require to code $2^{|B|}$ binary values (one for each possible combination of concepts in B). If we have l instances to code, then the structure cost per instance is $2^{|B|}/l$.

We get the following evaluation function f for the dependence between two set of attributes (equation 1):

$$f(A, B) = H(A) - H(A|B) - 2^{|B|}/l \tag{1}$$

Let A be fixed. If $f(A, B)$ is high, then $H(A|B)$ is low and $|B|$ is small. Thus B can be considered minimal, because if a concept in B add no information, then a subset of B would have the same conditional entropy, while a lower structural cost, and then get a better score. Thus, f is a reasonable metric to measure the dependence between attribute sets. We rely upon it to define our graph semantic.

Graph definition. Some definitions based on f are required to build our graph semantic. Given a concept A, we call *partial parent sets* a concept sets B with a positive measure $f(A, B)$. For each concept A, we accept at most n partial parent sets. We call *parent set* of concept A the union of all (accepted) partial parent sets. We say that a concept B is one of the *parents* of the concept A when B belongs to the parents set of A. The *dependence graph* is the graph where each concept is a node, and where each edges $a \leftarrow b$ exists iff b is a parent of a. We $f(A, B)$ value is called *score*. The dependence graph score is the sum over the graph of all partial parent sets scores.

2.2   Display Principle

Graph structure visualization is a complex problem. We consider two different approaches. The first one defines and maximize an appearance criteria. The main advantage is that we know which properties our structure has. The main drawback is the computation cost whens using such metric. The second approach is to use construction methods that implicitly implies some nice visualization feature. We have no control on the appearance criteria, but we do not need to compute it. To display our graph, we chose the second approach: a specific SOM (Self-Organizing Map) produces position of each node.

Using SOM to display maps. Self Organizing Maps (SOM) are introduced by Kohonen [1] It consists in an unsupervised discrete approximation method of a distribution. It is mainly used to display data items, to perform classification and clustering. In this paper, knowledge is extracted and represented as a network, and the SOM approach is used to display it. SOMs have already been successfully used to display graphs [2]. The SOM computes the position of each node in the visualization space. This method relies on the distribution approximation and the metric preservation properties to ensure appearance criteria. The distribution approximation property ensures that the distance between any two neighbor edges is approximately the same, and that edges tend to use all the available space (avoiding hole creation). Neighbors in the graph will likely be neighbors in the visualization space, because of the metric preservation property. Thus, it reduces the number of crossing links in the graph. However this method requires having the final graph to display.

Dynamics SOM. SOM graph visualization methods suppose that the graph to display is given, and find optimal node positions. What happens if we do not freeze it ? Let us make the assumption that in each iteration, the graph may be slightly different (i.e. the structure is dynamic). Unchanged parts of the graph are not directly affected by the modifications, and converges to better position. As soon as no more changes occur, normal convergence starts. But the unchanged parts already started the convergence process. Thus, it is reasonable to begin iterating before the exact structure is known . In the worst case, only the recently touched parts of the graph need a full iteration number. When using dynamics SOM, it is possible to display the current graph while we compute it. This way, the user always has some result to watch.

2.3   Graph Computation and Display Integration

We have previously defined our graph semantic using a score on edges. To compute our graph, we need to find edges with the best score. Thus, our graph building problem is a search problem. Among all possibles graphs, we search for the graph with the best overall score. Hopefully, the score can be computed on each node independently. However, the number of possible parent sets is exponential. The only way to restrict the search space size is to limit the number of possible parents we will consider, using some heuristic [3]. We choose to build a heuristic that produces graphs easy to visualize.

As we compute the graph and display it at once, the position of each node on the screen is known. Given a concept, we can find its neighbor on the screen and propose them as possible parent sets first. Thus, new edge are likely to be found between concepts who are close on the screen. This heuristic introduces a display bias in the search process. If two edges have the same score, the shorter is more likely to be found and added to the graph. Thus, the graph is to compute the display, which in turn is an heuristic used to compute the graph. To implement this principle, we just add a local graph optimization step (i.e. on a single node) in the dynamic SOM iteration.

3   Methods and Algorithms

3.1   Metric Approximation

Entropy computation is costly, so we use a stochastic approximation of it in order to avoid full computation. The approximation is based on the difference between instances (i.e. the set of concepts that are presents in one (and only one) of the pair of instances).

Fano's inequality gives :

$$H(P_e) + P_e . \log(|\xi| - 1) \geq H(X|Y) \qquad (2)$$

where P_e is the probability of error while predicting X using Y, and $|\xi|$ is the number of different possible values for X. In our context, X is a binary attribute (concept present or absent), so $\log(|\xi| - 1) = 0$: $H(P_e) \geq H(X|Y)$ Consequently, the conditional entropy is approximated by the entropy of the error of the prediction. We now express this error by using sets of equal attributes[1].

$$P_e = 1/2 - 1/2 . \sum_Y P(Y) . \sqrt{2 . P(X_= | Y) - 1)} \qquad (3)$$

The $\sum$ term describe the mean value of $\sqrt{2 . P(X_= | Y) - 1}$. We approximate it by the square root of the mean value : $\simeq 1/2 - 1/2\sqrt{2 . P(X_= | Y_=) - 1}$

We note that $P(X_= | Y_=) = P(\{X \cup Y\}_=) / P(Y_=)$. Thus, the information required to compute our approximation of conditional entropy $H(X|Y)$ is the count of identical attributes sets in pair of instances. This count is much easier to compute that every entropy measure, and can be stored in a more efficient way. Moreover, only a small sampling of all possible pairs is necessary. More information on this method can be found in [4].

3.2   Iterative Display

One interesting property of our approach is the ability to provide a graphical result at any iteration step. Thus, the current state of extraction is always available to the user. The progress of extraction is displayed on screen in real-time.

---

[1] Given two instances A_1, A_2 of a random variable A, we note $A_=$ the event $A_1 = A_2$

Algorithm 1 Visualization guided graph extraction

1: **repeat**
2:    get $x(t) \in [0,1] \times [0,1]$
3:    $j \leftarrow \text{argmin}_i \|x(t) - m_i\|$
4:    update C_j partial parent sets score
5:    update C_j partial parent set list using C_j neighbor as candidates
6:    move C_j and its neighbor toward $x(t)$
7: **until** convergence

Data used to compute the graph score can easily be upgraded. New data usually becomes available during treatment. It is necessary to have an incremental property to handle data on the fly.

If new data arise, they are handled as follow :

1. Incoming textual data are parsed and added to the data repository.
2. Relevant statistical result are upgraded according to the new data.
3. Occurrence count are updated.
4. If required, new nodes are added to the graph structure as concept arise, and placed randomly in the visualization space.

No additional action is needed. As an iteration occurs, partial parent set scores are updated according to the new metric. The already computed positions are reused, avoiding restarting from scratch. Thus, the algorithm presented here is incremental.

3.3   Complexity Issues

Evaluation of this algorithm requires to know the cost per iteration and the number of iteration. The number of iteration is addressed in section 4. We discuss here the cost per iteration. The most costly step is the partial parent optimization. It is a search among an exponential number of possibilities in the number of node. We reduce it by limiting the search to a small number of nodes (using the display as a heuristic), and by bounding the size of the set: The score we compute has two parts , the first one is the ability of the model to predict data, and the second is the size cost of the structure. While the first part $(H(a) - H(a|B))$ is bounded (by $H(a)$), the second grows exponentially $(2^{|B|}/l)$. As the metric is required to be greater than 0, there is a size limit for B, given by $2^{|B|} < l.H(a)$. If the size of a partial parent set is bigger than this limit, it will have a negative score, even if it defines a functional dependency $(H(a|B) = 0 = P_e)$. This property provides an efficient way to ensure that the complexity is not beyond a selected degree, by adjusting the structural cost l.

4   Experimental Results

4.1   Results on Corpus

First, we apply our approach to discover knowledge and to visualize it from two different sets of texts. In this first steps, we do not consider any dynamic aspect of the data .We assume that files are full and available. The main objective of these two tests is to show what kind of knowledge it is possible to extract from text, using unsupervised probabilistic network structure learning, and now to display the extracted knowledge. Let us now present the text data we focused on :

WWW-HOWTO. This how-to is included in many Linux distribution. It deals with WWW access and servicing. It is a typical technical document, using specific words. It would not be easy to analyze it using natural language text processing, because it would lack a specialized thesaurus. Its length is more than 14000 words. This is enough to perform statistical analysis.

In figure (2), we show the result of our unsupervised analyze method. By following the links, it is possible to recognize familiar computer domain words association, such as *ftp, downloaded, network, man, hosts, virtual, machine* ... . We can also distinguish some connected component such as *computer, domain, enable, restart, message, send.* Thus, it is possible to extract reduced lexical field automatically.

DNA Corpus. At opposite from the WWW-HOWTO file stand the DNA Corpus. This corpus has been presented and studied in the International Journal of Corpus Linguistics ([5]). Initial study was based on a linguist collocational network, in order to extract emergent use of new patterns of word in the scientific sublanguage associated to molecular biology applied to parasitic plants. Automated probabilistic networks construction may be usefull to linguist, even if the relation between collocational networks and probabilistic ones is not clear yet. We give here a textual summary of the extracted graph.

deletion ← gene contains kb similar evolutionary substitutions
evolutionary ← gene plant involved necessary deletion remains phylogenetic organisms hemiparasite properly introns
hybridizes ← chloroplast intact genes codons families stop lack leaf relate altered
intact ← functional species genes templates hybridizes leaf relate barley altered
remains ← gene plant plastids living involved hemiparasite reduction
sites ← protein site gel size homology sequencing
study ← trnas trna sequence isolated single content tests

Characterization of the linguistic relation between a word and its parents requires an expert of the domain. Being able to get any relation without knowing its nature was one of our requirements in this study. Interpretation of the relation is an other research topic, and a possible extension of this work.

4.2   Convergence Problem

In figure (1d), we draw the score augmentation per 1000 iteration step on the WWW-HOWTO file. As an experimental result, we see that the curve may be bounded by a decreasing exponential. This result is in accordance with the convergence property of the presented algorithm : score is strictly growing, because partial parent set may be replaced only by better partial parent set. The score is bounded, because there is only a finite number of possible graphs. The growing and bounded score suit therefore converges, and difference between consecutive scores tends to 0, as suggested by the figure (1d). We ensure graph score convergence, but what about graph xonstructionconvergence ? The score converges and depends only on finite set of variables. From a given iteration step, the score is constant. Structure change only if a better partial parent set has been found. but it is not possible if score is constant. Then no better partial parent set may be found, and structure do not evolve.

4.3   Effect of Initial Position on Result

The objective of this data set (Mail-HOWTO) is to study the dependence between initial position and graph score after numerous (100000) iteration steps. We run our program using the same data set and three different initial position of nodes in the visualization space. Results are shown in figure (1a), where each curve represents the score evolution for a given initialization of words positions in the visualization space . Although individual curves behavior is somewhat stochastic, it appears that distance between them is always lower than 1 unit. As the values are around 20, the relative error is 5 percent. Thus, the dependence of the curve evolution to the initial position is low.

4.4   Effect of New Data Insertion

In this experiment, initial data set has been cut into 4 segments. Every 50000 iteration step, a new segment has been transmitted to the program. The resulting graph curve is given in figure (1b). The most important effect of each new addition is to invalidate previous evaluation function. This has two immediate effect: Firstly, current structure is evaluated using the new notation function. Thus, score may increase or decrease very fast. It decreases if the graph is less useful given the new data set, and increase if new data fit the already built model. One interpretation of score decrease is that method learned on a restricted set of data, and was too close to these data, and no more able to generalize. This problem is also called over-fitting. Secondly, convergence process speed grows : . unless new data set may be predicted using current model, the model quality may increase by taking new data into account.

4.5   Influence of Data Order

This data set (Mail-HOWTO) has been cut into tree segments : A_1, A_2 and A_3. We present these data to our program in two different orders. *order 1:* segment A_1, A_2 and then A_3; *order 2:* segment A_3, A_2 and then A_1. In both experiments, we sent a new data segment every 10000 iteration step. Figure (1c) presents the score curves at each step for order 1 and order 2. In the first period (0-10000), order 1 discovered graph score is lower than the score of the one extracted

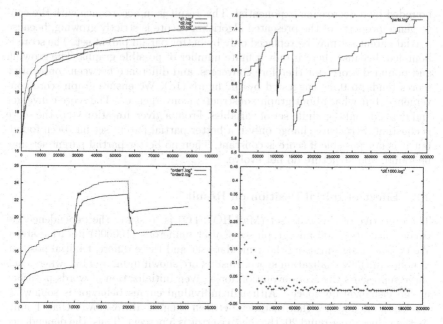

Fig. 1. a,b and c : score per iteration; d score augmentation per iteration

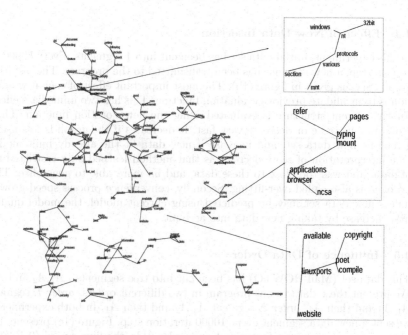

Fig. 2. WWW-HOWTO analysis and zooms

considering the order 2. We deduce from this observation that segment A_1 is harder to model than segment A_3. In the second period, the curves associated with both order 1 and order 2 grows rapidly. Consequently, segment A_2 seems to be the easiest to model. Networks that were well fitted for segment A_1 and A_3 get an even better not when A_2 is added. A_2 structure certainly encompass A_1 and A_3. In the third period, order 1 becomes better than order 2. but difference between the two curves is roughly one unit. As we have find such difference on curves that differs only in the initial nodes position, we cannot say that, in this case, data order had a great influence on final result.

5 Conclusion

In this paper, we have presented an original approach to deal with text mining in document collection. The resulting algorithms and methods have be implemented and produce dynamic and incremental graph structure extraction and visualization. These Methods have been experimented using two different and specific domains. Using visualization data (i.e. node position) for guiding extraction process has proved fruitful, and could be applied in other domains. Mixing mining and visualization is valuable for both aspects, as exploration needs heuristics, and dynamic display quality benefits from this particular heuristics. This work can be extended in order to handle the problem of web mining. For example, mining search result (such as provided by search engine like google, lycos etc..) provides specific domain knowledge which is useful when needed to reformulate the query.

References

1. Kohonen, T.: Self-Organizing Maps. Springer-Verlag (1994)
2. Meyer, B.: Self-organizing graphs – a neural network perspective of graph layout (1998)
3. Friedman, N., Nachman, I., Pe'er, D.: Learning bayesian network structure from massive datasets: The "sparse candidate" algorithm. In: Proceedings of the Fifteenth Annual Conference on Uncertainty in Artificial Intelligence (UAI–99), San Francisco, CA, Morgan Kaufmann Publishers (1999) 196–205
4. Dubois, V., Quafafou, M.: Discovering graph structures in high dimensional spaces. In: Data Mining II. (2000)
5. Williams, G.C.: Collocational networks: Interlocking patterns of lexis in a corpus of plant biology research articles. International Journal of Corpus Linguistic **3** (1998) 151–171

A Logic Framework for the Integration of Databases*

Gianluigi Greco, Sergio Greco, and Ester Zumpano

DEIS, Univ. della Calabria, 87030 Rende, Italy
{ggreco, greco,zumpano}@deis.unical.it

Abstract. In this paper we present a logic programming based framework for the integration of databases. Our framework is based on a logic language obtained by extending Datalog with several constructs such as choice, set constructors, aggregates. We show that the extended language can be profitable used to easily implement most of the integration techniques defined in the literature and define more general techniques.

1 Introduction

Data integration aims to provide a uniform integrated access to multiple heterogeneous information sources, which were designed independently for autonomous applications and whose contents are strictly related. The integration of knowledge from multiple sources is an important aspect in several areas such as data warehousing, database integration and active reactive databases. However, the database obtained from the merging of different sources could contain inconsistent data and thus it must be considered the possibility of constructing an integrated consistent database by replacing inconsistent tuples.

In this paper we propose a general framework which, given a set of n conflicting tuples $(t_{1,1}, ..., t_{1,m})$, ..., $(t_{n,1}, ..., t_{n,m})$, first replaces the n tuples having arity m, with a tuple $(f_1(\{t_{1,1}, ..., t_{n,1}\}), ..., f_m(\{t_{1,m}, ..., t_{n,m}\}))$, where f_i is a polynomial function which is applied to a set of n elements and returns a ('complex') term for each set. Next a polynomial function g combines the complex terms to construct the output standard tuples.

The specialization of the functions f_i and g permits us to express most of the integrating techniques and operators defined in literature. For instance, the merging by majority technique [14] is obtained by specializing all f_i to select the element which occurs a maximum number of times in the set. In other case the function f_i computes a value such as the maximum, minimum, average, etc.

The framework here proposed can be easily implemented by means of a logic language obtained by extending Datalog with set constructors, aggregates, nondeterministic choice. Moreover, the use of an (extended) Datalog program for

---

* Work partially supported by a MURST grants under the projects "Data-X" and "D2I". The second author is also supported by ISI-CNR.

integrating databases makes the merging process more flexible with respect to the use of predefined operators defined in the literature since it gives us the possibility to write ad hoc operators, ("business rules") reflecting the real user needs.

2 Sets, Bugs, Lists and Aggregate Functions

We assume familiarity with disjunctive logic program and disjunctive deductive databases [9,15] and introduce, in this section, an extension of Datalog to manage complex terms such as sets, bugs and lists. We also introduce standard SQL functions which are applied to complex terms and a nondeterministic function which selects (nondeterministically) one element from complex term.

Bugs and sets. A (ground) *bug term* S is of the form $\{s_1, ..., s_n\}$, where s_j $(1 \leq j \leq n)$ is a constant and the sequence in which the elements are listed is immaterial. Moreover, a bug term $\{s_1, ..., s_n\}$ is called *set term* if the number of occurrences of every s_j is immaterial. Thus, the three bugs $\{a, b\}$, $\{b, a\}$ and $\{b, a, b\}$ coincide, while the two bugs $\{a, b\}$ and $\{b, a, b\}$ are different.

We point out that the enumeration of the elements of a set term can be given either directly or by specifying the conditions for collecting them(*grouping variables*). Grouping variables may occur in the head of clauses with the following format

$$p(x_1, ..., x_h, <y_1>, ..., <y_k>, \ll y_{k+1} \gg, ..., \ll y_m \gg) \leftarrow B_1, ..., B_n$$

where $B_1, ..., B_n$ are the goals of the rules, p is the head predicate symbol with arity $h + m$, y_i for $1 \leq i \leq m$, is a grouping variable, and $x_1, ..., x_h$ are the other arguments (terms or other grouping variables). To the grouping variable $\ll Y \gg$ (resp. $<Y>$) will be assigned the bug (resp. set) $\{Y\theta \mid \theta$ is a substitution for r s.t. $B_1\theta, ..., B_n\theta$ are true$\}$. Note that grouping variable is similar to the construct *GROUP BY* of SQL.

Aggregate functions. Other than sets and bugs, we also consider built-in aggregate functions, such as $min, max, count, sum$ and avg which are applied to sets and bugs.

Definition 1. An aggregate term is of the form $f(S)$ where S is a grouping variable and $f \in \{min, max, count, sum, avg\}$ is an aggregate function.   □

Note that since grouping variables may only occur in the head of rules, aggregate terms only occur in the head of rules too. Observe that $min(\ll S \gg) = min(<S>)$ and $max(\ll S \gg) = max(<S>)$.

Nondeterministic predicates: list constructor and choice. A (*bounded*) *list term* L is a term of the form $[s_1, ..., s_n]$, where s_j $(1 \leq j \leq n)$ is a constant. We shall use the standard notation and the standard *cons* operator so that a not empty list can be denoted by $[X|L]$ where X is the head of the list and L is the tail; the empty list is denoted by $[]$. We also assume the existence of a list constructor which may occur in the head of clauses. Basically a list constructor is of the form $\ll Y \gg_I$ and its semantics is that the elements in the bug $\ll Y \gg$ are ordered with respect to the values of I. Clearly, the variable I must take values from a linearly ordered domain and the result may be nondeterministic since there could be more than one possible ordering.

Example 1. For the previous example, the rule $p(X, \ll Z \gg_Y) \leftarrow q(X, Y, Z)$ computes two facts: $p(a, [x, y])$ and either $p(b, [x, z, y])$ or $p(b, [z, x, y])$. The rule $p(X, \ll Y \gg_Z) \leftarrow q(X, Y, Z)$ computes two facts: $p(a, [2, 3])$ and $p(b, [4, 7, 4])$.   □

Other than classical aggregate operators, we also consider a nondeterministic function, called *choice*, which selects nondeterministically one element from a set, bug or list. A choice term is of the form $choice(S)$ where S is a grouping variable. Clearly, $choice(<S>) = choice(\ll S \gg) = choice(\ll S \gg_I)$.

Example 2. Consider the database $D = \{q(a, 2, x), q(a, 3, y), q(b, 4, x), q(b, 7, y), q(b, 4, z)\}$ and the program P consisting of the rule $p(X, choice(<Y>)) \leftarrow q(X, Y, Z)$. The program has four minimal models: $M_1 = \{p(a, 2), p(b, 4)\}$, $M_2 = \{p(a, 2), p(b, 7)\}$, $M_3 = \{p(a, 3), p(b, 4)\}$ and $M_4 = \{p(a, 3), p(b, 7)\}$.   □

In the following we assume sets, bugs and list constructors do not appear inside recursive rules and that aggregates functions can also be applied to lists.[1] We also assume the existence of the standard predicates $member(X, L)$, where X is a variable or a constant and L is a ground set, bug or list [20]; the predicate assigns to X the elements in the ground term L.

3   The Database Integration Problem

Integrating data from different sources consists of two main steps: the first in which the various relations are merged together and the second in which some tuples are removed (or inserted) from the resulting database in order to satisfy *integrity* constraints. Before formally introducing the database integration problem let us introduce some basic definitions and notations.

Let R be a relation name, then we denote by: i) *attr(R)* the set of attributes of R, ii) *key(R)* the set of attributes in the primary key of R, iii) $fd(R)$ the set of functional dependencies of R, and iv) *inst(R)* the instance of R (set of tuples). Given a tuple $t \in inst(R)$, *key(t)* denotes the values of the key attributes of t whereas, for a given database D, $fd(D)$ denotes the set of functional dependencies of D and *inst(D)* denotes the database instance.

---

[1]   Lists are basically ordered bugs.

We assume that relations associated with the same class of objects have been homogenized with respect to a common ontology, so that attributes denoting the same concepts have the same name [19]. We say that two homogenized relations R and S, associated with the same concept, are *overlapping* if $key(R) = key(S)$. In the following we assume that relations associated with the same class of objects have the same primary key.

The database integration problem is as follows: given n databases $D_1 = \{R_{1,1}, ..., R_{1,k}\}, ..., D_n = \{R_{n,1}, ..., R_{n,k}\}$, computes a database $D = \{T_1, ..., T_k\}$, where each T_j, $1 \le j \le k$, is derived from $R_{1,j}, ... R_{n,j}$ and $R_{1,j}, ... R_{n,j}$ refer to the same class of objects. Thus, the database integration problem consists in the integration of n relations $R_{1,j}, ... R_{n,j}$ into a relation T_j by means of a merge (binary) operator $\diamond$, i.e. computes $T_j = R_{1,j} \diamond ... \diamond R_{n,j}$. In the following we assume that each database D_i is identified by a unique index i, with $1 \le i \le n$ where n denotes the number of databases to be merged.

The merge operator. We introduce a general unification framework which permits us to define a generic merge operator by means of a logic program; before showing the technique, we need some preliminary definition and to formally define the desiderable properties of merging operators.

Definition 2. Given two relations R and S such that $attr(R) \subseteq attr(S)$ and two tuples $t_1 \in inst(R)$ and $t_2 \in inst(S)$, we say that t_1 is *less informative* than t_2 ($t_1 \ll t_2$) if for each attribute a in $attr(R)$, $t_1[A] = t_2[A]$ or $t_1[A] = \perp$, where $\perp$ denotes the null value. Moreover, given two relations R and S, we say that $R \ll S$ if $\forall t_1 \in inst(R)$ $\exists t_2 \in inst(S)$ s.t. $t_1 \ll t_2$. □

Definition 3. Let R and S be two relations, a binary operator $\diamond$ such that:

1. $attr(R \diamond S) = attr(R) \cup attr(S)$,
2. $R \bowtie S \ll R \diamond S$,
3. $R \diamond S = S \diamond R$ (*commutativity*),
4. $(R \diamond S) \diamond R = (R \diamond S) \diamond S = R \diamond S$ (*idempotency*).

is called *merge operator*. Moreover, a merge operator $\diamond$ is said to be

- *lossless*, if for all R and S, $R \ll (R \diamond S)$ and $S \ll (R \diamond S)$;
- *dependency preserving*, if for all R and S, is $(R \diamond S) \models (fd(R) \cap fd(S))$;
- *associative*, if $(R \diamond S) \diamond T = R \diamond (S \diamond T)$. □

Note that integrating more than two relations by means of a not associative merge operator, may give different results, if the merge operator is applied in different orders. Thus even if the associative property is deriderable, it is not satisfied by several operators defined in the literature.

In order to compare different merge operators we introduce the following definition.

Definition 4. Given two lossless merge operators $\diamond_1$ and $\diamond_2$, we say that $\diamond_1$ is
i) *content preferable* to $\diamond_2$ ($\diamond_1 \prec_C \diamond_2$) if, for all R and S, $|R \diamond_1 S| < |R \diamond_2 S|$; and
ii) *dependency preferable* to $\diamond_2$ ($\diamond_1 \prec_{FD} \diamond_2$) if, for all R and S, the number of
tuples in $(R \diamond_1 S)$ which violate the $fd(R) \cap fd(S)$ are less than the number of
tuples in $(R \diamond_2 S)$ which violate the $fd(R) \cap fd(S)$. $\qquad\square$

4   Database Integration

In this section we introduce a general framework for the merging of overlapping
relations. The framework is based on the collection of tuples with the same value
for the key attributes into a 'nested' tuple in which each non key attribute, say A,
contains a complex term of the form $f_i([a_1, ..., a_n])$ where $a_1, ..., a_n$ are the values
of the attribute A of the different tuples which have to be merged. The merged
relation is obtained by applying a functions g to each nested tuple identifying the
set of tuples in the source relations having the same key. It is worth nothing that
before collecting tuples with the same value for the key attributes, the relations
to be merged must be first *reconciled* so that they have the same schema and
the same set of key values.

Definition 5. Let $S_1, ..., S_n$ be a set of overlapping relations, K be the key
of the relations, then the set of *reconciled* relations $S'_1, ..., S'_n$ is such that the
generic S'_i is defined as follows:

1. the schema contains all attributes of all homogenized relations,
   i.e. $attr(S'_i) = \bigcup_{j=1}^{n} attr(S_j)$,
2. the instance is constructed as follows:
   a) it contains all tuples $t \in S_i$ completed with $\perp$ for all attributes belonging
      to $attr(S'_i) - attr(S_i)$;
   b) $\forall t' \in S_j$ with $j \neq i$ such that there is no tuple $t'' \in S_i$ with $t'[K] = t''[K]$,
      it contains a tuple t consisting of $t[K]$ completed with $\perp$ for all attributes
      belonging to $attr(S'_i) - K$ $\qquad\square$

Observe that $\pi_K(S'_i) = \pi_K(S'_j)$; moreover, if $S_1, ..., S_n$ are consistent, then $|S'_i| =
|S'_j| = |\pi_K(S'_i)| = |\pi_K(S'_j)|$, for all $i \neq j$. In the following, for the sake of
simplicity, we assume source relations are consistent, although the extension for
not consistent relations is trivial.

Example 3. Consider the following three overlapping relations S_1, S_2 and S_3:

Name	Dept	Salary
Greg	Admin	10000
Jones	Sales	20000
Smith	Sales	$\perp$

S_1

Name	City	Salary
Greg	NY	25000
Jones	WA	20000
Taylor	WA	30000
Smith	WA	25000

S_2

Name	Dept	Salary
Greg	Sales	20000
Jones	Sales	30000

S_3

The reconciled relations S'_1, S'_2 and S'_3 associated to S_1, S_2 and S_3 are:

Name	Dept	City	Salary
Greg	Admin	⊥	10000
Jones	Sales	⊥	20000
Smith	Sales	⊥	⊥
Taylor	⊥	⊥	⊥

S_1'

Name	Dept	City	Salary
Greg	⊥	NY	25000
Jones	⊥	WA	20000
Smith	⊥	WA	25000
Taylor	⊥	WA	30000

S_2'

Name	Dept	City	Salary
Greg	Sales	⊥	20000
Jones	Sales	⊥	30000
Smith	⊥	⊥	⊥
Taylor	⊥	⊥	⊥

S_3'

Let $S_1, ..., S_n$ be a set of consistent reconciled relations with key attributes K and let $T = S_1 \cup ... \cup S_n$. Let k be a key value in $\pi_K(T)$, then $T^k = [t_1, ..., t_n]$ denotes the list of tuples in T with key k such that $t_i \in S_i$ and is called *cluster* with key value k.

Definition 6. A merge function f is a polynomial function operating on a set of reconciled relations $S_1, ..., S_n$ producing a new set of tuples $R = f(S_1, ..., S_n)$ s.t.

1. $attr(R) = \cup_i attr(S_i)$;
2. $S_1 \bowtie \cdots \bowtie S_n \ll f(S_1, ..., S_n)$;
3. $S_i \ll f(S_1, ..., S_n)$ for all i;
4. $\pi_K(R) = \pi_K(S_1 \cup ... \cup S_n)$ where K is the key of $S_1, ..., S_n$.

Moreover, we say that f is *decomposable* if it can be applied to the different clusters of $S_1 \cup ... \cup S_n = T$, i.e. $R = f(T^{k_1}) \cup ... \cup f(T^{k_m})$, where $\{k_1, ..., k_m\} = \pi_K(T)$ is the set of keys in T. □

In the following we only consider decomposable functions which guarantee that tuples in different clusters are not 'combined' to produce new tuples.

Definition 7. Let $S_1, ..., S_n$ be a set of consistent reconciled relations with schema $(K, A_1, ..., A_m)$ and key K, then, every decomposable integrating function f operating on a cluster T^k of $T = S_1 \cup ... \cup S_n$ can be decomposed into $m + 1$ polynomial functions $f_1, ..., f_m, g$ s.t.

1. $f(T^k) = g(\{(k, f_1(L_1), ..., f_m(L_m)))\}$ with
   $L_i^k = [S_1^k, ..., S_n^k] = [\pi_{A_i}(S_1^k), ..., \pi_{A_i}(S_n^k)], \forall i$,
2. $|f_i(L_i^k)| \le |L_i^k|, \forall i$, and
3. g operates on nested tuples and gives, as result, a set of standard tuples (integrated relation), such that $|g(T^k)| \le |L_1 \times ... \times L_n|$. □

Definition 8. A generic function f is said to be *canonical* if i) $f([\bot, ..., \bot]) = \bot$, and ii) $f(L) = z$ if z is the unique not null value in L. □

Example 4. Consider the reconciled relations S_1', S_2' and S_3' introduced in the previous example. Applying a generic merge function, the general template of the integrated relation is of the following type:

Name	Dept	City	Salary
Greg	f_1([Admin,⊥,Sales])	f_2([⊥,NY,⊥])	f_3([10000,25000,20000])
Jones	f_1([Sales,⊥,Sales])	f_2([⊥,WA,⊥])	f_3([20000,20000,30000])
Smith	f_1([Sales,⊥,⊥])	f_2([⊥,WA,⊥])	f_3([⊥,25000,⊥])
Taylor	f_1([⊥,⊥,⊥])	f_2([⊥,WA,⊥])	f_3([⊥,30000,⊥])

T

If each f_i is a canonical function the template can be simplified as follows:

Name	Dept	City	Salary
Greg	f_1([Admin,⊥,Sales])	NY	f_3([10000,25000,20000])
Jones	Sales	WA	f_3([20000,20000,30000])
Smith	Sales	WA	25000
Taylor	⊥	WA	30000

T □

5   A Logic Programming Approach

In this section we show that the integration of relations can be easily implemented by means of a logic language such as the one presented in Section 3. In particular, we show first that most of the relevant merging techniques proposed in the literature can be expressed in terms of a logic program and next that logical rules define a powerful mechanism to implement more general integration techniques.

5.1   Implementing Merge Operators

We assume the function g returns the set of tuples which can be constructed by combining the values supplied by f_i functions in all possible ways. Moreover we suppose the input relations $S_1, ..., S_n$ to be stored by means of a global set of facts with schema $(i, k, e_1, ..., e_m)$, where i denotes the input relation, k the set of attributes corresponding to a key and $e_1, ...e_m$ the remaining attributes.

The following program computes a relation f integrating a set of relations $S_1, ..., S_n$.

```
allAtt(K, ≪E₁≫I, ..., ≪Eₘ≫I) ← s(I, K, E₁, ..., Eₘ).
f(K, E₁, ..., Eₘ)              ← allAtt(K, L₁, ..., Lₘ), f₁(L₁, E₁), ..., fₘ(Lₘ, Eₘ).
```

Here the predicate f_i (for all $1 \leq i \leq m$) receives in input a list of elements L_i and returns an element E_i which is used to build output tuples.

Example 5. The content of the predicate *allAttr* for the homogenized relations S'_1, S'_2 and S'_3 of Example 3 is the following

Name	Dept	City	Salary
Greg	[Admin,⊥,Sales]	[⊥,NY,⊥]	[10000,25000,20000]
Jones	[Sales,⊥,Sales]	[⊥,WA,⊥]	[20000,20000,30000]
Smith	[Sales,⊥,⊥]	[⊥,WA,⊥]	[⊥,25000,⊥]
Taylor	[⊥,⊥,⊥]	[⊥,WA,⊥]	[⊥,30000,⊥]

The body of the second rule implements the different functions f_i. The predicates f_i returns a value; the combination of the different values is used to construct the output tuple.   □

To implement the merge operators analyzed in the following, it is sufficient to specialize the predicates $f_1, ..., f_m$. Moreover, since all predicates have the same behaviour, we shall use a unique predicate called *mergeAttr*.

Match-join operator. The technique proposed in [19] makes use of an operator ⋈, called *Match Join*, to manufacture tuples in the global relation. This operator consists of the outer-join of the *ValSet* of each attribute, where the *ValSet* of an attribute A is the union of the projections of each database source on $\{K, A\}$. Therefore, the application of the Match Join operator produces tuples containing associations of values that may be not present in any original database.

The predicate *mergeAttr* returns not null values if the input list contains at least one not null value, otherwise it returns a null value. The formalization of the predicate *mergeAttr* is the following:

```
mergeAttr(L,T) ← member(T,L), T ≠ ⊥ .
mergeAttr(L,⊥) ← null(L).
```

where $null(L)$ is satisfied if all elements in L are null values.

Merging by majority. In the integration of different databases, an alternative approach, taking the disjunction of the maximal consistent subsets of the union of the databases, has been proposed in [5]. A refinement of this technique has been presented in [14] which proposed taking into account the majority view of the knowledge bases in order to obtain a new relation which is consistent with the integrity constraint. The "merging by majority" technique, proposed by Lin and Mendelson, tries to remove the conflicts maintaining the (not null) value which is present in the majority of the knowledge bases. However, it does not resolve conflicts in all cases since information is not always present in the majority of the databases and, therefore, it is not always possible to choose among different alternative values.

The formalization as logic program is the following:

```
mergeAttr(L, ⊥)            ←  null(L).
mergeAttr(L, X)            ←  countOcc(L, X, N),  ¬moreFrequent(L, X, N).
countOcc(L, X, count(≪X≫)) ← member(X, L), X ≠ ⊥ .
countOcc(L, X, N)          ← countOcc(L, X, N), countOcc(L, X, N₁), N₁ > N.
```

where the predicate $countOcc(L, X, N)$ assigns to N the number of occurrences of X in L.

The Merge Operator. Given a set of homogenized relations $S_1, S_2, ...S_n$, the *merge operator*, introduced in [11], integrates the information provided by each source relation by performing the full outer join and extending tuples coming from each relation S_i replacing null values appearing in a given tuple of such relation with values appearing in some correlated (i.e. with the same key) tuple of all other relations S_j, with $j \neq i$.

The implementation of the operator is showed in the next subsection.

The Prioritized Merge Operator. In order to satisfy preference contraints, we introduce an asymmetric merge operator, called *prioritized merge operator* $\lhd$, which gives preference to data coming from the left relation when conflicting tuples are detected. The prioritized merge operator includes all tuples of the left relation and only the tuples of the right relation whose key does not identify any tuple of the left relation. Moreover, only tuples 'coming' from the left relation are extended since tuples coming from the right relation, which join tuples coming from the left relation, are not included. When integrating relations conflicting on the key attributes, the prioritized merge operator gives preference to the tuples of the left side relation and completes them with values taken from the right side relation.

Thus, given two relations S_1 and S_2, let S_1' and S_2' be the homogenized relations corresponding, respectively, to S_1 and S_2. Then, $S_1 \lhd S_2$ is obtained by extending the tuples of S_1' with the information coming from S_2'. Clearly, this operator is not associative and we assume that operators are applied from left to right, i.e. $S_1 \lhd S_2 \lhd S_3$ is equal to $(S_1 \lhd S_2) \lhd S_3$.

The logic program expressing the prioritized merge operation is:

```
mergeAttr([X], X).
mergeAttr([X|L], X)   ← X ≠ ⊥ .
mergeAttr([⊥ |L], X) ← L ≠ [].
```

5.2   Database Integration by Logical Rules

The use of a (stratified) logic program for integrating databases makes the merging process more flexible with respect to predefined operators such as the ones introduced here and the others defined in the literature [19]. In particular, we describe some more complex examples of merging where the function f can be directly implemented.

Prioritized merge operator. Let S_1 and S_2 be two homogenized relations over the key K, the prioritized merge operation $R = S_1 \lhd S_2$ is given by the following logic program:

```
r(K, A₁, ..., Aₘ) ← s₁(K, B₁, ..., Bₘ), s₂(K, C₁, ..., Cₘ), max(B₁, C₁, A₁), ..., max(Bₘ, Cₘ, Aₘ).
max(⊥, C, C).
max(B, C, B)   ← B ≠ ⊥ .
```

Having one more relation to merge, say S_3, the program can be reused using the tuples of r, obtained by the merging of S_1 and S_2, as the left relation and S_3 as the right relation.

The Merge Operator. Let S_1 and S_2 be two homogenized relations over the key K, the merge operation $R = f(S_1, S_2)$ is defined as:

$r(K, A_1, ..., A_m) \leftarrow s_1(K, B_1, ..., B_m), s_2(K, C_1, ..., C_m), \max(B_1, C_1, A_1), ..., \max(B_m, C_m, A_m)$.
$r(K, A_1, ..., A_m) \leftarrow s_2(K, B_1, ..., B_m), s_1(K, C_1, ..., C_m), \max(B_1, C_1, A_1), ..., \max(B_m, C_m, A_m)$.

the merging of n homogenized relations can be implemented by using the associative property of the operator; thus, the merging of three relations $f(S_1, S_2, S_3)$ can be defined applying iteratively the above rules since $f(S_1, S_2, S_3) = f(f(S_1, S_2), S_3)$.

More General Techniques

Example 6. We want to merge relations S_1, S_2 and S_3 in Example 3, in a way more flexible with respect to the result obtained with the traditional merge operators. In particular, having two conflicting tuples, if the value of *Dept* is the same we want to obtain the average value of the *Salary*, while if an employee is registered in two different department we take the sum of all values of such attribute. Moreover, we assume to give no importance to conflicts on the attribute *city*.

$\text{salary}(\text{Name}, \text{Dept}, \text{avg}(\ll\text{Sal}\gg)) \leftarrow s(\text{I}, \text{Name}, \text{Dept}, \text{City}, \text{Sal})$.
$r(\text{Name}, \ll\text{Dept}\gg, \text{sum}(\ll\text{Sal}\gg)) \leftarrow \text{salary}(\text{Name}, \text{Dept}, \text{Sal}), s(\text{I}, \text{Name}, \text{Dept}, \text{City}, \text{S})$.

□

Example 7. Consider the two relations R and S denoting oriented weighted graphs whose schemata are $(From, To, Length)$ where the pair of attributes $(From, To)$ is a key. The following program P computes first the union of the two relations and next selects arcs (a, b, c) such that there is no path from a to b with length $c' < c$.

```
rs(From, To, Length)        ← r(From, To, Length).
rs(From, To, Length)        ← s(From, To, Length).
closure(From, To, Length) ← rs(From, To, Length).
closure(From, To, Length) ← rs(From, X, L1)), closure(X, To, L2), Length = L1 + L2.
tc'(From, To, Length)       ← rs(From, To, Length), closure(From, To, L), L < Length.
tc(From, To, Length)        ← rs(From, To, Length), ¬tc'(From, To, Length).
```

□

References

1. Abiteboul, S., Hull, R., Vianu, V. *Foundations of Databases*. Addison-Wesley, 1994.
2. Agarwal, S., Keller, A. M., Wiederhold, G., Saraswat, K., Flexible Relation: an Approach for Integrating Data from Multiple, Possibly Inconsistent Databases. *Proc. Int. Conf. on Data Engineering*, 1995.
3. Arenas, M., Bertossi, L., Chomicki, J., Consistent Query Answers in Inconsistent Databases. *PODS Conf.*, 1999.

4. Arenas, M., Bertossi, L., Chomicki, J., Specifying and Querying Database repairs using Logic Programs with Exceptions. *FQAS Conf.*, pp 27-41, 2000.
5. Baral, C., Kraus, S., Minker, J., Combining Multiple Knowledge Bases. *IEEE-TKDE*, Vol. 3, No. 2, pp. 208-220, 1991.
6. Baral, C., Kraus, S., Minker, J., Subrahmanian, V. S., Combining Knowledge Bases Consisting of First Order Theories. *Proc. ISMIS Conference*, pp. 92-101, 1991.
7. Bry, F., Query Answering in Information System with Integrity Constraints, *IFIP 11.5 Working Conf.*, 1997.
8. Dung, P. M., Integrating Data from Possibly Inconsistent Databases. *CoopIS Conf.*,pp. 58-65, 1996.
9. Gelfond, M., Lifschitz, V. The Stable Model Semantics for Logic Programming, *ICLP Conf.* pp. 1070–1080, 1988.
10. Grant, J., Subrahmanian, V. S., Reasoning in Inconsistent Knowledge Bases. *IEEE-TKDE*, Vol. 7, No. 1, pp. 177-189, 1995.
11. Greco, S., Zumpano E., Querying Inconsistent Database *LPAR Conf.*, pp. 308-325, 2000.
12. Kanellakis, P. C., Elements of Relational Database Theory. *Handbook of Theoretical Computer Science*, Vol. 2, J. van Leewen (ed.), North-Holland, 1991.
13. Lin, J., A Semantics for Reasoning Consistently in the Presence of Inconsistency. *Artificial Intelligence*, Vol. 86, No. 1, pp. 75-95, 1996.
14. Lin, J., Mendelzon, A. O., Knowledge Base Merging by Majority, in *Dynamic Worlds: From the Frame Problem to Knowledge Management*, R. Pareschi and B. Fronhoefer (eds.), Kluwer, 1999.
15. Lloyd, J., *Foundation of Logic Programming*. Spinger-Verlag, 1987.
16. Pradhan, S., J. Minker, J., Subrahmanian, V.S., Combining Databases with Prioritized Information *JIIS*, 4(3), pp. 231-260, 1995.
17. Subrahmanian, V. S., Amalgamating Knowledge Bases. *ACM-TODS*, Vol. 19, No. 2, pp. 291-331, 1994.
18. Ullman, J. K., *Principles of Database and Knowledge-Base Systems*, Vol. 1, Computer Science Press, 1988.
19. Yan, L.L., Ozsu, M.T., Conflict Tolerant Queries in Aurora. In *CoopIS Conf.*, pp. 279–290,1999.
20. Zaniolo, C., Arni, N., Ong, Q., The LDL++ system *TKDE*, 1992.

Inference for Annotated Logics over Distributive Lattices*

James J. Lu[1], Neil V. Murray[2], Heydar Radjavi[3], Erik Rosenthal[3], and
Peter Rosenthal[5]

[1] Department of Mathematics and Computer Science, Emory University Atlanta, GA 30322,
USA, jlu@mathcs.emory.edu
[2] Department of Computer Science, State University of New York, Albany, NY 12222, USA,
nvm@cs.albany.edu
[3] Department of Mathematics, Dalhousie University Halifax, Nova Scotia B3H 3J5, Canada,
radjavi@mscs.dal.ca
[4] Department of Mathematics, University of New Haven, West Haven, CT 06516, USA,
brodsky@charger.newhaven.edu
[5] Department of Mathematics, University of Toronto, Toronto, Ontario M5S 3G3, Canada,
rosent@math.toronto.edu

Abstract. The inference rule $\mho$-resolution was introduced in [18] as a technique
for developing an SLD-style query answering procedure for the logic programming
subset of annotated logic. This paper explores the properties of $\mho$-resolution in
the general theorem proving setting. In that setting, it is shown to be complete and
to admit a linear restriction. Thus $\mho$-resolution is amenable to depth-first control
strategies that require little memory. An ordering restriction is also described
and shown to be complete, providing a promising saturation-based procedure for
annotated logic. The inference rule essentially requires that the lattice of truth
values be *ordinary*. Earlier investigations left open the question of whether all
distributive lattices are ordinary; this is answered in the affirmative here.

1   Introduction

The inference rule $\mho^1$-resolution was developed [18,23,19] for application to *annotated
logics*, which were introduced by Subrahmanian [30], Blair and Subrahmanian [2], and
Kifer et al. [13,14,32], largely for knowledge representation and logic programming.
Previously, annotated resolution and reduction were used for inference with these logics.
The reduction rule is required because annotated resolution by itself is insufficient. But
this is less than satisfactory, in part because a linear restriction, convenient for logic
programming, is not really possible, and in part because these two inference rules perform
similar operations that can be redundant. The $\mho$-resolution rule is an elegant solution,
with the added advantage of pruning the search space. The $\mho$-operator requires that the
lattice of truth values be *ordinary* (see Section 3 for the definition). Heretofore it was
not known how large the class of ordinary lattices is. More than three years ago [18], the

---

* This research was supported in part by the National Science Foundation under grant CCR-
9731893.
[1] The usual pronunciation of this symbol, which is an upside-down Ω, is "mo"la long O.

authors conjectured that complete distributive lattices are ordinary, the truth of which would validate the inference rule by ensuring that it is widely applicable. But a proof remained elusive until one insight led to the simple proof presented here.

Prior work on $\mho$-resolution focused on Horn sets, which are typically employed within logic programming. In this paper, it is explored in the general theorem proving setting. It is shown to be complete and to admit a linear restriction. Thus $\mho$-resolution is amenable to depth-first control strategies that require little memory. An ordering restriction is also described and shown to be complete, providing a promising saturation-based procedure for annotated logic.

Space limitations limits the summary of the basics of signed formulas and annotated logics presented in Section 2, and most proofs have been omitted altogether.[2] The main results are presented in Section 3, and some concluding remarks and suggestions for future work are made in Section 4.

2   Signed Logics

Signed logics [22,10] provide a general[3] framework for reasoning about multiple-valued logics (MVL's). They evolved from a variety of work on non-standard computational logics, including [2,5,7,8,9,15,16,20,27,31]. The key is the attachment of *signs*|subsets of the set of truth values|to formulas in the MVL.

Given a language Λ and a set Δ of truth values, a *sign* is a subset of Δ, and a *signed formula* is an expression of the form $S : \mathcal{F}$, where S is a sign and $\mathcal{F}$ is a formula in Λ. A formula in Λ_S is defined to be Λ-*atomic* if whenever $S : A$ is a literal in the formula, then A is an atom in Λ.

An interpretation I over Λ assigns to each literal, and therefore to each formula $\mathcal{F}$, a truth value in Δ, and the corresponding Λ-consistent interpretation I_c is defined by $I_c(S:\mathcal{F}) = true$ if $I(\mathcal{F}) \in S$; $I_c(S:\mathcal{F}) = false$ if $I(\mathcal{F}) \notin S$. Let I_c be a Λ-consistent interpretation, let A be an atom and $\mathcal{F}$ a formula in Λ, and let S_1 and S_2 be signs. Then $I_c(\emptyset:\mathcal{F}) = false$; $I_c(\Delta:\mathcal{F}) = true$; $S_1 \subseteq S_2$ if and only if $S_1:\mathcal{F} \models_\Lambda S_2:\mathcal{F}$ for all formulas $\mathcal{F}$; there is exactly one $\delta \in \Delta$ such that $I_c(\{\delta\}:A) = true$; and finally, $S_1 : A \wedge S_2 : A \equiv_\Lambda (S_1 \cap S_2) : A$ and $S_1 : A \vee S_2 : A \equiv_\Lambda (S_1 \cup S_2) : A$.

Attention is focused on the ground case; the results lift in the usual way.

2.1   Signed Resolution

Signed resolution is a means of adapting resolution to signed formulas. Consider a Λ-atomic formula $\mathcal{F}$ in Λ_S in CNF. Let $C_j, 1 \leq j \leq r$, be clauses in $\mathcal{F}$ that contain, respectively, Λ-atomic literals $\{S_j:A\}$. Thus we may write $C_j = K_j \vee \{S_j:A\}$. Then the *resolvent* R of the C_j's is defined to be the clause $\left(\bigvee_{j=1}^r K_j\right) \vee \left(\left(\bigcap_{j=1}^r S_j\right):A\right)$.

---

[2] Greater detail can be found in [27,18,22], and proofs of the theorems in Section 2.2 can be found in [18]. A much more comprehensive version of this paper is available in [26], which can be found at URL http://www.cs.albany.edu/ by clicking on "Technical Reports."

[3] Hähnle and Escalada-Imaz [11] have an excellent survey encompassing deductive techniques for a wide class of MVL's, including (properly) signed logics.

The rightmost disjunct is called the *residue* of the resolution; it is unsatisfiable if its sign is empty and satisfiable if it is not. In the former case, it may simply be deleted from R.

Assume now that the set of truth values Δ is not simply an unordered set of objects but instead forms a complete distributive (the supremum and infimum operators each distribute over the other) lattice under some ordering $\preceq$. The greatest and least elements of Δ are denoted $\top$ and $\bot$, respectively, and Sup and Inf denote, respectively, the supremum (least upper bound) and infimum (greatest lower bound) of a subset of Δ.[4]

Let $(P; \preceq)$ be any partially ordered set, and let $Q \subseteq P$. Then $\uparrow Q = \{\rho \in P | (\exists \mu \in Q)\ \mu \preceq \rho\}$. Note that $\uparrow Q$ is the smallest *upset* containing Q (see [6]). If Q is a singleton set $\{\mu\}$, then we simply write $\uparrow\mu$. We say that a subset Q of P is *regular* if for some $\mu \in P$, $Q = \uparrow\mu$ or $Q = (\uparrow\mu)'$ (the set complement of $\uparrow\mu$). We call μ the *defining element* of the set. In the former case, we call Q *positive*, and in the latter *negative*. Observe that both Δ and $\emptyset$ are regular since $\Delta = \uparrow\bot$ and $\emptyset = \Delta'$. Observe also that if $\zeta = \mathrm{Sup}\{\mu, \rho\}$, then $\uparrow\mu \cap \uparrow\rho = \uparrow\zeta$. A signed formula is regular if every sign that occurs in it is regular. We may assume that no regular signed formulas have any signs of the form $(\uparrow\mu)'$, where $\mu = \bot$, since in that case $(\uparrow\mu)' = \emptyset$. An *annotated logic* is a signed logic in which only regular signs are allowed.

A regular sign is completely characterized by its defining element and its *polarity* (whether it is positive or negative). Thus a positive regular signed atom may be written $\uparrow\mu : A$, and the corresponding negative atom would be $(\uparrow\mu)' : A$. Observe that $(\uparrow\mu)' : A = \sim (\uparrow\mu : A)$; that is, the signed atoms are complementary with respect to Λ-consistent interpretations. With annotated logics, the most common notation is $\mathcal{F} : \mu$ and $\sim \mathcal{F} : \mu$. There is no particular advantage to one or the other, and it is perhaps unfortunate that both have arisen. We will follow the $\uparrow\mu : \mathcal{F}$ convention when dealing with signed logics and use $\mathcal{F} : \mu$ for annotated logics.

2.2 Signed Resolution for Annotated Logics

A sound and complete resolution proof procedure was defined for clausal annotated logics in [15]. The procedure contains two inference rules that we will refer to as *annotated resolution* and *reduction*.[5] These two inference rules correspond to disjoint instances of signed resolution. It is straightforward to see that the two inference rules are both captured by signed resolution. In particular, annotated resolution corresponds to an application of signed resolution (to regular signed clauses) in which the signs of the selected literals are disjoint. Reduction on the other hand, corresponds to an application of signed resolution in which the signs of the selected literals are both positive and thus have a non-empty regular intersection. For more details, see [18,19,26].

Theorem 1. Suppose that $\mathcal{F}$ is a set of annotated clauses and that $\mathcal{D}$ is a deduction of $\mathcal{F}$ using annotated resolution and reduction. Then $\mathcal{D}$ is a signed deduction of $\mathcal{F}$.

---

[4] The formulation of annotated logic in [15] does not restrict Δ to distributive lattices. However, most applications of annotated logics employ distributive lattices (see for example, [21,3,4]).

[5] Kifer and Lozinskii refer to their first inference rule simply as resolution. However, since we are working with several resolution rules in this paper, appropriate adjectives will be used to avoid ambiguity.

In particular, if $\mathcal{F}$ is an unsatisfiable set of annotated clauses, then there is a signed refutation of $\mathcal{F}$.   □

Theorem 2. Suppose $S_1, \ldots, S_n$ are regular signs whose intersection is empty, and suppose that no proper subset of $\{S_1, \ldots, S_n\}$ has an empty intersection. Then exactly one sign is negative; i.e., for some $j, 1 \leq j \leq n, S_j = (\uparrow\mu_j)'$, and for $i \neq j, S_i = \uparrow\mu_i$, where $\mu_1, \ldots, \mu_n \in \Delta$.   □

Theorem 3. A signed deduction of a regular formula is regular if and only if the sign of every satisfiable residue is produced by the intersection of two positive regular signs. □

Theorem 4. Let $\mathcal{D}$ be a sequence of annotated clauses. Then $\mathcal{D}$ is an annotated deduction if and only if $\mathcal{D}$ is a regular signed deduction.   □

Corollary. Suppose $\mathcal{F}$ is an unsatisfiable set of regular signed clauses. Then there is a regular signed deduction of the empty clause from $\mathcal{F}$.   □

These observations indicate that the restriction to regular signs is likely to improve performance, and the results in [24] seem to bear this out.

3   Resolution for Regular Signed Logics

For regular signed logics|equivalently, for annotated logics|signed resolution provides greater flexibility than annotated resolution and reduction. However, the restriction to regular signs often yields better performance. The objective is to discover a rule of inference that offers both.

3.1   Ordinary Lattices

Given annotated literals $\sim p : \mu$ and $p : \rho$, where μ is not less than or equal to ρ, the intersection of $(\uparrow \mu)'$ and $\uparrow \rho$ is simply not regular and cannot be represented by an annotation. Signed resolution would produce the goal $((\uparrow \mu)' \cap \uparrow \rho) : p$. However, since this goal can be soundly deduced, so can any goal of the form $S : p$, where $S \supseteq ((\uparrow \mu)' \cap \uparrow \rho)$. The key to maintaining regular deductions, then, is to determine an annotation γ such that $(\uparrow \gamma)'$ is the "smallest" regular set that contains $((\uparrow \mu)' \cap \uparrow \rho)$.

A solution is $\mho$-resolution. To define it, some notation and concepts are required. Given $\mu, \rho \in \Delta$, we use $\mathcal{M}(\mu, \rho)$ to denote the set of annotations for which the least upper bound of ρ with an element of the set is greater than or equal to μ. Formally, $\mathcal{M}(\mu, \rho) = \{\gamma \in \Delta, | \operatorname{Sup}\{\gamma, \rho\} \succeq \mu\}$. For the lattice FOUR in Figure 1, if $\mu = \top$, and $\rho = \mathbf{t}$, $\mathcal{M}(\mu, \rho) = \{\mathbf{f}, \top\}$.

Given $\mu, \rho \in \Delta$, the $\mho$-operator is defined by $\mho(\mu, \rho) = \operatorname{Inf} \mathcal{M}(\mu, \rho)$. A lattice Δ is said to be *ordinary* if $\mu, \rho \in \Delta$ implies $\mho(\mu, \rho) \in \mathcal{M}(\mu, \rho)$. To simplify the notation, given $\mu, \rho_1, \ldots, \rho_m$, for the expression $\mho(\mho(\ldots\mho(\mho(\mu, \rho_1), \rho_2)\ldots), \rho_m)$, we write $\mho(\mu, \rho_1, \ldots, \rho_m)$. Notice that the lattice FOUR is an ordinary lattice, while the lattice $M3$ (Figure 1) is not an ordinary lattice since the set $\mathcal{M}(\mu, \rho) = \{2, 3, \top\}$ has no least element in the set.

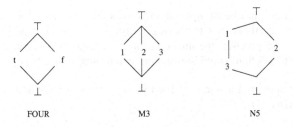

Fig. 1. Lattices FOUR, M3, and N5

Lemma 1. If Δ is ordinary, then so is any complete sublattice of Δ.

Proof. Let Γ be a complete sublattice of Δ, and let $\mu, \rho \in \Gamma$. Consider $\mathcal{M}^\Gamma(\mu, \rho)$ ($\mathcal{M}$ defined over Γ). The sublattice Γ is closed under Inf and Sup, so $\mathrm{Inf}(\mathcal{M}^\Gamma(\mu, \rho)) \in \Gamma$, and $\mathcal{M}^\Gamma(\mu, \rho) \subseteq \mathcal{M}(\mu, \rho)$. But then $\mathrm{Inf}(\mathcal{M}^\Gamma(\mu, \rho)) \succeq \mathrm{Inf}(\mathcal{M}(\mu, \rho))$. As a result, $\mathrm{Sup}(\mathrm{Inf}(\mathcal{M}^\Gamma(\mu, \rho)), \mu) \succeq \mu$ and is in $\mathcal{M}^\Gamma(\mu, \rho)$ by definition. Thus Γ is ordinary. □

The next theorem is the key result that ordinary and distributive lattices are the same.

Theorem 5. A complete lattice is distributive if and only if it is ordinary.

Proof. Let Δ be a complete lattice, and assume first that it is distributive. Without loss of generality, we may assume that Δ is a lattice of sets under union and intersection ([6], Theorem 10.3). Then, given $\mu, \rho \in \Delta$, $\mathcal{M}(\mu, \rho) = \{\gamma \in \Delta \mid \gamma \cup \rho \supseteq \mu\}$. Let $M = \mathcal{M}(\mu, \rho)$, and $\phi = \mathrm{Inf}(M)$. Then ϕ is the intersection of the elements of M. We must show that $\phi \in M$; i.e., that $\mu \subseteq \rho \cup \phi$. Let $x \in \mu$. If $x \in \rho$, we're done, so suppose it's not. For every $\gamma \in M$, $x \in \gamma$ since $\mu \subseteq \rho \cup \gamma$. Then $x \in \phi = \bigcap M$.

Suppose now that Δ is ordinary, and let $N5$ be the lattice shown in Figure 1. Neither it nor $M3$ is ordinary. Thus, by Lemma 1, Δ cannot contain $M3$ or $N5$ as a sublattice. But every non-distributive lattice must contain $M3$ or $N5$ as a sublattice (see [6], page 134, the $M3 - N5$ Theorem), so Δ must be distributive. □

The next lemma and Lemma 4 are useful for proving that $\mho$-resolution is complete.

Lemma 2. Let Δ be an ordinary lattice. Then $\mho(\mu, \rho_1, ..., \rho_m) = \perp$ if and only if $\mu \preceq \rho$, where $\rho = \mathrm{Sup}\{\rho_1, ..., \rho_m\}$. □

3.2 $\mho$-Resolution

The objective is to develop a resolution rule that can be used without reductions. Consider the annotated literals $\sim p : \mu$ and $p : \rho$, which are equivalent to $(\uparrow \mu)' : p$ and $\uparrow \rho : p$, respectively. Suppose $\mu \npreceq \rho$ and hence not annotated resolvable. Then to maintain a regular deduction, it is necessary to determine a regular sign S_0 that contains $(\uparrow \mu)' \cap \uparrow \rho$, and to resolve to a residue $\mathcal{R}$, whose annotation represents S_0.

In general there may be multiple minimal signs satisfying the above two conditions. Fortunately, the next theorem states that if Δ is distributive, complete, and hence ordinary, then $(\uparrow \mho(\mu, \rho))'$ is precisely the smallest negative regular set that contains $(\uparrow \mu)' \cap \uparrow \rho$. This will lead to a definition of $\mho$-resolution with residue $\sim p : \mho(\mu, \rho)$.

Theorem 6. Suppose Δ is ordinary. Then $(\uparrow \mho(\mu, \rho))'$ is the smallest negative regular sign that contains $(\uparrow \mu)' \cap \uparrow \rho$.   □

Definition. Given the annotated clauses $(\sim A : \mu \lor D_1)$ and $(A : \rho \lor D_2)$, then the $\mho$-*resolvent* of the two clauses on the annotated literals $\sim A : \mu$ and $A : \rho$ is $\sim A : \mho(\mu, \rho) \lor D_1 \lor D_2$.

The soundness of $\mho$-resolution follows from Theorem 6.

3.3   Completeness

The literal set $L = \{A : \mu_1, A : \mu_2, \ldots, A : \mu_m, \sim A : \mu_{m+1}, \ldots, \sim A : \mu_{m+r}\}$ is unsatisfiable if $m, r > 0$ and, for some $j, m+1 \leq j \leq m+r, \mathrm{Sup}\{\mu_1, \ldots, \mu_m\} \geq \mu_j$; i.e., L is unsatisfiable if the intersection of the signs in L is empty. Then L is *minimally unsatisfiable* if the removal of any member of L results in a satisfiable literal set. In light of Theorem 2, $r = 1$ for any minimally unsatisfiable annotated literal set.

A literal in a set S of annotated clauses is said to be *pure* if it does not belong to any minimally unsatisfiable set of literals in which distinct literals occur in distinct clauses. In that case, the clause containing the pure literal is also said to be pure.

Lemma 3 (Annotated Pure Rule). Let S be a set of annotated clauses in which the clause C contains the pure literal l. Then S is unsatisfiable if and only if $S' = S - \{C\}$ is unsatisfiable.   □

The next lemma is useful for proving the completeness of $\mho$-resolution.

Lemma 4. Let $S = \{C_0, C_1, C_2, \ldots, C_k\}$ be a minimally unsatisfiable set of annotated clauses (i.e., no proper subset of S is unsatisfiable), and suppose $C_0 = \{l\} \cup \{l_1, l_2, \ldots, l_n\}, n \geq 0$. Obtain S' from S by deleting every occurrence of l in S. Then S' is unsatisfiable, and every minimally unsatisfiable subset of S' contains $C_0' = \{l_1, \ldots, l_n\}$. Moreover, each such subset of S' contains all clauses C_i' such that the corresponding C_i in S contained l. For the proof, see [26].   □

Corollary. Let $S = \{C_0, C_1, C_2, \ldots, C_k\}$ be a minimally unsatisfiable set of annotated clauses and suppose $C_0 = \{l\} \cup \{l_1, l_2, \ldots, l_n\}, n \geq 0$. Let $S' = (S - \{C_0\}) \cup \{\{l\}\}$. Then S' is unsatisfiable, and every minimally unsatisfiable subset of S' contains $\{l\}$. □

The following theorem is from [23]; its corollary demonstrates a nice property of the $\mho$-operator.

Theorem 7 (Order Independence). Suppose Δ is ordinary, and suppose $\mu, \rho_1, \rho_2 \in \Delta$. Then $\mathcal{M}(\mho(\mu, \rho_1), \rho_2) = \mathcal{M}(\mho(\mu, \rho_2), \rho_1)$.   □

Thus the result of applying $\mho$ to two elements, ρ_1 and ρ_2, is order independent. A simple corollary to the theorem is that for a given μ, the result of applying $\mho$ to two elements, ρ_1 and ρ_2, is order independent.

Corollary. Suppose Δ is ordinary. Then for any $\mu, \rho_1, \rho_2 \in \Delta$, $\mho(\mho(\mu, \rho_1), \rho_2) = \mho(\mho(\mu, \rho_2), \rho_1)$. □

The next theorem establishes the completeness of $\mho$-resolution.

Theorem 8. If S is an unsatisfiable set of annotated clauses, then there is a refutation of S using $\mho$-resolution (with merging). □

The linear restriction is one of the most widely used strategies in classical resolution, in part because of its importance in logic programming. In essence, annotated resolution and reduction do not admit linear deductions.

Theorem 9. Suppose $\mathcal{F}$ is an unsatisfiable set of annotated clauses. Then there is a linear $\mho$-refutation of $\mathcal{F}$. (For the proof, see [26]. □

3.4 Ordered $\mho$-Resolution

Ordered resolution for classical logic is attributed to J. Reynolds [28]; variations have been proven complete by Kowalski and Hayes [17] and by Joyner [12]. More recent investigations include Bachmair and Ganzinger [1]. It is of interest because it significantly reduces the search space by ordering the predicates and activating only links that connect head literals.

For annotated logic, the set of signed atoms can be partially ordered by first selecting any total ordering on the set of predicates. Then, for a given predicate p, all positive signed atoms $p : \rho$ precede all negative signed atoms $\sim p : \mu$. Finally, atoms with the same predicate and sign are not comparable.

The term *head literal* of a clause denotes a maximal literal in the clause. Since the ordering is not total, a clause may have more than one head literal. However, all head literals will have the same predicate, and all will be positive or all will be negative.

Given clauses $A = \{\sim p : \mu\} \cup C$ and $B = \{p : \rho\} \cup D$, where $\sim p : \mu$ and $p : \rho$ are head literals, the clause $E = \{\sim p : \mho(\mu, \rho)\} \cup C \cup D$ is said to be an *ordered $\mho$-resolvent* of A and B. The procedure that requires every $\mho$-resolvent be ordered is called *ordered $\mho$-resolution*.

Theorem 10 below states that ordered $\mho$-resolution is complete. The proof of that theorem employs Lemma 5 plus an interesting variation of the excess literal argument.

Lemma 5. Let S be an unsatisfiable set of annotated clauses in which every literal is a head literal. Then there is an ordered $\mho$-resolution refutation of S. □

Theorem 10. Let S be an unsatisfiable set of annotated clauses. Then there is an ordered $\mho$-resolution refutation of S. □

It is important to realize that the corollary of Theorem 7 assures us that ordered $\mho$-resolution can be applied to the clauses with positive head literals in any order, and that the only clauses needed have positive annotations that would be relevant; none would be pruned by employing the $\mho$ operator as a pruning device in the usual way.

4 Discussion

The careful reader will have noticed that $\mho$-resolution prunes the search space significantly in two ways. First, the reduction inference defined initially for annotated logics is unnecessary. Given $n + 1$ clauses containing a negative literal and n positive literals on which resolutions may be performed, we need only select one order in which to $\mho$-resolve the positive ones against the negative literal. Of course, the use of reduction can also be curtailed to avoid redundant permutations.

A more important advantage of $\mho$-resolution is the way in which the $\mho$-operator detects certain "bad" steps that are to be avoided. These steps occur precisely when $\mho(\mu, \rho) = \mu$, where μ is the annotation of the negative literal, and ρ is the annotation of the positive literal. Suppose we have the annotated clauses $(\sim A : \mu \vee D_1)$ and $(A : \rho \vee D_2)$, where $\mho(\mu, \rho) = \mu$. Notice that the $\mho$-*resolvent* of the two clauses on the annotated literals $\sim A : \mu$ and $A : \rho$ is $(\sim A : \mu \vee D_1 \vee D_2)$. The first of the two parents will necessarily subsume the resolvent, rendering the step unnecessary. (This is true at the first order level also.)

Even if $\uparrow \rho \not\subseteq (\uparrow \mu)'$, by Theorem 6, the smallest regular sign that contains $\uparrow \rho \cap (\uparrow \mu)'$ is $(\uparrow \mu)'$. This means that the literal $A : \rho$ cannot contribute to any inference that ultimately resolves away $A : \mu$. But this redundancy is not readily detectable when performing reduction steps between this literal and other positive literals.

Intuitively, the $\mho$-operator allows annotated logic proofs to have the flavor of classical resolution-based proofs. There is one basic inference mechanism that operates on a pair of literals, one positive and one negative. Theorem 9 establishes completeness for the linear restriction, which requires retention of few clauses but considerable time in backtracking. Theorem 10 assures completeness for a saturation-based strategy. We expect that other saturation-based strategies, such as set-of-support and hyperresolution will prove to be applicable to $\mho$-resolution.

References

1. Bachmair, L. and Ganzinger, H., Rewrite-based equational theorem proving with selection and simplification. *Journal of Logic and Computation*, 4(3):217–247, 1994.
2. Blair, H.A. and Subrahmanian, V.S., Paraconsistent logic programming, *Theoretical Computer Science* 68, 135-154, 1989.
3. Calmet, J., Jekutsch, S., Kullmann, P., and Schü, J., A system for the integration of heterogeneous information sources, *Proc. ISMIS*, 1997.
4. Calmet, J. and Kullmann, P., Meta web search with KOMET, *Proceedings of the IJCAI-99 Workshop on Intelligent Information Integration*, Stockholm, July, 1999.
5. Carnielli, W.A., Systematization of finite many-valued logics through the method of tableaux. *J. of Symbolic Logic* 52(2):473-493, 1987.
6. Davey, B.A. and Priestley, H.A., *Introduction to Lattices and Order*, Cambridge Math, 1990.
7. Doherty, P., *NML3 — A Non-Monotonic Formalism with Explicit Defaults*, Linköping Studies in Sci. and Tech., Diss. 258, Dept. of CIS, Linköping University, 1991.
8. Fitting, M., First-order modal tableaux, *J. Automated Reasoning* 4:191-213, 1988.
9. Hähnle, R., *Automated Deduction in Multiple-Valued Logics*, International Series of Monographs on Computer Science, vol. 10. Oxford University Press, 1994.

10. Hähnle, R., Tableaux methods for many-valued logics, *Handbook of Tableau Methods* (M d'Agostino, D. Gabbay, R. Hähnle and J. Posegga eds.), Kluwer, Dordrecht, 1999.
11. Hähnle, R. and Escalada-Imaz, G., Deduction in many-valued logics: a survey, *Mathware & Soft Computing*, IV(2), 69-97, 1997.
12. Joyner, W.H., Resolution strategies as decision procedures, *JACM* **23(1)**, 398-417, 1976.
13. Kifer, M. and Li, A., On the semantics of rule-based expert systems with uncertainty, *Proc. the 2nd Int. Conf. on Database Theory*, 102-117, 1988.
14. Kifer, M. and Lozinskii, E.L., RI: a logic for reasoning in inconsistency, *Proceedings of the Fourth Symposium of Logic in Computer Science*, Asilomar, 253-262, 1989.
15. Kifer, M. and Lozinskii, E., A logic for reasoning with inconsistency, *JAR* 9, 179-215, 1992.
16. Kifer, M. and Subrahmanian, V.S., Theory of generalized annotated logic programming and its applications, *J. of Logic Programming* 12, 335-367, 1992.
17. Kowalski, R. and Hayes, P.J. Semantic trees in automatic theorem proving. In *Machine Intelligence* **4**, 87–101, Edinburgh University Press, 1969. Reprinted in [29].
18. Leach, S.M., Lu, J.J., Murray, N.V., and Rosenthal, E., ℧-resolution: an inference for regular multiple-valued logics,. *Proc. JELIA'98*, IBFI Schloss Dagstuhl, *Lecture Notes in Artificial Intelligence* **1489**, Springer-Verlag, 154-168, 1998.
19. Leach, S.M., Lu, J.J., Murray, N.V., and Rosenthal, E., ℧-resolution and hybrid knowledge bases, *Journal of The Franklin Institute* (Special issue on AI), **338 (5)**, 583-600, 2001.
20. Lu, J.J., Henschen, L.J., Subrahmanian, V.S., and da Costa, N.C.A., Reasoning in paraconsistent logics, *Automated Reasoning: Essays in Honor of Woody Bledsoe* (R. Boyer ed.), Kluwer Academic, 181-210, 1991.
21. Lu, J.J., Nerode, A., and Subrahmanian, V.S. Hybrid Knowledge Bases, *IEEE Transactions on Knowledge and Data Engineering*, 8(5):773-785, 1996.
22. Lu, J.J., Murray, N.V., and Rosenthal, E., A Framework for Automated Reasoning in Multiple-Valued Logics, *J. of Automated Reasoning* **21**,*1* 39-67, 1998.
23. Lu, J.J., Murray, N.V., and Rosenthal, E., A foundation for hybrid knowledge bases, *Proc. 19th Int. Conf. on Foundations of Software Technology & Theoretical Computer Science*, Chennai, India, *Lecture Notes in Computer Science* **1738**, Springer-Verlag, 155-167, 1999.
24. Lu, J.J., Murray, N.V., and Rosenthal, E., Annotated hyperresolution for non-Horn regular multiple-valued logics, *Proc. ISMIS-2000, Lecture Notes in Artificial Intelligence* **1932**, Springer-Verlag, 301-310.
25. Lu, J.J., Murray, N.V., and Rosenthal, E., Non-Horn clause annotated logic deduction over distributive lattice truth domains, Tech. Report TR 01-3, SUNY at Albany, 2001.
26. Lu, J.J., Murray, N.V., Radjavi, H., Rosenthal, E., and Rosenthal, P. Search strategies for annotated logics over distributive lattices, Tech. Report TR 02-1, SUNY at Albany, 2002.
27. Murray, N.V. and Rosenthal, E., Adapting classical inference techniques to multiple-valued logics using signed formulas, *Fundamenta Informaticae* 21:237-253, 1994.
28. Reynolds, J. Unpublished seminar notes, Stanford University, Palo Alto, CA, 1966.
29. Siekmann, J. and Wrightson, G., editors. *Automation of Reasoning: Classical Papers in Computational Logic 1967–1970*, volume 2. Springer-Verlag, 1983.
30. Subrahmanian, V.S., On the Semantics of Quantitative Logic Programs, in: *Proceedings of the 4th IEEE Symposium on Logic Programming*, Computer Society Press, 1987.
31. Subrahmanian, V.S., Paraconsistent Disjunctive Databases, *Theoretical Computer Science*, 93, 115-141, 1992.
32. Thirunarayan, K. and Kifer, M., A Theory of Nonmonotonic Inheritance Based on Annotated Logic, *Artificial Intelligence*, 60(1):23-50, 1993.

Disjunctive Logic Programs with Inheritance Revisited
(A Preliminary Report)

Stefania Costantini[1], Ramón P. Otero[2], Alessandro Provetti[3], and Tran C. Son[4]

[1] Università degli Studi di L'Aquila
Dipartimento d'Informatica
Via Vetoio, Loc. Coppito, I-67100 L'Aquila - Italy
stefcost@univaq.it
[2] University of Corunna
AI Lab Dep. da Computacion
E-15071 Corunna, Galicia, Spain
otero@dc.fi.udc.es
[3] Università degli Studi di Messina
Dip. di Fisica
Salita Sperone 31, I-98166 Messina - Italy
ale@unime.it
[4] Department of Computer Science
New Mexico State University
PO Box 30001, MSC CS
Las Cruces, NM 88003, USA
tson@cs.nmsu.edu

Abstract. We argue for a semantical modification of the language DLP$^<$. We show by examples that the current DLP$^<$ representation in some cases does not provide intuitive answers, in particular when applied to inheritance reasoning. We present and discuss an initial modification of DLP$^<$ that yields the expected answers in some examples that we consider significant

1 Introduction

The disjunctive logic program language DLP$^<$ was introduced in [1] for knowledge representation and non-monotonic reasoning. It has been advocated that inheritance reasoning (see e.g. [2,4]) can be dealt with under the DLP$^<$ framework. Using DLP$^<$, an inheritance network could be represented by a DLP$^<$ program and the answer set semantics of this program specifies the entailment relation of the original network. We demonstrate this by means of an example, written in the DLP$^<$ syntax (precise definitions are in the next section). Consider a taxonomy of animals with their locomotion properties such as *walks*, *swims*, *flies*, or *creeps*. This can be described by the following DLP$^<$ rules:

$animal\{\ walks(A) \lor swims(A) \lor flies(A) \lor creeps(A) \leftarrow is\_a(A, animal).$
$\qquad blood\_circulation(A) \leftarrow is\_a(A, animal).\}$
$is\_a(pingu, animal).$

According to the DLP$^<$ semantics, this program has four answer sets [3], in each one *pingu* has exactly one locomotion method.

M.-S. Hacid et al. (Eds.): ISMIS 2002, LNAI 2366, pp. 294–302, 2002.

Let us consider a subclass of *animal*, say *bird*, specified by the following rules:

$bird : animal\{swims(B) \vee flies(B) \vee creeps(B) \leftarrow is\_a(B, bird).\}$

$is\_a(pingu, bird).$

Intuitively, the rule describing birds locomotion is more specific than that describing animal locomotion. Thus, the combined theory should have only three answer sets, where *pingu* either swims or flies or creeps, exclusively. On the other hand, in all three answer sets we have *blood_circulation(pingu)*. The DLP$^<$ semantics also yields this conclusion.

In this paper, we propose several semantically modifications for DLP$^<$ that enhances its usability in inheritance reasoning. In this paper, however, we argue that, for improving the usability of the language, some generalizations should be made, and some unwanted behavior avoided. In particular, we propose some semantic modifications for DLP$^<$ that enhance its usability in inheritance reasoning. The proposed modifications are motivated and illustrated by means of examples. We will begin with a short overview of DLP$^<$. Afterward, we discuss the weakness of DLP$^<$ in knowledge representation, especially in inheritance reasoning, and discuss our initial proposal semantic fix for DLP$^<$.

2   Syntax and Semantics of DLP$^<$

In this section we review the basic definitions of DLP$^<$ [1]. Let us assume a set $\mathcal{V}$ of *variables,* a set Π of *predicates,* a set Λ of *constants,* and a finite partially ordered set of symbols $(\mathcal{O}, <)$, where $\mathcal{O}$ is a set of strings, called *object identifiers,* and $<$ is a strict partial order (i.e., the relation $<$ is irreflexive and transitive).

The definitions of *term, atom,* and *literal* are the standard ones, where function symbols are not considered, and $\neg$ is the strong *negation* symbol. A term, atom, literal, rule, or program is *ground* if no variable appears in it. Two literals are *complementary* iff they are of the form p and $\neg p$, for some atom p. Given a literal L, $\neg \cdot L$ denotes[1] the opposite literal. For a set $\mathcal{L}$ of literals, $\neg \cdot \mathcal{L}$ denotes the set $\{\neg \cdot L \mid L \in \mathcal{L}\}$.

A rule r is an expression of the form:

$a_1 \vee \ldots \vee a_n \leftarrow b_1, \ldots, b_k, \; not \; b_{k+1}, \ldots, \; not \; b_m$

where $a_1 \ldots a_n, b_1, \ldots, b_m$ are literals, and *not* is the *negation as failure* symbol. The disjunction $a_1 \vee \ldots \vee a_n$ is the *head* of r, while the conjunction $b_1, \ldots, b_k, \; not \; b_{k+1}, \ldots, \; not \; b_m$ is the *body*. $b_1, \ldots, b_k$, is called the *positive* part of the body of r, and $not \; b_{k+1}, \ldots, \; not \; b_m$ is called the *NAF (negation as failure)* part of the body of r. We often denote the sets of literals appearing in the head, in the body, in the positive part of the body, and in the NAF part of the body of a rule r by *Head(r)*, *Body(r) Body$^+$(r)*, and *Body$^-$(r)*, respectively.

Let an *object* o be a pair $\langle oid(o), \Sigma(o) \rangle$ where $oid(o)$ is an object identifier in $\mathcal{O}$ and $\Sigma(o)$ is a (possibly empty) set of rules associated to it.

A *knowledge base* on $\mathcal{O}$ is a set of objects, one for each element of $\mathcal{O}$. Given a knowledge base $\mathcal{K}$ and an object identifier $o \in \mathcal{O}$, the DLP$^<$ *program for o on* $\mathcal{K}$ is the set of objects

$\mathcal{P} = \{(o', \Sigma(o')) \in \mathcal{K} \mid o = o' \text{ or } o < o'\}$

The relation $<$ induces a partial order on $\mathcal{P}$ in the standard way.

---

[1] Elsewhere the contrary literal is denoted $\overline{L}$.

Informally, a knowledge base can be viewed as a set of *objects* embedding the definition of their properties specified through disjunctive logic rules, organized in a *is_a* (inheritance) hierarchy (induced by $<$). A program $\mathcal{P}$ for an object o on a knowledge base $\mathcal{K}$ consists of the subset of $\mathcal{K}$ *reachable from* o in the is_a-net.

Thanks to the inheritance mechanism, $\mathcal{P}$ incorporates the knowledge explicitly defined for o plus the knowledge inherited from the higher objects. If a knowledge base admits a *bottom* element (i.e., an object less than all the other objects, by the relation $<$), we call it a *program*, since it is equal to the program for the bottom element. In order to represent the membership of a pair of objects (resp., object identifiers) (o_2, o_1) to the transitive reduction of $<$ the notation $o_2 : o_1$ is used, to signify that o_2 is a *sub-object* of o_1.

2.1 The Semantics of DLP$^<$

Assume that a knowledge base $\mathcal{K}$ is given and an object o has been fixed. Let $\mathcal{P}$ be the DLP$^<$ program for o on $\mathcal{K}$. The *Universe* $U_\mathcal{P}$ of $\mathcal{P}$ is the set of all constants appearing in the rules. The *Base* $B_\mathcal{P}$ of $\mathcal{P}$ is the set of all possible ground literals that can be constructed from the predicates appearing in the rules of $\mathcal{P}$ and the constants occurring in $U_\mathcal{P}$. Note that, unlike in traditional logic programming the base $B_\mathcal{P}$ of a DLP$^<$ program contains both positive and negative literals. Given a rule r occurring in $\mathcal{P}$, a *ground instance* of r is a rule obtained from r by replacing every variable X in r by $\sigma(r)$ where σ is a mapping from the variables occurring in r to the constants in $U_\mathcal{P}$. *ground*($\mathcal{P}$) denotes the (finite) multi-set of all instances of the rules occurring in $\mathcal{P}$

A function *obj_of* is defined, from ground instance of rules in *ground*($\mathcal{P}$) onto the set O of the object identifiers, associating with a ground instance $\bar{r}$ of r the (unique) object of r.

A subset of ground literals in $B_\mathcal{P}$ is said to be *consistent* if it does not contain a pair of complementary literals. An *interpretation* $\mathcal{I}$ is a consistent subset of $B_\mathcal{P}$. Under an interpretation $\mathcal{I} \subseteq B_\mathcal{P}$, a ground literal L *is true* if $L \in \mathcal{I}$, *false* otherwise.

Given a rule r in *ground*($\mathcal{P}$), the head of r is *true* in $\mathcal{I}$ if at least one literal of the head is true w.r.t $\mathcal{I}$. The body of r is true in $\mathcal{I}$ if:

(i) every literal in *Body*$^+(r)$ is true w.r.t. $\mathcal{I}$, and

(ii) every literal in *Body*$^-(r)$ is false v.r.t. $\mathcal{I}$.

Rule r is *satisfied* in $\mathcal{I}$ if either the head of r is true in $\mathcal{I}$ or the body of r is not true in $\mathcal{I}$.

The semantics of overriding. To deal with explicit contradictions, the following definitions – taken from [1] – are needed.

Definition 1. *Given two ground rules r_1 and r_2, we will say that r_1 threatens r_2 on literal L if 1. $L \in Head(r_1)$, 2. $\neg \cdot L \in Head(r_2)$, and 3. obj_of($r_1$) $<$ obj_of(r_2).*

Equivalently, one can say that r_1 and r_2 are conflicting on L (or r_1 and r_2 are in conflict on L).

Definition 2. *Given an interpretation $\mathcal{I}$ and two ground rules r_1 and r_2 such that r_1 threatens r_2 on literal L, we say that r_1 overrides r_2 on L in $\mathcal{I}$ if:*

1. $\neg \cdot L \in \mathcal{I}$ and 2. the body of r_2 is true in $\mathcal{I}$.

A rule r in ground($\mathcal{P}$) is overridden in $\mathcal{I}$ if for each L in Head(r) there exists r_1 in ground($\mathcal{P}$) such that r_1 overrides r on L in $\mathcal{I}$.

The notion of overriding takes care of conflicts arising between conflicting rules. For instance, suppose that both a and $\neg a$ are derivable in $\mathcal{I}$ from rules r and r', respectively. If r is more specific than r' in the inheritance hierarchy, then r' is overridden. As a result, a should be preferred to $\neg a$ because it is derivable from a rule, r, which is more specific and therefore *more descriptive* of the object itself than r'.

Definition 3. *Let $\mathcal{I}$ be an interpretation for $\mathcal{P}$. $\mathcal{I}$ is a model for $\mathcal{P}$ if every rule in ground($\mathcal{P}$) is either satisfied or overridden in $\mathcal{I}$. Moreover, $\mathcal{I}$ is a minimal model for $\mathcal{P}$ if no (proper) subset of $\mathcal{I}$ is a model for $\mathcal{P}$.*

Definition 4. *Given an interpretation $\mathcal{I}$ for $\mathcal{P}$, the reduction of $\mathcal{P}$ w.r.t. $\mathcal{I}$, denoted $G(\mathcal{I}, \mathcal{P})$, is the set of rules obtained from ground($\mathcal{P}$) by removing 1. every rule overridden in $\mathcal{I}$; 2. every rule r such that $Body^-(r) \neq \emptyset$; 3. the negative part from the bodies of the remaining rules.*

The reduction of a program is simply a set of ground rules. Given a set S of ground rules, $pos(S)$ denotes the positive disjunctive program (called the *positive version of S*), obtained from S by renaming each negative literal $\neg p(X)$ as $p'(X)$.

Definition 5. *Let $\mathcal{M}$ be a model for $\mathcal{P}$. We say that $\mathcal{M}$ is a DLP$^<$ answer set for $\mathcal{P}$ if it is a minimal model of the positive version $pos(G(\mathcal{M}, \mathcal{P}))$ of $pos(G(\mathcal{M}, \mathcal{P}))$. Clearly, $\mathcal{M}$ is inconsistent if it contains both $p(X)$ as $p'(X)$.*

3   Knowledge Representation with DLP$^<$

In [1] it has been argued that DLP$^<$ is a suitable knowledge representation language for default reasoning with exceptions. The usefulness of DLP$^<$ in different tasks in knowledge representation and non-monotonic reasoning has been demonstrated by the encoding of classical examples of non-monotonic reasoning. The most interesting feature of DLP$^<$, as advocated in [1], is the addition of inheritance into the modeling of knowledge. For example, the famous Bird-Penguin example can be represented in DLP$^<$ without the conventional *abnormality predicate* as follows.

Example 1. Consider the following program $\mathcal{P}$ with $O(\mathcal{P})$ consisting of three objects *bird, penguin* and *tweety,* such that *penguin* is a sub-object of *bird* and *tweety* is a sub-object of *penguin:*

  $bird\{flies\}$ $penguin : bird\{\neg flies\}$ $tweety : penguin\{\}$

The only model of the above DLP$^<$ program contains $\neg flies$.

Unlike in traditional logic programming, the DLP$^<$ language supports two types of negation, that is *strong negation* and *negation as failure*. Strong negation is useful to express negative pieces of information under the complete information assumption. Hence, a negative fact (by strong negation) is true only if it is explicitly derived from the rules of the program. As a consequence, the head of rules may contain also such negative literals, and rules can be conflicting on some literals. According to the inheritance principles, the ordering relationship between objects can help us to assign different levels of acceptance to the rules, allowing us to avoid the contradiction that would otherwise arise.

3.1 Default Inheritance in DLP$^<$

As pointed out in [1], the syntax and semantics of DLP$^<$ allow us to capture forms of non-monotonic reasoning and knowledge representation, including inertia and *is*-nets in a rather straightforward way.

For improving its usability however, we believe that some generalization should be made, and some unwanted behavior avoided. The modifications that we propose to DLP$^<$ are illustrated by means of the following examples.

Consider again the knowledge base that defines animals and their possible ways of motion. For birds, the possible ways of locomotion must be defined, which constitute a subset of general ones. Following Buccafurri et al., [1] we define the following knowledge base:

$$P_1 = \begin{cases} animal & \{l_1 : walk \vee swim \vee run \vee fly \leftarrow \} \\ bird : animal \{ & \neg swim \leftarrow \qquad \neg run \leftarrow \} \end{cases}$$

The two DLP$^<$ models of this program are $\{\neg swim, \neg run, walk\}$ and $\{\neg swim, \neg run, fly\}$ which implies that a bird either walks or flies but does not swim and does not run. That is, in order to represent the fact that birds swim or fly, it is necessary to state what birds *do not* do, with respect to the general disjunctive rules. Cases that are left, define implicitly what birds are allowed to do, i.e. walk or fly (or maybe both).

We submit that an improvement is needed here, since:

- in many practical cases it is far more concise to list what the features of the object at hand *are*, rather than what they are not;
- a detailed knowledge of ancestor object definition should not be required;
- unwanted behavior arises if one formalizes the example in the intuitive way, as shown by the first example below, and
- unwanted behavior arises in case of multiple inheritance, as illustrated by the second example below.

To illustrate our point, let us consider the direct, intuitive encoding:

$$P_2 = \begin{cases} animal & \{l_1 : walk \vee swim \vee run \vee fly \leftarrow \} \\ bird : animal \{l_2 : walk \vee fly \leftarrow & \} \end{cases}$$

the latter formulation may appear conceptually equivalent to the former one, and one would expect the semantics to be the same, which is not the case though. Under the DLP$^<$ semantics, P_2 has two models $\{walk\}$ and $\{fly\}$ which indicate that a bird either walks or flies. Notice that these two models can be obtained from the two models of P_1 by removing the negative literals from them. We believe that given the hierarchical property of objects one would prefer P_2 over P_1 for its intuitiveness and that it conforms to the downward refinement technique one uses in software engineering. After all, we are still able to conclude that a bird walks or fly, which is also the intuitive answer.

What happens if we follow the downward refinement technique in describing penguins? Consider the addition of the following, more specific, definitions:

$$penguin : bird \quad \{ \quad \neg fly \leftarrow . \quad \neg walk \leftarrow wounded. \quad \neg walk \leftarrow newborn \}$$
$$pimpi : penguin \{ \quad newborn \leftarrow \qquad \qquad \qquad \qquad \qquad \}$$
$$pingu : penguin \{ \qquad \qquad \qquad \qquad \qquad \qquad \qquad \qquad \qquad \}$$

Consider *pingu*, a penguin, who is neither newborn nor wounded. From $walk \lor fly$ in *bird* and $\neg fly$ in *penguin*, we conclude $walk$, which also satisfies l_1. In this case, we say that rule l_1 is *de facto overridden* by l_2. Thus, for *pingu*, DLP$^<$ concludes that it $walk$ and $\neg fly$, which is what we expected.

The fact that rule l_2 cannot override l_1 (Definition 2) since they are not in conflict, gives rise to some unwanted consequences, which we now discuss.

Consider the penguin *pimpi* who is a newborn. From the rule in *penguin*, we can conclude that *pimpi* does not walk and does not fly, i.e., $\neg walk$ and $\neg fly$. Thus, rule l_2 is overridden by the rules in *penguin*. Rule l_1 will not be overridden because there exists no conflicting rule with l_1 on every literal $L \in head(l_1) \setminus head(l_2)$, which are required to override l_1 (Definition 2). This means that we will have answer sets where *pimpi* runs or swims. Even though the semantics of DLP$^<$ would entail $\neg walk$ and $\neg fly$ for *pimpi*, the existence of answer sets in which *pimpi* runs or swims seems not reasonable in this situation.

As a result, we believe that in this example rule l_2 should override l_1. In general, *disjunctive rules should override those rules in ancestors of which they are a special case.* Moreover, when describing specializations, new knowledge may be added, which is not present in the ancestor. I.e., rule l_2 could for instance be:

$$walk \lor fly \lor run$$

assuming that run is not included in l_1. Still, we think that l_1 should be overridden.

4 A Semantics Fix for Default Inheritance

The counter-intuitive results seen for the newborn penguin example above, can be avoided by slight changes in the semantics of overriding. What is being enforced by the new definition of overriding presented here is the fact that *specificity should never be context-independent,* rather, it should always be evaluated w.r.t. interpretations. Some new definitions are in order now.

Definition 6. *A ground rule r_1 is a specialization of rule r_2 if 1. $obj\_of(r_1) < obj\_of(r_2)$, 2. $Head(r_1) \cap Head(r_2) \neq \emptyset$, and 3. $Body(r_1) \subseteq Body(r_2)$.*

It is easy to see that in P_2, l_2 is a specialization of l_1.

Definition 7. *For an interpretation $\mathcal{I}$, and two conflicting ground rules r_1, r_2 in $ground(\mathcal{P})$ such that $L \in Head(r_2)$ (and $/.L \in Head(r1)$) we say that r_1 overrides r_2 on L in $\mathcal{I}$ if: 1. $obj\_of(r_1) < obj\_of(r_2)$, 2. $\neg \cdot L \in \mathcal{I}$, and 3. the body of r_2 is true in $\mathcal{I}$.*

The definition below is a stricter version of the original definition of overriding presented earlier on. The second condition is new and disallows the newborn penguin counterexample.

Definition 8. *A rule r in $ground(\mathcal{P})$ is overridden in $\mathcal{I}$ if one of the following conditions holds:*

(i) *either for each $L \in Head(r)$ there exists r_1 in $ground(\mathcal{P})$ such that r_1 overrides r on L in $\mathcal{I}$;*

(ii) *or, there exists a specialization r' of r and r' is overridden in $\mathcal{I}$.*

Going back to *pimpi*'s example, we see that rule l_2 is overridden according to condition (i) but under the new definition, also l_1 is because l_2 is a specialization of l_1 and l_2 is overridden (Condition (ii)). Therefore, the new definition ensures that *overriding a rule in an object implies overriding all its less specific ancestors*. Namely, since *pimpi* does not fly nor walks (which is what birds usually do), it won't any more be supposed to perform any less specific form of locomotion (run, swim, etc.). The general conclusion we draw from this example and discussion is that whenever we have two rules whose relation is similar to that of l_1 and l_2 above, which was called de facto overriding, we should make sure that overriding of l_2 also causes overriding of l_1. Hence, no redundant answer set should be generated.

4.1 Multiple Inheritance

The knowledge representation style required by DLP$^<$ as it is now, may yield some unwanted behavior when multiple inheritance and updates are used. This section provides another example of how weak DLP$^<$ is in this task. Consider the knowledge base of objects with their color and shapes with the following rules[2]:
$colored\_object$
$\{color(X, red) \lor color(X, yellow) \lor color(X, green) \lor color(X, blue) \leftarrow object(X)\}$
$shaped\_object$
$\{$
$shape(X, cube) \lor shape(X, sphere) \lor shape(X, cone) \leftarrow object(X)$
$volume(X, V) \leftarrow object(X), shape(X, S), formula(X, S, V).$
$formula(X, cube, V) \leftarrow edge(X, L), V = L \times L \times L$
$formula(X, sphere, V) \leftarrow radius(X, R), V = (4 \times L \times L \times L \times \Pi)/3$
$formula(X, cone, V) \leftarrow radius(X, R), height(X, H), V = (H \times R \times R \times \Pi)/3$
$\}$
$colored\_cube : colored\_object, shaped\_object$
  $\{object(c_1).\ shape(c_1, cube).\ edge(c_1, 4).\}$
$green\_object : colored\_object$ $\{color(X, green)\}$
$red\_object : colored\_object$ $\{color(X, red)\}$
At the top of this knowledge base, objects are defined in terms of their color, and the definition of objects in terms of their shape. The shape of an object allows one to compute its volume, by applying the appropriate formula. Then, as a particular case there is a cube, denoted as c_1, defined in terms of its shape. In our view, as discussed above, the specification $shape(c_1, cube)$ should override the general disjunctive definition, while the color is still one of those defined in the parent object. In this case, the object inherits from parent objects both the (disjunctive) specification of the possible colors it might assume, and the way of computing the volume.

Now, let us consider defining objects in terms of their color. The disjunctive specification of color should no longer be applicable, while the various choices about shape, and the corresponding formulas for computing the volume, are inherited. However, in DLP$^<$ as it is now, this example should be defined as follows:
  $green\_object:colored\_object\{\neg color(X, red) \leftarrow\ \neg color(X, yellow) \leftarrow\ \neg color(X, blue) \leftarrow\}$
  $red\_object : colored\_object\{\neg color(X, green) \leftarrow\ \neg color(X, yellow) \leftarrow\ \neg color(X, blue) \leftarrow\}$

---

[2] For the easy of reading, we use the formulas for computing the volume instead of representing them in LP's notation.

Not only is this definition longer and less readable, but it also yields counter intuitive results when augmented for instance by the following definition:

$redgreen\_radius\_object : green\_object, red\_object, shaped\_object$
$\{object(s_1) \leftarrow \quad shape(s_1, sphere) \leftarrow \quad radius(s_1, 3) \leftarrow$
$\quad object(p_1) \leftarrow \quad shape(p_1, cone) \leftarrow \quad radius(p_1, 2) \leftarrow \quad\quad height(p_1, 3) \leftarrow\}$

Here, there is an object (called $redgreen\_radius\_object$) specifying instances of spheres (namely, s_1) and cones (namely, p_1) which are either red or green. In our view, the inheritance should lead to create, in this object, the disjunctive rule

$$color(X, red) \vee color(X, green).$$

In fact, inheriting the same attribute by multiple sources, means that the attribute may have multiple values (provided they are not mutually inconsistent).

In DLP$^<$ as it is, $redgreen\_radius\_object$ inherits all definitions from its parent objects, i.e.:

$\{\neg color(X, red) \leftarrow \quad \neg color(X, yellow) \leftarrow \quad \neg color(X, blue) \leftarrow \quad \neg color(X, green) \leftarrow\}$

With respect to their union, the general disjunctive rule is completely overridden, and therefore $redgreen\_radius\_object$ turns out to have *no color.*

In the next section, we propose a semantic fix for this problem. We will show that a knowledge base written in this more general and concise form can be transformed into a DLP$^<$ knowledge base, so as to reuse the semantics and the implementation. The difference is in the easier, more intuitive style for the programmer. Consistency and adequacy of the resulting DLP$^<$ knowledge base are guaranteed by the system.

4.2 Addressing Multiple Inheritance

In what follows we propose a strengthening of DLP$^<$ that allows us to deal with multiple inheritance. We first define a concept called *sibling rules* as follows.

Definition 9. *Two ground rules r_1, r_2 are siblings if:*

1. *$obj\_of(r_1) \not< obj\_of(r_2)$ and $obj\_of(r_2) \not< obj\_of(r_1)$,*
2. *r_1 and r_2 are both the specialization of another rule r, and*
3. *$Body(r_1) = Body(r_2)$.*

Intuitively, two rules are siblings if they describe the properties of two (possibly disjoint) sub-classes of an object.

Definition 10. *Given program $\mathcal{P}$, the corresponding enhanced program $\mathcal{P}'$ is defined as follows. Given objects o, o_1, o_2, $o_i = (oid(o_i), \Sigma(o_i))$ where $o < o_1$ and $o < o_2$ and $o_1 \not< o_2$ and rules $r_1 \in \Sigma(o_1)$, $r_2 \in \Sigma(o_2)$ are siblings, add to $\mathcal{P}$ the rule: $Head(r_1) \vee Head(r_2) \leftarrow Body(r_1)$ (where, by definition, $Body(r_1) = Body(r_2)$)*

In the above example, we would add to $redgreen\_radius\_object$ the rule $color(X, red) \vee color(X, green)$ by merging the sibling rules $color(X,red)$ and $color(X,green)$ (each one with empty body) as we wanted to do. Notice that an interpretation for $\mathcal{P}$ is also an interpretation for $\mathcal{P}'$, since no new atoms are added. Then, a model for $\mathcal{P}$ is obtained as a model of the enhanced version $\mathcal{P}'$.

Definition 11. *Let $\mathcal{I}$ be an interpretation for $\mathcal{P}'$. $\mathcal{I}$ is a model for $\mathcal{P}$ if every rule in ground($\mathcal{P}'$) is satisfied or overridden in $\mathcal{I}$. $\mathcal{I}$ is a minimal model for $\mathcal{P}$ if no (proper) subset of $\mathcal{I}$ is a model for $\mathcal{P}$.*

Accordingly, we have to consider $\mathcal{P}'$ instead of $\mathcal{P}$ when performing the reduction.

Definition 12. *Given an interpretation $\mathcal{I}$ for $\mathcal{P}$, the reduction of $\mathcal{P}$ w.r.t. $\mathcal{I}$, denoted $G(\mathcal{I}, \mathcal{P})$, is the set of rules obtained from ground($\mathcal{P}'$) by removing 1. every rule overridden in $\mathcal{I}$; 2. every rule r such that $Body^-(r) \neq \emptyset$; 3. the negative part from the bodies of the remaining rules.*

5   Conclusions

In this paper we argued, mainly by examples, that to become a viable knowledge representation language that combines the expressiveness of disjunctive logic programming and the convenience of inheritance, DLP$^<$ needs improvements. We showed that overriding in DLP$^<$ is too weak to accommodate a straightforward encoding of classical examples of non-monotonic reasoning. The same is true for the treatment of multiple inheritance. We proposed the strengthening of DLP$^<$ by modifying the notion of overriding and introducing the concept of specialization. To deal with multiple inheritance, we defined the concept of siblings and enhanced programs. The new semantics provides the correct answers in the discussed examples, but we need more work on the actual range of application of DLP$^<$.

References

1. Buccafurri F., Faber W. and Leone N., 1999. *Disjunctive Logic Programs with Inheritance.* Proc. of ICLP'99, pp. 79–93. Long version submitted for publication.
2. Dung P.M. and Son T.C., 1995. *Nonmonotonic inheritance , argumentation, and logic programming.* In Proc. of the 3th Int'l Conference on Logic Programming and Non-Monotonic Reasoning (LPNMR'95), pp. 316–329.
3. Gelfond, M. and Lifschitz, V., 1991. *Classical Negation in Logic Programming and Disjunctive Databases,* New Generation Computing 9, 1991: 365–385.
4. Horty J.F., 1994. Some direct theories of non-monotonic inheritance. In D. Gabbay, C. Hogger, and J. Robinson, editors, *Handbook of Logic and Artificial Intelligence and Logic Programming*, pages 111–187. Oxford Uni., 1994.

Knowledge Constructions for Artificial Intelligence

Ahti Pietarinen

Department of Philosophy, University of Helsinki
P.O. Box 9, FIN-00014 University of Helsinki
`pietarin@cc.helsinki.fi`

Abstract. Some new types of knowledge constructions in epistemic logic are defined, and semantics given by combining game-theoretic notions with modal models. One such notion introduced is focussed knowledge, which arises from imperfect information in quantified epistemic logics. This notion is useful in knowledge representation schemes in artificial intelligence and multi-agent systems with uncertainty. In general, in all the logics considered here, the imperfect information is seen to give rise to partiality, including partial common and partial distributed knowledge. A game-theoretic method of creating non-monotonicity will then be suggested, based on the partialised notion of 'only knowing' and inaccessible possible worlds. The overall purpose is to show the extent in which games combine with a given variety of knowledge constructions.

1 Introduction

The underlying motivation for this work can perhaps be illustrated by noting that classical logic is a logic of perfect information transmission. This fact is of course true of propositional and predicate logics, but it is also true of intensional modal logics and logics of epistemic notions (knowledge and belief). By perfect information transmission, it is meant that in transmitting semantic information from one logical component to another, that information is never lost.

The aim is to show that once we adopt semantics that is suitable not only for the received logics with perfect information, we are able to produce new logics with new, expressive resources that capture an interesting variety of constructions of knowledge. Some of such constructions are needed in representing knowledge of multi-agent systems. The distinction between perfect and imperfect information transmission can be made precise within the framework of game-theoretic semantics (GTS, see e.g. [3,7,8]), which operationalises a semantic game between two players, the team of Verifiers (V, ∃loise) and the team of Falsifiers (F, ∀belard). These semantic games provide an evaluation method that can be defined for a variety of logics.

Research in epistemic logic and reasoning about knowledge has played an important role in AI, and uncertainty has been a major topic in reasoning even longer. The purpose of this paper is to combine the two. It is argued that logics of knowledge can represent multi-agent uncertainty, and it is suggested how

M.-S. Hacid et al. (Eds.): ISMIS 2002, LNAI 2366, pp. 303–311, 2002.

a unifying semantics based on the notion of games can be defined to a wide variety of knowledge constructions. These notions include focussed, common and distributed knowledge, and the nonmonotonic notion of 'only knowing'.

Epistemic logics with imperfect information are partial, that is, there are sentences that are neither true nor false. Partiality itself has game-theoretic roots: if the associated semantic games are non-determined, all attempts of trying to verify or falsify a formula can be defeated. In contrast to received partial modal logics [5], games give rise to partiality even if the underlying models are complete.

One outcome is that some new multi-agent logics for notions of knowledge that need games for their interpretation will be available. Far from being a purely technical enterprise, these logics are motivated by those knowledge representation schemes in multi-agent systems that virtually necessitate the introduction of new knowledge constructions. For example, focussed knowledge involves inherent uncertainty, and is argued to play an important role in representing knowledge in multi-agent systems where agents, such as communicating processors, do not always know the content of a message that has been sent to them.

2   From Perfect to Imperfect Information: Knowledge and Multi-agent Systems

The inauguration of epistemic logic [2] has led to a proliferation of knowledge in logic, philosophy, computer science and artificial intelligence. Nowadays we find notions like common, shared and distributed knowledge. Furthermore, the distinction between *de dicto* and *de re* knowledge is widely spread.

The well-formed formulas of ordinary propositional epistemic logic $\mathcal{L}$ are constructed by $\phi ::= p \mid \varphi \vee \psi \mid \neg \varphi \mid K_i \varphi$. $K_i \varphi$ is read 'an agent i knows φ'.

Let φ, ψ be formulas of classical propositional epistemic logic $\mathcal{L}$. A model is $M = \langle \mathcal{W}, R, g \rangle$, where g is a total valuation function $g \colon \mathcal{W} \to (\Phi \to \{\text{True}, \text{False}\})$, assigning to each proposition letter a subset of a set of possible worlds $\mathcal{W} = \{w_0 \ldots w_n\}$ for which $\{w_i \mid g(w)(p) = \text{True}, w \in \mathcal{W}\}$. $R = \{\rho_1 \ldots \rho_n\}$ is a set of accessibility relations for each $i = 1 \ldots n$, $\rho_i \subseteq \mathcal{W} \times \mathcal{W}$. Let $w_1 \in [w_0]_{\rho_i}$ denote that a possible world w_1 is i-accessible from w_0.

$\langle M, w \rangle \models p$ iff $\{w_i \mid g(w)(p) = \text{True}, w \in \mathcal{W}\}, p \in \Phi$.

$\langle M, w \rangle \models \neg \varphi$ iff $\langle M, w \rangle \not\models \varphi$.

$\langle M, w \rangle \models \varphi \vee \psi$ iff $\langle M, w \rangle \models \varphi$ or $\langle M, w \rangle \models \psi$.

$\langle M, w \rangle \models K_i \varphi$ iff $\langle M, w' \rangle \models \varphi$, for all $w' \in [w]_{\rho_i}$.

Let $K_j \psi$ be an $\mathcal{L}$-formula, and let $A = \{K_1 \ldots K_n\}, K_i \in A, i \in \{1 \ldots n\}$ such that K_j is in the syntactic scope of K_i. Now if $B \subseteq A$, then $(K_j / B) \psi \in \mathcal{L}^*, K_j \notin B$. For example, $K_1 (K_2 / K_1) \varphi$ and $K_1 (\varphi \wedge (K_2 / K_1) \psi)$ are wffs of $\mathcal{L}^*$.

Every $\mathcal{L}^*$-formula φ defines a game $\mathcal{G}(\varphi, w, g)$ on a model M between two teams of players, the team of falsifiers $F = \{F_1 \ldots F_n\}$ and the team of verifiers $V = \{V_1 \ldots V_k\}$, where w is a world and g is an assignment to the propositional letters. The game $\mathcal{G}(\varphi, w, g)$ is defined by the following rules.

(G.¬) If $\varphi = \neg\psi$, V and F change roles, and the next choice is in $\mathcal{G}(\psi, w, g)$.

(G.∨) If $\varphi = (\psi \vee \theta)$, V chooses Left or Right, and the next choice is in $\mathcal{G}(\psi, w, g)$ if Left and $\mathcal{G}(\theta, w, g)$ if Right.

(G.K_i) If $\varphi = K_i\,\psi$, and the game has reached w, $F_j \in F$ chooses $w_1 \in [w]_{\rho_i}$, and the next choice is in $\mathcal{G}(\psi, w_1, g)$.

(G.(K_i/B)) If $\varphi = (K_i/B)\,\psi$, $K_i \notin B$, and the game has reached w, then $F_l \in F$ chooses $w_1 \in \mathcal{W}$ 'independently' of the choices made for the elements in B.

(G.at) If φ is atomic, the game ends, and V wins if φ true, and F wins if φ false.

The formulas $(K_i/B)\,\psi$ signal imperfect information: player choosing for K_i on the left-hand side of the slash is not informed of the choices made for the elements in B earlier in the game. Nothing is said about the accessibility relation, since we want to leave the interpretation of these modalities open.

The purpose of V is to show that φ is true in M ($\langle M, w \rangle \models^+ \varphi$), and the purpose of F is to show that φ is false in M ($\langle M, w \rangle \models^- \varphi$). If $\langle M, w \rangle \models^+ \varphi$, V wins, and if $\langle M, w \rangle \models^- \varphi$, F wins. A strategy for a player in $\mathcal{G}(\varphi, w, g)$ is a function assigning to each non-atomic subformula a member of the team, outputting a possible world, a value in $\{\mathsf{Left}, \mathsf{Right}\}$ (the connective information), or an instruction to change roles (negation). A winning strategy is a strategy by which a player can make operational choices such that every play results in a win for him or her, no matter how the opponent chooses.

Let φ be an $\mathcal{L}^*$-formula. For any $M, w \in \mathcal{W}$, $\langle M, w \rangle \models^+ \varphi$ iff a strategy exists which is winning for V in $\mathcal{G}(\varphi, w, g)$, and $\langle M, w \rangle \models^- \varphi$ iff a strategy exists which is winning for F in $\mathcal{G}(\varphi, w, g)$. A game is determined, iff for every play on φ, either V has a winning strategy in $\mathcal{G}$ or F has a winning strategy in $\mathcal{G}$. It is easy to see that games for $\mathcal{L}^*$ are not determined. From non-determinacy it follows that the law of excluded middle $\varphi \vee \neg\varphi$ fails in $\mathcal{L}^*$. This is a common thing to happen in logics with imperfect information.

Non-determinacy is related to partiality. A partial model is a triple $M = \langle \mathcal{W}, R, g \rangle$, where g is a partial valuation function $g \colon \mathcal{W} \to (\Phi \to \{\mathsf{True}, \mathsf{False}\})$, assigning to each proposition letter in Φ a subset $g(\Phi)$ of a set of possible worlds $\mathcal{W} = \{w_0 \ldots w_n\}$. Partiality means that

$$\langle M, w \rangle \models^+ K_i\varphi \text{ iff } \langle M, w' \rangle \models^+ \varphi \text{ for all } w \in \mathcal{W}, w' \in [w]_{\rho_i}.$$
$$\langle M, w \rangle \models^- K_i\varphi \text{ iff } \langle M, w' \rangle \models^- \varphi \text{ for some } w \in \mathcal{W}, w' \in [w]_{\rho_i}.$$

An alternative way to approach partiality is by GTS of imperfect information, where partiality arises at the level of complex formulas, dispensing with partial models. One consequence is that semantic games generalise received partial modal logics [5] to complete models.

3   Focussed Knowledge and Multi-agent Systems

There are important non-technical motivations as to why one should be interested in combining games with various modalities. For one thing, in quantified extensions the combination gives rise to focussed knowledge.

3.1 Language and Semantics

Let the syntax for first-order epistemic logic $\mathcal{L}_{\omega\omega}$ consist of a signature, a logical vocabulary, and rules for building up formulas: $\phi ::= P \mid K_i\varphi \mid \forall x\varphi \mid \exists x\varphi \mid \varphi \vee \psi \mid \neg\varphi \mid x \simeq y$.

Let $Q\psi, Q \in \{\forall x_j, \exists y_j, K_i\}$ be an $\mathcal{L}_{\omega\omega}$-formula in the syntactic scope of the elements in $A = \{K_1 \ldots K_n, \forall x_k, \exists y_k\}$. Then $\mathcal{L}_{\omega\omega}^*$ consists of wffs of $\mathcal{L}_{\omega\omega}$ together with: if $B \subseteq A$, then $(Q/B)\,\psi$ is an $\mathcal{L}_{\omega\omega}^*$-formula, $Q \notin B$. For example, $K_1 \exists y (K_2/K_1 y)\,Sxy \in \mathcal{L}_{\omega\omega}^*$. This hides the information about the choice for K_1 and y at K_2.

Models and valuations have to take the world-boundedness of individuals into account. A non-empty world-relative domain consisting of aspects of individuals is D_{w_j}. We skip the formal definitions here.

The semantics needs to be enriched by a finite number of identifying functions (world lines), which extend the valuation g to a (partial) mapping from worlds to individuals, that is, to $g\colon X \to D_{w_i}^{\mathcal{W}}$, such that if $w \in \mathcal{W}$ and g is an identifying function, then $g(w) \in D_w$. These functions imply that individuals have local manifestations in any possible world.

The interpretation of the equality sign $\simeq$ (identifying functional) is:

$$\langle M, w_0, g\rangle \models x \simeq y \text{ iff for some } w_i, w_j \in \mathcal{W}, \exists f \exists h \text{ such that } f(w_i) = h(w_j).$$

That is, two individuals are identical iff there are world lines f and h that pick the same individuals in w_i and in w_j. World lines can meet at some world but then pick different individuals in other worlds: the two-place identifying functional operation spells out when they meet. Individuals within a domain of a possible world are local and need to be cross-identified in order to be global and specific.

The informal game rules for $\mathcal{L}_{\omega\omega}^*$ are:

(G.$\exists x \ldots K_i$) If K_i is in the syntactic scope of $\exists x$ and the game has reached w, the individual picked for x by a verifying player V has to be defined and exist in all worlds accessible from the current one.

This rule is motivated by the fact that the course of the play reached at a certain point is unbeknownst to F choosing for K_i. This approach leads to the notion of specific focus.

(G.$K_i \ldots \exists x$) If $\exists x$ is in the scope of K_i, the individual picked for x has to be defined and exist in the world chosen for K_i.

This leads to the notion of non-specific focus. Finally, the rule for the hidden information says that

(G.Q/B) If $\varphi = (Q/B)\,\psi, Q \in \{\forall x, K_i\}$, and the game has reached w, then if $Q = \forall x$, $F_1 \in F$ chooses an individual from D_{w_1}, where w_1 is the world from which the first world in B has departed. The next choice is in $\mathcal{G}(\psi, w, g)$. If $Q = K_1$ then $F_1 \in F$ chooses a world w_1 'independently' of the choices made for the elements in B, and the next choice is in $\mathcal{G}(\psi, w_1, g)$. Likewise for $V_1 \in V$.

The notion of choosing independently is explained below. Other game rules are ordinary.

Independent modalities mean that the player choosing for K_i is not informed of the choices made for K_j, and hence K_i's are exempted from the syntactic scope of K_j. This can be captured by taking hints from the theory of games. We will apply a partitional information structure $(I_i)_{i \in N}$ in the corresponding extensive-form games, which partitions sequences of actions (histories) $h \in H$ into equivalence classes $\{S_j^i \mid S_j^i \in (I_i)_{i \in N}, h \sim_i h' \in S_j^i, h, h' \in H\}$. The purpose of equivalence classes is to denote which histories are indistinguishable to players.

Payoff functions $u_i(h)$ associate a pair of truth-values in $\{1, -1\}$ to terminal $h \in H$. Strategies are functions $f_i: P^{-1}(\{i\}) \to A$ from histories where players move to sequences of actions in A. If i is planning his decisions within the equivalence class S_j^i annotated for him, his strategies are further required to be uniform on indistinguishable histories $h, h' \in S_j^i$, that is, $f_i(h) = f_i(h'), i \in N$.

This leads to an informal observation: tracing uniform strategies along the game histories reveals in which worlds the specific focus is located. To see this, it suffices to correlate information sets of an extensive game with world lines.

The clause 'choosing independently' that appeared in the above game rules now means that players' strategies have to be uniform on indistinguishable histories, that is, on worlds that players cannot distinguish.

The notion of uniformity puts some constraints on allowable models. At any modal depth (defined in a standard way) there has to be the same number of departing worlds. If we assume that players can observe the set of available choices, the uniformity of strategies also requires that the departing worlds have to coincide for all indistinguishable worlds. Independent K_i's can either refer to simultaneous worlds accessible from the current one, or to detached submodels of M. In the latter case we evaluate formulas in $\langle M, (w_0^1, w_0^2 \ldots w_0^n), g \rangle$. The models would break into concurrent submodels, whence the designated worlds in each submodel become independent.

3.2   A Case for Imperfect Information in Multi-agent Systems

Understanding knowledge of communicating multi-agent system benefits from the kind of concurrency outlined above. Suppose a process U_2 sends a message x to U_1. We ought to report this by saying that 'U_2 knows what x is', and 'U_1 knows that *it* has been sent' (U_1 might knows this because a communication channel is open). This is already a rich situation involving all kinds of knowledge. However, the knowledge involved in this two-agent system cannot be captured in ordinary (first-order) epistemic logic.

In this system, what is involved is 'U_2 knows what has been sent', as well as 'U_1 knows that something has been sent'. However, what is not involved is 'U_1 knows that U_2 knows', nor 'U_2 knows that U_1 knows'. How do we combine these clauses? It is easy to see that the three formulas $\exists x K_{U_2} \mathsf{Mess}(x) \wedge K_{U_1} \exists y \mathsf{Mess}(y)$, $K_{U_1} \exists x (\mathsf{Mess}(x) \wedge K_{U_2} \mathsf{Mess}(x))$, and $\exists x (K_{U_2} \mathsf{Mess}(x) \wedge K_{U_1} \exists y \mathsf{Mess}(y) \wedge x \simeq$

y) all fail. So does an attempt that distinguishes between a message whose content is known ('Cont(x)'), and a message that has been sent ('Sent(y)'): $\exists x \exists y ((K_{U_1} \mathsf{Cont}(x) = y) \wedge K_{U_2} \mathsf{Sent}(x))$. For now U_2 comes to know what has been sent, which is too strong.

Hence, what we need is information hiding:

$$\exists x K_{U_2} (K_{U_1}/K_{U_2} x)(\exists y/K_{U_2} x)\,(\mathsf{Mess}(x) \wedge x \simeq y). \tag{1}$$

In concurrent processing for quantified multi-modal epistemic logic, the notion of focussed knowledge is thus needed.

4   Further Knowledge Constructions and Semantic Games

Here we move back to propositional logics and observe how games can be applied to various other constructions of knowledge. What we get is a range of partial logics for different modalities. The purpose is to show that (i) GTS is useful for epistemic logics in artificial intelligence as it unifies the semantic outlook to different notions of knowledge; (ii) if games are non-determined, one gets partialised versions of these logics; (iii) if the possible-worlds semantics is augmented with inaccessible worlds, non-monotonic epistemic logic can be built upon game-theoretic principles.

4.1   Partial Only Knowing

Let us begin with the logic of only knowing, partialise it, and then define semantics game rules for it. 'Only knowing' ($O_i\,\varphi$, or 'exactly knowing') means that we do not have worlds in a model where φ could be true other than the accessible ones [4,6]. Informally, such a description picks a model where the set of possible worlds is as large as possible. This is because the larger set of possible worlds, the less knowledge an agent has.

To partialise the logic of only knowing, we define

$\langle M, w \rangle \models^+ O_i\,\varphi$ iff $\langle M, w' \rangle \models^+ \varphi \Leftrightarrow w' \in [w]_{\rho_i}$, for all $w' \in W$.
$\langle M, w \rangle \models^- O_i\,\varphi$ iff $\langle M, w' \rangle \models^- \varphi \Leftrightarrow w' \in [w]_{\rho_i}$, for some $w' \in W$.

Let a logic based on these be $\mathcal{L}^O$. The operator O_i can also be understood in terms of another operator N_i: $O_i\,\varphi ::= K_i\varphi \wedge N_i\neg\varphi$.

$\langle M, w' \rangle \models^+ N_i\,\varphi$ iff for all $w' \in \overline{W}, \langle M, w' \rangle \models^+ \varphi$,
$\langle M, w' \rangle \models^- N_i\,\varphi$ iff for some $w' \in \overline{W}, \langle M, w' \rangle \models^- \varphi$,

where $\overline{W}$ is the set of inaccessible worlds, $W = W^* \cup \overline{W}$, W^* is the set of accessible worlds.

A game $\mathcal{G}(\varphi, w, g)$ for $\mathcal{L}^O$-formulas φ, with a world $w \in W$ and an assignment g to the propositional letters is defined as a set of classical rules plus:

(G.O_i) If $\varphi = O_i\,\psi$, and the game has reached $w \in W$, F chooses between $K_i\psi$ and $N_i\neg\varphi$, and the game continues with respect to that choice.

(G.N_i) If $\varphi = N_i \neg\psi$, and the game has reached $w \in W$, F chooses $w' \in \overline{W}$, and the next choice is in $\mathcal{G}(\neg\psi, w', g)$.

(G.at) If φ is atomic, the game ends. F wins, if $\langle M, w' \rangle \models^+ \varphi, w' \in \overline{W}$, or if not: $\langle M, w \rangle \models^+ \varphi, w \in W^*$. V wins, if $\langle M, w' \rangle \models^- \varphi, w' \in \overline{W}$, or if $\langle M, w' \rangle \models^+ \varphi, w \in W^*$.

Strategies will operate on all worlds, including inaccessible ones. In general, we dispense with the accessibility relation and assume that also inaccessible worlds can be chosen. This is natural, because player knowledge and agent knowledge mean different things. (Further restrictions can be that any such inaccessible world can be chosen only once within a play of the game, etc.) Letting φ be an $\mathcal{L}^O$-formula, then for any model M, a valuation g, and $w \in W$, φ is true iff there exists a strategy which is winning for V in $\mathcal{G}(\varphi, w, g)$, and false iff there exists a strategy which is winning for F in $\mathcal{G}(\varphi, w, g)$.

By imposing the uniformity condition on strategies, the logic of only knowing becomes partial and the underlying games non-determined, even if the propositions were completely interpreted. Traditionally, the logic of only knowing was developed in order to create semantic non-monotonicity by using stable sets [6]. An alternative game-theoretic method of creating non-monotonicity can thus be obtained by assuming that players can choose inaccessible worlds in addition to the accessible ones.

4.2 Partial Common Knowledge

The modal operator $E_I \varphi$ means that 'everyone in the group of agents $I \subseteq$ Ag (the set of all agents) knows φ', and $C_I \varphi$ means that 'it is common knowledge among the group of agents I that φ'. The partialised version of the logic augmented with these operators has

$\langle M, w \rangle \models^+ E_I \varphi$ iff $\langle M, w' \rangle \models^+ K_i \varphi$ for all $i \in I$.

$\langle M, w \rangle \models^- E_I \varphi$ iff $\langle M, w' \rangle \models^- K_i \varphi$ for some $i \in I$.

Let $E_I^* \varphi$ be a reflexive and transitive closure on $E_I^0 \varphi \cup E_I^1 \varphi \cup \cdots \cup E_I^{k+1} \varphi$, where $E_I^0 \varphi = \varphi$, $E_I^1 = E_I \varphi$, and $E_I^{k+1} \varphi = E_I E_I^k \varphi$. Hence:

$\langle M, w \rangle \models^+ C_I \varphi$ iff $\langle M, w' \rangle \models^+ E_I^* \varphi$.

$\langle M, w \rangle \models^- C_I \varphi$ iff $\langle M, w' \rangle \models^- K_i \varphi$ for some $i \in I$.

A game-theoretisation of common knowledge is this. A world w' is I-reachable from w if there exists a sequence of worlds $w_1 \ldots w_k, w_1 = w, w_k = w'$ and for all $j, 0 \leq j \leq k - 1$, there is $i \in I \subseteq$ Ag for which $w_{j+1} \in [w_j]_{\rho_i}$ for some $k \geq 0$ [1]. A game $\mathcal{G}(\varphi, w, g)$ for formulas of $\mathcal{L}^C$, with a world w and an assignment g to the propositional letters has two additional rules. (The latter is to have duality. Since there can be infinite plays in the game tree, winning strategies are to be slightly modified in order to account for this.)

(G.C_I) If $\varphi = C_I \psi$, and the game has reached w, F chooses some w' that is I-reachable from w, and the game continues as $\mathcal{G}(\psi, w', g)$.

(G.$\neg C_I \neg$) If $\varphi = \neg C_I \neg\psi$, and the game has reached w, V chooses some w' that is I-reachable from w, and the game continues as $\mathcal{G}(\psi, w', g)$.

By letting φ be an $\mathcal{L}^C$-formula, then for any model M, a valuation g, and $w \in W$, φ is true iff there exists a strategy which is winning for V in $\mathcal{G}(\varphi, w, g)$, and false iff there exists a strategy which is winning for F in $\mathcal{G}(\varphi, w, g)$. This is how we bring GTS to bear on common knowledge, certainly an important notion both in AI and Game Theory.

It is known that common knowledge cannot be attained if communication is not taken to be reliable. It should be noted that any reference to communication pertains to agents' knowledge, not to the information players have, and hence it is safe for us to consider partialised common knowledge.

4.3   Partial Distributed Knowledge

Let the operator $D_I \varphi$ mean 'it is distributed knowledge among the group of agents I that φ'. Partial distributed knowledge based on this notion can be defined as follows:

$$\langle M, w \rangle \models^+ D_I \varphi \text{ iff } \langle M, w' \rangle \models^+ \varphi \text{ for each } w' \in \bigcap_{i \in I} [w]_{\rho_i}.$$
$$\langle M, w \rangle \models^- D_I \varphi \text{ iff } \langle M, w' \rangle \models^- \varphi \text{ for some } w' \in \bigcap_{i \in I} [w]_{\rho_i}.$$

A game $\mathcal{G}(\varphi, w, g)$ for $\mathcal{L}^{C+D}$, with a world w and an assignment g to the propositional letters has two additional rules:

(G.D_I) If $\varphi = D_I \psi$, and the game has reached w, F chooses some $w' \in \bigcap_{i \in I} [w]_{\rho_i}$, and the game continues as $\mathcal{G}(\psi, w', g)$.

(G.$\neg D_I \neg$) If $\varphi = \neg D_I \neg \psi$, and the game has reached w, V chooses some $w' \in \bigcap_{i \in I} [w]_{\rho_i}$, and the game continues as $\mathcal{G}(\psi, w', g)$.

This definition amounts to partiality, as games for $\mathcal{L}^{C+D}$ are non-determined.

4.4   Some Further Variations

Finally, some further knowledge constructions can be envisaged, by a combination of previous systems. For instance, we can have a logic with 'only common knowledge' ($C_I^O \varphi$). To see this, let us start with the notion of 'everybody only knows' ($E_I^O \varphi$):

$$\langle M, w \rangle \models^+ E_I^O \varphi \text{ iff } \langle M, w \rangle \models^+ O_i \varphi \text{ for all } i \in I.$$
$$\langle M, w \rangle \models^- E_I^O \varphi \text{ iff } \langle M, w \rangle \models^- O_i \varphi \text{ for some } i \in I.$$

'Only common knowledge' is now closure on 'everybody only knows', along the lines already described. For falsification, it suffices that 'only knowing' fails. Thus:

$$\langle M, w \rangle \models^+ C_I^O \varphi \text{ iff } \langle M, w \rangle \models^+ E_I^* \varphi, \text{ for all } i \in I.$$
$$\langle M, w \rangle \models^- C_I^O \varphi \text{ iff } \langle M, w \rangle \models^- O_i \varphi, \text{ for some } i \in I.$$

One can then devise games for these in a straightforward way. Also other combinations are possible. In general, we can have 'non-standard' partiality:

$$\langle M, w \rangle \models^+ K_i^\circ \varphi \text{ iff } \langle M, w' \rangle \models^+ \varphi \text{ for all } w' \in W, w' \in [w]_{\rho_i}.$$
$$\langle M, w \rangle \models^- K_i^\circ \varphi \text{ iff } \text{not } \langle M, w' \rangle \models^+ \varphi \text{ for some } w' \in W, w' \in [w]_{\rho_i}.$$

$\langle M, w \rangle \models^+ K_i^{\#} \varphi$ iff not $\langle M, w' \rangle \models^- \varphi$ for all $w' \in \mathcal{W}, w' \in [w]_{\rho_i}$.

$\langle M, w \rangle \models^- K_i^{\#} \varphi$ iff $\langle M, w' \rangle \models^- \varphi$ for some $w' \in \mathcal{W}, w' \in [w]_{\rho_i}$.

The formula $K_i^{\circ} \varphi$ captures the idea that the sentence is true when φ is true in all accessible worlds, and false when φ is not true in some accessible world. $K_i^{\#} \varphi$, on the other hand, says that the sentence is true when φ is not false in every accessible worlds, and false when φ is false in some accessible world. Clearly the standard interpretation subsumes the truth-conditions for $K_i^{\circ} \varphi$ and the falsity-conditions for $K_i^{\#} \varphi$. The duals L_i° and $L_i^{\#}$ are defined accordingly.

Games for non-standard clauses change the rules for winning conditions to weaker ones. For ∘-modalities and #-modalities we have, respectively:

(**G.at°**) If φ atomic, game ends. V wins if φ true, and F wins if φ not true.

(**G.at#**) If φ atomic, game ends. V wins if φ not false, and F wins if φ false.

5 Concluding Remarks

Our approach is useful for sentences using non-compositional information hiding. The general perspective is that games unify the semantics for modalities, and that their imperfect information versions partialise logics extended with new operators.

Further uses and computational aspects of the above knowledge constructions have to be left for future occasions. In general, areas of computer science and AI where these constructions and GTS may turn out to be useful include uncertainty in AI and in distributed systems, intensional dimensions of knowledge representation arising in inter-operation, unification of verification languages for multi-agent systems [9], reasoning about secure information flow, strategic meanings of programs, modularity, and other information dependencies.

References

1. Fagin, R., Halpern, J.Y., Moses, Y., Vardi, M.Y.: Reasoning about Knowledge. Cambridge: MIT Press (1995)
2. Hintikka, J.: Knowledge and Belief. Cornell University Press, Ithaca (1962)
3. Hintikka, J., Sandu, G.: Game-theoretical semantics. In: van Benthem, J., ter Meulen, A. (eds): Handbook of Logic and Language. Elsevier, Amsterdam (1997) 361–410
4. Humberstone, I.L.: Inaccessible worlds. Notre Dame Journal of Formal Logic **24**. (1981) 346–352
5. Jaspars, J., Thijsse, E.: Fundamentals of partial modal logic. In: Doherty, P. (ed.): Partiality, Modality, and Nonmonotonicity. Stanford, CSLI (1996) 111–141
6. Levesque, H.J.: All I know: A study in autoepistemic logic. Artificial Intelligence **42**. (1990) 263–309
7. Pietarinen, A.: Intentional identity revisited. Nordic Journal of Philosophical Logic **6**. (2001) 147–188
8. Sandu, G., Pietarinen, A.: Partiality and games: Propositional logic. Logic Journal of the IGPL **9**. (2001) 107–127.
9. Wooldridge, M.: Semantic issues in the verification of agent communication languages. Journal of Autonomous Agents and Multi-Agent Systems **3**. (2000) 9–31

Validation and Reparation of Knowledge Bases

R. Djelouah[1, 2], B. Duval[1], and S. Loiseau[1]

[1]LERIA, Université d'Angers, 2 bd Lavoisier, 49045 ANGERS Cedex 01 France
{djelouah, bd, loiseau}@info.univ-angers.fr
[2]ISAIP-ESAIP, 18 rue du 8 Mai 45, 49180 St Barthélémy France

Abstract: Two properties characterize the quality of a knowledge base (KB): coherency and completeness. In our work, the completeness of the KB is evaluated on a set of test cases. The incompleteness is revealed by test cases that cannot be proved, called deficiencies. We also use test cases to check the coherency of the KB: we propose a new notion, called C_coherency, that extends previous definitions of coherency. The situations that reveal the C_incoherency of the KB are called conflicts. When the problems in a KB have been identified, our aim is to restore the validity of this base. For each conflict and each deficiency, we determine which modifications of the KB can suppress this problem without introducing new deficiencies or conflicts in the KB.

1 Introduction

Two kinds of properties are searched to measure the quality of a knowledge base (KB): the coherency and the completeness. An incoherency is equivalent to finding a valid input from which we can infer, with the knowledge, contradictory results. An incompleteness is equivalent to finding a valid input which must give a result, that is not inferred by the KB. One difficult point is to define formal properties that enable to characterize an incoherency or an incompleteness. The research in this area has proposed many such properties [1, 6, 8, 9, 10, 11]. We must remark that, except when we have a complete and coherent model of the knowledge represented in the KB, these formal properties are necessarily limited.

The contribution of this paper is two folds. First, we propose a new definition for the validity of a KB relatively to a set of test cases. The *C_coherency* property that we present formalizes the KB coherency and extends previous definitions [4, 7, 11]. It defines a valid input as an input fact base satisfying some constraints, these constraints are given with the KB or come from the test cases. Then, a KB is C_coherent if the results inferred from any input satisfying the constraints are not contradictory with the KB and the test cases. Besides, a KB is *T_complete* if the output of each test case can be inferred with the KB and the input part of the test case. Finally, a KB is said to be CT_valid if it is C_coherent and T_complete.

The second contribution of this paper is to propose a solution to restore the validity of a CT_invalid KB. The first step towards reparation is to provide proofs of invalidities of the KB. The proofs of C_incoherency are called *conflicts*. The proofs of T_incompleteness are called *deficiencies*. The second step is to propose actions that make a simple modification to the KB in order to improve its validity. To each proof of invalidity, is associated one or several sets of actions to revise the KB; the application of the actions of such a set, called a *revision plan*, makes the invalidity disappeared.

M.-S. Hacid et al. (Eds.): ISMIS 2002, LNAI 2366, pp. 312–320, 2002.

2 Validity of a Knowledge Base

2.1 Assumptions

We consider that a KB is a rule base *RB*, made up of a set of revisable rules *rb* and a set of constraints *RC* that are considered as valid knowledge. An integrity constraint is a constraint whose conclusion is the inconsistency noted "⊥". The KB designer defines the set of input literals: they are the only literals that can occur in a input fact base, and they cannot appear in rule conclusions. A fact base is a set of literals, logically equivalent to the conjunction of its literals. This work uses a formalism based on propositional logic. To a rule noted "If L1 ∧ ... ∧ Ln then Lm" is associated the formula "L1 ∧ ... ∧ Ln → Lm". The rules are supposed to be triggered in a forward chaining and the deduction scheme that relies on Modus Ponens is noted by the symbol ⊢$_{MP}$. We suppose that the KB designer provides a set of reliable test cases <F$_{test}$, O> where F$_{test}$ is an input fact base, and O is a non-input fact that should be deducible from F$_{test}$. The fact base F$_{test}$ of each test is necessarily a valid input, and all the facts from F$_{test}$ are necessary to infer the result O. Each test case can be represented by a logical association between the input F$_{test}$ and the output fact O and this logical association is considered as a constraint associated to the test case.

Definition 1 Let t=<{f1, ..., fn}, O> be a test case. The formula " If f1 ∧ ... ∧ fn then O" is *the constraint associated to the test case t*. Let T$_{test}$ be a set of test cases, we call *RC$_{test}$* the set of constraints associated to the test cases of T$_{test}$.

2.2 Coherency

A rule base is coherent if and only if no contradictory results can be inferred from any valid input. Two main problems have to be solved in order to formalize this notion of coherency. The first problem is to characterize a valid input. In our approach, an input fact base is considered as valid if it satisfies a set of contraints. The second problem is to find a way to infer results from any such valid input. We use the knowledge contained in the rule base and in the test cases to infer results, and to see if they are contradictory. This approach leads to the following definitions.

Definition 2 Let RC$_{test}$ be the constraints associated with a set of tests T$_{test}$. An input fact base F$_i$ *satisfies the constraints* RC∪ RC$_{test}$ if F$_i$ ∪RC∪ RC$_{test}$ ⊬$_{MP}$⊥.

Definition 3 Let T$_{test}$ be a set of test cases and RC$_{test}$ the constraints associated to T$_{test}$. *RB is C_coherent with respect to the set T$_{test}$* if for each input fact base F$_i$ satisfying the constraints RC ∪ RC$_{test}$, F$_i$ ∪ RB ∪ RC$_{test}$ ⊬$_{MP}$ ⊥.

The C_coherency generalizes and improves the VT_coherency given in [4] that generalizes and improves the properties of [7, 11]. The difference between C_coherency and VT_coherency is that, in VT_coherency, the final consistency test of "F$_i$ ∪ RB ∪ RC$_{test}$ ⊬$_{MP}$ ⊥" is only made on "F$_i$ ∪ RB ⊬$_{MP}$⊥".

Example This example will be followed all along the article.
Suppose that RB is composed of revisable rules r1, r2, r3, r4, r5 and constraints Cons1, Cons2. The set of input literals is {Rich, Shareholder, Poor, Withoutcharge, Homeless, Foreign, Incomeless}.

r1: if Rich∧ Shareholder ∧ Withoutcharge *then* Taxable
r2: if Taxable *then* ¬Helped   *r3: if* Poor *then* Helped
r4: if Incomeless *then* Helped   *r5: if* Poor ∧ Homeless ∧Foreign *then* ¬Helped
Cons1: if Rich∧ Poor *then* ⊥   *Cons2: if* Poor ∧ Homeless ∧ Incomeless *then* ⊥
Consider that we have the following set T_{test} of test cases:
T1: < {Rich, Shareholder, Withoutcharge}, ¬Helped>
T2: <{Poor,Homeless}, ¬Helped>   *T3:* <{Shareholder}, Taxable>
T4:<{Incomeless}, Helped>
RC_{test} is composed of the four constraints associated to T1, T2, T3, T4 (*if* Rich∧ Shareholder ∧ Withoutcharge *then* ¬ Helped, ...). RB is C_incoherent with respect to T_{test}. For instance, on one hand, the input fact base {Incomeless,Shareholder} satisfies the constraints $RC \cup RC_{test}$ ({Incomeless,Shareholder} $\cup$ Cons1 $\cup$ Cons2 $\cup RC_{test}$ $\nvdash_{MP} \perp$) and on the other hand, with the test T3 and the rules r2 and r4, this input fact base allows to infer the contradictory results ¬Helped and Helped. Note that this incoherency that is found with T3 cannot be detected with the VT_coherency.

2.3 Completeness and Validity

A KB is complete if and only if with each valid input that provides a result, the KB can infer this result. As it is difficult to know all the valid inputs with their attended results, the notion of completeness will be only partially tackled by way of the set of tests. This notion agrees with the completeness definition used in the subfield of machine learning interested in theory refinement [2, 8].

Definition 4 *A rule base RB is T_complete with respect to a set of test cases* T_{test} *if for each test case* <F_{test}, O> *of* T_{test}, $F_{test} \cup RB \vdash_{MP}$ O.

Example RB is not T_complete. With the input fact base {Poor, Homeless} of T2, the rule base does not deduce ¬Helped, hence T2 is not proved by RB. On the same way, the test T3 is not proved by RB.

Our process of reparation of the KB uses test cases to complete missing knowledge but also requires that the modified KB satisfies the property of C_coherency. Finally, we propose the following definition of CT_validity.

Definition 5 *A rule base RB is CT_valid with respect to a set of test cases* T_{test} *if RB is C_coherent and T_complete with respect to* T_{test}.

3 Characterization of Anomalies in a Knowledge Base

This section presents the conflicts (resp. the deficiencies) that are the proofs of the KB incoherency (resp. incompleteness) and explain how they can be computed.

3.1 Conflicts

Definition 6 A *conflict is a couple* <F_c, br_c>, *such that (i)* F_c *is an input fact base that satisfies the constraints* $RC \cup RC_{test}$, *(ii)* $br_c \subset rb$, *(iii)* $F_c \cup br_c \cup RC_{test} \cup RC \vdash_{MP} \perp$.

We must note that in the conflict, appear only the factual knowledge F_c and the revisable part br_c that, with the constraints and the tests, lead the deduction of ⊥. The tests and the constraints do not appear in the definition of a conflict because they are considered as non revisable knowledge. We consider only the minimal proofs of incoherency that are the interesting conflicts.

Definition 7 *A conflict* $<F_c, br_c>$ *is minimal if and only if there does not exist another conflict* $<F_c', br_c'>$ *such that* $br_c' \subseteq br_c$ *and* $F_c' \subseteq F_c$.

The existence of a conflict may result of one of the following reasons. Either the fact base F_c, that satisfies the constraints, is not really a valid entry, which means that some constraints are missing in the set RC; or F_c is a valid entry and the conflict means that some rules from br_c need to be modified or suppressed. Note that if the fact base F_c of a conflict $<F_c, br_c>$ is included in the condition part of a test case $<F_{test}, O>$, F_c is a valid entry since the tests are certified reliable. Such a conflict, called a strong conflict, means that necessarily some rules from br_c have to be modified.

Definition 8 *A strong conflict is a minimal conflict* $<F_c, br_c>$ *for which there exists a test* $<F_{test}, O>$ *of* T_{test} *such that* $F_c \subseteq F_{test}$.

Example $C1=<\{Poor, Homeless\},\{r3\}>$ is a minimal conflict for RB and T_{test}, because the fact base $\{Poor, Homeless\}$ leads to the deduction of Helped with the rule r3 while the test T2 associates these facts with the deduction ¬Helped. C1 is a strong conflict since $\{Poor, Homeless\}$ is the fact base of the test T2.

3.2   Deficiencies

Definition 9 *A deficiency is a test* $<F_{test}, O>$ *from* T_{test} *such that* $F_{test} \cup RB \nvdash_{MP} O$.

So the set of tests T_{test} is divided into two parts. On one hand, the tests that cannot be proved are called deficiencies and are the basis for the completion of the KB. On the other hand, the tests that are proved by the given KB are called the *true positive tests*, and we shall note T_{true} this set of tests.

Example The set of test cases contains two deficiencies T2 and T3. The input fact base of T2, $\{$ Poor,Homeless$\}$, does not enable to deduce ¬Helped with the rules of RB, and the same is true for T3. T1 is true positive. In fact, the input fact base of T1, $\{$Rich, Shareholder, Withoutcharge$\}$and the rules r1 and r2 of RB leads to the deduction of ¬Helped that is the output part of T1. T4 is also true positive.

3.3   Computation of Conflicts and Deficiencies

The computation of conflicts is made in two steps with an adaptation of ATMS [5]. Let us recall that, given a set of *hypotheses* and a set of *implications*, ATMS computes for each literal a *label* that is a formula E1∨E2∨...∨En in disjunctive normal form. Each clause Ei of the label, called an *environment*, is a conjunction composed only of the hypotheses given to ATMS. Each environment of the label of a literal L enables to deduce L by Modus Ponens with the use of the implications.
The first step of our method computes a reformulation of the integrity constraints which uses only the input literals. We note ICS this new formulation of constraints that defines all the inconsistent input fact bases. In the second step, ATMS computes for each literal L its label E1∨... ∨En, where E_i can be decomposed into a set of facts

E_i^{Facts}, a set of rules E_i^{Rules} and a set of test cases E_i^{Tests} such that $E_i^{Facts} \cup E_i^{Rules} \cup E_i^{Tests} \vdash L$. Moreover, E_i^{Facts} is a consistent fact base (according to ICS). The minimal conflicts are obtained from the label of $\bot$.

This exhaustive computation of the labels also enables to obtain easily the deficiencies. A test $<F_{test}, O>$ is proved by RB if the label of $O = E_1 \vee ... \vee E_i ... \vee E_n$ contains a E_i such that $E_i^{Facts} \subseteq F_{test}$ and $E_i^{Tests} = \varnothing$.

Example For our example, the first step of the computation returns the set ICS= {Rich∧Poor), (Poor∧Homeless∧Incomeless), (Rich∧Shareholder∧Withoutcharge∧ Incomeless). A fact base F satisfies RC $\cup$ RC$_{test}$ if F contains no environment of ICS. The second step computes the label of each literal. Label(¬Helped) = (Rich∧ Shareholder ∧Withoucharge ∧r1 ∧r2) $\vee$ (Poor∧ Homeless ∧Foreign ∧r5)∨ (Rich ∧ Shareholder ∧Withoucharge ∧T1)∨(Poor∧Homeless ∧T2)∨(Shareholder ∧r2∧T3); ...
For instance, the environment E=(Rich∧Shareholder∧Withoucharge∧r1∧r2) corresponds to E^{Facts} = {Rich, Shareholder, Withoucharge}; E^{Rules} ={r1,r2}; E^{Tests}= { }. The label of $\bot$ is particularly interesting because it gives the conflicts.
Label($\bot$)= (Poor∧Homeless∧r3∧T2) $\vee$ (Incomeless∧Shareholder∧r2∧r4∧T3) $\vee$ (Poor∧Shareholder∧r2∧r3∧T3) $\vee$ (Poor∧Homeless∧Foreign∧r5∧r3) $\vee$ (Incomeless∧Shareholder∧ r2∧T3∧T4).
So, the minimal conflicts are C1:<{Poor,Homeless},{r3}>, C2:<{Incomeless, Shareholder}, {r2}> and C3:<{Poor,Shareholder},{r2,r3}>. C1, C2, C3 correspond respectively to the first, the fifth and the third environments in the label of $\bot$. The second and the fourth environments correspond to conflicts that are not minimal. C1 is the sole strong conflict.
We have found that label(¬Helped) is composed of five environments. For the first environment E_1, we have E_1^{Facts} = {Rich,Shareholder,Withoucharge}, and E_1^{Tests}={ }. So this environment proves that the test T1 = <{Rich, Shareholder, Withoucharge}, ¬Helped> is true positive. On the contrary, T2 = <{Poor, Homeless}, ¬Helped> is a deficiency because the label of ¬Helped does not contain an environment E_i such that $E_i^{Facts} \subseteq$ {Poor, Homeless}and $E_i^{Tests} = \varnothing$.

4   Reparation of a Knowledge Base

For each conflict or deficiency, we propose one (or several) set(s) of actions of revision of the KB, called revision plan(s), such that if the actions of revision of the plan (resp. of one of the plans) are applied to the KB, the conflict or the deficiency disappears. One important point is that we guarantee that the application of actions of a set not only solves the conflict or the deficiency, but also does not provide new problem, i.e. new conflict or deficiency.

4.1   Revision Actions and Revision Plans

In the following, we shall note RB the initial rule base and [A](RB) the rule base obtained after the application of the action A. When it makes sense (A is not the suppression of a rule), we also note [A](r) the rule r modified by the action A.

Definition 10 Let RB be a KB and T$_{test}$ a set of tests. *An action A is conservative for RB and T$_{test}$* if [A](RB) does not contain any deficiencies that are not present in RB. *An action A is admissible for RB and T$_{test}$* if [A](RB) does not contain any conflicts that are not present in RB.

We say that a set of actions is conservative (resp. admissible) if the application of these actions to KB does not introduce new deficiencies (resp. new conflicts) in KB.

Definition 11 *A revision plan P for a conflict (resp. a deficiency)* is a minimal set of actions such that *(i)* P solves the conflict (resp. the deficiency), *(ii)* P is conservative, *(iii)*P is admissible.

In the following, we explain how we propose solutions to repair a conflict or a deficiency. We present the revision plans that we consider and some properties to check whether these plans are conservative and admissible.

4.2 Revision for a Conflict

To remove a minimal conflict $<F_c, br_c>$, we consider three types of revision plans.

1) A plan can be composed of a unique action that is the suppression of a rule r belonging to br_c, this action will be noted *Supp_rule(r)*. The minimality of the conflict guarantees that only one rule suppression is sufficient to remove it. A rule suppression is admissible because this suppression reduces the possible deductions and then cannot introduce new conflict. So we have to test which rule suppressions are conservative, which can be done according to the following proposition.

Proposition 1 The action Supp_rule(r) is conservative if for every test $<F_{test},O>$ from T_{true}, the label of O contains an environment $E_i=< E_i^{Facts}, E_i^{Rules}, \{\}>$ such that $E_i^{Facts} \subseteq F_{test}$ and $r \notin E_i^{Rules}$.

Example Let us consider the conflict C1=< {Poor, Homeless}, r3>. The action Supp_rule(r3) is conservative; in fact, we can check that the tests T1 et T4 are still proved if we suppress r3 from RB. In the label of ¬Helped, the environment that proves that T1 is true positive is (Rich∧ Shareholder∧ Withoutcharge∧ r1∧r2) and it does not use r3. On the same way, the environment (Incomeless∧r4) in the label of Helped proves that T4 is true positive and it does not use r3.

2) If Supp_rule(r) is not a revision action, this means that the rule r is necessary to make a test t true positive. In this case, one possible plan to solve the conflict is to specialize the rule r by adding, to its premises, literals that belong to the true positive tests. In fact, the idea that supports this proposition is that the information contained in a test is relevant for the deduction of the conclusion. We note *Add_Prem(r, P)* the action that adds to the premises of the rule r the literal P. We notice, as in the preceding case, that such a specialization of the rule is admissible. The following proposition precises how a premise P must be chosen to ensure that the action Add_Prem(r, P) is conservative.

Proposition 2 The action Add_Prem(r, P) is conservative if P is an input literal such that, for each true positive test $<F_{test},O>$ such that $F_{test} \cup (BR -\{r\}) \vdash_{MP} O$, P belongs to F_{test}.

Furthermore, in order to remove a conflict C=$<F_c, br_c>$, it may be necessary to associate in a plan several premise additions. It is interesting to combine several premise additions to the rules of br_c until the conjunction of the premises of these modified rules gives a fact base forbidden by the constraints. So we consider a plan P={Add_Prem(r_1,P_1), ... Add_Prem(r_k,P_k)} such that $F_c \cup \{P_1, ...P_k\}$ is an input fact base that does not satisfy the constraints. As the combination of two conservative actions is not necessarily conservative, we must check whether such a proposed plan does not introduce new deficiencies. This verification is often easy because of the following property.

Theorem 1 Let A_1=Add_Prem(r_1, P_1), ..., A_n=Add_Prem(r_n, P_n) be n conservative actions. If each true positive test has a unique proof in RB, then the association of the n conservative actions A_1, ..., A_n is conservative.

Example Let the conflict C2=<{Incomeless, Shareholder}, {r2}>. Supp_rule(r2) is not conservative since the only possible proof for T1 uses r2. According to proposition 2, we can add to r2 a premise that is a literal belonging to T1. So Proposition 2 guarantees that the actions Add_Prem(r2,Rich) and Add_Prem(r2, Withoutcharge) are conservative. Let us notice that a modification of r2 has no effect for the true positive test T4. Moreover, the constraints ICS computed by ATMS show that the fact base{Rich, Shareholder, Withoutcharge, Incomeless} does not satisfy the constraints. So to repair the conflict C2, we can propose the plan P = {Add_Prem(r2, Rich), Add_Prem(r2, Withoutcharge)}, which is conservative according to theorem 1 because T1 and T4 have a unique proof in RB.

3) When <F_c, br_c> is not a strong conflict, a third type of plan can be considered. This plan contains the sole action, noted Add_IC(F_c), that adds to the KB a constraint that forbids the fact base F_c of the conflict. Adding a constraint is admissible because it reduces the possible deductions and moreover it is conservative when <F_c, br_c> is not a strong conflict (the fact base of the conflict is not included in the base of a test).

Example: to solve the conflict C2, the plan Add_IC({Incomeless, Shareholder}) is possible.

4.3   Revision for a Deficiency

If a test <F_{test}, O> is a deficiency, that means that the current rules do not enable to construct a proof of O from the facts of F_{test}. So a revision plan may propose to generalize some rules in order to obtain a proof of O from F_{test}. The type of generalization action that we consider is noted *Supp_Prem(r, P)*, it consists to suppress an input literal from the premises of a rule. A procedure that compares F_{test} to the fact parts of the environments of the label of O is used to compute all the minimal sets of premises that are missing in F_{test} to prove O (these sets are minimal for inclusion). This procedure also determines which rules have introduced these literals in the label of O. Such a minimal set of premises {P_1, ... P_n} leads to a plan that associates all the actions Supp_Prem(r_{ki},P_k) (where P_k is included in the rule r_{ki} who appears in the label of the literal O). Such a plan is always conservative because each test that is true positive in a KB remains true positive when this KB is generalized. But we have to study the admissibility of such a revision plan.
First, we consider the possible effects of an action A= Supp_Prem(r, P) on the set of conflicts. If this action gives a new conflict in [A](RB), then this conflict necessarily involves this modified rule [A](r). As the computation of conflicts with ATMS is a greedy process, we try to limit the amount of computation necessary after a modification of the KB. The following theorem characterizes situations where new conflicts may appear after the suppression of a premise in a rule.

Theorem 2 Let $r = P \wedge P_1 \wedge \ldots \wedge P_n \rightarrow Q$ be a rule of rb and $A = Supp\_Prem(r, P)$.
$[A](RB)$ contains a new conflict $<F_c, [A](r) \cup br_c>$ not present in RB only if the label of Q in RB is different from the label of Q in $[A](RB)$ and only if the fact base $F_c \cup \{P\}$ does not satisfy the constraints $RC \cup RC_{test}$.

This theorem allows to determine that some actions $Supp\_Prem(r,P)$ are admissible without a recomputation of the labels by the ATMS. In fact, the theorem states that an action $Supp\_Prem(r, P)$ may introduce new conflicts only if there exists a potential fact base $F_c \cup \{P\}$ that does not satisfy the constraints. So in the case where the premise P does not appear in the constraints, the action $Supp\_Prem(r,P)$ is admissible. In the other cases, if we want to consider this action, we have to compute the update of labels induced by this action.

A plan composed of several admissible actions is not necessarily admissible, and the following proposition examines the situations where new conflicts can appear.

Proposition 3 Let $A_1 = Supp\_Prem(r_1, P_1)$, ..., $A_n = Supp\_Prem(r_n, P_n)$ be n admissible actions. The plan $P = \{A_1, \ldots, A_n\}$ introduces a new conflict $C = <F_c, \{[A_1](r), \ldots, [A_n](r_n)\} \cup br_c>$ not present in RB only if the fact base $F_c \cup \{P_1\} \cup \{P_2\} \cup \ldots \cup \{P_n\}$ is forbidden by the constraints in RB.

Example: The test T2: $<\{Poor, Homeless\}, \neg Helped>$ is a deficiency. Comparing the label of $\neg Helped$ with the fact base $\{Poor, Homeless\}$ gives only one possible revision plan, that is $\{Supp\_Prem(r5, Foreign)\}$. As Foreign does not occur in any input constraint of ICS, we are sure that there exists no input fact base F_c such that $F_c \cup \{Foreign\}$ is forbidden by the constraints $RC \cup RC_{test}$; so theorem 1 enables to conclude that the action $Supp\_Prem(r5, Foreign)$ (and then the plan) is admissible without any computation of the conflicts that may appear in $[A](RB)$.

When no admissible plan, composed of premise suppressions, can be obtained to solve a deficiency (F_{test}, O) , we propose to solve the deficiency by adding into the rule base a rule corresponding to the test. This action is noted $Add\_Test(F_{test} \rightarrow O)$. Such an action constitutes a plan that is obviously conservative and also admissible. In fact, this modification cannot create new conflicts since our definition of C_coherency takes into account the tests to determine all the potential conflicts in the KB.

Example: T3: $<\{Shareholder\}, Taxable>$ is a deficiency. The label of Taxable suggests only one possible revision plan, that is $\{Supp\_Prem(r1, Withoutcharge), Supp\_Prem(r1, Rich)\}$. We have to study the admissibility of the action $A = Supp\_Prem(r1, Withoutcharge)$. The literal Withoutcharge occurs in the input constraint(*if* Rich $\wedge$ Shareholder $\wedge$ Withoutcharge $\wedge$ Incomeless *Then* $\perp$); so theorem 1 does not apply to this situation and we have to determine the effects of the action A on the set of conflicts. The constraint containing Withoutcharge indicates that any fact base containing $F_c = \{Rich, Shareholder, Incomeless\}$ is a potential source of a new conflict in $[A](RB)$. A forward chaining deduction from the fact base $\{ Rich, Shareholder, Incomeless\}$ in $[A](RB)$ leads to the contradiction between Helped and $\neg Helped$. So we conclude that $[A](RB)$ contains a new conflict $C = <\{Rich, Shareholder, Incomeless\}, \{[A](r1), r2, r4\}>$, and so this action A is not admissible.
As the only possible plan formed of premise supressions is not a good candidate, the sole solution for this deficiency is to propose to add the test T3 to our KB.

To summarize the example, let us recall the different repair plans that are proposed to the user. The plans for conflicts are {Supp_rule(r3)} for C1 and C3, and {Add_Prem(r2,Rich), Add_Prem(r2,Withoutcharge)} for C2. The plans for deficiencies are *{Supp_Prem(r5,Foreign)}* or *{Add_Test(T2)}* for T2, and *{Add_Test(T3)}* for T3.

5 Conclusion

This paper presents a method to validate and refine a theory expressed as a set of rules. To check the completeness of the KB, we use a set of test cases certified as reliable by an expert. Our approach also uses the information contained in these test cases to check the coherency of the rule base. So the CT_validity property that we propose is a better evaluation of the quality of a KB.

The KB inconsistency is revealed by the presence of conflicts, while its incompleteness is characterized by deficiencies. The first step of our method deals with the computation of conflicts and the determination of deficiencies. Then we propose for each problem one or several reparation plans, that are sets of modifications that suppress the problem from the KB. As our aim is to obtain a rule base that is both coherent and complete, we define the notions of conservative and admissible actions; an action is conservative (resp. admissible) when it contributes to solve a conflict (resp. a deficiency) without introducing new deficiencies (resp new conflicts). We present some properties that enable to check whether an action is admissible or conservative. We then propose to the user for each conflict (resp deficiency) a set of reparation plans. Each plan is a set of actions that remove the conflict (resp deficiency) without providing other conflicts or deficiencies.

References

1. Beauvieux A, Dague P. A General Consistency checking and restoring Engine for Knowledge Bases, ECAI, p. 77-82, 1990.
2. Boswell R., Craw S. Organising Knowledge refinement operators. In Proc of EUROVAV. p.149-161. Kluwer Academic Publishers. 1999.
3. Bouali F, Loiseau S, Rousset MC. Rule Base Debugging, ITCAI, p. 166-169, 1996.
4. Bouali F, Loiseau S, Rousset MC. Revision of rule base , EUROVAV, p. 193-203, 1997.
5. De Kleer J. An assumption-based truth maintenance system, AI.28, p. 127-224, 1986.
6. Ginsberg A. Knowledge-base reduction: a new approach to checking knowledge bases for inconsistency and redundancy, AAAI, p. 585-589, 1988.
7. Loiseau S. Refinement of KB based on Consistency, ECAI, p. 845-849, 1992.
8. Mooney R.J, Ourston D. A multistrategy approach to theory refinement, Machine Learning. Vol IV, p. 141-164, 1994.
9. Nguyen T.A., Perkins W.A., Laffey T.J., Pecora D. Checking an expert system knowledge base for consistency and completeness, IJCAI, p.375-379 1985.
10. Preece A.D, Talbot S, Vignollet L, Evaluation of verification tools for knowledge-based systems; Int. J. Human-Computer Studies 47 p. 629-658 1997.
11. Rousset MC. On the consistency of KB: the COVADIS system, ECAI, p.79-84, 1988.

Automated Discovery of Decision Rule Chains Using Rough Sets and Medical Diagnostic Model

Shusaku Tsumoto

Department of Medicine Informatics, Shimane Medical University, School of Medicine,
89-1 Enya-cho Izumo City, Shimane 693-8501 Japan
tsumoto@computer.org

Abstract. One of the most important problems on rule induction methods is that they cannot extract rules, which plausibly represent experts' decision processes. On one hand, rule induction methods induce probabilistic rules, the description length of which is too short, compared with the experts' rules. On the other hand, construction of Bayesian networks generates too lengthy rules. In this paper, the characteristics of experts' rules are closely examined and a new approach to extract plausible rules is introduced, which consists of the following three procedures. First, the characterization of decision attributes (given classes) is extracted from databases and the classes are classified into several groups with respect to the characterization. Then, two kinds of sub-rules, characterization rules for each group and discrimination rules for each class in the group are induced. Finally, those two parts are integrated into one rule for each decision attribute. The proposed method was evaluated on a medical database, the experimental results of which show that induced rules correctly represent experts' decision processes.

1 Introduction

One of the most important problems in developing expert systems is knowledge acquisition from experts[4]. In order to automate this problem, many inductive learning methods, such as induction of decision trees[3,10], rule induction methods[7,10,11] and rough set theory[8,14,18], are introduced and applied to extract knowledge from databases, and the results show that these methods are appropriate.

However, it has been pointed out that conventional rule induction methods cannot extract rules, which plausibly represent experts' decision processes[14, 15]: the description length of induced rules is too short, compared with the experts' rules. For example, rule induction methods, including AQ15[7] and PRIMEROSE[14], induce the following common rule for muscle contraction headache from databases on differential diagnosis of headache[15]:

$$[location = whole] \wedge [\text{Jolt Headache} = no] \wedge [\text{Tenderness of M1} = yes]$$
$$\rightarrow \text{muscle contraction headache.}$$

This rule is shorter than the following rule given by medical experts.

M.-S. Hacid et al. (Eds.): ISMIS 2002, LNAI 2366, pp. 321–332, 2002.

[Jolt Headache = no]
$\wedge$([Tenderness of M0 = yes] $\vee$ [Tenderness of M1 = yes] $\vee$ [Tenderness of M2 = yes])
$\wedge$[Tenderness of B1 = no] $\wedge$ [Tenderness of B2 = no] $\wedge$ [Tenderness of B3 = no]
$\wedge$[Tenderness of C1 = no] $\wedge$ [Tenderness of C2 = no] $\wedge$ [Tenderness of C3 = no]
$\wedge$[Tenderness of C4 = no]
        $\rightarrow$ muscle contraction headache

where [Tenderness of B1 = no] and [Tenderness of C1 = no] are added.

These results suggest that conventional rule induction methods do not reflect a mechanism of knowledge acquisition of medical experts.

In this paper, the characteristics of experts' rules are closely examined and a new approach to extract plausible rules is introduced, which consists of the following three procedures. First, the characterization of each decision attribute (a given class), a list of attribute-value pairs the supporting set of which covers all the samples of the class, is extracted from databases and the classes are classified into several groups with respect to the characterization. Then, two kinds of sub-rules, rules discriminating between each group and rules classifying each class in the group are induced. Finally, those two parts are integrated into one rule for each decision attribute. The proposed method is evaluated on medical databases, the experimental results of which show that induced rules correctly represent experts' decision processes.

2   Background: Problems with Rule Induction

As shown in the introduction, rules acquired from medical experts are much longer than those induced from databases the decision attributes of which are given by the same experts. This is because rule induction methods generally search for shorter rules, compared with decision tree induction. In the case of decision tree induction, the induced trees are sometimes too deep and in order for the trees to be learningful, pruning and examination by experts are required. One of the main reasons why rules are short and decision trees are sometimes long is that these patterns are generated only by one criteria, such as high accuracy or high information gain. The comparative study in this section suggests that experts should acquire rules not only by one criteria but by the usage of several measures. Those characteristics of medical experts' rules are fully examined not by comparing between those rules for the same class, but by comparing experts' rules with those for another class. For example, a classification rule for muscle contraction headache is acquired from medical experts, as shown above. This rule is very similar to the following classification rule for disease of cervical spine:

[Jolt Headache = no]
$\wedge$([Tenderness of M0 = yes] $\vee$ [Tenderness of M1 = yes] $\vee$ [Tenderness of M2 = yes])
$\wedge$([Tenderness of B1 = yes] $\vee$ [Tenderness of B2 = yes] $\vee$ [Tenderness of B3 = yes]
$\vee$[Tenderness of C1 = yes] $\vee$ [Tenderness of C2 = yes] $\vee$ [Tenderness of C3 = yes]
$\vee$[Tenderness of C4 = yes])
        $\rightarrow$ disease of cervical spine

The differences between these two rules are attribute-value pairs, from tenderness of B1 to C4. Thus, these two rules can be simplified into the following form:

$$a_1 \wedge A_2 \wedge \neg A_3 \rightarrow muscle\ contraction\ headache$$
$$a_1 \wedge A_2 \wedge A_3 \rightarrow disease\ of\ cervical\ spine$$

The first two terms and the third one represent different reasoning. The first and second term a_1 and A_2 are used to differentiate muscle contraction headache and disease of cervical spine from other diseases. The third term A_3 is used to make a differential diagnosis between these two diseases. Thus, medical experts firstly selects several diagnostic candidates, which are very similar to each other, from many diseases and then make a final diagnosis from those candidates.

In the next section, a new approach for inducing the above rules is introduced. The differences between these two rules are attribute-value pairs, from tenderness of B1 to C4. Thus, these two rules can be simplified into the following form:

3 Rough Set Theory and Probabilistic Rules

3.1 Rough Set Notations

In the following sections, we use the following notations introduced by Grzymala-Busse and Skowron[12], which are based on rough set theory[8]. These notations are illustrated by a small database shown in Table 1, collecting the patients who complained of headache.

Let U denote a nonempty, finite set called the universe and A denote a nonempty, finite set of attributes, i.e., $a : U \rightarrow V_a$ for $a \in A$, where V_a is called the domain of a, respectively. Then, a decision table is defined as an information system, $A = (U, A \cup \{d\})$. For example, Table 1 is an information system with $U = \{1, 2, 3, 4, 5, 6\}$ and $A = \{age, location, nature, prodrome, nausea, M1\}$ and $d = class$. For $location \in A$, $V_{location}$ is defined as $\{occular, lateral, whole\}$.

The atomic formulae over $B \subseteq A \cup \{d\}$ and V are expressions of the form $[a = v]$, called descriptors over B, where $a \in B$ and $v \in V_a$. The set $F(B, V)$ of formulas over B is the least set containing all atomic formulas over B and closed with respect to disjunction, conjunction and negation. For example, $[location = occular]$ is a descriptor of B.

For each $f \in F(B, V)$, f_A denote the meaning of f in A, i.e., the set of all objects in U with property f, defined inductively as follows.

1. If f is of the form $[a = v]$ then, $f_A = \{s \in U | a(s) = v\}$
2. $(f \wedge g)_A = f_A \cap g_A; (f \vee g)_A = f_A \vee g_A; (\neg f)_A = U - f_a$

For example, $f = [location = whole]$ and $f_A = \{2, 4, 5, 6\}$. As an example of a conjunctive formula, $g = [location = whole] \wedge [nausea = no]$ is a descriptor of U and f_A is equal to $g_{location,nausea} = \{2, 5\}$.

By the use of the framework above, classification accuracy and coverage, or true positive rate is defined as follows.

Table 1. An Example of Database

	age	loc	nat	prod	nau	M1	class
1	50...59	occ	per	no	no	yes	m.c.h.
2	40...49	who	per	no	no	yes	m.c.h.
3	40...49	lat	thr	yes	yes	no	migra
4	40...49	who	thr	yes	yes	no	migra
5	40...49	who	rad	no	no	yes	m.c.h.
6	50...59	who	per	no	yes	yes	psycho

DEFINITIONS: loc: location, nat: nature, prod: prodrome, nau: nausea, M1: tenderness of M1, who: whole, occ: occular, lat: lateral, per: persistent, thr: throbbing, rad: radiating, m.c.h.: muscle contraction headache, migra: migraine, psycho: psychological pain,

Definition 1.
Let R and D denote a formula in $F(B, V)$ and a set of objects which belong to a decision d. Classification accuracy and coverage(true positive rate) for $R \to d$ is defined as:

$$\alpha_R(D) = \frac{|R_A \cap D|}{|R_A|}(= P(D|R)), \text{ and } \kappa_R(D) = \frac{|R_A \cap D|}{|D|}(= P(R|D)),$$

where $|S|$, $\alpha_R(D)$, $\kappa_R(D)$ and $P(S)$ denote the cardinality of a set S, a classification accuracy of R as to classification of D and coverage (a true positive rate of R to D), and probability of S, respectively.

In the above example, when R and D are set to $[nau = 1]$ and $[class = migraine]$, $\alpha_R(D) = 2/3 = 0.67$ and $\kappa_R(D) = 2/2 = 1.0$.

3.2 Probabilistic Rules

According to the definitions, probabilistic rules with high accuracy and coverage are defined as:

$$R \xrightarrow{\alpha, \kappa} d \text{ s.t. } R = \vee_i R_i = \vee \wedge_j [a_j = v_k], \alpha_{R_i}(D) \geq \delta_\alpha \text{ and } \kappa_{R_i}(D) \geq \delta_\kappa,$$

where δ_α and δ_κ denote given thresholds for accuracy and coverage, respectively. For the above example shown in Table 1, probabilistic rules for m.c.h. are given as follows:

$$[M1 = yes] \to m.c.h. \ \alpha = 3/4 = 0.75, \ \kappa = 1.0,$$
$$[nau = no] \to m.c.h. \ \alpha = 3/3 = 1.0, \ \kappa = 1.0,$$

where δ_α and δ_κ are set to 0.75 and 0.5, respectively.

3.3   Characterization Sets

In order to model medical reasoning, a statistical measure, coverage plays an important role in modeling, which is a conditional probability of a condition (R) under the decision $D(P(R\text{---}D))$. Let us define a characterization set of D, denoted by L(D) as a set, each element of which is an elementary attribute-value pair R with coverage being larger than a given threshold, δ_κ. That is,

$$L_{\delta_\kappa} = \{[a_i = v_j] | \kappa_{[a_i = v_j]}(D) \geq \delta_\kappa$$

Then, three types of relations between characterization sets can be defined as follows:

Independent type: $L_{\delta_\kappa}(D_i) \cap L_{\delta_\kappa(D_j)} = \phi$,
Boundary type: $L_{\delta_\kappa}(D_i) \cap L(D_j)_{\delta_\kappa} \neq \phi$, and
Positive type: $L_{\delta_\kappa}(D_i) \subseteq L_{\delta_\kappa}(D_j)$.

All three definitions correspond to the negative region, boundary region, and positive region[4], respectively, if a set of the whole elementary attribute-value pairs will be taken as the universe of discourse. For the above example in Table 1, let D_1 and D_2 be m.c.h. and migraine and let the threshold of the coverage is larger than 0.6. Then, since

$$
\begin{aligned}
L_{0.6}(m.c.h.) &= \{[age = 40 - 49], [location = whole], [nature = persistent], \\
&\quad [prodrome = no], [nausea = no], [M1 = yes]\}, \text{ and} \\
L_{0.6}(migraine) &= \{[age = 40 - 49], [nature = throbbing], \\
&\quad [nausea = yes], [M1 = no]\},
\end{aligned}
$$

the relation between m.c.h. and migraine is boundary type when the threshold is set to 0.6. Thus, the factors that contribute to differential diagnosis between these two are: $[location = whole], [nature = persistent], [nature = throbbing], [prodrome = no], [nausea = yes], [nausea = no], [M1 = yes], [M1 = no]$. In these pairs, three attributes: nausea and M1 are very important. On the other hand, let D_1 and D_2 be m.c.h. and psycho and let the threshold of the coverage is larger than 0.6. Then, since

$$
\begin{aligned}
L_{0.6}(psycho) &= \{[age = 50 - 59], [location = whole], [nature = persistent], \\
&\quad [prodrome = no], [nausea = yes], [M1 = yes]\},
\end{aligned}
$$

the relation between m.c.h. and psycho is also boundary. Thus, in the case of Table 1, age, nausea and M1 are very important factors for differential diagnosis.

According to the rules acquired from medical experts, medical differential diagnosis is a focusing mechanism: first, medical experts focus on some general category of diseases, such as vascular or muscular headache. After excluding the possibility of other categories, medical experts proceed into the further differential diagnosis between diseases within a general category. In this type of reasoning, subcategory type of characterization is the most important one. However, since medical knowledge has some degree of uncertainty, boundary type with high overlapped region may have to be treated like subcategory type. To check this boundary type, we use rough inclusion measure defined below.

3.4   Rough Inclusion

In order to measure the similarity between classes with respect to characterization, we introduce a rough inclusion measure μ, which is defined as follows.

$$\mu(S,T) = \frac{|S \cap T|}{|S|}.$$

It is notable that if $S \subseteq T$, then $\mu(S,T) = 1.0$, which shows that this relation extends subset and superset relations. This measure is introduced by Polkowski and Skowron in their study on rough mereology[9]. Whereas rough mereology firstly applies to distributed information systems, its essential idea is rough inclusion: Rough inclusion focuses on set-inclusion to characterize a hierarchical structure based on a relation between a subset and superset. Thus, application of rough inclusion to capturing the relations between classes is equivalent to constructing rough hierarchical structure between classes, which is also closely related with information granulation proposed by Zadeh[17]. Let us illustrate how this measure is applied to hierarchical rule induction by using Table 1. When the threshold for the coverage is set to 0.6,

$$\mu(L_{0.6}(m.c.h.), L_{0.6}(migraine)) = \frac{|\{[age=40-49]\}|}{|\{[age=40-49],[location=whole],...\}|} = \frac{1}{6}$$

$$\mu(L_{0.6}(m.c.h.), L_{0.6}(psycho))$$
$$= \frac{|\{[location=whole],[nature=persistent],[prodrome=no],[M1=yes]\}|}{|\{[age=40-49],[location=whole],...\}|} = \frac{4}{6} = \frac{2}{3}$$

$$\mu(L_{0.6}(migraine), L_{0.6}(psycho)) = \frac{|\{[nausea=yes]\}|}{|\{[age=40-49],[nature=throbbing],...\}|} = \frac{1}{4}$$

These values show that the characterization set of m.c.h. is closer to that of psycho than that of migraine.

Therefore, if the threshold for rough inclusion is set to 0.6, the characterization set of m.c.h. is roughly included by that of psycho. On the other hand, the characterization set of migraine is independent of those of m.c.h. and psycho. Thus, the differential diagnosis process consists of two process: the first process should discriminate between migraine and the group of m.c.h. and psycho. Then, the second process discriminate between m.c.h and psycho. This means that the discrimination rule of m.c.h. is composed of (discrimination between migraine and the group)+ (discrimination between m.c.h. and psycho). In the case of L0.6, since the intersection of the characerization set of m.c.h and psycho is $\{[location = whole], [nature = persistent], [prodrome = no], [M1 = yes]\}$, and the differences in attributes between this group and migraine is nature, M1. So, one of the candidates of discrimination rule is

$$[nature = throbbing] \wedge [M1 = no] \rightarrow migraine$$

The second discrimination rule is derived from the difference between the characterizaton set of m.c.h. and psycho: So, one of the candidate of the second discrimination rule is: $[age = 40 - 49] \rightarrow m.c.h.$ or $[nausea = no] \rightarrow m.c.h.$ Combining these two rules, we can obtain a diagnostic rule for m.c.h as:

$$\neg([nature = throbbing] \wedge [M1 = no]) \wedge [age = 40 - 49] \rightarrow m.c.h.$$

4   Rule Induction

Rule induction(Fig 1.) consists of the following three procedures. First, the characterization of each given class, a list of attribute-value pairs the supporting set of which covers all the samples of the class, is extracted from databases and the classes are classified into several groups with respect to the characterization. Then, two kinds of sub-rules, rules discriminating between each group and rules classifying each class in the group are induced(Fig 2). Finally, those two parts are integrated into one rule for each decision attribute(Fig 3).[1]

procedure *Rule Induction (Total Process)*;
   var
      $i : integer$; $M, L, R : List$;
      $L_D : List$; /* A list of all classes */
   begin
      Calculate $\alpha_R(D_i)$ and $\kappa_R(D_i)$ for each elementary relation R and each class D_i;
      Make a list $L(D_i) = \{R|\kappa_R(D) = 1.0\}$) for each class D_i;
      while $(L_D \neq \phi)$ **do**
        begin
          $D_i := first(L_D)$; $M := L_D - D_i$;
          while $(M \neq \phi)$ **do**
            begin
              $D_j := first(M)$;
              if $(\mu(L(D_j), L(D_i)) \leq \delta_\mu)$ **then** $L_2(D_i) := L_2(D_i) + \{D_j\}$;
             $M := M - D_j$;
            end
          Make a new decision attribute D_i' for $L_2(D_i)$;
          $L_D := L_D - D_i$;
        end
      Construct a new table $(T_2(D_i))$for $L_2(D_i)$.
      Construct a new table$(T(D_i'))$ for each decision attribute D_i';
          Induce classification rules R_2 for each $L_2(D)$; /* Fig.2 */
          Store Rules into a List $R(D)$
          Induce classification rules R_d for each D' in $T(D')$; /* Fig.2 */
          Store Rules into a List $R(D')(= R(L_2(D_i)))$
      Integrate R_2 and R_d into a rule R_D; /* Fig.3 */
   end *{Rule Induction }*;

Fig. 1. An Algorithm for Rule Induction

---

[1] This method is an extension of PRIMEROSE4 reported in [16]. In the former paper, only rigid set-inclusion relations are considered for grouping; on the other hand, rough-inclusion relations are introduced in this approach. Recent empirical comparison between set-inclusion method and rough-inclusion method shows that the latter approach outperforms the former one.

procedure *Induction of Classification Rules*;
  var
    $i : integer$; $M, L_i : List$;
  begin
    $L_1 := L_{er}$; /* L_{er}: List of Elementary Relations */
    $i := 1$; $M := \{\}$;
    for $i := 1$ **to** n **do**   /* n: Total number of attributes */
    begin
      while ($L_i \neq \{\}$) **do**
        begin
          Select one pair $R = \wedge[a_i = v_j]$ from L_i;
          $L_i := L_i - \{R\}$;
          if $(\alpha_R(D) \geq \delta_\alpha)$ **and** $(\kappa_R(D) \geq \delta_\kappa)$
            then do $S_{ir} := S_{ir} + \{R\}$; /* Include R as Inclusive Rule */
          else $M := M + \{R\}$;
        end
      $L_{i+1} :=$ (A list of the whole combination of the conjunction formulae in M);
    end
  end {*Induction of Classification Rules* };

Fig. 2. An Algorithm for Classification Rules

procedure *Rule Integration*;
  var
    $i : integer$; $M, L_2 : List$; $R(D_i) : List$; /* A list of rules for D_i */
    $L_D : List$; /* A list of all classes */
  begin
    while($L_D \neq \phi$) **do**
    begin
      $D_i := first(L_D)$; $M := L_2(D_i)$;
      Select one rule $R' \rightarrow D'_i$ from $R(L_2(D_i))$.
      while ($M \neq \phi$) **do**
      begin
        $D_j := first(M)$;
          Select one rule $R \rightarrow d_j$ for D_j;
          Integrate two rules: $R \wedge R' \rightarrow d_j$.
        $M := M - \{D_j\}$;
      end
      $L_D := L_D - D_i$;
    end
  end {*Rule Combination*}

Fig. 3. An Algorithm for Rule Integration

Example

Let us illustrate how the introduced algorithm works by using a small database in Table 1. For simplicity, two thresholds δ_α and δ_μ are set to 1.0, which means that only deterministic rules should be induced and that only subset and superset relations should be considered for grouping classes.

After the first and second step, the following three sets will be obtained: $L(m.c.h.) = \{[prod = no], [M1 = yes]\}$, $L(migra) = \{[age = 40...49], [nat = who], [prod = yes], [nau = yes], [M1 = no]\}$, and $L(psycho) = \{[age = 50...59], [loc = who], [nat = per], [prod = no], [nau = no], [M1 = yes]\}$. Thus, since a relation $L(psycho) \subset L(m.c.h.)$ holds (i.e., $\mu(L(m.c.h.), L(psycho)) = 1.0$), a new decision attribute is $D_1 = \{m.c.h., psycho\}$ and $D_2 = \{migra\}$, and a partition $P = \{D_1, D_2\}$ is obtained. From this partition, two decision tables will be generated, as shown in Table 2 and Table 3 in the fifth step.

Table 2. A Table for a New Partition P

	age	loc	nat	prod	nau	M1	class
1	50...59	occ	per	0	0	1	D_1
2	40...49	who	per	0	0	1	D_1
3	40...49	lat	thr	1	1	0	D_2
4	40...49	who	thr	1	1	0	D_2
5	40...49	who	rad	0	0	1	D_1
6	50...59	who	per	0	1	1	D_1

Table 3. A Table for D_1

	age	loc	nat	prod	nau	M1	class
1	50...59	occ	per	0	0	1	m.c.h.
2	40...49	who	per	0	0	1	m.c.h.
5	40...49	who	rad	0	0	1	m.c.h.
6	50...59	who	per	0	1	1	psycho

In the sixth step, classification rules for D_1 and D_2 are induced from Table 2. For example, the following rules are obtained for D_1.

$[M1 = yes]$ $\rightarrow D_1$ $\alpha = 1.0$, $\kappa = 1.0$,   supported by $\{1,2,5,6\}$
$[prod = no]$ $\rightarrow D_1$ $\alpha = 1.0$, $\kappa = 1.0$,   supported by $\{1,2,5,6\}$
$[nau = no]$ $\rightarrow D_1$ $\alpha = 1.0$, $\kappa = 0.75$, supported by $\{1,2,5\}$
$[nat = per]$ $\rightarrow D_1$ $\alpha = 1.0$, $\kappa = 0.75$, supported by $\{1,2,6\}$
$[loc = who]$ $\rightarrow D_1$ $\alpha = 1.0$, $\kappa = 0.75$, supported by $\{2,5,6\}$
$[age = 50...59] \rightarrow D_1$ $\alpha = 1.0$, $\kappa = 0.5$,   supported by $\{2,6\}$

In the seventh step, classification rules for m.c.h. and psycho are induced from Table 3. For example, the following rules are obtained from m.c.h..

$[nau = no]$ $\rightarrow m.c.h.$ $\alpha = 1.0$, $\kappa = 1.0$,   supported by $\{1,2,5\}$
$[age = 40...49] \rightarrow m.c.h.$ $\alpha = 1.0$, $\kappa = 0.67$, supported by $\{2,5\}$

In the eighth step, these two kinds of rules are integrated in the following way. Rule $[M1 = yes] \rightarrow D_1$, $[nau = no] \rightarrow m.c.h.$ and $[age = 40...49] \rightarrow m.c.h.$ have a supporting set which is a subset of $\{1,2,5,6\}$. Thus, the following rules are obtained:

$$[M1 = yes] \ \& \ [nau=no] \quad \rightarrow m.c.h. \ \alpha = 1.0, \ \kappa = 1.0, \ \text{supported by } \{1,2,5\}$$
$$[M1 = yes] \ \& \ [age=40...49] \rightarrow m.c.h. \ \alpha = 1.0, \ \kappa = 0.67, \text{supported by } \{2,5\}$$

5   Experimental Results

The above rule induction algorithm is implemented in PRIMEROSE4.5 (Probabilistic Rule Induction Method based on Rough Sets Ver 4.5), [2] and was applied to databases on differential diagnosis of headache, whose training samples consist of 1477 samples, 20 classes and 20 attributes.

This system was compared with PRIMEROSE4[16], PRIMEROSE[14], C4.5[10], CN2[5], AQ15[7] and k-NN[2] [3] with respect to the following points: length of rules, similarities between induced rules and expert's rules and performance of rules.

In this experiment, length was measured by the number of attribute-value pairs used in an induced rule and Jaccard's coefficient was adopted as a similarity measure[6]. Concerning the performance of rules, ten-fold cross-validation was applied to estimate classification accuracy.

Table 4 shows the experimental results, which suggest that PRIMEROSE4.5 outperforms PRIMEROSE4(set-inclusion approach) and the other four rule induction methods and induces rules very similar to medical experts' ones.

Table 4. Experimental Results

Method	Length	Similarity	Accuracy
		Headache	
PRIMEROSE4.5	8.8 ± 0.27	0.95 ± 0.08	$95.2 \pm 2.7\%$
PRIMEROSE4.0	8.6 ± 0.27	0.93 ± 0.08	$93.3 \pm 2.7\%$
Experts	9.1 ± 0.33	1.00 ± 0.00	$98.0 \pm 1.9\%$
PRIMEROSE	5.3 ± 0.35	0.54 ± 0.05	$88.3 \pm 3.6\%$
C4.5	4.9 ± 0.39	0.53 ± 0.10	$85.8 \pm 1.9\%$
CN2	4.8 ± 0.34	0.51 ± 0.08	$87.0 \pm 3.1\%$
AQ15	4.7 ± 0.35	0.51 ± 0.09	$86.2 \pm 2.9\%$
k-NN (7)	6.7 ± 0.25	0.61 ± 0.09	$88.2 \pm 1.5\%$

k-NN (i) shows the value of i which gives the highest performance in k ($1 \leq k \leq 20$).

---

[2] The program is implemented by using SWI-prolog [13] on Sparc Station 20.
[3] The most optimal k for each domain is attached to Table 4.

6   Conclusion

In this paper, the characteristics of experts' rules are closely examined, whose empirical results suggest that grouping of diseases are very important to realize automated acquisition of medical knowledge from clinical databases. Thus, we focus on the role of coverage in focusing mechanisms and propose an algorithm on grouping of diseases by using this measure. The above experiments show that rule induction with this grouping generates rules, which are similar to medical experts' rules and they suggest that our proposed method should capture medical experts' reasoning. The proposed method was evaluated on three medical databases, the experimental results of which show that induced rules correctly represent experts' decision processes.

Acknowledgments. This work was supported by the Grant-in-Aid for Scientific Research on Priority Areas(B) (No.759) "Implementation of Active Mining in the Era of Information Flood" by the Ministry of Education, Science, Culture, Science and Technology of Japan.

References

1. Agrawal, R., Imielinski, T., and Swami, A., Mining association rules between sets of items in large databases, in *Proceedings of the 1993 International Conference on Management of Data (SIGMOD 93)*, pp. 207-216, 1993.
2. Aha, D. W., Kibler, D., and Albert, M. K., Instance-based learning algorithm. *Machine Learning*, 6, 37-66, 1991.
3. Breiman, L., Freidman, J., Olshen, R., and Stone, C., *Classification And Regression Trees*, Wadsworth International Group, Belmont, 1984.
4. Buchnan, B. G. and Shortliffe, E. H., *Rule-Based Expert Systems*, Addison-Wesley, New York, 1984.
5. Clark, P. and Niblett, T., The CN2 Induction Algorithm. *Machine Learning*, 3, 261-283, 1989.
6. Everitt, B. S., *Cluster Analysis*, 3rd Edition, John Wiley & Son, London, 1996.
7. Michalski, R. S., Mozetic, I., Hong, J., and Lavrac, N., The Multi-Purpose Incremental Learning System AQ15 and its Testing Application to Three Medical Domains, in *Proceedings of the fifth National Conference on Artificial Intelligence*, 1041-1045, AAAI Press, Menlo Park, 1986.
8. Pawlak, Z., *Rough Sets*. Kluwer Academic Publishers, Dordrecht, 1991.
9. Polkowski, L. and Skowron, A.: Rough mereology: a new paradigm for approximate reasoning. Intern. J. Approx. Reasoning **15**, 333–365, 1996.
10. Quinlan, J.R., *C4.5 - Programs for Machine Learning*, Morgan Kaufmann, Palo Alto, 1993.
11. *Readings in Machine Learning*, (Shavlik, J. W. and Dietterich, T.G., eds.) Morgan Kaufmann, Palo Alto, 1990.
12. Skowron, A. and Grzymala-Busse, J. From rough set theory to evidence theory. In: Yager, R., Fedrizzi, M. and Kacprzyk, J.(eds.) *Advances in the Dempster-Shafer Theory of Evidence*, pp.193-236, John Wiley & Sons, New York, 1994.
13. SWI-Prolog Version 2.0.9 Manual, University of Amsterdam, 1995.

14. Tsumoto, S. and Tanaka, H., PRIMEROSE: Probabilistic Rule Induction Method based on Rough Sets and Resampling Methods. *Computational Intelligence*, **11**, 389-405, 1995.
15. Tsumoto, S., Automated Induction of Medical Expert System Rules from Clinical Databases based on Rough Set Theory. *Information Sciences* **112**, 67-84, 1998.
16. Tsumoto, S. Extraction of Experts' Decision Rules from Clinical Databases using Rough Set Model *Intelligent Data Analysis*, 2(3), 1998.
17. Zadeh, L.A., Toward a theory of fuzzy information granulation and its certainty in human reasoning and fuzzy logic. *Fuzzy Sets and Systems* **90**, 111-127, 1997.
18. Ziarko, W., Variable Precision Rough Set Model. *Journal of Computer and System Sciences.* 46, 39-59, 1993.

Inheriting Parents Operators: A New Dynamic Strategy for Improving Evolutionary Algorithms[*]

María-Cristina Riff[1] and Xavier Bonnaire[2]

[1] Department of Computer Science, Universidad Técnica Federico Santa María,
Valparaíso, Chile, mcriff@inf.utfsm.cl
[2] Laboratoire d'Informatique Paris VI, Université Pièrre et Marie Curie, Paris,
France, Xavier.Bonnaire@lip6.fr

Abstract. Our research has been focused on developing techniques for solving binary constraint satisfaction problems (CSP) using evolutionary algorithms, which take into account the constraint graphs topology. In this paper, we introduce a new idea to improve the performance of evolutionary algorithms, that solve complex problems. It is inspired from a real world observation: The ability to evolve for an individual in an environment that changes is not only related to its genetic material. It also comes from what has learned from it parents. The key idea of this paper is to use its inheritance to dynamically improve the way the algorithm creates a new population using a given set of operators. This new dynamic operator selection strategy has been applied to an evolutionary algorithm to solve CSPs, but can be easily extended to other class of evolutionary algorithms. A set of benchmarks shows how the new strategy can help to solve large NP-hard problems with the 3-graph coloring example.

1 Introduction

Designing genetic algorithms to tackle a complex problem is a time consuming task. It requires to create a new algorithm for each specific problem, [2]. Roughly speaking, we need to define at least the following: a representation, some especially designed operators, and the "best" parameters values or, a control strategy to them.

In the evolutionary algorithms community we can find many papers proposing new algorithms with new strategies that work better than others. However, they are usually completely different from the original ones. In order to obtain good comparisons other researchers use public benchmarks to establish if a new algorithm is more efficient than another one. In particular Craenen et al. in [1] present an evaluation of some specialized operators to solve Constraint Satisfaction Problems. In this work they identify which is the best operator for a given problem connectivity, according to the constraints graph topology. Adaptation

---

[*] Partially supported by CNRS/CONICYT Collaboration Project France-Chile

M.-S. Hacid et al. (Eds.): ISMIS 2002, LNAI 2366, pp. 333–341, 2002.
© Springer-Verlag Berlin Heidelberg 2002

of the parameters and operators in evolutionary algorithms is an important research area as it tunes the algorithm to the problem while solving it. There are many publications related to the subject of adaptation in evolutionary algorithm, all of them agree to include an adaptation strategy which can improve the performance of the algorithm, [10], [14], [19], [9].

On the other hand, in [6] the subject of parameter control has been addressed to try to improve the performance of evolutionary algorithms. This research concluded that the best way to determine the parameters values of an evolutionary algorithm is to use a parameters control strategy instead of a parameters tuning strategy. This suggests that the best way to find good parameters values could be to make self-adaptive algorithms where the control strategy is included in the algorithm itself. Therefore, we naturally expect that the algorithm could also be able to auto-identify which operator should give better results according to the parents inheritance.

Our goal in this paper is to define some strategies to guide the algorithm to choose the best operator to be applied according to a set of criteria, for an evolutionary algorithm that have a pool of genetic operators.

We apply this strategy on an evolutionary algorithm to solve binary constraints satisfaction problems. Constraints problems embodies a class of general problems which are both important in theory and in practice. Constraint problems can be considered as search problems, i.e. given a finite search space composed by a set of configurations. They are usually NP-hard. This paper deals with one class of methods: evolutionary algorithms.

In this context, we introduce a strategy that can help the evolutionary algorithm to choose the most appropriate operator to be used in a generation. It takes into account the evolution of the population and the selected individuals, in order to be able to generate individuals with better fitness. This idea can also help the algorithm to discard some operators that don't have good performance. Computational tests are carried out of an NP-hard problem: the 3-graph coloring. Experimental evidence shows the benefits of the strategy to solve hard instances of a set of sparse graphs. The results are compared with those obtained by the algorithm without the operator selection strategy.

2   Constraint Satisfaction and Evolutionary Algorithms

The involved problem is a constraint satisfaction problem (CSP) defined in the sense of Mackworth [11], which can be stated briefly as follows: We are given a set of variables, a domain of possible values for each variable, and a conjunction of constraints. Each constraint is a relation defined over a subset of the variables, limiting the combination of values that the variables in this subset can take. The goal is to find one consistent assignment of values to the variables so that all the constraints are satisfied simultaneously.

CSP's are usually NP-complete and some of them are NP-hard [4]. Thus, a general algorithm designed to solve any CSP will necessarily require exponential time in problem size in the worst case.

2.1   Notions on CSP

A *Constraint Satisfaction Problem* (CSP) is composed of a set of *variables* $V = \{X_1, \ldots, X_n\}$, their related *domains* $D_1, \ldots, D_n$ and a set θ containing η *constraints* on these variables. The domain of a variable is a set of values to which the variable may be instantiated. The domain sizes are $m_1, \ldots, m_n$, respectively, and we let **m** denote the maximum of the m_i. Each variable X_j is *relevant* to a subset of constraints $C_{j_1}, \ldots, C_{j_k}$ where $\{j_1, \ldots, j_k\}$ is a subsequence of $\{1, 2, \ldots, \eta\}$. A constraint which has exactly one relevant variable is called a *unary constraint*. Similarly, a *binary constraint* has exactly two relevant variables. A binary CSP is associated with a constraint graph, where nodes represent variables and arcs represent constraints. If two values assigned to variables that share a constraint are not among the acceptable value-pairs of that constraint, this is an *inconsistency* or constraint violation.

2.2   Evolutionary Algorithms for CSP

Evolutionary Algorithms for CSP can be divided into two classes: EAs using adaptive fitness functions and EAs using heuristics, [7], [8], [12], [18], [16], [17]. We consider four very known heuristics based operators implemented in evolutionary algorithms for CSPs.

1. Asexual Heuristic Operator: This operator was proposed by Eiben et al. in [8]. It selects a number of variables in a given individual, and then selects new values for these variables. The best parameters reported for this operator are $(\#, r, b)$, that means, one fourth of the variables to be changed ($\#$), choosing them randomly (r), and selects the values for these variables which maximize the number of constraints that become satisfied.

2. Local Search Operator: This operator is inspired of the Minton et al. work.[13]. It is a hill climbing procedure. The operator chooses a variable randomly in a given individual, and then selects a new value for this variable which improve the number of constraints that become satisfied.

3. Arc-crossover Operator: We introduced in [17], [15] a EA for solving CSPs which uses information about the constraint network in the fitness function and in the genetic operators. The fitness function is based on the notion of *error evaluation* of a constraint. The error evaluation of a constraint is the number of variables of the constraint and the number of variables that are connected to these variables in the CSP graph. It is used as a measure of the connectivity of the network and as a indicator of how important it is to satisfy the constraint. The fitness function of an individual is the sum of error evaluations of all the violated constraints in the individual. The crossover operator selects randomly two parents and builds a child by means of an iterative procedure over all the constraints of the CSP. Constraints are ordered according to their error-evaluation function value. For the two variables of a selected constraint c, say v_i, v_j, the following cases are distinguished: If one of the two variables are instantiated yet in the offspring under construction, and none of the parents satisfies c, then a combination of values for

the variables from the parents is selected which minimizes the sum of the error evaluations of the constraints containing v_i and v_j whose other variables are already instantiated in the offspring. If there is one parent which satisfies c, then that parent supplies the value for the child. If both parents satisfy c, then the parent which has the higher fitness provides its values for the variables. If only one variable, is not instantiated in the offspring under construction, its value is selected from the parent minimizing the sum of the error-evaluations of the constraints involving the variable. If both variables are instantiated in the offspring under construction, then the next constraint (in the order described above) is selected.

4. Constraint Dynamic Adapting Crossover: It uses the same idea of arc-crossover, that is there are not fixed points to make crossover. This operator uses a dynamic constraints priority. The dynamic constraint priority does not only take into account the network structure, but also the current values of the parents. The priority is built using the following procedure: First, it identifies the *number of violations*, **nv**, that means, between both parents selected, how many are violating the current constraint. Then, it classifies the constraints in one of the following three categories : 0, 1 or 2 number of violations. And finally, within each category (0,1 or 2 number of violations), the constraints are ordered according to their contribution to the fitness function. To make crossover the operator uses two *partial fitness functions*. The first one is the *partial crossover fitness function*, **cff**, which allows us to guide the selection of a combination of variable values by constraint. The second one is the *partial mutation fitness function* **mff** to choose a new variable value. The whole process is introduced, in details, in [17].

3   Dynamic Operators Selection Strategy

We have used all the previous operators presented above in an evolutionary algorithm, where we now introduce as Dynamic Selection Strategy of Operators. Usually, the more time-consuming operators are the crossover ones, thus we focus on the selection of a crossover operator. Given two selected parents, how to find the most appropriate operator of the pool that could be generate potentially a best offspring?. It requires some heuristics in order to define what "most appropriate" means. The original representation uses real values, where each gene represents a variable value. Our key idea is to extend this representation to include a new gene, that records which operator has been used to generate this individual. Therefore, the offspring will not only inherit the variables values from its parents, but it could also inherit the operator that has been used to create one of them. The inheritance process is shown in figure 1

4   Tests

The goal of the following benchmarks is to evaluate the effect of including a dynamic operator selection into the constraints-graph based evolutionary algorithm, and to compare it with the traditional approach. The algorithm has

```
Begin /* Procedure Dynamic Operator Selection Strategy */
Parent 1 = select(population(t))
Parent 2 = select(population(t))
if both parents have been generated by the same crossover operator
cross-op then
    Generate the offspring using cross-op
if only one parent have been generated by a crossover operator
cross-op then
    Generate the offspring using cross-op
if the parents have been created by different crossover operators
cross-op-1, cross-op-2 then
    Generate the offspring using the crossover operator from
    the best of the two parents.
Include the applied crossover operator information in the child
End /* procedure */
```

Fig. 1. Dynamic Operator Selection Strategy

been tested with randomly generated 3-coloring graphs, subject to the constraint that adjacent nodes must be colored differently. We used the 3-coloring graphs because it is a well known problem in the research community, there are benchmarks available in the litterature and we can also easily generate hard problems.

We used the Joe Culberson library, [5] to generate the random graphs. We have tested both algorithms for 3-coloring problems with solution, which are related to a sparse graph. This kind of graphs are known to be as the most difficult to solve [4]. For each number of constraints we have generated 500 random 3-coloring graph problems. In order to discard the "easy problems" we have applied DSATUR [3] to solve them. Then, we have selected the problems not solved by DSATUR. DSATUR is one of the best algorithms to solve this kind of problems. It is important to remark that it is easy to find problems not solved by DSATUR in the hard zone [4], which is not the case with others connectivities.

4.1   Hardware

The hardware platform for the experiments was a PC Pentium IV, 1.4Ghz with 512 MB RAM under the LINUX operating system. The algorithm has been implemented in C.

4.2   Results

Both algorithms use the following parameters, which are the best reported values for the operators considered in this paper, [8], [17]: Mutation probability = 0.7,

Crossover probability = 0.8, Asexual propability = 0.5. We have fixed a maximum number of generations of 10000. The problems analyzed are shown in the following table:

Number-Constraints	CPU-time[s] without	CPU-time[s] with
30	3	3
45	15.3	15.25
60	85.09	62.23
90	2854	2278
120	20080	13145
150		18758

From this table we can conclude that for small problem instances (30-60 constraints) both algorithms have the same performance. However when the problem is larger the new strategy helps the algorithm to converge.

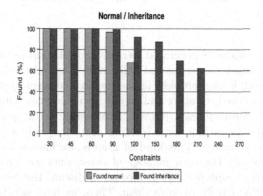

Fig. 2. Solved Problems using operator selection and without

Figure 2 and 3 shown the results obtained. The inclusion of dynamic operators selection strategy helps the algorithm to solve more problems with a lower number of generations than the initial approach. With 120 or a higher number of constraints the inheritance strategy is really better than the traditional approach. The more constraints we have for this type of problems (sparses graphs), the more efficient will be the inheritance strategy because it automatically selects the most efficient operator.

We known that between these two operators the best one is Constraint Dynamic Adaptive Crossover (CDAC) [17]. Figure 4 and 5 shown that the CDAC have been significantly more used by the algorithm to create new individuals. At the beginning of the execution, both operators are used by the algorithm with the same probability, but the better efficiency of the CDAC is quickly propagated through the inheritance mechanism when it starts to produce several individuals which become the best fit ones.

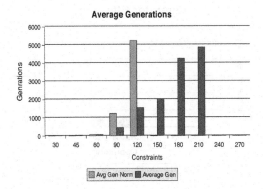

Fig. 3. Number of Generations

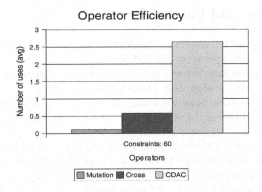

Fig. 4. Average number of uses of each operator to find the bestfit individual by graph for 60 constraints

The results for 90 constraints show even more efficiency of the CDAC front of the crossover operator. The difference of 4.54 instead of 2.06 for the 60 constraints problems clearly brings out that CDAC is much powerfull and leads to find a solution with less generations and less CPU time. We can expect that the difference will be higher between the two operators as the number of constraints increases. Thus, the algorithm has auto-detected the operator which was expected to be the best one to solve this problem. This auto-detection prevents the user from running several executions of the algorithm with different probabilities for each crossover operators trying to find which is the best one regarding to the number of solved problems. Our algorithm is able to do it itself with a single execution.

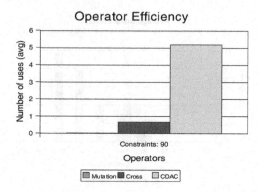

Fig. 5. Average number of uses of each operator to find the bestfit individual by graph for 90 constraints

5 Discussion and Further Issues

We have obtained better results by including a dynamic operator selection strategy for two crossover operators applied to a classical NP-hard problem. We are motivated to explore new ways of selecting operators. We are going towards to give to the evolutionary algorithm some heuristics in order to be able of discard some no good operators. Now we would like to develop some strategies for the Travel Salesman Problem, because it is a classical problem and there are a lot of proposed operators in the litterature.

The code included in the algorithm in the worst case correspond a $O(n)$, thus it is not an expensive strategy in computational time. However, its uses could give an important improvement for the algorithm performance. When we try to solve NP-complete problems algorithm performance means be able to find more solutions of the problem in a reasonable time.

6 Conclusion

Our research allows us to conclude that using an evolutionary algorithm with operator selection strategy we are able to solve around 85% of the problems that are in the hard zone. The results suggest that our technique is a good option to improve the performance of an evolutionary algorithm.

There is a variety of ways in which the techniques presented here can be extended. The principal advantage of our method is that it is general, i.e., the approach is not related to a particular algorithm.

References

[1]   B. Craenen, A. Eiben, E. Marchiori. Solving Constraint Satisfaction Problems with Heuristic-based Evolutionary Algorithms. In Proceedings of the Congress on Evolutionary Computation, (CEC2000),pages 1571-1577, IEEE Press.

[2]   Michalewicz Z., Genetic Algorithms + Data Structures = Evolution Programs. Ed. Springer Verlag, Artificial Intelligence Series, 1994.

[3]   Brelaz, New methods to color vertices of a graph. Communications of the ACM, 22,pp. 251-256, 1979.

[4]   Cheeseman P.,Kanefsky B., Taylor W., Where the Really Hard Problems Are. Proceedings of IJCAI-91, pp. 163-169, 1991

[5]   Culberson, J. http://web.cs.ualberta.ca/ joe/.

[6]   Eiben A.E., Hinterding R., and Michalewicz Z. Parameter Control. Evolutionary Computation 2: Advanced Algorithms and Operators, pages 170-187, Institute of Physics Publishing, 2000.

[7]   G. Dozier, J. Bowen, and Homaifar, Solving Constraint Satisfaction Problems Using Hybrid Evolutionary Search, IEEE Transactions on Evolutionary Computation, Vol. 2, No. 1, 1998.

[8]   A.E. Eiben, J.I. van Hemert, E. Marchiori, A.G. Steenbeek. Solving Binary Constraint Satisfaction Problems using Evolutionary Algorithms with an Adaptive Fitness Function. Fifth International Conference on Parallel Problem Solving from Nature (PPSN-V), LNCS 1498, pp. 196-205, 1998.

[9]   Hinterding, R. Self-adaptation using Multi-chromosmes. Proceedings of the 4th IEEE International Conference on Evolutionary Computation, 1997.

[10]   Smith, J.E. and Fogarty T.C. Operator and Parameter Adaptation in Genetic Algorithms. pp81–87, Soft Computing , 1:2, June 1997. Springer Verlag

[11]   Mackworth A.K., Consistency in network of relations. Artificial Intelligence, 8:99-118, 1977.

[12]   Marchiori E., Combining Constraint Processing and Genetic Algorithms for Constraint Satisfaction Problems. 7th International Conference on Genetic Algorithms (ICGA97), 1997.

[13]   Minton S., Integrating heuristics for constraint satisfaction problems: A case study. Proceedings of the Eleventh National Conference on Artificial Intelligence, 1993.

[14]   Smith, J.E. and Vavak, F. Replacement strategies in steady state genetic algorithms: dynamic environments, p 49-60 Journal of Computing and Information Technology, Special Issue on Evolutionary Computing. Vol. 7 No. 1. March 1999

[15]   Riff M.-C., From Quasi-solutions to Solution: An Evolutionary Algorithm to Solve CSP. Constraint Processing (CP96), Ed. Eugene Freuder, pp. 367-381, 1996.

[16]   Riff M.-C., Evolutionary Search guided by the Constraint Network to solve CSP. Proc. of the Fourth IEEE Conf on Evolutionary Computation, Indianopolis, pp. 337-342, 1997.

[17]   Riff M.-C., A network-based adaptive evolutionary algorithm for CSP, In the book "Metaheuristics: Advances and Trends in Local Search Paradigms for Optimisation", Kluwer Academic Publisher, Chapter 22, pp. 325-339, 1998.

[18]   Tsang, E.P.K., Wang, C.J., Davenport, A., Voudouris, C., Lau,T.L., A family of stochastic methods for constraint satisfaction and optimization, The First International Conference on The Practical Application of Constraint Technologies and Logic Programming (PACLP), London, pp. 359-383, 1999

[19]   Smith, J.E. Modelling GAs with Self Adaptive Mutation Rates, pp 599-606 in Proceedings of the Genetic and Evolutionary Computation Conference, GECCO-2001. San Francisco, CA: Morgan Kaufmann Publishers.

An Intelligent Web Recommendation System: A Web Usage Mining Approach

Hiroshi Ishikawa[1], Toshiyuki Nakajima[2], Tokuyo Mizuhara[3], Shohei Yokoyama[1],
Junya Nakayama[1], Manabu Ohta[1], and Kaoru Katayama[1]

[1] Tokyo Metropolitan University
[2] NTT Data Corporation
[3] Hitachi Software Engineering Co., Ltd.

Abstract. As an increasing number of Web sites consist of an increasing number of pages, it is more difficult for the users to rapidly reach their own target pages. So the intelligent systems supporting the users in navigation of the Web contents are in high demand. In this paper, we describe an intelligent recommendation system called the system L-R, which constructs user models by mining the Web access logs and recommends the relevant pages to the users based both on the user models and the Web contents. We have evaluated the prototype system and have obtained the positive effects.

1 Introduction

As an increasing number of Web sites consist of an increasing number of pages, it is more difficult for the users to rapidly reach their own target pages. So the systems supporting the users in navigation of the Web contents such as [7] are in high demand. In this paper, we describe a recommendation system called the system L-R (Log-based Recommendation), which constructs user models by mining the user access logs (e.g., IP addresses and access time) and recommends the relevant pages to the users based both on the user models and the Web contents [5]. In other words, the system L-R recommends based on collaborative filtering [7].

In this paper, we explain the functional aspects of the system L-R in Section 2, describe the experiment and evaluation of the system in Section 3, and discuss implementation issues and related work in Section 4.

2 System L-R

Indeed, the recommendation systems [7] are very helpful in directing the users to the target pages. However, applying recommendation systems to existing Web sites requires a large amount of work and knowledge. So we propose a recommendation system that assumes no detailed knowledge about the recommendation system and that can be adapted to any existing Web sites without rewriting the contents.

The proposed system has the following merits:

M.-S. Hacid et al. (Eds.): ISMIS 2002, LNAI 2366, pp. 342–350, 2002.

(1) It is easy for the Web site administrator to incorporate the recommendation facility because the system utilizes only Web usage logs. The system doesn't impose the users to explicitly input their profiles.
(2) It is possible for the Web site administrator to provide multiple recommendation methods by considering the objective of the site and the tendency of the users.
(3) It is possible for the users to interactively choose their favorite recommendation methods.

The system is intelligent in that it can automatically mine the Web log data and construct the user model based on the Web usage and recommend the pages fit for the user.

2.1 Extraction of Web Usage Logs

Our system recommends the relevant pages to the users based on the probability of the user's transition from one page to another, which is calculated by using the Web access logs. First, we delete the unnecessary log data left by so-called Web robots (i.e., sent by search engines) by heuristically finding them in Web access logs [3]. In general, robots are recommended to have access to a file "robots.txt" created by the Web site administrator as the Web policy about the robot access. Moreover, since robots leave their own names in the Web log as host names or user agents, we prepare the list of robots in advance. Thus, we can find most robots in the Web logs by checking access to the robots text or searching in the robot list. Please note that there is small possibility that non-human data log, such as brand-new robots and page scanning tools, remain in the Web.

Second, we correct the genuine (i.e., human) Web logs by deleting the transition caused by pushing the back button in Web browsers. For example, assume that the user browses the page A and the page B and browses again the page A by pushing the back button and then the page C. We change the transition from B to A to C into the transition from B to C (See Fig.1).

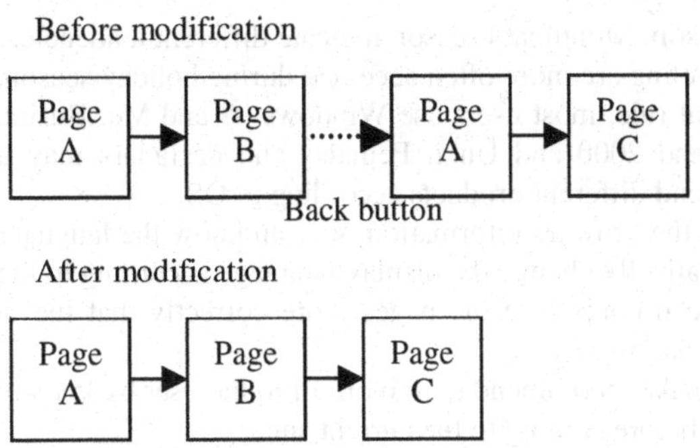

Before modification

Back button

After modification

Fig. 1. Log modification w.r.t. back transition

Lastly, we calculate the probability of the transition from the page A to the page B denoted by $P_{A\text{->}B}$ based on the modified Web log as follows:

$P_{A\to B}$ = (the total number of transitions from A to B) / (the total number of transitions from A).

Note that the transition probability of the path from A to B to C which we denote by A->B->C (where the length of the path is two) is calculated as follows: $P_{A\to B\to C} = P_{A\to B} * P_{B\to C}$.

2.2 Classification of Users

We classify the Web users by using information extracted from the Web access logs. The information includes IP addresses, domain names, host names, access time, OS, browser names, refers (i.e. the site just previously visited by the user), and keywords for retrieval. We describe the methods of classification based on such kinds of information. We construct user models by applying the methods of classification to the modified Web log data and realize the recommendation fit for the users based on the user models. We show the viewpoints of classification based on the Web log data as follows:

(1) IP address. We count the same IP address to get the number of access times. We recommend pages to the user according to their frequency of access to the Web site. For example, the frequent users are likely to browse the frequently updated pages. New comers are likely to browse "getting started" pages.

(2) Domain and host name. The names of user domains and hosts indicate the place from which the users are accessing the Web site. We classify the users according to the places. For example, the users from companies may browse the company information of EC sites while the general users may browse the product pages

(3) Access time. The users have different tendencies according to the time when the users are accessing the Web site. During the daytime, the housewives and businesspersons often access the site. At midnight, students often access the site.

(4) Day of the week. The weekday and weekend indicate different tendencies. For example, the pages about the leisure information are more often accessed on weekends than weekdays.

(5) Month and season. Month and season indicate different tendencies. For example, the pages about traveling are more often accessed during holiday seasons.

(6) OS. As a general rule, most users use Windows 98 and Me. Business users often use Windows NT and 2000 and Unix. Females and designers may use Mac. It is possible to recommend different products according to OS.

(7) Browser. From the browser information, we can know the language that the user uses. We can automatically change the display language according to the browser.

(8) Keyword. We can conjecture the pages more correctly that the user intends to access by user-input keywords.

(9) Refer. We can make recommendation more fit to the user by knowing the site that the user visited just before coming to the current site.

Of course, we can know other information such as the types of requests (e.g., get, put) and the size of transferred data from the Web logs, too. However, for the moment, we don't know the effect of the classification based on these kinds of information.

2.3 Recommendation

We provide various methods for recommendation, which can be classified into two groups: pure probability-based methods and weighted probability-based methods.

(1) Pure-probability-based methods. The following recommendation methods are based solely on the transition probabilities calculated from the Web log data.

- Path recommendation. The whole path with high transition probability such as pages A, B, and C is recommended to the user (See Fig.2). The recommended path reflects the series of pages, which are usually browsed in sequence such as instructions stretching over manual pages. Of course, the path longer than two can also be recommended.

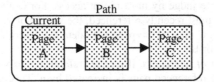

Fig. 2. Path recommendation

- History-based recommendation. Based on the pages visited before coming to the current page, the next page with high probability is recommended. In other words, even if the current page is the same, the next recommended pages differ depending on such histories. For example, either C if A->B or E if D->B is recommended (See Fig.3). Of course, the history path older than two can be utilized too.

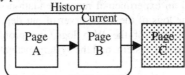

Fig. 3. History-based recommendation

- Future prediction-based recommendation. A page ahead by more than one link is recommended based on the path transition probability. This can let the user know what exists ahead in advance. Any link ahead (i.e., any future path farer than two) can be recommended, but it is also possible that the user may miss their true target between the current page and the page far ahead. For example, if the path A->B->C has the highest probability, then the user at A is recommended C (See Fig.4).

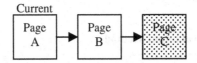

Fig. 4. Future prediction-based recommendation

- *Shortcut recommendation.* The transition by the back button is viewed insignificant and then the path is shortcut. For example, there is a path A->B->A->C where B->A is done by the back button. Then the path is shortened to A->C.

(2) Weighted probability-based methods. The following recommendation methods are done based on the probability weighted by other aspects such as the time length of stay, the Web policy, and the Web content structures:

- *Weighted by time of stay.* The page where the user stays longest is recommended. It can be known by using the Web log data. For example, if there is a path A->B->C where C is longest referenced, the weight of A and B with respect to C is increased by one. Then C is recommend at A or B.
- *Weighted by most recent access.* The probability is weighted by the importance of the target pages that we judge by most recent access. For example, if there is a path A->B->C where C is most recently referenced, the weight of A and B with respect to C is increased by one. C may be the page with detailed description of products. Then C is recommend at A or B.
- *Weighted by number of references.* If n pages reference a page within the same site, then the weight of the referenced page is increased by n. This method is validated by the observance that many pages link the important pages, which is similar to authorities and hubs in WWW [2].

3   Experiment and Evaluation

We have implemented an experimental recommendation system and have evaluated the system by using the logs of the Web server of our department. In this section, we describe the statistical data of the Web logs, the problems and the method for evaluation, the experimental system, and the system evaluation in sequence.

3.1 Statistics

First, we show the statistical information about the Web log data used for the experiments as follows:

Access logs: 384941 records; Web Pages: about 170 HTML files; Log duration: from June to December 2000; Subjects: five In-campus (knowledgeable) students and five out-campus (less knowledgeable) students

Please note that we have excluded non-HTML files such as GIF, JPEG because they need to be handled separately.

3.2 Problems and Evaluation Method

Before evaluation, we have prepared problems corresponding to the possible objectives of the users visiting the department Web site. They include the following problems:

Problem 1. Find the major field of Prof. Ishikawa.
Problem 2. Find the contents of the course "electric circuit I".
Problem 3. Find the contact information of the member of faculty doing the research on "efficient implementation of pipeline-adaptable filter".
Problem 4. Find the contents of Phd theses for 1995.
Problem 5. Find the contact information of the member of faculty teaching the course on "communication network theory ".

Next, we describe the method for evaluating the experimental system. We instruct the subjects to write down the number of transitions (i.e., clicks) and the time to reach the target pages as answers to the above problems. We evaluate the experimental system based on the figures. Each subject solves different problems by different recommendation methods.

3.3 Experimental System

For this time of evaluation, we have implemented the following four recommendation methods effective for our department site:

(1) Recommendation with back button transitions
(2) Recommendation without back button transitions
(3) Future prediction-based recommendation
(4) Recommendation Weighted by number of references

Please note that both (1) and (2) are simple methods which recommend the next page based on pure transition probability. They are used just for the purpose of comparison with our methods (3) and (4). We use two user groups based on IP addresses: In-campus students and out-campus students.

We have implemented the recommendation system by using two page frames. The upper frame displays the original Web page and the lower frame displays the recommendation page. Both of the frames change in an interrelated manner. When the user moves from one page to another based on the recommendation, the recommendation page is changed accordingly. The home page allows the user to select favorite recommendation methods. The recommendation page frame displays titles, URLs, and ranks of the recommended pages. The ranks are based on the transition probability calculated from the Web logs. At most five pages are recommended to the user. The user either may or may not accept the recommendation.

3.4 Evaluation

We illustrate the graphs indicating the average clicks and time required for solving the five problems (See Fig.5). 1, 2, 3, 4, and 5 indicate no recommendation, recommendation with back button transitions, recommendation without back button transitions, future prediction-based recommendation, and recommendation weighted by number of references, respectively.

First of all, the result shows the positive effect of recommendation because all methods (2-5) decrease the clicks and time in comparison with no recommendation

(1). Recommendation without back button transitions (3) is better than recommendation with them (2), so we think that the modified Web logs reflect user access histories more correctly. Future prediction-based recommendation (4) is a little bit worse than recommendation without back button transitions (3). This is probably because the former can skip the user's target mistakenly. Recommendation weighted by number of references (5) is the best of all although recommendation without back button transitions (3) is a little bit better in the number of clicks.

The fact that there is difference between in-campus students and out-campus students suggests that we need to classify the user groups. The difference can be shortened by our recommendation system. This indicates that our system is more effective for less-knowledgeable people such as out-campus students.

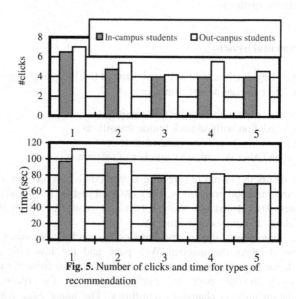

Fig. 5. Number of clicks and time for types of recommendation

4   Conclusion

We have proposed an experimental recommendation system L-R based on both Web usage mining and Web site structures. From the result of the evaluation of the system L-R, we have been able to indicate the following findings:

(1) The recommendation based on Web usage mining is positively effective. All recommendations based on modified Web logs in respect to back button transitions are more effective than that based on pure Web logs.
(2) The recommendation based on user classification is positively effective. We have found that the amount of knowledge about the Web site affects the number of clicks and the time to the target pages. Recommendation is more helpful for the less-knowledgeable people. So the classification from the viewpoint is valid.

(3) The recommendation based on Web page structures is positively effective. The one based on the modified Web logs and Web page structures is the most effective.

However, we also have found remaining issues, in particular, in the system implementation as follows.

4.1 Issues in Implementation

We will discuss issues in the current implementation of our recommendation system. First, we have copied the original Web site and Web logs to the virtual site from the experiment and evaluation. So we must rewrite the contents for the virtual site, such as modification of URL. Moreover, the contents in the virtual site are not completely synchronized with those in the original site. However, simple solution such as just incorporating the recommendation system to the original site is also problematic because the user access according to the recommendation modifies the access logs.

Second, the current classification of the users is quite naive, so the recommended contents are less sensitive to individual users. So we have some room to adopt different classification of users. At the extreme end, there is identification of individuals based on IP addresses. Moreover, there is any room for considering automatic clustering of the users in addition to classification.

Third, the size of the Web logs is no so large that we could not implement the other methods such as path recommendation. This is because the multiplication of the probabilities tends to be quite small in the small-sized Web logs.

The number of problems and subjects is not so large enough to give very confident results; it is difficult to prepare as distinctive types of problems as possible.

4.2 Future Plan

First, we will improve the evaluation result by the following ways without changing the system:

(1) Increasing the problems and subjects
(2) Increasing the size of the Web logs by using the longer duration of the logs
(3) Classifying users into groups form different viewpoints

Second, we will generalize our recommendation system as follows:

(1) Adapting the system to different sites
(2) Adapting the system to non-HTML contents such c, MPEG, MP3
(3) Constricting the user models based on automatic clustering of the users

The above three ways to generalization can require the system to change more or less.

4.3 Related Work

We will compare our work with relevant works. Perkowits et al. [6] have proposed Adaptable Web Sites as a method for providing index pages suitable for the users based on Web access logs. They have implemented the algorithm to extract user access patterns from the access logs. They provide virtual sites adapted to individual users by determining the links and their ranks (order) in the index pages based on the algorithm. The Adaptable Web Sites automatically recommend different pages depending individuals while our system recommends pages in several ways chosen by both the Web site administrator and the users.

Mobasher et al. [4] have proposed a method for recommending pages weighted by mining the user access logs. The system recommends pages according to the user access recorded in "cookies" while our system allows the user to choose among several recommendation methods and takes page structures into consideration. The recommended pages change depending on the current page but not on the cookies.

Kiyomitsu et al. [1] [8] have proposed a system for displaying different link structures according to the user access logs and a mechanism for the administrator to easily change the contents. They change pages according to the user access logs while we keep the original contents intact and allow any site to add on recommendation. Their mechanism is solely intended for the Web site administrators. Our recommendation is intended for both the users and the Web site administrators in that several recommendation methods can be chosen by both of them.

Acknowledgements. This work is partially supported by the Ministry of Education, Culture, Sports, Science and Technology, Japan under a grant 13224078.

References

1. H. Kiyomitsu, A. Takeuchi, and K.Tanaka.: Dynamic Web Page Reconfiguration Based on Active Rules, IPSJ Sig Notes, vol.2000, no.69 (2000-DBS-122), pp.383-390, 2000 (in Japanese).
2. J. Kleinberg: Authoritative sources in a hyperlinked environment. Proc. 9th ACM-SIAM Symposium on Discrete Algorithms, 1998.
3. T. Mizuhara, T. Nakajima, M. Ohta, and H. Ishikawa: Web Log Data Analysis for Recommendation System, Proc. IPSJ National Convention, 4W-3, 2001 (in Japanese).
4. B.Mobasher, R.Cooley, and J.Srivastava: Automatic Personalization Based on Web Usage Mining, CACM, vol.43, no.8, pp.142-151, 2000.
5. T. Nakajima, T. Mizuhara, M. Ohta, and H. Ishikawa: Recommendation System Using User Models based on Web Logs, Proc. IPSJ National Convention, 4W-4, 2001 (in Japanese).
6. M. Perkowittz and O.Etzioni: Adaptive Web Sites, CACM, vol43, no.8, pp.152-158, 2000.
7. J. Schafer, J. Konstan, and J. Riedl: Recommender Systems in E-Commerce. Proc. ACM Conference on Electronic Commerce (EC-99), pp.158-166, 1999.
8. A. Takeuchi, H. Kiyomitsu, and K.Tanaka.: Access Control of Web Content Based on Access Histories, Aggregations and Meta-Rules, IPSJ Sig Notes, vol.2000, no.69 (2000-DBS-122), pp.315-322, 2000 (in Japanese).

Porphyry 2001: Semantics for Scholarly Publications Retrieval

Aurélien Bénel[1,2], Sylvie Calabretto[1], Andréa Iacovella[2], and Jean-Marie Pinon[1]

[1] LISI – INSA Lyon
Bâtiment Blaise Pascal, 69621 Villeurbanne CEDEX, France
Firstname.Surname@lisi.insa-lyon.fr

[2] French School of Archaeology (EFA)
6 Didotou street, 10680 Athens, Greece
Firstname.Surname@efa.gr

Abstract. We describe the design and algorithms of *Porphyry 2001*, a scholarly publication retrieval system. This system is intended to meet library user studies which advocate human interpretation and social interactions. The metaphors we used are annotations and publication (making public). We first discuss about different philosophical approaches to semantics and choose the more suited to scholarly work: the one considering a transitory, hypothetical and polemical knowledge construction. Then we propose an overview of *Porphyry 2001*: an hypertext system based on a dynamic structure of user annotations. The visualization and evolution of the structure (a dynamic directed acyclic graph) is made more efficient by the use of an *ad hoc* browsing algorithm.

Keywords. Patron-augmented digital libraries, user interfaces and visualization systems, semantic nets, browsing/reading/annotating.

1   Introduction

Our study is related to a digitalization project by the French school of archaeology in Athens[1]. This project aims at giving online access to one of its main periodical publications: *"La Chronique des fouilles"*, an archeological excavations and findings yearly survey. This corpus has been chosen since although its size is reasonable (about 12,000 pages), it is nearly exhaustive in regards to the past 80 years of archaeological activity in Greece and Cyprus. Besides, the *"Chronique"* is daily read in libraries throughout the world.

We must stress that the information retrieval problem is not new concerning the *"Chronique"*. Publishers have tried for 80 years to make it easier to consult. It is made of small independent parts (about 50,000) which are hierarchically structured and indexed according to artifact location, dating and typology. Archaeologists who have tried retrieval systems based on automatic indexing or manual indexing using thesauri

---

[1] Ecole française d'Athènes (http://www.efa.gr)

M.-S. Hacid et al. (Eds.): ISMIS 2002, LNAI 2366, pp. 351-361, 2002.

are satisfied by none of them. The former is said to be inadequate because it deals with out-of-context terms. The latter is considered to be hard to manage over time by the indexing team since it needs periodic updates of both thesauri and indexes in order to reflect science progress. As a first example, there has been several years ago a polemic between two archaeologists about determining in ambiguous cases whether the border of a mosaic was black or white. An automatic indexing system would have extracted only the point of view in the text. Moreover, without knowing whom point of view it is, the index could not have been interpreted. As a second example, when the Copper Age has been inserted in the chronology between the Neolithic Period and the Bronze Age, a thesaurus-based system would have needed plenty of documents to be reinterpreted and re-indexed. Therefore, we had to study the most theoretical aspects of information retrieval (even philosophical aspects), to find an alternative for our system.

2   From Semantics Theories to Workstations

Information retrieval (IR) as defined by Cornelis J. van Rijsbergen [19] aims at matching relevant documents with user information needs. In order to be "computed", this matching has to be transmuted from the *content* space into the *form* space. Since computers cannot match the *meaning* of the information needs with the meaning of the documents, IR techniques tend to translate information needs into *formal* queries and documents into *formal* descriptions (also called "logical views" [1]). So one of the challenges in IR should be to minimize the gap due to this translation: the gap between *signifiers* and *signified*. This question is a central one in linguistic semantics.

2.1   Linguistic Theroies of Semantics

As stated by the French linguist François Rastier [13], there have been, among the various theories of semantics, mainly two streams: the first one (widely spread) from the logic community, the second one (nearly unknown) from the hermeneutic community. Whereas the former focuses on *representation*, the latter focuses on *communication*. Whereas, in the former, properties of a sign occurrence are inferred from relations between types (see "type hierarchies" in John F. Sowa [15]), in the latter, there are only "source occurrences" and "revisited occurrences". Whereas the former makes the Aristotelian assumption of an *ontology* (from the Greek word "ontos" for "being"), the latter considers a transitory and hypothetical knowledge construction.

Since the system we want to design is for scientists, we will adopt the hermeneutical view of semantics (see our prior work [3]). Indeed, this approach is more adapted to modern science by highlighting the constructivist nature of scientific knowledge (see Karl R. Popper [12] and Thomas S. Kuhn [10]).

It is worth noting that the need for both interaction and communication has been highlighted in experimental studies about traditional library users.

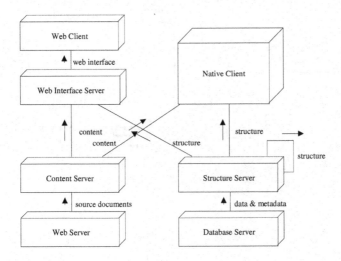

Fig. 1. Corpus consulting through Porphyry multi-tiers architecture.

Kenton O'Hara *et al.* [8] studied the document–related research activities of PhD students during a working day. The induced model characterized the work carried out by university library users as going beyond the traditional searching and retrieving of information. In that way, note making, photocopying, bibliographic searching, reading, annotating, information reviewing, and documents writing should be considered as a whole.

In a different setting, Andreas Paepcke [11] interviewed engineers involved for example in customer support or in design in order to learn about their information needs and habits. He concluded that even if retrieving information is central, it is interwoven with discovering, managing, interpreting and sharing information and that all of these activities need the communication between humans.

But oddly enough, very few digital library systems at this time support social interactions [17] and patron-augmentation [7] (see [14] also).

Because science carries more than interactions among individuals, systems should go one step further by supporting groups. Scientific groups (from working groups to colloquiums) are important for knowledge construction in the process of becoming more objective.

Knowing the knowledge of each individual, the question becomes: "What is the knowledge of the group?" Expressed in a different way: "How do we get a syntactic and semantic coherence from these different (and even contradictory) models?" If these questions are opened for Knowledge Managing in general, they have got an answer for years in the scientific praxis: publication.

In the traditional publication process, the "publishers" (real publishers, reviewers, committees...) check submitted papers regarding form and contents in order to ensure its validity for the group. Then the authority given to the publishers is transferred to the papers themselves.

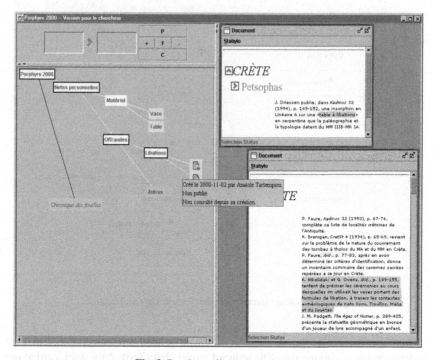

Fig. 2. Porphyry client screenshot.

As a result we propose that in our system scientists can choose to join groups headed by "publishers" they consider as authorities and that their knowledge representations can be "published" through a reviewing process just like in the physical world.

2.2 Porphyry 2001 Overview[2]

Porphyry 2001 is a client-server system aiming at creating, retrieving and sharing documents and annotations. Its architecture (see Figure 1) is grounded on the distinction between content and structure.

The *content server* is a classic web server with an *ad hoc* "servlet". Given extraction parameters, it is able to deliver fragments from web accessible documents (only plain-text and JPEG images for now).

The *structure server* use a database server to store and retrieve data and meta-data. Both are handled in the same way: they are filtered by the *structure server* and formalized through the same directed acyclic graph model. In this model, if, for two descriptors D_1 and D_2, $D_1 \rightarrow D_2$, then any document described by D_2 is described by D_1 too. It is worth mentioning that only edges and nodes have significance for the

---

[2] The Porphyry Project Page: http://lisi.insa-lyon.fr/projets/descrippr27.htm

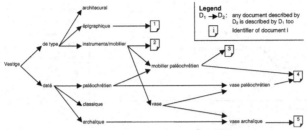

Fig. 3. – Sample index structure.

system. But, so that users can interpret the graph, we store labels too. Node labels contain short descriptions and edge labels contain information (see the edge popup label in Figure 2 at the center) about their creation (user, date) and publication (group, date). As long as the formal signification of this framework is kept, users are free to use it in order to represent (see Figure 3): specialization, composition, attributes, attribute values, relations.... The graph being accessed by a user can be split into different sub-graphs depending on their ownership and performance considerations.

Context and structure are combined either by the *native client* (see Figure 2) or by the *web interface server* (so that a classic web client can access it). Although the web interface is dedicated on browsing, the *native client* allow the researcher to upload new documents, to define new fragments, and to modify also his/her own corpus structure.

3   Scenario of User Interactions

In this section, we will trace step by step an example of computer-human interactions involved in document retrieval. Our schema (Figure 4) will show both the annotation graph as displayed by *Porphyry 2001* and the user actions. As shown in the Figure 4, let us navigate in the Figure 3 indexing graph…

- **Step #1.**   The global corpus deals with "*vestige typé*". More specialized corpora exist dealing with "*daté*" or "*épigraphique*" or "*instrumenta/mobilier*" but not with "*architectural*" (since this descriptor corresponds to no document). When the user selects "*instrumenta/mobilier*", the system jumps to step #2.
- **Step #2.**   The selected corpus deals with "*vestige de type instrumenta/mobilier*". This describes exactly the document which has the identifier "2". More specialized corpora deal with "*mobilier paléochrétien*" or "*vase*" but neither with "*architectural*" nor with "*épigraphique*". When the user selects "*vase*", the system jumps to step #3.
- **Step #3.**   The selected corpus deals with both "*vestige de type vase (instrumenta/mobilier)*" and "*vestige daté*". Please note that "*daté*" is automatically inferred (since all documents dealing with "*vase*" deals also with "*daté*"). More specialized corpora deal with "*mobilier paléochrétien*", "*vase paléochrétien*", "*vase archaïque*", "*paléochrétien*" or "*archaïque*" but not with "*architectural*", "*épigraphique*", "*classique*" or "2". When the user selects "*archaïque*", the system jumps to step #4.

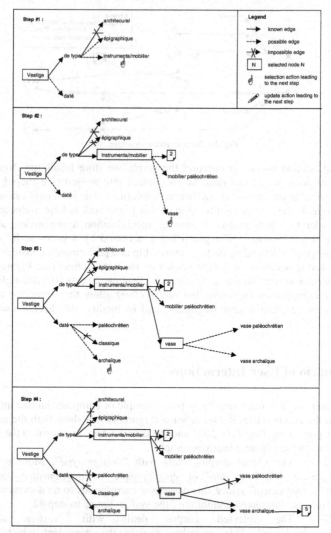

Fig. 4. – Retrieval scenario (see index structure in Figure 3).

- **Step #4.** The selected corpus deals with *"vestige de type vase (instrumenta/mobilier) daté de l'époque archaïque"*. This corpus contains only one document, the one with *"5"* as its identifier.

4   Algorithms

In the two preceding scenari, the annotation graph was filtered. As a matter of fact, most of interactive information retrieval systems (see Marti Hearst [9]) focus on reducing cognitive load by filtering information. In our system, the filtering algorithm is a valuable help in navigating through corpora. Since searching and indexing are both corpora discriminations, our filter can be seen as an assistant for both refining a query and reusing descriptors for a new indexing. We will now explain our algorithm in detail.

Gerard Salton in the late 60's [15] defined a set-theoretical model of information retrieval. It deals with a set of "descriptors" and a set of documents. In that way, we can draw the corpus inclusion (see Figure 5) and the request conjunction graphs (see Figure 6). Then, from the mapping of documents with descriptors (see Table 1), we can deduce the mapping of requests with documents corpora (see Table 2). From that point, we can figure out that several corpora can't be obtained by any request (e.g. {B,C}) and that the same corpus can be obtained by different requests (e.g. request *a* AND *b* with request *b*). Although these results are widely known, they have been, as far as we know, rarely used as interaction media.

Table 1. Sample mapping of documents A, B, C, D with descriptors a, b, c.

		Descriptors		
		a	b	c
Documents	A	X		X
	B	X	X	
	C			X
	D	X		

Table 2. Mapping of requests with documents corpora (computed from Table 1).

TRUE	{A,B,C,D}
a	{A,B,D}
b	{B}
c	{A,C}
a AND b	{B}
b AND c	∅
c AND a	{A}
a AND b AND c	∅

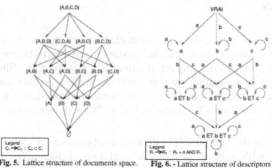

Fig. 5. Lattice structure of documents space.   **Fig. 6.** - Lattice structure of descriptors

Claudio Carpineto *et al.* [6] used Boolean logic results by removing from the corpus inclusion graph every inaccessible corpora in order to get a static generalization/specialization diagram of documents classes (see Figure 7).

In our approach (see our prior works [2] for more details) we preferred to join together, in the requests graph, requests which describe the same corpus. By doing so, we get a state-chart diagram (see Figure 8) in which states correspond to corpora and transitions correspond to elementary requests. These one-descriptor-requests on transient corpora can be seen as the addition of a descriptor to the global request: a kind of query refinement.

Owing to the preceding state-chart, in a given state (result of the selection of a set of descriptors) any refinement can be said:

- *Impossible*: if it leads from the current corpus to the empty corpus (e.g. descriptor *c* in state *{B}* see Figure 8),
- *Known*: if it leads from and to the current corpus (e.g. descriptor *a* in state *{B}*, descriptor *b* in state *{B}* see Figure 8),

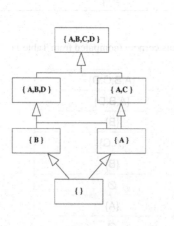

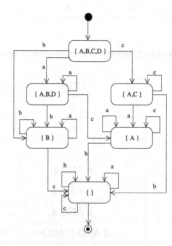

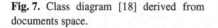

Fig. 7. Class diagram [18] derived from documents space.   **Fig. 8.** State-chart diagram [18] derived from descriptors space.

- *Possible*: otherwise.

The filter consists in showing only known descriptors and their "children" and in assigning its corresponding state to any showed descriptor. The scenari shown in Figure 4 illustrates the use of this filter on a simple example. We can also have a look at real size examples in Figure 1.

5 Discussion

At this point, a few aspects should be discussed about *Porphyry 2001* system.

5.1 Starting from Scratch

The digital library system we have presented is based on patron-augmentation. But, for such an evolutionary approach, the question is: "Evolution? From what?". Can we give an "empty box" to users? If document retrieving is based on annotations, how could the first annotator of a document retrieve it?

As a matter of fact, some information can be automatically loaded in the descriptor graph:
- The title hierarchy of the semi-structured document (since this structure *describes* each section),
- Manual (or intellectual?) controlled indexes stored in document appendices,
- Automatically extracted key-words or key-phrases (structured for example regarding alphabetical order or formal clusters).

One should note that there are neither thesauri, nor "ontologies", nor even concepts which are approved by the whole archaeological community. Therefore we cannot reuse them as a bootstrap for our sytem. But, on the contrary, the collaborative use of *Porphyry 2001* system could lead archaeologists to normalize such definitions. From an archeological point of view, this is one of the main challenge of using the system.

5.2 Combinatory Explosion

Another important question deals with the algorithmic complexity of our graph filter. On the one hand the system must give results in less than a few seconds (in order to remain usable in an interactive process). On the other hand it is difficult to evaluate the theoretic complexity of the algorithm since there are a very few constraints on the partial order structure.

To find a practical answer, we must consider the use of the system. As we saw, the graph which is browsed by a given user, is made of its personal graph and the graphs from the groups he/she has registered.

Firstly, these graphs are connected only by the "root" descriptor and by identifiers. They are independent indexing dimensions. That is what information sciences call *"facets"*. Because of their independence, the complexity of n groups is only n times the complexity of 1 group and, moreover, the algorithm can be run in parallel on n servers (one per group) so that the computing time for n graphs is nearly the same as for 1 graph.

Secondly, the nature of personal graphs and group graphs are quite different. The latter are rather bigger than the former and is updated much less often (only during the *publication* process). So it is interesting to make pre-computation of the group graphs. In fact the involved algorithms consist in recursively deducing relations and in doing basic set operations. We chose to do in advance recursive computations only and to do "on the fly" set operations (database management systems are good for it). It seems to be a good compromise between mass memory use and response time.

The two proposed optimizations (multiple servers and pre-computation) have been implemented and used. We plan for the next months to test them with huge real data.

5.3   Evaluating Interactive Information Retrieval

Let us study a few epistemological aspects. Since science is based on *falsification* (see Karl R. Popper [12]), a theory must be *testable* to be said "scientific". A test is an experiment that can make the theory getting false (by deduction *modus tollens*). A test result is *particular* but not *singular*: it must be obtained and obtained again at anytime by anybody at anyplace. A succeeding test result is a result that "breaks" the theory. Moreover, since methods are based on the domain paradigms (see Thomas S. Kuhn [10]), testing protocols must be validated by the scientific community.

We would like to stress a few points. First, the scientist must *propose* a test but shouldn't *lead* the test. The *community* should test it. A testable theory is "objective" and doesn't need anymore the subject who have invented it. By the way, it is psychologically difficult for a human to break his/her own work... On the contrary, it is so great to break somebody else's work! Second, because we work on *interactive* information retrieval and so with human individuals, it seems to be difficult to get *particular* results. Does it make sense to compare the activity of two users, especially when each of them is the world expert in his/her domain? Does it make sense to compare activities of a same user with two interactive systems (knowing that he/she may have learned "something" during the first activity)?

For us, it would be important if this kind of methodological aspects were discussed by the IR community. If these points were clearer, then we could ask the community to validate or invalidate the following protocol.

Our protocol (its setup is in progress) relies on the "reality" of the test: real users doing their own activities with real information and for a long time. Firstly, we propose to compare two interfaces to access the same data (250,000 records of archeological photographs descriptions): the classical QBE interface (query by example) and ours. Secondly, we propose to log over time the growing of the descriptors graph (for "*La Chronique des fouilles*") in order to know if the evolution we hope for is real or not.

6   Conclusion

The system we have presented proposes a framework for free descriptors created either by machines (words or phrases occurrences...) or by human (categories, annotations...). Most of all, owing to collaboration and dynamics, it can be used as a debate media. Every annotation is dated and authored, so that it can be interpreted, contradicted by another annotation, or considered as obsolete.

We aim at giving the user a system just like the "memex" Vannevar Bush [5] dreamt of. The reader could retrieve his/her former mind "trails" and others' ones (colleagues, tutors, librarians…). The automatic system would be there to assist the reader in his task by ridding him of repetitive aspects of his/her activity, so that he/she could focus on creative and intuitive aspects of his/her work.

References

[1]   Baeza-Yates, R., and Ribeiro-Neto, B. Modern Information Retrieval, ACM Press and Addison Wesley, 1999.

[2]   Bénel, A., Calabretto, S., Pinon, J.-M., and Iacovella, A. Vers un outil documentaire unifié pour les chercheurs en archéologie. In: Actes du XVIIIe congrès INFORSID, 2000. pp.133-145. In French.

[3]   Bénel, A., Egyed-Zsigmond, E., Prié Y., Calabretto, S., Mille, A., Iacovella, A., Pinon, J.-M. Truth in the digital library: from ontological to hermeneutical systems. In: Proceedings of the fifth European Conference on Research and Advanced Technology for Digital Libraries, LNCS #2163, Springer-Verlag, 2001. pp.366-377.

[4]   Berleant, D. Models for reader interaction systems. In: Proceedings of the Ninth ACM Conference on Information and Knowledge Management, 2000.

[5]   Bush, V. As we may think. In: The Atlantic Monthly. July 1945.

[6]   Carpineto, C., and Romano, G. Dynamically bounding browsable retrieval spaces: an application to Galois lattices. In: RIAO'94 conference proceedings, "Intelligent Multimedia Information Retrieval Systems and Management", 1994.

[7]   Goh, D., Leggett, J. Patron-augmented digital libraries. In: Proceedings of the Fifth ACM Conference on Digital Libraries, 2000.

[8]   O'Hara, K., Smith, F., Newman, W., and Sellen, A. Student readers' use of library documents: implications for library technologies. In: ACM Conference Proceedings on Human Factors in Computing Systems, 1998.

[9]   Hearst, M. User interfaces and visualization. In: [1].

[10] Kühn, T.S. The Structure of Scientific Revolutions. University of Chicago Press, 1962.

[11] Paepcke, A. Digital libraries: Searching is not Enough. What we learned on-site. In: D-Lib Magazine. May 1996.

[12] Popper, K.R. Objective Knowledge: an Evolutionary Approach. Clarendon Press, 1972.

[13] Rastier, F. Sens et signification. In: Jacob, A. Encyclopédie philosophique universelle, Presses Universitaires de France, 1999. In French.

[14] Röscheisen, M., Mogensen, C., and Winograd, T. Beyond browsing: shared comments, soaps, trails and on-line communities. In the Third International World Wide Web Conference, "Technology, Tools and Applications", 1995.

[15] Salton, G. Automatic Information Organization and Retrieval. Chapter: "Retrieval models". Computer Sciences series, McGrow-Hill Inc., 1968.

[16] Sowa J.F. Semantic networks. In: Shapiro, S.C. Encyclopedia of Artificial Intelligence, Wiley, New York, 1992.

[17] Tochtermann, K. A first step toward communication in virtual libraries. In the Proceedings of the First Annual Conference on the Theory and Practice of Digital Libraries, 1994.

[18] UML Notation Guide. OMG, 1997.

[19] van Rijsbergen, C.J. A new theoretical framework for information retrieval. In: Proceedings of 1986 ACM Conference on Research and Development in Information Retrieval, 1986.

Preprocessor to Improve Performance of GA in Determining Bending Process for Sheet Metal Industry

Chitra Malini Thanapandi[1], Aranya Walairacht[2], Thanapandi Periasamy[3], and Shigeyuki Ohara[1]

[1] Department of Electronics, School of Engineering,
Tokai University, Japan
chitra_pandi@hotmail.com; ohara@keyaki.cc.u-tokai.ac.jp
[2] Department of Computer Engineering, Faculty of Engineering,
King Mongkut's Institute of Technology Ladkrabang, Thailand
kwaranya@kmitl.ac.th
[3] Amada Co.Ltd, Isehara, Kanagawa, Japan
pandi@amtec-amada.co.jp

Abstract. In manufacturing fabricated sheet metal parts, the required shape has to be bent from the flat 2-D layouts. In this bending process, the most complex and critical work is determining the bend sequence and assigning appropriate tools for each bend. Determining the bend sequence is itself a combinatorial problem and this when coupled with tool assignment leads to a huge combination and clearly shows an exhaustive approach is impossible and we propose Genetic Algorithm (GA), an adaptive algorithm to solve the problem. Information regarding the operator knowledge and operator desire are input to the system to generate efficient bending process. And moreover, in order to improve the performance of GA, a preprocessor is being implemented which searches combinable bends and thereby reduce search space and solve the problem in time-economic way.

1   Introduction

In the sheet metal industry, the most important and process is to bend the flat sheet metal layout into required shape using tools by means of CNC (Computer Numerically Controlled) machines, mostly operated by human operators. With the economic reasons the need to manufacture small sized batches and shorter delivery times are inevitable. Hence the process planning departments have to generate more process plans in a shorter period of time. With complex parts it becomes tedious as it involves combinatorial (non-polynomial, exponential) problem, which cannot be solved within the required time.

This paper is concerned with techniques for generating bend sequences and assigning tools for each bend. The feasible solution is based on collision detection, a filtering parameter detecting if there is any collision between part and part, part and tool .The filtered solutions which also satisfies the operator-desire and

M.-S. Hacid et al. (Eds.): ISMIS 2002, LNAI 2366, pp. 362–373, 2002.
© Springer-Verlag Berlin Heidelberg 2002

simple process are searched to generate a process that is more friendly with the operator. And moreover, a preprocessor is implemented which checks for bend lines that can be combined based on its attributes to improve the performance of GA in generating simple process and fasten the search. A prototype system is developed for generating the bending process and the system architecture is also described. The advantage of this approach is that the operator is able to give his own knowledge about tool selection and desire to the system in generating the bending process. And with the preprocessor we reduce the search space making the process simple and faster.

2   Related Works

The bending process being a complex and a combinatorial problem, many researches approach it by using heuristics along with AI techniques to solve it.L.Cser et al [1] classifies the sheet metal parts with semantic net and uses case based learning in generating the bending process. As these works are based on case learning depending on features and it becomes impossible when a new part with different feature is involved. L.J.de.Vin [2] have developed a process planning system to find the optimal bending sequence without part-tool collision and focuses on accuracy and tolerance constraints. Heuristic rules are being used to reduce the search space. "Local ordered depth-first search" a heuristic technique is being used to merge the rules for product handling and positioning. Radin, .B [3] uses two-stage algorithm to determine the bending sequence and tool assignment. The algorithm finds a feasible solution based on collision avoidance heuristics in first stage and rapidly finds an alternative solution with low cost in its second stage. It uses A* algorithm to obtain an optimal solution through heuristic functions to achieve a solution that does not exceed time limitations. J.R.Duflou [4] uses heuristic rules to downsize the problem and applies constraint solving and branch- and- bound algorithm to identify potential solutions. It is characterized by a dynamic updated penalty system, knowledge obtained through the analysis of partial sequences. As the heuristics are based on the part geometry, parts with new feature have more probability to fail in planning the bending process.

In all these researches, the feasible solution are based on collision detection and importance to operators desire are not given much importance and are decided by the system to some extend. But since the role of the operator is inevitable in bending process they should be given importance and their desire, knowledge and a simple process have to be considered in evaluating the process.

3   System Architecture

Fig. 1 illustrates the system architecture of the bending process planning using genetic algorithms. The system consists of two main components :Operators interface and Processing Kernel. The Operators interface again consists of two components Operator Desire and Part Data. Operator Desire component helps the operator to input his knowledge depending on the Part Data and Tool

Database information. And moreover he is able to input his desire as explained in Section.6 and based on it the system decides the bending process. Part Data has the information regarding the part to be bent such as the length, width, and bend line details like the type of the bend its angle. The Tool Database contains the details regarding the punches and dies available such as its length, width, radius, bent type and the angle to be bent. The Processing kernel also composes of two components the Preprocessor and the Genetic Algorithm embedded with Collision Detection kernel. The Preprocessor gets the part information from the Part Data and searches for the combinable bend lines and this information along with the tool information is feed into the Genetic Algorithm where it generates the bend sequence and tool assignment without collision using the collision detection kernel. The generating process keeps continuing till a bend sequence and tool selection for each bent is generated without collision and satisfying operator's desire. Bonus is granted when the chromosomes satisfy above allowing the better chromosomes to be in the population.

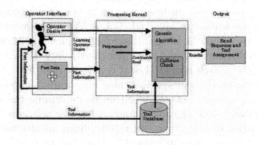

Fig. 1. System Architecture

4   Bend Sequence Generation and Tool Assignment in Bending Process

In the bending problem, the flat 2-D layout has to be bent along its bend lines to get the required shape. Bending sequence has to be determined and to bend them proper tools have to be assigned for each bend. The tools are a set of punch and die having their own attributes. The punch can be defined and differentiated from other punches by its attributes the angle, the type it can bend and its bend radius. The type of bend means the shape it can bend (V, R, U...) as shown in Fig. 2. The angle and the type of the bend and depth it can support ,define the die.

4.1   Complexity of Bending Process

Having tools of varying type, angle and radius any tools cannot be selected for any bend line. As bending can be done in a single stage and several stages tools

Fig. 2. Types of Bend

having the same angle or tools having angle less than the bend line and belonging to same bend type is only eligible. So considering all tools is meaning less and makes the search space so wider and time consuming. Tools to be selected for a bend line can be determined by the angle of the bend line. Hence all tools having angles ≤ the angles of bend line can be grouped and are eligible to be selected. Hence for a product with N bend lines and n varying angles and t number of eligible tools for each angle then the combination order of the tools will be

$$\sum_{i=1}^{n} ni * ti!$$

And this when combined with bending sequence results to huge combination of

$$N! * \left(\sum_{i=1}^{n} ni * ti! \right)$$

If there is a product with 7 bend lines with all 3 different angles and the number of eligible tools for each angle is 5,then the combination will be 4233600 combinations. Its common to find parts with 8-10 bends lines and complex parts have maximum of 36-40 bend lines and the complexity increases with the bend lines and available tools.

4.2   Problem Definition

Closely viewing this problem we can see two problems are being embedded in it. The determination of bend sequence is a sequencing problem and assigning tools to each bend line is a scheduling problem. Thus the problem can be defined as: Given a set of bend lines for a desired shape, bend sequence has to be generated and tools have to be assigned for each bend in such a way that there is no collision between the part-part, part-tool, part-machine and also satisfies the operator desire.

5   Genetic Algorithms for Bending Process

Genetic Algorithms (GA) is an evolutionary intelligent search algorithm [6] working well with the combinatorial explosion problems and hence we apply GA for our research.

5.1   Structure of the Chromosome

The chromosome is a combination of three components, bend sequence, punch and die to be assigned. The length of each component of the chromosome is dependent and limited to the number of bend lines of the part. Fig. 3 shows the chromosome structure of a problem of a part with 3 bend lines. Bend chromosome (BC) is composed by genes of bend lines (BL), which are to be sequenced. It is represented by its attributes such as bend line number, bend angle, bend type, Part Orientation (the side aligned under the punch) and Part Insertion. The bend line number is randomly selected and Part Orientation is set to default as top. The Part Insertion is set to right. The bend angle and bend type information is read from the part data. The punch (PC) and the die (DC) chromosome represent the genes of punch (P) and the die (D) to be selected for the respective bend line in the bend sequence chromosome. A detailed explanation regarding the structure of chromosomes can be found in [7]. The preprocessor depending on the attributes of bend lines combines the bend lines and is explained in the following section.

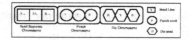

Fig. 3. Multi-component chromosome structure

5.2   Preprocessor to GA

Preprocessor is an engine, which process the part data before its send to the GA for determining bending process. When the bend lines share the same bend radius, bend angle, bend direction and with a common bend axis they can be bend together and considered as a single collinear bend. By combining the bends we can make the process simple by reducing the rotations and process to be faster by decreasing bend lines. The preprocessor, inspects the part data for the collinear bends and if they are available they are combined to a single bend and then input to the GA for further processing. Hence if the part has collinear bends as shown in Fig. 8(a), then the bend lines are grouped, thereby the genes are also grouped and considered as a single gene In the part Data_008 we can find that the bend lines 1,2,3 and 4,5,6 are collinear bends and the structure of the bend chromosome will be as in Fig. 4. Depending on the bend chromosomes the Punch and Die chromosomes are generated and has 4 genes respectively.

5.3   Selection

The chromosomes are evaluated by their fitness value and checked whether feasible solution exists. If there are no feasible solutions generated then, these chromosomes are selected for reproduction. Roulette selection method is used to select the chromosomes for reproduction to have a diversity in the solution.

Fig. 4. Bend Chromosome of the Part Data_008C having 2 Collinear bends

5.4 Crossover

The chromosomes selected are given a chance to crossover to create new chromosomes with variation. As no bend lines can be repeated or omitted (bend lines numbers have to be maintained) in bending problem traditional crossover cannot be applied. Hence a single point position based crossover is being used. To parent chromosomes A and B, and a crossover point in which the genes have to be exchanged are selected randomly. If gene of A and B are same no exchange is done. Otherwise, the genes are exchanged and the repeated genes are replaced by exchanging. Position based crossover is shown in Fig. 5(a). If the crossover point selected by random is 2,then the bend line 1 and 2 are exchanged. As no bend line can be repeated or omitted bend line 2 in Chromosome A is replaced with 1 and bend line 1 in Chromosome B is replaced with 2, as shown in Fig. 5(b). Double lines show the exchange of bend lines and single lines shows the replaced positions. Continuing in this same fashion the final offspring looks like as shown in Fig. 5(c). Depending on the bend lines the punch and the die are also exchanged in the same way. This is shown in the following example with the 4 bend lines as in Fig. 4.

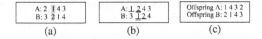

(a)   (b)   (c)

Fig. 5. Crossover process

If the random point selected is 3,then after crossover the chromosomes look like Fig. 6. The bend lines are exchanged on position basis and depending on the bend lines the punch and die are also exchanged. The chromosomes are done crossover at a probability (p_c) of 0.8 per generation.

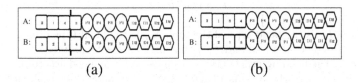

(a)   (b)

Fig. 6. Chromosomes before and after crossover

5.5   Mutation

The chromosomes and the genes to be mutated or flipped are selected randomly. And with the bend sequence component ,the gene that is selected for mutation, its characteristics are flipped. The bend sequence component's characteristic Part Orientation and Part Insertion are flipped. On mutation, Part Orientation is flipped from the default setting of top to bottom and the Part Insertion is also flipped from right to left. With the tools (Punch and Die), another tool with the same angle but different property is selected randomly. The chromosomes are done mutation at a probability (p_m) of 0.1 per generation.

5.6   Fitness Function

The chromosomes of the bending problem are evaluated based on the fitness function, which is a combination two-fitness function. The first and the filtering fitness function is collision detection function and the second is Operator Desire function and they are explained in the following function.

6   Operator Desire and Fitness Function

With the present researches focusing on generating feasible solution based on collision avoidance consideration of user desire is neglected. Bending operations as a manufacturing activity distinguish themselves from many other processes because of the physical effort that is required from the side of the machine operator. Even with the sophisticated CNC machine tools, robot systems still the need for the operator is *conditio sine qua non* as in [5].

6.1   Operator Desire

- *Minimize Process Timing*
  Flat part is bent using a set of Punch and Die, which are mounted to the press-brake in NC machines. Punches and Dies are selected for a bend line according to the properties of the bend, bend shape and angle of the bend line. Having tools of varying type, angle and radius, the tool T is eligible to be selected if it satisfies the following condition.

  $$if\ (T_{bt} = B_{bt}\ ;bt \in \{\ V,R\ \}$$
  $$\{$$
  $$if\ (T_a <= B_a)$$
  $$T = eligible,$$
  $$\}$$

  where T_{bt} is the bend type of the tool, B_{bt} is the bend type of bend line, T_a is the angle of the tool and B_a is the angle of the bend line.
  During the bending process the tools have to be changed according to above conditions, which consumes time. So with less number of tool changes the time taken for the process is also reduced. So the Process Timing Reduction, PTR is calculated when

$$T_n \leq N \; ; n \in \{ \; 1...N\text{-}1, \; \}$$

where T_n is the number of tools used and N is the number of bend lines as in worst case each bent can be assigned different tool. When the above desire is satisfied bonus is granted relatively to the less number of tools used and are evaluated according to the Eq. 1.

$$F_{PTR} = (C + (N - T_n) * RB, \tag{1}$$

where C is constant and RB is called the relative bonus.

– **Risk**

Another problem in bending process is the shape precision, which affects the accuracy A of the product. A product that lacks accuracy cannot be used for manufacturing resulting waste of material and time. This is due to the improper tooling and can be avoided by selecting accurate tools .The accuracy of the product can be evaluated by Eq. 2.

$$F_A = \begin{cases} 1 \; if\{(T_a \pm \Theta_s) == B_a\}, \\ 0 \; otherwise, \end{cases} \tag{2}$$

where T_a is the angle of the tool selected, B_a is the angle of bend line and Θ_s is the spring back.

– **Operator's Knowledge**

Operator's knowledge, K regarding the tool selection fastens the search process. Deciding and implementing operators knowledge is very difficult, but our system uses the fitness function and easily adapts it to the system. The operator's knowledge is given preference according to their level of knowledge. The levels of knowledge are classified into Excellent, Good, Normal and none. And Bonus are given relatively according to the level the operator selects his knowledge. With none, decision is left to the system and Eq. 3 evaluates the operator's knowledge.

$$F_K = \begin{cases} 3 \; if\{ST == OT\} \wedge \{l = 1\}, \\ 2 \; if\{ST == OT\} \wedge \{l = 2\}, \\ 1 \; if\{ST == OT\} \wedge \{l = 3\}, \\ 0 \; if\{ST == OT\} \wedge \{l = 4\}, \end{cases} \tag{3}$$

where ST is the selected tool by the system, OT is the tool selected by the operator and l is the level of knowledge of the operator.

– **Safety**

This is with the part handling while bending the part. It depends on the distance between the bend line and the back gauge d_{bb} and distance between the bend line and the operator d_{bo} while bending. The smallest distance should be kept with the back gauge to have safety process S and is evaluated by Eq. 4. Bonus is granted if the equation is satisfied and if not satisfied penalty is given.

$$F_S = \begin{cases} 1 \; if(d_{bb} < d_{bo}), \\ -1 \; otherwise. \end{cases} \tag{4}$$

6.2   Simple Process

To ease the bending process simple process should be a must condition. And a process can be said simple if the number of part rotations are kept minimum. And rotations can be defined as position based rotation and safety-based rotation.

- **Position Based Rotation**
  Bend lines can be bend in two directions either forward F or backward B, which needs part reversing and is shown in Fig. 7. This part reversing becomes a tedious job with the size of the part making the part handling very hard. So by bending the bend lines in the same direction the number of part reversions can be kept minimum enabling a simple process. The Eq. 5 can evaluate this.

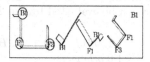

Fig. 7. Different positions in a part with 3 bend lines

$$F_P = \begin{cases} 1 & if(bd_i == bd_{i-1}), \\ -1 & otherwise, \end{cases} \tag{5}$$

where P is Position based Rotation, bd_i is the bend direction of bend i. The chromosomes, which satisfy the above are given bonus, and penalty is given when its not satisfied.

- **Safety Based Rotation**
  In the flat layout, the bend lines lie in different axis and related to the bend sequence, the part has to be rotated when the axis changes. The sheet metal is hold by the back gauge before bending and the part should be placed in such a way it can be held by the back gauge. Back gauge can hold the part only in the following conditions:
  $$if(d_{bb} < d_{bo}) \vee if\{(p_l \vee p_r) \neq bend\},$$
  where p_l is the left side of the part to be bend, is the p_r right side of the part to be bend. In case if the left or the right side of the part has a bend then the side which doesn't have the bend has to be holded by the back gauge. But in case if both the sides have bend then the part with the least distance has to be holded by the back gauge.
  So the bend sequence should be generated in such a way the part rotation is minimized. Bonus is granted in satisfying the above conditions else penalty is given and is evaluated by Eq. 6.

$$F_{SR} = \begin{cases} 1 & if(d_{bb} < d_{bo}) \vee if\{(p_l \vee p_r) \neq bend\}, \\ -1 & otherwise, \end{cases} \tag{6}$$

where SR is the Safety based rotation.

6.3   Operator Desire Fitness Function

So the Operator-Desire OP can be evaluated as a fitness function as expressed in following equation.

$$F_{OP} = F_{PTR} * Cost_{PTR} + F_A * Cost_A + F_K * Cost_K + F_S * Cost_S + F_P * Cost_P + F_{SR} * Cost_{SR},$$

where $Cost_{PTR}, Cost_A, Cost_K, Cost_S, Cost_P$, and $Cost_{SR}$ are the given costs for process time reduction, accuracy, knowledge, safety, position based rotation and safety based rotation, respectively. Depending on the selection of operator desire, the cost of the selected desire is doubled.

6.4   Collision Detection Function

It is a function that checks whether the candidate solution generated by the GA has a collision. 2-D graphic approach is being used to check collision. The flange folded ff, flange unfolded fu and the punch and die Ti selected for the relative bend i are considered as objects. The areas A of these objects are calculated and check is made if there is any intersection in these areas and Eq. 7 evaluates it.

$$F_C = \begin{cases} 1 & if(Aff \cap Afu \cap AT_i = NULL), \\ -1 & otherwise. \end{cases} \tag{7}$$

And finally, the following equation evaluates fitness value of each chromosome.

$$FitnessOfTheChromosome = F_C + F_{OP}.$$

7   Implementation and Evaluation

The above ideas were implemented in the BBST system (**B**est **B**ending **S**equence and **T**ool selection) and evaluated with the real part data having 7 and 8 bend lines.

The part geometry, tool library (database) in dxf.files and operator's desire are input to the system. The data are processed for collinear bends by the preprocessor and uses GA to generate the best bending process. The real part (Data_008C) and (Data_007C) as shown in Fig. 6 and Fig. 7 were tested with the above ideas and its results are explained below. The part has 8 and 7 bend lines respectively and we used the tool database, which has 15 tools to generate the best bending sequence and tool selection. If the above data were to be handled by the operator, which has 1.15E+17 possible combinations, it would not be possible to obtain results within the required time.

With the implementation of the preprocessor and operator desire the search space is considerably reduced improving the performance of the system by enhancing a simple process and fastening the search. We were able to get the solutions converged from its 15th generation.

A population of 100 chromosomes was maintained in the generation and with stable results being continuing for 50 generations the search was stopped and we

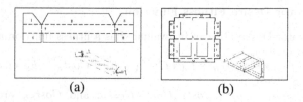

Fig. 8. Sample part (Data_008C,Data_007C) unfolded and folded for evaluation

were able to seek our solutions within 35 generations. And we can find the system with the preprocessor converges quickly than simple GA. The system was tested with both preprocessor and simple GA and was able to get better results making the process simpler by reducing the angle of rotation. A comparison between the system performance with and without preprocessor was done and the results are shown in Table 1. The system was tested on Dell Computer pentium III 600 MHz and took 1.7 seconds for part (Data_008C), as shown in Fig. 8(a) and 1.5 seconds for part (Data_007C), as shown in Fig. 8(b) to complete its search as shown in Fig. 9(a) and Fig. 9(b) but took just 1 second and 0.7 seconds respectively using preprocessor, which shows its efficiency. The solution that was obtained with and without preprocessor is being explained below.

(Data_008C): Without Preprocessor: 2-5-1-8-7-3-4-6

With Preprocessor:(1,2,3)-(4,5,6)-8-7

(Data_007C): Without Preprocessor: 3-6-5-1-2-7-4

With Preprocessor:(1,2)-6-(3,4)- 5-7

Table 1. Comparison of performance of GA with and without Preprocessor

Number of bend lines	Angle of Rotation Without Preprocessor	Angle of Rotation With Preprocessor
8	720°	450°
7	540°	270°

8   Conclusion

In this paper, we proposed a new approach for bending problem. We reduce the search space by grouping the genes in the preprocessor and use GA to generate the bending process. The feasible solution is based on collision detection and satisfying operator's desire. The operator's desire is defined and its fitness function is described. These ideas were implemented for real part data with 7 and 8 bend lines and the results are evaluated. In our future research, we are planning it to be implemented and get our expected results with complicated parts. We

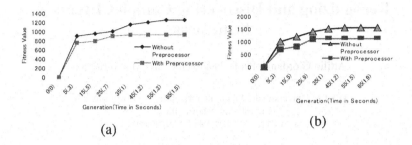

(a)   (b)

Fig. 9. Convergence and performance of the solution for the sample part (Data_008C)

are also considering of using knowledge database, which learns and stores the knowledge of the operator on bend sequencing and tool selection to fasten the bending process.

References

1. Cser,L., Geiger,M., Greska,W., and Hoffmann: Three Kinds of case-based learning in sheet metal manufacturing. Computers in Industry, Vol. 17, 195–206
2. Devin, J.deVries, A.H.Streppel,. J.W.Klaassen and H.J.J.Kals: The generation of bending sequences in a CAPP System for sheet metal components. Journal of materials processing technology, Vol. 41 (1994) 331–339
3. Radin, B. and Shpitalni, M.: Two-Stage Algorithm for determination of the bending sequence in sheet metal products. Proceedings of the ASME Design Automation Conference, Irvine, CA, (1996) USA, 1–12
4. J.R.Duflou, D.Van Oudheusden, J.P.Kruth and D.Cattrysee: Methods for sequencing of sheet metal bending operations. International Journal of Production Research, Volume 37, (1999) 3185–3202
5. J.R.Duflou: Ergonomics based criteria for manufacturability and process plan evaluation for bending processes. Proceedings of the 4th International Conference on Sheet Metal, Enschede, Vol. 1 (1996) 105–116
6. D.E.Goldberg: Genetic Algorithms in search, optimization and Machine Learning Addison Wesley, Massachusetts, (1989)
7. Chitra Thanapandi, Aranya Walairacht and Shigeyuki OHARA Genetic Algorithm for Bending Process in Sheet Metal Industry. CCECE,Toronto, Canada, (2001)

Recognizing and Discovering Complex Events in Sequences

Attilio Giordana[1], Paolo Terenziani[1], and Marco Botta[2]

[1]DISTA, Università del Piemonte Orientale, C.so Borsalino 54
15100 Alessandria, Italy
{attilio,terenz}@mfn.unipmn.it

[2]Dipartimento di Informatica, Università di Torino,
C.so Svizzera 185, 10149 Torino, Italy
botta@di.unito.it

Abstract. Finding complex patterns in long temporal or spatial sequences from real world applications is gaining increasing interest in data mining. However, standard data mining techniques, taken in isolation, seem to be inadequate to cope with such a task. In fact, symbolic approaches show difficulty in dealing with noise, while non-symbolic approaches, such as neural networks and statistics show difficulty in dealing with very long subsequences where relevant episodes may be interleaved with large gaps. The way out we suggest is to integrate the logic approach with non-symbolic methods in a unified paradigm, as it has been already done in other Artificial Intelligence tasks. We propose a framework where a high level knowledge representation is used to incorporate domain specific knowledge, to focus the attention on relevant episodes during the mining process, and flexible matching algorithms developed in the pattern recognition area are used to deal with noisy data. The knowledge extraction process follows a machine learning paradigm combining inductive and deductive learning, where deduction steps can be interleaved with induction steps aimed at augmenting a weak domain theory with knowledge extracted from the data. Our framework is formally characterized and then is experimentally tested on an artificial dataset showing its ability at dealing with noise and with the presence of long gaps between the relevant episodes.

1 Introduction

Discovering knowledge from long temporal or spatial sequences is a task attracting increasing attention in the literature owing to its significance in many real word applications. However, the task is not easy and the difficulty increases along with the length of the sequences and patterns to be discovered.

In this paper we propose a framework aimed at supporting the process of discovering the occurrence of complex events in long sequences. We assume that a complex event is a partially ordered set of short chains (episodes) of elementary events (*instants*) interleaved with gaps where irrelevant facts may occur. Moreover, we assume the presence of noise in the instances occurring in real world sequences, which can make the events hard to recognize. Episodes are represented as strings of

M.-S. Hacid et al. (Eds.): ISMIS 2002, LNAI 2366, pp. 374–382, 2002.

symbols, being a symbol a label assigned to an instant. Then, noise may be modeled as insertion, deletion and substitution errors according to a common practice followed in Pattern Recognition.

The typical approaches used in Pattern Recognition to learn and match patterns in sequences affected by such a kind of errors (e.g. dynamic time warping and hidden Markov Models [12]) are based on dynamic programming algorithms. Alternative approaches, such as Time Delay [13] and recurrent neural networks [8] have also been developed inside the neural network paradigm. However, all mentioned approaches have troubles to deal with very long sequences and, in particular, suffer from the presence of long gaps occurring among episodes.

We propose to combine a dynamic programming approach with a restricted first order logic language, in order to deal with the presence of both gaps and noise at the same time. The structure of a complex event is represented in the logic language, as a collection of episodes localized in different regions of a possibly long sequence according to a given set of constraints. From this point of view, episodes are seen as logical constants and for this reason will be referred to as *atomic events* in the following. Dynamic programming deals with the problem of matching episodes on a sequence affected by noise finding the most plausible instances. At the logical level, a plausibility measure accounts for the degree of matching. Logic resolution and dynamic programming strictly cooperate: the former provides information about the regions where dynamic programming matching (DP-matching) must be activated, the latter provides a quantitative plausibility estimate. The above framework recalls Michalski's *two tiered concept representation* and *flexible matching* [3], where DP-matching plays the role of flexible matching. Moreover, it differs from the approach by Bettini et al., [4] because in their approach both the structure of a complex event and the event types are given, whereas in our approach we aim to learn the structure of a complex event, event types and constraints among them.

In the first part of the paper we describe the logic language and we show how DP-matching can be integrated with logic resolution implementing a plausible reasoning paradigm. Afterwards, we show how it is possible to start with incomplete event description and learn missing knowledge from positive and negative examples. The learning procedure strictly follows an integrated deductive and inductive paradigm in the line of [2,11]. At a first step, a partial event description is deduced from imperfect domain knowledge. Then, the partial description is completed through an induction step. We show how DP-matching is a good method to also cope with an imperfect domain knowledge as well as with noisy data.

The paper is organized as follows. Section 2 presents the description language. Section 3 discusses the integration of DP-matching with logical resolution. Section 4 discusses the problem of learning part of a complex event description from the positive and negative examples. Finally, Section 5 gives a perspective above possible developments originating from the proposed framework.

2   The Description Language

The Description Language (DL) contains a set of logical predicates that model in a symbolic (explicit) way the structure of the domain knowledge and (in part) the description of the searching and learning tasks. We distinguish among five main types of concepts: **Events**, **Tasks**, **Contexts**, **Locations**, and **Constraints**.

376   A. Giordana, P. Terenziani, and M. Botta

Each (instance of) event takes place (*Happens* predicate) in a specific **location**. A location can be specified as a pair of natural numbers, representing the distance (the number of instants) of the starting point (function *Start*) and ending point (function *End*) of the event from a reference point (the beginning of the string where the event is found/learned).

Events can be either **atomic** (*AtomicEvent* predicate), or **composite** (*CompositeEvent* predicate). Atomicity is a domain-dependent property deriving from an initial abstraction step: whenever a knowledge engineer starts to describe a domain, s/he is free to choose which events are regarded to be atomic and which are not. In the following, atomic events are fully characterized by a string representing a chain of instants, and are referred to by using a name.

On the other hand, the description of a composite event consists of two main parts:

- the definition of its components
- the definition of the **constraints** between the components

The first part of the description is given by means of the *HasPart* predicate (which is a binary predicate operating on a composite event and an event, which may be composite or not). Currently, we focus our work on descriptions in which only conjunctions of HasPart predicates can be used (i.e., we do not consider events with alternative components). The second part constrains the relative location of the components, and is specified via the *Distance* predicate.

As an example, let us consider the domain knowledge represented in a graphical form in Figure 1. The (composite) event CE_3 is composed by CE_1 and CE_2, which are constrained as follows (indicated by the label α in the figure and in the following):

$$\alpha: Distance(Start(CE_2),End(CE_1),[10,20]) \land$$
$$Distance(End(CE_2),End(CE_1),[15,100]). \qquad (1)$$

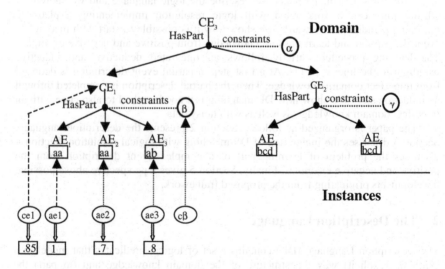

Fig. 1. Example of domain knowledge describing a complex event.

In turn, CE_1 is composed by the (atomic) events AE_1, AE_2 and AE_3, and CE_2 is composed by the (atomic) events AE_4 and AE_5. β and γ are conjunctions of Distance constraints among AE_1, AE_2, AE_3 and between AE_4, AE_5 respectively. Dashed arcs represent InstanceOf predicates, whereas block arrows represent plausibilities.

In our formalism, such knowledge can be described as follows:

CompositeEvent(CE_1) $\wedge$ CompositeEvent(CE_2) $\wedge$ CompositeEvent(CE_3) $\wedge$
AtomicEvent (AE_1,"aaa") $\wedge$ AtomicEvent (AE_1,"aa") $\wedge$ AtomicEvent (AE_1,"aba") $\wedge$
AtomicEvent (AE_1,"bcde") $\wedge$ AtomicEvent (AE_1,"bcd") $\wedge$ HasPart(CE_3,CE_1) $\wedge$ (2)
HasPart(CE_3,CE_2) $\wedge$ HasPart(CE_1,AE_1) $\wedge$ HasPart(CE_1,AE_2) $\wedge$
HasPart(CE_1,AE_3) $\wedge$ HasPart(CE_2,AE_4) $\wedge$ HasPart(CE_2,AE_5) $\wedge \alpha \wedge \beta \wedge \gamma$

In particular, a specific instance ce1 of the composite event CE_1 can be represented as follows:

InstanceOf(ce1,CE_1) $\wedge$ Happens(ce1,[10,29]) $\wedge$ Plausibility(ce1,0.85) $\wedge$
HasPart(ce1,ae1) $\wedge$ HasPart(ce1,ae2) $\wedge$ HasPart(ce1,ae3) $\wedge$
InstanceOf(ae1,AE_1) $\wedge$ Happens(ae1,[10,12]) $\wedge$ Plausibility(ae1,1.0) $\wedge$ (3)
InstanceOf(ae2,AE_2) $\wedge$ Happens(ae2,[15,17]) $\wedge$ Plausibility(ae2,0.7) $\wedge$
InstanceOf(ae3,AE_3) $\wedge$ Happens(ae3,[26,29]) $\wedge$ Plausibility(ae3,0.8)

The Plausibility predicate reflects the fact that we also take into account partial matching of events (see Section 3).

Although our approach is basically independent of the specific constraint framework adopted in order to represent spatial/temporal constraints between events, some comments about our adoption of the Distance predicate are in order. First of all, notice that the notion of distance is very flexible: for instance, it can be either interpreted as temporal or spatial distance. Secondly, the literature about constraints in the AI field has widely shown that the distance primitive is very powerful [6, 7]. For instance, in the temporal area, two main frameworks based on distance constraints (also called "bounds on differences" [6, 7]) have been used. The STP framework only takes into account conjunctions (sets) of distances [7], and can be used to model *precise* or *imprecise* temporal locations (dates), durations, delays between points, and different forms of qualitative temporal constraints between time points and/or time intervals (see [5, 10]). In the TCSP framework, also disjunctions of distances are allowed, to represent disjunctive temporal constraints, at the price of exponential algorithms for consistency checking [7].

Basically, we distinguish between two main types of **tasks**: finding and learning. Although they differs significantly from the operational point of view, both of them can be characterized in terms of at least four parameters (which might be optionally missing): the task location, its plausibility, the object of the task (which may be an event or a context), and the contexts in which the task is "eligible".

3   Detecting a Complex Event in Presence of Noise

Instances of a composite event are searched by instantiating task Find(). Instead of requiring exact matching between the string bound to an instance and the nominal description of an atomic event, we accept partial matching. Plausibility is a numeric value in the interval [0,1], which reflects the degree of matching.

Plausible instances in a sequence of a composite event are searched by means of a two level algorithm based on dynamic programming. At the first level, possible instances of atomic events (strings) are found generating a redundant lattice of atomic hypotheses. At the second level, global instances are selected choosing the best atomic instances that meet all the constraints.

3.1 Flexible Matching of Atomic Events

Algorithms for computing partial matching between strings have been widely investigated in Pattern Recognition and are extensively used for DNA analysis [9] and for automated text correction. The basic idea is that the effect of noise on a string "$x_1 x_2 x_3 ... x_n$" can be fully described by means of a set of rewriting rules corresponding to three types of errors: insertion errors (a spurious element x is introduced), deletion errors (an element 'x_i' is canceled), and substitution errors (an element 'x_i' is replaced by another element 'y').

Any string S_1 can be transformed into a string S_2 by applying a proper sequence of such transformations. However, every transformation T_i decreases the plausibility that S_2 is an instance of S_1, of an amount Δ. As many alternative sequences may exist, a sequence requiring the minimum number of transformations, and then corresponding to the maximum plausibility, is searched using a Dynamic Programming algorithm [9].

3.2 "Find" Algorithm

For the sake of space, we will describe just the basic version of the algorithm, being aware that many optimizations are possible in order to reduce the complexity both in time and space. In the first step, the input sequence S is scanned left-to-right. Every instant 'x_t' (a symbol in S) may be the start of any atomic event AE_i, defined in the domain knowledge. Then, for every event AE_i, the algorithm evaluates the plausibility of having AE_i an instance initiating in 'x_t'. All instances having non-null plausibility are included into a set **G**, where the constraints among the atomic events define a partial order. Therefore, the set **G** is a graph where each node g_i is a possible instance of an atomic event AE_i.

The second step searches for the most plausible global instance of the whole "context", i.e. of the complex event including all the instantiated atomic events. This is accomplished by finding a path of maximum plausibility on **G** containing an instance for every atomic event AE_i. The plausibility of a path $<g_1, g_2, ... g_n>$ is computed as a function $PL(<pl(g_1), pl(g_2), ... pl(g_n)>)$ of the plausibility of the single atomic instances. Being **G** acyclic, if function PL can be put into the form:

$$PL(<pl(g_1), ... pl(g_i), pl(g_{i+1})>) = PL(PL(<pl(g_1), ... pl(g_i)>), pl(g_{i+1})) \qquad (4)$$

where the plausibility at step i+1 only depends on the plausibility at step i and on the plausibility of node g_{i+1}, a maximum plausibility path can be found using a dynamic programming algorithm such as Dijkstra algorithm. Otherwise the computation of this step may be exponential.

3.3 Flexible Matching versus Resolution

Given the example of Figure 1, a dataset D^+ of 240 sequences containing at least one positive instance of the complex event CE_3 has been generated. The gaps between atomic events have duration chosen at random, according to the given constraints. Gaps are filled with symbols randomly chosen from the alphabet {a,b,c,d,e,f}. Moreover, a dataset D^- of 240 random sequences not containing instances of CE_3 has also been generated. All sequences in D^+ and D^- have a length of 40 symbols.

Finally, starting from CE_3, two new event descriptions, CE_3' and CE_3'', have been constructed being CE_3' very similar to CE_3 (see Table 1) and CE_3'' somewhat different. In any case, both CE_3' and CE_3'' do not have any perfect model in the dataset D^+. The question was how well flexible matching allows CE_3 to be discriminated from CE_3' and CE_3''.

Table 1. Description of the complex event used for the experiment reported in Table 2. As the three complex events differ only for the strings characterizing AE1, AE2, AE3, AE4 and AE5, the constraints have not been reported.

Event	Description (abbreviated in D)
CE_3	D(AE1, aaa); D(AE2, aa); D(AE3, aba); D(AE4, bcde); D(AE5,bcd)
CE_3'	D(AE1, aa); D(AE2, aaa); D(AE3, aba); D(AE4, bcd); D(AE5, bcde)
CE_3''	D(AE1, aa); D(AE2, aba); D(AE3, aba); D(AE4, aaa); D(AE5, bcd)

The distribution of the plausibility found for CE_3, CE_3', and CE_3'' on D^+ has been computed and threshold τ has been set on plausibility in the minimal classification error point between two distribution peaks. The results are reported in Table 2. For comparison, the error rate obtained using classical logic is also reported. It is worth noting that classical logic and flexible matching give the same result when the noise level is 0. Nevertheless, as soon as noise is introduced, the performances of classical logic drop dramatically (the evaluation fails for all three description), whereas flexible matching exhibits a good robustness.

Table 2. Error rate obtained by classical logic evaluation and by flexible matching on the task of discriminating CE_3 from CE_3' and CE_3'' on dataset D^+.

Matching	Events	Noise level						
		0	5%	10%	20%	30%	40%	50%
Logic	CE_3 vs CE_3'	0.0	0.27	0.43	0.46	0.48	0.49	0.50
	CE_3 vs CE_3''	0.0	0.25	0.42	0.46	0.48	0.49	0.50
DP	CE_3 vs CE_3'	0.0	0.19	0.27	0.29	0.35	0.39	0.44
	CE_3 vs CE_3''	0.0	0.03	0.07	0.15	0.17	0.25	0.33

4 Learning Part of the Description

Task Learn() accomplishes the extraction of new knowledge from data in order to complete a partial description CE of a composite event CE. The basic assumption is that a set D of sequences classified by a "teacher" is available; i.e., for every sequence S_i in the set D it is known if CE has an instance in D (is a positive example of CE) or not (is a negative example of CE). We also assume that D contains a balanced amount of positive and negative examples.

The learning procedure basically consists of three steps:

(a) For every sequence S_i belonging to set D, the most plausible instance $I_{CE}(S_i)$ of partial description CE is found by applying flexible matching.
(b) A new learning set D_{CE} is constructed where every example is a pair $<I_{CE}(S_i), S_i>$ containing the best instance $I_{CE}(S_i)$ in S_i for CE, and the sequence S_i itself. The instance $I_{CE}(S_i)$ is necessary in order to state the constraints the learned knowledge has to meet.
(c) An induction algorithm is used to learn from D_{CE} the knowledge CE' missing from CE. In particular, on examples belonging to D_{CE}, the instance of $I_{CE'}(S_i)$, must complete $I_{CE}(S_i)$ in such a way that S_i is correctly classified.

Given algorithm Find(), the first two steps are straightforward. It is worth noting that, a priori deciding if an instance $I_{CE'}(S_i)$ completes the most plausible partial instance $I_{CE}(S_i)$ is a strong assumption that in some cases may prevent the learning algorithm from finding the correct inductive hypothesis. In fact, the most plausible partial instance may be no longer such, after that a new piece of knowledge has been added by the learning step. On the contrary, other instances, apparently less plausible, could be better at the very end. However, this assumption is necessary in order to keep the complexity manageable. A viable improvement could be to consider the k-most plausible partial hypotheses. In this case, for every sequence S_i, the second step would generate k alternative learning examples. Then, the learning task could be posed in the form of *learning from multiple instances* framework. The problem, up to now, has been investigated in its simplest formulation only.

4.1 Learning Missing Knowledge

Depending on the knowledge declared missing in CE, the learning problem may present different difficulties. In our formalism, missing knowledge may be explicitly declared using symbol "?" meaning *undefined*. As an example, expression:

CompositeEvent(CE₁) ∧ CompositeEvent(CE₂) ∧ CompositeEvent(CE₃) ∧
AtomicEvent (AE₁,"aaa") ∧ AtomicEvent (AE₂,"aa") ∧
AtomicEvent (AE₃,"aba") ∧ AtomicEvent (AE₄,?) ∧ AtomicEvent (AE₅,?) ∧   (5)
HasPart(CE₃,CE₁) ∧ HasPart(CE₃,CE₂) ∧ HasPart(CE₁,AE₁) ∧ HasPart(CE₁,AE₂) ∧
HasPart(CE₁,AE₃) ∧ HasPart(CE₂,AE₄) ∧ HasPart(CE₂,AE₅) ∧ α ∧ β ∧ ?

has been obtained from expression (2) by declaring unknown the description of events AE_4, AE_5, and constraint γ.

In the simplest case, the problem is to learn missing constraints among some atomic events (e.g. constraint γ). Given the atomic instances found in the sequences, the problem may be solved by means of a classical relational learning (or ILP) algorithm. The problem is more difficult when also the descriptions for atomic events are to be learned because no algorithms specific for this task are available in the literature. The solution we adopted relies on a genetic algorithm G-NET* derived from G-NET [1], which has been adapted to the specific task, and which is able to deal with constraint, a-priori supplied to the system.

In G-NET*, the genetic search explores the hypothesis space by generating new solutions to the problem evolving a population of existing solutions by means of mutation and crossover. Every new solution is evaluated on all the examples in the given dataset D by means of flexible matching. Then, the plausibility distribution on positive and negative examples is computed, and a threshold on the plausibility is set in order to discriminate the positive from the negative instances. The fitness function trades-off the error rate and the complexity of the solutions (more details can be found in [1]). The constraints set by the instantiation I_{CE} of the partial description *CE* are handled by algorithm Find(), which, in any positive example begin the matching step on S_i starting from the partial model $I_{CE}(S_i)$.

Notice that the description language we presented only allows conjunctive descriptions. This enforces a learner to only produce conjunctive descriptions. However, if a complex event cannot be described by a single conjunctive description, a learner can generate a set of alternative conjunctive descriptions, each one covering a subset of the positive examples.

4.2 Experimental Evaluation

In the following we will show how G-NET* can complete a partial description *CE* rediscovering from the data a description, which, in general, is very similar to the original one. To this aim, a set of experiments has been done using the artificial dataset introduced in Section 3.

The results concerning the first set of experiments are reported in Table 3. The first experiment consisted in learning the description of atomic events AE_4 and AE_5 (formula (5) plus constraints γ). The second experiment consisted in learning the information missing in formula (5). The third one consisted in learning the global description of CE starting from the information that CE was consisting of five atomic events. Nothing was said about the description of the atomic events or about the constraints among them.

G-NET* failed to produce a single description only when the noise level reached 30%. In this case, three alternative descriptions quite different from the nominal one have been found.

Table 3. Results obtained by G-NET* on the artificial dataset. In column 2 to 5, the first value indicates the number of symbols in the nominal description, the second indicates the number of symbols in the learned description, and the third one indicates the number of Atomic Events added by the learning algorithm.

Initial CE	Number of symbols different from the Nominal Description			
	Noise = 0%	Noise = 10%	Noise = 20%	Noise = 30%
Formula (5)+γ	7, 7, 2	7, 7, 2	7, 7, 2	7, 10, 2
Formula (5)	7, 7, 2	7, 8, 2	7, 9, 2	7, 11, 2
The template of CE	15, 15, 5	15, 17, 6	15, 19, 7	-

5 Conclusions

A new multi-strategy approach for discovering complex events in long sequences has been proposed. The most important novelty is combining a logical description language with a string matching algorithm based on dynamic programming (DP-matching) to deal with gaps and noise in sequences. The robustness of the method and the advantages with respect to a purely logic approach have been experimentally demonstrated. However, the method also presents many advantages with respect to pure DP-matching. In fact, even if it is possible to account for gaps in DP-matching, the known methods lack the flexibility necessary to deal with very complex events as the one we considered in this paper (see [8] for a discussion).

In the paper, we have also shown how it is possible to learn substantial parts of an event description. To this aim, we revisited several ideas developed in the past that nicely cooperate to solve the considered task. DP-matching can be seen as a reformulation of flexible matching proposed in the two tiered concept representation [3]. Moreover, the general task of learning missing knowledge from an initial event description can be seen as a problem of combining deductive and inductive learning, where substantial work done in the past can be exploited. It is worth noting that DP-matching deals in the same way with noise in the data and noise in the domain knowledge, providing an elegant solution to a difficult problem that has been investigated by many researchers.

However, the results presented here are only preliminary ones, and an amount of substantial work is needed in order to fully develop the ideas we proposed.

References

1. C. Anglano, A. Giordana, G. Lobello, L. Saitta, "An experimental Evaluation of Coevolutive Concept Learning, *Proceedings of the 15th International Conference on Machine Learning*, (Madison ,WI, 1998), pp. 19-23.
2. F. Bergadano and A. Giordana, "Guiding Induction with Domain Theories", in *Machine Learning: An Artificial Intelligence Approach, vol. III*, R.S. Michalsky and Y. Kodratoff (Eds.), Morgan Kaufmann, 474-492, 1990.
3. F. Bergadano, S. Matwin, R.S. Michalski, J. Zhang, "Learning Two-Tiered Descriptions of Flexible Concepts: The POSEIDON System", *Machine Learning* , 8(1), 5- 44, 1992.
4. C. Bettini, S. Wang, S. Jajodia, J. Lin, "Discovering Frequent Event Patterns with Multiple Granularities in Time Sequences", IEEE Trans. on TKDE, 10(2), 222-237, 1998.
5. L. Console, P. Terenziani, "Efficient processing of queries and assertions about qualitative and quantitative temporal constraints", *Computational Intelligence 15(4)*, 442-465, November 1999.
6. E. Davis, "Constraint Propagation with Interval Labels", *Artificial Intelligence 32*, 281-331, 1987.
7. R. Dechter, I. Meiri, J. Pearl, "Temporal Constraint Networks", *Artificial Intelligence 49*, 61-95, 1991.
8. P. Frasconi, M. Gori, M. Maggini, G. Soda, "Representation of Finite State Automata in Recurrent Radial Basis Function Networks", *Machine Learning, 23*, 5-32, 1996.
9. D. Gussfield, "Algorithms on Strings, Trees, and Sequences", Cambridge University Press, 1997.
10. I. Meiri, "Combining Qualitative and Quantitative Constraints in Temporal Reasoning", *Proc. of the National Conference on Artificial Intelligence*, pp. 260-267, 1991.
11. M.J. Pazzani, D. Kibler, "The utility of knowledge in Inductive Learning", *Machine Learning, 9*, 57-94, 1992.
12. L.R. Rabiner, "A tutorial on hidden Markov models and selected applications in speech recognition", *Proc. IEEE, 77 (2)*, 257-286, 1989.
13. A. Waibel, T. Hanazawa, G. Hinton, K. Shikano, K. Lang, "Phoneme Recognition Using Time-Delay Neural Networks", *IEEE Transactions on acoustics, speech and signal processing*, 328-339, March, 1989.

Why to Apply Generalized Disjunction-Free Generators Representation of Frequent Patterns?

Marzena Kryszkiewicz and Marcin Gajek

Institute of Computer Science, Warsaw University of Technology
Nowowiejska 15/19, 00-665 Warsaw, Poland
{mkr,gajek}@ii.pw.edu.pl

Abstract. Frequent patterns are often used for discovery of several types of knowledge such as association rules, episode rules, sequential patterns, and clusters. Since the number of frequent itemsets is usually huge, several lossless representations have been proposed. Frequent closed itemsets and frequent generators are the most useful representations from application point of view. Discovery of closed itemsets requires prior discovery of generators. Generators however are usually discovered directly from the data set. In this paper we will prove experimentally that it is more beneficial to compute the generators representation in two phases: 1) by extracting the generalized disjunction-free generators representation from the database, and 2) by transforming this representation into the frequent generators representation. The respective algorithm of transitioning from one representation to the other is proposed.

1 Introduction

Frequent patterns are often used for discovery of several types of knowledge such as association rules, episode rules, sequential patterns, and clusters [5]. As the number of frequent itemsets is usually huge, it is important to apply concise, preferably lossless, representations of frequent itemsets. By lossless we mean a representation that allows derivation and support determination of all frequent itemsets without accessing the database. Recently, five lossless representations of frequent patterns have been investigated. They are based on the following families of itemsets: closed itemsets (see e.g. [2-3]), generators (see e.g. [3,7]), disjunction-free sets [4], disjunction-free generators [7] and generalized disjunction-free generators [8]. As proved in [8], the generalized disjunction-free generators representation is more concise than the other representations except for closed itemsets, in which case it may be more or less concise depending on data. In practice, in the case of highly-correlated data, it is much more concise than the closed itemsets representation as well [8].

From application point of view, the most useful representations are frequent closed itemsets and frequent generators. Their usefulness has been demonstrated e.g. in the case of discovery of representative rules [6] and minimal non-redundant association rules [2] that constitute concise lossless representations of all strong association rules. In the case of highly correlated data to be mined these representations amount to 1% of all rules. The characteristic feature of these rule representations is that no patterns except for closed itemsets and generators are involved in the process of their discovery. In particular, in the case of representative association rules [6] as well as generic basis and informative basis [2], rule's antecedent is a generator, while its consequent is a closed itemset diminished by the items present in the antecedent.

M.-S. Hacid et al. (Eds.): ISMIS 2002, LNAI 2366, pp. 383–392, 2002.

Discovery of closed itemsets always requires prior discovery of generators. Generators however are usually discovered directly from the data set. In this paper we will prove experimentally that it is more beneficial to compute the generators representation in two phases: 1) by determining the generalized disjunction-free generators representation from the database, and 2) by transforming this representation into the frequent generators representation. The algorithm realizing phase 1 was proposed in [8]; the respective algorithm of passing from the generalized disjunction-free generators representation to the generators one is offered here.

2 Basic Notions and Properties

2.1. Itemsets, Frequent Itemsets

Let $I = \{i_1, i_2, ..., i_m\}$, $I \neq \emptyset$, be a set of distinct literals, called *items*. In the case of a transactional database, a notion of an item corresponds to a sold product, while in the case of a relational database an item will be an (*attribute,value*) pair. Any non-empty set of items is called an *itemset*. An itemset consisting of k items will be called *k-itemset*. Let D be a set of transactions (or tuples, respectively), where each transaction (tuple) T is a subset of I. (Without any loss of generality, we will restrict further considerations to transactional databases.) *Support* of an itemset X is denoted by $sup(X)$ and defined as the number of transactions in D that contain X. The itemset X is called *frequent* if its support is greater than some user-defined threshold *minSup*. F will denote the set of all frequent itemsets:

$$F = \{X \subseteq I | sup(X) > minSup\}.$$

Property 2.1.1 [1]. If $X \in F$, then $\forall Y \subset X$, $Y \in F$.

2.2 Closures, Closed Itemsets, and Generators

Closure of an itemset X is denoted by $\gamma(X)$ and is defined as the greatest (w.r.t. set inclusion) itemset that occurs in all transactions in D in which X occurs. Clearly, $sup(X) = sup(\gamma(X))$. The itemset X is defined *closed* iff $\gamma(X) = X$. The set of all closed itemsets will be denoted by C, i.e.

$$C = \{X \subseteq I | \gamma(X) = X\}.$$

Let X be a closed itemset. A minimal itemset Y satisfying $\gamma(Y) = X$ is called a *generator* of X. By $G(X)$ we will denote the set of all generators of X. The union of generators of all closed itemsets will be denoted by G, i.e.

$$G = \bigcup \{G(X) | X \in C\}.$$

Example 2.2.1. Let D be the database from Table 1. To make the notation brief, we will write itemsets without brackets and commas (e.g. *ABC* instead of $\{A,B,C\}$).

Table 1. Example database D

Id	Transaction
T_1	{A,B,C,D,E,G }
T_2	{A,B,C,D,E,F}
T_3	{A,B,C,D,E,H,I},
T_4	{A,B,D,E}
T_5	{A,C,D,E,H,I}
T_6	{B,C,E }

The itemset *ABCDE* is closed since $\gamma(ABCDE) = ABCDE$. The itemset *ABC* is not closed as $\gamma(ABC) = ABCDE \neq ABC$. Clearly, $sup(ABC) = sup(ABCDE) = 3$. The itemset *ABC* is a minimal subset the closure of which equals to *ABCDE*. Hence, $ABC \in G(ABCDE)$.

Support of a generator differs from supports of its proper subsets:

Property 2.2.1 [3]. Let $X \subseteq I$. $X \in G$ iff $sup(X) \neq \min\{sup(X\backslash\{A\})| A \in X\}$.

On the other hand, support of any itemset equals to support of some generator:

Property 2.2.2 [7]. Let $X \subseteq I$. $sup(X) = \min\{sup(Y)| Y \in G \wedge Y \subseteq X\}$.

The next property states that all subsets of a generator are generators.

Property 2.2.3 [3,7]. Let $X \in G$. Then, $\forall Y \subset X, Y \in G$.

2.3 Generalized Disjunctive Rules and Generalized Disjunction-Free Sets

The notions of *generalized-disjunctive rules* and *generalized disjunction-free sets* were introduced in [8]. Let us remind them.

Let $Z \subseteq I$. $X \Rightarrow A_1 \vee...\vee A_n$ is defined as a *generalized disjunctive rule based on Z* (and Z is *the base of* $X \Rightarrow A_1 \vee...\vee A_n$) if $X \subset Z$ and $A_i \in Z\backslash X$ for $i = 1..n$.

Support of $X \Rightarrow A_1 \vee...\vee A_n$, denoted by $sup(X \Rightarrow A_1 \vee...\vee A_n)$, is defined as the number of transactions in D in which X occurs together with A_1 or A_2, or...or A_n.

Confidence of $X \Rightarrow A_1 \vee...\vee A_n$, denoted by *conf*, is defined in usual way:

$$conf(X \Rightarrow A_1 \vee...\vee A_n) = sup(X \Rightarrow A_1 \vee...\vee A_n) / sup(X).$$

$X \Rightarrow A_1 \vee...\vee A_n$ is defined a *certain rule* if $conf(X \Rightarrow A_1 \vee...\vee A_n) = 1$. So, $X \Rightarrow A_1 \vee...\vee A_n$ is certain if each transaction containing X contains also A_1 or A_2, or ... or A_n.

An itemset X is defined *generalized disjunctive* if there are $A_1,...,A_n \in X$ such that $X\backslash\{A_1,...,A_n\} \Rightarrow A_1 \vee...\vee A_n$ is a certain rule. Otherwise, the itemset is called *generalized disjunction-free*. The set of all generalized disjunction-free sets will be denoted by *GDFree*, i.e.

$$GDFree = \{X \in I| \neg\exists A_1,...,A_n \in X, conf(X\backslash\{A_1,...,A_n\} \Rightarrow A_1 \vee...\vee A_n) = 1, n \geq 1\}.$$

Example 2.3.1. Let us consider the database D from Table 2. Let us list all itemsets followed by subscript informing on their support: $\varnothing_7$, A_4, B_4, C_4, AB_2, AC_2, BC_2, ABC_1. Table 3 presents all generalized disjunctive rules based on ABC. The set ABC is generalized disjunction-free since there is a generalized disjunctive rule based on ABC (namely, $\varnothing \Rightarrow A \vee B \vee C$), which is certain.

Table 2. Example database D

Id	Transaction
T_1	{A,B,C}
T_2	{A,B}
T_3	{A,C}
T_4	{A}
T_5	{B,C}
T_6	{B}
T_7	{C}

Table 3. Generalized disjunctive rules based on ABC

$r: X \Rightarrow A_1 \vee...\vee A_n$	$sup(X)$	$sup(r)$	certain?
$AB \Rightarrow C$	2	1	no
$AC \Rightarrow B$	2	1	no
$BC \Rightarrow A$	2	1	no
$A \Rightarrow B \vee C$	4	3	no
$B \Rightarrow A \vee C$	4	3	no
$C \Rightarrow A \vee B$	4	3	no
$\varnothing \Rightarrow A \vee B \vee C$	7	7	yes

Property 2.3.1 [8]. If $X \Rightarrow A_1 \vee...\vee A_n$ is certain, then $\forall Z \supset X, Z \Rightarrow A_1 \vee...\vee A_n$ is certain.

Supersets of a generalized disjunctive set are generalized disjunctive, and subsets of a generalized disjunction-free set are generalized disjunction-free:

Property 2.3.2 [8]. Let $X \subseteq I$. If $X \notin GDFree$, then $\forall Y \supset X, Y \notin GDFree$. Otherwise, if $X \in GDFree$, then $\forall Y \subset X, Y \in GDFree$.

Let Y be an itemset such that $Y = \{A_1,...,A_n\}$. In the sequel, the disjunction $A_1 \vee...\vee A_n$ will be denoted by $\vee Y$. Support of a generalized disjunctive rule, say $X \Rightarrow \vee Y$, can be determined from the supports of itemsets Z such that $X \subset Z \subseteq X \cup Y$:

Property 2.3.3 [8]. Let $X,Y \subset I$ and $X \Rightarrow VY$ be a generalized disjunctive rule. Then:

$$sup(X \Rightarrow VY) = \{\Sigma_{i=1..|Y|} (-1)^{i-1} \times [\Sigma_{i\text{-itemsets } Z \subseteq Y} sup(X \cup Z)]\}.$$

Corollary 2.3.1 [8]. Let $X,Y \subset I$ and $X \Rightarrow VY$ be a generalized disjunctive rule. Then:

$$sup(X \cup Y) = (-1)^{|Y|} \times \{-sup(X \Rightarrow VY) + \Sigma_{i=1..|Y|-1} (-1)^{i-1} \times [\Sigma_{i\text{-itemsets } Z \subset Y} sup(X \cup Z)]\}.$$

Clearly, if the rule $X \Rightarrow VY$ is certain, then $sup(X \Rightarrow VY) = sup(X)$ and the equation from Corollary 2.3.1, can be rewritten as follows:

$$sup(X \cup Y) = (-1)^{|Y|} \times \{-sup(X) + \Sigma_{i=1..|Y|-1} (-1)^{i-1} \times [\Sigma_{i\text{-itemsets } Z \subset Y} sup(X \cup Z)]\}.$$

The formula on the right-hand side of the equation above can be treated as a *hypothetical support* of $X \cup Y$ driven by the rule $X \Rightarrow VY$: Hypothetical support of base $X \cup Y$ w.r.t. $X \Rightarrow VY$ is denoted by $HBSup(X \Rightarrow VY)$ and defined as follows:

$$HBSup(X \Rightarrow VY) = (-1)^{|Y|} \times \{-sup(X) + \Sigma_{i=1..|Y|-1} (-1)^{i-1} \times [\Sigma_{i\text{-itemsets } Z \subset Y} sup(X \cup Z)]\}.$$

Let us note that $HBSup(X \Rightarrow VY)$ is determinable from the supports of the itemsets Z such that $X \subseteq Z \subset X \cup Y$.

Property 2.3.4. $X \Rightarrow VY$ is a certain generalized rule iff $sup(X \cup Y) = HBSup(X \Rightarrow VY)$.

Thus, $X \Rightarrow VY$ is certain if and only if the support of $X \cup Y$ equals to the hypothetical support of $X \cup Y$ w.r.t. $X \Rightarrow VY$. Clearly, for any $Z \supset X$, if $X \Rightarrow VY$ is certain, then $Z \Rightarrow VY$ is also certain and thus $sup(Z \cup Y)$ can be calculated as $HBSup(Z \Rightarrow VY)$.

2.4 Generators versus Generalized Disjunction-Free Sets and Disjunctive Rules

Property 2.4.1 [7]. $X \in G$ iff $\neg \exists A \in X$ such that $X \setminus \{A\} \Rightarrow A$ is a certain rule.

Property 2.4.2 [8].

a)   Each generalized disjunction-free set is a generator.

b)   1-itemsets that are generators and $\varnothing$ are generalized disjunction-free sets.

Corollary 2.4.1. Length of a generalized disjunction-free generator is at least 2.

3 Generators Representation and Generalized Disjunction-Free Generators Representation

3.1 Generators Representation

Generators are commonly used as an intermediate step for discovery of closed itemsets. However, the generators themselves can constitute a concise lossless representation of frequent itemsets [7]. *Frequent generators (FG)*, are defined as:

$$FG = F \cap G.$$

Negative generators border (GBd⁻) is defined as follows:

$$GBd^- = \{X \in G \mid X \notin F \wedge (\forall Y \subset X, Y \in FG)\}.$$

GBd^- consists of all minimal (w.r.t. set inclusion) infrequent generators.
Generators representation (GR) is defined as:

- the set FG enriched by the information on support for each $X \in FG$,
- the border set GBd^-.

GR is sufficient to determine all frequent itemsets and their supports [7].

3.2 Generalized Disjunction-Free Generators Representation

The *generalized disjunction-free generators representation* was introduced in [8] and is defined by means of the following notions:

Generalized disjunction-free generators (*GDFreeG*) are defined as follows:

$$GDFreeG = GDFree \cap G.$$

Generalized frequent disjunction-free generators (*FGDFreeG*) are defined as below:

$$FGDFreeG = GDFreeG \cap F.$$

Property 3.2.1 [8]. Let $X \in FGDFreeG$. Then, $\forall Y \subset X$, $Y \in FGDFreeG$.

Generalized infrequent generators border, denoted by $IGDFreeGBd^-$, is defined as:

$$IGDFreeGBd^- = \{X \in G \mid X \notin F \wedge (\forall Y \subset X, Y \in FGDFreeG)\}.$$

$IGDFreeGBd^-$ consists of all minimal (w.r.t. subset inclusion) infrequent generators the proper subsets of which are frequent generalized disjunction-free generators.

Generalized frequent generators border (*FGDFreeGBd^-*) is defined as beneath:

$$FGDFreeGBd^- = \{X \in G \mid X \in F \wedge X \notin GDFreeG \wedge (\forall Y \subset X, Y \in FGDFreeG)\}.$$

$FGDFreeGBd^-$ consists of all minimal (w.r.t. subset inclusion) frequent generalized disjunctive generators. Let us note that $IGDFreeGBd^- \cap FGDFreeGBd^- = \varnothing$.

Generalized disjunction-free generators representation (GDFGR) is defined as:

- *FGDFreeG* enriched by the information on support for each $X \in FGDFreeG$,
- *FGDFreeGBd^-* enriched by information on support for each $X \in FGDFreeGBd^-$
- *IGDFreeGBd^-*.

GDFGR is sufficient to determine all frequent itemsets and their supports [8].

4 Relationships among GR, GDFGR, and Other Representations

It follows immediately by definitions of components in GDFGR and GR that the frequent components of GDFGR are contained in the frequent component of GR and the infrequent GDFGR component is contained in the infrequent GR component:

Property 4.1. (GDFGR $\subseteq$ GR).

$$FGDFreeG \cup FGDFreeGBd^- \subseteq FG \text{ and } IGDFreeGBd^- \subseteq GBd^-.$$

Let us observe that for each generator in GR "missing" in GDFGR, i.e. in GR\GDFGR, all its proper subsets are frequent generators, and at least one of its proper subsets belongs to the frequent border part $FGDFreeGBd^-$:

Proposition 4.1.

a) $FG \setminus (FGDFreeG \cup FGDFreeGBd^-) = \{X \in FG \mid (\forall Y \subset X, Y \in FG) \wedge$
$(\exists Y \subset X, Y \in FGDFreeGBd^-)\}$,

b) $GBd^- \setminus IGDFreeGBd^- = \{X \in G \mid X \notin F \wedge (\forall Y \subset X, Y \in FG) \wedge (\exists Y \subset X, Y \in FGDFreeGBd^-)\}$,

c) $GR \setminus DFGR = \{X \in G \mid (\forall Y \subset X, Y \in FG) \wedge (\exists Y \subset X, Y \in FGDFreeGBd^-)\}$,

d) $GR \setminus DFGR = \{X \in G \mid (\forall Y \subset X, Y \in FG) \wedge (\exists Y \subset X, |Y| = |X|-1 \wedge Y \notin GDFree)\}$.

Proof: Ad. a) By Properties 2.1.1 and 2.2.3, $FG = \{X \in G \mid X \in F \wedge (\forall Y \subset X, Y \in FG)\}$, and by definitions of GDFGR components and Property 3.2.1, $FGDFreeG \cup FGDFreeGBd^- = \{X \in FG \mid \forall Y \subset X, Y \in FGDFreeG\}$. Hence, $FG \setminus (FGDFreeG \cup FGDFreeGBd^-) = \{X \in FG \mid (\forall Y \subset X, Y \in FG) \wedge (\exists Y \subset X, Y \in FG \wedge Y \notin GDFree)\}$. Since $FGDFreeGBd^-$ consists of all minimal $Y \in FG$ such that $Y \notin GDFree$, then $FG \setminus (FGDFreeG \cup FGDFreeGBd^-) = \{X \in FG \mid (\forall Y \subset X, Y \in FG) \wedge (\exists Y \subset X, Y \in FGDFreeGBd^-)\}$.

Ad. b) By definitions of GBd^- and $IGDFreeGBd^-$: $GBd^- \setminus IGDFreeGBd^- = \{X \in G \mid X \notin F \wedge (\forall Y \subset X, Y \in FG)\} \setminus \{X \in G \mid X \notin F \wedge (\forall Y \subset X, Y \in FGDFreeG)\} = \{X \in G \mid X \notin F \wedge (\forall Y \subset X, Y \in FG) \wedge (\exists Y \subset X, Y \in FG \wedge Y \notin GDFree)\}$. Since

FGDFreeGBd⁻ consists of all minimal $Y \in FG$ such that $Y \notin GDFree$, then *GBd⁻*
\ *IGDFreeGBd⁻* = $\{X \in G|\, X \notin F \wedge (\forall Y \subset X,\, Y \in FG) \wedge (\exists Y \subset X,\, Y \in FGDFreeGBd⁻)\}$.
Ad. c) Follows immediately from Proposition 4.1a-b.
Ad. d) By Proposition 4.1c, Property 2.3.2, and by the fact that *FGDFreeGBd⁻*
consists of all minimal frequent generators that are generalized disjunctive.

Corollary 4.1.
a)   Each missing generator X in GR\GDFGR is a generalized disjunctive set.
b)   If *FGDFreeGBd⁻* = $\varnothing$, then GR = GDFGR.
Proof: Immediate by Proposition 4.1c and Property 2.3.2.

   Actually, GDFGR constitutes a subset not only of GR, but also of *the disjunction-free generators representation* (DFGR) (proposed in [7]), and *the disjunction-free sets representation* (DFSR) (proposed in [4]), namely GDFGR $\subseteq$ DFGR $\subseteq$ DFSR [7-8].

5 Transitioning GDFGR Representation into GR Representation

In this section we offer the *GDFGR-to-GR* algorithm for computing the generators representation from the generalized disjunction-free generators representation. In the algorithm we use the following notation:
*   *FGDFreeG$_k$*, *FGDFreeGBd⁻$_k$*, *IGDFreeGBd⁻$_k$*, – k-itemsets in the respective components of the generalized disjunction-free generators representation;
*   *C$_k$* – candidate generalized disjunction-free k-sets (potential missing generators).
   Itemsets are assumed ordered. The following fields are associated with an itemset c:
*   *sup* – support of c;
*   *minSubSup* – minimum of the supports of all $(|c|-1)$-subsets of c;
*   *c.ruleCons* – items in the consequent of a certain generalized disjunctive rule based on X or **NULL** if there is no such rule.

   GDFGR-to-GR starts with initializing GR border with infrequent itemsets in GDFGR. If there are no generalized disjunctive itemsets in GDFGR, then GR = GDFGR (by Corollary 4.1b) and the algorithm stops. Otherwise, the *GDisRuleCons* function (described later) is called for each frequent generalized disjunctive generator $Y \in FGDFreeGBd⁻$ to determine the consequent ($Y.ruleCons$) of a certain generalized disjunctive rule based on Y. Next, the length l of a shortest itemset in *FGDFreeGBd⁻* is determined (lengths of missing generators are greater than l). The frequent generators in GDFGR initialize *FG*. The *AprioriGDisGGen* function (described shortly) creates $(l+1)$-candidates, which are generalized disjunctive sets, from *FG$_l$*. The function not only creates the candidates, but also determines the consequents (*consRule*) of certain rules based on the candidates and minimum (*minSubSup*) of the supports of their l-subsets. The following steps are performed level-wise for all k-candidates, $k > l$:
1.   For each candidate k-itemset c, its support is determined as the hypothetical base support *HBSupCount(c\c.ruleCons$\Rightarrow$\c.ruleCons)* based on supports of c's subsets, which belong to $\cup_{i<k} FG_i$.
2.   The k-candidates whose supports differ from the supports of their $(k-1)$-subsets ($c.sup \neq c.minSubSup$) are found generators (by Property 2.2.1).
3.   The frequent candidate k-generators are added to *FG$_k$*, while the infrequent candidate k-generators are added to the negative border *GBd⁻$_k$*.

4. *AprioriGDisGGen* is called to generate $(k+1)$-candidates, which are generalized disjunctive sets, from the frequent k-generators FG_k, and to determine the candidates' fields: *consRule* and *minSubSup*.

The algorithm ends when there are no more candidates to evaluate.

Algorithm *GDFGR-to-GR(FGDFreeG,*
  FGDFreeGBd⁻, IGDFreeGBd⁻);

$GBd^- = IGDFreeGBd^-$;
if $FGDFreeGBd^- = \{\}$ **then** $FG = FGDFreeG$
else begin
  /* Determine certain rules for g in FGDFreeGBd⁻ */
  forall $g \in FGDFreeGBd^-$ **do**
    $g.ruleCons = GDisRuleCons(g, FGDFreeG)$;
  l = the length of a shortest itemset in $FGDFreeGBd^-$;
  $FG = FGDFreeG \cup FGDFreeGBd^-$;
  $C_{l+1} = AprioriGDisGGen(FG_l)$;
  for $(k = l+1; C_k \neq \{\}; k++)$ **do begin**
    forall candidates $c \in C_k$ **do begin**
      $s = c.ruleCons$;   // $c\backslash s \Rightarrow \forall s$ is certain
      $c.sup = HBSupCount(c\backslash s \Rightarrow \forall s)$;
      if $c.sup \neq c.minSubSup$ **then**   // c is a generator
        if $c.sup > minSup$ **then** add c to FG_k
        else add c to GBd^-_k;
    endfor;
    $C_{k+1} = AprioriGDisGGen(FG_k)$
  endfor;
endif;
return $<\cup_k FG_k, \cup_k GBd^-_k>$;

---

function *GDisRuleCons(c, FGDFreeG)*;

---

forall $i=2$ to $|c|$ **do**
  forall i-itemsets $s \subseteq c$ **do**
    if $X.sup = HBSupCount(c\backslash s \Rightarrow \forall s)$ **then return** Y;
return NULL;

---

function *AprioriGDisGGen(FG_k)*;

---

forall $f, h \in FG_k$ **do**
  if $f[1] = h[1] \wedge ... \wedge f[k-1] = h[k-1]$
    $\wedge f[k] < h[k]$
    /* Optional pruning strategies: */
    /* $\wedge c \notin FGDFreeGBd^-_{k+1}$ (A) */
    /* $\wedge c \notin IGDFreeGBd^-_{k+1}$ (B) */
  then begin
    $c = f[1] \bullet f[2] \bullet ... \bullet f[k] \bullet h[k]$;
    $c.ruleCons = $ NULL;
    add c to C_{k+1};
  endif;
  /* Pruning */
forall $c \in C_{k+1}$ **do begin**
  forall k-itemsets $s \subset c$ **do**
    if $s \notin FG_k$ **then**
      /* c is not a generator */
      delete c from C_{k+1}
    else begin
      $c.minSubSup = $
        $min(c.minSubSup, s.sup)$;
      if $c.ruleCons = $ NULL **then**
        $c.ruleCons = s.ruleCons$;
    endif;
    if $c.ruleCons = $ NULL **then**
      /* c is not gen. disjunctive */
      delete c from C_{k+1}
endfor;
return C_{k+1};

Determining Certain Rules for Generalized Disjunctive Sets. The first argument (c) of the *GDisRuleCons* function is assumed a frequent generalized disjunctive generator belonging to the border *FGDFreeGBd⁻*. The second one is the set *FGDFreeG* of all frequent generalized disjunction-free generators. Thus c, by definition of a border element, has all proper subsets in *FGDFreeG*, the supports of which are known. Since c is a generator, then no rule $X\backslash\{a\} \Rightarrow a$ is certain (by Property 2.4.1). However, c is generalized disjunctive, so there is a corresponding certain rule $c\backslash s \Rightarrow \forall s$, $s \subseteq c$ and $|s| \geq 2$, based on c. *GDisRuleCons* creates and evaluates (possibly) all such rules. Each rule $c\backslash s \Rightarrow \forall s$ is evaluated as follows:

The hypothetical support $HBSup(c\backslash s \Rightarrow \forall s)$ of c is calculated from the supports of c's subsets in *FGDFreeG*. If $HBSup(c\backslash s \Rightarrow \forall s) = sup(c)$, then $c\backslash s \Rightarrow \forall s$ is found certain (by Property 2.3.4). The *GDisRuleCons* function returns the items occurring in the consequent of the first generalized rule based on c that was found as certain.

Creating candidate missing generators. The task is performed by the *AprioriGDisGGen* function. According to Proposition 4.1d, all proper subsets of a missing generator c are frequent generators and at least one ($|c|-1$)-subset of c is a frequent generalized disjunctive generator. Hence, *AprioriGDisGGen* builds $(k+1)$-

candidates by merging only frequent generators. (For efficiency reasons, we use the technique applied in the *Apriori* algorithm [1] for ordered itemsets, which restricts itemsets' merging only to k-itemsets that differ on last item. The technique guarantees that the obtained candidates will contain all missing $(k+1)$-generators). The candidates that do not have all their k-subsets among FG_k, are discarded as invalidating Proposition 4.1d. While examining if a candidate c has all its k-subsets among FG_k, *AprioriGDisGGen* copies the subsets' *ruleCons* fields to *c.ruleCons*, until *c.ruleCons* becomes non-**NULL**. This happens when a k-subset s of c is generalized disjunctive. Then, $s\backslash s.ruleCons \Rightarrow \backslash s.ruleCons$ is a certain rule based on s, and by Property 2.3.1, $c\backslash s.ruleCons \Rightarrow \backslash s.ruleCons$ is a certain rule based on c and thus c is generalized disjunctive. In this case, *s.ruleCons* is assigned to the *c*'s field *ruleCons*. If none of k-subsets of c among FG_k is generalized disjunctive (i.e. if *c.ruleCons* remains **NULL**), then c is discarded as invalidating Proposition 4.1d. As a side effect, *AprioriGDisGGen* computes the value of the *minSubSup* field for each candidate c as the minimum from the supports of $(|c|-1)$-subsets of X.

The number of candidates created by *AprioriGDisGGen* can be additionally reduced by discarding the itemsets already present in $FGDFreeGBd^-_{k+1} \cup IGDFreeGBd^-_{k+1}$. We decided to test experimentally whether this optional pruning is useful. We compared four versions of *AprioriGDisGGen*: 1) with no additional pruning, 2) with additional pruning of candidates present in $FGDFreeGBd^-_{k+1}$ (condition A), 3) with additional pruning of candidates present in $IGDFreeGBd^-_{k+1}$ (condition B), 4) with additional pruning of candidates present in $FGDFreeGBd^-_{k+1} \cup IGDFreeGBd^-_{k+1}$ (both A and B conditions). The results are presented in Section 6.

6 Experimental Results

The results of the experiments, we will present, were obtained for the very dense *Connect-4* data consisting of 67557 transactions, each of the length 43, $|I|=129$ (http://www.ics.uci.edu/~mlearn/MLRepository.html). (Similar results were obtained for the *Mushroom* data, nevertheless lack of space does not allow us to present them.)

Figure 1 presents the execution times of extracting: 1) GR from the database D, 2) GDFGR from D, 3) GR from GDFGR, 4) the total time of 2) + 3).

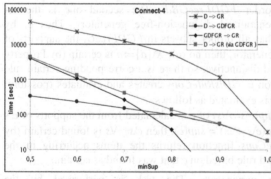

Table 4. Differences in time of transitioning *Connect-4* GDFGR into GR, when using or not frequent and infrequent parts of the GDFGR border

Pruning	-	A	B	A∧B
minSup	[sec]	[sec]	[sec]	[sec]
50%	3967	3961	3952	4047
60%	1069	1066	1066	1124
70%	264	264	263	274
80%	37	39	37	37
90%	1	1	1	1
99%	0	0	0	0

Fig. 1. Time of extracting: GR directly from D, and GR from D via GDFGR

As follows from Fig. 1, the execution time of the two step calculation of frequent generators with the use of GDFGR is up to two orders of magnitude less than the direct discovery of GR from the database. In addition, Table 4 shows that the use of the borders *FGDFreeGBd⁻* and *IGDFreeGBd⁻* during candidate generators pruning only slightly influences the time of calculating GR from GDFGR.

Table 5 shows the execution time of extracting GR: 1) directly from the *Connect-4* database, 2) via DFGR (the disjunction-free generators representation [7]), and 3) via GDFGR. It turns out that GDFGR, which is more concise than DFGR, is also a competitive indirect form of discovery of frequent generators.

Table 5. Discovering *Connect*-4 GR: 1) directly from D, 2) via DFGR, 3) via GDFGR

	D → GR	D → DFGR → GR			D → GDFGR → GR		
		D → DFGR	DFGR → GR	Total	D → GDFGR	GDFGR → GR	Total
minSup	[sec]	[sec]	[sec]	[sec]	[sec]	[sec]	[sec]
50%	44713	588	4107	4695	330	3967	4297
60%	23346	303	1128	1431	229	1069	1298
70%	12240	160	298	458	146	264	410
80%	5297	98	40	138	98	37	135
90%	1166	54	1	55	54	1	55
99%	32	18	0	18	18	0	18

GR could be also calculated from DFSR (the disjunction-free sets representation [4]) as follows: 1) extract DFSR from D, 2) yield DFGR from DFSR, 3) transform DFGR into GR. Ad. 1) The discovery of DFSR and the discovery of DFGR are similarly time-consuming [8]. Ad. 2) DFGR and DFSR differ only on frequent parts of their negative borders [7]. Determining DFGR from DFSR would consist in discarding from DFSR the border itemsets that are not generators. Hence, the overall time of extracting GR via DFSR would be longer than extracting GR via DFGR.

7 Conclusions

Frequent generators and closed itemsets are the most useful brief form for discovery of association rules. Closed itemsets are commonly determined from generators. In the paper, we examined the critical step of discovering frequent generators. We proposed the algorithm transforming GDFGR into GR. We proved experimentally, that GDFGR, which is more concise than GR, DFSR and DFGR, is currently the best intermediate form for obtaining GR. In fact, GR can be calculated up to 2 orders of magnitude more quickly via GDFGR, than directly from the database.

References

[1] Agrawal, R., Mannila, H., Srikant, R., Toivonen, H., Verkamo, A.I.: Fast Discovery of Association Rules. In: Advances in KDD. AAAI, Menlo Park, California (1996) 307-328
[2] Bastide, Y., Pasquier, N., Taouil, R., Stumme, G., Lakhal, L.: Mining Minimal Non-redundant Association Rules Using Frequent Closed Itemsets. CL (2000) 972-986
[3] Bastide, Y., Taouil, R., Pasquier, N., Stumme, G., Lakhal, L.: Mining Frequent Patterns with Counting Inference. ACM SIGKDD Explorations, Vol. 2(2). (2000) 66-75
[4] Bykowski, A., Rigotti, C.: A Condensed Representation to Find Frequent Patterns. In: Proc. of the 12th ACM SIGACT-SIGMOD-SIGART PODS' 01 (2001)
[5] Han, J., Kamber, M.: Data Mining: Concepts and Techniques. Morgan Kaufmann (2000)

[6] Kryszkiewicz, M.: Closed Set based Discovery of Representative Association Rules. In: Proc. of IDA '01. Springer (2001) 350-359

[7] Kryszkiewicz, M.: Concise Representation of Frequent Patterns based on Disjunction-Free Generators. In: Proc. of ICDM '01. IEEE (2001) 305-312

[8] Kryszkiewicz, M., Gajek, M.: Concise Representation of Frequent Patterns based on Generalized Disjunction-Free Generators, PAKDD '02, to appear in a Springer volume

Trading-Off Local versus Global Effects of Regression Nodes in Model Trees

Donato Malerba, Annalisa Appice, Michelangelo Ceci, and Marianna Monopoli

Dipartimento di Informatica, Università degli Studi di Bari
via Orabona 4, 70125 Bari, Italy
{malerba, appice, ceci, monopoli}@di.uniba.it

Abstract. Model trees are an extension of regression trees that associate leaves with multiple regression models. In this paper a method for the top-down induction of model trees is presented, namely the Stepwise Model Tree Induction (SMOTI) method. Its main characteristic is the induction of trees with two types of nodes: regression nodes, which perform only straight-line regression, and split nodes, which partition the sample space. The multiple linear model associated to each leaf is then obtained by combining straight-line regressions reported along the path from the root to the leaf. In this way, internal regression nodes contribute to the definition of multiple models and have a "global" effect, while straight-line regressions at leaves have only "local" effects. This peculiarity of SMOTI has been evaluated in an empirical study involving both real and artificial data.

1 Introduction

Regression trees are well-known tree-based prediction models for numerical variables [1]. As in the case of decision trees, they are generally built top-down by recursively partitioning a feature space $\mathcal{X}$ spanned by m independent (or predictor) variables x_i (both numerical and categorical). The main difference is that the dependent (or response) variable y to be predicted is continuous. Therefore, each leaf in the tree is associated with a numerical value, and the underlying model function $y=g(\mathbf{x})$ is approximated by means of a piecewise *constant* one. *Model trees* generalize the concept of regression trees in the sense that they approximate the function above by a piecewise *linear* function, that is they associate leaves with multiple models. The problem of inducing model trees from a training set has received attention both in statistics [2,7,10] and in machine learning. Some of the model tree induction systems developed are: M5 [9], RETIS [4], M5' [13], TSIR [5], and HTL [11,12]. In most of them the multiple model associated with a leaf is built on the basis of those training cases falling in the corresponding partition of the feature space. Therefore, models in the leaves have only a "local" validity and do not consider the "global" effects that some variables might have in the underlying model function. Such global effects can be represented by variables that are introduced in the multiple models at higher levels of the model trees. However, this requires a different tree-structure, where internal nodes can either define a further partitioning of the feature space or introduce some regression variables in the models to be associated to the leaves.

M.-S. Hacid et al. (Eds.): ISMIS 2002, LNAI 2366, pp. 393–402, 2002.

In this paper we present the current state of the art of the research on top-down induction of model trees and we motivate the stepwise construction of models associated with the leaves. A new method, named Stepwise Model Tree Induction (SMOTI), is presented. SMOTI is characterized by the construction of tree models with both regression and split nodes. Regression nodes perform straight-line regression, while split nodes partition the sample space. The multiple linear model associated with each leaf is obtained by composing the effect of regression nodes along the path from the root to the leaf. Therefore, variables of the regression nodes selected at higher levels in the tree have a "global" effect, since they affect several multiple models associated with the leaves.

The state of the art of model tree induction is described in the next section, while in Section 3 the method SMOTI is introduced, and its computational complexity is analyzed. Finally, in Section 4 some experimental results are reported and the trade-off between "local" and "global" effects is discussed.

2 Induction of Model Trees: State of the Art

The induction of model trees can be reformulated as a search problem in the space of all possible model trees that can be built with m independent variables. Since an exhaustive exploration of this space is not possible in practice, several heuristics (*evaluation functions*) have been proposed to solve this problem. In CART [1], the quality of the (partially) constructed tree T is assessed by means of the mean square error $R^*(T)$, whose sample estimate is:

$$R(T) = \frac{1}{N} \sum_{t \in \tilde{T}} \sum_{x_i \in t} (y_i - \bar{y}(t))^2$$

where N is the number of training examples $(\mathbf{x}_i, y_i)$, $\tilde{T}$ is the set of leaves of the tree, and $\bar{y}(t)$ is the sample mean of the response variable, computed on the observations in the node t. By denoting with $R(t)$ and $s^2(t)$ the resubstitution estimate of risk and the sample variance at a node t, respectively, $R(T)$ can be rewritten as:

$$R(T) = \sum_{t \in \tilde{T}} R(t) = \sum_{t \in \tilde{T}} \frac{N(t)}{N} s^2(t) = \sum_{t \in \tilde{T}} p(t) s^2(t)$$

where $N(t)$ is the number of observations in the node t and $p(t)$ is the probability that a training case reaches the leaf t. When the observations in a leaf t are partitioned into two groups, we obtain a new tree T', where t is an internal node with two children, say, t_L and t_R. Different splits generate distinct trees T', and the choice of the best split is made by minimizing the corresponding $R(T')$, that is, by minimizing $p(t_L)s^2(t_L) + p(t_R)s^2(t_R)$, the contribution to $R(T')$ given by the split.

This heuristic criterion, initially conceived for regression trees, has also been used for model trees. In the system HTL the evaluation function is the same as that reported above, while in M5 the sample variance $s^2(t)$ is substituted by the sample standard deviation $s(t)$. The problem with these evaluation functions, when used in model tree induction, is that they do not take into account the models associated with the leaves of the tree. In principle, the optimal split should be chosen depending on how well each model fits the data. In practice, many model tree induction systems choose the optimal split on the basis of the spread of observations with respect to the *sample mean*. However, a model associated with a leaf is generally more sophisticated than the sample mean. Therefore, *the evaluation function is incoherent with respect to the model tree being built*. Consequently, the induced tree may fail to discover the underlying model, as exemplified in [6]. This problem is due to the neat separation of the *splitting* stage from the *predictive* one. The partitioning of the feature space (splitting stage) does not take into account the multiple regression models that can be associated with the leaves. Moreover, the association of models with the leaves (prediction stage) takes place only when the partition of the feature-space has been fully defined; therefore, it is difficult to establish whether a variable has a more global effect involving several regions of the feature space.

This problem does not occur in regression tree induction, since the models are the sample means which are used in the computation of $R(T)$. Moreover, the choice of a constant function (the sample mean) as the type of model in the leaves explicitly prevents the differentiation between global and local effects of variables in the models. For different reasons, the same problem cannot potentially occur in RETIS, whose heuristic criterion is to minimize $p(t_L)s^2(t_L) + p(t_R)s^2(t_R)$, where $s^2(t_L)$ ($s^2(t_R)$) is now computed as the mean square error with respect to the regression plane g_L (g_R) found for the left (right) child:

$$s^2(t_L) = \frac{1}{N(t_L)} \sum_{x_i \in t_L} (y_i - g_L(x_i))^2 \qquad \left(s^2(t_R) = \frac{1}{N(t_R)} \sum_{x_i \in t_R} (y_i - g_R(x_i))^2 \right)$$

In practice, for each possible partitioning the best regression planes at leaves are chosen, so that the selection of the optimal partitioning can be based on the result of the prediction stage.

The weakness of the RETIS heuristic evaluation function is its high computational complexity, especially when all independent variables are continuous. In particular, it can be proven that the choice of the first split takes time $O(N(N-1)m(m+1)^2)$, which is cubic in m and square in N [6]. In addition to the high computational cost, RETIS is characterized by models that can take into account only local decisions.

A solution to both problems is the stepwise construction of multiple linear models by intermixing regression steps with partitioning steps, as done in TSIR. TSIR has two types of node: split nodes and regression nodes. The former perform a boolean test on a variable and have two children. The latter compute a single variable regression, $Y = a+bX$, and pass down to its *unique* child the residuals $y_i - (a+bx_i)$ as new values of the response variable. Thus, descendants of a regression node will operate on a modified training set. Lubinsky claims that "each leaf of the TSIR tree corresponds to a different multiple linear regression," and that "each regression step adds one variable and its coefficients to an incrementally growing model" [5].

However, this interpretation is not correct from a statistical point of view, since the incremental construction of a multiple linear regression model is made *by removing the linear effect of the introduced variables each time a new independent variable is added to the model* [3]. For instance, let us consider the problem of building a regression model $Y=a+bX_1+cX_2$ through a sequence of straight-line regressions. We start regressing Y on X_1, so that the model $Y = a_1+b_1X_1$ is built. This fitted equation does not predict Y exactly. By adding the new variable X_2, the prediction might improve. Instead of starting from scratch and building a model with both X_1 and X_2, we can build a linear model for X_2 given X_1:

$X_2 = a_2 + b_2 X_1$,

then compute the residuals on X_2:

$X'_2 = X_2 - (a_2 + b_2 X_1)$,

and finally regress Y on X'_2 alone:

$Y = a_3 + b_3 X'_2$.

By substituting the equation of X'_2 in the last equation we have:

$Y = a_3 + b_3 X_2 - a_2 b_3 - b_2 b_3 X_1$.

It can be proven that this last model coincides with the first model built, that is $a=a_3-a_2b_3$, $b=-b_2b_3$ and $c=b_3$. Therefore, when the first regression line of Y on X_1 is built we do not pass down *the residuals of Y* but *the residuals of the regression of X_2 on X_1*. This means we remove the linear effect of the variables already included in the model (X_1) from those variables to be selected for the next regression step (X_2). TSIR operates in a different way, so that it is not possible to assert that the composition of straight-line models found along a path from the root to a leaf is equivalent to a multiple linear model associated with the leaf itself. In fact, the only correct interpretation is that the subtree of a regression node is in turn a model tree that aims at predicting the residuals of the regression performed in the node.

The above problem does not occur in the system SMOTI, which removes the effect of the variable selected by a regression node before passing down training cases to deeper levels. However, this adjustment must be accompanied by a look-ahead strategy when regression nodes and split nodes are compared for selection. This has been also taken into account in the design of SMOTI, as explained in the next section.

3 Induction of Model Trees in SMOTI

In SMOTI, the development of a tree structure is not only determined by a recursive partitioning procedure, but also by some intermediate prediction functions.

This means that there are two types of node in the tree: regression nodes and split nodes. The former performs only straight-line regressions, while the latter partitions the feature space. They pass down observations to their children in two different ways. For a split node t, only a subgroup of the $N(t)$ observations in t is passed to each child, and no change is made on the variables. For a regression node t, all the observations are passed down to its only child, but the values of the independent variables not included in the model are transformed, to remove the linear effect of those variables already included. Thus, descendants of a regression node will operate on a modified training set.

The validity of either a regression step on a variable X_i or a splitting test on the same variable is based on two distinct evaluation measures, $\pi(X_i,Y)$ and $\sigma(X_i,Y)$ respectively. The variable X_i is of a continuous type in the former case, and of any type in the latter case. Both $\pi(X_i,Y)$ and $\sigma(X_i,Y)$ are mean square errors,[1] therefore they

---

[1]   This is different from TSIR, which minimizes the absolute deviation between a median (the model) and the Y values of the cases. Actually, the minimization of absolute deviation is more robust with respect to the presence of outliers and skewed distributions. However, SMOTI coherently minimizes the least squares both when a straight-line regression has to be built and when two different alternatives have to be compared.

can be actually compared to choose between either growing the model tree by adding a regression/split node t, or stopping the tree's growth at node t.

As pointed out in Section 2, the evaluation measure $\sigma(X_i,Y)$ should be coherently defined on the basis of the multiple linear model to be associated with each leaf. In the case of SMOTI it is sufficient to consider a straight-line regression associated with each leaf t_R (t_L), since regression nodes along the path from the root to t_R (t_L) already define partially a multiple regression model (see Figure 1a-b).

If X_i is continuous and α is a threshold value for X_i then $\sigma(X_i,Y)$ is defined as:

$$\sigma(X_i,Y) = \frac{N(t_L)}{N(t)}R(t_L) + \frac{N(t_R)}{N(t)}R(t_R)$$

where $N(t)$ is the number of cases reaching t, $N(t_L)$ ($N(t_R)$) is the number of cases passed down to the left (right) child, and $R(t_L)$ ($R(t_R)$) is the resubstitution error of the left (right) child, computed as follows:

$$R(t_L) = \sqrt{\frac{1}{N(t_L)} \sum_{j=1}^{N(t_L)} (y_j - \hat{y}_j)^2} \quad \left(R(t_R) = \sqrt{\frac{1}{N(t_R)} \sum_{j=1}^{N(t_R)} (y_j - \hat{y}_j)^2} \right)$$

The estimate $\hat{y}_j = a_0 + \sum_{s=1}^{m} a_s x_s$ is computed by combining the straight-line regression associated with the leaf t_L (t_R) with all univariate regression lines associated with regression nodes along the path from the root to t_L (t_R).

If X_i is discrete, SMOTI partitions attribute values into two sets, so that binary trees are always built. Partitioning is based on the same criterion applied in CART [1, pp. 247], which reduces the search for the best subset of categories from 2^{k-1} to $k-1$, where k is the number of distinct values for X_i.

The evaluation of the effectiveness of a regression step $Y=a+bX_i$ at node t cannot be naïvely based on the resubstitution error $R(t)$:

$$R(t) = \sqrt{\frac{1}{N(t)} \sum_{j=1}^{N(t)} (y_j - \hat{y}_j)^2}$$

where the estimator $\hat{y}_j$ is computed by combining the straight-line regression associated with t with all univariate regression lines associated with regression nodes along the path from the root to t. This would result in values of $\eta(X_i,Y)$ less than or equal to values of $\sigma(X_i,Y)$ for some splitting test involving X_i. Indeed, the splitting test "looks-ahead" to the best multiple linear regressions after the split on X_i is performed,

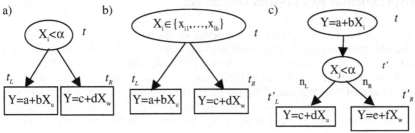

Fig. 1. a) A continuous split node. b) A discrete split node. c) An example of regression node.

while the regression step does not. A fairer comparison would be growing the tree at a further level in order to base the computation of $\pi(X_i, Y)$ on the best multiple linear regressions after the regression step on X_i is performed (see Figure 1c).

Let t' be the child of the regression node t, and suppose that it performs a splitting test. The best splitting test in t' can be chosen on the basis of $\sigma(X_j, Y)$ for all possible variables X_j, as indicated above. Then $\pi(X_i, Y)$ can be defined as follows:

$$\pi(X_i, Y) = min \{ R(t), \ \sigma(X_j, Y) \ for \ all \ possible \ variables \ X_j \}.$$

Having defined both $\pi(X_p, Y)$ and $\sigma(X_p, Y)$, the criterion for selecting the best node is fully characterized as well. A weight w $(1-w)$ is associated with split (regression) nodes, so as to express the user preference for model trees with splitting tests (regression steps). Therefore, SMOTI actually compares the weighted values $w \ \sigma(X_p, Y)$ and $(1-w) \pi(X_p, Y)$ while selecting a node. At each step of the model tree induction process, SMOTI chooses the apparently most promising node according to a greedy strategy. A continuous variable selected for a regression step is eliminated from further consideration, so that it can appear only once in a regression node along a path from the root to a leaf.

In SMOTI three different stopping criteria are implemented. The first uses the partial F-test to evaluate the contribution to the model of a new independent variable [3]. The second requires the number of cases in each node to be greater than a minimum value. The third stops the induction process when all continuous variables along the path from the root to the current node are used in regression steps and there are no discrete variables in the training set.

The computational complexity of the model tree induction algorithm is highly dependent on the choice of the best splitting test or regression step for a given node. For regression steps, the worst case complexity is $O(NmlogN)$, where N is the number of examples in the training set and m is the number of independent variables. For splitting tests, the worst case complexity is $O(N+NlogN)$, where the component $NlogN$ is due to the quicksort algorithm. Therefore, the worst case complexity for the selection of any node is $O(Nm^2 logN)$, since there are m independent variables.

It is noteworthy that SMOTI is more efficient than RETIS at building model trees and defines the best partitioning of the feature space coherently with respect to the model tree being built. Moreover, the use of both regression and split nodes permits the system to consider both global and local effects of variables in the various regression models. This is evident in the experimental results reported below.

4 Experimental Results and Discussion

SMOTI has been implemented as a module of the knowledge discovery system KDB2000 (www.di.uniba.it/~malerba/software/kdb2000/) and has been empirically evaluated on six datasets taken from UCI Machine Learning Repository (www.ics.uci.edu/~mlearn/MLRepository.html) and the site of the system HTL (www.ncc.up.pt/~ltorgo/Regression/DataSets.html). They are: a) *Abalone*, with 2889 cases and 8 attributes (7 continuous and 1 discrete); b) *Auto* with 398 cases and 8 attributes (5 continuous and 3 discrete); c) *Housing* with 506 cases and 14 continuous attributes;

d) *Machine CPU* with 209 cases and 6 discrete attributes; e) *Pyrimidines* with 74 cases and 27 continuous attributes; f) *Price* with 159 cases and 16 attributes (15 continuous and 1 discrete). Each dataset is analyzed by means of a 10-fold cross-validation, that is, the dataset is first divided into ten blocks of near-equal size and with near-equal distribution of class values, and then, for every block, SMOTI is trained on the remaining blocks and tested on the hold-out block. The system performance is evaluated on the basis of both the average resubstitution error and the average number of leaves. For pairwise comparison of methods, the non-parametric Wilcoxon signed rank test is applied [8], where the summations on both positive and negative ranks, namely W+ and W-, are used to determine the winner. In all experiments reported in this empirical study, the significance level α is set to 0.05.

4.1 Effect of Node Weighting

The first experiment aims at investigating the effect of node weighting on the predictive accuracy and complexity of the tree. A weight greater than 0.5 prefers splitting tests, while a weight lower than 0.5 favors the selection of regression nodes. It is noteworthy that, for higher weight values, regression nodes are often selected near the leaves of the tree, so that they can give only a local contribution to the approximation of the underlying function with a model tree. On the contrary, for lower values of the weight regression node they tend to be selected at the root, so that they give a global contribution to the approximation of the underlying function. In other words, the weight represents the trade-off between global regression models that span the whole feature space and are built using all training cases and local regression models, which fit fewer data falling in smaller portions of the feature space.

The weighting factor also affects the predictive accuracy of the induced model, as reported in Table 1. In each of the ten trials per dataset, predictive accuracy is estimated by the mean square error, computed on the corresponding validation set. Experimental results show that by increasing the weight, that is favoring the selection of split nodes, it is possible to obtain more accurate model trees. Moreover, we also observed that for weight values higher than 0.6 the situation does not change with respect to the case w=0.6, while for weight values lower than 0.5 the accuracy is lower than that observed with w=0.5. The conclusion is that, in almost all the data sets considered, local effects of regression variables are preferred.

Table 1. Results of the Wilcoxon signed rank test on the accuracy of the induced model. The best value is in boldface, while the statistically significant values ($p \leq \alpha/2$) are in italics

Data set	0.5 vs 0.52			0.5 vs 0.56			0.5 vs 0.6		
	p	*W+*	*W-*	*P*	*W+*	*W-*	*p*	*W+*	*W-*
Abalone	0.083	45	**10**	*0.004*	54	*1*	*0.004*	54	*1*
Auto	0.556	34	**21**	0.492	35	**20**	1.000	28	**27**
Housing	0.492	**20**	35	0.275	39	**16**	0.432	36	**19**
Machine	0.064	46	**9**	0.064	46	**9**	0.064	46	**9**
Price	0.083	45	**10**	0.232	**40**	15	0.432	36	**19**
Pyrimidines	*0.002*	55	*0*	0.106	11	**44**	0.064	46	**9**

SMOTI has also been compared to two other TDMTI systems, namely a trial version of Cubist and M5'. Experimental results, which are reported in [6] and are unfavorable to SMOTI, seem to confirm the presence of a common factor to many of the data sets used in the experiments on regression and model trees: no general behavior was noted for the underlying function to be approximated, and it can be better represented as a composition of many definite local behaviors.

4.2 Experiments on Artificial Data Sets

SMOTI was also tested on artificial data sets randomly generated for seven different model trees. These model trees were automatically built for learning problems with nine independent variables (five continuous and four discrete), where continuous variables take values in the unit interval [0,1], while discrete variables take values in the set {A,B,C,D,E,F,G}. The model tree building procedure is recursively defined on the maximum depth of the tree to be generated. The choice of adding a regression or a split node is random and depends on a parameter $\theta \in [0,100]$: the probability of selecting a split node is $\theta\%$; conversely, the probability of selecting a regression node is $(100-\theta)\%$. Therefore, the returned model trees have a variable number of regression/split nodes and leaves, while the depth of the tree is kept under control. In the experiments reported in this paper θ is fixed to 0.5, while the depth is set to 5.

Ten data points are randomly generated for each leaf, so that the size of the data set associated with a model tree depends on the number of leaves in the tree itself. Data points are generated according to the different multiple linear models associated with the leaves. The error added to each model is distributed normally, with zero mean and variance σ^2, which is kept constant for all leaves. The value of σ^2 set for the experimentation is 0.001, which means that for almost 90% of generated data points the effect of the error is ±0.095, according to Chebyshev's inequality. It is noteworthy that the effect of the error is not marginal, given that both independent variables and their coefficients range in the unit interval.

Each dataset was analyzed by means of a 10-fold cross-validation. In order to study the effect of the weight, two different values were considered: $w=0.5$ and $w=0.55$. Experimental results are reported in Table 2. The number of leaves of the original model trees (T. #leaves) is compared to the corresponding property of the induced tree (denoted by the initial I).The last three columns list the average mean square error reported by SMOTI and M5´. Results show that SMOTI over-partitions the feature space, since the number of leaves in the induced trees is always greater than the number of leaves in the theoretical model tree. This is true even in the case of $w=0.5$. Interestingly, in many cases SMOTI outperforms M5´ with respect to average MSE.

Table 2. Results for the model tree built with parameters θ=0.5, depth=5, and σ^2=0.001.

T. depth	T. # leaves	I. # leaves w=0.5	I. # leaves w=0.55	Av. MSE SMOTI w=0.5	Av. MSE SMOTI w=0.55	Av. MSE. M5'
5	5	7	9	0.24	0.61	0.35
5	7	10	10	0.2	0.15	0.36
5	8	11	12	0.19	0.17	0.3
5	6	10	10	0.53	0.32	0.27
5	8	12	10	0.56	0.68	0.24
5	1	1	1	0.16	0.16	0.29
5	6	17	18	0.15	0.16	0.25

Results on a more extensive experimentation are reported in Table 3. They are obtained by keeping θ=0.5, σ^2=0.001, and by varying both the number of training cases per leaf (10, 20, 30 items) and the depth of the tree (5,6,7). Three main conclusions can be drawn from Table 4: first, SMOTI performs better than M5′ when split nodes are slightly preferred to regression nodes, that is, local decisions are favored; second, by increasing the number of training cases per leaf, no difference is observed in the trading-off between local and global effects[2]; third, the depth of the tree has no clear effect on the predictive accuracy of the induced model tree.

Table 3. Results of the Wilcoxon signed rank test on the accuracy of the induced model tree built with parameters θ=0.5 and σ^2=0.001. The best value is in boldface, while the statistically significant values ($p \le \alpha/2$) are in italics.

Data set	Depth	M5' vs. SMOTI (w=0.5)			M5' vs. SMOTI (w=0.55)		
		P	*W+*	*W-*	*p*	*W+*	*W-*
10 items per leaf	5	0.937	15	**13**	1	14	14
	6	0.46	9	19	0.937	**13**	15
	7	*0.078*	*3*	25	1	14	14
20 items per leaf	5	*0.047*	*2*	26	0.6875	17	**11**
	6	*0.047*	*2*	26	*0.07812*	25	*3*
	7	0.93	**13**	15	0.2969	21	**7**
30 items per leaf	5	1	14	14	0.375	20	**8**
	6	0.218	**6**	22	0.5781	18	**10**
	7	0.687	**11**	17	*0.0312*	27	*1*

5 Conclusions

In the paper, a novel method, called SMOTI, has been presented. The main advantage of SMOTI is that it efficiently generates model trees with multiple regression models in the leaves. Model trees generated by SMOTI include two types of nodes: regression nodes and split node. A weight associated to the type of node permits the user to express a preference for either local regression or global regression.

Experimental results on UCI data sets proved that in most of them, local effects of regression variables are preferred. An empirical comparison with M5′ on artificial data sets proved that SMOTI could induce more accurate model trees when both global and local behaviors are mixed up in the underlying model. In the future, we plan to investigate the effect of pruning model trees. To date, no study on the simplification techniques for model trees has been presented in the literature. There are several possible approaches, some based on the direct control of tree size, and others based on the extension of the set of tests considered. Both a theoretical and an empirical evaluation of these approaches in terms of accuracy and interpretability would be helpful in practical applications.

---

[2] In a personal communication, Tom Mitchell hypothesized that the importance of taking into account "global" effects might vanish with larger training sets. This hypothesis is not evident in our results.

Acknowledgments. This work is part of the MURST COFIN-1999 project on "Statistical Models for Classification and Segmentation of Complex Data Structures: Methodologies, Software and Applications." The authors thank Valentina Tamma and Domenico Pallotta for their collaboration and Tom Mitchell for his valuable comments on a preliminary version of this paper.

References

1. Breiman L., Friedman J., Olshen R., & Stone J.: *Classification and regression tree*, Wadsworth & Brooks, 1984.
2. Ciampi A.: Generalized regression trees, *Computational Statistics and Data Analysis*, 12, pp. 57-78, 1991.
3. Draper N.R., & Smith H.: *Applied regression analysis*, John Wiley & Sons, 1982.
4. Karalic A.: Linear regression in regression tree leaves, in *Proceedings of ISSEK '92 (International School for Synthesis of Expert Knowledge)*, Bled, Slovenia, 1992.
5. Lubinsky D.: Tree Structured Interpretable Regression, in *Learning from Data*, Fisher D. & Lenz H.J. (Eds.), Lecture Notes in Statistics, 112, Springer, pp. 387-398, 1994.
6. Malerba D., Appice A., Bellino A., Ceci M., & Pallotta D.: Stepwise Induction of Model Trees. In F. Esposito (Ed.), *AI*IA 2001: Advances in Artificial Intelligence*, Lecture Notes in Artificial Intelligence,2175, Springer, Berlin, Germany, pp. 20-32, 2001.
7. Morgan J.N., & Sonquist J.A.: Problems in the analysis of survey data, and a proposal, in *American Statistical Association Journal*, pp. 415-434, 1963.
8. Orkin, M., Drogin, R.: *Vital Statistics*, McGraw Hill, New York (1990).
9. Quinlan J. R.: Learning with continuous classes, in Proceedings AI'92, Adams & Sterling (Eds.), World Scientific, pp. 343-348, 1992.
10. Siciliano R., & Mola F.: Modelling for recursive partitioning in variable selection, in *COMPSTAT '94*, Dutter R., & Grossman W. (Eds.), Physica-Verlag, pp. 172-177, 1994.
11. Torgo L.: Kernel Regression Trees, in *Poster Papers of the 9th European Conference on Machine Learning (ECML 97)*, M. van Someren, & G. Widmer (Eds.), Prague, Czech Republic, pp. 118-127, 1997.
12. Torgo L.: Functional Models for Regression Tree Leaves, in *Proceedings of the Fourteenth International Conference (ICML '97)*, D. Fisher (Ed.), Nashville, Tennessee, pp. 385-393, 1997.
13. Wang Y., & Witten I.H.: Inducing Model Trees for Continuous Classes, in *Poster Papers of the 9th European Conference on Machine Learning (ECML 97)*, M. van Someren, & G. Widmer (Eds.), Prague, Czech Republic, pp. 128-137, 1997.

An Efficient Intelligent Agent System for Automated Recommendation in Electronic Commerce

Byungyeon Hwang[1], Euichan Kim[1], and Bogju Lee[2]

[1] Dept. of Computer Engineering, The Catholic University of Korea
43-1 Yokkok 2-dong, Wonmi-gu, Puchon City, Kyonggi-do
420-743, Korea
byhwang@catholic.ac.kr, eckim@songsim.cuk.ac.kr
[2] Dept. of Computer Engineering, Dankook University
Hannam-dong, Yongsan-gu, Seoul, 140-714, Korea
blee@dankook.ac.kr

Abstract. Recently, many solutions and sites related to the intelligent agent are created in order to provide good services for customers. Moreover, some new proposals including the collaborative filtering are put forward in the field of electronic commerce (EC) solutions. However, these proposals are lack of the add-on characteristics. In fact, it seems that only a few intelligent systems could provide the recommendations to the customers for the items that they really want to purchase, by means of the collaborative filtering algorithm based on their previous evaluation data. In this paper, we propose the CLASG (Clustering And Similarity Grouplens) collaborative filtering agent algorithm. The CLASG algorithm is the one that uses both the GroupLens algorithm and the clustering method. We have evaluated its performance with enough experiments, and the results show that the proposed method provides more stable recommendations than GroupLens does. We developed the MindReader, which makes it possible to have the correct predictions and recommendations with less response time than ever, as an automated recommendation system that includes both of CLASG algorithm and WhoLiked agent. It can be readily integrated into the existing EC solutions since it has an add-on characteristic, which is lacked in the past solutions.

1 Introduction

Internet provides good environments for the commercial transactions such as Electronic Commerce (EC). Most EC sellers are conscious of the necessities of turning the internet visitors into buyers, maximizing the chances of purchases per each visitor, and maintaining the relationships with the visitors for a long time[1, 2, 3]. For the past few years, the necessities of turning the traditional commerce into EC and the following effects have been the issues. These days, there are many successful EC solutions and EC web sites, and so the issues are changed to the competitions in EC. Also, most recent solutions provide good services and make more profits[4, 5, 6].

M.-S. Hacid et al. (Eds.): ISMIS 2002, LNAI 2366, pp. 403-411, 2002.
© Springer-Verlag Berlin Heidelberg 2002

The site, Amazon, provides 'Who bought[7]' service and automated recommendation service. When a user search a book, 'Who bought' service shows the bestseller among the buyers who bought the searched book. Automated recommendation service recommends the books based on buyers' evaluations. EC sites that have the item recommendation functions, using intelligent agents, are successful. However, most sites do not use collaborative filtering algorithm. These sites use only the rule based matching, which is the old style in the automated recommendations. For example, the site (Aladdin.co.kr) has 'Who bought' function, but not the ones that recommend the suitable items according to the buyers' evaluation history that reflects the preferences and satisfactions.

Now, more sellers require real collaborative filtering agent systems. It is likely that the intelligent agent system which has both the collaborative filtering function and 'Who bought' would become successful. Collaborative filtering agent systems need the following two conditions to be the specialized collaborative filtering agents and add-on systems[8]. First, the systems should have better performance than other products (ex. NetPerception), to be marketable. Second, the systems should be the package type and connected with the major EC platforms (ex. COM, EJB, CORBA). These requirements make collaborative filtering agent systems to be the add-on systems, which could work with the existing EC solutions and sites.

In this paper, we propose the CLASG (CLustering And Similarity Grouplens) collaborative filtering agent algorithm. The CLASG algorithm is the one that uses both the GroupLens algorithm and the clustering method[9, 10, 11]. We have evaluated the performances with a number of experiments. Also, we propose the MindReader system, a collaborative filtering agent system, that uses the CLASG algorithm proposed in this paper. It also uses CORBA to have a distributed structure[12], to get expandability, and to be an add-on product. In addition, it has the component-based structure so that it could provide the recommendations quickly and suitably.

This paper is organized as follows. Section 2 describes GroupLens. Section 3 proposes CLASG algorithm and shows the performance evaluations in comparison with the GroupLens algorithm. Section 4 explains MindReader system. Finally, section 5 is the conclusion and future works.

2   GroupLens

GroupLens[13, 14] was made for individualized recommendations in Netnews. GroupLens stores user profile in a server with the numerical evaluation results. GroupLens has two ways of evaluations. One is the evaluation by the users, and the other is the estimation by the similarity with other users' profiles.

The rating database records the user's reaction after watching a movie. Table 1 shows the results. The empty cell shows that the user did not yet watch the movie. The question mark, ?, means that the user has watched the movie, but not yet evaluated it. GroupLens gets the value of evaluation for the movie Cube, which Sam has not yet evaluated, with the use of Pearson correlation coefficient, which ranges from -1 to 1. The correlation coefficients of Sam with others are: 0.57 with David, 0.74 with Mary,

0.12 with Mark, and –0.85 with Annie. With those values, we may get the predicted value of the evaluation that Sam would mark for the movie, Cube. We may get the value of 2.5 by the formula from [15, 16]. We may get the values for other question marks, ?.

Table 1. Evaluation about items of each user

		Movies					
		Titanic	Matrix	Hall	Mask	Jurassic	Cube
Users	David	5	3	1	4	4	4
	Mary	3	5	2	3	5	3
	Mark	2	4			3	2
	Annie	4	4		1	2	5
	Sam	3	3	2		5	?

We need enough data, user evaluations, to estimate each user's value by GroupLens. Less evaluation data would produce poor predictions. Therefore, GroupLens requires users certain amount of tasks. GroupLens does the predictions through the calculations of the correlation coefficients between a user and the others for an item, but the CLASG algorithm of this paper groups the users by their similarities, chooses N most-similar users from the group in which the given user is included, and then gets the correlation coefficients between the given user and the N users so as to predict and recommend for the given item. GroupLens did not experiment on the correctness of the prediction score. So, we tested the correctness of GroupLens, in addition to comparing it with the CLASG algorithm proposed in this paper.

3   Improved Collaborative Filtering Agent

3.1   CLASG Algorithm

In this study, CLASG algorithm was proposed to improve the accuracy of the recommendations as follows:

Step 1) Initialize mincost to infinity and i to 1. Set numlocal and maxneighbor by inputs. The numlocal is the number of choosing k representative users randomly and the maxneighbor is the max number of comparisons to find out the neighbor node that has the lowest exchange cost to the k random representative users.

Step 2) Choose k random representatives out of all the users and set these as a current node.

Step 3) Initialize j to 1.

Step 4) Select the neighbor of a given node, which is composed of k random representative users. For a given node, its neighbor is another node that has only one different user from it.

Step 5) Calculate the cost for the exchange of the current node and its neighbor. If the cost is negative, replace the current node with its neighbor and go to Step 3.

Step 6) If (j++ < maxneighbor) then go to Step 4.

Step 7) If (cost of the current node < mincost) then mincost := cost of the current node. The 'cost of the current node' is the cost to create k clusters by putting the objects that are neither the representative of the current node nor chosen to the nearest representative ones.

Step 8) If (i++ < numlocal) then go to Step 2.

Step 9) Choose N most-similar users from the cluster of the given user.

Step 10) Calculate the estimated evaluation value for the item of the given user by the Pearson correlation coefficient for the N users and the evaluation formula and then recommend by the value.

3.2 Performance Evaluation

We experimented on CALSG algorithm with the data set, which U.S. Digital Company provided us, and which the company collected for the recommendation service of EachMovie. We evaluated the performance by comparing the correctness of CLASG algorithm with that of GroupLens algorithm.

The data set is divided in terms of the number of movies evaluated by user into five user groups, and the number of items evaluated by optional users is set about one fifth for each of the five groups. The user group, u1, has less than 10 items (12958 people); u2, 20 items (11649 people); u3, 40 items (14664 people); u4, 80 items (11974 people); and u5 has more than 80 items (10020 people). On the same way, movie group, m1, has less than 50 people (322 items); m2, 200 people (360 items); m3, 650 people (324 items); m4, 1900 people (313 items); and m5 has more than 1900 people (304 items).

1) Experiment on GroupLens algorithm
GroupLens algorithm selects 100 user/item pairs at random. Then, we compute the error rate of the pairs. We estimated an appraised value without the real value, which the user evaluated, and compared it with the real value. We got error rates in this way. The error rates of each group by GroupLens algorithm are shown in Fig. 1 (a). It has taken 7158 seconds to recommend total 2500 user/item pairs (25 groups × 100 pairs). The average of the error rates is 1.15284, and the standard deviation of the error rates is 0.2889.

2) Experiment on CLASG algorithm
We clustered with k (an integer) medoids, which are computed by CLARANS algorithm. We computed five medoids. We then assigned the rest users to the most similar medoid. To get the appraised value of a user, we picked up the most similar n users who belong to the same cluster as the user after comparing with the medoid of the cluster. We could get the appraised value by the relationship between the user and the n users. The error rates of each group by CLASG algorithm are shown in Fig. 1 (b).

These error rates are much lower than those of Fig. 1 (a). It took 1045 seconds for CLASG to recommend; the error rates were averaged as 0.51772; and the standard deviation of the error rates was 0.11902.

These two graphs tell that CLASG algorithm in this paper has better performance.

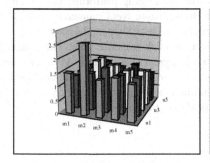 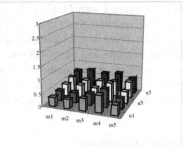

Fig. 1. (a) The error rate graph of GroupLens algorithm by group is left. (b) The error rate graph of CLASG algorithm by group is right

We summarized the results in Table 2. The average error rate of CLASG algorithm is lower than that of GroupLens algorithm as much as 0.63512. Also, the standard deviation is lower as much as 0.16988. Moreover, CLASG finished 6104 seconds earlier.

Table 2. Experiment results

	Average error rate	Error rate standard deviation	Runtime (second)
GroupLens	1.15284	0.2889	7158
CLASG	0.51772	0.11902	1045

4 MindReader System

4.1 System Functions and Characteristics

MindReader system grasps visitor's taste and recommends suitable items. It is composed of the collaborative filtering engine and the WhoLiked engine. At first, the collaborative filtering engine recommends suitable items dynamically based on each visitor's purchasing history, evaluation information, and behaviors. This helps to estimate each user's taste. Also, it can recommend items in a specific category. If a user selects an item and other customers favored the same item, WhoLiked engine recommends other most favorite items of them. It can also recommend other related items such as other books written by the same author, or other goods produced by the same company.

Followings are the characteristics of the system. First, exact and quick estimations and recommendations, which are made possible by the advanced collaborative filtering algorithm. Second, easy integrations with the leading platforms. For example, it could be integrated with One-To-One of BroadVision, Net.Commerce of IBM, Site Server of Microsoft, ICS of Oracle, I-Commerce of InterShop, and Commerce21 of E-Net, and etc. Third, a great extensibility and a quick response time: The system has distributed structure and uses CORBA, so it has great extensibility. Also, it responses quickly regardless of the number of users at one moment. Fourth, easy and quick implementations, and fast outcomes: We can implement easily and quickly, and add the system to the existing system. Thus, we could save time and expenses.

4.2 System Architecture

MindReader system has open architecture, using CORBA and DB Middleware for add-on function. Owing to CORBA, it has the distributed structure and the extensibility. Server is coded with C++. It is easy to integrate the system with other ones because the system uses the middleware such as Orbix and Roguewave. It is also easy to modify or add new modules because of the object broker. If we develop CORBA based object server modules with the share library, objects will be loaded automatically when the CORBA server starts up.

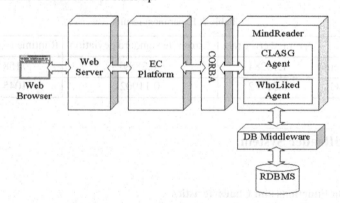

Fig. 2. MindReader System Architecture

4.3 Modules

There are two modules: the main engine module, Fig. 3, and the data processing engine module, Fig. 4.

The main engine module has the collaborative filtering engine and WhoLiked engine. We can divide the collaborative filtering engine into Predictor part and Recommender part. Predictor part evaluates the likeability of a specific user for a specific item. Recommender part recommends suitable items to users. When a user chooses an item, WhoLiked engine can recommend other items related with it.

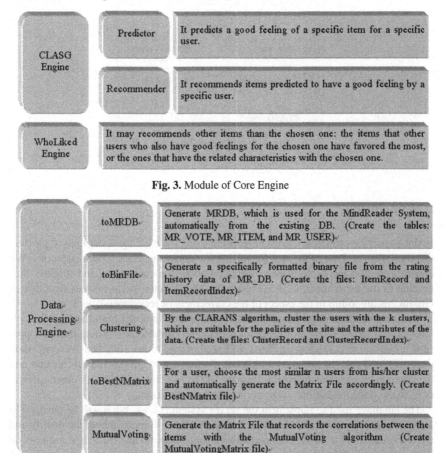

Fig. 3. Module of Core Engine

Fig. 4. Module of Data Processing Engine

Data processing engine has five modules: toMRDB, toBinFile, Clustering, toBestNMatrix, and MutualVoting. toMRDB module creates MR_DB for MindReader system automatically in a regular DBMS. toBinFile module creates a binary file, having a specific format, with evaluation data, which are in MR_DB. Clustering module clusters users with k clusters, which suit with the site policies or the data attributes, by the CLARANS algorithm. toBestNMatrix module picks up the most similar Best N users of each user, and makes Matrix file automatically. MutualVoting module finds the relationships between items with the MutualVoting algorithm and writes on a new Matrix file. Fig. 5 is the flow chart of modules in MindReader system.

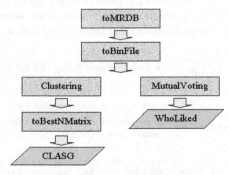

Fig. 5. Flow Chart of Modules

5 Conclusion

In this paper, we proposed CLASG algorithm using the existing GroupLens algorithm, the similarity, and the clustering for raising the correctness of recommendations. We experimented on the performance evaluation about the correctness and runtime. According to the experiment, CLASG algorithm shows better performances than that of GroupLens algorithm in the aspect of the correctness of recommendations.

Next, we developed the MindReader system which includes both the CLASG collaborative filtering agent and the WhoLiked agent. MindReader system makes it possible to have the correct predictions and recommendations with less response time than ever, and easy integrations with other platforms through the add-on function and the component-based architecture. Because of the easy integration with other applications in the implementations stage, we may reduce the costs.

The language used to implement the server system is C++, but it will be changed to Java so that the system could be integrated well. We will improve both the quality and the response time for the recommendations through continuous researches and tests on the intelligent collaborative filtering agent algorithm. Also, to improve the quality of the recommendations, we will collect actions of users, and continue the study of weighting value allowances for each action.

References

1. Ma, M.: Agents in E-Commerce. Communications of the ACM, Vol. 42, No. 3 (1999) 79-80
2. Maes, P., Guttman, R., Moukas, A.G.: Agents That Buy and Sell. Communications of the ACM, Vol. 42, No. 3 (1999) 81-91

3. Lee, R.S.T., Liu, J.N.K.: iJADE eMiner – A Web-Based Mining Agent Based on Intelligent Java Agent Development Environment (iJADE) on Internet Shopping. In Proceedings of the fifth Pacific-Asia Conference on Knowledge Discovery and Data Mining, Hong Kong, China (2001) 28-40
4. Maes, P.: Agent that Reduce Work and Information Overload. Communications of the ACM, Vol. 37, No. 7 (1994) 30-40
5. Oracle, Oracle iMarketing Release 3i, http://www.oracle.com
6. Schafer, J.B., Konstan, J., Riedl, J.: Recommender Systems in E-Commerce. In Proceedings of the ACM Conference on Electronic Commerce, November 3-5 (1999) 158-166
7. Mirkin, B.: Mathematical Classification and Clustering. Kluwer Academic Publisher (1996) 428
8. Bassett, J.K., Jong, K.A.D.: Evolving Behaviors for Cooperating Agents. In Proceedings of 12th International Symposium on Methodologies for Intelligent Systems, Charlotte, NC, USA (2000) 157-165
9. Kaufman, L., Rousseeuw, P.: Finding Groups in Data : an Introduction to Cluster Analysis. Wiley Series in Probability and Mathematical Statistics (1990) 342
10. Resnic, P., Iacocou, N., Sushak, M., Bergstrom, P., Riedl, J.: GroupLens : An Open Architecture for Collaborative Filtering of Netnews. In Proceedings of the Computer Supported Collaborative Work Conference (1994)
11. O'Conner, M., Herlocker, J.: Clustering items for Collaborative Filtering. In Proceedings of the ACM SIGIR Workshop on Recommender Systems, Berkeley, CA, USA (1999)
12. Tanaka, K., Higashiyama, M., Ohsuga, S.: Problem Decomposition and Multiagent System Creation for Distributed Problem Solving. In Proceedings of 12th International Symposium on Methodologies for Intelligent Systems, Charlotte, NC, USA (2000) 237-246
13. Konstan, J., Miller, B., Maltz, D., Herlocker, J., Gordon, L., Riedl, J.: GroupLens : Applying Collaborative Filtering to Usenet News. Communications of the ACM, Vol. 40, No. 3 (1997) 77-87
14. Lyengar, V.S., Zhang, T.: Empirical Study of Recommender Systems Using Linear Classifiers. In Proceedings of the fifth Pacific-Asia Conference on Knowledge Discovery and Data Mining, Hong Kong, China (2001) 16-27
15. Herlocker, J., Konstan, J., Borchers, A., Riedl, J.: An Algorithmic Framework for Performing Collaborative Filtering. In Proceedings of the Conference on Research and Development in Information Retrieval (1999) 230-237
16. Chee, S.H.S., Han, J., Wang, K.: RecTree: An Efficient Collaborative Filtering Method. In Proceeding of the Conference on Data Warehouse and Knowledge Discovery, Munich, Germany (2001) 141-151

Matching an XML Document against a Set of DTDs

Elisa Bertino[1], Giovanna Guerrini[2], and Marco Mesiti[2]

[1] Dipartimento di Scienze dell'Informazione
Università degli Studi di Milano, Italy
bertino@dsi.unimi.it
[2] Dipartimento di Informatica e Scienze dell'Informazione
Università degli Studi di Genova, Italy
{guerrini,mesiti}@disi.unige.it

Abstract. *Sources of XML documents are proliferating on the Web and documents are more and more frequently exchanged among sources. At the same time, there is an increasing need of exploiting database tools to manage this kind of data. An important novelty of XML is that information on document structures is available on the Web together with the document contents. However, in such an heterogeneous environment as the Web, it is not reasonable to assume that XML documents that enter a source always conform to a predefined DTD in the source. In this paper we address the problem of document classification by proposing a metric for quantifying the structural similarity between an XML document and a DTD. Based on such notion, we propose an approach to match a document entering a source against the set of DTDs available in the source, determining whether a DTD exists similar enough to the document.*

1 Introduction

XML [10] has recently emerged as the most relevant standardization effort for document representation and exchange on the Web. It offers the possibility of defining tags and modeling nested document structures. XML documents, thanks to semantic tags, are self-describing. Thus, with the advent of XML, information on document structures (provided through the tags embedded in a document) are available on the Web. These information can obviously be used in order to improve document retrieval. XML also offers the possibility of defining document types (called DTDs -*Document Type Definitions*) that describe the structure of documents. An XML DTD essentially is a grammar constraining the tags and the structure of a document. A document whose structure conforms to a DTD is called *valid* in XML terminology. Obviously, the presence of a DTD allows one to take advantage of the knowledge about document structures for storing, querying, and indexing a set of documents.

In such an heterogeneous and flexible environment as the Web, however, we cannot assume that documents related to the same topic, that is, "talking of the same things", exactly have the same structure. Thus, we cannot fix a certain set

M.-S. Hacid et al. (Eds.): ISMIS 2002, LNAI 2366, pp. 412–422, 2002.
© Springer-Verlag Berlin Heidelberg 2002

of predefined DTDs and then only handle XML documents that are valid for a DTD in that set. Similarly, if we aim at developing an XML-based search engine capable of extracting from the Web those (portions of) documents dealing with given semantic structural properties, and we express the user query as a DTD, we cannot retrieve only the documents valid for that DTD.

We thus address the problem of matching documents against a set of DTDs even when such documents do not fully conform to any DTD in such set. Specifically, we allow some attributes and subelements specified for an element in the DTD to be missing in the corresponding element of the document, and, viceversa, we allow the document to contain some additional attributes and subelements not appearing in the DTD. Moreover, we allow elements/attributes in the document to follow a different order w.r.t. the one specified in the DTD (i.e. we are focusing on data-centric documents). Finally, document and DTD tags could not be exactly the same, provided they are *stems* or are similar enough according to a given Thesaurus. In matching a document against a DTD the goal is then to quantify, through an appropriate measure, the structural similarity between the document and the DTD.

The scenario we refer to consists of a number of heterogeneous sources of XML documents able to exchange documents among each other. Each source stores and indexes the local documents according to a set of local DTDs. An XML document entering a source is matched against the DTDs in the source. If a DTD exists in the source to which the document conforms according to the usual notion, then the document is accepted as valid for this DTD. Otherwise, the proposed metric is used for selecting the DTD, among the ones in the source, that best describes the document structure.

The matching process is performed against a tree representation of both documents and DTDs. This representation can be easily obtained from their declarations. Though our technique handles all the features of XML documents, in the paper we will focus on the most meaningful *core* of the approach, thus we restrict ourselves to a subset of XML documents and to tag equality. We will only briefly sketch how the approach generalizes to arbitrary XML documents and how tag similarity is handled, and we refer the interested reader to [2] for the treatment of the general case.

Our proposal is, to the best of our knowledge, the first one addressing the issue of measuring the structural similarity of XML documents and DTDs, and it has relevant potential applications for structural clustering of documents and for document retrieval based on conditions on the document structure. Our work benefits from previous work developed in the context of automatic object classification [1] and of heterogeneous information integration (both at the data [6] and at the schema [3] levels).

The remainder of the paper is structured as follows. Section 2 presents our tree representation of XML documents and DTDs. Section 3 presents the similarity measure and the matching process. Finally, Section 4 concludes the work, by discussing extensions and applicability of the proposed technique.

```
<product>                                  <!DOCTYPE product [
  <name>Deliver</name>                       <!ELEMENT product(name,urls+,description,
  <urls>                                                    (author*|vendor),version?)>
    <download>                               <!ELEMENT name (#PCDATA)>
      http://.../deliver.tgz                 <!ELEMENT urls(download*, homepage)>
    </download>                              <!ELEMENT description ANY>
    <homepage>                               <!ELEMENT author (fName, mName?, lName)>
      http://.../index.html                  <!ELEMENT vendor (#PCDATA)>
    </homepage>                              <!ELEMENT version (#PCDATA)>
  </urls>                                    <!ELEMENT download (#PCDATA)>
  <description>Mail... </description>        <!ELEMENT homepage (#PCDATA)>
  <author>                                   <!ELEMENT fName (#PCDATA)>
    <fName>Chip</fName>                       <!ELEMENT mName (#PCDATA)>
    <lName>Salzenberg</lName>                 <!ELEMENT lName (#PCDATA)>
  </author>                                  ]>
  <version>2.1.13</version>
</product>

            (a)                                          (b)
```

Fig. 1. An example of document and DTD

2 Documents and DTDs as Trees

Fig. 1(a) shows an example of XML document describing software products whereas Fig. 1(b) shows a possible corresponding DTD. The example shows that, in a DTD, for each subelement it is possible to specify whether it is optional ('?'), whether it may occur several times ('*' or '+' with the usual meaning), and whether some subelements are alternative with respect to each other ('|'). As we have anticipated in the introduction, we will focus on a subset of XML documents. In particular, we will only consider elements (that can have a nested structure) disregarding attributes (that can be seen as a particular case of elements). Since we disregard attributes, we will only consider nonempty elements. Moreover, since we focus on data-centric documents, we disregard the order of subelements. In the matching process, we represent both DTDs and XML documents through labeled trees. The document representation is compliant wit the tree representation of DOM [9]. By contrast, the representation of DTDs we adopt facilitates the description of the algorithms we propose. In this section we discuss this representation.

2.1 Tree Representation of Documents

An XML document is represented as a labeled tree. Our representation is based on the classical definition of labeled tree.[1] In our representation of documents each node represents an element or a value. The label associated with a node represents the corresponding tag name or value. The labels used to label the tree belong to a set of element tags $(\mathcal{EN})$ and to a set of values that the data content of an element can assume $(\mathcal{V})$. In each tree that represents an XML document the

---

[1] Given a set $\mathcal{N}$ of nodes, a tree is defined by induction as follows: $v \in \mathcal{N}$ is a tree; if $T_1, \ldots, T_n$ are trees, then $(v, [T_1, \ldots, T_n])$ is a tree. A label is then associated with each node of the tree from a set $\mathcal{A}$ of labels.

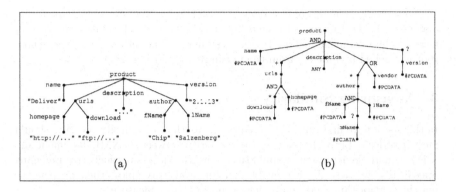

Fig. 2. Tree representations of a document and a DTD

root label belongs to $\mathcal{EN}$ (it is the document element name). Moreover, all nodes labeled by values in $\mathcal{V}$ are tree leaves. Fig. 2(a) shows the tree representation of the XML document of Fig. 1(a).[2]

2.2   Tree Representation of DTDs

A DTD is also represented as a labeled tree. In the tree representation, in order to represent optional elements, repeatable elements, and alternative of elements, the set of operators $\mathcal{OP} = \{$AND, OR, ?, $*\}$ is introduced. The AND operator represents a sequence of elements, the OR operator represents an alternative of elements, the ? operator represents an optional element, and the $*$ operator represents repeatable elements (0 or more times). We remark that there is no need to introduce the + operator because an element type declaration like <!ELEMENT a (b)+> can be replaced by the equivalent one <!ELEMENT a (b,b*)>.

In our representation of DTDs each node corresponds to an element tag, to an element type, or to an operator. In each tree that represents a DTD there is a single edge outgoing from the root, and the root label belongs to $\mathcal{EN}$ (it is the name of the main element of documents described by the DTD). Moreover, there can be more than one edge outgoing from a node, only if the node is labeled by AND or OR. Finally, all nodes labeled by types are leaves of the tree. Fig. 2(b) shows the tree representation of the **product** DTD of Fig. 1(b).

We remark that the introduction of operators $\mathcal{OP} = \{$AND, OR, ?, $*$, $+\}$ allows us to represent the structure of all kinds of DTDs. The introduction of the AND operator is required in order to distinguish between an element containing an alternative between sequences (e.g. <!ELEMENT a(b|(c1,c2))>) and an element containing the alternative between all the elements in the sequence (e.g. <!ELEMENT a(b|c1|c2)>).

---

[2] Explicit direction of edges is omitted. All edges are oriented downward.

Note finally that not only a document/DTD is a tree, but any element of a document/DTD is a tree, subtree of the document/DTD. For instance, element name of the document in Fig. 1(a) corresponds to the leftmost subtree, whose root is reached by an edge from the product node in Fig. 2(a).

3   Measuring Similarity

In this section we first outline the requirements that a similarity measure should meet in order to properly evaluate the similarity between an XML document and a DTD, and then present a similarity measure addressing such requirements. Specifically, we describe the evaluation function we employ, then present the matching algorithm, and finally define the similarity measure.

3.1   Requirements for a Similarity Measure

We briefly introduce the requirements for a metric to measure the structural similarity between a document and a DTD.

Common, Plus, and Minus Elements. The similarity measure should consider: elements appearing both in the document and in the DTD, referred to as *common* elements; elements appearing in the document but not in the DTD, referred to as *plus* elements; elements appearing in the DTD but not in the document, referred to as *minus* elements. Obviously, to achieve the best similarity, plus and minus elements should be minimized and common elements should be maximized.

Repeatable Elements. There can be many ways in which a document can be matched against a DTD. Because of alternative and repeatable elements, indeed, a DTD describes different possible document structures. When matching a document against a DTD, a structure, among those possible structures, must be identified, that is the most adequate for the document. In case of repeatable elements, the similarity measure must identify the best number of repetitions, that is, the one that maximizes common elements and minimizes plus and minus elements. Note that an higher number of repetitions can allow every element in the document to match with an element in the DTD (no plus) but can increase the number of unmatched elements in the DTD (minus).

Level of an Element. Elements in a document are not all "equivalent": elements at higher levels in the document structure are more relevant than subelements deeply nested in the document structure. The similarity measure should catch the intuition that the elements at a higher level in a document are more relevant than the elements at a lower level.

We thus introduce the notion of level of an element, related to the depth of the corresponding tree. Given a tree T in a tree representing a document, the level of T is its depth as a tree, that is, the number of nodes along the longest maximal path (that is, a path from the root to a leaf) in T. By contrast, given a tree T in a tree representing a DTD, its level is the number of nodes, not labeled by an operator, along the longest maximal path in T. Nodes labeled by operators in DTD trees, indeed, only influences the breadth of the corresponding document trees, not their depths. In the following, given a tree T, $label(T)$ denotes the label of the root of T.

Definition 1. *(Function Level). Let $T = (v, [T_1, \ldots, T_n])$ be a subtree of a document or a DTD. Function Level is defined as follows:*

$$Level(T) = \begin{cases} 1 + max_{i=1}^n Level(T_i) & \text{if } label(T) \in \mathcal{EN} \\ max_{i=1}^n Level(T_i) & \text{if } label(T) \in \mathcal{OP} \\ 0 & \text{otherwise} \end{cases} \qquad \square$$

Example 1. Let T denote the tree of Fig. 2(b), then $Level(T) = 3$. $\qquad \bigcirc$

Now we can assign a different weight to elements at different levels of the tree. Let $l = Level(T)$ be the level of a document/DTD tree T, the root of T will have weight γ^l, and the weight is then divided by γ when going down a level. Thus, γ^{l-i} is the weight of a generic level i of T. $\gamma \in \mathbb{N}$ is a parameter of our technique, that allows one to specify the relevance of information at higher levels in the document with respect to information at lower levels. By taking $\gamma = 1$ all the information are considered equally relevant, and thus the fact that elements appear at different levels in the nested structure is not taken into account. In what follows, we will consider $\gamma = 2$. In this way, the relevance of each node is double than the relevance of its children.

Weight of an Element. The similarity measure should also take into account the fact that an element with a more complex structure can appear in the document when a simple data element is declared in the DTD, or that, by contrast, the element in a document can have a structure simpler than the one specified for the corresponding element in the DTD.

The similarity measure should consider the structure of plus and minus elements. In case of minus elements, however, the structure is not fixed. Our idea is to consider, as structure of the minus elements, the simplest structure associated with that portion of DTD. Thus, the measure should not take into account optional or repeatable elements and, in case of alternative, the measure should take into account only one of the alternative elements (the one with the simplest structure).

We thus introduce function $\mathcal{W}eight$ to evaluate a subtree of a document or of a DTD. This function is used to measure the "unmatched" components (plus and minus) in the matching process. Given a subtree of the document and a weight w, function $\mathcal{W}eight$ multiplies the number of elements in each level for the weight associated with the level. The resulting values are then summed. Given a subtree of the DTD and a weight w, function $\mathcal{W}eight$ works as on a document, but it takes into account only mandatory elements in the DTD. That is, the function does not consider optional elements or repeatable elements. Moreover, in case of OR labeled nodes, the weights associated with the possible alternatives are evaluated and the minimal value is chosen. The choice of the minimal value corresponds to select the subtree with the simplest structure.

Definition 2. *(Function $\mathcal{W}eight$). Let T be a subtree of a document or a DTD, and w_l be the weight associated with the level of T in D. Function $\mathcal{W}eight$ is defined as follows:*

$$Weight(T, w_l) = \begin{cases} w_l & \text{if } label(T) \in \mathcal{V} \cup \mathcal{ET} \\ 0 & \text{if } label(T) \in \{*, ?\} \\ \sum_{i=1}^{n} Weight(T_i, w_l) & \text{if } label(T) = \text{AND}, \ T = (v, [T_1, \dots, T_n]) \\ min_{i=1}^{n} Weight(T_i, w_l) & \text{if } label(T) = \text{OR}, \ T = (v, [T_1, \dots, T_n]) \\ \sum_{i=1}^{n} Weight(T_i, \frac{w_l}{\gamma}) + w_l & \text{otherwise, where } T = (v, [T_1, \dots, T_n]) \end{cases}$$

□

Example 2. Let T denote the tree of Fig. 2(b), recall that we consider $\gamma = 2$, $Weight(T, 8) = 20$. Note that, in this example, the level weight 8 is 2^3, where 3 is the number of levels of the DTD.   ○

3.2   Evaluation Function

Having outlined the requirements of the similarity measure, we introduce an evaluation function that allows one to quantify the similarity degree between a document and a DTD. The function takes as input a triple of integer values (p, m, c). The (p, m, c) triple represents the evaluation of plus, minus, and common elements, taking also into account their different levels in the document and in the DTD. These three values are combined to obtain a similarity evaluation.

Definition 3. *(Function $\mathcal{E}$).* Let (p, m, c) be a triple of natural numbers and α, β be real numbers s.t. $\alpha, \beta \geq 0$. Function $\mathcal{E}$ is defined as follows:

$$\mathcal{E}((p, m, c)) = \frac{c}{\alpha * p + c + \beta * m}$$

□

Function $\mathcal{E}$, defined according to the *ratio model* [8], is based on two parameters α, β and returns a value between 0 and 1. Depending on the value assigned to these parameters, the function gives more relevance to *plus* elements w.r.t. *minus* elements, or vice-versa. For example, if $\alpha = 0$ and $\beta = 1$ the function does not take into account *plus* elements in measuring similarity. Therefore, a document with only extra elements w.r.t. the ones specified in the DTD has a similarity measure equal to 1. By contrast, if $\alpha = 1$ and $\beta = 0$ the evaluation function does not take into account *minus* elements in the similarity measure. In the following examples we assume that $\alpha = \beta = 1$, thus giving the same relevance to *plus* and *minus* elements.

3.3   Matching Algorithm

An algorithm, named $\mathcal{M}atch$, that allows one to assign a (p, m, c) triple to a pair of trees $(document, DTD)$ has been defined [2]. Such algorithm is based on the idea of locally determining the best structure for a DTD element, for elements containing alternatives or repetitions, as soon as the information on the structure of its subelements in the document are known.

The algorithm is general enough to evaluate the similarity between any kind of XML documents and DTDs. In this paper, however, we focus on the most meaningful *core* of the algorithm, based on the assumption that, in the declaration of an element, two subelements with the same tag are forbidden. That is, element declarations such as <!ELEMENT a (b*, (c|b))> are not considered. The general version of the algorithm is briefly discussed in Section 4 and all the details can be found in [2].

Given a document D, and a DTD T, algorithm $\mathcal{Match}$ first checks whether the root labels of the two trees are equal. If not, then the two structures do not have common parts, and a null triple is returned. If the root labels are equal, the maximal level l between the levels of the two structures is determined, and the recursive function $\mathcal{M}$ is called on: (1) the root of the document, (2) the first (and only) child of the DTD, (3) the level weight (2^{l-1}) considering the fact that function $\mathcal{M}$ is called on the second level of the DTD structure, (3) a flag indicating that the current element (the root element) is not repeatable.

Function $\mathcal{M}$ recursively visits the document and the DTD, at the same time, from the root to the leaves, to match common elements. Specifically, two distinct phases can be distinguished:

1. in the first phase, moving down in the trees from the roots, the parts of the trees to visit through recursive calls are determined, but no evaluation is performed;
2. when a terminal case is reached, on return from the recursive calls and going up in the trees, the various alternatives are evaluated and the best one is selected.

Intuitively, in the first phase the DTD is used as a "guide" to detect the elements of the document that are covered by the DTD, disregarding the operators that bind together subelements of an element. In the second phase, by contrast, the operators used in the DTD are considered in order to verify that elements are bound as prescribed by the DTD, and to define an evaluation of the missing or exceeding parts of the document w.r.t. the DTD. Terminal cases are the following: a leaf of the DTD is reached, or an element of the DTD not present in the document is found. In these cases a (p, m, c) triple is returned. Therefore, the second phase starts and the evaluation of internal nodes is performed, driven by their labels.

For lack of space, we do not include the definition of function $\mathcal{M}$, rather we illustrate its behavior on the document and the DTD in Fig. 3(a,b). For sake of clarity, in the discussion of the algorithm, we denote the element of the document labeled by a as a_D, and the element of the DTD labeled by a as a_T.

During the first phase, function $\mathcal{M}$, driven by the label of the current DTD node, is called on subtrees of the document and the DTD. For example, on the first call of $\mathcal{M}$ on (a_D, AND_T), recursive calls on a_D and all the subtrees of AND_T are performed (i.e., on (a_D, b_T), and (a_D, AND_T)). Recursive calls are performed disregarding the operators in the DTD and moving down only when an element declared in the DTD is found in the document as child of the current node. Moreover, in such cases, the weight level is divided by γ in order to determine the level weight of the underlying level. Fig. 3(a,b) shows the recursive calls

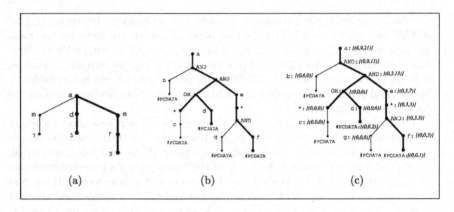

Fig. 3. Execution of function $\mathcal{M}$

performed. An edge (v, v') of the tree is bold if a recursive call of function $\mathcal{M}$ has been made on the subtree rooted at v'. Note that no recursive calls have been made on b_T, c_T, and g_T because such elements are not present in the document. Note also that m_D has not been visited by function $\mathcal{M}$, because this element is not required in the DTD.

When a terminal case is reached, a (p, m, c) triple is produced. For example, when function $\mathcal{M}$ is called on $(f_D, \#PCDATA_T)$, the triple $(0, 0, 1)$ is generated, because the DTD requires a data content for f_D and, actually, such element has a textual content. By contrast, when function $\mathcal{M}$ is called on (a_D, b_T), the triple $(0, 6, 0)$ is generated, because the DTD requires an element tagged b, but such element is missing in the document. Therefore, function $Weight$ is called on b_T and, since the current level weight is 4, the value 6 is returned as weight of the missing subtree.

On return from the recursive calls, the operators and the repeatability of the node are considered in order to select the best choice among the possible ones for binding together subelements. For example, returning from the evaluation of subtrees of the OR element, which is not repeatable, the triples $(0, 0, 0)$ and $(0, 0, 6)$ obtained for the evaluation of subtrees are considered. The best one is selected relying on the $\mathcal{E}$ evaluation function. By contrast, returning from the evaluation of subtrees of an AND element, which is not repeatable, the obtained evaluations are summed in order to determine the evaluation of the sequence of elements. The behavior of the algorithm is much more articulated when elements are repeatable. In such cases, indeed, not only a triple is generated, but a list of triples. The lists of triples are combined in order to evaluate internal nodes.

The intermediate evaluations are reported in Fig. 3(c). If an edge is bold the label is followed by the (p, m, c) triple obtained from the evaluation of the corresponding subtree. If an edge is not bold, but the label is followed by a (p, m, c) triple, it represents the evaluation of minus elements of the subtree.

3.4   Similarity Measure

The similarity measure between a document and a DTD is defined as follows.

Definition 4. *(Similarity Measure). Let D be a document and T a DTD. The similarity measure between D and T is defined as follows:*

$$\mathcal{S}(D,T) = \mathcal{E}(\mathcal{M}atch\langle D,T\rangle) \qquad \qquad \square$$

Example 3. Let D and T be the document and the DTD of Fig. 3(a,b). Their similarity degree is $\mathcal{S}(D,T) = \mathcal{E}(\mathcal{M}atch\langle D,T\rangle) = \mathcal{E}(\langle 6,9,21\rangle)$=0.58.   ○

The following proposition states the relationship between the notion of validity and our similarity measure.

Proposition 1. *Let D be a document, T a DTD, and α, β the parameters of function $\mathcal{E}$. If $\alpha, \beta \neq 0$ the following properties hold:*

- *If D is valid w.r.t. T, then $\mathcal{S}(D,T) = 1$;*
- *If $\mathcal{S}(D,T) = 1$, then D is valid w.r.t. T, disregarding the order of elements.*   △

4   Discussion

Though we have presented a *core* of the algorithm that works for a subset of XML documents, the approach can handle arbitrary XML documents [2]. Attribute handling does not raise new relevant issues. Subelements with the same tags are handled by considering and evaluating all the possible matching between different subelements with the same tag in the DTD and an element with that tag in the document. A matrix is built for each element in the DTD with some direct subelements with the same tag. This matrix has a column for each of the subelements of an element with the same tag, and it contains a row for each of the possible ways in which the elements with that tag at that level in the document can be matched with them. The similarity measure is evaluated for all these possible matching, and the best one is then selected.

Tag similarity can be evaluated relying on a Thesaurus [5], containing a set of terminological relationship, among which, for instance, SYN and USE. Different affinity values $\delta \in [0,1]$ can be assigned to each terminological relationship. In the similarity measure, when matching two element tags, the value $1 - \delta$ is added to the component m of the subtree evaluation. In this way we capture the missing tag equality.

The complexity of the algorithm we have presented in Section 3 is polynomial in the number of nodes of the document and of the DTD. Each node in the document and each node in the DTD is indeed visited only once, and for each node in the DTD, in the worst case, some operations that are quadratic in the number of nodes of the document and DTD are performed. In the general case discussed above, however, the algorithm is exponential. Thus, there is an obvious trade-off between the efficiency of the matching process and the strictness of the similarity requirements. Details on the algorithm complexity are reported in [2].

The described algorithm as well as its extensions discussed above have been implemented in Java, using the DOM libraries [9]. To validate the proposed technique we have performed some experiments over "real data", gathered from the Web, and "synthetic data", randomly generated. Because of space limitations, we cannot report on these experiments here and we refer to [2]. In both the experiments, however, we obtained that for each document D, and for each pair of DTDs T_1, T_2 such that D is not valid neither for T_1 nor for T_2, whenever $\mathcal{S}(D, T_1) > \mathcal{S}(D, T_2)$, D actually is more similar to T_1 than to T_2.

The work described in this paper can be extended in different directions. First, we are investigating how to use the feedback information of the matching algorithm to obtain a set of DTDs describing in the most accurate way the structure of the considered XML documents. Another direction we are investigating is the integration of structure-based retrieval with classical content-based retrieval. The goal is to express and evaluate queries containing both filters on the document structure and on the document content. In this context, we also plan to investigate how the defined structural similarity measure can be employed for structural clustering of XML documents.

References

1. E. Bertino, G. Guerrini, I. Merlo, and M. Mesiti. An Approach to Classify Semi-Structured Objects. In *Proc. European Conf. on Object-Oriented Programming*, LNCS 1628, pp. 416–440, 1999.
2. E. Bertino, G. Guerrini, and M. Mesiti. Measuring the Structural Similarity among XML Documents and DTDs, 2001. http://www.disi.unige.it/person/MesitiM.
3. S. Castano, V. De Antonellis, M. G. Fugini, and B. Pernici. Conceptual Schema Analysis: Techniques and Applications. *ACM Transactions on Database Systems*, 23(3):286–333, Sept. 1998.
4. M. N. Garofalakis, A. Gionis, R. Rastogi, S. Seshadri, and K. Shim. XTRACT: A System for Extracting Document Type Descriptors from XML Documents. In *Proc. of Int'l Conf. on Management of Data*, pp. 165–176, 2000.
5. A. Miller. WordNet: A Lexical Database for English. *Communications of the ACM*, 38(11):39–41, Nov. 1995.
6. T. Milo and S. Zohar. Using Schema Matching to Simplify Heterogeneous Data Translation. In *Proc. of Int'l Conf. on Very Large Data Bases*, pp. 122–133, 1998.
7. S. Nestorov, S. Abiteboul, and R. Motwani. Extracting Schema from Semistructured Data. In *Proc. of Int'l Conf. on Management of Data*, pp. 295–306, 1998.
8. A. Tversky. Features of Similarity. *J. of Psychological Review*, 84(4):327–352, 1977.
9. W3C. Document Object Model (DOM), 1998.
10. W3C. Extensible Markup Language 1.0, 1998.

Decision Tree Modeling with Relational Views

Fadila Bentayeb and Jérôme Darmont

ERIC – Université Lumière Lyon 2
5 avenue Pierre Mendès-France
69676 Bron Cedex
France
{bentayeb | jdarmont}@eric.univ-lyon2.fr

Abstract. Data mining is a useful decision support technique that can
be used to discover production rules in warehouses or corporate data.
Data mining research has made much effort to apply various mining
algorithms efficiently on large databases. However, a serious problem in
their practical application is the long processing time of such algorithms.
Nowadays, one of the key challenges is to integrate data mining methods within the framework of traditional database systems. Indeed, such
implementations can take advantage of the efficiency provided by SQL
engines.
In this paper, we propose an integrating approach for decision trees
within a classical database system. In other words, we try to discover
knowledge from relational databases, in the form of production rules,
via a procedure embedding SQL queries. The obtained decision tree is
defined by successive, related relational views. Each view corresponds
to a given population in the underlying decision tree. We selected the
classical Induction Decision Tree (ID3) algorithm to build the decision
tree. To prove that our implementation of ID3 works properly, we
successfully compared the output of our procedure with the output of
an existing and validated data mining software, SIPINA. Furthermore,
since our approach is tuneable, it can be generalized to any other similar
decision tree-based method.

Keywords: Integration, Databases, Data Mining, Decision trees, Relational views.

1 Introduction

Recently, an important research effort has been made to apply data mining
operations efficiently on large databases. Indeed, data mining tool vendors tend
to integrate more and more database features in their products. However, in
practice, the long processing time required by data mining algorithms remains a
critical issue. Current systems consume minutes or even hours to answer simple
mining queries on very large databases. On the other hand, database vendors
recently began to integrate data mining methods in the heart of their systems.
Hence, integrating data mining algorithms within the framework of traditional

M.-S. Hacid et al. (Eds.): ISMIS 2002, LNAI 2366, pp. 423–431, 2002.
© Springer-Verlag Berlin Heidelberg 2002

database systems [2] becomes one of the key challenges for research in both the databases and data mining fields.

A first step in this integration process has been achieved by the rise of data warehousing, whose primary purpose is decision support rather than reliable storage. A closely related area is called On-Line Analytical Processing (OLAP) [3]. There has also been an impressive amount of work related to association rules, their generalization, and their scalability [6,11]. Relatively, less work has been done in the context of other classical data analysis techniques from the machine learning field, e.g., clustering or classification. In this area, most research focused on scaling data mining techniques to work with large data sets [1,4].

To truly integrate data mining methods into their systems, database vendors recently developed extensions to SQL and Application Programming Interfaces (APIs) [5,7,9,12]. These tools allow client applications to explore and manipulate existing mining models and their applications through an interface similar to that used for exploring tables, views and other first-class relational objects.

In this paper, we propose to integrate classical data analysis techniques (namely, decision tree-based methods) within relational database systems. To achieve this goal, we only use existing structures, namely, relational views that we exploit through SQL queries.

To illustrate our approach, we chose to integrate the ID3 decision tree-based method [10], which is a supervised learning method generating knowledge in a production rule-set form. We selected ID3 mainly because it is quite simple to implement. However, we plan to take other, more elaborate methods into account, since our approach is now validated.

Such algorithms as ID3 generate a decision tree that is a succession of smaller and smaller partitions of an initial training set. Our key idea comes from this very definition. Indeed, we can make an analogy between building successive, related partitions (different populations) and creating successive, related relational views. Each node of the decision tree is associated with the corresponding view. Since SQL database management systems provide a rich set of primitives for data retrieval, we show that data mining algorithms can exploit them efficiently, instead of developing all requirement functionality from scratch.

To achieve this goal, we designed a PL/SQL stored procedure that uses SQL queries to generate the decision tree. Note that the views that are successively created can be stored and thus queried or analyzed after the tree is generated, if needed. The main differences between our approach and the existing ones are: (1) existing methods extend SQL to support mining operators when our approach only uses existing SQL statements and structures; (2) existing methods use APIs when our approach does not; and (3) existing methods store the obtained mining models into an extended relational table as in [8]. In our approach, the mining model we obtain is defined as a traditional table representing the decision tree and a set of successive, related views representing the nodes of the tree.

The remainder of this paper is organized as follows. Section 2 explains the principle of our approach. Section 3 details our implementation of ID3 and the functionality of our stored procedure. Section 4 presents the experiments we performed to validate our approach. We finally conclude this paper and discuss research perspectives in Section 5.

2   Principle of Our Approach

Induction graphs are data mining tools that produce "if-then"-like rules. They take as input a set of objects (tuples, in the relational databases vocabulary) described by a collection of attributes. Each object belongs to one of a set of mutually exclusive classes. The induction task determines the class of any object from the values of its attributes. A training set of objects whose class is known is needed to build the induction graph. Hence, an induction graph building method takes as input a set of objects defined by predictive attributes and a class attribute, which is the attribute to predict.

Then, these methods apply successive criteria on the training population to obtain groups wherein the size of one class is maximized. This process builds a tree, or more generally a graph. Rules are then produced by following the paths from the root of the tree (whole population) to the different leaves (groups wherein the one class represents the majority in the population strength). Figure 1 provides an example of decision tree with its associated rules, where p(Class #i) is the probability of objects to belong to Class #i.

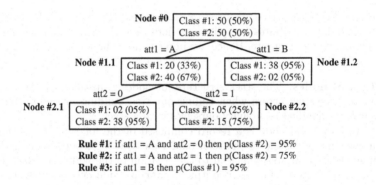

Fig. 1. Example of decision tree

In our approach, the root node of the decision tree is represented by a relational view corresponding to the whole training dataset. Since each sub-node in the decision tree represents a sub-population of its parent node, we build for each node a relational view that is based on its parent view. Then, these views are used to count the population strength of each class in the node with simple GROUP BY queries. These counts are used to determine the criteria that helps either partitioning the current node into a set of disjoint sub-partitions based on the values of a specific attribute or concluding that the node is a leaf, i.e., a terminal node. To illustrate how these views are created, we represented in Figure 2 the SQL statements for creating the views associated with the sample decision tree from Figure 1. This set of views constitutes the decision tree.

```
Node #0:    CREATE VIEW v0 AS SELECT att1, att2, class FROM training_set
Node #1.1: CREATE VIEW v11 AS SELECT att2, class FROM v0 WHERE att1='A'
Node #1.2: CREATE VIEW v12 AS SELECT att2, class FROM v0 WHERE att1='B'
Node #2.1: CREATE VIEW v21 AS SELECT class FROM v11 WHERE att2=0
Node #2.2: CREATE VIEW v22 AS SELECT class FROM v11 WHERE att2=1
```

Fig. 2. Relational views associated with sample decision tree

3   Implementation

We used Oracle 8i to implement the ID3 method, under the form of a PL/SQL stored procedure named BuildTree. Its full, commented code, installation and de-installation scripts, the sample datasets we used to validate our code, and a short user manual are freely available on-line[1].

3.1   Data Structures

To build a decision tree, we need to manage: (1) the nodes of the tree; and (2) the candidate attributes for splitting a node, and the associated new nodes each attribute would generate. Hence, we implemented the following data structures.

Stack of nodes. The stack structure for nodes is justified by the fact we encountered system errors when coding our tree building procedure recursively. Hence, we handled recursivity ourselves with a stack.

An individual node is a record composed of the following fields: num, node number; nview, name of the relational view that is associated with the node; rule, the explicit rule that lead to the creation of the node, e.g., GENDER=FEMALE (this is only stored for result output); entrop, node entropy (which variation expresses the discriminating power of an attribute); and pop, node population strength.

List of candidates. Our list of candidates must contain a set of attributes, the information gain associated with these attributes (expressed as a difference in entropy weighted averages), and a list of the nodes that would be generated if the current attribute was selected for splitting the current node. Hence, we need a list of lists. Such a data structure is impossible to achieve with the usual PL/SQL collections. The solution we adopted in this first implementation is using the extented relational features of Oracle. We used a relational table as our principal list, with an embedded table (collection) as the list of nodes.

As a consequence, our table of candidates is composed of the following fields: att_name, considered attribute name; gain, information gain; and nodes, embedded list of associated nodes.

---

[1] http://eric.univ-lyon2.fr/~jdarmont/download/buildtree.zip

3.2 Algorithm

Input parameters. The input parameters of our algorithm are given in Table 1.

Pseudo-code. We suppose we can call a procedure named `Entropy()` that computes both the entropy and the population strength of a node. These data are used when computing the information gain. `Entropy()` has actually been coded in PL/SQL. Our algorithm pseudo-code for the `BuildTree` procedure is provided in Figure 3.

Table 1. Algorithm input parameters

Parameter	Name	Default value
Data source table name	table_name	—
Class attribute (attribute to predict)	class	—
Result table name	res_name	BTRES
(Strict) minimum information gain for node building	min_gain	0
Root node view name	root_view	BTROOT
Clean-up views after execution (True/False)	del	TRUE

3.3 Result Output

The output of our stored procedure, namely a decision tree, is stored into a relational table whose name is specified as an input parameter. The table structure reflects the hierarchical structure of the tree. Its fields are: **node**, node ID number (primary key, root node is always #0 — note that there is a direct link between the node ID and the associated view name); **parent**, ID number of parent node in the tree (foreign key, references a node ID number); **rule**, the rule that lead to the creation of this node, e.g., GENDER=FEMALE; and for each value V of attribute E, a field labelled **E_V**, population strength for the considered value of the attribute in this node.

Such a table is best queried using Oracle SQL hierarchical statements. The result is directly a textual description of the output decision tree. A sample query is provided in Figure 4. From this representation, it is very easy to deduce the corresponding set of production rules.

4 Tests and Results

The aim of these experiments is to prove our implementation of the ID3 decision tree generation method functions properly. For this sake, we compared the output of our procedure with the output of a validated data mining tool,

```
Create result table
Create root node using the data source table
Compute root node entropy and population strength
Push root node
Update result table with root node
While the stack is not empty do
    Pop current node
    Clean candidate list
    For each attribute but the class attribute do
        Create a new candidate
        For each possible value of current attribute do
            Build new node and associated relational view
            Compute new node entropy and population strength
            Update information gain
            Insert new node into current candidate node list
        End for (each value)
    End for (each attribute)
    Search for maximum information gain in candidate list
    For each candidate do
        If current attribute bears the greater information gain then
            For each node in the list of nodes do
                Push current node
                Update result table with current node
            End for (each node)
        Else
            For each node in the list of nodes do
                Destroy current node
            End for (each node)
        End if
    End for (each candidate)
End while (stack not empty)
```

Fig. 3. Pseudo-code for the BuildTree stored procedure

```
SELECT LEVEL, node, parent, rule, E_1, E_2, ... FROM btres
CONNECT BY node = parent START WITH node = 0
```

Fig. 4. Hierarchical SQL query for decision tree display

SIPINA [13], which can be configured to apply ID3 as well, on several datasets. Due to space constraints, we only present here our most significant experiment. However, the full range of our experiments is available on-line[1].

The dataset we selected is designed to test decision tree building methods. It is aimed at predicting which classes of passengers of the Titanic are more likely to survive the wreck. The attributes are: CLASS = {1ST | 2ND | 3RD | CREW}; AGE = {ADULT | CHILD}; GENDER = {FEMALE | MALE}; and SURVIVOR = {NO | YES} (class attribute). There are 2201 tuples. Since the CLASS attribute has four modalities (distinct values), it can generate numerous nodes, and thus a relatively dense tree.

The results provided by our procedure, `BuildTree`, are provided in Figure 5. Note that we added in our result query the computation of the relative populations in each node (in percentage). Due to the tree width, the results provided by SIPINA are split-up in Figures 6 and 7. The common point in these two figures is the root node. As expected, the results provided by SIPINA and `BuildTree` are the same.

LEVEL	NODE	PARENT	RULE	SURVIVOR_NO	P_NO	SURVIVO_YES	P_YES
1	0			1490	68%	711	32%
2	1	0	GENDER=FEMALE	126	27%	344	73%
3	13	1	CLASS=CREW	3	13%	20	87%
3	14	1	CLASS=1ST	4	3%	141	97%
4	21	14	AGE=CHILD	0	0%	1	100%
4	22	14	AGE=ADULT	4	3%	140	97%
3	15	1	CLASS=2ND	13	12%	93	88%
4	19	15	AGE=CHILD	0	0%	13	100%
4	20	15	AGE=ADULT	13	14%	80	86%
3	16	1	CLASS=3RD	106	54%	90	46%
4	17	16	AGE=CHILD	17	55%	14	45%
4	18	16	AGE=ADULT	89	54%	76	46%
2	2	0	GENDER=MALE	1364	79%	367	21%
3	3	2	CLASS=CREW	670	78%	192	22%
3	4	2	CLASS=1ST	118	66%	62	34%
4	11	4	AGE=CHILD	0	0%	5	100%
4	12	4	AGE=ADULT	118	67%	57	33%
3	5	2	CLASS=2ND	154	86%	25	14%
4	9	5	AGE=CHILD	0	0%	11	100%
4	10	5	AGE=ADULT	154	92%	14	8%
3	6	2	CLASS=3RD	422	83%	88	17%
4	7	6	AGE=CHILD	35	73%	13	27%
4	8	6	AGE=ADULT	387	84%	75	16%

Fig. 5. `BuildTree` result for TITANIC

5   Conclusion and Perspectives

Major database vendors have all started to integrate data mining features into their systems, through extensions of the SQL language and APIs. In this paper, we presented a slightly different approach for integrating data mining operators into a database system. Namely, we implemented the ID3 method, which we selected for its simplicity, as a stored procedure that builds a decision tree by

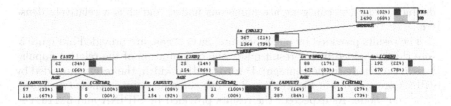

Fig. 6. SIPINA result for TITANIC (`GENDER=MALE`)

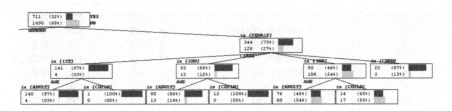

Fig. 7. SIPINA result for TITANIC (`GENDER=FEMALE`)

associating each node of the tree with a relational view. It is very easy to deduce a set of production rules from the output of our procedure. This approach has three advantages over the "black box" tools currently proposed by database vendors: (1) no extension of the SQL language is needed; (2) no programming through an API is required; and (3) the views associated with the nodes of a decision tree can be stored for further analysis (descriptive statistics or clustering on the sub-population, deployment of a new decision tree from this node, etc.). The concurrent splitting alternatives could even be retained if needed.

We sucessfully checked that the results provided by our implementation of ID3 were correct by comparing the output of our procedure to the output of the SIPINA software, which is a well-known and reliable data mining platform, on several test datasets of growing complexity.

The perspectives opened by this study are numerous. From a technical point of view, the performance of our solution could be improved at least at two levels. First, there is room for code optimization, e.g., by replacing the relational table with an embedded collection by more efficient, in-memory data structures. Second, a more global optimization scheme could be achieved by indexing the source table so that building and exploiting the views is faster.

We also need to test the results obtained by `BuildTree` on very large databases. This would help us determining how well our procedure scales up. We also plan to compare the performances (i.e., response time) of `BuildTree` and SIPINA on such very large databases (that do not fit into a computer's main memory) in order to check out that our approach indeed takes advantage of the host DBMS capabilities.

Eventually, we chose to first implement a very simple decision tree building method (ID3). It would be interesting to enrich our stored procedure with other, more elaborate methods. Our idea is to make them available through simple parameterization and keep the tree building as transparent to the user as possible. We could also integrate other procedures for helping users to complete the machine learning process, e.g., scoring and cross-validation procedures.

References

1. R. Agrawal, H. Mannila, R. Srikant, H. Toivonen, and A. Verkamo. Fast discovery of association rules. In *Advances in Kowledge Discovery and Data Mining*, pages 307–328, 1996.
2. S. Chaudhuri. Data mining and database systems: Where is the intersection? *Data Engineering Bulletin*, 21(1):4–8, 1998.
3. E. F. Codd. Providing olap (on-line analytical processing) to user-analysts: An it mandate. Technical report, E.F. Codd and Associates, 1993.
4. J. Gehrke, R. Ramakrishnan, and V. Ganti. Rainforest - a framework for fast decision tree construction of large datasets. In *24th International Conference on Very Large Data Bases (VLDB 98), New York City, USA*, pages 416–427. Morgan Kaufmann, 1998.
5. IBM. Db2 intelligent miner scoring.
   http://www-4.ibm.com/software/data/iminer/scoring, 2001.
6. R. Meo, G. Psaila, and S. Ceri. A new sql-like operator for mining association rules. In *22th International Conference on Very Large Data Bases (VLDB 96), Mumbai, India*, pages 122–133. Morgan Kaufmann, 1996.
7. Microsoft. Introduction to ole-db for data mining.
   http://www.microsoft.com/data/oledb, July 2000.
8. A. Netz, S. Chaudhuri, J. Bernhardt, and U. Fayyad. Integration of data mining and relational databases. In *26th International Conference on Very Large Data Bases (VLDB 00), Cairo, Egypt*, pages 719–722. Morgan Kaufmann, 2000.
9. Oracle. Oracle 9i data mining. White paper, June 2001.
10. J. R. Quinlan. Induction of decision trees. *Machine Learning*, 1:81–106, 1986.
11. S. Sarawagi, S. Thomas, and R. Agrawal. Integrating mining with relational database systems: Alternatives and implications. In *ACM SIGMOD International Conference on Management of Data (SIGMOD 98), Seattle, USA*, pages 343–354. ACM Press, 1998.
12. S. Soni, Z. Tang, and J. Yang. Performance study microsoft data mining algorithms. Technical report, Microsoft Corp., 2001.
13. D. A. Zighed and R. Rakotomalala. Sipina-w(c) for windows: User's guide. Technical report, ERIC laboratory, University of Lyon 2, France, 1996.

Discovering Sequential Association Rules with Constraints and Time Lags in Multiple Sequences*

Sherri K. Harms[1], Jitender Deogun[2], and Tsegaye Tadesse[3]

[1] Department of Computer Science and Information Systems
University of Nebraska-Kearney, Kearney NE 68849 harmssk@unk.edu,
http://faculty.unk.edu/h/harmssk
[2] Department of Computer Science and Engineering
University of Nebraska-Lincoln, Lincoln NE 68588-0115
[3] National Drought Mitigation Center
University of Nebraska-Lincoln, Lincoln NE 68588

Abstract. We present *MOWCATL*, an efficient method for mining frequent sequential association rules from multiple sequential data sets with a time lag between the occurrence of an antecedent sequence and the corresponding consequent sequence. This approach finds patterns in one or more sequences that precede the occurrence of patterns in other sequences, with respect to user-specified constraints. In addition to the traditional frequency and support constraints in sequential data mining, this approach uses separate antecedent and consequent inclusion constraints. Moreover, separate antecedent and consequent maximum window widths are used to specify the antecedent and consequent patterns that are separated by the maximum time lag.

We use multiple time series drought risk management data to show that our approach can be effectively employed in real-life problems. The experimental results validate the superior performance of our method for efficiently finding relationships between global climatic episodes and local drought conditions. We also compare our new approach to existing methods and show how they complement each other to discover associations in a drought risk management decision support system.

1 Introduction

Discovering association rules in sequences is an important data-mining problem that is useful in many scientific and commercial domains. Predicting events and identifying sequential rules that are inherent in the data help domain experts to learn from past data and make informed decisions for the future. Several different approaches have been investigated for sequential data mining [1], [2], [3], [4], [5]. Algorithms for discovering associations in sequential data [2], and episodal

---

* This research was supported in part by NSF Digital Government Grant No. EIA-0091530 and NSF EPSCOR, Grant No. EPS-0091900.

M.-S. Hacid et al. (Eds.): ISMIS 2002, LNAI 2366, pp. 432–441, 2002.

associations [1], [3] use all frequent episodes. The entire set of association rules is produced and significance criterion such as J-measure for rule ranking are used to determine the valuable rules [2]. An approach that uses temporal constraints on transactional sequences was presented in [5]. Our earlier methods, *Gen-FCE* and *Gen-REAR*, use inclusion constraints with a sliding window approach on event sequences to find the frequent closed episodes and then generate the representative episodal association rules from those episodes. We propose a generalized notion of episodes where the antecedent and consequent patterns are separated by a time lag and may consist of events from multiple sequences.

In this paper, we present a new approach that uses Minimal Occurrences With Constraints And Time Lags (*MOWCATL*), to find relationships between sequences in the multiple data sets. In addition to the traditional frequency and support constraints in sequential data mining, *MOWCATL* uses separate antecedent and consequent inclusion constraints, along with separate antecedent and consequent maximum window widths, to specify the antecedent and consequent patterns that are separated by a maximum time lag. The *MINEPI* algorithm was the first approach to find minimal occurrences of episodes [3].

Our approach is well suited for sequential data mining problems that have groupings of events that occur close together, but occur relatively infrequently over the entire dataset. They are also well suited for problems that have periodic occurrences when the signature of one or more sequences is present in other sequences, even when the multiple sequences are not globally correlated. The analysis techniques developed in this work facilitate the evaluation of the temporal associations between episodes of events and the incorporation of this knowledge into decision support systems. We show how our new approach complements the existing approaches to address the drought risk management problem.

2   Events and Episodes

For mining, sequential datasets are normalized and discretized to form subsequences using a *sliding window* [2]. With a sliding window of size δ, every normalized time stamp value at time t is used to compute each of the new sequence values $y_{t-\delta/2}$ to $y_{t+\delta/2}$. Thus, the dataset is divided into segments, each of size δ. The discretized version of the time series is obtained by using a clustering algorithm and a suitable similarity measure [2]. We consider each cluster identifier as a single *event type*, and the set of cluster labels as the *class of events* E. The new version of the time series is called an event sequence. Formally, an *event sequence* is a triple $(t_B, t_D, \mathcal{S})$ where t_B is the beginning time, t_D is the ending time, and $\mathcal{S}$ is a finite, time-ordered sequence of events [3], [6]. That is, $\mathcal{S} = (e_{t_B}, e_{t_{B+1p}}, e_{t_{B+2p}}, \ldots e_{t_{B+dp}} = e_{t_D})$, where p is the step size between events, d is the total number of steps in the time interval from $[t_B, t_D]$, and $D = B + dp$. Each e_{t_i} is a member of a class of events E, and $t_i \leq t_{i+1}$ for all $i = B, \ldots, D - 1p$. A sequence of events $\mathcal{S}$ includes events from a single class of events E.

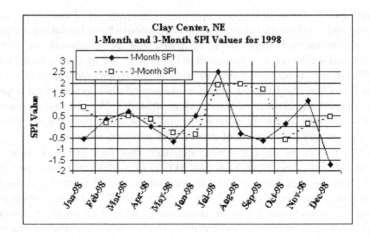

Fig. 1.   Example multiple event sequences

Example 1. Consider the event sequences of 1-month and 3-month Standardized Precipitation Index (SPI) values from Clay Center, Nebraska from January to December 1998 shown in Figure 1. SPI values show rainfall deviation from normal for a given location at a given time [7]. For this application, a sliding window width of 1 month was used, and the data was clustered into 7 clusters: A. Extremely Dry ($SPIvalue \leq -2.0$), B. Severely Dry ($-2.0 < SPIvalue \leq -1.5$), C. Moderately Dry ($-1.50 < SPIvalue \leq -0.5$), D. Normal ($-0.5 < SPIvalue < 0.5$), E. Moderately Wet ($0.5 \leq SPIvalue < 1.5$), F. Severely Wet ($1.5 \leq SPIvalue < 2.0$, and G. Extremely Wet ($SPIvalue \geq 2.0$).

When multiple sequences are used, each data set is normalized and discretized independently. The time granularity is then converted to a single (finest) granularity [1] before the discovery algorithms are applied to the combined sequences.

An episode in an event sequence is a partial order defined on a set of events [3], [6]. It is said to occur in a sequence if events are consistent with the given order, within a given time bound (window width). Formally, an *episode P* is a pair ($V, type$), where V is a collection of events. An episode is of type *parallel* if no order is specified and of type *serial* if the events of the episode have a fixed order. An episode is *injective* if no event type occurs more than once in the episode.

3   The *MOWCATL* Method

The *MOWCATL* method shown in Figure 2, finds minimal occurrences of episodes and relationships between them and requires a single database pass as in *MINEPI* algorithm[3]. Larger episodes are built from smaller episodes by joining episodes with overlapping minimal occurrences, which occur within the specified window width. However, our approach has additional mechanisms for: (1) constraining the search space during the discovery process, (2) allowing a time lag between the antecedent and consequent of a discovered rule, and (3) working with episodes from across multiple sequences. Our focus is on finding episodal rules where the antecedent episode occurs within a given maximum window width win_a, the consequent episode occurs within a given maximum window width win_c, and the start of the consequent follows the start of the antecedent within a given maximum time lag. This allows us to easily find rules such as "if A and B occur within 3 months, then within 2 months they will be followed by C and D occurring together within 4 months."

```
1)   Generate Antecedent Target Episodes of length 1 (ATE_1,B);
2)   Generate Consequent Target Episodes of length 1 (CTE_1,B);
3)   Input sequence S, record occurrences of ATE_1,B and CTE_1,B episodes;
4)   Prune unsupported episodes from ATE_1,B and CTE_1,B;
5)   k = 1;
6)   while (ATE_k,B ≠ ∅) do
7)       Generate Antecedent Target Episodes ATE_k+1,B from ATE_k,B
8)       Record each minimal occurrence of the episodes less than win_a;
9)       Prune the unsupported episodes from ATE_k+1,B;
10)      k++;
11)  Repeat or execute in parallel, Steps 5 - 11 for
         consequent episodes, using CTE_k+1,B and win_c;
12)  Generate combination episodes CE_B from ATE_B × CTE_B;
13)  Record the combination's minimal occurrences that occur within lag;
14)  Return the supported lagged episode rules in CE_B
         that meet the min_conf threshold;
```

Fig. 2. *MOWCATL* Algorithm.

Our approach is based on identifying minimal occurrences of episodes along with their time intervals. Given an episode α and an event sequence S, we say that the window $w = [t_s, t_e)$ is a *minimal occurrence* of α in S, if: (1) α occurs in the window w, and (2) α does not occur in any proper subwindow of w. The maximal width of a minimal occurrence for both the antecedent and the consequent are fixed during the process, and will measure the interestingness of the episodes.

The sequence S can be a combination of multiple sequences $S_1, S_2, \ldots, S_k$. An episode can contain events from each of the k sequences. Additionally, *combination events* are created with events from different sequences that occur together at the same timestamp. When finding minimal occurrences, a combination event is considered as a single event. The *support* of an episode α is the number of minimal occurrences of α. An episode α is considered *frequent* if its support meets or exceeds the given minimum support threshold min_sup. After the frequent episodes are found for the antecedent and the consequent independently, we combine the frequent episodes to form an episode rule.

Definition 1. An *episode rule* r is defined as an expression $\alpha[win_a] \Rightarrow_{lag} \beta[win_c]$, where α and β are episodes, and win_a, win_c, and lag are integers.

For each frequent antecedent episode α we join its minimal occurrences with each minimal occurrence of each frequent consequent episode β, as long as the starting time of the minimal occurrence for β is after the starting time of the minimal occurrence of α and no later than the ((starting time of α) + lag). The occurrence of α must end before the occurrence of β ends. The number of events in episodes α and β may differ. The informal interpretation of the rule is that if episode α has a minimal occurrence in the interval $[t_s, t_e)$, with $t_e - t_s \leq win_a$, and β has a minimal occurrence in the interval $[t_r, t_d)$, with $t_d - t_r \leq win_c$, and t_r is in the range $[t_{s+1}, t_{s+lag}]$, and $t_e < t_d$, then the rule r has a minimal occurrence in the interval $[t_s, t_d)$.

The *confidence* of an episode rule $r = \alpha[win_a] \Rightarrow_{lag} \beta[win_c]$ in a sequence S with given windows win_a, win_c, and lag is the conditional probability that β occurs, given that α occurs, under the time constraints specified by the rule. The *support* of the rule is the number of times the rule holds in the database.

Example 2. The *MOWCATL* method generates minimal occurrences and episodal rules shown in Table 1 when applied to event sequences S given in Figure 1, with $win_a = 3$, $min\_sup = 2$, $win_c = 3$, $lag = 1$, with the SPI1 sequence as the antecedent and the SPI3 sequence as the consequent for parallel episodes. The events are the cluster labels described in Example 1.

Table 1. Sample *MOWCATL* episodes, minimal occurrences, and rules

Episode/Rule	Minimal occurrences	Support	Confidence
1C	1-1, 5-5, 9-9	3	
1D	2-2, 4-4, 6-6, 8-8, 10-10	5	
1E	3-3, 11-11	2	
3D	2-2, 3-3, 4-4, 5-5, 6-6, 11-11, 12-12	7	
3F	7-7, 8-8, 9-9	3	
1C,1D	1-2, 4-5, 5-6, 8-9, 9-10	5	
1C,1E	1-3, 9-11	2	
1D,1E	2-3, 3-4, 10-11	3	
3D,3F	6-7, 9-11	2	
1C,1D,1E	1-3, 3-5, 9-11	3	
1C,1D $\Rightarrow_{lag=1}$ 3D,3F	(5-6,6-7), (8-9,9-11)	2	.4
1C,1D $\Rightarrow_{lag=1}$ 3D	(1-2,2-2), (4-5,5-5), (5-6,6-6)	3	.6
1D,1E $\Rightarrow_{lag=1}$ 3D	(2-3,3-3), (3-4,4-4), (10-11, 11-11)	3	1
1C $\Rightarrow_{lag=1}$ 3D	(1-1,2-2), (5-5,6-6)	2	.67
1D $\Rightarrow_{lag=1}$ 3D	(2-2,3-3), (4-4,5-5), (10-10, 11-11)	3	.6
1D $\Rightarrow_{lag=1}$ 3F	(6-6,7-7), (8-8,9-9)	2	.4
1E $\Rightarrow_{lag=1}$ 3D	(3-3,4-4), (11-11,12-12)	2	1

4   The *Gen-FCE* and the *Gen-REAR* Methods

Previously, we presented the *Gen-FCE* and *Gen-REAR* methods for the drought risk management problem [8]. *Gen-FCE*, defines a *window* on an event sequence S as an event subsequence $W = \{e_{t_j}, \ldots, e_{t_k}\}$, where $t_B \leq t_j$, and $t_k \leq t_D + 1$ as in the *WINEPI* algorithm[3], [6]. The width of the window W is $width(W) = t_k - t_j$. The set of all windows W on $\mathcal{S}$, with $width(W) = win$ is denoted as $\mathcal{W}(\mathcal{S}, win)$. The window width is pre-specified. The *frequency* of an episode is defined as the fraction of windows in which the episode occurs. Given an event sequence S, and a window width win, the frequency of an episode P of a given type in $\mathcal{S}$ is:

$$fr(P, \mathcal{S}, win) = \frac{\mid \boldsymbol{w} \in \mathcal{W}(\mathcal{S}, win) : P \ occurs \ in \ \boldsymbol{w} \mid}{\mid \mathcal{W}(\mathcal{S}, win) \mid}$$

Given a frequency threshold min_fr, P is *frequent* if $fr(P, \mathcal{S}, win) \geq min\_fr$. Closure of an episode set X, denoted by $closure(X)$, is the smallest closed episode set containing X and is equal to the intersection of all frequent episode sets containing X. *Gen-FCE* generates frequent closed target episodes with respect to a given set of Boolean target constraints B, an event sequence S, a window width win, an episode type, a minimum frequency min_fr, and a window step size p. We use the set of frequent closed episodes FCE produced from the *Gen-FCE* algorithm to generate the *representative episodal association rules* (REAR) that cover the entire set of association rules [9].

Using our techniques on multiple time series while constraining the episodes to a user-specified target set, we can find relationships that occur across the sequences. Once the set of representative association rules is found, the user may formulate queries about the association rules that are covered (or represented) by a certain rule of interest for given support and confidence values. These techniques can be employed in many problem domains, including drought risk management.

5   Drought Risk Management – An Application

Drought affects virtually all US regions and results in significant economic, social, and environmental impacts. According to the National Climatic Data Center, the losses due to drought are more than any other severe weather disaster. Given the complexity of drought, where the impacts from a drought can accumulate gradually over time and vary widely across many sectors, a well-designed decision support system is critical to effectively manage drought response efforts.

This work is part of a Digital Government project at UNL that is developing and integrating new information technologies for improved government services in the USDA Risk Management Agency (RMA) and the Natural Resources Conservation Service. We are in the process of developing an advanced Geospatial Decision Support System (GDSS) to improve the quality and accessibility of drought related data for drought risk management [10]. Our objective is to integrate spatio-temporal knowledge discovery techniques into the GDSS using a combination of data mining techniques applied to geospatial time-series data.

6   Experimental Results and Analysis

Experiments were designed to find relationships between drought episodes at the automated weather station in Clay Center, NE, and other climatic episodes, from 1949-1999. There is a network of automated weather stations in Nebraska that can serve as long-term reference sites to search for key patterns and link to climatic events. We use historical and current climatology datasets, including 1) Standardized Precipitation Index (SPI) data from the National Drought Mitigation Center (NDMC), 2) Palmer Drought Severity Index (PDSI) from the National Climatic Data Center (NCDC), 3) North Atlantic Oscillation Index (NAO) from the Climatic Research Unit at the University of East Anglia, UK, 4) Pacific Ocean Southern Oscillation Index (SOI) and Multivariate ENSO Index (MEI) available from NOAA's Climate Prediction Center, and 5) Pacific/North American (PNA) Index and Pacific Decadal Oscillation (PDO) Index available from the Joint Institute for the Study of the Atmosphere and Ocean.

The data for the climatic indices are grouped into seven categories, i.e. extremely dry, severely dry, moderately dry, near normal, moderately wet, severely wet, and extremely wet. In our study, the 1-month, 3-month, 6-month, 9-month, 12-month SPI, and the PDSI values are grouped into the same seven categories to show the precipitation intensity relative to normal precipitation for a given location and a given month. The SOI, MEI, NAO, PDO, and PNA categories are based on the standard deviation from the normal and the negative values are considered to show the dry periods.

After normalizing and discretizing each dataset using the seven categories above, we performed experiments to find whether the method discovers interesting rules from the sequences, and whether the method is robust. Several window widths, minimal frequency values, minimal confidence values, and time lag values for both parallel and serial episodes were used. We specified droughts (the three dry categories in each data source) as our target episodes. For *MOWCATL*, we used the global climatic indices (SOI, MEI, NAO, PDO, and PNA) as our antecedent data sets, and the local precipitation indices (SPI1, SPI3, SPI6, SPI9, SPI12, and PDSI) as our consequent data sets. The experiments were ran on a DELL Optiplex GX240 2.0GHz PC with 256 MB main memory, under the Windows 2000 operating system. Algorithms were coded in C++.

Episodes with time lags from *MOWCATL* are useful to the drought risk management problem when trying to predict future local drought risk considering the current and past global weather conditions. Table 2 represent performance statistics for finding frequent drought episodes with various support thresholds using the *MOWCATL* algorithm. *MOWCATL* performs extremely well when finding the drought episodes. At a minimum support of .020 for parallel episodes, the algorithm only needs to look through the 212 candidate drought episodes to find the 109 frequent drought episodes. Whereas, using no constraints it would need to look through 3892 candidate episodes to find 2868 total frequent episodes.

Gen-FCE episodes are useful to the drought risk management problem when considering events that occur together, either with order (serial episodes), or without order specified (parallel episodes). Table 3 represent performance statistics for finding frequent closed drought episodes with various frequency thresholds using the *Gen-FCE* algorithm. As shown, the number of frequent closed

Table 2. Performance characteristics for parallel and serial drought episodes and rules with $MOWCATL$, Clay Center, NE drought monitoring database, $win_a = 4$ months, $win_c = 3$ months, and $lag = 2$ months, and $min\_conf = 25\%$.

Min. support	Parallel				Serial			
	Total cand.	Freq. episodes	Distinct rules	Total time (s)	Total cand.	Frequent episodes	Distinct rules	Total time (s)
0.005	930	732	98	3	9598	1125	174	34
0.007	716	575	41	3	6435	621	58	33
0.010	452	288	10	2	4144	275	15	32
0.013	332	192	7	1	3457	168	6	32
0.016	254	142	1	1	2805	109	1	31
0.020	212	109	1	1	2637	83	1	30

episodes decreases rapidly as the frequency threshold increases as expected from the nature of drought.

Tables 2 and 3 also show the number of distinct rules generated for these algorithms. As shown, the number of rules between global climatic drought episodes and local drought at Clay Center, NE decreases rapidly as the frequency and support levels increase. In fact, there was only one parallel drought rule out of 1954 total rules at a 25% confidence level for a support threshold of 0.020 using the $MOWCATL$ algorithm.

Examples of how the window widths influence the results are shown in Table 4. The $MOWCATL$ algorithm finds a significant number of patterns and relationships for all window widths specified. In general, wider combined window widths win_a, win_c, produce more patterns and relationships, but with less significant meaning. With a 2 month lag in time, the $MOWCATL$ algorithm discovers 142 parallel drought episodal rules and 199 serial drought episodal rules, using $win_a = 3$ and $win_c = 3$. $MOWCATL$ discovers more relationships at higher confidence values than the $Gen\text{-}REAR$ approach. These examples indicate that there is a delay in time after global climatic drought indicators are recognized, before local drought conditions occur. This is encouraging, since knowing this time difference will allow drought risk management experts time to plan for the expected local drought conditions.

Table 3. Performance characteristics for parallel and serial drought episodes and rules with $Gen\text{-}FCE$ and $Gen\text{-}REAR$, Clay Center, NE drought monitoring database, window width 4 months and a $min\_conf = 25\%$.

Min. freq.	Parallel				Serial			
	Total cand.	Freq. episodes	Distinct rules	Total time (s)	Total cand.	Frequent episodes	Distinct rules	Total time (s)
0.02	1891	93	175	4	3002	327	9	10
0.04	650	265	41	1	1035	139	1	6
0.08	297	68	10	0	494	33	0	1
0.12	154	28	1	0	310	16	0	0
0.16	108	15	1	0	226	13	0	0
0.20	75	10	0	0	160	10	0	0
0.24	51	7	0	0	112	7	0	0

Table 4. Performance characteristics for parallel and serial drought episodes and rules for the Clay Center, NE drought monitoring database, with varying window widths. Parameters include $lag = 2$, $min\_sup = 0.005$, $min\_fr = 0.02$, and $min\_conf = 25\%$.

		MOWCATL				Gen-FCE/Gen-REAR			
		Parallel		Serial		Parallel		Serial	
win or		Freq.	Distinct	Freq.	Distinct	Freq.	Distinct	Freq.	Distinct
win_a	win_c	episodes	rules	episodes	rules	episodes	rules	episodes	rules
1	1	135	44	101	45	40	0	40	0
1	2	319	64	387	55				
1	3	532	72	741	58				
2	1	199	84	212	134	149	4	55	0
2	2	383	127	498	176				
2	3	596	154	852	189				
3	1	252	79	331	140	400	45	183	1
3	2	436	121	596	184				
3	3	649	142	951	199				
4	1	335	60	485	125	930	175	327	9
4	2	519	86	771	164				
4	3	732	98	1125	174				
4	4	1056	104	1596	198				

Finding the appropriate time lag is an iterative process. Using the parameters from Table 2, but decreasing the time lag to one month, reduces the number of rules to 24 parallel drought rules and 62 serial drought rules at a minimal support of 0.005. By increasing the time lag to three months, we get 275 parallel drought rules and 506 serial drought rules. As the time lag increases, more rules are discovered, but again with decreased significant meaning.

Clearly, the results produced by these methods need to be coupled with human interpretation of the rules and an interactive approach to allow for iterative changes in the exploration process. Using our methods, the drought episodes and relationships are provided quickly and without the distractions of the other non-drought data. These are then provided to the drought risk management expert for human interpretation. We provide the user with the J-measure [2] for ranking rules by interestingness, rather than using the confidence value alone. Similarly, our method can be employed in other applications.

7   Conclusion

This paper presents a new approach for generating episodal association rules in multiple data sets. We compared the new approach to the *Gen-FCE* and the *Gen-REAR* approaches, and showed how the new approach complements these techniques in addressing complex real-life problems like drought risk management. As demonstrated by the experiments, our methods efficiently find relationships between climatic episodes and droughts by using constraints, time lags, closures and representative episodal association rules.

Other problem domains could also benefit from this approach, especially when there are groupings of events that occur close together in time, but occur relatively infrequently over the entire dataset. Additional suitable problem domains are when the entire set of multiple time series is not correlated, but there are periodic occurrences when the signature of one sequence is present in other sequences, with possible time delays between the occurrences. The analysis techniques developed in this work facilitate the evaluation of the temporal associations between episodes of events and the incorporation of this knowledge into decision support systems. Currently, there is no commercial product that addresses these types of problems.

For future work, we plan to extend these methods to consider the spatial extent of the relationships. Additionally, we are incorporating these approaches into the advanced geospatial decision support system for drought risk management mentioned above.

References

1. Bettini, C., Wang, X.S., Jajodia, S.: Discovering frequent event patterns with multiple granularities in time sequences. IEEE Transactions on Knowledge and Data Engineering **10** (1998) 222–237
2. Das, G., Lin, K.I., Mannila, H., Ranganathan, G., Smyth, P.: Rule discovery from time series. In: Proceedings of the Fourth International Conference on Knowledge Discovery and Data Mining [KDD 98], New York, NY (1998) 16–22
3. Mannila, H., Toivonen, H., Verkamo, A.I.: Discovery of frequent episodes in event sequences. Technical report, Department of Computer Science, University of Helsinki, Finland (1997) Report C-1997-15.
4. Srikant, R., Vu, Q., Agrawal, R.: Mining association rules with item constraints. In: Proceedings of the Third International Conference on Knowledge Discovery and Data Mining [KDD97]. (1997) 67–73
5. Zaki, M.: Sequence mining in categorical domains: Incorporating constraints. In: Proceedings of the Ninth International Conference on Information and Knowledge Management [CIKM2000], Washington D.C., USA (2000) 422–429
6. Mannila, H., Toivonen, H., Verkamo, A.I.: Discovering frequent episodes in sequences. In: Proceedings of the First International Conference on Knowledge Discovery and Data Mining [KDD 95], Montreal, Canada (1995) 210–215
7. McGee, T.B., Doeskin, N.J., Kliest, J.: Drought monitoring with multiple time scales. In: Proceedings of the 9th Conference on Applied Climatology, Boston, MA (1995) 233–236 American Meteorological Society.
8. Harms, S.K., Deogun, J., Saquer, J., Tadesse, T.: Discovering representative episodal association rules from event sequences using frequent closed episode sets and event constraints. In: Proceedings of the 2001 IEEE International Conference on Data Mining, San Jose, California, USA (2001) 603–606
9. Kryszkiewicz, M.: Fast discovery of representative association rules. In: Lecture Notes in Artificial Intelligence. Volume 1424., Proceedings of RSCTC 98, Springer-Verlag (1998) 214–221
10. Harms, S.K., Goddard, S., Reichenbach, S.E., Waltman, W.J., Tadesse, T.: Data mining in a geospatial decision support system for drought risk management. In: Proceedings of the 2001 National Conference on Digital Government Research, Los Angelos, California, USA (2001) 9–16

Mining Association Rules in Preference-Ordered Data

Salvatore Greco[1], Roman Slowinski[2], and Jerzy Stefanowski[2]

[1] Faculty of Economics, University of Catania, 95129 Catania, Italy
salgreco@mbox.unict.it
[2] Institute of Computing Science, Poznan University of Technology,
60-965 Poznan, Poland
{Roman.Slowinski, Jerzy.Stefanowski}@cs.put.poznan.pl

Abstract. Problems of discovering association rules in data sets containing semantic information about preference orders on domains of attributes are considered. Such attributes are called criteria and they are typically present in data related to economic issues, like financial or marketing data. We introduce a specific form of association rules involving criteria. Discovering such rules requires new concepts: semantic correlation of criteria, inconsistency of objects with respect to the dominance, credibility index. Properties of these rules concerning their generality and interdependencies are studied. We also sketch the way of mining such rules.

1 Introduction

Mining association rules is an important research and application area in knowledge discovery, see e.g. review in [4]. Several algorithms for discovering association rules from data have been already proposed for various types of attributes (nominal, numerical, etc.) [1,5,6]. However, these algorithms do not take into account semantic information often present in data sets, that is information about *preference order* in attribute domains. For example, when considering persons applying for a credit to a bank, an attribute like "salary" has a clear preference scale – the more, the better. The attributes with preference–ordered domains are called *criteria*. When several criteria are present in data, any reasonable regularity to be discovered have to take into account a *semantic correlation* between criteria. For example, in decision about credit granting, where two criteria are considered, "month salary" and "evaluation of bank risk concerning payment of a credit", these criteria are semantically correlated in the following sense: an improvement of month salary should not deteriorate the evaluation of bank risk. This semantic information is often present in data related to cost or quality, like in financial data; however, it is neglected by today's data mining tools.

The paper introduces consideration of criteria in association rules. Some of basic concepts have been inspired by dominance-based decision rules of *multiple criteria classification problems* introduced in [3]. In multiple criteria classification

M.-S. Hacid et al. (Eds.): ISMIS 2002, LNAI 2366, pp. 442–450, 2002.

problems criteria are semantically correlated with preference–ordered decision classes. This results in a special syntax and semantics of decision rules [3,7].

The paper is organized as follows. In the next section we present basic concepts of the proposed approach. The syntax of association rules is defined in section 3. Quality measures and properties of association rules, concerning their generality and interdependencies, are also studied in this section. In section 4, we sketch the way of mining such rules. Final section presents conclusions.

2   Semantically Correlated Criteria in Data Tables

Formally, a *data table* is a pair $DT = (U, A)$, where U is a nonempty finite set of objects called *universe*, A is a nonempty finite set of *attributes* such that $a : U \to V_a$ for every $a \in A$. The set V_a is a domain of a. Let $a(x)$ denotes the value of attribute $a \in A$ taken by object $x \in U$. The domains of attributes may be preference–ordered or not. In the first case the attributes are called *criteria*, while in the latter case we call them *regular attributes*. The domains of criteria are called preference scales (increasing or decreasing). Scales may be either ordinal or cardinal depending whether the strength of preference is meaningful for the scale or not. A preference scale of each criterion a induces a weak preference relation being a complete preorder (i.e. a strongly complete and transitive binary relation) $\succeq_a$ on set V_a. For values $\alpha, \beta \in V_a$, $\alpha \succeq_a \beta$ means that α is at least as good as β. The asymmetric part of $\succeq_a$ is denoted by $\succ_a$, while the symmetric part is denoted by $\sim_a$. In other words, object x is *preferred* to object y on criterion a if $a(x) \succ_a a(y)$ and x is *indifferent* to y if $a(x) \sim_a a(y)$.

Definition 2.1:
Let P be a subset of criteria A. The object x *dominates* object y with respect to subset P (denotation $x \gg_P y$) iff $a(x) \succeq_a a(y)$ for all $a \in P$.

Definition 2.2:
Let $a_i, a_j \in A$, $x, y \in U$ and $a_i(x), a_i(y) \in V_{ai}$, $a_j(x), a_j(y) \in V_{aj}$. If the following conditions are supposed to hold:
$$a_i(x) \succeq_{ai} a_i(y) \Rightarrow a_j(x) \succeq_{aj} a_j(y)$$
$$a_i(x) \preceq_{ai} a_i(y) \Rightarrow a_j(x) \preceq_{aj} a_j(y)$$
then criteria a_i and a_j are in the relation of *semantic correlation* (denotation $a_i SC a_j$).

Notice that relation SC is not necessarily complete in the set of criteria A.

Example:
Let us illustrate the above definitions. Consider a data table including 4 criteria $\{a_1, a_2, a_3, a_4\}$ and 10 objects $\{x_1, \ldots, x_{10}\}$ corresponding to persons applying for a credit to a bank. The criteria are: a_1 is the monthly salary with the increasing cardinal scale, e.g. counted in dollars; a_2 is an evaluation of the debt defined on the ordinal scale of three values: none $\succ$ small $\succ$ high; a_3 refers to amount of the requested credit with ordinal scale: small $\prec$ medium $\prec$ high; a_4 is an evaluation of bank risk concerning payment of a credit with ordinal scale: low $\succ$ medium $\succ$ high.

Table 1. Example of a bank data table

Object	a_1	a_2	a_3	a_4
x_1	3000	small	medium	low
x_2	5000	small	medium	medium
x_3	10000	none	high	low
x_4	7500	small	low	medium
x_5	5000	high	medium	high
x_6	10000	none	high	low
x_7	3000	high	low	high
x_8	7500	none	high	low
x_9	5000	high	low	high
x_{10}	7500	small	medium	medium

Remark that debt ratio a_2 is in SC relation with bank risk a_4. This means that with increase of the debt ratio we expect an increase of the bank risk. We assume that the following SC relations also hold: $a_1 SC a_3, a_1 SC a_4, a_2 SC a_3, a_3 SC a_4$.

3   Association Rules for Semantically Correlated Criteria

Let (a_i, l_i, u_i) denote an atomic formula defined in $A \times V_{a_i} \times V_{a_i}$, where criterion (or attribute) a_i takes value not worse than l_i and not better than u_i. If a_i is a regular attribute, then $l_i = u_i$. In this atomic formula a_i is treated as a variable.

Let $I_R = \{(a_i, l_i, u_i) : \exists x \in DT$ such that $a_i(x) \sim_a l_i$ and/or $a_i(x) \sim_a u_i$, for all $a_i \in A\}$, i.e. set I_R is composed of such atomic formulas that all values l_i and u_i exist in the data table DT for all $a_i \in A$.

Let C be a subset of I_R such that each criterion a_i is represented in at most one atomic formula. We will assume that in association rules formulas from C will be represented in a conjunction form. $[C] = \{a_i : (a_i, l_i, u_i) \in C\}$ is a set of criteria represented in C.

Definition 3.1:
Object $x \in U$ *supports* the conjunction of atomic formulas from set C if for all $(a_i, l_i, u_i) \in C$ $a_i(x) \succeq_{ai} l_i$ and $a_i(x) \preceq_{ai} u_i$.

Let $x\_supp(C)$ denote a set of objects x supporting C, while $support(C) = card(x\_supp(C))$ will denote the cardinality of $x\_supp(C)$, shortly called *support* of C.

Definition 3.2:
An *association rule* is an implication of the form $C \rightarrow D$, where $C \subset I_R, D \subset I_R$ and $[C] \cap [D] = \emptyset$.

The rule $C \rightarrow D$ is characterized by support and confidence:

$$support(C \rightarrow D) = support(C \cup D)$$
$$confidence(C \rightarrow D) = support(C \cup D)/support(C).$$

In other words, the confidence of rule $C \to D$ is a percentage of objects in DT supporting C that also support D.

Remark that the syntax of association rules defined above is similar to generalized association rules proposed by Sirkant and Agrawal [6]. The main difference between our rules and the generalized association rules lies in their semantics. In our atomic formulas "$\preceq$" means a *preference relation*, while in generalized association rules "$\geq$" means simple relation between quantities.

Notice that atomic formulas $(a_i, l_i, u_i) \in C \cup D$ should be read as "$(a_i \succeq_{ai} l_i)$ and $(a_i \preceq_{ai} u_i)$". If l_i or u_i is an extreme value on preference scale of a_i and the other value is not, then the elementary condition boils down to either $(a_i \succeq_{ai} l_i)$ or $(a_i \preceq_{ai} u_i)$. For simplicity of further notation we skip index a_i in the symbol of the complete preorder $\succeq$.

Let us assume, without loss of generality, that criteria from sets $[C]$ and $[D]$ are numbered consecutively from 1 to p and $p+1$ to r, respectively, $p < r$, i.e. $[C] = \{a_1, \ldots, a_p\}$ and $[D] = \{a_{p+1}, \ldots, a_r\}$. Also, from now, we assume that domains of these criteria are recorded with the same direction of preference. The association rule may have one of three following forms:

(i) $(a_1 \succeq l_{a_1}) \wedge \ldots \wedge (a_p \succeq l_{a_p}) \to (a_{p+1} \succeq l_{a_{p+1}}) \wedge \ldots \wedge (a_r \succeq l_{a_r})$

(ii) $(a_1 \preceq u_{a_1}) \wedge \ldots \wedge (a_p \preceq u_{a_p}) \to (a_{p+1} \preceq u_{a_{p+1}}) \wedge \ldots \wedge (a_r \preceq u_{a_r})$

(iii) $(l_{a_i} \preceq a_1 \preceq u_{a_1}) \wedge \ldots \wedge (l_{a_p} \preceq a_p \preceq u_{a_p}) \to (l_{a_{p+1}} \preceq a_{p+1} \preceq u_{a_{p+1}}) \wedge \ldots \wedge (l_{a_r} \preceq a_r \preceq u_{a_r})$

We will require the association rule to be *robust*. This means that for association rule (i), there must exist an object x in data table DT such that $a_1(x) \sim l_{a_1}, \ldots, a_p(x) \sim l_{a_p}, a_{p+1}(x) \sim l_{a_{p+1}}, \ldots a_r(x) \sim l_{a_r}$. Similarly, for association rule (ii) there must exist an object x in data table DT such that $a_1(x) \sim u_{a_1}, \ldots, a_p(x) \sim u_{a_p}, a_{p+1}(x) \sim u_{a_{p+1}}, \ldots a_r(x) \sim u_{a_r}$. Finally, for association rule (iii) there must exist two objects $x, y \in U$ such that $a_1(x) \sim l_{a_1}, \ldots, a_p(x) \sim l_{a_p}, a_{p+1}(x) \sim l_{a_{p+1}}, \ldots a_r(x) \sim l_{a_r}$ and $a_1(y) \sim u_{a_1}, \ldots, a_p(y) \sim u_{a_p}, a_{p+1}(y) \sim u_{a_{p+1}}, \ldots a_r(y) \sim u_{a_r}$. Such supporting objects will be called *basic objects* of the robust association rules.

Concepts of robust rules and their basic objects permits to interpret the syntax of rules in terms of objects existing in the data table rather than of some "artificial" ones obtained by combining the attribute values describing other objects from the data table.

If C and D do not contain semantically correlated criteria split between the two sets, then the association rule $C \to D$ does not need to fulfill any additional condition in comparison with the case of regular attributes.

If, however, rule $C \to D$ involves at least two semantically correlated criteria, one in C and another in D, then it has to be checked for inconsistency of supporting objects. More formally, let us consider rule $C \to D$, $a_i \in [C]$, $a_j \in [D]$ and $a_i S C a_j$. If the *confidence*$(C \to D) < 1$ (or 100%), then there is a difference between sets $x\_supp(C \cup D)$ and $x\_supp(C)$ denoted by Y. In other words, Y is composed of objects y that support C but not $C \cup D$. We will now define the concept of inconsistency using the concept of dominance introduced in Definition 2.1.

Definition 3.3:
Object $y \in Y$ is *inconsistent* with an object x supporting rule $C \to D$ if either $(x \gg_{[C]} y$ and $y \gg_{[D]} x)$ or $(y \gg_{[C]} x$ and $x \gg_{[D]} y)$.

Inconsistency of some objects from Y with some other objects supporting the rule $C \to D$ means that there exist an object dominating the rule basic object on criteria from the antecedent part while being dominated by the basic object on criteria from the consequent part of the rule. Such an object clearly weakens the credibility of the regularity expressed by the rule.

For this reason we introduce a new quality measure for association rules called *credibility* and defined as follows:

$$credibility(C \to D) = confidence(C \cup D) - \alpha \cdot (INC\{W, Y\}/support(C))$$

where $\alpha \in [0, 1]$ is a parameter controlling the accepted level of inconsistency in the association rule, $W = x\_supp(C \cup D)$ and $INC(W, Y)$ is the cardinality of the set of objects from W being inconsistent with some objects from Y.

The parameter $\alpha = 1$ corresponds to exclusion of all inconsistent objects from the support of the rule, while $\alpha = 0$ makes $credibility(C \to D) = confidence(C \to D)$. The user should tune the value α with respect to his tolerance of inconsistent objects in the rule support. If the credibility of the association rule is smaller than user's defined threshold *mincredibility*, the rule will be deleted from the set of discovered rules.

Continuation of the example:
To illustrate the above definitions let us come back to the example. Consider the following conjunction C, which could be generated from data shown in Table 1: $(a_1 \succeq 5000)(a_2 \succeq small)(a_3 \succeq medium)$. The above conjunction can be expressed as a statement saying *"month salary at least \$5000, debt none or small, credit medium or high"*. Its support is equal to 50% as $x\_supp(C \cup D) = \{x_2, x_3, x_6, x_8, x_{10}\}$.

Let us consider the following candidate for a rule $C \to D$: $(a_1 \succeq 5000)(a_2 \succeq small) \to (a_3 \succeq medium)$. This rule says *if an applicant have month salary at least \$5000 and debt none or small, then he gets credit medium or high*. It is supported by 50% objects. As $x\_supp(C) = \{x_2, x_3, x_4, x_6, x_8, x_{10}\}$, the rule confidence is equal to $5/6 \cdot 100\% = 83.3\%$. Let us remind that in this rule a_1SCa_3 and a_2SCa_3.

The object x_4 (with description \$7500, *small, low, medium*) supports the antecedent of the rule but does not support the consequence of this rule, therefore $Y = \{x_4\}$. One should check possible inconsistencies of object x_4 with all other objects from $x\_supp(C \to D)$. There are two inconsistencies of object x_4 with objects x_2 (with description \$5000, *small, medium, medium*) and object x_{10} (with description \$7500, *small, medium, medium*), i.e. $x_4 \gg_{[C]} x_2$ but $x_2 \gg_{[D]} x_4$, $x_4 \gg_{[C]} x_{10}$ but $x_{10} \gg_{[D]} x_4$. In other words, object x_4 is evaluated better than object x_2 or evaluated the same as object x_{10} with respect to amount of salary and debt but gets smaller credit than these objects. We intuitively may expect that the better assessment of object x_4 on the first criteria from $[C]$ should imply its better assessment of the criterion a_3. However, the examples $\{x_2, x_{10}\}$ show that these better values of a_1 and a_2 implied deterioration of value for a_3, what finally makes our doubtful as to the credibility of the presented rule. Therefore, if we want to consider complete influence of inconsistent objects x_2 and x_{10} on the quality of the rule, we determine $\alpha = 1$. In such a case, the rule credibility is equal to 83.3% – (2/6)*100% = 50%.   □

Besides the above discussed inconsistency of objects supporting the rule, it is necessary to consider two next problems for discovered association rules, i.e.:
- redundancy of some rules,
- interdependency between two rules.

First problem refers to relations between two rules, where one rule contains more general antecedent and more precise consequent than the other rule. In such a case one is not interested in accepting both rules but prefers to stay with the more general (more informative) rule and to reject the less general one. The concept of more general rule is defined below.

Definition 3.4:
Given two rules $C \rightarrow D$ and $C' \rightarrow D'$, where $C \cup D = \{(a_1, l_1, u_1), \ldots, (a_m, l_m, u_m)\}$ and $C' \cup D' = \{(b_1, l'_1, u'_1), \ldots, (b_n, l'_n, u'_n)\}$, the rule $C' \rightarrow D'$ is *more general* than the rule $C \rightarrow D$ if the following conditions are satisfied:

1. $[C'] \subseteq [C]$ and $[D] \subseteq [D']$;
2. $\forall a_i \in [C]$ and $\forall b_i \in [C']$ where $a_i = b_i$ we have $l'_i \preceq l_i \preceq u_i \preceq u'_i$;
3. $\forall a_i \in [D]$ and $\forall b_i \in [D']$ where $a_i = b_i$ we have $l_i \preceq l'_i \preceq u'_i \preceq u_i$;
4. $confidence(C \cup D) \leq confidence(C' \cup D')$.

If one of the above conditions is not fulfilled, one cannot determine which rule is redundant and could be removed.

The second problem concerns *interdependency of rules*. Let us illustrate it by considering a simple example of two rules: $(a \preceq 3) \rightarrow (b \preceq 4)$ and $(a \succeq 2) \rightarrow (b \succeq 2)$. Informally speaking these rules have intersected elementary conditions. These rules can be synthesized into $(2 \preceq a \preceq 3) \rightarrow (2 \preceq b \preceq 4)$ if the support, confidence and credibility of the resulting rule is satisfactory.

Definition 3.5:
Two rules $C \rightarrow D$ and $C' \rightarrow D'$ are *interdependent*, if $[C] = [C']$ and $[D] = [D']$ and $\forall a_i \in [C] \cup [D]$ $l_i \preceq u'_i$ or $l'_i \preceq u_i$.

To deal with this situation we propose to add a new (intersected) rule with elementary conditions defined as $(a_i, max\{l, l'\}, min\{u, u'\})$. Moreover, for the rule created in this way one has to check its support, confidence and credibility.

Continuation of the example.
Let us illustrate the problem of redundant rules by means of two rules, which could be generated from examples represented in Table 1:

$r_1 : (a_1 \preceq \$3000) \rightarrow (a_2 \preceq small)$ with support=10% and confidence=100%
$r_2 : (a_1 \preceq \$5000) \rightarrow (a_2 \preceq small)$ with support=50% and confidence=100%

The rule r_2 is more general than rule r_1 because the antecedent part of r_2 covers more examples than that of r_1, while the consequence parts of both rules and their confidence ratios are the same. Therefore, rule r_1 is removed.

Then, compare the rule r_2 with another rule r_3 of the following form:
$r_3 : (a_1 \preceq \$5000) \rightarrow (a_2 \preceq \text{high})$ with support=30% and confidence=60%
One can easily notice that rule r_3 is not more general than rule r_2 because both
rules r_2 and r_3 satisfy conditions 1,2 and 3 of Definition 3.4, but they do not
satisfy condition 4. In fact, rule r_3 has worse confidence, so one should stay with
both rules.

Intersection of rules will be illustrated by means of two other rules that can
be generated from examples presented in Table 1.
$r_4 : (a_2 \preceq \text{small}) \rightarrow (a_1 \leq \$7500) \wedge (a_3 \preceq \text{medium})$ with support = 70% and
confidence = 100%
$r_5 : (a_2 \succeq \text{small}) \rightarrow (a_1 \geq \$5000) \wedge (a_3 \succeq \text{medium})$ with support = 50% and
confidence = 71%
These two rules can be synthesized in a new rule:
$r_6 : (a_2, \text{small,small}) \rightarrow (a_1, \$5000, \$7500) \wedge (a_3, \text{medium,medium})$ or shortly
written as $(a_2 \sim \text{small}) \rightarrow (\$5000 \preceq a_1 \preceq \$7500) \wedge (a_3 \sim \text{medium})$.   □

Given a data table, the problem of mining association rules is now the following:

1. Find all association rules that have support, confidence and credibility at
   least equal to the user specified thresholds *minsupp*, *minconf* and *mincredbility* (minimum accepted support, confidence and credibility, respectively).
2. Check the redundancy and interdependency of these rules.

4   Algorithm of Mining Association Rules

We propose to induce the new kind of association rules by an algorithm which is
an extension of "original" Agrawal et al. algorithm [2]. The problem of mining
such rules is decomposed into two subproblems:

1. Find all conjunctions of elementary conditions (also called itemsets) that
   have support at least equal to the required *minsupp* parameter; they are
   shortly called frequent itemsets.
2. Use the frequent itemsets to generate the rules having evaluation measures
   not less than user's defined parameters *minsupp*, *minconf* and *mincredbility*.

Due to the limited size of this paper we can only sketch this algorithm stressing
the main extensions. In the first phase single conditions are defined as $(a_i \preceq u_i)$
or $(a_i \succeq l_i)$, respectively. If a criterion is defined on the ordered set of values
$\{v_i^1, v_i^2, \ldots, v_i^{n-1}, v_i^n\}$, then the following elementary conditions are considered
$(a_i \preceq v_i^1)$, $(a_i \preceq v_i^2)$, $\ldots$, $(a_i \preceq v_i^{n-1})$ and $(a_i \succeq v_i^2)$, $(a_i \succeq v_i^3)$, $\ldots$, $(a_i \succeq v_i^n)$.
Only these elementary conditions that have support not less than *minsupp* be-
come frequent itemsets of size 1 (denoted as L_1). Then, in a subsequent pass,
say pass k, the frequent itemsets L_{k-1} (found in k-1 pass) are used to create
candidate itemsets C_k (see the description of *Apriorigen* function in [2]). However, combinations of conditions referring to the same criterion are not allowed.
Moreover, we require to select only robust itemsets. Any itemset defined by con-
ditions $(a_i \succeq r_{ai})$ or $(a_i \preceq r_{ai})$, where $a_i \in C \subseteq A$, is robust iff $\exists x \in DT$

such that $\forall a_i\ a_i(x) \sim r_{ai}$. While combining conditions for criteria having the same direction of preference, we also require use of the same type of preference operator either $\preceq$ or $\succeq$. While performing *join* and *prune* steps of *Apriorigen* function we use proper lexicographic order of candidates C_k, where we may use properties of dominance between different combinations of conditions. It means that for instance given two combinations $(a_1 \succeq r_1)$, $(a_2 \succeq r_2)$, ..., $(a_k \succeq r_k)$ and $(a_1 \succeq p_1)$, $(a_2 \succeq p_2)$, ..., $(a_k \succeq p_k)$, where $\forall i\ p_i \succeq r_i$, if the first candidate is not frequent, then also the second will not be frequent.

The generating rule phase extends the schema of *ap_genrules* procedure defined in [2]. For every frequent itemset we generate rules starting from consequence with one element, then with two elements, etc. The modifications include operations performed in the following order:

1. For each rule with SC criteria and confidence below 100% check consistency of supporting objects. Calculate the credibility of the rule. Delete rules with credibility less than *mincredibility*.
2. For all rules test their generality.
3. Test possible interdependency of rules.

Let us comment that this extended algorithm is more time consuming than its original version. The most complex part is the operation of checking consistency of supporting objects. In the first phase of *Apriori* candidate generation procedure the number of considered values for each attribute is a crucial issue. If one has to consider too many values, the discretization of criterion scales may be applied in early phase of the algorithm - see also discussion of similar problems for mining quantitative association rules [5,6]. Here, we should stress the role of robust items which limit the allowed combinations of conditions to objects existing in data tables. We have also experimentally checked that it can significantly reduce the number of frequent itemsets and final rules. Obviously, the proper choice of minimal support, confidence and credibility, depending on the considered data, is quite important.

5   Conclusions

The novelty of the approach to Knowledge Discovery proposed in this paper is the handling of preference information in data. Preference information is a fundamental concept of Decision Theory and it is well known that, in particular, multiple criteria decision problems have no solution unless this information is taken into account. Nowadays methods of Knowledge Discovery do not take into account the preference information present in data and thus they may lead to wrong conclusions. For instance, they may discover a rule that says "the higher the month salary, the more risky the credit payment for the bank", because in the data there were objects supporting this statement and not identified as inconsistent.

The present proposal is based on a specific understanding of the association rules that handles inconsistency between objects with respect to semantically correlated criteria.

This proposal was applied to real data concerning technical diagnostics for motor vehicles. We compared it with typical approach for mining association rules that do not take into account criteria. For chosen values of rule parameters, we observed that 78% of typical association rules were not consistent if preference ordered scales of criteria and semantically correlation between criteria were considered.

The presented approach can be combined with methods handling "imperfect" character of data like missing or imprecise values of attributes and criteria. Moreover, other future research topics could concern defining specific rule interest measures for selecting the most relevant results among the quite large number of rules inferred from data. Yet another important problem is evaluation of the computation cost of the proposed approach on various data sets. We are also interested in developing applications of the association rules on preference ordered data in some real life problems (e.g. financial markets).

Acknowledgment. The authors wish to acknowledge financial support from State Committee for Scientific Research, research grant no. 8T11F 006 19, and from the Foundation for Polish Science, subsidy no. 11/2001. Moreover, the first author has been supported by MIUR (Italian Ministry of Education, University and Research).

References

1. Agrawal R., Imelinski T., Swami A.: Mining association rules between sets of of items in large databases. In: Proc. of ACM SIGMOD Conf. on Management Data, 1993, 207–216.
2. Agrawal R., Mannila H., Srikant R., Toivinen H., Verkamo I.: Fast discovery of association rules. In: Fayyad U.M. et al. (eds): Advances in Knowledge Discovery and Data Mining, AAAI Press, 1996, 307–328.
3. Greco S., Matarazzo B., Slowinski R.: Rough sets theory for multicriteria decision analysis. European Journal of Operational Research, 2001, **129** (1), 1–47.
4. Han J., Kamber M.: Data mining: Concepts and techniques. Morgan Kaufmann, 1999.
5. Miller R.J., Yang Y.: Association rules over interval data. In Proc. of ACM SIGMOD Conf. on Management Data, 1997.
6. Sirkant R., Agrawal R.: Mining generalized association rules in large relational tables. In: Proc. of ACM SIGMOD Conf. on Management Data, 1996.
7. Slowinski R., Stefanowski J, Greco, S., Matarazzo B.: Rough sets processing of inconsistent information, Control and Cybernetics, 2000, **29** (1), 379–404.

Unknown Attribute Values Processing by Meta-learner

Ivan Bruha

McMaster University, Dept. Computing & Software
Hamilton, Ont., Canada L8S4K1
bruha@mcmaster.ca

Abstract. Real-world data usually contain a certain percentage of unknown (missing) attribute values. Therefore efficient robust data mining algorithms should comprise some routines for processing these unknown values. The paper [5] figures out that each dataset has more or less its own 'favourite' routine for processing unknown attribute values. It evidently depends on the magnitude of noise and source of unknownness in each dataset. One possibility how to solve the above problem of selecting the right routine for processing unknown attribute values for a given database is exhibited in this paper. The covering machine learning algorithm CN4 processes a given database for six routines for unknown attribute values independently. Afterwards, a meta-learner (meta-combiner) is used to derive a meta-classifier that makes up the overall (final) decision about the class of input unseen objects.
The results of experiments with various percentages of unknown attribute values on real-world data are presented and performances of the meta-classifier and the six base classifiers are then compared.

1 Introduction

If machine learning algorithms induce decision trees or decision rules from real-world data, many various aspects are to be taken into account. One important aspect in particular is the processing of *unknown* (*missing*) attribute values. This topic has been discussed and analyzed by several researchers in the field of machine learning [3], [4], [5], [14].

[15] surveys and investigates quite a few techniques for unknown attribute values processing for the TDIDT (Top Down Induction Decision Trees) family and analyzes seven combinations of their placement in the learning algorithm.

The paper [5] firstly discusses the sources of 'unknownness' and then in detail introduces five routines for processing unknown attribute values in the covering machine algorithm CN4 [6], [7], a large extension of the well-known algorithm CN2 [2], [10], [11]. In its analysis, it concludes that each dataset needs more or less its own 'favourite' routine for processing unknown attribute values. It evidently depends on the magnitude of noise and source of unknownness in each dataset, measured e.g. by methodology in [13]. [5] also suggested (but not investigated) how to select a favourite routine for a given database: All routines should be independently run on a small subset (window) of the given database and the suitable routine is to be selected according to their classification accuracies.

This paper describes another way of processing unknown attribute values. We were inspired by the idea of multiple knowledge, multi-strategy learning, and meta-learning, particularly by the concept of *combiner* and *stack generalizer* [12].

M.-S. Hacid et al. (Eds.): ISMIS 2002, LNAI 2366, pp. 451–461, 2002.

Our approach utilizes the above concept of the combiner as follows. The algorithm CN4 processes a given database for each of six routines for unknown attribute values independently. (The sixth routine was added to CN4 lately.) We can thus view the CN4 algorithm with various routines as independent *base learners*. Consequently, we obtain six independent, so called *base classifiers*. Also, a *meta-database* is derived from the results of base classifiers and the *meta-learner* induces a *meta-classifier*. We call the entire system *meta-combiner*, namely *Meta-CN4* because the base learners are formed by the CN4 algorithm.

Hence, if an unknown object is to be classified, then each base classifier yields its decision (class of the input unseen object) and the meta-classifier combines their results in order to produce the final (over-all) decision about the class of the given input object.

In order to compare various machine learning algorithms we also implemented another meta-combiner, *Meta-ID3* in the same way. The base classifiers utilize the well-known algorithm ID3 [9] (the version designed and implemented by the author) with the equivalent six routines for processing unknown attribute values.

Section 2 of this paper surveys the methodology of the CNx family of covering algorithms. The way CN4 processes unknown attribute values are briefly presented in Section 3. Section 4 presents the principle of the meta-combiner. Experiments exhibiting the performance of Meta-CN4 and Meta-ID3 are introduced in Section 5, together with their comparison with C4.5 [16] . The results are analyzed in Section 6.

2 The CNx Family

The inductive algorithms of the CNx family comprise two main procedures: the top procedure that repeatedly controls the search for decision rules, and the search procedure that performs the beam search to find the best complex for a portion of the training set.

The inductive algorithm generates decision rules from a set of K training examples (objects), each accompanied by its desired class C_r, $r = 1,...,R$. Examples (objects) are formally represented by N attributes which are either discrete (symbolic) or numerical (continuous). A discrete attribute A_n comprises J(n) distinct values $V_1,...,V_{J(n)}$; a numerical attribute may attain any value from a continuous interval[1]. The algorithm yields either an *ordered* or an *unordered* list of decision rules of the form

Rule: if *Cmplx* then class is C_r

A complex[2] *Cmplx* is evaluated according to a user-specified heuristic evaluation function which is one of the three: either (negative) entropy, Laplacian

---

[1]   There exist several procedures for discretizing numerical attributes. The one implemented in CN4 is described in [7]. An off-line discretization (KEX-preprocessor) [1] can be applied to various symbolic algorithms, including CN4, too.

[2]   A *complex* is a conjunction of attribute pairs of the form $A_n = V_j$ for a symbolic attribute, or $A_n = Int_j$ for a numerical attribute (*Int$_j$* is a numerical discretized interval).

criterion for expected accuracy, or m-probability [5], [8]. The larger the value of the evaluation function, the better the complex.

The flow chart of the top-level learning procedure for the ordered mode looks as follows (here T is a training set, SEARCH is the search procedure that performs the beam search to find the best complex):

procedure CN$x(T)$
> Let *ListOfRules* be an empty list
> **Until** T is empty **do**
>> 1. Let *Cmplx* be the best complex found by the search procedure SEARCH(T) for the given set T and the user-selected heuristic
>> 2. **If** *Cmplx* is not nil then
>>> Let T' f T be examples covered by *Cmplx*
>>> Let T become $T \setminus T'$
>>> Add the rule if *Cmplx* then class is C to the end of *ListOfRules* where C is the majority class in T'
>>> **else** break (quit the loop)
> **enddo**
> Add the default rule If *true* then class is *majority class* to the end of *ListOfRules*
> Return *ListOfRules*

3 Unknown Attribute Value Processing

To deal with real-world situations, it is necessary to process incomplete data, i.e. data with unknown attribute values. Six routines for processing of unknown attribute values were designed for CN4 [5].

The following natural ways of dealing with unknown attribute values were incorporated:

(i)   ignore the example (object) with unknown values (routine *Ignore*),

(ii)   consider the unknown value as an additional regular value for a given attribute (routine *Unknown*), or

(iii)   substitute the unknown value for matching purposes by a suitable value which is either

- the most common value (routine *Common*), or
- a proportional fraction (routine *Fraction*), or
- a random value from the probabilistic distribution (routine *Random*), or
- any value of the known values of the attribute that occur in the training set (routine *Anyvalue*).

Treating unknown attribute values is determined by the following statistical parameters (here the classes are subject to the index r$=1,...,R$, attributes A_n for $n=1,...,N$, their values j$=1,...,$J(n)):

- the *over-all absolute* frequencies $F_{n,j}$ that express the number of examples exhibiting the value V_j for each attribute A_n ;
- the *class-sensitive absolute* frequencies $F_{r,n,j}$ that express the number of examples of the class C_r exhibiting the value V_j for each attribute A_n ;
- the *over-all relative* frequencies $f_{n,j}$ of all known values V_j for each attribute A_n ;

- the *class-sensitive relative* frequencies $f_{r,n,j}$ of all known values V_j for each attribute A_n and for a given class C_r .

The underlying idea for learning relies on the class distribution; i.e., the class-sensitive frequencies are utilized. As soon as we substitute an unknown value by a suitable one, we take the desired class of the example into consideration in order not to increase the noise in the data set. On the other hand, the over-all frequencies are applied within classification.

(A)   Routine Ignore: Ignore Unknown Values. This strategy simply ignores examples with at least one unknown attribute value before learning. Consequently, this approach does not contribute to any enhancement of processing noisy or partly specified data.

(B)   Routine Unknown: Unknown Value as a Regular One. An unknown value is considered as an additional attribute value. Hence, the number of values is increased by one for each attribute that depicts an unknown value in the training set. Note that some special arrangements have to be done for a numerical attribute if processed by this routine [5].

(C)   Routine Common: The Most Common Value. This routine needs the class-sensitive absolute frequencies $F_{r,n,j}$ to be known before learning and the over-all frequencies $F_{n,j}$ before classification. An unknown value of a discrete attribute A_n of an example belonging to the class C_r is replaced by the *class-sensitive common* value which maximizes the Laplacian formula
$\{F_{\{func \{r,n,'j\}\}}\text{'\+'}1\}$ over $\{F_{\{func \{n,'j\}\}}\text{'\+''}R\}$ over j for the given r and n. An unknown value within classification is replaced by the *over-all common* value which maximizes $F_{n,j}$ over subscript j . We use here the Laplacian formula within learning because it prefers those attribute values that are more predictive for a given class in the contrary to the conventional 'maximum frequency' scheme. Again, some special arrangements have to be done for a numerical (continuous) attribute if processed by this routine [5].

(D)   Routine Fraction: Split into Proportional Fractions. The learning phase requires that the relative frequencies $f_{r,n,j}$ above the entire training set be known. Each example **x** of class C_r with an unknown value of a discrete attribute A_n is substituted by a collection of examples before the actual learning phase as follows: unknown value of A_n is replaced by all known values V_j of A_n and C_r. The weight of each split example (with the value V_j) is

$$w_j = w(\mathbf{x}) * f_{r,n,j} , \quad j=1,...,J(n)$$

where $w(\mathbf{x})$ is the weight of the original example **x** .
If a training example involves more unknown attribute values, then the above splitting is done for each unknown value. Again, special arrangements are done for numerical attributes [5].

(E)   Random Value. An unknown attribute value is replaced by one of the values of the given attribute by utilizing a random number generator; it yields a random number in the range <0; 1> which is exploited to select corresponding value by utilizing the distribution of its attribute values. In the learning phase, the distribution is formed by the class-sensitive relative frequencies $f_{r,n,j}$ of all known values V_j for each attribute A_n and for a given class C_r . In classification phase, the over-all relative frequencies $f_{n,j}$ are used.

(F)   Routine Anyvalue: Any Value Matches. An unknown value matches any existing attribute value of an example (object), both in learning and classification. This routine in fact emulates the situation that a designer of a training database does not care about a value of a certain attribute for a given example (so-called *dont-care* scenario).

4 Meta-learner

Following [12] in spirits, we exploit the meta-learning (multistrategy learning) in order to process unknown attribute values in a database-independent fashion. Each of the six *base learners* (CN4 with different routines for processing unknown attribute values) generates a *base classifier*. Afterwards, the decisions of the base classifiers form a *meta-database*, a set for training *meta-objects* (examples) for the *meta-learner*. The meta-learner then generates a *meta-classifier*. The meta-classifier does not select the best base classifier (routine for processing unknown attribute values) but rather combines the decisions (predictions, classes) of all the base classifiers. In the classification phase, the base classifiers first derive their predictions (classes, decisions); then a meta-object is derived from these predictions which is then classified by the meta-learner.

More precisely, the *meta-combiner* consists of two phases: meta-learning and meta-classifying; we will now define both these phases in detail.

A training set is split for the meta-learning purposes into two subsets: the *genuine-training* and *examining* ones. The genuine-training subset is applied for inducing the base classifiers; the examining one for generating a meta-database.

Let q be the q-th base classifier, $q=1...,Q$ (where Q is the number of the base classifiers; in our project $Q=6$).Each example of the examining subset (examining example) **x** generates a meta-object of the meta-database as follows. Let z_q be the decision (class) of the q-th base classifier for the examining object **x**; then the corresponding meta-object of the meta-database looks as follows:

$$[z_1, \ldots, z_Q, Z]$$

where z_q, $q=1...,Q$ is the decision the of q-th base classifier, Z is the desired class if the input examining object. This rule is denoted as *class-combiner* [12].

Let T be a training set of K training examples, S be an integer in the range $<2; K>$. Let us assume to have Q different base learners. The flow chart of the meta-learner looks as follows (here):

procedure Meta-Learning-Phase(T, S)
1. Partition the training set T randomly into S disjoint subsets of equal size (as equal as possible). Let T_s be the s-th such subset, $s=1,...,S$, card(T_s) the number of its objects (examples).
2. Form S pairs $[T_s, T \setminus T_s]$, $s=1...,S$.
3. Let *MetaDatabase* be empty.

---

[3] The splitting (partition) procedure has to preserve the original distribution of classes as in T.
[4] For each s, $T \setminus T_s$ is the genuine-training subset and T_s the examining one, generated from the training set T.

4. **for** s=1,...,S **do**

Train all base learners using the genuine-training subset $T \setminus T_s$; result is Q base classifiers.

Classify the examining objects from T_s by these base classifiers.

Generate card(T_s) meta-objects using the above class-combiner rule and add them to *MetaDatabase*

enddo

5. Train the meta-learner using the meta-database *MetaDatabase*. The result is a meta-classifier

6. Generate the base classifiers using the entire training set T which will be used in the following meta-classification

Similar scenario is applied for the classifying an unseen object **x**:

procedure Meta-Classifying-Phase(**x**)

1. Classify the unseen object **x** by all Q base classifiers (generated in the step 6 of the above meta-learning phase); let the output of the q-th base classifier be z_q , q=1,...,Q .

2. Generate the corresponding meta-object $[z_1, ..., z_Q]$ by utilizing the class-combiner rule.

3. Classify the above meta-object by the meta-classifier; its result (decision) is the class to which the given input object **x** is classified.

The number S of split subsets is crucial for this system. Therefore, we call it *S-fold meta-learner* or *S-fold meta-combiner*. The paper [12] introduces two architectures of their meta-system: combiner and stacked generalization. Their combiner corresponds to the 2-fold and stacked generalized to the K-fold meta-learner.

5 Experiments

This section describes the experiments that have been carried out in order to compare the above meta-combiner Meta-CN4 of the six routines for unknown attribute value processing in the CN4 algorithm. Following [12], we selected the promising 4-fold meta-combiner ($S=4$). As we already explained, we also designed and implemented for the comparison purposes the meta-combiner Meta-ID3 for the 'traditional' ID3 machine learning algorithm. The over-all results are also compared with the performance of the machine learning algorithm C4.5. Namely, the following algorithms were experimentally tested[5]:

a) Meta-CN4 ($S=4$),

b) Meta-ID3 ($S=4$),

---

[5]   The parameters of CN4 were set up to their default values (i.e. ordered mode, Laplacian formula for evaluation, star size equal to 5, parameter for Π^2-distribution equal to 0.025). The parameters of other algorithms were also set up to their default values.

c) the original CN4 with the routine Unknown,
d) that with the routine Common,
e) that with the routine Anyvalue,
f) C4.5

Only the above three routines for unknown attribute value processing were selected in cases c) to e) because they exhibit the best performance, which was analyzed in [5].

All above systems were tested on four databases. Each database was randomly split to two sets (70% training, 30% testing) and this scenario has been executed 20 times for each combination. The following tables thus involve in each slot an average of classification accuracy (of testing sets) acquired from 20 runs.

We have to realize that the above splitting procedure has nothing common with that in the meta-learner. The 70% of training examples are furthermore split within the 4-fold meta-learner into a genuine-training subset of the size 52.5% and a examining subset of the size 17.5% of the original database.

The fours AI databases are as follows:

- **ThyroidGland**: This task of diagnosis of thyroid gland disease has been provided by the Institute of Nuclear Medicine of Inselspital, Bern, Switzerland. The database has been used at the Dept. of Advanced Mathematics, University of Bern, and also in the project CN4. The entire set involves 269 patients' data. Each patient is described by 19 attributes, 5 of them are numerical attributes, the rest are symbolic ones; the average number of values per symbolic attribute is 4.9 . About 30% of attribute values are unknown. The task involves two classes; the frequency of the majority class is 72%.

- **BreastTumor**: This dataset has been provided by the Jozef Stefan Institute, the research group of Prof. Dr. I. Bratko, Ljubljana. It involves 288 examples and two classes. Each attribute is represented by 10 attributes, 4 of them are numerical; symbolic attributes exhibit on average 2.7 values per attribute. 0.7% of attribute values are unknown. The majority class has frequency 80%.

- **Onco**: The oncological data were used for testing in the Czech Academy of Sciences, Prague, Czechland, and also in the project CN4 [6]. The entire set involves 127 examples. Each example is represented by 8 attributes; 7 of them are numerical attributes, the only symbolic one involves 3 values. All attribute values are known. The task involves three classes; the frequency of the majority class is 50%.

- **Soybean**: This well-known data has been used in many various experiments in machine learning, namely within the AQ family. The set available to the authors of this paper involves 290 training examples and 15 classes. Each example is characterized by 24 attributes, all are symbolic ones with average 2.9 values per attribute. The set exhibits 3.7% unknown attribute values. There are 4 classes exposing the maximum frequency (14%).

To achieve extensive and comprehensive comparison of the above routines' behaviour we decided to find how classification accuracy depends on various percentage of unknown attribute values in databases.

458   I. Bruha

However, only the database *ThyroidGland* exhibits a reasonable size of 'unknownness'. Therefore, we performed three experiments with this database for various number of attributes:
- set with all 19 attributes (there is 30% unknown values),
- set with 10 most informative attributes[6] (there is 20% unknown values),
- set with 5 most informative attributes (there is 15% unknown values).

As for the remaining databases, to emulate various number of unknown values, we have run the original data through a filter which randomly changes attribute values to unknown ones. The filter procedure ('unknownizer') has the percentage of unknown attribute values as its parameter.

Tab. 1 to 4 comprise the average classification accuracy (in %) for all four datasets for various percentage of unknown values. Fig. 1 then depicts the above classification accuracies averaged above all datasets.

Table 1. Average classification accuracy (in %) as a function of unknownness for the dataset *ThyroidGland*

	Meta-CN4	Meta-ID3	CN4 Unknown	CN4 Common	CN4 Anyvalue	C4.5
15%	91	88	90	85	88	84
20%	92	86	91	85	92	84
30%	92	86	91	85	92	84

Table 2. Average classification accuracy (in %) as a function of unknownness for the dataset *BreastTumor*

	Meta-CN4	Meta-ID3	CN4 Unknown	CN4 Common	CN4 Anyvalue	C4.5
5%	88	85	86	85	84	83
10%	87	85	85	85	84	84
20%	84	83	83	83	83	83
30%	84	83	82	83	83	82

Table 3. Average classification accuracy (in %) as a function of unknownness for the dataset *Onco*

	Meta-CN4	Meta-ID3	CN4 Unknown	CN4 Common	CN4 Anyvalue	C4.5
5%	77	76	75	74	75	75
10%	75	74	74	74	75	73
20%	74	74	71	71	72	72
30%	73	73	71	70	72	71

---

[6] Informativity of attributes were measured by the information gain, see e.g. [14].

Table 4. Average classification accuracy (in %) as a function of unknownness for the dataset *Soybean*

	Meta-CN4	Meta-ID3	CN4 Unknown	CN4 Common	CN4 Anyvalue	C4.5
5%	77	75	75	74	75	74
10%	76	73	74	74	75	73
20%	73	72	71	71	72	71
30%	73	71	71	70	72	70

6 Analysis

The aim of this research paper was to project, implement, and experimentally compare the meta-learner Meta-CN4 with its base classifiers, i.e. the CN4 algorithm for six routines for processing of missing attribute values. Furthermore, we also used Meta-ID3 and C4.5 for comparison. The only, but widely used criterion in our experiments was the classification accuracy acquired from testing sets.

By analyzing the results of our experiments we came to the following:

- The meta-learner Meta-CN4 became a winner in comparison with the other learning algorithms. We can see it from the results portrayed on the above tables and the Fig. 1. We can also perceive tis statement at Tab. 5 which depicts the statistical results of the t-test (with the confidence level 0.05) for both Meta-CN4 and Meta-ID3.
- The reason why the C4.5 algorithm was not so successful is that it uses only the equivalent of the routine Common.
- We did not use the stack generalizer (fold $S=K$) because it is much more time consuming; the paper [12] indicates that the timing cost for the stack generalizer is much more larger than that for the meta-combiner for relatively small parameter S.

Table 5. Results of the t-tests of comparing Meta-CN4 and Meta-ID3 with the single 'non-combiners'.

Here the following symbols mean:

+   significantly better
!   significantly worse
0   cannot decide

compared with	Meta-CN4	Meta-ID3	CN4 Unknown	CN4 Common	CN4 Anyvalue	C4.5
Meta-CN4		+	+	+	+	+
Meta-ID3	!		0	+	0	+

For the future research, we plan to investigate the way of generating and processing the meta-databases. Such a database usually contains many contradictory examples (objects).

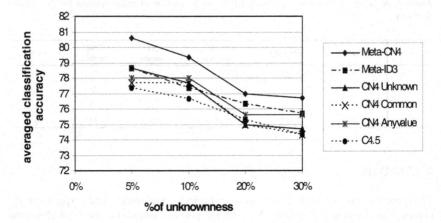

Fig. 1. Averaged classification accuracy vs. percentage of unknownness for six algorithms

References

1. Berka, P. and Bruha, I.: Various discretizing procedures of numerical attributes: Empirical comparisons. 8th European Conference Machine Learning, Workshop Statistics, Machine Learning, and Knowledge Discovery in Databases, Heraklion, Crete (1995), 136-141
2. Boswell, R.: Manual for CN2, version 4.1. Turing Institute, Techn. Rept. P-2145/Rab/4/1.3 (1990)
3. Brazdil, P.B. and Bruha, I.: A note on processing missing attribute values: A modified technique. Workshop on Machine learning, Canadian Conference AI, Vancouver (1992)
4. Bruha, I.: Unknown attribute values processing utilizing expert knowledge on attribute hierarchy. 8th European Conference on Machine Learning, Workshop Statistics, Machine Learning, and Knowledge Discovery in Databases, Heraklion, Crete (1995), 130-135
5. Bruha, I. and Franek, F.: Comparison of various routines for unknown attribute value processing: Covering paradigm. International Journal Pattern Recognition and Artificial Intelligence, 10, 8 (1996), 939-955
6. Bruha, I. and Kockova, S.: Quality of decision rules: Empirical and statistical approaches. Informatica, 17 (1993), 233-243
7. Bruha, I. and Kockova, S.: A support for decision making: Cost-sensitive learning system. Artificial Intelligence in Medicine, 6 (1994), 67-82
8. Cestnik, B.: Estimating probabilities: A crucial task in machine learning. ECAI-90 (1990)
9. Cestnik, B., Kononenko, I., Bratko, I.: ASSISTANT 86: A knowledge-elicitation tool for sophisticated users. In: Bratko, I. and Lavrac, N. (eds.): Progress in machine learning. Proc. EWSL'87, Sigma Press (1987)
10. Clark, P. and Boswell, R.: Rule induction with CN2: Some recent improvements. EWSL'91, Porto (1991), 151-163
11. Clark. P. and Niblett, T.: The CN2 induction algorithm. Machine Learning, 3 (1989), 261-283
12. Fan, D.W., , Chan, P.K., Stolfo, S.J.: A comparative evaluation of combiner and stacked generalization. Workshop Integrating Multiple Learning Models, AAAI, Portland (1996)

13. Kononenko, I. and Bratko, I.: Information-based evaluation criterion for classifier's performance. Machine Learning, 6 (1991), 67-80
14. Quinlan, J.R.: Induction of decision trees. Machine Learning, 1 (1986), 81-106
15. Quinlan, J.R.: Unknown attribute values in ID3. International Conference ML (1989), 164-8
16. Quinlan, J.R.: C4.5 programs for machine learning. Morgan Kaufmann (1992)

Intelligent Buffer Cache Management in Multimedia Data Retrieval

Yeonseung Ryu[1]*, Kyoungwoon Cho[2], Youjip Won[3]**, and Kern Koh[2]

[1] Division of Information and Communication Engineering, Hallym University, Korea
ysryu@hallym.ac.kr
[2] School of Computer Engineering, Seoul National Univeristy, Korea
{cezanne, kernkoh}@oslab.snu.ac.kr
[3] Division of Electrical and Computer Engineering, Hanyang University, Korea
yjwon@ece.hanyang.ac.kr

Abstract. In this paper, we present an intelligent buffer cache management algorithm in multimedia data retrieval called *Adaptive Buffer cache Management (ABM)*. The proposed ABM scheme automatically detects the reference pattern of each file and intelligently switches between different buffer cache management schemes on per-file basis. According to our simulation based experiment, the ABM scheme yields better buffer cache miss ratio than the legacy buffer cache schemes such as LRU or interval based scheme. The ABM scheme manifests itself when the workload exhibits not only sequential but also looping reference patterns.

Keywords: Buffer Cache, Multimedia File System, Looping Reference

1 Introduction

The multimedia streaming workload is generally characterized as sequential access of the data. Multimedia technology is being applied in various fields, e.g. entertainment, education, tele-collaboration to list a few. Recently some studies showed that users may not sequentially access the files in on-line educational media server [8,1,7,5]. In on-line education system, students can access the particular segment of video clips repeatedly to review the materials they were not able to understand properly. Thus, it is possible that some users scan the file sequentially while the others repeatedly view the particular segment of the same file. In this case, aggregated file access workload may exhibit mixture of widely different access characteristics. The buffer cache replacement scheme should be able to change the policy dynamically depending on the workload characteristics.

In this paper, we propose a buffer cache replacement algorithm called *Adaptive Buffer cache Management (ABM)*, which automatically detects the reference pattern of each file and intelligently applies an appropriate policy per-file basis.

---

* This work was supported by the Research Fund 2001 at Hallym University.
** The work of this author was supported by KOSEF through Statistical Research Center for Complex System at Seoul National University.

M.-S. Hacid et al. (Eds.): ISMIS 2002, LNAI 2366, pp. 462–471, 2002.

The proposed ABM scheme maintains a metric called *Looping Reference Indicator* for each opened files which denotes whether there exist looping reference patterns and how *effective* they are. The loop is said to be *effective* if the data blocks in the loop can be entirely loaded in the buffer cache. The ABM scheme periodically monitors the reference pattern and applies different buffer replacement policies depending on whether the current workload exhibits sequential or looping reference characteristics. Simulation study shows that the ABM scheme can significantly improve the buffer cache miss ratio, especially when the underlying workload exhibits not only sequential but also looping reference property.

The remainder of this paper is organized as follows. In Sect. 2, we discuss the buffer replacement schemes for multimedia server. In Sect. 3, we describe *Adaptive Buffer Cache Management* algorithm. Section 4 presents results of performance analysis and verifies that the proposed algorithm behaves as expected. Finally, we conclude with a summary in Sect. 5.

2   Buffer Cache Schemes for Multimedia File System

When a stream accesses the file in sequential fashion, it is unlikely that recently accessed data block is to be referenced by the same stream in the near future. Rather, it will be referenced by different streams which access the same file with a certain time interval. Thus, as the age of the data block gets older, it is more likely that the block is to be accessed sooner. In this environment, the interval based caching policy looks promising way of minimizing the buffer cache miss ratio.

A number of articles proposed the interval based cache replacement schemes and showed that they deliver better buffer cache performance in multimedia streaming environment than the legacy LRU buffer cache replacement scheme [4, 3,6,9]. Dan *et al.* proposed *Interval Caching* algorithm [4,3]. It exploits temporal locality between streams accessing the same file, by caching *intervals* between successive streams. Özden *et al.* presented *DISTANCE* algorithm [6]. It also caches the blocks in *distance* of successive streams accessing the same media file.

The interval based replacement schemes maintain information about intervals (or distances) of consecutive streams accessing the same file. When there are only sequential references, intervals between consecutive streams do not change normally. However, if there exist looping references, intervals can be changed whenever loop begins. After intervals are changed, the interval based schemes are going to change contents of cache space gradually. That is, when new block needs to be read into the buffer cache, the interval based schemes must determine which blocks to cache and which blocks to replace using the newly created (or modified) interval sets. In order to maximize the number of streams accessing data from the buffer cache, the interval based schemes cache data blocks from the shortest intervals.

Recently, a number of research results have been published regarding the workload analysis of educational media servers [8,1,7,5]. In on-line education system, the user watches lecture on-line and the lecture materials and instructor's annotation appears on the same screen synchronized what speaker is saying. We carefully suspect that the users may exhibit *more than* sequential behavior in this environment. Aimeida *et al.* showed that for short files, interactive requests like jump backwards are common [1]. Rowe *et al.* addressed that students access the video clips to review the materials they were not able to understand properly during the class [8]. In this situation, it is possible that the user accesses particular segment of the video repeatedly rather than sequentially scans the file from the beginning to the end. We call the reference pattern where there exists repetitive sequence of reference pattern as *looping reference*.

Looping reference can be thought as temporally localized or sequential depending on the time scale of interest. The time scale of interest depends on the amount of buffer cache available. If the buffer cache is large enough to hold the entire data blocks in the loop, we can think that the workload exhibits temporal locality. Otherwise, it is regarded as sequential workload. The LRU policy is known optimal in temporal localized reference pattern [2].

The victim selection mechanism of the LRU and the interval based scheme is opposite to each other. The LRU selects the least recently used block as a victim while the interval based schemes select the block from the largest interval. The DISTANCE scheme, for example, actually chooses the youngest data block in the buffer cache which belongs to the largest interval. Thus, it is not possible to find the compromising solution between these two. If the buffer cache is large enough to hold all data blocks in the loop (the loop becomes *effective*), the LRU may be the right choice. Otherwise, the interval based schemes will be more appropriate. We will examine the relationship between the size of the loop and the size of buffer cache for each replacement scheme in more detail in Sect. 4.

3   Intelligenet Buffer Cache Management

3.1   Characterizing the Degree of Looping Reference

We propose a metric called *Looping Reference Indicator* to denote whether there exist looping reference patterns for a given file and how strong it is. The objective of this metric is to decide which of the two buffer replacement schemes to use: interval based caching or LRU. In this work, we choose the DISTANCE policy as interval based caching scheme.

Let u and $U_t(i)$ be the user id and the set of users who access the file i at time t. $|U_t(i)|$ is the number of members in $U_t(i)$. Let $N_i(R_t(u))$ be the logical block number of file i which is accessed by the user u at t. Let $SU_t(i)$ be the set of users in $U_t(i)$ who sequentially access the file i at t. That is, $SU_t(i) = \{ u \mid N_i(R_t(u)) = N_i(R_{t-1}(u)) + 1$ and $u \in U_t(i) \}$. And the set of users who do not sequentially access the file i at t is denoted by $SU_t(i)^c$. Let $B_t(i)$ be the number of data blocks of file i in the buffer cache at time t. When u is accessing the file in looping reference at t, let $L_t(u)$ denote the length of the loop in terms of the number of data blocks. The length of the loop becomes available when

user accesses a certain segment of a file repeatedly. Also, it is not unreasonable
to assume that user can mark the looping interval, i.e. segment of interest and
pass the information of the looping reference to file system.

A loop is said to be *effective* if the number of buffer cache pages allocated
to user u is greater than the length of the loop, $L_t(u)$. Let $EU_t(i)$ be a set of
users in $SU_t(i)^c$ who have effective looping reference at t. These are the set of
users whose subsequent I/O requests can be most likely serviced from the buffer
cache.

$$EU_t(i) = \{u | L_t(u) \le \frac{B_t(i)}{|U_t(i)|} \ and \ u \in SU_t(i)^c\} \tag{1}$$

Given all these, we define the *looping reference indicator* $\delta_t(i)$ of file i at time
t as in Eq. 2.

$$\delta_t(i) = \frac{\int_{t-\theta}^{t} |EU_s(i)| ds}{\int_{t-\theta}^{t} |EU_s(i)| ds + \int_{t-\theta}^{t} |SU_s(i)| ds} \tag{2}$$

Large $\delta_t(i)$ means that there are many effective loop requests to the file i
and thus data blocks in loop area can be served from buffer cache. On the other
hand, small $\delta_t(i)$ implies that relatively larger fraction of the users are accessing
the file i in sequential fashion or non-effective loop requests are often occurred.

In Eq. 2, θ is the update interval for δ. For every θ second, system collects
$EU_s(i)$ and $SU_s(i)$ during past θ second and recomputes δ. To analyze the
reference patterns more elaborately, we can distinguish the update interval θ and
the window length $\mathcal{W}$. System can recompute the looping reference indicator for
every θ seconds based on the past $\mathcal{W}$ sec's samples.

3.2   Buffer Management Method

The proposed ABM scheme applies buffer replacement policy per file basis. When
the file is first referenced, the ABM applies the DISTANCE policy to that file.
This is based on the assumption that streaming workload normally accesses
the file in sequential fashion. The ABM scheme monitors the looping reference
indicator of the files periodically. When the looping reference indicator of the
file becomes large, the ABM switches to the LRU scheme for that file.

As a selection criteria to determine which of the two buffer cache replacement
policies, the ABM uses the threshold value δ^*. If the looping reference indicator
of file is smaller than δ^*, the DISTANCE policy is applied to that file. Otherwise,
the LRU policy is applied.

Figure 1 shows the architecture of the ABM cache manager. The ABM cache
manager consists of three components: system buffer manager, DISTANCE manager and LRU manager. The system buffer manager executes the ABM algorithm
and controls the allocation of buffer space.

The system buffer manager computes the looping reference indicator of
opened files and compares them with threshold value, δ^*. If the looping reference indicator of a file is greater than or equal to δ^*, then the file is allocated

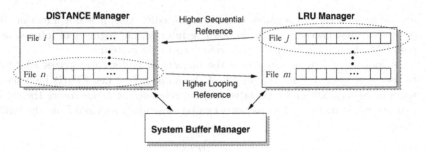

Fig. 1. Structure of Adaptive Buffer Cache Management Scheme

to the LRU manager. Otherwise, the file remains under the DISTANCE manager's control. When the file is determined to transfer to the LRU manager, the data blocks allocated to that file become controlled by the LRU manager. On the contrary, if the file is transferred from the LRU manager to the DISTANCE manager, the data blocks are also transferred to the DISTANCE manager.

It is very important to assign appropriate amount of buffers to each category, elaborate modelling of which is rather complicated. In this subsection, we propose a method of buffer allocation to each manager. The DISTANCE manager and the LRU manager periodically request for additional buffer pages to the system buffer manager. The system buffer manager examines whether it can acquire the buffer pages from the other manager. The system buffer manager maintains information about the total amount of buffer pages allocated to each manager and the respective number of users. The system buffer manager computes the amount of data blocks per user for each manager. The basic idea is to evenly allocate the data blocks to individual streaming sessions. When the DISTANCE manager requests for additional buffer pages, the system buffer manager examines if the users controlled by the DISTANCE manager is allocated smaller number of pages than the users in the LRU manager's control. If so, the system buffer manager requests for the buffer pages to the LRU manager. And then the LRU manager selects the buffer pages using its replacement policy and transfers them to the DISTANCE manager.

4   Simulation Study

In this section, we present the simulation results of legacy buffer cache replacement schemes and verifies the effectiveness of the ABM scheme. We use the synthetic workload. A loop is characterized by three attributes: interval between loops(IBL), length of loop, and loop count. For example, loop parameter of (100, 50, 3) means that (i) the distance between the completion of the one looping reference and the beginning of the following looping reference is 100 second on the average, (ii) length of single iteration is 50 blocks and (iii) loop is repeated for 3 times. Interarrival times of clients are exponentially distributed and average interarrival time is 100 seconds. We assume that every client consumes one block per service round with same playback rate. 20 media files are serviced with an access skew parameter of 0.271 and each file has a length of 60 minutes. The prime performance metric is buffer cache miss ratio. Simulation took more than 8 hours to obtain various numbers: the number of cache hits, the number of block requests and etc.

4.1 Performance Analysis: DISTANCE and LRU

We vary the average interval between the loops to examine the effect of frequency of looping accesses. Figure 2(a) and 2(b) illustrate the effects of varying IBL on the cache misses when the average length of loop are 20 seconds and 40 seconds, respectively. The loop count is set to 5. In the legend of figures, symbols L and D represent LRU and DISTANCE respectively. Numbers shown in the legend represent IBL. Let us look into the graph more closely. With sequential reference pattern, the miss ratios of LRU range from 95% to 99% and remain high even if the cache size increases. The miss rate of DISTANCE is much lower than LRU and decreases as the cache size increases. There is not much difficulty in finding that the DISTANCE is better choice for buffer replacement scheme under sequential reference pattern.

When sequential and looping reference co-exist, miss rate of LRU changes depending on IBL, the length of loop and the cache size. In Fig. 2(a), when IBL is greater than 500 and the cache size is 6000, the miss ratio of LRU is higher than that of DISTANCE. On the other hand, when IBL is 100, the LRU scheme exhibits lower miss ratio at 30% compared to the DISTANCE scheme. However, it is noted that when the cache size is relatively small(for instance, the cache size is 1000), the miss ratio of LRU is higher than that of DISTANCE. This is because the loops become *ineffective* when the cache size is small. As the cache space is big enough to accommodate the blocks accessed by looping, the miss ratios of LRU decrease rapidly and are lower than DISTANCE (See Fig. 2(b)). In summary, the LRU scheme outperforms the DISTANCE scheme when there exist effective looping reference patterns in continuous media streams.

Fig. 3 illustrates the effects of varying the length of loop from 20 blocks to 100 blocks. Average interval between loops is 100 seconds and loop count is 5. Numbers in legend of the figure represent the size of cache. The figure shows that varying the length of loop has little impact on the DISTANCE scheme, but has much impact on the LRU scheme. The LRU yields lower miss ratio as the length of loop decreases. This figure also shows that the cache size has significant impact on the miss ratio especially when the cache is managed by the LRU scheme. When the cache size is large enough to hold the entire loop, the LRU scheme exhibit better cache miss ratio.

Fig. 4 illustrates miss ratios with varying the loop count, 3, 5, and 10, respectively. The average length of loop is 20 blocks and the size of cache is 4000. Numbers appeared in the legend represent IBL. The miss ratios of LRU drop as the loop count increases.

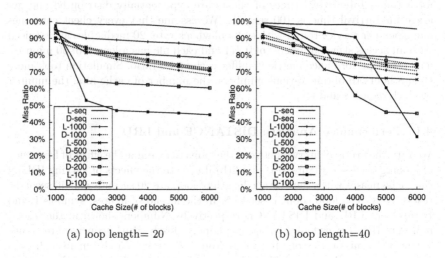

(a) loop length= 20   (b) loop length=40

Fig. 2. Effects of varying the frequency of looping reference via Interval Between the Loops factor

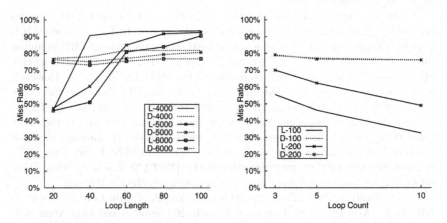

Fig. 3. Effects of the loop length   **Fig. 4.** Effects of the loop count

4.2   Performance of Adaptive Buffer Cache Management Scheme

In order to investigate the performance of the ABM scheme, we generate a number of different looping reference patterns for each file. There are 20 files in total. Figures in Fig. 5 describes the various workload used in our experiments and illustrate the respective simulation results. **IBL**(i) denotes the average interval between loops of clients accessing file i. N and $L(i)$ denotes the total number of

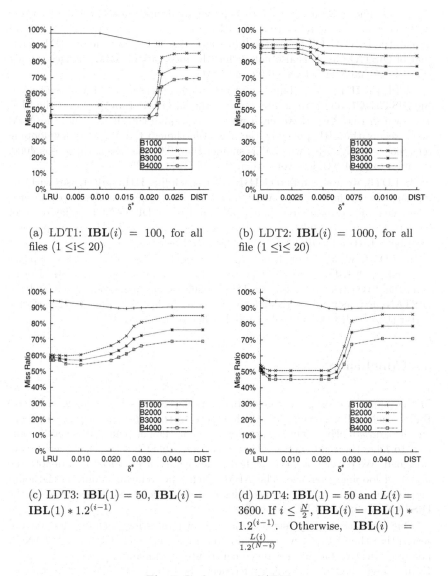

(a) LDT1: **IBL**(i) = 100, for all files ($1 \leq i \leq 20$)

(b) LDT2: **IBL**(i) = 1000, for all file ($1 \leq i \leq 20$)

(c) LDT3: **IBL**(1) = 50, **IBL**(i) = **IBL**$(1) * 1.2^{(i-1)}$

(d) LDT4: **IBL**(1) = 50 and $L(i)$ = 3600. If $i \leq \frac{N}{2}$, **IBL**(i) = **IBL**$(1) * 1.2^{(i-1)}$. Otherwise, **IBL**(i) = $\frac{L(i)}{1.2^{(N-i)}}$

Fig. 5. Performance of ABM

files and the length of file i, respectively. In all LDT, we set the average length of loop and the loop count to 20 blocks and 5 times, respectively.

Fig. 5(a) summarizes the result of experiment with LDT1. Be reminded that when IBL is 100(Fig. 2(a)), the LRU scheme exhibits better performance than DISTANCE scheme. Let us examine the cache size of 4000 blocks. If δ^* is smaller than 0.02, The ABM applies the LRU policy to all files. Hence, the miss ratio of ABM becomes the same as that of LRU. If δ^* is greater than 0.025, the ABM applies the DISTANCE policy to all files and thus, the miss ratio of ABM equals that of DISTANCE. It is also noted that the miss rate of ABM changes rapidly when δ^* is changing between 0.02 and 0.025.

In LDT2, **IBL**(i) for all file is set to 1000. In this case, the ABM should select the DISTANCE policy to all files because the DISTANCE outperforms the LRU as shown in Fig. 2(a). However, if we use very small threshold value, the ABM may execute the LRU policy to the files even though the files have few looping references. In Fig. 5(b), when δ^* is smaller than 0.01 and the cache size is 4000, the miss ratio of ABM is worse than that of DISTANCE.

In LDT3, we assign different **IBL**(i)'s to each file. **IBL**(i) decreases with the increase of i. In this case, the ABM applies the LRU policy to files whose looping reference indicator is greater than δ^* and applies the DISTANCE policy to other files. In fig. 5(c), consider the size of cache is 4000. the ABM can outperform than both LRU and DISTANCE if it uses 0.01 as δ^*.

In LDT4, we partition files into two groups. Files in the first group are assigned small IBL and files in the second group are assigned large IBL. In this case, the ABM tries to apply the LRU policy to the first group's files and the DISTANCE policy to the second group's files. In fig. 5(d), the ABM performs better than both LRU and DISTANCE when δ^* is 0.01 or 0.02.

5   Conclusion

In this paper, we propose a novel buffer replacement scheme called Adaptive Buffer cache Management(ABM) that detects the *effective* looping reference pattern and adaptively applies appropriate replacement policy. It is very important to have the right metric which effectively quantifies the characteristics of workload. We develop a metric called *looping reference indicator* to denote the *degree* of looping reference. The ABM scheme periodically monitors the looping reference indicator of opened files and dynamically switches between the DISTANCE and the LRU on per-file basis.

Our simulation study reveals a number of interesting phenomenon. We observed that the LRU policy can yield lower cache miss rate than the DISTANCE policy if effective looping reference constitutes dominant fraction of workload. Even though there exist looping references, the LRU policy may not work properly if the buffer cache can not accommodate the entire data blocks in the loop. We also observed that the ABM scheme exhibits better cache hit rate than both the LRU and the DISTANCE when the threshold value of looping reference indicator is properly established. The ABM scheme changes the buffer cache management algorithm dynamically depending on the ongoing workload characteristics and henceforth is possible to deliver superior buffer cache miss ratio. The dynamic and intelligent nature of the ABM manifests itself when the underlying workload exhibits both sequential and looping reference access pattern.

References

1. Jussara M. Aimeida, Jeffrey Krueger, Derek L. Eager, and Mary K. Vernon. Analysis of educational media server workloads. In *Proceedings of International Workshop on Network and Operating System Support for Digital Audio and Video*, Port Jefferson, NY, USA, June 2001.
2. E. G. Coffman, Jr. and P. J. Denning. *Operating Systems Theory*. Prentice–Hall, Englewood Cliffs, New Jersey, 1973.
3. A. Dan, Y. Heights, and D. Sitaram. Generalized interval caching policy for mixed interactive and long video workloads. In Proc. of SPIE's Conf. on Multimedia Computing and Networking, 1996.
4. Asit Dan and Dinkar Sitaram. Buffer Management Policy for an On-Demand Video Server. Technical Report IBM Research Report RC 19347, IBM Research Division, T.J. Watson Research Center, Yorktown Heights, NY 10598, 1993.
5. N. Harel, V. Vellanki, A. Chervenak, G. Abowd, and U. Ramachandran. Workload of a media-enhanced classroom server. In *Proceedings of IEEE Workshop on Workload Characterization*, Oct. 1999.
6. Banu Özden, Rajeev Rastogi, and Abraham Silberschatz. Buffer replacement algorithms for multimedia storage systems. In *International Conference on Multimedia Computing and Systems*, pages 172–180, 1996.
7. J. Padhye and J. Kurose. An empirical study of client interactions with a continuous-media courseware server. In *Proceedings of International Workshop on Network and Operating System Support for Digital Audio and Video*, July 1998.
8. Lawrence A. Rowe, Diane Harley, and Peter Pletcher. Bibs: A lecture webcasting system. Technical report, Berkeley Multimedia Research Center, UC Berkeley, June 2001.
9. Youjip Won and Jaideep Srivastava. "smdp: Minimizing buffer requirements for continuous media servers". *ACM/Springer Multimedia Systems Journal*, 8(2):pp. 105–117, 2000.

A Logical Formalization of Semistructured Data Models

Antonio Badia

Computer Engineering and Computer Science Department
University of Louisville, Louisville KY 40292
abadia@louisville.edu

Abstract. Semistructured data has attracted much attention in
database research lately. New data models, query languages and systems have been developed. However, very little research has been done
on *formally defined semantics* for the new data models and query languages. As a consequence, some aspects of the meaning of expressions
in the database and answers to queries are not completely understood.
In this paper we propose a semantics for semistructured data based on
a modal logic framework used to give semantics to feature structures.
A semistructured database is seen as inducing a certain model, which
is then used to evaluate queries posed to the database in a first-order
language. The main advantage of this approach is to give a formal basis
for analyzing some possibly conflicting views of semistructured data as
a model for *partial information.*

1 Introduction

Semistructured data has attracted much attention in database research lately
([1]), due in part to the influence of the Web and its growing importance as a
data repository, which suggests new directions in database development ([15]).
New data models, query languages and systems have been developed ([13]).
Most data models are essentially directed, labeled graphs. However, very little
research has been done on *formally defined semantics* for the new data models
and query languages. The meaning of databases and queries is usually explained
intuitively, trough examples. However, such a situation leaves the door open for
misunderstandings and ambiguities.

In this paper we propose a semantics for semistructured data based on a
modal logic framework used to give semantics to feature structures ([12]). The
main advantage of this approach is to give a formal basis for analyzing some
possibly conflicting views of semistructured data as a model for *partial information* and clearing up the exact meaning of queries, especially those involving
negation. In the next section we introduce the semistructured data model and
a representative query language, in order to make the paper self-contained. In
subsection 2.1 we point out some of the issues that motivate a formalization
of the data model. One such formalization is presented next, in section 3. The
formalization is then used to analyze the issues previously considered. Finally,
we close with some conclusions and indications for further research.

M.-S. Hacid et al. (Eds.): ISMIS 2002, LNAI 2366, pp. 472–481, 2002.

2   Background and Motivation

Semistructured data is assumed not to have a strict type, but to posses irregular, partial organization ([1]). Because, in addition, the data may evolve rapidly, the schema for such data is usually large, dynamic, and is not strictly respected. Data models have been proposed that try to adapt to those characteristics. Several of them have in common that they can be thought of as directed, labeled graphs (for many applications, the graph is actually a tree). The schema information is maintained in the *labels* of the graph which describe the data (i.e. they correspond to the attribute names of a relational schema). Because of the labels, the data is considered *self-describing* (we note that, since the graph also contains the data elements, this blurs the distinction between *schema* and data in traditional databases). Nodes in the graph contain the data; they are seen as *objects* in more traditional object-oriented databases. Nodes with no outgoing edges (or leaves on a tree) are seen as atomic objects, while nodes with outgoing edges correspond to complex objects. The value of an atomic object is simply a string labeling the node; the value of a complex object is the subgraph that has the complex object as root. The objects contained in such a value are *subobjects* of the root object. Given an object or node o, `attributes(o)` is the set of labels in outgoing edges of o, and `roles(o)` is the set of labels in ingoing edges of o (if o denotes an atomic object, `attributes(o)` = $\emptyset$). For instance, objects in the *Object Exchange Model* (OEM) ([14]) are defined, formally, as 4-tuples *(label, type, value, oid)*, where *label* is a string, identifying the object; *type* refers to the data type, and can be either *atomic* or *complex* (in the latter case, it is either a set or a list); the *value* of an atomic object is drawn from one of the basic atomic types (integer, real, string, gif,...), while the value of a complex object is a set or list of atomic values or oids. Finally, the *oid* is a unique identifier. By allowing oids to appear in the value field (i.e. in a set or list of oids), we obtain nesting and complex object structure. *Names* are special labels; they are used as entry points in the database. Figure 1 shows an example of an OEM database, drawn as a graph; object identifiers are not shown for simplicity. It is assumed that semistructured databases are *rooted* graphs, i.e. that a distinguished node called the *root* of the graph exists and that queries are evaluated by starting any traversal of the database at this point ([13]). This is the node called Library in the figure, and it is customarily considered to have an incoming edge (even though such an edge has no origin node).

Query languages for semistructured data models combine techniques from database query languages, navigation interfaces (like Web browsers) and information retrieval. Since data can be seen as a graph, navigating the data is seen as moving through the graph, starting at certain nodes considered *entry points* (usually the *root* in the case of a tree). Vertical traveling of the graph (going down from the entry point) is usually done through *path expressions*. Paths expressions are strings of labels that indicate a path in the data. Usually *regular expressions* are allowed to specify paths. Conditions in semistructured query languages involve, as in their counterparts for structured data, comparisons of constants and attributes, and Boolean combinations of simpler conditions, but

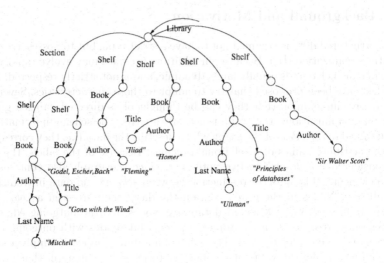

Fig. 1. An OEM database

in addition to simple attribute names, paths can be used. Pattern matching is used to determine which paths in the data are indicated by path expressions in a query. The paths in the data are said to be *realizations* of the path expression.

Several query languages have been proposed. Lorel ([13]) is similar to OQL ([6]) in that it extends SQL-like `SELECT ... FROM ... WHERE` syntax by allowing subqueries anywhere, and having the ability to return complex (and heterogeneous) types in an answer. In this paper we will use Lorel for our examples; however, the issues and solutions examined can be adapted to other query languages. Queries expressed in English are written in *emphasis* font and queries expressed in Lorel are written in `typewriter` font. As an example, consider the query

```
Select R.LastName from Library.*.Author R where R.address.zipcode
= 92310
```

which obtains author's names in a given zipcode. The zipcode may be represented as an integer (as the query does) or as a string. The Lore system ignores these differences in type, and automatically tries to convert between types (a feature called *coercion*) to make the query syntactically correct. Some authors may have several zipcodes (or even several addresses!), some may have no zipcode at all. Again, the Lore system ignores these differences. This is achieved by assuming all properties are set-valued. Then the empty set (not zipcodes) and the singleton (only one address) are just special cases. As a consequence, authors without zipcodes do not cause an error.

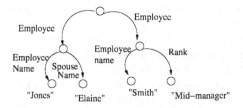

Fig. 2. A semistructured database

2.1   Query Language Issues

Because the semistructured data model has no formal semantics, the interpretation of data in a semistructured database is intuitive. This has consequences in the design of query languages and the definition of what constitutes an answer. As an example, consider the following situation: we want to capture information about employees in a company. Employee Jones is married to Elaine and (because of a restructuring) his present rank in unknown, while employee Smith is single and is a middle manager. Such a situation can be modeled by the semistructured database of figure 2. Thanks to the freedom offered by the model, each node labeled **Employee** can have only those attributes (outgoing edges) which are required by the given information. However, since both nodes have the same role, one would expect to see a similar structure. In particular, how should one interpret the *absence* of certain edges? In one case, an **Employee** node lacks a **Rank** edge that the other has. This absence is due to the fact that the rank of the employee is currently unknown. In another case, an **Employee** node lacks a **Spouse-Name** edge that the other has. This absence is due to the fact that the employee does not need such edge at all. Thus, two very different situations are modeled by the absence of an edge. This has consequences when querying the data[1]. Recall that all attributes are considered set-valued, so no edge translates into an empty set, and equality is changed to set membership. Thus, the query

(1)   `Select Employee-name From EMPLOYEE Where spouse-name = ''Elaine''`

will retrieve Jones, but not Smith. On the other hand, the SQL query

(2)   `Select Employee-name From EMPLOYEE Where spouse-name ≠ ''Elaine''`

will retrieve Smith, but not Jones In fact, the query

(3)   `Select Employee-name From EMPLOYEE Where spouse-name = ''Elaine'' or spouse-name ≠ ''Elaine''`

---

[1] It should be pointed out that exactly the same issues appear in the relational model of data, where *nulls* would be used, leading to the same kind of problem that we show here ([16]).

will retrieve both Jones and Smith. This can be considered intuitively incorrect if we take into account that Smith is single, so he really has no spouse (named Elaine or otherwise). On the other hand, the query

(4) `Select Employee-name From EMPLOYEE Where rank = mid-manager` will retrieve Smith and not Jones; the query

(5) `Select Employee-name From EMPLOYEE Where rank ≠ mid-manager` will retrieve Jones but not Smith, and the query

(6) `Select Employee-name From EMPLOYEE Where rank = mid-manager or rank ≠ mid-manager`
will retrieve both Jones and Smith. In this case, it can be argued that, since Jones does have a rank, the answer is intuitively correct. However, nothing seems to distinguish this case from the previous one involving spouses.

3   The Modal Logic Approach

In this section we describe formally a model for semistructured data as a graph. We then give formal semantics to graphs using (a simplified form of) *Kripke structures*, formal structures used to provide meaning to formulas in modal logic ([7]). We then define different notions of answer that the semantics make possible, and show how this helps solve the problems posed in the previous section.

Consider given a *signature* $< L, V >$, where L is a non-empty set of *attributes* and V a set of *atomic values* (called the *domain*). A signature denotes the vocabulary or set of non-logical names used in a database. Graphs are defined over a signature.

Definition 1. A *graph* over the signature $< L, V >$ is a tuple $< N, E, val >$, where

- N is a nonempty set of *nodes*, each one having a different *name*;
- $E \subseteq N^2 \times L$.
- $val : N \rightarrow V$.

Moreover,

- E is asymmetric on N^2 (i.e. for no $l \in L$ it is the case that $E(n_1, n_2, l)$ and $E(n_2, n_1, l)$).
- E is functional on N^2 (i.e. if $E(n_1, n_2, l)$ and $E(n_1, n_2, l')$, then $l \neq l'$).
- $val(n)$ is defined only if $\{x \mid \exists l \ E(n, x, l)\} = \emptyset$

Intuitively, $E(n_1, n_2, l)$ means that there is an edge from node n_1 to node n_2 with label l. Requiring E to be asymmetric captures the fact that the graph is directed. Requiring E to be functional captures the fact that we do not deal with multigraphs. The final requirement implies that val gives values to the nodes representing atomic objects. For any $n \in N$, $out(n) = \{x \mid \exists l \ E(n, x, l)\}$, represents the set of nodes pointing to n, while $in(n) = \{x \mid \exists l \ E(x, n, l)\}$ represents the set of nodes being pointed at from n. If $out(n) = \emptyset$, the node is given a value by val since it represents an *atomic object* (a *sink* in graph terms). Other nodes represent *complex objects* (*internal modes* in graph terms). As before, $roles(n) = \{l \mid \exists x \; E(x, n, l)\}$ and $attributes(n) = \{l \mid \exists x \; E(n, x, l)\}$. This model is not different from others already defined in the literature ([11]). In particular, there is a perfect correspondence between OEM databases and graphs as defined above: nodes are objects, object labels are the labels of incoming edges ($roles(n)$); object types are implicit (simple objects are sinks and complex objects are internal nodes); object values are either the values $val(n)$ for simple objects or the set of nodes reachable from the given node ($out(n)$) for complex objects; and object identifiers (oids) are node names. As an example, the graph of Figure 1 adjusts to our definition (except for the edge denoting the entry point or root).

Definition 2. For any node n in graph $\mathcal{G} = <\; N, E, val\; >$, $n/l = \{x \mid E(n, x, l)\}$.

Two issues must be pointed out about this definition. First, it is possible that n/l is empty; in fact $n/l = \emptyset$ iff $l \notin attributes(n)$ (i.e. there is no outgoing edge labeled l out of n). Second, there can be two edges out of node n, both with the same label (for instance, a book may have several authors). Moreover, such edges may lead to atomic objects in one case and complex objects in others. Thus, n/l truly may be a set, and its elements are not necessarily atomic objects.

In the context of the relational data model, it is customary to give semantics to query language expressions by identifying a relational database with a (relational) structure (in the logical sense), and expressing the query language in (a variant of) first order logic. Then the standard definitions of satisfaction and variable substitution can be used to define the answer to a query. This allows the well-understood, rigorously defined semantics of first order logic to be applied to databases ([16]). It is possible to export these ideas to the realm of semistructured data by identifying graphs (semistructured databases) with *Kripke models* ([7]). Our strategy will be to use this identification to provide formal semantics to the semistructured database and the query language.

Definition 3. A structure $\mathcal{A}$ for signature $< L, V >$ is a tuple $< W, \{R_l \mid l \in L\}, f >$, where W is a nonempty set of elements called *states*, $R_l \subseteq W^2$ for each $l \in L$, and $f : V \to \mathcal{P}(W)$.

Intuitively, f is a valuation which maps every atomic value to the set of states in which it is true, while each R_l gives us the *accessibility relation* associated with label l. We can identify a semistructured database (graph) with a structure since, given graph $\mathcal{G} = < N, E, val >$, a structure $\mathcal{A} = < W, \{R_l \mid l \in L\}, f >$ can be generated as follows:

- $W = N$;
- for all $l \in L$, $R_l(n_1, n_2)$ iff $E(n_1, n_2, l)$.
- $f(v) = \{n \mid val(n) = v\}$.

$\mathcal{A}$ is called *the structure generated by* $\mathcal{G}$, in symbols $gen(\mathcal{G})$. Thus, we identify a semistructured database $\mathcal{G}$ with the structure generated by $\mathcal{G}$. For simplicity, and to make the present work widely applicable, we do not define a particular query language; instead, we focus on a definition of *condition*, which attempts to capture the usual WHERE clauses used in many (semistructured) query languages. The $\models$ relationship will be limited to conditions; additional semantics for the rest of the query language can be provided.

Definition 4. The language $\mathcal{C}$ is defined as follows:

1. expressions of the form $A = a$ $(a \in V, A \in L)$ are in $\mathcal{C}$.
2. $A_1, \ldots A_n = a$ (with $a \in V$, $A_i \in L$, $1 \leq i \leq n$) is in $\mathcal{C}$.
3. If φ, φ_1, φ_2 are in $\mathcal{C}$, then so are $\neg\varphi$, $\varphi_1 \wedge \varphi_2$, $\varphi_1 \vee \varphi_2$.

A *condition* is an expression in the language $\mathcal{C}$. Expressions formed by (1) are called *atomic conditions*. Expressions formed by (2) are called *path conditions*. Expressions formed by (3) are called *complex conditions*.

Given graph $\mathcal{G}$, node $n \in \mathcal{G}$, condition c, we define three relationships: $gen(\mathcal{G}), n \models_{support} c$ ($\mathcal{G}$ supports c), $gen(\mathcal{G}), n \models_{cont} c$ ($\mathcal{G}$ contradicts c), and $gen(\mathcal{G}), n \models_{compat} c$ ($\mathcal{G}$ is compatible with c)[2]. The basic issue is the treatment of atomic conditions.

Definition 5. The relations $\models_{support}$, $\models_{compat}$ and $\models_{cont}$, between structures and atomic conditions, are defined as follows:

- $gen(\mathcal{G}), n \models_{support} A = a$ iff $\exists n'(n' \in n/A \wedge n' \in f(a))$.
- $gen(\mathcal{G}), n \models_{compat} A = a$ iff $n/A = \emptyset$.
- $gen(\mathcal{G}), n \models_{cont} A = a$ iff $n/A \neq \emptyset$ and $\forall n'(n' \in n/A \rightarrow n' \notin f(a))$.

In our database of figure 2, the employee node with name "Jones" supports Spouse-name = ''Elaine'' and is compatible with Rank = ''mid-manager'', while the employee node with name "Smith" supports Rank = ''mid-manager'' and is compatible with Spouse-name = ''Elaine''. Compatibility can be seen as stating that there is no information to decide an issue, for or against.

Note that the definition implies that n' is a simple object. Therefore, when n' is a complex object the clauses are not satisfied. This corresponds to the case where a path in a query is *understated* ([3]); for instance, a query with condition Employee = ''Jones'' over the database of figure 2 would return an empty answer because all Employee nodes correspond to complex objects, and the condition assumes the node denoted by Employee is atomic and thus has an atomic value. Note also that when a node n has two attributes labeled A, one going to an atomic node with value a and another one going to an atomic node with value $b \neq a$, the condition $A = a$ is satisfied for that node, but so is $A \neq a$. This is a consequence of the set valued approach; it corresponds, for instance, to an employee with multiple phone numbers. If employee Jones had two phone numbers, "112234" and "556678", a query asking for employees with

---

[2] The following definitions must be interpreted as making the root node of the graph (database) explicit.

phone number "112234" should include Jones, but a query asking for employees with a phone number *different from* "112234" should also include Jones.

The treatment of complex conditions, as well as path expressions, is not shown for lack of space; the interested reader is referred to [2]. Here we simply show the behavior of our previous example. In our database of figure 2, the employee node with name "Jones" contradicts Spouse-name $\neq$ ``Elaine'' but is compatible with Rank $\neq$ ``mid-manager'', while the employee node with name "Smith" contradicts Rank $\neq$ ``mid-manager'' and is compatible with Spouse-name $\neq$ ``Elaine''.

The above analysis provides two alternative semantics for negation, a *narrow* one and a *wide* one. In a standard setting, the relations $\models_{supports}$ and $\models_{cont}$ are complementary of each other, in the sense that $\models_{cont}$ is $\not\models_{support}$; for each formula φ, it is always the case that one of the following holds: $gen(\mathcal{G})_{DB} \models_{supports} \varphi$ or $gen(\mathcal{G})_{DB} \models_{cont} \varphi$. The reason for this is that perfect information is assumed; the structure tells you everything there is to know about the domain of discourse, and therefore any statement is either true (and supported) or false (and contradicted) (note the relationship with the *Closed World assumption* in traditional databases, and with the *law of excluded middle* in classical reasoning). But in environments with less then perfect information, the symmetry is lost. Thus, there are two possible definitions of answer:

1. an answer to $\varphi(\boldsymbol{x})$ in $gen(\mathcal{G})$ is $\{\boldsymbol{a} \mid gen(\mathcal{G}) \models_{support} \varphi[\boldsymbol{x}/\boldsymbol{a}]\}$. This is identical to the standard definition; we call it the *narrow definition*.

2. an answer to $\varphi(\boldsymbol{x})$ in $gen(\mathcal{G})$ is $\{\boldsymbol{a} \mid gen(\mathcal{G}) \models_{support} \varphi[\boldsymbol{x}/\boldsymbol{a}]\} \cup \{\boldsymbol{a} \mid gen(\mathcal{G}) \models_{comp} \varphi[\boldsymbol{x}/\boldsymbol{a}]\}$. This is called the *wide definition*, as it includes more than its narrow counterpart, namely information which does not contradict $\varphi[\boldsymbol{x}/\boldsymbol{a}]$. We call $\{\boldsymbol{a} \mid gen(\mathcal{G}) \models_{comp} \varphi[\boldsymbol{x}/\boldsymbol{a}]\}$ the *extended answer*.

Thus, in our previous example, query (1) would return Jones, but Smith would be part of an extended answer; query (2) would return an empty answer but would offer Smith as part of an extended answer; and query (3) would again retrieve Jones in the (standard) answer and Smith in the extended answer. Moreover, query (4) would retrieve Jones, and would have Smith in the extended answer; query (5) would return an empty standard answer, but would keep Smith in the extended answer; finally query (6) would return Smith in the standard answer and Jones in the extended answer. Deciding which answer (wide or narrow) best fits a given context, or how to present the information to the user is beyond the scope of this paper; what we argue is that, at a minimum, *the possibility should exist to distinguish between the two possible answers*.

4   Conclusion and Further Research

This paper attempts to bring modal logic and its theory to shed light on some issues of modeling and querying semistructured data. Obviously, the present work is just a first step and a lot of work remains; several issues deserve further consideration.

One possibly counter-intuitive consequence of the approach is that the set $\{a \mid gen(\mathcal{G}) \models_{compat} \varphi[x/a]\} \cap \{a \mid gen(\mathcal{G}) \models_{compat} \neg(\varphi[x/a])\}$ is not empty for any condition φ. Also, this information is *tentative* and may have to be retracted in the presence of further information (i.e. the situation is similar to that of *non-monotonic reasoning*). Therefore, the information in a wide answer must be presented to the user *separated* from the standard (narrow) answer, and its contingency must be pointed out. However, we argue that this still far superior than presenting the user with a standard answer alone, as it may be misleading to simply bring out an answer without any explanation. Indeed, the whole area of research known as *Cooperative Query Answering* ([8,9,10]) is built around the fact that plain communication of answers to a user in cases where assumptions are violated is simply not enough to ensure good communication. As pointed out above, the semantics should be extended to a whole query language. Issues may arise as to how to treat heterogeneous and/or complex collections of objects that can be returned as an answer in many of these languages. There is an obvious connection between the techniques proposed above and other techniques to deal with semistructured data as incomplete information ([11]) and to return *extended answers* in semistructured data ([3]). However, a general framework which connects these related projects is missing. Finally, a more faithful representation of semistructured data would include *oids* as first-class entities. There are some approaches which could be brought to shed some insight ([4]).

References

1. Serge Abiteboul, P. Buneman and D. Suciu *Data on the Web: From Relations to Semistructured Data and XML*, Morgan Kaufmann, 1999.
2. Badia, A. *A Logical Formalization of Semistructured Data Models*, Technical Report, available from http://date.spd.louisville.edu/badia/Research.html.
3. Badia, A. and Kumar Madria, S. *Cooperative Query Answering with Semistructured Data*, poster session in DASFAA'2000.
4. Blackburn, P. *Representation, Reasoning, and Relational Structures: A Hybrid Logic Manifesto*, Proceedings of the 1st Method for Modalities Workshop, Amsterdam, Areces, C., Franconi, E., Gore R., de Rijke, M., Schlingloff, H., editors. Also in Special Issue of the Logic Journal of the IGPL, to appear.
5. Buneman, P. and Davidson, S. and Fernandez, M. and Suciu, D., *Adding Structure to Unstructured Data*, in Proceedings of ICDT, 1997.
6. Catell, R. G., *Object Data Management*, Addison-Wesley, 1994.
7. Chellas, B. *Modal Logic: An Introduction*, Cambridge University Press, 1980.
8. Christiansen, H. and Larsen, H.L. and Andreasen, T., *Proceedings of the 1996 Workshop on Flexible Query Answering Systems*, Roskilde University Center, 1996.
9. Larsen, H.L. and Andreasen, T., *Proceedings of the 1994 Workshop on Flexible Query Answering Systems*, Roskilde University Center, 1994.
10. Gaasterland, T. and Godfrey, P. and Minker, J., *An Overview of Cooperative Answering*, Journal of Intelligent Information Systems, Kluwer Academic Publishers, 1, 1992
11. Kanza, Y. and Nutt, W. and Sagiv, Y., Incomplete Answers for Queries over Semistructured Data, Proceedings of KRDB, 1998

12. Kasper, J., *Feature Structures*, PhD. thesis, University of Michigan, 1987.
13. McHugh, J. and Abiteboul, S. and Goldman, R. and Quass, D. and Widom, J., *Lore: A Database Management System for Semistructured Data*, SIGMOD Record, volume 26, 1997.
14. Papakonstantinou, Y. and Garcia-Molina, H. and Widom, J., *Object Exchange Across Heterogeneous Information Sources*, in Proceedings of the 11th International Conference on Data Engineering, 1995.
15. Special Section on *Advanced XML Data Processing*, SIGMOD Record, vol. 30, n. 3, September 2001.
16. Ullman, A. *Principles of Database and Knowledge-Base Systems*, vol. 1, Computer Science Press, 1988.

Solving Travel Problems by Integrating WEB Information with Planning

David Camacho, José M. Molina, Daniel Borrajo, and Ricardo Aler

Universidad Carlos III de Madrid, Computer Science Department, Avenida de la
Universidad n° 30, CP 28911, Leganés, Madrid, Spain
{dcamacho, molina, dborrajo}@ia.uc3m.es, aler@inf.uc3m.es

Abstract. The evolution of the WEB has encouraged the development
of new information gathering techniques. In order to retrieve WEB information, it is necessary to integrate different sources. Planning techniques
have been used for this purpose in the field of information gathering. A
plan for information gathering is the sequence of actions that specify
what information sources should be accessed so that some characteristics, like access efficiency, are optimised. MAPWEB is a multiagent
framework that integrates Planning Agents and WEB Information Retrieval Agents. In MAPWEB, planning is not only used to integrate and
to select information sources, but also to solve actual planning problems
with information gathered from the WEB. For instance, in an travel assistant domain, plans represent the sequence of actions an user has to
follow to perform his/her trip. But also, each step in the plan informs
the WebAgents which information sources should be accessed. In this
paper we describe MAPWEB and study experimentally two information
retrieval characteristics: the average number of solutions retrieved depending on the WebAgents used and the allocated time limit, and the
number of problems solved (those travel assistant problems for which at
least one solution was retrieved).

1 Introduction

Traditional information retrieval tries to extract documents from a database related to a user query [10]. However, the evolution of the WEB has encouraged
the development of new information gathering techniques. Information in the
WEB is usually more structured than a simple document collection. Not only
documents in the WEB display more structure, but different information sources
contain different kinds of information. Therefore, in order to solve user queries,
it is necessary to integrate the different information sources. In other words,
information gathering intends to integrate a set of different information sources
with the aim of querying them as if they were a single information source [6,
7]. Also, because of the amount of information, efficiency considerations become
very important. For instance, it is very useful to select which information sources
will be queried. In order to both integrate and select the relevant information
sources different techniques can be used. A frequently used technique is planning [1,3]. In that case, every step in the plan represents an action to query an

M.-S. Hacid et al. (Eds.): ISMIS 2002, LNAI 2366, pp. 482–490, 2002.

information source. Figure 1 summarizes the discussion above about traditional information retrieval and the new WEB information gathering techniques.

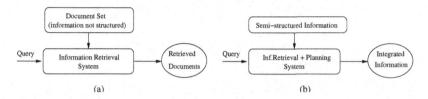

Fig. 1. (a) Traditional information retrieval and (b) plan based WEB information gathering.

There exist different actual systems for WEB information retrieval, the most close to the multi-agent system (MAS) presented in this paper is Heracles [9], in this case, instead of classical planning, a dynamic, hierarchical constraint propagation network is used the integration of the different information sources. Two assistant systems have been implemented: *The Travel Planning Assistant* (specialized in assisting tourists to plan their trips) and *The WorldInfo Assistant* (for a user-specified location, it integrates information from different information sources like weather, news, holidays, maps, airports, ...).

However, the information distributed in the WEB is heterogeneous in both content and format. This makes difficult to integrate different information sources to answer user queries. It would be better if all sources shared the same language so that standard techniques like planning could be directly applied. In order to solve this problem, wrappers are commonly used [2]. Furthermore, flexibility can be improved by having agents which are specialized in particular information sources [8].

In this paper we describe and study empirically MAPWEB [5] from the point of view of its information gathering skills. MAPWEB is a MAS which combines different kinds of agents that cooperate to solve problems. In this paper, the MAPWEB framework is applied to a travel planning assistant domain (e-tourism [4]),[1] where the user needs to find a plan to travel among several places. Each plan not only determines what steps the user should perform, but also which information sources should be accessed. For instance, if a step is to go from A to B by a plane of a given airline, then it is also known that the WEB server of that airline has to be accessed for further flight information.

MAPWEB will be analyzed empirically by taking into account its information retrieval abilities. Basically, two aspects will be studied: the number of solutions recalled depending on the time allocated to the system and agent topology, and the number of actual problems solved using these retrieved solutions.

This paper is structured as follows. First, MAPWEB architecture will be described. Three main points will be addressed: MAPWEB MAS based archi-

---

[1] This domain is a modified version of the Logistics domain.

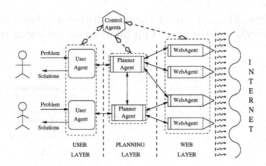

Fig. 2. MAPWEB three-layer architecture.

tecture, how planning is used by MAPWEB to gather information and to solve problems, and the role of the specialized WebAgents. Next, the experimental results about recall will be shown. Finally, conclusions will be summarized.

2   MAPWEB System Architecture

As Figure 2 shows, MAPWEB is structured into three layers: the *user layer* (which contains UserAgents), the *planning layer* (with the PlannerAgents), and the WEB *access layer* (made of specialized WebAgents). Next, each one of the three types of agents will be described:

- **UserAgents**: They pay attention to user queries and display to users the solution(s) found by the system. When an UserAgent receives problem queries from the users, it passes them to the PlannerAgents and when they answer back with the plans, they provide them to the user.
- **PlannerAgents**: They receive an user query, build an abstract representation of it, and solve it by means of planning. Then, the PlannerAgents fill in the information details by querying the WebAgents. The planner that has been used for this work by the PlannerAgents is PRODIGY4.0 [11].
- **WebAgents**: Their main goal is to fill in the details of the abstract plans obtained by the PlannerAgents. They obtain that information from the WEB.

In addition, MAPWEB contains **ControlAgents** to handle several control functions like the insertion and deletion of agents in the system and communication management.

3   The PlannerAgents

The goal of MAPWEB is to deal with problems that require planning to be solved and access to WEB information to validate and complete the plans obtained previously. For instance, as described in Section 1, in the e-tourism domain [4] if a step in a plan is to go from A to B by plane, then it is also known

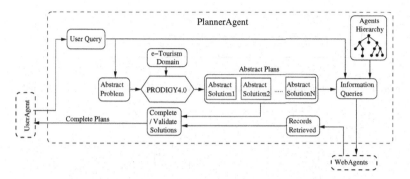

Fig. 3. Planning Process developed by the PlannerAgent.

that a WEB server with flight information must be accessed to complete the details for that step.

MAPWEB decouples the problem solving task by splitting it between the PlannerAgents and the WebAgents. Figure 3 displays the inner workings of a PlannerAgent.[2] The planning process works as follows. First, the PlannerAgent receives a query from any UserAgent. This query is analyzed and translated into an abstract planning problem by removing some details from the user query. Second, the PlannerAgent uses a planner (PRODIGY4.0 [11]) and tries to solve it. If the solving process is successful, the PlannerAgent generates a set of abstract solutions (abstract plans). However, the solutions obtained (abstract plans) lack the details. Therefore, each step in the plans has to be completed. To do so, the PlannerAgent builds a set of information queries for every step in every abstract plan. In order to build the queries, some of the details supplied by the user that were removed previously are also required. Then, each query is sent to the most appropriate WebAgent according to hierarchy. This hierarchy classifies the different WebAgents into categories, depending on the kind of information sources they are able to access. Finally, the PlannerAgent integrates all the specific information with the abstract solutions to generate the final solutions that will be sent to the UserAgent.

To illustrate the previous process, let us suppose that an user wants to travel from Madrid (airport) to Barcelona (train station). After removing unnecessary details, an abstract problem would be generated and subsequently solved. One of the possible abstract plans is shown in Figure 4.

Each step in the plan of Figure 4 would generate a set of information queries. The set corresponding to the `travel-by-airplane` would be sent to WebAgents that can retrieve flight information. Likewise for the `move-by-local-transport` set of queries.

---

[2] A more detailed description of this process can be found in [5].

```
Abstract plan:

<travel-by-airplane user1 plane0 airport0 airport1>
<move-by-local-transport user1 lbus0 bustop1 trainstat1 city1>
```

Fig. 4. Abstract solutions generated by PRODIGY4.0 for Leg 1 with 0-Transfers.

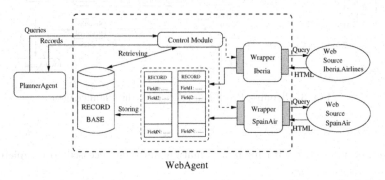

WebAgent

Fig. 5. WebAgents Architecture.

4   The WebAgents

The purpose of the WebAgents is to receive queries from the PlannerAgents, transform them into actual WEB queries, query the WEB source associated with the WebAgent, and return the information to the PlannerAgent in a standard format. The translation of the information in the WEB, which can be stored in many different formats, into a common format is performed by Wrappers [2].

Figure 5 displays the WebAgent architecture. A WebAgent is made of three main components: a control module, a record database, and one or several Wrappers. When a WebAgent receives a query from a PlannerAgent, its control module tries to fulfill the query by retrieving the appropriate records from the database. If there is no such record, the WebAgent access its WEB sources through the Wrappers. The Wrappers return a set of records which are first stored in the database, and then returned to the PlannerAgent.

For instance, the queries in the previous subsection would be answered by the WebAgents with the three records shown in Table 1.

Finally, the PlannerAgent receives all the retrieved information from the different WebAgents and uses these templates to instantiate the abstract plans. Those plans in which one or several steps received either no answer or an empty answer are rejected. Therefore, only fulfillable plans are sent back to the UserAgent. Every abstract plan will be instantiated into many different actual plans.

Table 1. Retrieved WebAgent Information.

Information-Flights	flight1	flight2	flight3
air-company	Iberia	Iberia	Spanair
http-address	www.iberia.es	www.iberia.es	www.spanair.com
flight-id	323	450	null
ticket-fare	38200	21850	43700
currency	ESP	ESP	ESP
flight-duration	null	null	null
airport-departure-city	MAD	MAD	MAD
departure-date	03-06-01	03-06-01	03-06-01
airport-arrival-city	BCN	BCN	BCN
return-date	06-06-01	06-06-01	06-06-01
number-of-passengers	1	1	1

5   Experimental Setup and Results

The aim of this section is to carry out several experiments with MAPWEB to evaluate its performance. The main aspect we want to evaluate in this paper is the number of plans (solutions) retrieved depending on the allowed time limit and the set of WebAgents used. To achieve this goal we followed the following steps:

- Three categories of problems were considered: national trips (within Spain), European trips, and Intercontinental trips. 10 planning problems were randomly generated for each category.
- Then, all the possible combinations of WebAgents were generated and tested by considering four specialized WebAgents[3]: Amadeus-Flights (AMF), 4airlines (4AL), Iberia (IBE), and Avianca (AVI). Amadeus-Flights and 4airlines are metasearchers: they can search information from many airplane companies. Iberia and Avianca can only search information about their own flights.
- Finally, we have plotted the number of solutions retrieved depending on the allocated time limit for the combination that retrieves the largest number of plans.

Table 2 shows the number of problems solved for the topologies that use only an isolated WebAgent, and the problems solved for the best topology tested for the different possible WebAgents combinations. As it is shown in Table 2 the best isolated WebAgents are the metasearcher engines (AMF and 4AL) given that these agents are able to retrieve information from different companies.

Table 2 shows that using different specialized WebAgents is useful to solve more problems: the best single agent configuration (AMF) solves 15 problems of 0 transfers and 25 of 1 transfer, whereas the four agent configuration (AMF-4AL-IBE-AVI) manages to solve 29 out of the 30 problems. However, adding more agents (3 and 4 agent topologies) is not always beneficial with respect to solving problems: a simple 2 agent configuration already fulfills 17/28 problems.

---

[3] *Amadeus:* http://www.amadeus.net, *4airlines:* http://www.4airlines.com, *Iberia:* http://www.iberia.com *Avianca:* http://www.avianca.com.

Table 2. Number of solved problems (out of 30) using different topologies.

Topology type	Selected topology	Problem type 0 Transfers	1 Transfer
1 WebAgent	AMF	15	25
	4AL	11	24
	IBE	5	14
	AVI	2	2
2 WebAgents	AMF-4AL	17	28
	AMF-IBE	17	28
3 WebAgents	AMF-4AL-IBE	17	28
4 WebAgents	AMF-4AL-IBE-AVI	18	29

But larger topologies usually find more solutions per problem, which can be useful if the user wants to choose a solution from a set of many possible plans according to some personal preferences (like travel time, cost, etc.). This can be seen in Figure 6, which shows the average number of plans per problem found for each of the three categories described in the experimental setup.

6 Discussion and Conclusions

Three main points will be addressed: the total number of solutions found, the time required to obtain them, and finally the effect of integrating complementary information sources.

Number of solutions: Figure 6 shows that there is a large difference between the 0-transfer and 1-transfer problems: the later always returns many more different solutions. This is due to existing many more indirect flights than direct flights.

Time required to obtain the maximum number of solutions (transient time): it can be seen that for the three categories (national, European, and international) of 0-transfer problems, this time is usually small (less than 3 minutes). The reason is that when only 0 transfers are considered, the number of queries and the number of retrieved solutions is small. On the other hand, 1-transfer problems require at least 5 minutes to retrieve all the solutions. This is because many more solutions are found. Also, this time increases from the national problems (5 minutes) and the European problems (10 minutes), to the international problems (15 minutes). In this case, the cause is not the higher number of solutions (there are fewer solutions for international problems) but the high number of WEB queries. WebAgents send more queries for international problems because many more cities are involved. Fewer solutions for international flights are found because some queries return no solution, or redundant solutions are found.

Finally, the more WebAgents there are in the system, the more solutions are found. It is remarkable that when two 2-WebAgent configurations are combined into a 3-WebAgent configuration (i.e. from AMF-4AL and AMF-IBE to AMF-4AL-IBE), the number of solutions of the 3-WebAgent configuration (AMF-4AL-IBE) is usually higher than the sum of solutions of the two 2-WebAgent configurations (AMF-4AL and AMF-IBE), even though many solutions found

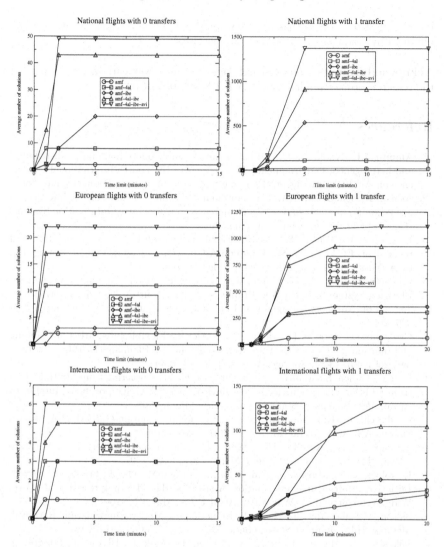

Fig. 6. Average number of solutions for 0 and 1 transfers.

by AMF-4AL and AMF-IBE might be the same. This is because new solutions are found by integrating the three information sources. Also, introducing new WebAgents in the configuration does not significantly increase response time even though there is a single PlannerAgent to process all the solutions found by all the WebAgents.

So far, we have only used WebAgents for airplane companies. However, MAPWEB is very well suited for integrating information coming from heterogeneous WEB sites (like taxi, bus, trains, etc.). In the future we plan to integrate these kind of sources, so that new solutions are achieved, which are not usually obtained by traditional travel WEB applications.

Acknowledgements. The research reported here was carried out as part of the research project funded by CICYT TAP-99-0535-C02.

References

1. Ambite, J.L., Knoblock, C.A.: Flexible and scalable query planning in distributed and heterogeneous environments. Proceedings of the Fourth International Conference on Artificial Intelligence Planning Systems. Pittsburgh, Pennsylvania (1998).
2. Ashish, N., Knoblock, C.A.: Semi-automatic Wrapper Generation for Internet Information Sources. Second IFCIS Conference on Cooperative Information Systems (CoopIS).Charleston, South Carolina.1997.
3. Bergmann, R., Wilke, W.: PARIS: Flexible plan adaptation by abstraction and refinement. ECAI (1996) Workshop on Adaptation in Case-Based Reasoning. Ed. by A. Voss et al. Published by John Wiley & Sons, Ltd.
4. Camacho, D., Borrajo, D., Molina, J.M.: Intelligent Travel Planning: A MultiAgent Planning System to Solve Web Problems in the e-Tourism Domain. International Journal on Autonomous Agents and Multiagent Systems. Vol. 4, num. 4, pp. 385-390, 2001.
5. Camacho, D., Borrajo, D., Molina, J.M., Aler,R.: Flexible Integration of Planning and Information Gathering. European Conference on Planning (ECP-01). September, 2001. pp. 73-84. Springer-Verlag. Toledo (Spain).
6. Fan, Y., Gauch, S.:Adaptive Agents for Information Gathering from Multiple, Distributed Information Sources. Proceedings of 1999 AAAI Symposium on Intelligent Agents in Cyberspace, Stanford University, March 1999.
7. Lambrecht, E., Kambhampati, S.: Planning for Information Gathering: A tutorial Survey. ASU CSE Techincal Report 96-017. May (1997).
8. Knoblock, C.A., Ambite, J.L.: Agents for Information Gathering. In Software Agents. Ed. by AAAI/MIT Press. Menlo Park, CA. (1997).
9. Knoblock, C.A., Minton, S., Ambite, J.L., Muslea, M., Oh, J., Frank, M.: Mixed-Initiative, Multi-source Information Assistants. The Tenth International World Wide Web Conference (WWW10). ACM Press. May 1-5. (2001).
10. Salton, G., and McGill, M. J.: Introduction to Modern Information Retrieval. McGraw-Hill Computer Science Series. New York: McGraw-Hill.1983.
11. Veloso, M., Carbonell, J., Perez, A. Borrajo, D., Fink, E., Blythe, J.: Integrating planning and learning: The Prodigy architecture. Journal of Experimental and Theoretical AI. Volume 7 (1995) 81–120.

A Framework for Generating Task Specific Information Extraction Systems

Cécile Aberg and Nahid Shahmehri

Department of Computer and Information Science, Linköpings universitet, Sweden
{cecab,nahsh}@ida.liu.se

Abstract. Information extraction helps in building advanced tools for text processing applications such as electronic publishing and information retrieval. The applications differ in their requirements on the input text, output information, and available resources for information extraction. Since existing IE technologies are application specific, extensive expert work is required to meet the needs of each new application. However, today, most users do not have this expertise and thus need a tool to easily create IE systems tailored to their needs. We introduce a framework that consists of (1) an extensible set of advanced IE technologies together with a description of the properties of their input, output, and resources, and (2) a generator that selects the relevant technologies for a specific application and integrates these into an IE system. A prototype of the framework is presented, and the generation of IE systems for two example applications is illustrated. The results are presented as guidelines for further development of the framework.

1 Introduction

With the Internet, electronic text has become an important resource for information. As a result, there are a growing number of applications that need to perform information extraction tasks. During the last ten years, advanced information extraction technology has been developed for tasks with specific requirements (e.g. message understanding [1], web mining [9] [5]). However, little effort has been invested to support the choice and adaptation of solutions provided by this technology for new tasks with specific requirements. In this paper we describe how such support can be provided.

Information extraction tasks can be described in terms of their input, output, and a set of requirements where the input is a collection of texts, the output is the set of pieces of text that contain information relevant to the task, and the set of requirements describe practical constraints on the processing of the texts and the characteristics of the input and output. Examples of requirements are the quality of the results expressed in terms of precision and recall, the time spent on the processing, the resources available, etc.

One important example of information extraction tasks is defined by the Message Understanding Conferences (MUC). During MUC, state of the art information extraction systems are evaluated. The tasks are designed to explore specific

M.-S. Hacid et al. (Eds.): ISMIS 2002, LNAI 2366, pp. 491–502, 2002.

problems such as the identification of noun entities or solving coreferences. The information extraction task for the 7th conference (MUC-7) is described in table 1. The requirements of the task influence the strategies adopted to build the information extraction systems. For example:

- The fact that the text is written in correct language allows the information extraction systems to do direct look ups of words and exploit predefined rules of the language's syntax.
- The extraction of composite information requires the identification of relations between atomic pieces of information.
- The training requires that the trainers have linguistic knowledge and are familiar with the process of building grammars for natural language.

Table 1. Input, output, and requirements of the MUC-7 task

- input: 200 texts from the New York Times News Service.
- output: A set of (attribute, value)-pairs that describe an *air vehicle launch report or update* for a predefined set of attributes. For instance (`vehicle_owner`, ``NASA'') is a possible pair for the attribute `vehicle_owner`.
- requirements:
  - Characteristic of the input: the text is correct in spelling and grammar usage.
  - Characteristic of the output: Composite information.
  - Training requirement: One single initial step of training.
    Each participant had one month to provide an information extraction system for the task. They were provided with 200 texts from the New York Times News Service and very specific descriptions of the set of (attribute, value)-pairs to extract.
  - Resource requirement: Any domain and language specific knowledge could be used by the participants.
  - Usage requirement: One single run.
    The systems are run on the 200 input texts on the day of the conference. No adjustment of the system is allowed between the processing of two texts.

Systems developed for MUC-7 have reasonable performance and are viable solutions for tasks that share similar requirements. However, the strategies adopted by these systems do not suit information extraction tasks with different requirements. The following lists some examples of these requirements:

- **Characteristic of the input:** *the input text is incorrect in spelling or grammar usage.*
  Web pages, emails and chat logs are examples of text where the writers are not always careful with the quality of their writing. As a result, robust syntactic and semantical analysis must be performed.
- **Characteristic of the output:** *the information to extract is atomic.*
  Producing a composite output requires computational efforts to identify the different components. Tasks whose output is atomic do not require this effort.

- **Information Description Acquisition requirement:** *there exists no large corpus to train the system in one unique step.*
  For some tasks there is little or no corpus and acquiring a corpus that is large enough to train a system could take too much time. For instance, for an electronic journal or a newsletter, the corpus consists of the texts submitted for publication, and its size can be only augmented with each publication. In the case of a monthly publication, it can take months to acquire a corpus large enough for training. For such applications, waiting for a corpus is not reasonable and a new strategy for acquiring the description of the information to extract must be designed[1].

In the remaining sections of this paper we describe a framework that takes the requirements of tasks into account to generate task-specific information extraction systems. In section 2 we introduce the framework. In sections 3 and 4 we illustrate the usage of the framework. In section 5 we provide guidelines for using the framework. We discuss related work in section 6 and finally we conclude in section 7.

2 The Framework

As pointed out by Hobbs in [10], "an information extraction system is a cascade of [...] modules that at each step add structure and often lose information, hopefully irrelevant [...]". Thus we can say that current information extraction technology is composed of a set of *modules* and a set of *strategies* to assemble the modules into a complete system. Different modules that share the same functionality (e.g. sentence splitting) can have different *requirements*. For instance, a robust sentence splitter can process incorrect text while an ordinary sentence splitter can only process correct text. Moreover, depending on the strategy, the number and order of the modules that are needed to compose a system vary. For instance, in LaSIE [7] the *gazeeter lookup* module is immediately after the *sentence splitter* module, while in LaSIE-II [11], it is immediately after the *tokenizer* module. Our framework provides an environment for automating the creation of information extraction systems according to the requirements of a given task. The framework is sketched in figure 1. It is comprised of:

- a knowledge management toolkit (i.e. KMT) that documents existing information extraction modules.
- a generator of information extraction systems that selects, orders, and assembles information extraction modules according to the requirements of a given task.

The KMT is composed of a knowledge base and a management functionality. The knowledge base is defined as the quadruplet $(M, R, S, \gg)$ where:

---

[1] Resampling methods can be used for incrementally acquiring this description.

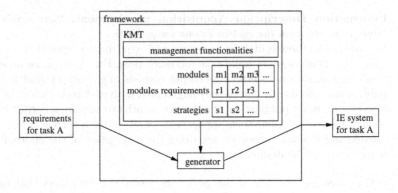

Fig. 1. The Framework

- $M = \{(m_i, Rm_i)|(m_i$ is an information extraction module$) \wedge (Rm_i = \{r|r$ is a requirement for $m_i\})\}$
  We use the term *module-representation* for the pairs (m_i, Rm_i).
- $R = \bigcup Rm_i$
- $S = \{(id_i, M_i, Rs_i)|\ (id_i$ is a unique identifier$) \wedge (M_i \subset M) \wedge$
  $(Rs_i = \{r|r$ is a non-module-specific requirement for $s_i\})\}$
- $\gg$ is a partial order that defines a *preference relation* on S: $\forall s_i, s_j \in S, s_i \gg s_j$ iff s_i is preferred to s_j.
  As an abbreviation we write $s_i \gg S'$ where $S' \subset S$, iff $\forall s_j \in S', s_i \gg s_j$.

The management functionality of the KMT provides the following operations:

- adding a new module-representation to the knowledge base.
- deleting a module-representation from the knowledge base.
- adding a new strategy in the knowledge base.
- deleting a strategy from the knowledge base.

Given the KMT, and R_A the set of requirements for the task A such that $R_A \subset R$, the generator proceeds through the following steps:

1. Builds the set of candidate module-representations M_A:
   $M_A = \{(m_i, R_i)|(m_i, R_i) \in M \wedge (R_i$ is compatible with $R_A)\}$
   If $M_A = \emptyset$ then the framework can not generate any system for the task.
2. Selects a maximally preferred strategy $s_i = (id_i, M_i, Rs_i)$ such that $(M_i \subset M_A)$, $(Rs_i$ is compatible with $R_A)$ and all tasks requirements are satisfied by the combination of the module and strategy requirements.
   If no strategy can be found then the framework can not generate any system for the task.
3. Integrates the modules according to s_i.
4. Returns the system.

To study the feasibility of this framework we created a prototype for a particular category of information extraction tasks. The prototype framework is described in next section.

3   The Prototype Framework

When building the prototype we considered a subset of information extraction tasks that we call *pattern identification tasks* and that we have studied in our previous work (see [4] and [3]). These tasks share the following requirements:

- The input text can be written in incorrect English with respect to spelling and grammar usage.
- The output is atomic information that we call *pattern.*
- There is little to no initial corpus.
- The users of the task do not have any linguistic knowledge nor are they experts in grammar development.
- The users are able to distinguish relevant from irrelevant patterns in the text.

We have designed an information extraction system for one such task. It is sketched in figure 2. The principle consists in parsing the text with a *grammar*

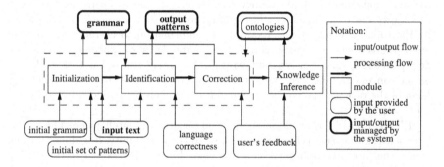

Fig. 2. Example of information extraction system for a pattern identification task.

describing the relevant patterns. The grammar is automatically built by generalizing examples of patterns as described in [4] and [3][2]. The grammar can be initialized either with an initial grammar or with an initial set of patterns. Moreover the grammar is updated after the processing of each text. These updates allow the system to begin with incomplete knowledge and offer an alternative to the unique step training used in MUC-7 systems.

The modules that make up the system must be adapted to the specific requirements of different pattern identification tasks. We automate this adaptation process with our prototype framework by defining a KMT. The requirements (R), modules (M) and strategies (S) of the KMT are given in table 2. The preference relationship $(\gg)$ on the strategies implements the combination of two heuristics:

---

[2] Examples of relevant patterns are rewritten to provide a description of a set of relevant patterns.

(1)the more modules the strategy uses, the more the strategy is preferred, and
(2) given two strategies s_i and s_j, $s_i \gg s_j$ if the set of requirements of M_j is a
subset of the set of requirements of M_i. As a result we get the following order on
the strategies: $s_{06} \gg \{s_{04}, s_{05}\} \gg s_{03} \gg \{s_{01}, s_{02}\} \gg s_{12} \gg \{s_{10}, s_{11}\} \gg s_{09} \gg$
$\{s_{07}, s_{08}\} \gg s_{14} \gg s_{13} \gg s_{16} \gg s_{15}$. We note that $\{r_3, r_5, r_6\}$ is the minimal
set of requirements that have to be satisfied to create an information extraction
system in the prototype framework,. We also point out that the system in figure
2 follows strategy s_{06}.

The next section illustrates the usage of our prototype framework.

4   Illustration

We used the framework to build parsers for two specific tasks that we call
Elfwood-FAQ and ETAI.

Elfwood-FAQ: Elfwood is a web site dedicated to the publication and teaching of art and literature in the domain of fantasy and science fiction. In the
live help system for Elfwood described in [2], part of the task of the human
assistant consists of looking through the log of her dialogues with users to identify the pieces of discussions addressing problems that are good candidates to
be the topic of FAQ[3] items. Examples of information to extract are problem
descriptions such as "where can I find tutorials of guides on the net
for photoshop and general drawing?". The *input text* of the task is the log
of one conversation between an assistant and a user of the site. The *output patterns* of the task are the pieces of text that express problems encountered by the
user.

ETAI: ETAI [6] is an electronic journal for artificial intelligence. The review
of articles submitted to the journal is open to the community. It is done through
emails that are then published on a web page. In this process, one of the editing
operations that the editor of the journal performs is to transform the pieces of
email that cite articles (e.g. "in the IJCAI paper of Harris") into links to
the actual articles. The references can be expressed in several ways (e.g. "in my
paper", [Harris-Jones96], etc.). The *input text* of the task is a review email.
The *output patterns* are the citations of articles in the email.

Table 3 provides the description of the tasks in terms of the requirements
$r_i \in R$ from the KMT. Given these requirements, the generator goes through
the following steps:

1. Builds the set of candidate modules:
   $M_{ETAI} = \{m_{ident1}, m_{ident2}, , m_{corr}, m_{ki}\}$.
   $M_{Elfwood-FAQ} = \{m_{ident1}, m_{corr}, m_{ki}\}$.
2. Selects a maximally preferred strategy:
   - Among the possible strategies for M_{ETAI} (i.e. $s_{13}, s_{14}, s_{15}, s_{16}$), the preferred strategy according to the preference relation is s_{14}.
   - Among the possible strategies for $M_{Elfwood-FAQ}$ (i.e. $s_{13}, and s_{15}$), the
   preferred strategy is s_{13}.

---

[3] FAQ stands for Frequently Asked Question.

Table 2. The requirements, modules, and strategies of the prototype framework

$\mathbf{R} = \{r_1, r_2, r_3, r_4, r_5, r_6\}$:

$r_1 =$ "there is an initial set of pattern", $r_2 =$ "there is an initial grammar", $r_3 =$ "there is a domain specific ontology", $r_4 =$ "there is a grammatical ontology", $r_5 =$ "the language is correct/incorrect in spelling and grammar usage". $r_6 =$ "there is an oracle (e.g. user) able to tell which patterns are relevant to the task".

$\mathbf{M} = \{init1, init2, init3, ident1, ident2, ident3, corr, ki\}^a$:

module	module description	R_i
m_{init1}	"Take the initial set of pattern to initialize the parsing grammar."	$\{r_1\}$
m_{init2}	"Take the initial grammar to initialize the parsing grammar."	$\{r_2\}$
m_{init3}	"Take the initial set of pattern and grammar to initialize the parsing grammar."	$\{r_1, r_2\}$
m_{ident1}	"Parse the text with the grammar to generate a set of patterns. Use the ontology to annotate the text. Adapt the robustness of the parser to the correctness of the language."	$\{r_3, r_5\}$
m_{ident2}	"Parse the text with the grammar to generate a set of patterns. Use the domain specific and grammatical ontologies to annotate the text. Adapt the robustness of the parser to the correctness of the language."	$\{r_3, r_4, r_5\}$
m_{corr}	"Integrate the corrections provided by the oracle in terms of forgotten and wrongly identified patterns, and modify the grammar accordingly."	$\{r_6\}$
m_{ki}	"Detect new concepts specific to the task. If there is an ontology, it is augmented. Otherwise a new ontology is created from scratch. The intuition behind this module is described in [3]."	$\emptyset$

$\mathbf{S}$ is the set of strategies $s_i = (id_i, M_i, Rs_i)$ listed below:

s_i	id_i	M_i	$Rs_i{}^b$
s_{01}	01	$\{init1, ident1, corr, ki\}$	order($init1, ident1, corr, ki$)
s_{02}	02	$\{init2, ident1, corr, ki\}$	order($init2, ident1, corr, ki$)
s_{03}	03	$\{init3, ident1, corr, ki\}$	order($init3, ident1, corr, ki$)
s_{04}	04	$\{init1, ident2, corr, ki\}$	order($init1, ident2, corr, ki$)
s_{05}	05	$\{init2, ident2, corr, ki\}$	order($init2, ident2, corr, ki$)
s_{06}	06	$\{init3, ident2, corr, ki\}$	order($init3, ident2, corr, ki$)
s_{07}	07	$\{init1, ident1, corr\}$	order($init1, ident1, corr$)
s_{08}	08	$\{init2, ident1, corr\}$	order($init2, ident1, corr$)
s_{09}	09	$\{init3, ident1, corr\}$	order($init3, ident1, corr$)
s_{10}	10	$\{init1, ident2, corr\}$	order($init1, ident2, corr$)
s_{11}	11	$\{init2, ident3, corr\}$	order($init2, ident2, corr$)
s_{12}	12	$\{init3, ident2, corr\}$	order($init3, ident2, corr$)
s_{13}	13	$\{ident1, corr, ki\}$	order($ident1, corr, ki$)
s_{14}	14	$\{ident2, corr, ki\}$	order($ident2, corr, ki$)
s_{15}	15	$\{ident1, corr\}$	order($ident1, corr$)
s_{16}	16	$\{ident2, corr\}$	order($ident2, corr$)

[a] *init* is short for initialization, *ident* is short for identification, *corr* is short for correction, *ki* is short for knowledge inference.

[b] The requirements on the strategies describe the order in which the modules must be assembled, e.g. order(*ident2, corr*) says that in the final system, the modules are assembled so that the output of *ident2* is input to *corr*.

Table 3. Requirements for tasks ETAI and Elfwood-FAQ

r_i	$r_i =$" there is/are ..."	r_i for ETAI	r_i for Elfwood-FAQ
r_1	initial patterns	false	false
r_2	initial grammar	false	false
r_3	domain specific ontology	**true**	**true**
r_4	grammatical ontology	**true**	false
r_5	correct language	**true**	false
r_6	oracle	**true**	**true**

3. Integrates the modules according to the strategy.
   - For ETAI, s_{14} requires an order on the modules: m_{ident2} before m_{corr} before m_{ki}.
   - For Elfwood-FAQ, s_{13} requires an order on the modules: m_{ident1} before m_{corr} before m_{ki}.
4. Returns one system for each task.
   The two parsers generated are shown in figure 3. They differ in one unique module: the identification module for Elfwood-FAQ must be more robust and must work with little or no domain knowledge (until the inference knowledge module has produced enough concepts).

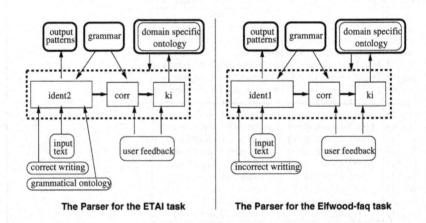

The Parser for the ETAI task   **The Parser for the Elfwood-faq task**

Fig. 3. Parser generated for two specific applications

5   Guidelines

As long as the IE community designs new modules and strategies, the framework is bound to evolve. Based on our experience building and using a prototype framework, we provide the following guidelines for the usage and the development of the knowledge base.

Adding a new strategy: The addition of a new strategy does not always imply the addition of modules. A new strategy can express a new way to assemble existing modules. A new strategy can also require a modification of the preference relation.

Adding a new module: The granularity of the requirements used to describe the module may influence the behavior of the generator dramatically. The lower the granularity, the more flexible the generator will be. A low granularity can be interesting for generating approximative systems with reasonable performance. This is illustrated by *Case A* in table 4. However, a low granularity can be risky since it can allow the creation of systems that do not perform well. This is illustrated by *Case A* in table 5. For the tasks whose requirements can not all be satisfied within the KMT, new modules and strategies must be designed. A high granularity eases the identification of such tasks. This is illustrated by the cases B in table 4 and 5.

Deleting modules and strategies: The constant evolution of the framework can lead to the obsolescence of some information extraction technology. As a result, some modules and strategies will cease to be selected by the generator. It should be possible to delete them from the framework. A simple example of a deletion rule is to delete the modules that are not used by any strategies[4].

6   Related Work

The issue of automatic generation of information extraction systems is quite new and there has not been much work addressing it yet. In [8], the authors argue that GATE[5] is a good environment for "detailed comparative evaluation of alternative approaches to IE subtasks" and "flexible adaptation of IE systems to new users and domains". However, no support for the automatic creation of systems is provided. One other important initiative to ease the adaptation of existing IE systems to new tasks consists of automating the creation of *dictionaries of extraction patterns* (i.e. structures having a function similar to our *grammar* for pattern identification tasks). Notable systems are AutoSlogTS[15] and the method of "Multi Level Bootstrapping"[16] that refines the dictionaries generated by AutoSlog. These approaches are still task specific in the sense that

---

[4] A consequence of this rule is that deleting a strategy can trigger the deletion of a set of modules.

[5] GATE was originally built as a software environment for research on, and development of, Language Engineering systems. GATE provides a solid environment for testing and integrating alternative language engineering technologies.

Table 4. ETAI task: the granularity influences the description of the task

---

Two users defined two different ETAI tasks by not agreeing on one characteristic of the output:
- User1 wants to identify all the patterns expressing references to articles.
- User2 wants to identify one reference per article in each email.
Let us consider the requirement r_1 = "no double output patterns".
Case A) <u>low granularity</u>:
Let us consider a framework F1 with the same knowledge base $(M, R, S, \gg)$ as our prototype's.
R does not provide the means to describe the difference between the tasks.
As a result the generator of F1 produces the same system for both tasks.
The following table shows the performance for the systems after processing three email reviews (37 emails[a]):

	User1	User2
precision	90%	62%
recall	72%	64%

Case B) <u>high granularity</u>:
Let us consider a framework F2 with the knowledge base $(M, R \cup \{r_1\}, S, \gg)$.
It is now possible to express the difference between the tasks.
Consequently, no strategy is found to match the requirements of user2 and no system is produced for her.

---
[a] For applications that acquire text slowly, a good recall and precision after processing a small collection of text is significant.

Table 5. Elfwood-FAQ task: the granularity influences the description of the task

---

In the prototype framework, the *corr* module uses a biased version of the pattern generalization algorithm described in [4][a]. This bias does not allow the generation of good grammar for patterns composed of long phrases.
Moreover, the patterns to extract for Elfwood-FAQ are composed of long phrases[b].
Let us consider the requirement r_2 = "the patterns do not contain long phrases".
Case A) <u>low granularity</u>:
Let us consider a framework F1 with the same knowledge base $(M, R, S, \gg)$ as our prototype's.
The generated system is not able to provide a good grammar and, consequently, can not identify the patterns relevant to the task.
Case B) <u>high granularity</u>:
Let us consider a framework F3 with the knowledge base $(M, R \cup \{r_2\}, S, \gg)$.
No system is generated.

---
[a] The bias: disallowing the generalization of a sequence of tokens into a "<phrase>", a "<verb>" or a "<noun>"
[b] E.g."`where can I find tutorials of guides on the net for photoshop and general drawing?`"

---

they require the existence of large training corpus (e.g. 772 texts were used for a task in [15], 4160 and 1500 texts for tasks in [16]) and that the texts are correct with respect to spelling and grammar.

On the other hand, much work has been done recently to develop technology for *pattern identification tasks*. We integrated our approach in the prototype framework. Products such as the Data Detectors of Apple [13] and the Selection Recognition Agent of Intel[14] are addressing ad hoc pattern identification tasks such as the identification of email addresses, urls, or meeting data. Their *grammars* are defined once for all and are not directly tailored to the user and her task. KPS [9] addresses several non ad hoc tasks of pattern identification for the web by exploiting resources specific to web pages such has html tags. While our approach strives to hide the definition of the grammar in the normal workflow of the user's task, Grammex [12] allows the user to actively participate in the creation of the grammar. Grammex is an alternative for our initialization modules.

7   Conclusion and Future Work

We have introduced a framework to automate the creation of information extraction systems adapted to specific tasks. The tasks presented to the framework are described in terms of the requirements on their input, output, and available resources. The framework is based on a knowledge management toolkit that is composed of a knowledge base of information extraction technology and a management functionality. The later allows the framework to continually integrate new information extraction technology. We have demonstrated the feasibility of the framework by building a prototype and illustrating its usage on two tasks. We also gave guidelines based on our experience in using the prototype.

Future work will address further analysis of some features of the framework such as the preference relation on the strategies and the granularity of the requirements. Moreover, we will use the framework to study information extraction tasks and propose modules and strategies for the tasks that are not covered by the current technology.

Acknowledgments. The authors would like to thank Patrick Lambrix and Lena Strömbäck for their valuable comments on earlier versions of this paper. We are also grateful for the detailed and helpful comments provided by the ISMIS reviewers on the submitted version of this paper.

References

1. *Proceedings of the 7th Message Understanding Conference (MUC-7)*.   1998. http://www.itl.nist.gov/iaui/894.02/related_projects/muc/index.html.
2. Johan Aberg and Nahid Shahmehri. An Empirical Study of Human Web Assistants: Implications for User Support in Web Information Systems. In *Proceedings of the CHI Conference on Human Factors in Computing Systems*, pages 404–411, 2001.

3. Cécile Boisson-Aberg. Applying Similarity Measures for Management of Textual Templates. In *Proceedings of the Student Workshop of the 38th Annual Meeting of the Association for Computational Linguistics*, pages 463–473, 2000.
4. Cécile Boisson-Aberg and Nahid Shahmehri. Template Generation for Identifying Text Patterns. In *Proceedings of the International Symposium on Methodologies for Intelligent Systems*, pages 8–15, 2000.
5. M. Craven, D. DiPasquo, D. Freitag, A. McCallum, T. Mitchell, K. Nigam, and S. Slattery. Learning to Extract Symbolic Knowledge from the World Wide Web. In *Proceedings of the 15th National Conference on Artificial Intelligence (AAAI)*, 1998.
6. ETAI. Electronic Transactions on Artificial Intelligence. http://www.ida.liu.se/ext/etai/, 1997.
7. R. Gaizauskas, T. Wakao, K. Humphreys, H. Cunningham, and Y. Wilks. Description of LaSIE System as used for MUC-6. In *Proceedings of the 6th Message Understanding Conference (MUC-6)*, pages 207–220, 1995.
8. R. Gaizauskas and Y. Wilks. *Natural Language Information Retrieval*, chapter 8. LaSIE Jumps the GATE. Kluwer Academic: Berlin, 1999.
9. Tao Guan and Kam-Fai Wong. KPS: a Web Information Mining Algorithm. In *Proceedings of the 8th International WorldWideWeb Conference (WWW8)*, pages 417–429, 1999.
10. Jerry R. Hobbs. Generic Information Extraction System. In *Proceedings of the 5th Message Understanding Conference (MUC-5)*, 1993.
11. K. Humphreys, R. Gaizauskas, S. Azzam, C. Huyck, B. Mitchell, H. Cunningham, and Y. Wilks. Description of the University of Sheffield LaSIE-II System as used for MUC-7. In *Proceedings of the 7th Message Understanding Conference (MUC-7)*, 1998.
12. Henry Lieberman, Bonnie A. Nardi, and David Wright. Training Agents to Recognize Text by Example. In *Proceedings of the 3rd International Conference on Autonomous Agents*, pages 116–122, 1999.
13. Bonnie A. Nardi, James R. Miller, and David J. Wright. Collaborative, Programmable Intelligent Agents. *Communication of the ACM*, 41(3):96–104, 1998.
14. Milind S. Pandit and Sameer Kalbag. The Selection Recognition Agent: Instant Access to Relevant Information and Operations. In *Proceedings of the International Conference on Intelligent User Interfaces*, pages 47–52, 1997.
15. Ellen Riloff. Automatically Generating Extraction Patterns from Untagged Text. In *Proceedings of the 13th National Conference on Artificial Intelligence (AAAI)*, pages 1044–1049, 1996.
16. Ellen Riloff and Rosie Jones. Learning Dictionaries for Information Extraction by Multi-Level Boostrapping. In *Proceedings of the 16th National Conference on Artificial Intelligence (AAAI)*, 1999.

A Formal Framework for Reasoning on UML Class Diagrams

Andrea Calì, Diego Calvanese, Giuseppe De Giacomo, and Maurizio Lenzerini

Dipartimento di Informatica e Sistemistica
Università di Roma "La Sapienza"
Via Salaria 113, I-00198 Roma, Italy
lastname@dis.uniroma1.it

Abstract. In this paper we formalize UML class diagrams in terms of a logic belonging to Description Logics, which are subsets of First-Order Logic that have been thoroughly investigated in Knowledge Representation. The logic we have devised is specifically tailored towards the high expressiveness of UML information structuring mechanisms, and allows one to formally model important properties which typically can only be specified by means of qualifiers. The logic is equipped with decidable reasoning procedures which can be profitably exploited in reasoning on UML class diagrams. This makes it possible to provide computer aided support during the application design phase in order to automatically detect relevant properties, such as inconsistencies and redundancies.

1   Introduction

There is a vast consensus on the need for a precise semantics for UML [9,12], in particular for UML class diagrams. Indeed, several types of formalization of UML class diagrams have been proposed in the literature [8,9,10,6]. Many of them have been proved very useful with respect to the task of establishing a common understanding of the formal meaning of UML constructs. However, to the best of our knowledge, none of them has the explicit goal of building a solid basis for allowing automated reasoning techniques, based on algorithms that are sound and complete wrt the semantics, to be applicable to UML class diagrams.

In this paper, we propose a new formalization of UML class diagrams in terms of a particular formal logic of the family of Description Logics (DL). DLs[1] have been proposed as successors of semantic network systems like KL-ONE, with an explicit model-theoretic semantics. The research on these logics has resulted in a number of automated reasoning systems [13,14,11], which have been successfully tested in various application domains (see e.g., [17,18,16]). Our long term goal is to exploit the deductive capabilities of DL systems, and show that effective reasoning can be carried out on UML class diagrams, so as to provide support during the specification phase of software development.

In DLs, the domain of interest is modeled by means of *concepts* and *relationships*, which denote classes of objects and relations, respectively. Generally speaking, a DL is formed by three basic components:

---

[1] See http://dl.kr.org for the home page of Description Logics.

M.-S. Hacid et al. (Eds.): ISMIS 2002, LNAI 2366, pp. 503–513, 2002.

- A *description language*, which specifies how to construct complex concept and relationship expressions (also called simply concepts and relationships), by starting from a set of atomic symbols and by applying suitable constructors,
- a *knowledge specification mechanism*, which specifies how to construct a DL knowledge base, in which properties of concepts and relationships are asserted, and
- a set of *automatic reasoning procedures* provided by the DL.

The set of allowed constructors characterizes the expressive power of the description language. Various languages have been considered by the DL community, and numerous papers investigate the relationship between expressive power and computational complexity of reasoning (see [7] for a survey).

Several works point out that DLs can be profitably used to provide both formal semantics and reasoning support to formalisms in areas such as Natural Language, Configuration Management, Database Management, Software Engineering. For example, [5] illustrates the use of DLs for database modeling. However, to the best of our knowlegde, DLs have not been applied to the Unified Modeling Language (UML) (with the exception of [3]). The goal of this work is to present a formalization of UML class diagrams in terms of DLs. In particular, we show how to map the constructs of a class diagram onto those of the EXPTIME decidable DL $\mathcal{DLR}$ [2,4]. The mapping provides us with a rigorous logical framework for representing and automatically reasoning on UML class specifications. The logic we have devised is specifically tailored towards the high expressiveness of UML information structuring mechanisms, and allows one to formally model important properties which typically can only be specified by means of constraints. The logic is equipped with decidable reasoning procedures which can be profitably exploited in reasoning on UML class diagrams. This makes it possible to provide computer aided support during the application design phase, in order to automatically detect relevant properties, such as inconsistencies and redundancies.

2 Classes

In this paper we concentrate on class diagrams for the conceptual perspective. Hence, we do not deal with those features that are relevant for the implementation perspective, such as public, protected, and private qualifiers for methods and attributes.

A *class* in an UML class diagram denotes a *sets of objects* with common features. The specification of a class contains the *name* of the class, which has to be unique in the whole diagram, and the *attributes* of the class, each denoted by a name (possibly followed by the *multiplicity*, between square brackets) and with an associated *class*, which indicates the domain of the attribute values. The specification contains also the *operations* of the class, i.e., the operations associated to the objects of the class. An operation definition has the form:

$$operation\text{-}name(parameter\text{-}list): (return\text{-}list)$$

Observe that an operation may return a *tuple* of objects as result.

An UML class is represented by a $\mathcal{DLR}$ concept. This follows naturally from the fact that both UML classes and $\mathcal{DLR}$ concepts denote *sets of objects*.

An UML *attribute* a of type C' for a class C associates to each instance of C, zero, one, or more instances of a class C'. An optional *multiplicity* $[i..j]$ for a specifies that a associates to each instance of C, at least i and most j instances of C'. When the multiplicity is missing, $[1..1]$ is assumed, i.e., the attribute is *mandatory* and *single-valued*.

To formalize attributes we have to think of an attribute a of type C' for a class C as a binary relation between instances of C and instances of C'. We capture such a binary relation by means of a binary relation a of $\mathcal{DLR}$. To specify the type of the attribute we use the assertion:

$$C \sqsubseteq \forall[1](a \Rightarrow (2:C'))$$

Such an assertion specifies precisely that, for each instance c of the concept C, all objects related to c by a, are instances of C'. Note that an attribute name is not necessarily unique in the whole diagram, and hence two different classes could have the same attribute, possibly of different types. This situation is correctly captured by the formalization in $\mathcal{DLR}$.

To specify the multiplicity $[i..j]$ associated to the attribute we add the assertion:

$$C \sqsubseteq (\geq i\,[1]a) \sqcap (\leq j\,[1]a)$$

Such an assertion specifies that each instance of C participates at least i times and at most j times to relation a via component 1. If $i = 0$, i.e., the attribute is *optional*, we omit the first conjunct, and if $j = *$ we omit the second one. Observe that for attributes with multiplicity $[0..*]$ we omit the whole assertion, and that, when the multiplicity is missing the above assertion becomes:

$$C \sqsubseteq \exists[1]a \sqcap (\leq 1\,[1]a)$$

An operation of a class is a function from the objects of the class to which the operation is associated, and possibly additional parameters, to tuples of objects. In class diagrams, the code associated to the operation is not considered and typically, what is represented is only the signature of the operation.

In $\mathcal{DLR}$, we model operations by means of $\mathcal{DLR}$ relations. Let

$$f(P_1, \ldots, P_m) : (R_1, \ldots, R_n)$$

be an operation of a class C that has m parameters belonging to the classes $P_1, \ldots, P_m$ respectively and n return values belonging to $R_1, \ldots, R_n$ respectively. We formalize such an operation as a $\mathcal{DLR}$ relation, named $\mathrm{op}_{f(P_1,\ldots,P_m):(R_1,\ldots,R_n)}$, of arity $m+n+1$ among instances of the $\mathcal{DLR}$ concepts $C, P_1, \ldots, P_m, R_1, \ldots, R_n$. On such a relation we enforce the following assertions:

- An assertion imposing the correct types to parameters and return values:

$$C \sqsubseteq \forall[1](\mathrm{op}_{f(P_1,\ldots,P_m):(R_1,\ldots,R_n)} \Rightarrow$$
$$((2:P_1) \sqcap \cdots \sqcap (m+1:P_m) \sqcap (m+2:R_1) \sqcap \cdots \sqcap (m+n+1:R_n))$$

Fig. 1. Binary association and aggregation in UML

- Assertions imposing that invoking the operation on a given object with given parameters determines in a unique way each return value (i.e., the relation corresponding to the operation is in fact a function from the invocation object and the parameters to the returned values):

$$(\textbf{fd } \mathsf{op}_{f(P_1,\ldots,P_m):(R_1,\ldots,R_n)} \ 1, \ldots, m+1 \to m+2)$$

$$\cdots$$

$$(\textbf{fd } \mathsf{op}_{f(P_1,\ldots,P_m):(R_1,\ldots,R_n)} \ 1, \ldots, m+1 \to m+n+1)$$

These functional dependencies are determined only by the number of parameters and the number of result values, and not by the specific class for which the operation is defined, nor by the types of parameters and result values.

The *overloading* of operations does not pose any difficulty in the formalization since an operation is represented in $\mathcal{DLR}$ by a relation having as name the whole signature of the operation, which consists not only the name of the operation but also the parameter and return value types. Observe that the formalization of operations in $\mathcal{DLR}$ allows one to have operations with the same name or even with the same signature in two different classes.

3   Associations and Aggregations

An *association* in UML is a relation between the instances of two or more classes. An association often has a related *association class* that describes properties of the association such as attributes, operations, etc. A binary association A between the instances of two classes C_1 and C_2 is graphically rendered as in the left hand side of Figure 1, where the class A is the association class related to the association, r_1 and r_2 are the *role names* of C_1 and C_2 respectively, i.e., they specify the role that each class plays within the relation R, and where the *multiplicity* $a..b$ specifies that each instance of class C_1 can participate at least a times and at most b times to relation A; $c..d$ has an analogous meaning for class C_2.

An *aggregation* in UML is a binary association between the instances of two classes, denoting a part-whole relationship, i.e., a relationship that specifies that each instance of a class is made up of a set of instances of another class. An aggregation is graphically rendered as shown in the right hand side of Figure 1, where the diamond indicates the *containing class*, opposed to the *contained class*. The multiplicity has the same meaning as in associations. As for associations, also for aggregation it is possible to define role names which denote the role each class plays in the aggregation.

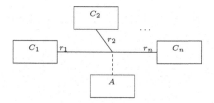

Fig. 2. Association in UML

Observe that names of associations and names of aggregations (as names of classes) are *unique*. In other words there cannot be two associations/aggregations with the same name.

Next we turn to the formalization in $\mathcal{DLR}$. An aggregation A as depicted in Figure 1, without considering multiplicities, is formalized in $\mathcal{DLR}$ by means of a binary relation A on which the following assertion is enforced:

$$A \sqsubseteq (1:C_1) \sqcap (2:C_2).$$

Note that, to distinguish between the contained class and the containing class, we simply use the convention that *the first argument of the relation is the containing class*. To express the multiplicity $n_l..n_u$ on the participation of instances of C_2 for each given instance of C_1, we use the assertion

$$C_1 \sqsubseteq (\geq n_l\,[1]A) \sqcap (\leq n_u\,[1]A)$$

We can use a similar assertion for a multiplicity on the participation of instances of C_1 for each given instance of C_2.

Observe that, in the formalization in $\mathcal{DLR}$ of aggregation, role names do not play any role. If we want to keep track of them in the formalization, it suffices to consider them as convenient abbreviations for the components of the $\mathcal{DLR}$ relation modeling the aggregation.

Next we focus on *associations*. Since associations have often a related association class, we formalize associations in $\mathcal{DLR}$ by reifying each association A into a $\mathcal{DLR}$ concept A with suitable properties. Let us consider the association shown in Figure 2. We represent it in $\mathcal{DLR}$ by introducing a concept A and n *binary* relations $r_1, \ldots, r_n$, one for each component of the association A[2]. Then we enforce the following assertion:

$$A \sqsubseteq \exists[1]r_1 \sqcap (\leq 1\,[1]r_1) \sqcap \forall[1](r_1 \Rightarrow (2:C_1)) \sqcap$$
$$\exists[1]r_2 \sqcap (\leq 1\,[1]r_2) \sqcap \forall[1](r_2 \Rightarrow (2:C_2)) \sqcap$$
$$\vdots$$
$$\exists[1]r_n \sqcap (\leq 1\,[1]r_n) \sqcap \forall[1](r_n \Rightarrow (2:C_n))$$

---

[2] These relations may have the name of the roles of the association if available in the UML diagram, or an arbitrary name if role names are not available. In any case, we preserve the possibility of using the same role name in different associations.

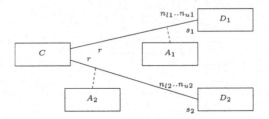

Fig. 3. Multiplicity in aggregation

where $\exists[1]r_i$ (with $i \in \{1,\ldots,n\}$) specifies that the concept A must have all components $r_1,\ldots,r_n$ of the association A, $(\leq 1\,[1]r_i)$ (with $i \in \{1,\ldots,n\}$) specifies that each such component is single-valued, and $\forall[1](r_i \Rightarrow (2:C_i))$ (with $i \in \{1,\ldots,n\}$) specifies the class each component has to belong to. Finally, we use the assertion

$$(\text{id } A\ [1]r_1,\ldots,[1]r_n)$$

to specify that each instance of A represents a *distinct* tuple in $C_1 \times \cdots \times C_n$.

We can easily represent in $\mathcal{DLR}$ a multiplicity on a binary association, by imposing a number restriction on the relations modeling the components of the association. Differently from aggregation, however, the names of such relations (which correspond to roles) are unique wrt to the association only, not the entire diagram. Hence we have to state such constraints in $\mathcal{DLR}$ in a slightly more involved way.

Suppose we have a situation like that in Figure 3. Consider the association A_1 and the constraint saying that for each instance of C there can be at least n_{l1} and at most n_{u1} instances of D_1 related by A_1 to it. We capture this constraint as follows:

$$C \sqsubseteq (\geq n_{l1}\,[2](r \sqcap (1:A_1))) \sqcap (\leq n_{u1}\,[2](r \sqcap (1:A_1)))$$

Observe that nothing prevents C to partecipate to a different association A_2 with the same role r but with different multiplicity $n_{l2}..n_{u2}$. Observe that this is modeled by the totally unrelated assertion:

$$C \sqsubseteq (\geq n_{l2}\,[2](r \sqcap (1:A_2))) \sqcap (\leq n_{u2}\,[2](r \sqcap (1:A_2)))$$

4   Generalization and Inheritance

In UML one can use *generalization* between a parent class and a child class to specify that each instance of the child class is also an instance of the parent class. Hence, the instances of the child class inherit the properties of the parent class, but typically they satisfy additional properties that in general do not hold for the parent class.

Generalization is naturally supported in $\mathcal{DLR}$. If an UML class C_2 generalizes a class C_1, we can express this by the $\mathcal{DLR}$ assertion:

$$C_1 \sqsubseteq C_2$$

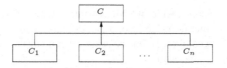

Fig. 4. A class hierarchy in UML

Inheritance between $\mathcal{DLR}$ concepts works exactly as inheritance between UML classes. This is an obvious consequence of the semantics of $\sqsubseteq$ which is based on subsetting. Indeed, given an assertion $C_1 \sqsubseteq C_2$, every tuple in a $\mathcal{DLR}$ relation having C_2 as i-th argument type may have as i-th component an instance of C_1, which is in fact also an instance of C_2. As a consequence, in the formalization, each attribute or operation of C_2, and each aggregation and association involving C_2 is correctly inherited by C_1. Observe that the formalization in $\mathcal{DLR}$ also captures directly inheritance among association classes, which are treated exactly as all other classes, and multiple inheritance between classes (including association classes).

Moreover in UML, one can group several generalizations into a class hierarchy, as shown in Figure 4. Such a hierarchy is captured in $\mathcal{DLR}$ by a set of inclusion assertions, one between each child class and the parent class:

$$C_i \sqsubseteq C \qquad \text{for each } i \in \{1, \ldots, n\}$$

We discuss in Section 5 how to formalize in $\mathcal{DLR}$ additional properties of a class hierarchy, such as mutual disjointness between the child classes, or covering of the parent class.

5 Constraints

In UML it is possible to add information to a class diagram by using *constraints*. In general, constraints are used to express in an informal way information which cannot be expressed by other constructs of UML class diagrams. We discuss here common types of constraints that occur in UML class diagrams and how they can be taken into account when formalizing class diagrams in $\mathcal{DLR}$.

Often, when defining generalizations between classes, we need to add additional constraints among the involved classes. For example, for the class hierarchy in Figure 4, a constraint may express that $C_1, \ldots, C_n$ are *mutually disjoint*. In $\mathcal{DLR}$, such a relationship can be expressed by the assertions $C_i \sqsubseteq \neg C_j$, for each $i, j \in \{1, \ldots, n\}$ with $i \neq j$.

In general, in UML, if not otherwise specified by a constraint, two classes may have common instances, i.e., they are *not disjoint*. If a constraint imposes the disjointness of two classes, say C and C', this can be formalized in $\mathcal{DLR}$ by means of the assertion $C \sqsubseteq \neg C'$.

Disjointness of classes is just one example of *negative information*. Again, by exploiting the expressive power of $\mathcal{DLR}$, we can express additional forms of negative information, usually not considered in UML, by introducing suitable assertions. For example, we can enforce that no instance of a class C has an attribute a by means of the assertion $C \sqsubseteq \neg \exists [1]a$. Analogously, one can assert that no instance of a class is involved in a given association or aggregation.

Turning again the attention to generalization hierarchies, by default, in UML a generalization hierarchy is open, in the sense that there may be instances of the superclass that are not instances of any of the subclasses. This allows for extending the diagram more easily, in the sense that the introduction of a new subclass does not change the semantics of the superclass. However, in specific situations, it may happen that in a generalization hierarchy, the superclass C is a covering of the subclasses $C_1, \ldots, C_n$. We can represent such a situation in $\mathcal{DLR}$ by simply including the additional assertion $C \sqsubseteq C_1 \sqcup \cdots \sqcup C_n$ Such an assertion models a form of *disjunctive information*: each instance of C is either an instance of C_1, or an instance of C_2, ... or an instance of C_n.

Other forms of disjunctive information can be modeled by exploiting the expressive power of $\mathcal{DLR}$. For example, that an attribute a is present only for a specified set $C_1, \ldots, C_n$ of classes can be modeled by suitably using union of classes: $\exists [1]a \sqsubseteq C_1 \sqcup \cdots \sqcup C_n$.

Keys are a modeling notion that is very common in databases, and they are used to express that certain attributes uniquely identify the instances of a class. We can exploit the expressive power of $\mathcal{DLR}$ in order to associate keys to classes. If an attribute a is a key for a class C this means that there is no pair of instances of C that have the same value for a. We can capture this in $\mathcal{DLR}$ by means of the assertion (**id** C [1]a). More generally, we are able to specify that a *set* of attributes $\{a_1, \ldots, a_n\}$ is a key for C; in this case we use the assertion (**id** C [1]$a_1, \ldots, [1]a_n$).

As already discussed in Section 4, constraints that correspond to the specialization of the type of an attribute or its multiplicity can be represented in $\mathcal{DLR}$. Similarly, consider the case of a class C participating in an aggregation A with a class D, and where C and D have subclasses C' and D' respectively, related via an aggregation A'. A *subset constraint* from A' to A can be modeled correctly in $\mathcal{DLR}$ by means of the assertion $A \sqsubseteq A'$, involving the two binary relations A and A' that represent the aggregations.

More generally, one can exploit the expressive power of $\mathcal{DLR}$ to formalize several types of constraints that allow one to better represent the application semantics and that are typically not dealt with in a formal way. Observe that this allows one to take such constraints fully into account when reasoning on the class diagram.

6   Reasoning on Class Diagrams

Traditional CASE tools support the designer with a user friendly graphical environment and provide powerful means to access different kinds of repositories that store information associated to the elements of the developed project. However, no support for higher level activities related to managing the complexity of the design is provided. In particular, the burden of checking relevant properties of class diagrams, such as consistency or redundancy (see below), is left to the responsibility of the designer.

Thus, the formalization in $\mathcal{DLR}$ of UML class diagrams, and the fact that properties of inheritance and relevant types of constraints are perfectly captured by the formalization in $\mathcal{DLR}$ and the associated reasoning tasks, provides the ability to reason on class diagrams. This represents a significant improvement and is a first step towards the development of modeling tools that offer an automated reasoning support to the designer in his modeling activity.

We briefly discuss the tasks that can be performed by exploiting the reasoning capabilities of a $\mathcal{DLR}$ reasoner [14,15], and that allow a modeling tool to take over tasks traditionally left to the responsibility of the designer. Such a tool may construct from a class diagram a $\mathcal{DLR}$ knowledge base, and manage it in a way completely transparent to the designer. By exploiting the $\mathcal{DLR}$ reasoning services various kinds of checks can be performed on the class diagram. [3]

Consistency of the class diagram. A class diagram is *consistent*, if its classes can be populated without violating any of the constraints in the diagram. Observe that the interaction of various types of constraints may make it very difficult to detect inconsistencies. By exploiting the formalization in $\mathcal{DLR}$, the consistency of a class diagram can be checked by checking the satisfiability of the corresponding $\mathcal{DLR}$ knowledge base.

Class Consistency. A *class* is *consistent*, if it can be populated without violating any of the constraints in the class diagram. The inconsistency of a class may be due to a design error or due to over-constraining. In any case, the designer can be forced to remove the inconsistency, either by correcting the error, or by relaxing some constraints, or by deleting the class, thus removing redundancy from the diagram. Exploiting the formalization in $\mathcal{DLR}$, class consistency can be checked by checking satisfiability of the corresponding concept in the $\mathcal{DLR}$ knowledge base representing the class diagram.

Class Equivalence. Two classes are *equivalent* if they denote the same set of instances whenever the constraints imposed by the class diagram are satisfied. Determining equivalence of two classes allows for their merging, thus reducing the complexity of the diagram. Again, checking class equivalence amounts to check the equivalence in $\mathcal{DLR}$ of the corresponding concepts.

Class Subsumption. A class C_1 is *subsumed by* a class C_2 if, whenever the constraints imposed by the class diagram are satisfied, the extension of C_1 is a subset of the extension of C_2. Such a subsumption allows one to deduce that properties for C_1 hold also for C_2. It is also the basis for a *classification* of all the classes in a diagram. Such a classification, as in any object-oriented approach, can be exploited in several ways within the modeling process [1]. Subsumption, and hence classification, can be checked by verifying subsumption in $\mathcal{DLR}$.

Logical Consequence. A property is a *logical consequence* of a class diagram if it holds whenever all constraints specified in the diagram are satisfied. As an example, consider the generalization hierarchy depicted in Figure 4 and assume that a constraint specifies that it is complete. If an attribute a is defined as mandatory for all classes $C_1, \ldots, C_n$

---

[3] A prototype design tool with such a kind of automated reasoning support is available at
http://www.cs.man.ac.uk/~franconi/icom/.

then it follows logically that the same attribute is mandatory also for class C, even if not explicitly present in the diagram. Determining logical consequence is useful on the one hand to reduce the complexity of the diagram by removing those constraints that logically follow from other ones, and on the other hand it can be used to explicit properties that are implicit in the diagram, thus enhancing its readability.

Logical consequence can be captured by logical implication in $\mathcal{DLR}$, and determining logical implication is at the basis of all types of reasoning that a $\mathcal{DLR}$ reasoning system can provide. In particular, observe that all reasoning tasks we have considered above can be rephrased in terms of logical consequence.

7 Conclusions

We have proposed a new formalization of UML class diagrams in terms of a particular formal logic of the family of Description Logics. Our long term goal is to exploit the deductive capabilities of DL systems, thus showing that effective reasoning can be carried out on UML class diagrams, so as to provide support during the specification phase of software development. As a first step, we have shown in this paper how to map the constructs of a class diagram onto those of Description Logics. The mapping provides us with a rigorous logical framework for representing and automatically reasoning on UML class specifications.

We have already started experimenting our approach. In particular, we have used FACT for representing and reasoning on class diagrams. Although FACT does not yet incorporate all features required by our formalization (e.g., keys), the first results are encouraging. In particular, we have been able to draw interesting, non-trivial inferences on class diagrams containing about 50 classes. More experiments are under way, and we plan to report on them in the near future.

In the future, we aim at extending our formalization in order to capture further aspects of the UML. Our first step in this direction will be to add to our formal framework the possibility of modeling and reasoning on objects and links (i.e., instances of classes and associations).

References

1. S. Bergamaschi and B. Nebel. Acquisition and validation of complex object database schemata supporting multiple inheritance. *Applied Intelligence*, 4(2):185–203, 1994.
2. D. Calvanese, G. De Giacomo, and M. Lenzerini. On the decidability of query containment under constraints. In *Proc. of PODS'98*, pages 149–158, 1998.
3. D. Calvanese, G. De Giacomo, and M. Lenzerini. Reasoning in expressive description logics with fixpoints based on automata on infinite trees. In *Proc. of IJCAI'99*, pages 84–89, 1999.
4. D. Calvanese, G. De Giacomo, and M. Lenzerini. Identification constraints and functional dependencies in description logics. In *Proc. of IJCAI 2001*, pages 155–160, 2001.
5. D. Calvanese, M. Lenzerini, and D. Nardi. Description logics for conceptual data modeling. In J. Chomicki and G. Saake, editors, *Logics for Databases and Information Systems*, pages 229–264. Kluwer Academic Publisher, 1998.

6. T. Clark and A. S. Evans. Foundations of the Unified Modeling Language. In D. Duke and A. Evans, editors, *Proc. of the 2nd Northern Formal Methods Workshop*. Springer-Verlag, 1997.

7. F. M. Donini, M. Lenzerini, D. Nardi, and A. Schaerf. Reasoning in description logics. In G. Brewka, editor, *Principles of Knowledge Representation*, Studies in Logic, Language and Information, pages 193–238. CSLI Publications, 1996.

8. A. Evans, R. France, K. Lano, and B. Rumpe. The UML as a formal modeling notation. In H. Kilov, B. Rumpe, and I. Simmonds, editors, *Proc. of the OOPSLA'97 Workshop on Object-oriented Behavioral Semantics*, pages 75–81. Technische Universität München, TUM-I9737, 1997.

9. A. Evans, R. France, K. Lano, and B. Rumpe. Meta-modelling semantics of UML. In H. Kilov, editor, *Behavioural Specifications for Businesses and Systems*, chapter 2. Kluwer Academic Publisher, 1999.

10. A. S. Evans. Reasoning with UML class diagrams. In *Second IEEE Workshop on Industrial Strength Formal Specification Techniques (WIFT'98)*. IEEE Computer Society Press, 1998.

11. V. Haarslev and R. Möller. Expressive ABox reasoning with number restrictions, role hierarchies, and transitively closed roles. In *Proc. of KR 2000*, pages 273–284, 2000.

12. D. Harel and B. Rumpe. Modeling languages: Syntax, semantics and all that stuff. Technical Report MCS00-16, The Weizmann Institute of Science, Rehovot, Israel, 2000.

13. I. Horrocks. Using an expressive description logic: FaCT or fiction? In *Proc. of KR'98*, pages 636–647, 1998.

14. I. Horrocks and P. F. Patel-Schneider. Optimizing description logic subsumption. *J. of Log. and Comp.*, 9(3):267–293, 1999.

15. I. Horrocks, U. Sattler, and S. Tobies. Practical reasoning for expressive description logics. In H. Ganzinger, D. McAllester, and A. Voronkov, editors, *Proc. of LPAR'99*, number 1705 in LNAI, pages 161–180. Springer-Verlag, 1999.

16. T. Kirk, A. Y. Levy, Y. Sagiv, and D. Srivastava. The Information Manifold. In *Proceedings of the AAAI 1995 Spring Symp. on Information Gathering from Heterogeneous, Distributed Enviroments*, pages 85–91, 1995.

17. D. L. McGuinness and J. R. Wright. An industrial strength description logic-based configuration platform. *IEEE Intelligent Systems*, pages 69–77, 1998.

18. U. Sattler. *Terminological Knowledge Representation Systems in a Process Engineering Application*. PhD thesis, LuFG Theoretical Computer Science, RWTH-Aachen, Germany, 1998.

A Biological Approach to the Development of Computer Autoimmune Systems

Kevin Deeb and Steven Lewis

Department of Information Technology, Barry University, 11415 NE 2nd Ave, Miami Shores, Florida, 33161
{kdeeb, lewiss}@mail.barry.edu

Abstract. Experiencing repeated computer virus attacks over the last decade has led to a number of intriguing technological challenges. The study of human immunology may help to solve these challenges and aid in the understanding of how and why computer viruses propagate. Current techniques employ heuristic systems to ferret the viral attacks and annihilate them. This technology is more suited for addressing known viruses and has been relatively successful. However, there remains a challenge as to how to deal with the virus problems of the near future, albeit unknown viral code. Ultimately, this paper will stimulate new innovations in anti-virus technology. This paper explores current research in the area of protection from computer viruses and suggests a possible framework for virus detection in such an autoimmune system. Hence, this paper exposes the mechanics of virus detection in the human immune system. Then it suggests techniques that could be used to identify or detect unknown viruses by distinguishing between "self" and foreigner.

1 Introduction

As recent history has reminded, anti-virus problems could threaten the freedoms enjoyed in the network economy, the information age and the Internet. Hence, the importance of finding alternative protection systems to reduce the potency of computer viral attacks.

Although it may be productive to translate the structure of the human immune system into a computer immune system, the goal is not to merely copy human immunology. Since biological solutions may not be directly applicable to computer systems, it is more productive to imitate the solutions to viral attacks. Hence, this paper exposes the mechanics of virus detection in the human immune system. Then it suggests techniques that could be used to identify unknown viruses. The first step in virus detection is the distinction between "self" and foreigner. This paper suggests techniques for virus detection that are inspired by the human immune system.

M.-S. Hacid et al. (Eds.): ISMIS 2002, LNAI 2366, pp. 514–525, 2002.

2 Review of Related Literature

There are a variety of complementary anti-virus techniques in common usage [1, 2]. Scanning monitors alert users to system activity patterns that are associated with viruses, not the normal byte code patterns of normal legitimate programs. Upon detection, the anti-virus system warns the user of suspicious patterns that have been detected. Virus scanners search files, boot records, memory, and other locations where executable code can be stored for characteristic byte patterns that occur in one or more known viruses. Scanners are essential for establishing the identity and location of a virus. This method has been effective at removing known viruses. The drawback of scanning and repair mechanisms is that they can only be applied to known viruses, or variants of them; this requires that scanners and repairers be updated frequently.

Whenever a new virus is discovered, it is very quickly distributed among an informal, international group of virus experts. Many such collectors are in the anti-virus software business, and they set out to obtain information about the virus, which enables detection of the virus, and restoration of an infected host program to its original uninfected state. Typically, an expert obtains this information by disassembling the virus and then analyzing the program code to determine the behavioral patterns and the method that it uses to attach itself to host programs. Then, the expert selects a sequence of perhaps 16 to 32 bytes that represents a sequence of instructions guaranteed to be found in each instance of the virus, and which (in the expert's estimation) is unlikely to be found in legitimate programs. This is called the virus' "signature". The signature can then be encoded into the scanner, and the knowledge of the attachment method can be encoded into the repairer. Such an analysis is tedious and time-consuming, sometimes taking several hours or days, and even the best experts have been known to select poor signatures ones that cause the scanner to report false alarms on legitimate programs.

As stated previously, the static scanner techniques that are prominent today are no match the future onslaught of malicious code. So, In 1995, researchers [19] were investigating dynamic detection of computer viruses. The technique used by researchers [19] was to employ an expert system programmed with certain rules to monitor system activity of a virtual PC. The rules encoded in the expert system helped to identify viruses from the monitored data. Although this technique offered an improvement over scanning and heuristics, it became evident that such a system could not develop the relationships and rules fast enough to keep up with frequent and unique virus attacks. In 1996, researchers at IBM [20] employed neural networks for detection of boot sector viruses. Although quite successful, their technique faced severe constraints on CPU, memory, and disk-space usage in the "average" PC. Hence researchers looked toward data mining to solve these problems. With regard to data mining as a technique against viruses, [18] researchers discussed systematic data mining methods for intrusion detection. Their method was to use data mining to discover program behavior patterns from the monitored data. This information would be useful in classification of anomalies and possibly intrusion. However the technique is not suited for complex computing environments because of the large volume of data that had to be analyzed. In the end it was stated that the intrusion detection technique was not sufficient because exploitable system weaknesses become more plentiful as the computing environment becomes more complex. The use of lightweight agents for intrusion detection was researched in [15]. In this study, researchers developed a prototype model for using intelligent agents to detect the presence of an intruder. The researchers discovered that in a distributed environment, centralized artificial intelligence intrusion detection was not very effective because the central agents would be required to pour through large amounts of data. This could increase latency and detection could take place after the damage has been done. As a result, they employed lightweight mobile agents for information retrieval, data transformation and knowledge discovery. The lightweight mobile agents were comprised of minimal code and were sent via the network to various areas to perform data transformation and knowledge discovery. Typically, the agents analyzed audit data and transformed it into information about the behavior of a computer system component through data mining. This distributed architecture has a fundamental similarity to the human immune system operation and it holds much promise to solve the problem of detecting malicious intrusion. In addition, researchers described the framework of a messaging system used for agents to communicate. Previous intrusion detection systems discovered system relationships and encoded these relationships as rules as an expert system. The system proposed in [15] is superior in that it is more dynamically capable of discovery. However, the distributed mobile agents required a cumbersome hierarchy for all distributed agents to communicate and share information. It is this author's opinion that the weakness of this technique is in the complexity of the hierarchical structure of the agents and their communication system. Complexity usually is accompanied by numerous opportunities for failure. While not a perfect solution, mobile agent technology goes a long way toward being able to realize the ideal behavior desired in an intrusion detection system.

3 The Mechanics of the Human Immune System

The task of extracting the essence or mechanics of the human immune system for creation of a useful digital immune system is a difficult one. The human immune system is complicated in its execution, due in part to its multi-layered approach. In spite of these difficulties, a study of the immune system reveals a useful set of principles of operation of the human immune system.

For instance, lymphocytes in the immune system are able to determine locally the presence of an infection. No central coordination takes place, which means there is no single point of failure. A distributed, mobile agent architecture for security was also proposed in [3]. In this work, the researchers first sought to analyze the human immune system to determine how it works. Then they classified it into its structural and procedural components at the cell level. Then similar architectures for a computer system were proposed that supposedly would allow the system to protect itself. Although it was remunerative to translate the human structure, care was taken not to blindly imitate the human system when applying concepts to computers. For example, the human system is not concerned with privacy, confidentiality, and protection of intellectual property, etc. as is a computer system. The work [3] merely analyzes the human immune system to expose the human security concepts that are devoid in the current computer anti virus systems. So, the human immune system provides a good example of a highly distributed architecture that greatly enhances robustness. The human immune system's detection and memory systems are distributed without central control that administers the collective response. In the human immune system, there are localized interactions with the unknown virus among the individual detectors. This is helped by variable cell reproduction rates that allow the immune system to regenerate cells where and when they are needed. In addition, the human body is resilient in that it allows entire organs, e.g. tonsils, spleen etc., to be deleted while being able to sustain immune system operation. The work done [3] sets the stage for adaptation of protection concepts found in the human immune system for application in a computer immune system. Where this work fell short is that it did not actually suggest a framework for the computer immune system based on the lessons learned from the human immune system. Hence, it is this papers objective to explain the important relevant workings of the human immune system and extract the important concepts followed by formulating methods or framework that adapts from the lessons learned from the human immune system.

4 The Human Immune System's Discovery of Foreign Material

The human immune system initiates a primary response comprised of new detectors such as B cells, Killer T cells and NK (natural killer) cells that are chosen for the type of infection found. This process uses two strategies. Firstly, distributed detection and, secondly learning. Killer T cells are an important part of the human immune system. In addition, there are several kinds of T cells that play different roles in the immune system.

4.1 The Detection Process

The detection system is flexible in that less specific lymphocytes can detect a wider variety of pathogens but will be less efficient at detecting any specific pathogen. However, they all have the ability to bind themselves to peptides from antigens. T cells that bind themselves to the body's own peptides are sent to an organ called the thymus. There, they are put through a maturation process. During the maturation process, the T cell is tested to ensure that it will not bind to its own peptides. All T cells that bind to the body's own peptides are killed off in a screening process. After maturation, the thymus releases only T cells that fail to bind to the body's peptides. When in circulation, if a T cell binds itself to an antigen, one can be reasonably assured that it has detected a foreign body. When the T cells are in circulation, they are said to be distributed detectors. The T cells are widely distributed throughout the body for distributed detection. The ability to detect intrusion of unfamiliar or foreign entities is an important feature of any security system.

4.2 The Learning Mode

The human immune system recognizes particular antigens (viruses and other undesirable foreign substances) by means of antibodies and immune cell receptors which bind to epitopes. The killer T cell receptors can see the inner portions of antigen, after the antigen has been consumed by a macrophage, which then presents pieces of the antigen on its surface, so they can be seen by other cells. It is worth mentioning that the immune system does not attempt an exact match when killer T cell receptors attempt to bind to the antigen. In the human immune system, a particular virus is not recognized via an exact match for a good reason. The ability to recognize variants of a virus is essential because viruses can mutate frequently. If an exact match were required, immunity to one variant of a virus would offer no protection against a slightly different variant.

After a foreign body is detected using distributed detection, the foreigner must be cordoned off in order for the immune system to "learn" its behavior. The human immune system focuses its attention on the protein fragments called peptides. There are two distinct detection responses. The cell-mediated response is suited for virus and other intra cellular intrusion. The human immune system response is also targeted at extra cellular intrusion from organisms like bacteria.

4.3 Self Replication

The human immune system replicates its detectors to deal with replicating pathogens. By contrast, computer systems do not replicate themselves and are subject to such attacks as denial-of-service attacks. In this case, the computer system has no way of replicating itself to deal with attacks on its resources. Servers being attacked with increasing demands are forced to shut down to deal with the onslaught. Mammalian immune systems handle this by placing more detectors into service to help locate foreign bodies.

5 Biologically Inspired Techniques for Anti Virus Systems

The recent onslaught of viral and worm attacks suggests that software designers must find ways of recognizing and removing discovered and undiscovered viruses. The human immune system already has extremely effective techniques for discovering and reacting to annihilate viruses. The human immune system topology has inspired the design of a digital autoimmune system for computers, [7]. The researchers after a thorough study of the human immune system gave illustrations of how the principles of immunology could be applied to computers. The illustrations were meant to admonish the intellectual movement toward robust, distributed protection techniques. Although researchers [7] laid the foundation by extracting the relevant protection mechanism found in the human immune system, it did not develop or apply the framework for the computer immune system. As stated previously, this paper seeks to apply current software technology thereby adapting immunology principles to computer systems.

Although there are many differences between the human organisms and computers, improvements to anti-virus systems can be achieved by designing computer systems that have the important properties found in the human immune system. These include a stable definition of "self", multi-layered protection, distributed detection and memory systems, inexact matching strategies, sensitivity to most new antigens, and methods of protecting the immune system itself from attack.

In a digital immune system, a similar arrangement could be used. Distributed detection could employ bots that are designed to fail to detect "self". The bots are to be deployed in different locations within the operating system to monitor the computer system. Whenever bots are activated, an anomaly has been detected and its operating system location would be known. Such bots can be tested "for maturation" using a theorem called the r-contiguous bits rule, [8]. This rule says the samples are matched if there are r-contiguous matches between symbols in corresponding positions. That is, for two strings A and B, match (A,B) is true if A and B agree at r contiguous locations. Hence the distributed bots would test the suspect using the r-contiguous test to detect the foreign code. As stated previously, this method is greatly improved if cryptography is employed.

Such bots could be generated at methodically by the operating system for various parts of the computer system (e.g. registry, Input/Output subsystem, system calls, etc). Then the bots compare test cases against self using the r-contiguous theorem. In this arrangement, careful thought must be given to the number of r-contiguous bits that are necessary for detection of "self". The number is actually dependent on the complexity of "self" and the acceptable false negative rate.

Again, the digital immune system must have a stable definition of "self", i.e. it must be able to differentiate between its behavior and that of foreign bodies. In the bio-chemical world, this is extremely complex. In a digital immune system definition of "self" could be achieved by establishing a local database that contains normal usage patterns of the operating system and user software architecture environment. In the event that a virus attempted certain system calls, the database would be queried for comparison and an alarm would be generated in the event no exact match is found. In this technique, the computer defines "self" by comparing current traces of normal system call behavior with the database, and follows by comparing the system call behavior of the intruder. In this technique, data mining of usage patterns is performed in real time on the computer. Statistically significant usage patterns or profiles would be stored for later query during investigation of a foreign entity. According to [14], the key advantages of this technique is that it can detect unknown intrusion since it requires no a previous knowledge of specific intrusions. However, defining and maintaining "normal" profiles is a nontrivial and error prone task. Inductively learned classification rules replace the manually encoded intrusion patterns and profiles. System features and measures are selected by considering the statistical patterns computed from the audit data. Further, meta-learning can be used to learn the correlation of intrusion evidence from multiple audit data sources, making it feasible to detect a full range of intrusions. Here, data mining agents use algorithms or statistical correlation to establish predictive rules about usage from the audit data contained in the database. However, there are physical challenges with this scenario. Such a database cannot grow in size to the point where its shear size presents a challenge to merely parse the data. The continuous data mining is likely to reduce performance, as it would consume computer resources such as processor threads and memory. Also, for data mining to be a successful remedy for definition of "self", the large volumes of data must be analyzed without offering performance restrictions to the monitored computer system. For these reasons data mining is typically performed on powerful servers. There is a good possibility that this technique of foreigner detection can produce good results when deployed in a networked environment with centralized data mining where all workstations are static clones or images.

Although this method does not provide a fail-safe way of detecting an intruder's behavior, its accuracy can be improved upon with the use of "digital certificates". The operating system and other software vendors can employ digital certificates for authentication. To reduce false alarms from the data mining technique, an attempt would be made to authenticate the suspected foreign code by checking its digital certificate.

As pointed out in the previous discussion of the mechanics of the human immune system, the T cell detectors are distributed throughout the body. This suggests that detectors or agents used for detection of foreigners are to be deployed throughout the computer system. This in envisioned as a distributed agent technique. These intelligent agents contain code and state and exist to perform detection tasks in their respective areas of the operating system. Others have suggested the use of intelligent agents to detect the presence of intruders, [15]. In this technique, the computer system is divided into its components and small intelligent agents are deployed in these areas. The agents are deployed with a specific purpose. ·The intelligent agents are used to intelligently process audit data at the sources instead of at a central location. Essentially, the distributed agents apply data mining techniques to the audit data and collaborate suspicious events with other agents. This technique requires the distributed agents to have established criteria that allow them to determine when to be suspicious. Distributed autonomous agents solve critical problems in detection and provide the framework that allows additional area specific agents to be added. Since these agents contain code, it is possible to upgrade them dynamically. This dynamic feature also makes them portable like mobile agents.

The agent computing paradigm raises several security concerns, which are one of the main obstacles to the widespread use and adaptation of this new technology. Agent security issues include: authentication, identification, secure messaging, certification, and resource control. In addition, the intelligent agent frameworks must be protected from attack itself.

6 Combining Intelligent Agents with a Virtual Environment

Once detected, the operating system can be designed to observe the behavior of the malicious code in a similar fashion as the human immune systems. This would require the immune system to contain a virtual environment or machine. The virtual operating system technique has been documented in recent software designs such as VMWare. The malicious code would be executed in the virtual environment to learn its behavior.

VMWare is a virtual machine environment that can be utilized to create virtual computers (guests) that run on top of Windows NT, Windows 2000, or Linux installations (hosts). A guest can run most variants of Windows, DOS, and Linux. A virtual machine is a software-imposed environment that encapsulates the operating system and applications running in the virtual machine so that when they try and interact with the hardware they believe is present, the virtual machine software intercepts the requests. The virtual machine software creates virtual devices that serve as carefully controlled surrogates to real hardware or virtual hardware [9]. In addition, with the advent of artificial intelligence, it is now possible to design anti-virus system models to include intelligent agents to perform the role of learning the behavior of the foreign code while it is executed in the virtual environment after it is detected. Subsequently, this information can be used to locally generate signature files.

In the currently deployed anti-virus systems, if the system detects an exact match to a signature for a known virus, it takes the analogous step of erasing or otherwise deactivating the file containing the virus. This is a valid approach. However, an important difference between computer viruses and biological viruses raises the possibility of a much gentler alternative.

From the body's point of view, cells are easily replaced. Even if biological viruses didn't destroy infected cells, an infected host cell would hardly be worth the trouble of saving; there are plenty of other cells around that can serve the same function. In contrast, each of the applications run by a typical computer user are unique in function and irreplaceable (unless backups have been kept, of course). A user would be likely to notice any malfunction. Consequently, it would be suicidal for a computer virus to destroy its host program, because the ensuing investigation would surely lead to its discovery and eradication. For this reason, all but the most ill conceived computer viruses attach themselves to their host in such a way that they do not destroy its function. The fact that host information is merely rearranged, not destroyed, allows one to construct repair algorithms for a large class of non-destructive viruses for which one has a precise knowledge of the attachment method.

Hence, after the virus is detected, any CPU or Input/Output processes assigned to the virus are to be halted while the learning process takes place. The learning process as described above will be successful in determining the modus operandi and "signature". This information can be used to repair any infected areas by reversing any changes that were made. Subsequently, the source virus must be removed from any infected files. To do this, the scanner anti-virus software would be loaded with the signature files generated during the learning stage.

In the initial detection stage, lightweight mobile intelligent agents as described in [17] would be employed to scan audit data and use data mining techniques suited to the local environment monitored to discover an intrusion. After detection, learning would take place in a virtual environment as depicted in Figure 1 to follow.

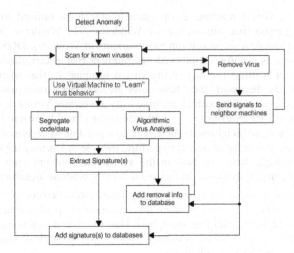

Fig. 1. Process Chart Of A Simple Virus Analysis Subsystem

7 Prevention of Virus Multiplication

As stated previously, viruses proliferate in a networked environment. In a biologically inspired digital immune system, steps must be taken to account for higher infection rates in a networked environment. The human immune system is remarkable in that it incorporates a memory feature. In the process of vaccination, a weakened strain of the target virus is injected into the body. The body responds by killing the virus, the body then generates anti bodies that are designed to annihilate the target virus. The anti bodies are then dispatched throughout the body to ensure that the virus is killed. In the event of re-infection with the known virus, remembering the anti body formula, the body dispatches anti bodies to fight and kill the virus. This method is very effective in combating viruses. The digital immune system must incorporate this distributed learning ability if it is to be successful in the fight against malicious code. There are good reasons for distributing the task of virus analysis, including increasing the amount of computing power available to the task, introducing redundancy of a critical component, reducing network latency and load balancing. It is necessary to incorporate features found in enterprise client server applications, namely, messaging. A messaging subsystem allows clients and servers to communicate via established format and network protocols. After detection, the message subsystem resident on the client would alert corresponding servers that a virus was detected. It would also indicate if it was known or unknown. Then, virus behavior learning takes place in the virtual machine, and the signature file would be generated. The messaging system would notify servers that virus definition files are available for upload. Servers, in turn, begin scanning using the definition files, and would broadcast the signature to other servers in its domain. In this way, servers are allowed to synchronize the results of virus analysis done in client computers.

8 Limited-Function Environments

In mammalian immune systems, a virus that targets a certain feature of a whale's anatomy may not affect humans. A viral disease that affects fish may have little effect on birds because the virus attacks a function or trait not found in birds. The lesson learned from nature here is that viruses attack the targeted function or biological components. To understand the point, consider that a virus targeted for the Japanese version of Microsoft Word will not spread in an English version of Microsoft Word. A separate replication environment is used for each format and language, to ensure that viruses in these formats and languages execute and spread properly in the virtual machines. Hence the programming environment may offer clues to stem the spread of viruses. In programming environments where it is virtually impossible for viruses to create, or modifying programs, then such a programming environment will be incapable of spreading viruses. The Java "sandbox" security model is a good example of this kind of protection. Unfortunately, developers and customers desire to extend limited-function languages to be more powerful and functional. Java is shedding its limited function sandbox by incorporating signed applets that allow the Java applications to extend their functionality and directly access system resources. Due to the continuing desire to make languages more powerful and fully functional, most major programming environments will remain functional enough to support viruses. In limited-function environments, a virus would not be able to exploit the system in order to spread. A possible application of this technique is in mobile phones, personal digital assistants or devices embedded with limited functioning operating systems or user applications. A way of preventing these programs from spreading virus threats is vital. Intelligent agents can be used to switch on this type of protection in the event a virus is detected. In this scenario, the virus will be given a limited functioning environment to execute or "live" in. In order for this to be effective, operating system and anti-virus system designers must decide the strategy and classify the functional areas for limiting access to create these new environments safely. This concept is already deployed in the Microsoft Windows operating system in a different form; namely the safe mode. In this mode, a limited set of files are loaded during operating system start for the purpose of troubleshooting operating errors. Provided a similar technique was incorporated into the operating system, the intelligent agents would simply request that the operating system impose this limited functioning environment on the virus, [10].

In the same manner, intelligent agents can be utilized to impose granular execution controls on the offending virus after it is detected. Traditional access controls, focusing on permissions to read, write and execute, are not successful in preventing viruses in current systems. This may be because they do not offer sufficient control of rudimental operations, tasks or processes. In other words, they do not offer granular control. A virus when executed operates like a trusted program that has full access to all system resources through the operating system. Granular execution controls seek to limit access to parts of the system, and tasks, that are critical to sustaining healthy operation, [11]. Hence, it may be possible to preclude unauthorized programs operating in a granular controlled environment from creating or modifying other files or programs, unless those programs are authorized to do so. This prevents the spread of a virus. Both Lotus Notes and Sun's Java incorporate this type of access control in their security model. Worth mention is the fact that few, if any, Java viruses exist!

9 Conclusion

This paper has explored the human immune system to expose the protection mechanisms. Although, the human immune system and computer systems are vastly different, lessons can be learned from the human mechanisms used. The paper reveals several philosophies that are yet to be incorporated into current anti virus systems. Techniques such as discovery of the inner portions of an antigen after consumption by macrophages inspires techniques that can be deployed in anti virus systems. In this example, a virtual machine or environment would be part of the anti virus strategy used solely for the purpose of developing active behavior learning. Also, the human immune system uses killer T cells to distinguish between "self" and "non-self". This paper provides a behavioral approach and cryptographic approach to distinguishing "self" from foreign bodies. The paper does not purport to offer the panacea to the virus problem, rather it suggests that techniques inspired by the biological immune system that should be investigated for inclusion in future anti virus systems.

10 Future Work

This paper serves to admonish anti virus system designers to delve into a new era of intelligent anti virus systems. The framework upon which these systems can be based has been presented herein. However, the author concedes that in the future, the operating system manufacturer should be encouraged to work with anti virus system and other software architects (such as VMWare virtual machine) to embed the type of framework provided in this report in the operating system in much the same way it is embedded in the human immune system. Hence, it is critical to the success of a computer immune system that future work be devoted to embedding the type or class of framework discussed in this paper in the operating system.

References

1. Spafford, E. H. 1991. Computer viruses: A form of artificial life? In D. Farmer, C. Langton, S. Rasmussen, and C. Taylor, eds., Artificial Life II. Studies in the Sciences of Complexity, 727-747. Redwood City: Addison-Wesley.
2. Kephart, Jeffrey O., Steve R. White, and David M. Chess. Computers and epidemiology. IEEE Spectrum, May 1993, 20-26.
3. Anil Somayaji, Steven Hofmeyr, Stephanie Forrest. Principles of a Computer Immune System. Department of Computer Science. University of New Mexico. Albuquerque, NM 87131
4. P. D'haeseleeer, S. Forrest, P. Helman. An Immunological Approach To Change Detection: Algorithms, Analysis and Implications. Preceedings Of The 1996 IEEE Symposium On Computer Security and Privacy. IEEE, 1996.
5. C.A. Janeway, P. Travers. Immunology: The Immune System In Health and Disease. Current Biology Ltd., London, 2nd edition, 1996.

6. Jeffrey O. Kephart. A Biologically Inspired Immune System, Artificial Life IV, Proceedings of the Fourth International Workshop on Synthesis and Simulatoin of Living Systems. MIT Press, Cambridge, Massachusetts, 1994, pp. 130-139.
7. Stephanie Forrest. Computer Immunology. University of Mexico, 1996
8. J.K. Percus, O. Percus, A.S. Perelson. Predicting The Size Of The Antibody Combining Region From Consideration Of Efficient self/nonself Discrimination. Proceedings Of The National Academy Of Science, 90:1691 1695, 1993.
9. http://vmware1.m0.net/m/s.asp?HB4162878203X1075673X73339X
10. Steve R. White. Open Problems in Computer Virus Research. Virus Bulletin Conference, Oct 22, 1998. Munich, Germany.
11. Martin Overton. Viruses and Lotus Notes: Have Virus Writers Finally Met Their Match. Proceedings of the Ninth International Virus Bulletin Conference, 1999, pp 149-174.
12. Maria Pozzo and Terence Gray. An Approach to Containing Computer Viruses. Computers and Security, v6n4, 1987, pp. 321-331.
13. David Aubrey-Jones. Combining Encryption with an Anti-Virus Strategy. Proceedings of the Eighth International Virus Bulletin Conference, October 1999, pp 205-234.
14. Wenke Lee, Salvatore J. Stolfo. Adaptive Intrusion Detection: a Data Mining Approach. Computer Science Department, Columbia University, 500 West 120th Street, New York, NY 10027.
15. Guy Helmer, Johnny S. K. Wong, Vasant Honavar, and Les Miller. Intelligent Agents for Intrusion Detection. Proceedings, IEEE Information Technology Conference, Syracuse, NY, September, 1998, pp. 121-124.
16. Guy Helmer, Johnny Wong, Mark Slagell, Vasant Honavar, Les Miller, and Robyn Lutz. Software Fault Tree and Colored Petri Net Based Specification, Design and Implementation of Agent-Based Intrusion Detection Systems. Submitted to ACM Transactions on Information and System Security (TISSEC).
17. Wayne Jansen, Peter Mell, Tom Karygiannis, Donald Marks. Mobile Agents in Intrusion Detection and Response. Proceedings of the 12th Annual Canadian Information Technology Security Symposium, Ottawa, Canada, June 2000.
18. Wenke Lee, Salvatore J. Stolfo. Data Mining Approaches for Intrusion Detection. Proceedings of the 7th USENIX Security Symposium, USENIX, 1998.
19. Baudouin Le Charlier, Abdelaziz Mounji, Morton Swimmer. Dynamic Detection And Classification Of Computer Viruses Using General Behavior Patterns. University Of Hamburg, Fachbereic Informatik Virus Test Center. Germany, July 2, 1995.
20. Gerald Tesauro, Jeffrey O. Kephart, Gregory B. Sorkin. Neural Networks for Computer Virus Recognition. IEEE Expert, vol. 11, no. 4, pp. 5-6, Aug. 1996.

Adaptive Layout Analysis of Document Images

Donato Malerba, Floriana Esposito, and Oronzo Altamura

Dipartimento di Informatica, Università degli Studi di Bari,
via Orabona 4, I-70126 Bari – Italy
{malerba, esposito, altamura}@di.uniba.it

Abstract. Layout analysis is the process of extracting a hierarchical structure describing the layout of a page. In the document processing system WISDOM++ the layout analysis is performed in two steps: firstly, the global analysis determines possible areas containing paragraphs, sections, columns, figures and tables, and secondly, the local analysis groups together blocks that possibly fall within the same area. The result of the local analysis process strongly depends on the quality of the results of the first step. In this paper we investigate the possibility of supporting the user during the correction of the results of the global analysis. This is done by allowing the user to correct the results of the global analysis and then by learning rules for layout correction from the sequence of user actions. Experimental results on a set of multi-page documents are reported.

1 Background and Motivations

Processing document images, that is bitmaps of scanned paper documents, is a complex task involving many activities, such as preprocessing, segmentation, layout analysis, classification, understanding and text extraction [6]. Those activities are all important, although, the extraction of the right layout structure is deemed the most critical. *Layout analysis* is the perceptual organization process that aims at detecting structures among blocks extracted by the segmentation algorithm. The result is a hierarchy of abstract representations of the document image, called the *layout structure* of the document. The leaves of the layout tree (lowest level of the abstraction hierarchy) are the blocks, while the root represents the set of pages of the whole document. A page may include several layout components, called *frames*, which are rectangular areas corresponding to groups of blocks.

Strategies for the extraction of layout analysis have been traditionally classified as *top-down* or *bottom-up* [10]. In top-down methods, the document image is repeatedly decomposed into smaller and smaller components, while in bottom-up methods, basic layout components are extracted from bitmaps and then grouped together into larger blocks on the basis of their characteristics. In WISDOM++ (www.di.uniba.it/~malerba/ wisdom++/), a document image analysis system that can transform paper documents into either HTML or XML format [1], the applied page decomposition method is hybrid, since it combines a top-down approach to segment the document image, and a bottom-up layout analysis method to assemble basic blocks into *frames*.

Some attempts of learning the layout structure from a set of training examples have also been reported in the literature [2,3,4,8,11]. They are based on ad-hoc learning algorithms, which learns particular data structures, such as geometric trees and tree

M.-S. Hacid et al. (Eds.): ISMIS 2002, LNAI 2366, pp. 526–534, 2002.

grammars. Results are promising although it has been proven that good layout structures could also be obtained by exploiting generic knowledge on typographic conventions [5]. This is the case of WISDOM++, which analyzes the layout in two steps:

1. A *global analysis* of the document image, in order to determine possible areas containing paragraphs, sections, columns, figures and tables. This step is based on an iterative process, in which the vertical and horizontal histograms of text blocks are alternately analyzed, in order to detect columns and sections/paragraphs, respectively.

2. A *local analysis* of the document to group together blocks that possibly fall within the same area. Generic knowledge on west-style typesetting conventions is exploited to group blocks together, such as "the first line of a paragraph can be indented" and "in a justified text, the last line of a paragraph can be shorter than the previous one".

Experimental results proved the effectiveness of this knowledge-based approach on images of the first page of papers published in either conference proceedings or journals [1]. However, performance degenerates when the system is tested on intermediate pages of multi-page articles, where the structure is much more variable, due to the presence of formulae, images, and drawings that can stretch over more than one column, or are quite close. The main source of the errors made by the layout analysis module was in the global analysis step, while the local analysis step performed satisfactorily when the result of the global analysis was correct.

In this paper, we investigate the possibility of supporting the user during the correction of the results of the global analysis. This is done by means of two new system facilities:

1. the user can correct the results of the layout analysis by either grouping or splitting columns/sections, automatically produced by the global analysis;

2. the user can ask the system to learn grouping/splitting rules from his/her sequence of actions correcting the results of the layout analysis.

The proposed approach is different from those that learn the layout structure from scratch, since we try to correct the result of a global analysis returned by a bottom-up algorithm. Furthermore, we intend to capture knowledge on correcting actions performed by the user of the document image processing system. Other document processing systems allow users to correct the result of the layout analysis; nevertheless WISDOM++ is the only one that tries to learn correcting actions from user interaction with the system.

In the following section, a description of the layout correction operations is reported, and the automated generation of training examples is explained. Section 3 briefly introduces the learning system used to generate layout correction rules and presents some preliminary experimental results.

2   Correcting the Results of the Global Analysis

Global analysis aims at determining the general layout structure of a page and operates on a tree-based representation of nested columns and sections. The levels of columns and sections are alternated, which means that a column contains sections, while a section contains columns. At the end of the global analysis, the user can only see the sections and columns that have been considered atomic, that is, not subject to further decomposition (Figure 1). The user can correct this result by means of three different operations:

- Horizontal splitting: a column/section is cut horizontally.
- Vertical splitting: a column/section is cut vertically.
- Grouping: two sections/columns are merged together.

The cut point in the two splitting operations is automatically determined by computing either the horizontal or the vertical histogram on the basic blocks returned by the segmentation algorithm. The horizontal (vertical) cut point corresponds to the largest gap between two consecutive bins in the horizontal (vertical) histogram. Therefore, splitting operations can be described by means of a binary function, namely, $split(X,S)$, where X represents the column/section to be split, S is an ordinal number representing the step of the correction process and the range of the split function is the set {$horizontal, vertical, no\_split$}.

The grouping operation, which can be described by means of a ternary predicate $group(A,B,S)$, is applicable to two sections (columns) A and B and returns a new section (column) C, whose boundary is determined as follows. Let ($left_X$, top_X) and ($bottom_X$, $right_X$) be the coordinates of the top-left and bottom-right vertices of a column/section X, respectively.[1] Then:

$$left_C = min(left_A, left_B), \quad right_C = max(right_A, right_B),$$
$$top_C = min(top_A, top_B), \quad bottom_C = max(bottom_A, bottom_B).$$

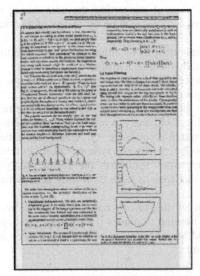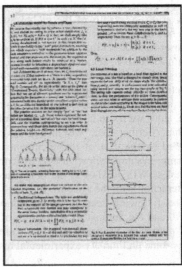

Fig. 1. Results of the global analysis process: one column (*left*) includes two sections (*right*). The result of the local analysis process (i.e., the frames) is in reported the background.

---

[1] The origin of the coordinate system is at the top left-hand corner; the abscissa increases from the leftmost to the rightmost column, while the ordinate increases from the uppermost to the lowest row.

Grouping is possible only if the following two conditions are satisfied:
1. *C* does not overlap another section (column) in the document.
2. *A* and *B* are nested in the same column (section).

After each splitting/grouping operation, WISDOM++ recomputes the result of the local analysis process, so that the user can immediately perceive the final effect of the requested corrections and can decide whether to confirm the correction or not.

From the user interaction, WISDOM++ implicitly generates some training observations describing when and how the user intended to correct the result of the global analysis. These training observations are used to learn correction rules of the result of the global analysis, as explained below.

3   Learning Rules for Layout Correction

The inductive learning problem to be solved concerns the concepts *split(X,S)= horizontal*, *split(X,S)=vertical* and *group(X,Y,S)=true*, since we are interested to find rules predicting both when to split horizontally/vertically a column/ section and when to group two columns/sections. No rule is generated for the case *split(X,S)=no_split* and *group(X,Y,S)= false*.

The definition of a suitable representation language for the global layout structure is a key issue. In this work, we restrict this representation to the lowest column and section levels in the tree structure extracted by the global analysis and we deliberately ignore other levels as well as their composition hierarchy. Nevertheless, describing this portion of the layout structure is not straightforward, since the columns and sections are spatially related and the feature-vector representation typically adopted in statistical approaches cannot render these relations. In this work the application of a first-order logic language has been explored. In this language, unary function symbols, called *attributes*, are used to describe properties of a single layout component (e.g., height and width), while binary predicate and function symbols, called *relations*, are used to express spatial relationships among layout components (e.g., part_of and on_top). An example of a training observation automatically generated by WISDOM++ follows:

```
split(c1,s)=horizontal, group(s1,s2,s)=false,
split(s1,s)=no_split, split(s2,s)=no_split ←
   step(s)=1,
   type(s1)=section, type(s2)=section, type(c1)=column,
   width(s1)=552, width(s2)=552, width(c1)=552,
   height(s1)=8, height(s2)=723, height(c1)=852,
   x_pos_centre(s1)=296, x_pos_centre(s2)=296,
   x_pos_centre(c1)=296,
   y_pos_centre(s1)=22, y_pos_centre(s2)=409,
   y_pos_centre(c1)=426,
   on_top(s1,s2)=true,
   part_of(c1,s1)=true, part_of(c1,s2)=true,
   no_blocks(s1)=2, no_blocks(s2)=108, no_blocks(c1)=110,
   per_text(s1)=100, per_text(s2)=83, per_text(c1)=84.
```

This is a multiple-head ground clause, which has a conjunction of literals in the head. It describes the first correction applied to a page layout, where two sections and one column were originally found (Figure 1). The horizontal splitting of the column is the first correction performed by the user (Figure 2), as described by the first literal, namely *step(s)=1*. This column is 552 pixels wide and 852 pixels high, has a center located at the point (296,426), and includes 110 basic blocks and the two sections *s1* and *s2*, which are one on top of the other. The percentage of the area covered by text blocks, enclosed by the column, is 84%. It is noteworthy that the multiple-head clause above also reports that the two sections *s1* and *s2* should be neither split (literals *split(s1,s)=no_split*   and   *split(s2,s)=no_split*)   nor   grouped   (literal *group(s1,s2,s)=false*) at the first correction step. Many other literals, such as *group(c1,s2,s)=false, group(s1,c1,s)=false,* and *group(c1,c1,s)=false,* have not been generated, since they do not represent admissible groupings according to the two constraints specified above.

Rules for the automated correction of the layout analysis can be automatically learned by means of a first-order learning system. In this work, the learning system ATRE has been used [9]. It solves the following learning problem:

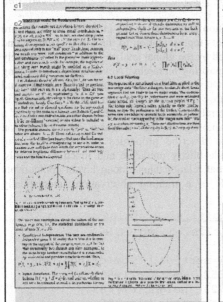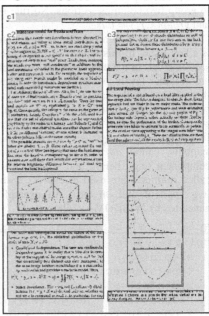

Fig. 2. Horizontal split of the column (*left*) and vertical split of column c2 (*right*). The result of the layout analysis process is in the background.

Given

- a set of concepts $C_1, C_2, ..., C_r$ to be learned,
- a set of observations O described in a language L_O,
- a background knowledge BK described in a language L_{BK},
- a language of hypotheses L_H,

- a generalization model Γ over the space of hypotheses,
- a user's preference criterion PC,

Find

a (possibly recursive) logical theory T for the concepts C_1, C_2, ..., C_r, such that T is complete and consistent with respect to O and satisfies the preference criterion PC.

The *completeness* property holds when the theory T explains all observations in O of the r concepts C_i, while the *consistency* property holds when the theory T explains no counter-example in O of any concept C_i. The satisfaction of these properties guarantees the correctness of the induced theory with respect to O.

In ATRE, observations are represented by means of ground multiple-head clauses, called *objects*. All literals in the head of the clause are called *examples* of the concepts C_1, C_2, ..., C_r. They can be considered either positive or negative according to the learning goal. In this application domain, the set of concepts to be learned are $split(X,S)=horizontal$, $split(X,S)=vertical$, $group(X,Y,S)=true$, since we are interested in finding rules which predict when to split horizontally/vertically or when to group two columns/sections. Therefore, no rule is generated for the case $split(X,S)=no\_split$ and $group(X,Y,S)=false$. Moreover, no background knowledge is available.

The generalization model provides the basis for organizing the search space, since it establishes when a hypothesis explains a positive/negative example and when a hypothesis is more general/specific than another. The generalization model adopted by ATRE, called *generalized implication*, is explained in [7].

The preference criterion PC is a set of conditions used to discard some solutions and favor others. In this work, short rules, which explain a high number of positive examples and a low number of negative examples, are preferred.

4 Experimental Results

To investigate the applicability of the proposed solution we considered thirteen papers published as either regular or short, in the IEEE Transactions on Pattern Analysis and Machine Intelligence, issues of January and February 1996. Each paper is a multi-page document; therefore we processed 109 document images in all, which were used for the training phase. The distribution of pages used for training purposes is reported in Table 1.

The number of training observations for ATRE corresponds to the final, corrected layout of each page (i.e., 109), plus the number of intermediate global layout structures, which are subject to corrections (i.e., 106). The total number of examples in the 215 training observations is 7786, which corresponds to the total number of literals in the multiple-head clauses. Given the set of concepts to be learned, only 106 out of 7786 examples are positive, which correspond to actual corrective actions performed by the user (vertical/horizontal splitting or grouping). The average number of corrections performed by the user is 0.97 (i.e., 106/109) per page. In fact, some intermediate pages of multi-page documents are the most critical and may require several operations to correct the column/section structure.

Table 1. Training set: Distribution of pages and examples per document.

Name of the multi-page document	No. of pages	No. of horizontal splits	No. of vertical splits	No. of groupings	Total no. of examples
TPAMI1	14	6	5	4	1004
TPAMI2	8	4	5	0	374
TPAMI5	6	1	3	0	402
TPAMI6	2	0	0	1	83
TPAMI7	7	0	0	1	328
TPAMI8	6	2	1	2	526
TPAMI9	5	1	1	0	114
TPAMI14	10	3	4	12	1035
TPAMI15	15	9	10	0	806
TPAMI16	14	1	4	2	965
TPAMI18	10	2	8	4	1464
TPAMI22	5	2	2	0	181
TPAMI23	7	3	2	1	504
Total (training)	109	34	45	27	7786

ATRE generated a theory with 44 clauses: 19 for vertical split, 11 for horizontal split and 14 for grouping. Some clauses for the three concepts are reported below:

```
1.   split(X1,S)=horizontal ← width(X1)∈[540..567],
         height(X1)∈[848..875], step(S)∈[1..1]
2.   split(X1,S)=vertical ← width(X1)∈[536..581],
         on_top(X1,X2)=true, x_pos_centre(X1)∈[467..467],
         step(S)∈[1..1]
3.   group(X1,X2,S)=true ← width(X1)∈[408..513],
         type(X1)=column, step(S)∈[1..6], type(X2)=column
```

The interpretation of these clauses is straightforward. The first clause states that «at the first correction step, columns/areas with width between 540 and 567 pixels and height between 848 and 875 pixels should be horizontally split». The second clause states that «at the first correction step, columns/areas with a width between 536 and 581 pixels, the baricentre at point 467 on the x axis and below another column/area should be vertically split». Finally, the third clause states that «at any step between 1 and 6, two columns can be grouped if the left one[2] has a width between 408 and 513». It is noteworthy that the second clause involves the relation *on_top* and could be generated only by learning systems that operate on first-order logic descriptions, such as ATRE.

From the examples above, it is evident that some of the induced clauses (e.g., the second) are clearly specific and have been generated by the system to explain a limited number of examples (sometimes only one). Specificity of clauses is due to two factors: firstly, the limited number of positive examples used in the training set, and secondly, the fact that ATRE is asked to generate a *complete* theory, that is a set of clauses that explain *all* positive examples. However, other clauses generated by ATRE are quite general, such as the first example above.

WISDOM++ uses the induced rules to automatically correct a page layout every time a document image is processed. This operation is quick and totally transparent to

---

[2] In this case the area is necessarily a column, since users can only group two columns or two sections.

the user. Data on the test set are reported in Table 2. They refer to ten additional papers published in the issues of January and February 1996 of the IEEE Transactions on Pattern Analysis and Machine Intelligence. Results of the test examples are reported in Table 3. *Omission* errors occur when correct actions on page layout are missed, while *commission* errors occur when wrong actions are "recommended" by a rule. In the case of horizontal (vertical) split, the number of possible commission errors, that is, 3189 (3200), is the sum of the number of examples of vertical (horizontal) split plus the number of no split, that is, 3153. In the case of grouping, possible commission errors equals the number of examples of *grouping(X,Y,S)=false*.

Table 2. Testing set: Distribution of pages and examples per document.

Name of the multi-page document	No. of pages	No. of horizontal splits	No. of vertical splits	No. of groupings	Total no. of examples
Total (testing)	109	47	36	12	7376

Table 3. Commission and omission errors performed by rules of various concepts.

Rule for	No. omission errors	No. commission errors
split(X,S)=horizontal	18/47	5/3189
split(X,S)=vertical	10/36	5/3200
grouping(X,Y,S)=true	10/12	14/4128

Unfortunately, the induced set of clauses missed most of the grouping operations, whereas it was able to correct some page layouts by performing horizontal and vertical splitting. The percentage of commission errors is very low, whereas the percentage of omission errors is quite high. This confirms our comments on the specificity of part of the learned theory, due to the reduced number of training observations with respect to the complexity of the learning task. It is also noteworthy that most of the errors occurred in few pages, where the correction process was quite complex.

5 Conclusions

This work presents a preliminary application of machine learning techniques to the problem of correcting the result of the global layout analysis process in WISDOM++. The proposed approach is alternative to inducing the complete layout structure from a set of training examples The learning problem to be solved has been introduced and the first-order logic representation of the corrections performed by the user has been illustrated. Experimental results on a set of multi-page documents showed that the proposed approach is able to capture relatively simple layout corrections. Inaccuracy for complex processes can be mainly attributed to the limited size of training documents. A more extensive experimentation is planned to confirm these initial conclusions. A further research issue to be investigated concerns the application of a learning system like ATRE, devised to solve classification problems, to a typical planning task. Finally, we intend to investigate the problem of incrementally refining the set of rules generated by ATRE, when new training observations are made available.

534   D. Malerba, F. Esposito, and O. Altamura

Acknowledgments. This work partially fulfills the research objectives set by the IST-1999-20882 project COLLATE (Collaboratory for Automation, Indexing and Retrieval of Digitized Historical Archive Material) funded by the European Union (http://www.collate.de)

References

1. Altamura O., Esposito F., & Malerba D.: Transforming paper documents into XML format with WISDOM++, *Int. Journal on Document Analysis and Recognition*, 4(1), pp. 2-17, 2001.
2. Akindele O.T., & Belaïd A.: Construction of generic models of document structures using inference of tree grammars, *Proc. of the 3rd Int. Conf. on Document Analysis and Recognition*, IEEE Computer Society Press, pp. 206-209, 1995.
3. Dengel A.: Initial learning of document structures, *Proc. of the 2nd Int. Conf. on Document Analysis and Recognition*, IEEE Computer Society Press, pp. 86-90, 1993.
4. Dengel A., & Dubiel F.: Clustering and classification of document structure – A machine learning approach, *Proc. of the 3rd Int. Conf. on Document Analysis and Recognition*, IEEE Computer Society Press, pp. 587-591, 1995.
5. Esposito F., Malerba D., & Semeraro G.: A Knowledge-Based Approach to the Layout Analysis, *Proc. of the 3rd Int. Conf. on Document Analysis and Recognition*, IEEE Computer Society Press, pp. 466- 471, 1995.
6. Esposito F., Malerba D., & Lisi F.A.: Machine learning for intelligent processing of printed documents, *Journal of Intelligent Information Systems*, 14(2/3), pp. 175-198, 2000.
7. Esposito F., Malerba D., & Lisi F.A.: Induction of recursive theories in the normal ILP setting: issues and solutions, in J. Cussens and A. Frisch (Eds.), *Inductive Logic Programming*, Lecture Notes in Artificial Intelligence, 1866, pp. 93-111, Springer: Berlin, 2000.
8. Kise K.: Incremental acquisition of knowledge about layout structures from examples of documents. *Proc. of the 2nd Int. Conf. on Document Analysis and Recognition*, IEEE Computer Society Press, pp. 668-671, 1993.
9. Malerba D., Esposito F., & Lisi F.A.: Learning recursive theories with ATRE, *Proc. of the 13th European Conf. on Artificial Intelligence*, John Wiley & Sons, pp. 435-439, 1998.
10. Srihari S.N., & Zack G.W.: Document Image Analysis. *Proc. of the 8th Int. Conf. on Pattern Recognition*, pp. 434-436, 1986.
11. Walischewski H.: Automatic knowledge acquisition for spatial document interpretation. *Proc. of the 4th Int. Conf. on Document Analysis and Recognition*, IEEE Computer Society Press, pp. 243-247, 1997.

A NLG-Based Presentation Method for Supporting KDD End-Users

Berardina De Carolis and Francesca A. Lisi

Dipartimento di Informatica, Università degli Studi di Bari
Via Orabona 4 – 70126 Bari – Italy
{decarolis | lisi}@di.uniba.it

Abstract. In this paper, we propose to provide KDD end-users with a tool which can not only discover the necessary knowledge for supporting their decision making processes but also present it in an immediately and intuitively understandable way. The presentation method is based on natural language generation (NLG) techniques. It has been implemented into the agent DM-PA which, starting from an XML representation of the discovered knowledge, can generate the description of the application of this knowledge to a specific decision context by using different presentation modalities. The presentation agent has been interfaced with INGENS, a prototypical GIS with capabilities of knowledge discovery. Results of the first integration prototype are discussed.

1   Introduction

Research and development in the rapidly growing area of knowledge discovery in databases (KDD) has led to a number of successful *KDD applications* [4]. They are characterized by (1) an initial laborious discovery of knowledge by someone who understands the application domain as well as specific data analysis techniques, (2) encoding of the discovered knowledge within a specific problem-solving architecture, and finally (3) application of the discovered knowledge in the context of a real world task by a well-defined class of end users (KDD end-users). It is noteworthy that each of these applications ultimately supports business people in a single task. When dealing with KDD end-users, an open issue is to find a suitable presentation of the discovered knowledge.

In this paper we propose a presentation method that relies on natural language generation (NLG) techniques. It has been implemented into the agent DM-PA [1] which, starting from an XML representation of the discovered knowledge, can generate the description of the application of this knowledge to a specific decision context by using different presentation modalities. To show the usefulness of the method, DM-PA has been interfaced with the inductive geographical information system INGENS [9]. INGENS can be seen as a KDD application that supports urban and land planners in one of their crucial activities, *map interpretation* [7]. Map interpretation is a knowledge-intensive task. In INGENS it has been automated by applying machine learning methods. Unfortunately, these inductive tools produce an output that can be hardly understood by those users who are not technologically

M.-S. Hacid et al. (Eds.): ISMIS 2002, LNAI 2366, pp. 535–543, 2002.
© Springer-Verlag Berlin Heidelberg 2002

sophisticated. By interfacing INGENS with DM-PA we provide an intelligent GIS which can not only extract the necessary knowledge for automating map interpretation but also reason on it and present it in a way that is immediately and intuitively understandable by KDD end-users.

The paper is structured as follows. Section 2 is devoted to the presentation method and its implementation in the agent DM-PA. Section 3 gives a short presentation of INGENS and its application to urban planning. Section 4 presents the results of the first integration prototype. Conclusions and future work are drawn in Section 5.

2   The Presentation Agent DM-PA

A presentation agent has the main goal of presenting more or less complex pieces of information to end-users in a way that is "suitable" to their needs and to the specific application domain. The Data Mining Presentation Agent (DM-PA) is an agent specialized in presenting knowledge discovered by a Data Mining (DM) tool. Most of DM tools on the market use visualization techniques to help users in understanding complex results. The purpose of visualization is to transform data in information that constitutes a critical component of the decision process by making, in this way, raw data easily understandable [13]. However, visualization *in se* is not the goal of DM-PA. Our goal is to generate a natural language or a multimodal comment accompanying the visualization of the result.

The architecture of DM-PA, illustrated in Figure 1, achieves these objectives in the following way. Given a DM result represented in XML (our agent is able to understand results expressed according to PMML 1.1: www.dmg.org) and a user-defined presentation goal, the agent: i) builds a presentation plan that is appropriate to the user features and goals; ii) selects a visualization form of the DM result that is adequate to the used DM model; iii) generates a comment (in natural language, as hypermedia, through an 'Animated Agent', …) which emphasizes the "added-value" of the extracted knowledge, starting from one or more discovered results in which there is a dependent variable that describes the subject 'classes', a set of independent variables that affect assignment of subjects to classes and a set of (eventually generated) images/graphics that illustrate the results.

As far as the adaptation of presentation is concerned, we consider only the following user requirements: his/her **role** in the KDD process and the related main goal in using the system; his/her **experience** in the domain and in working with computers or with the particular device available for accessing information; his/her **interests** towards particular aspects of the result. These factors influence the selection of particular presentation features such as: a) the presentation goal to trigger and, consequently, the discourse plan to build and, then, the content and structure of the provided comment; b) the visualization form; c) the media combination; and d) the degree of interactivity with the generated presentation.

As regards the possible presentation modalities, we consider the following modalities: i) multimedia, ii) hypermedia [2], and iii) Animated Agent [3].

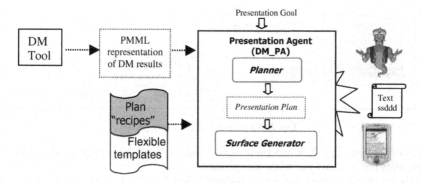

Fig. 1. DM-PA Architecture

Discourse Planning: as in most of the developed NLG systems, the first step of the generation process consists in the generation of a 'discourse plan' that allows achieving the communicative goals of the presentation. This plan can be either computed by a planning algorithm using a library of operators or retrieved/composed from a library of plans. In both cases, the output of the planner defines "what to present" (the content) and in "which order" (the structure) ensuring the coherence of the overall presentation. In this application, the Content Planner, according to the user goal, selects the most appropriate solution from a library of non-instantiated plans ("recipes"). The generic plan is, then, instantiated by filling the slots of its leaves with available data expressed as PMML document. This choice has been made after an analysis of the end-users requirements and of a set of DM results in the domain of urban and land planning. On this basis, taking the possible roles/goals of the user (querying, report reading, analysing, and so on), we have identified the following goals: **1) Goal1**: Illustrate how the dependent variable varies according to changes in the values of the independent variables. **2) Goal2**: Illustrate which independent variables influence belonging of a subject to a given category as requested by the user. **3) Goal3**: Given a "fully-described situation" (a combination of values of all independent variables) describe the value of the dependent variable (the category). **4) Goal4**: Given a "partially described situation", (a combination of values for a subset of independent variables) describe the value of the dependent variable (the category) by completing hypotheses about independent variables ("what-about" questions).

Each of these goals triggers an appropriate "plan recipe" for achieving it. The structure of the plan recipe we propose derives from the operationalization of the Rhetorical Structure Theory proposed in [10] and from the definition of discourse plan originally proposed in [11]. It is represented in XML according to the DPML language [1]. Briefly, a discourse plan is a hierarchy of nodes with the following attributes: **name** (node identification), **goal** (communicative goal attached to a node), **focus** (concept or object in focus in that discourse step), **RR** (rhetorical relation among the subtrees departing from the current node), **role** (role of a node in the RR of its parent node with possible values: root, nucleus, satellite).

An example of discourse plan for achieving Goal1 is shown in Figure 2. The main goal is associated to the root 'n1', it is then decomposed in subgoals and so on down to primitive communicative acts (leaves represented as boxes in the figure). These

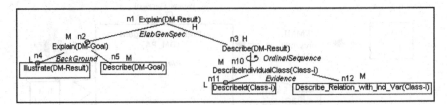

Fig. 2. An example of discourse plan

primitives acts are then rendered at the surface level according to the selected presentation modality and to the user features.

This plan explains the conditions influencing the belonging to a particular class: first it gives an overview of the case of interest of the DM process (n4, n5), then, additional details on each subject class in the result are provided (n11-n12).

Among the previously described goals, some of them are more appropriate for less expert users while others are more oriented to knowledgeable ones. We presume that the first goal is more adequate for end-users with no experience in the data mining field that are interested only in reading the final report about the result, while the last goal is more suitable for users that are interested in a particular aspects of the result.

Surface Generation: the DPML specification of the plan recipe, the PMML file describing DM results and the context model settings are the input to the Surface Generator. This module has the role of extracting, from this input, data that are relevant to the realisation of the user-adapted presentation and rendering the discourse plan leaves accordingly. We can identify three types of leaves in the plan tree with respect to their communicative function: *general*, *illustrative*, and *model-dependent*.

The first type corresponds to those primitive communicative goals that do not depend from the result itself but have the goal of giving global information to the user about the purpose of the communication (i.e. Describe(DM-Goal)). In this case, flexible templates, that are then filled with data from the domain KB, are used.

The second type of leaf corresponds to those primitive communicative goal that have the purpose of visualizing the result (of part of it). Illustrate(DM-result) is one example of it. In the case of decision tree, a tree visualization program will be called or a graphical metaphor, dependent on the domain application, can be used.

Finally, the third type of leaf is the one dependent on the model in the sense that the semantics implicit in the mining model is used to generate the comment. In the case of decision tree and rules, its structure drives the building of the sentence by avoiding redundancies, by emphasizing differences and dependencies. Indeed, the pure translation of the set of rules or decision tree structure in natural language would produce a redundant and "less-natural" text comment. In order to optimise the comment, the generator uses algorithms for grouping paths or attributes per class or for finding common portion of paths or group of attributes per class and NL or multimodal generation, according to the selected presentation modality.

3   The INGENS System

The system INGENS (INductive GEographic iNformation System) is a prototypical GIS which can be trained to recognize geographic objects that are not explicitly modeled in the GIS database (e.g., ravine or steep slopes). Training is based on the inductive learning from a set of examples and counterexamples (training examples) of these geographic objects. The training examples are provided by the user who detects them on stored maps by applying browsing, querying and displaying functions of the INGENS interface. Furthermore, they are described according to a first-order logic language by an automated feature extraction process from maps. Thus the inductive learning capability of INGENS consists in generating predictive models of geographic objects from the logical descriptions of training examples.

The software architecture of INGENS is three-layered. The upper layer implements a *Graphical User Interface* (GUI), which allows the system to be accessed by the following four categories of users:

- Administrators, who are responsible for GIS management.
- Map maintenance users, whose main task is updating the Map Repository.
- Sophisticated users, who can ask the system to learn operational definitions of geographic objects not explicitly modeled in the database.
- End users, who occasionally access the database and may need different information each time. They cannot train INGENS.

The GUI is an applet and can be run in any Java-enabled Web browser (see Figure 4).

The middle layer makes several facilities available to the four categories of INGENS users. In particular, the *Map Descriptor* is responsible for the automated generation of first-order logic descriptions of geographic objects according to a fixed set of operational descriptors. The *Learning Server* provides a suite of inductive learning systems that can be run concurrently by multiple users to train INGENS. In this paper, we are concerned with ATRE [8]. The knowledge discovery task accomplished by ATRE is the induction of recursive logical theories from a set of training examples. An example of logical theory is the following set of first-order definite clauses:

downtown(X) ← high_business_activity(X), onthesea(X).
residential(X) ← close_to(X,Y), downtown(Y), low_business_activity(X).
residential(X) ← close_to(X,Y), residential(Y), low_business_activity(X).

It expresses sufficient conditions for the two concepts of "main business center of a city" and "residential zone," which are represented by the unary predicates downtown and residential, respectively. Further details about the application of ATRE to geographic knowledge discovery are reported in [9]. It is noteworthy that the *Learning Server* supplies an operational definition to new non-operational descriptors of interest to the users. This allows any user to formulate queries in a first-order logic language that can contain both operational descriptors and non-operational descriptors whose operational definition has already been learned. It is responsibility of the *Query Interpreter* to deal with such advanced queries. The *Map Converter* is a suite of tools which support the acquisition of maps from external sources. Currently, INGENS can automatically acquire geographic objects from vectorized maps in the MAP87 format (Italian Military Geographic Institute, www.nettuno.it/fiera/igmi/igmit.htm). Since these maps contain static information on orographic, hydrographic and administrative boundaries alone, the *Map Editor* is required to integrate and/or modify this information.

The lowest layer manages resources like the *Map Repository* and the *Knowledge Repository*. The former is the database instance that contains the actual collection of maps stored in the GIS. Geographic data are organized according to an object-oriented data model and stored in the object-oriented DBMS ObjectStore 5.0 (Object Design, Inc.). The *Map Storage Subsystem* is involved in storing, updating and retrieving items in and from the map collection. As a resource manager, it represents the only access path to the data contained in the *Map Repository* and accessed by multiple, concurrent clients. The *Knowledge Repository* contains the operational definitions that have been induced by the *Learning Server*. In INGENS, different users can have different definitions of the same concept. Knowledge is expressed according to a first-order logic language and managed by a deductive relational DBMS. The inference engine of the deductive DBMS computes the answer set for a certain user query. It is invoked by the *Query Interpreter*, once that the objects that are involved in the query have been retrieved from the *Map Repository* and their logical descriptions have been generated by the *Map Descriptor*.

4   Interfacing DM-PA with INGENS: First Results

Recent trends in the use of GIS in urban and land planning propose the integration of multimedia [6] and virtual reality [5] to make the planners more aware of the planning problem that they are facing. Furthermore, the use of GIS in the Internet/Intranet environment (especially the World Wide Web) can facilitate the dissemination of planning information and enhance the public participation in the planning process [12]. Our aim, in interfacing DM-PA with INGENS, is to obtain an intelligent GIS which can not only extract the necessary knowledge for automating map interpretation but also reason on it and present it in a way that is immediately and intuitively understandable by end-users. The architecture of the first integration prototype encompasses the following software components: i) a *description component*, capable to deal with different map digital formats and to generate automatically a formal description of objects and relationships among objects in maps; ii) a *discovery component*, skilled in the extraction of relevant knowledge from these formal descriptions, and iii) a *presentation component* able to reason on the extracted knowledge and present it to the end user in a proper way. INGENS supplies the description and discovery components while DM-PA represents the presentation component. Their integration relies on an XML-based language that acts as a middle-ware component between the two systems.

The integration prototype has been tested on the recognition of four morphological patterns in topographic maps of the Apulia region, Italy, namely regular grid system of farms, fluvial landscape, system of cliffs and royal cattle track. Such patterns are deemed relevant for the environmental protection, and are of interest to town planners. Thus we refer to this application as an example of knowledge discovered by INGENS and presented by DM-PA in the field of automated map interpretation. As for the description component, training observations are pre-classified cells which have been represented by means of a given set of descriptors. As for the discovery component, a fragment of the logical theory induced by ATRE:

class(X1) = fluvial_landscape ← contain(X1,X2), color(X2)=blue,
    type_of(X2)=river,trend(X2)=curvilinear, extension(X2) ∈ [325.00..818.00].
class(X1) = fluvial_landscape ← contain(X1,X2), type_of(X2)=river,
    color(X2)=blue, relation(X3,X2)=almost_perpendicular,
    extension(X2) ∈ [615.16..712.37], trend(X3)=straight.

The two clauses explain all training observations of fluvial landscape. In particular, the former states that cells labeled as *fluvial_landscape* contain a long, curvilinear, blue object of type river, while the latter states that cells concerning a fluvial landscape may also present a straight object that is almost perpendicular to the river (presumably, a bridge).

To present these results, first the *Describe(Class-i)* leaf is instantiated with *Class-i=fluvial-landscape*, then the surface generator detects and groups the following features:

– *contain(X1,X2) and color(X2)=blue and type_of(X2)=river*
– *contain(X1,X2) and color(X2)=blue and type_of(X2)=river and*
  trend(X2)=curvilinear and extension(X2)∈[325.00..818.00]
– *contain(X1,X2) and color(X2)=blue and type_of(X2)=river and*
  relation(X3,X2)=almost_perpendicular and extension(X2)∈[615.16..712.37] and
  trend(X3)=straight

Let us consider a NL comment and an Animated Agent presentation.

Natural Language Comment
From this path structure the text generator returns the NL comment reported in Figure 3. The percentage of cases is used to generate grouping adjectives (large majority, rest of cases, most of the cases, and so on), while the tree structure is used to generate conjunctions, disjunctions, conditionals and differences. In particular, first the common portion of the left-side part of the rule is described in NL, by conjuncting all the common nodes, and then the different branches departing from it are emphasized by the OR and BUT connectives.

 The shown map-cell represents a *fluvial landscape* since it contains **a river** (the curvilinear blue line in the middle of the cell) with an extension between 325 and 818 linear meters. This may occur, as well, when the extension is between 615.16 and 712.37 **but** exists another object in the cell almost perpendicular to the river (presumably a bridge).

Fig. 3. An example of NL comment for INGENS

Animated Agent
In this case, the comment generated comment is expressed through a combination of verbal and non-verbal communicative acts that result in the animated agent behavior. What changes, respect to the NL comment, is the type of templates: in this case the Surface Generator uses enriched templates specifying concurrently verbal and non verbal acts (i.e, a deictic gesture and a text fragment) and their synchronization [3]. The model-dependent type of leaf is implemented by means of the same algorithms used for generating NL comments, in which, for instance, common attributes or differences are emphasized by the Animated Agent mimic capabilities. In addition, the Animated Agent can use deixis (by moving on or pointing to objects in the map or

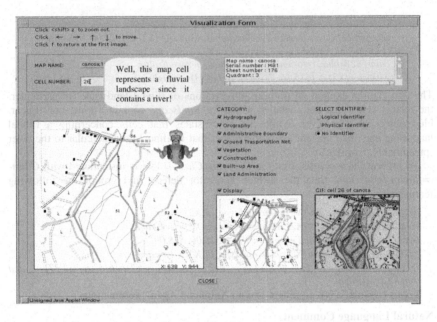

Fig. 4. An example of multimodal comment for INGENS.

eventually in a 3D representation of the map) while talking and explaining the discovered knowledge (Figure 4). A map cell labeled as fluvial landscape, by means of the aforementioned classification rules, is visualized in the GUI of INGENS.

The Agent appears on the map cell while providing the explanation. In this case, the comment is not provided at once but in subsequent explanation turns. In this example, the next agent move would be to point at the river and describe its identifying features (curvilinear, blue, extension, ...).

5   Conclusions and Future Work

In this paper, we have presented a proof-of-concept prototype that integrates two systems that were initially conceived as stand-alone applications, INGENS and DM-PA. Their integration offers several advantages to urban and land planners. In particular, generating natural language or multimodal comments to the rules for map interpretation extracted by INGENS makes the discovered knowledge easily understandable to end-users who are not familiar with first-order logic. From the implementation viewpoint, the middle-ware component between this two systems is based on XML which proves to be a useful technology for interfacing systems in a straightforward manner.

Besides refining the XML-based integration, we plan to extend the functionalities of the presentation component of the system by: i) describing more cells at a time, including the relations among them; ii) implementing tutoring strategies to train students in urban planning using the discovered knowledge; iii) using more realistic 3D images, related to the map-portion in the focus of the presentation, so as to make the rules explanation more comprehensible to non-expert users. Finally, it is necessary to empirically evaluate the effectiveness of the presentation method implemented in DM-PA and consequently the usability of the resulting INGENS user interface.

Acknowledgements. This work has been partially funded by the MURST '98 project "Agenti Intelligenti: Interazione e Acquisizione di Conoscenza", (Intelligent Agents: Interaction and Knowledge Acquisition), 1999-2000.

References

[1] Cassotta, M.T., De Carolis, B., de Rosis, F., Andreoli, C., De Cicco, M.L. (2001). User-Adapted Image Descriptions from Annotated Knowledge Sources. In Esposito, F. (Ed.): AI*IA 2001: Advances in Artificial Intelligence, Springer Verlag.

[2] De Carolis, B., de Rosis, F., Pizzutilo, S. (1997). Generating User-Adapted Hypermedia from Discourse Plans. In Lenzerini (ed.): Fifth Congress of the Italian Association of Artificial Intelligence (AI*IA 97).

[3] de Rosis, F., De Carolis, B., and Pizzutilo, S. (1999). Software documentation with Animated Agents. In Proc. of the 5th ERCIM Workshop on 'User Interfaces for All'.

[4] Fayyad, U.M., Piatetsky-Shapiro, G., Smyth, P., Uthurusamy, R. (Eds). Advances in knowledge discovery and data mining. AAAI Press/The MIT Press, 1996.

[5] Faust, N.L. (1995). The virtual reality of GIS. Environment and Planning B: Planning and Design, 22, 257-268.

[6] Fonseca, A., Gouveia, C., Camara, A., Silva, J.P. (1995), Environmental impact assessment with multimedia spatial information systems. Environment and Planning B: Planning and Design, 22, 637-648.

[7] Keats, J.S. (1996). Map understanding. Edinburgh: Longman.

[8] Malerba, D., Esposito, F., and Lisi, F.A. (1998). Learning Recursive Theories with ATRE. In H. Prade (Ed.), Proc. of the 13th European Conf. on Artificial Intelligence, Chichester: Wiley, 435-439.

[9] Malerba, D., Esposito, F., Lanza, A., and Lisi, F.A. (2000). Discovering geographic knowledge: The INGENS system. In Z.W. Ras and S. Ohsuga (Eds.), Foundations of Intelligent Systems, LNAI 1932, 40-48, Springer: Berlin.

[10] Mann, W. C., Matthiesen, C. and Thompson, S. (1989). Rhetorical structure theory and text analysis. ISI Research Report 89-242.

[11] Moore, J., D. (1995). Participating in Explanatory Dialogues. Interpreting and Responding to Question in Context. ACL-MIT Press series in NLP.

[12] Shiffer, M.J. (1995), Interactive multimedia planning system: moving from standalone systems to the World Wide Web. Environment and Planning B: Planning and Design, 22, 649-664.

[13] Tufte, E. (1990). Envisioning Information, Graphics Press, 126.

A Tool Supported Structured Method for Planning Domain Acquisition

R.M. Simpson and T.L. McCluskey

Department of Computing Science University of Huddersfield, UK
r.m.simpson@hud.ac.uk t.l.mccluskey@hud.ac.uk

Abstract. Knowledge engineering in AI planning is the process that deals with the acquisition, validation and maintenance of planning domain models, and the selection and optimisation of appropriate planning machinery to work on them. Our aim is to research and develop rigorous methods for the acquisition, maintenance and validation of planning domain models. We aim to provide a tools environment suitable for use by domain experts in addition to experts in the field of AI planning. In this paper we describe such a method and illustrate it with screen-shots taken from an implemented Graphical Interface for Planning with Objects system called GIPO. The GIPO tools environment has been built to support an object centred approach to planning domain modelling. The principal innovation we present in this paper is a process of specifying domain operators that abstracts away much of the technical detail traditionally required in their specification. Such innovations we believe could ultimately open up the possibility of bringing planning technology to a wider public.

1 Introduction

Most recent research in AI planning has largely focused on finding efficient algorithms for planning but as this has become more successful and with the fielding of large planning systems [7,8], knowledge engineering is becoming arguably as important a research topic as the algorithmic aspects of abstract planning engines. Knowledge engineering in planning has been defined as the process that deals with the acquisition, validation and maintenance of planning domain models, and with the selection and optimisation of appropriate planning machinery to work on them [5]. The problems of acquiring appropriate knowledge within a planning application, and of configuring an appropriate planner to form the target software are very acute when one deals with knowledge intensive applications. This is evidenced by the effort that has been spent on interfaces in large planning systems such as SIPE [1] and O-Plan [11].

In this paper we describe a development method and tools to support both the knowledge acquisition phase, perhaps to be carried out by domain experts rather than planning experts, and to support the phase of domain modelling and validation. In pursuit of this aim we recently released a "Graphical Interface for Planning with Objects' called GIPO [10] (pronounced GeePo). This is an experimental GUI and tools environment for building classical planning domain models, providing help for those involved in knowledge acquisition and the subsequent task of domain modelling. For the former, it provides an interface that abstracts away much of the syntactic details of encoding domains, and

M.-S. Hacid et al. (Eds.): ISMIS 2002, LNAI 2366, pp. 544–552, 2002.
© Springer-Verlag Berlin Heidelberg 2002

embodies validation checks to help the user remove errors early in domain development. To assist in the definition of domain operators, we have recently introduced, an induction engine that alleviates much of the problem of encoding operators. For the domain modeller, the new induction tool integrates with a range of planning tools within GIPO - plan generators, a stepper, an animator, a random task generator, a reachability analysis tool - all to help the user explore the domain encoding, eliminate errors, and determine the kind of planner that may be suitable to use with the domain. This paper's contribution is that it introduces a new process, based on induction and object-centred technology, that can be used to acquire operator and domain knowledge in AI Planning. We describe the operator induction method in the context of its use within GIPO. A beta version of the software is available from the GIPO web site *http://scom.hud.ac.uk/planform/GIPO*

2   The Object Centred Domain Acquisition and Validation Process

The knowledge acquisition method is designed on the assumption that the knowledge engineer will be trying to build descriptions of new domains using a method which imposes a loose sequence on the sub-tasks to be undertaken to develop an initial model. Once an initial rough model has been constructed development may proceed in a more iterative and experimental manner. The process of domain model development on which this is based is detailed in the literature, see references [6,4] for more details. Here we sketch the main steps of the knowledge acquisition process, showing how the supporting tool embodies this process. We outline two important steps of the knowledge acquisition process - acquiring domain structure and acquiring domain actions using the new induction tool.

2.1   Acquisition of Domain Structure

The central conception used to raise the level of abstraction in domain capture is that planning essentially involves changing properties and relationships of the objects that inhabit the domain. Consequently all knowledge is structured round describing the objects, their relationships and the changes they undergo as a result of the application of operators during plan execution. The process starts with the identification of the kinds of objects that characterise the domain. The method requires that distinct collections of objects, which we call *sorts*, can be organised into a hierarchy and object instances for each sort identified. Each object in a sort is assumed to have identical behaviour to any other object in the sort. To assist in this element of the conceptualisation we provide a visual tree editor. Once a tentative sort tree has been constructed the domain engineer should next describe the sorts by identifying predicates that characterise the properties of a typical object of each sort and relationships that hold between objects.

The next, and arguably most important, step in the object centred modelling process is to define sets of predicates that characterise each valid state of objects of sorts that are subject to change during the planning process. We refer to sorts subject to such change as *dynamic* where as the sorts where objects remain unchanged are *static*. Under classical assumptions each member of a sort may be in only one substate at any time, and that during plan execution the object goes through *transitions* which change its state.

A *substate* of an object (called here *'substate'* to distinguish it from a state of the world, which is formed from a collection of substates) is distinguished from other possible substates by all properties and relations referring to that object that are true. If we restrict the language to the sort we're interested in, and the set of predicates to those referring to that sort, then we are interested in specifying all the Herbrand interpretations that correspond to actual substates in the domain. To illustrate consider the *trunk* in Russell's *Flat Tyre World*, given properties *open*, *closed*, *locked* and *unlocked* referring to a trunk. There there are potentially 16 subsets of the Herbrand Base for an instance of sort Trunk called trunk-1, but only three that make sense in the case where the trunk cannot be both open and locked:

> open(trunk-1) and unlocked(trunk-1)
> closed(trunk-1) and locked(trunk-1)
> closed(trunk-1) and unlocked(trunk-1)

These three sets of predicates correspond to the only three Herbrand interpretations that model sensible states of that part of the world. If we parameterise each of these interpretations with variable "Trunk" we call them *substate* definitions (substate definitions are therefore akin to parameterised "possible worlds" restricted to one particular sort). In encoding the possible substates in this way the domain modeller is capturing the implicit negations holding between the predicates *open* and *closed* and between *locked* and *unlocked* as well as the contingent fact that the *trunk* cannot be *locked* when *open*.

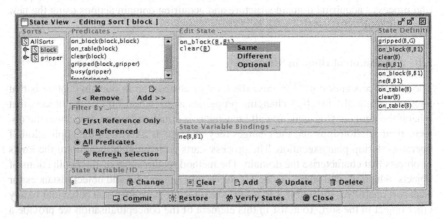

Fig. 1. Substate Editor Tool / Blocks World

Providing an editor to allow domain modellers to define such substate definitions appears straight forward in that essentially the user is only required to select from the list of already defined typed predicates a set for the selected object sort that will characterise a single substate and then repeat the process until all possible substates for the sort are defined. However this is complicated by the need in many instances to restrict the possible unification of variables of the same sort or between variables belonging to the same path in the sort tree hierarchy. This occurs for example in the "Blocks World" where one possible state of a block is that it is *clear* and that it stands on another block. Specifying a set of Herbrand interpretations with the expression $clear(Block) \wedge on(Block, Block)$ is not adequate, as we assume that any instantiation of a substate definition forms a valid ground substate. We require $clear(Block) \wedge on(Block, Other) \wedge Block \neq Other$ using the normal conventions for the unification of parameters. To achieve this on our graphical editor we allow the user to edit the names of variables. We provide a visual indication of possibly unifying variables and allow the user to select from a popup menu how an individual variable is to unify with a target variable and if the decision is that they must be distinct then the *not_equals* clause is automatically generated, see Figure 1. This strategy for dealing with the unification of variables becomes pervasive in the set of editor tools provided.

The substate definitions derived from this process specify the possible Herbrand interpretations determined by considering the domain and its constraints. These form the basis of much of the static validity checks that can be carried out on the developing domain specification.

2.2   Capturing Domain Operators

Though we provide editors to allow for the capture of other elements of domain structure the most important remaining task is to specify the domain operators. Operators in our object-centred language are conceptualised as sets of parameterised *transitions*, written $(S, O, LHS \Rightarrow RHS)$, where O is an object constant or variable belonging to sort S, and LHS and RHS are substate classes. This means that O moves from situation LHS to situation RHS. Transitions can be necessary, conditional or null. Null transitions are prevail conditions where O must be in LHS and stays in that situation after operator execution.

In the GIPO operator editor we provide a graph representation of an operator where the nodes are the LHS and RHS states of the object sorts involved in the operator. Each such node contains an editable state definition. The new operator induction method which we call *opmaker* provides a more user friendly alternative to the use of this editor.

Inducing Operator Descriptions.   The *opmaker* algorithm in the current version of GIPO is capable of generating operators for non-hierarchical domains. As an illustrative example we describe *the Hiking Domain*, a new planning domain with documentation and description on the GIPO resource page.

Two people (hikers) want to walk together a long clockwise circular route (over several days) around the Lake District of NW England. They do one "leg" each day, as they get tired and have to sleep in their tent to recover for the next leg. Their equipment is heavy, so they have two cars which can be used to carry their tent and themselves to the start/end of a leg.

We assume that we have been constructing our domain model and have reached the stage where we have a partial model with a valid sort tree, predicate definitions and substate definitions. In addition to run *opmaker* the user must specify, using the task editor, a well understood problem in the domain. A task specification allocates an initial state to every object in the problem and the desired state of a subset of these object as the goal state to be achieved. The user now supplies *opmaker* with a training sequence of actions. A snapshot of the *opmaker* interface is shown in figure 2. An action is simply

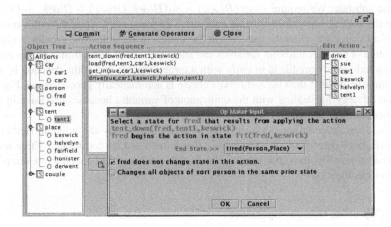

Fig. 2. A Screen Shot of *opmaker*

the chosen name for the action followed by the names of all objects that participate in the action. A good sequence of operators would ideally include instances of all operators required in the domain, though this is not required by *opmaker* and the sequence can be built up incrementally using different problem instances. For the Hiking domain a good sequence would be one that enabled the couple to complete the first leg of the tour, and be rested and ready to start the next with their cars in the correct place. Such a sequence would include all the operators required. A fragment of the sequence is shown below.

```
putdown tent1 fred keswick
load fred tent1 car1 keswick
getin sue keswick car1
drive sue car1 keswick helvelyn tent1
```

The user is encouraged to think of each action in terms of a sentence describing what happens. For example in the last action we think of this as "Sue drives car1 from Keswick to Helvelyn taking the tent with her." We sketch the algorithm for inducing the "drive" operator assuming that the earlier operators have been derived and that the specified start situation in the problem placed "Sue","Fred", the tent "tent1", and both cars in Keswick and that the tent was erected.

Prior to reaching the point of the derivation of the *drive* operator we initialise the *worldstate* to that of all objects as described in the initial state of the chosen task and then as each operator is derived we advance the *worldstate* by applying the operator to change the states of the affected objects. In considering the *drive* operator we detect that this is the first application of the operator. Therefore to create the *drive* operator we generate a new operator skeleton and set the parameterised name of the operator to $drive(sue, car1, keswick, helvelyn, tent1)$. We then iterate over the dynamic objects in the parameterised name, these are the objects of sorts for which substates have been defined. In this example it is all the objects excluding the two place arguments $keswick$ and $helvelyn$. For the first object to be considered sue we find her state as stored in the $worldstate$, which for the operator sequence given would be $in(sue, car1, keswick)$. This will form the basis of the left hand side of the transition for this object instance. We now query the user about the states of sue that results from applying the $drive$ operator. In the dialogue with the user we attempt to gather all the additional information required to correctly identify the transition made by the object. We ask whether or not sue does change state, if not we add a null transition to the operator. In our example case however sue will change state, and the user will select from a supplied list of possible states which will be the resulting state. The selected state will form the basis for the RHS element of the transition. As part of the dialog we also ask if any other object of sort person in the same prior state would make the same transition. Depending on the answer to this question we treat the transition either as a conditional change or as a required change of the operator and add the transition accordingly. When a transition is added as conditional the object name is removed from the operators parameter list. Only the objects referred to in the prevail and necessary sections are recorded in the parameter list.

Though we now have the main structure for the transition made by sue we still have some details to clarify. First we detect that $keswick$ is recorded as next to $helvelyn$ in a list of static facts provided as part of the initial domain model, we accordingly query the user again to ask if this is a required condition of applying the operator. That is, must the two places be recorded as $next$ to one another to enable the application of the $drive$ operator. If it is required then we add the fact to the LHS of the transition. In the example domain it is not required that sue can only drive between adjacent locations, she may drive to any location, hence the predicate will not be added to the LHS.

We continue the above process by iterating over the remaining dynamic objects $car1$ and $tent1$ The result is that we have a fully instantiated instance of the $drive$ operator. We generalise the operator by replacing the object names with variable names maintaining a one to one relationship between the object names and the variable names. Finally we apply the operator to the $worldstate$ to advance the state ready for consideration of the next operator and our derivation of the operator $drive$ is complete.

Using this procedure the algorithm induces the following necessary transition for objects of the sorts corresponding to sue and $car1$.
$(person, Person0, [in(Person0, Car0, Place0)] \Rightarrow [in(Person0, Car0, Place1)])$
$(car, Car0, [at(Car0, Place0)] \Rightarrow [at(Car0, Place1)])$
For $tent1$ the conditional transition
$(tent, Tent0, [loaded(Tent0, B, Place0)] \Rightarrow [loaded(Tent0, B, Place1)])$
The variables, starting with upper case letters, in the transitions above are all typed either explicitly in the transition or implicitly by their occurrence in the strongly typed predicates defining the transition.

After having been translated into PDDL by GIPO, the induced drive operator is as follows:

```
(:action drive
  :parameters ( ?x1 - person ?x2 - car
                ?x3 - place ?x4 - place)
  :precondition (and (in ?x1 ?x2 ?x3)(at ?x2 ?x3))
  :effect (and (in ?x1 ?x2 ?x4)(not (in ?x1 ?x2 ?x3))
               (at ?x2 ?x4)(not (at ?x2 ?x3))
               (forall ( ?x5 - tent)
                  (when (loaded ?x5 ?x2 ?x3)
                    (and (loaded ?x5 ?x2 ?x4)
                      (not (loaded ?x5 ?x2 ?x3)))))))))
```

3   Evaluation of GIPO

Evaluating any engineering method or tools environment is a hard, painstaking process. Experiments for rating effectiveness are difficult to set up and it is often hard to control their validity. This is because of the quasi-experimental nature of using people in such exercises with the complication of human factors. Nevertheless we have identified four steps to our of empirical evaluation:

1. internal evaluation using planning experts
2. internal evaluation using non-planning experts (students)
3. external evaluation using planning experts
4. external evaluation using non-planning experts

We have carried out step 1 and will be carry out step 2 this semester with a group of second year computing undergraduates. Following a demonstration of the tools environment at the ECP'01 conference we have placed the first version of GIPO on general release and have recorded approximately eighty downloads. For step 4 we plan to engage the help of our industrial partners on the project funding this work.

Step 1 involved two subtasks: First the input, manipulation and modelling of our existing published domain models, all available on the *GIPO* web page *http://scom.hud.ac.uk/planform/GIPO*. Secondly the creation of new domain(s) models. The first of these tasks resulted in a review of GIPO, as well as helping in the identification of some previously unnoticed bugs in the existing domain models. For the second subtask we developed a new domain called "The Hiking Domain", details of which are on the web site above. Both a non-conditional version and a version using conditional effects was built. The amount of effort required to build and debug this domain was of the order of one person day. Most gratifying is that at the time dynamic testing started our internal system planners were able to return solutions on their first run (i.e. it appeared that all syntax and semantic errors had been removed before this stage). This is in contrast to our normal experience of domain acquisition where one essentially uses a planner to debug the domain. Further, the PDDL produced from our object-centred domain model was input to an external planner (FF) [3] which was able to produce a (non-optimal) solution to the main task of the the Hiking Domain with 5 seconds of computation. Our internal planner, although generating an optimal plan, took approximately 150 minutes. The *opmaker* induction tool was further evaluated by:

1. comparing the accuracy of what was induced with hand crafted operator sets
2. comparing the robustness of the algorithm when input with different operator sequences.

Then the operators were induced using a sequence of actions to accomplish the first days walk as described above, a full operator set was generated, passing all local and global validation checks in the GIPO system. We have performed an initial evaluation with several variants of the Hiking Domain, as well as the standard Briefcase World, Rocket World and Tyre World with similar results. As regards varying the operator sequences, the algorithm as described is sensitive to order for operators having conditional effects, though we are working on removing this sensitivity by allowing a limited form of operator revision for such operators.

4   Scope of the GIPO Environment

Our intention in creating the GIPO Environment is not simply to develop a tool for the creation of planning domains in the internal object centred representation language but to promote the tool as a modelling tool irrespective of the final target language. Central to GIPO is the object centred internal representation of domains which is manipulated by all major tool elements. These elements are the set of editors, augmented by *opmaker*, to create the domain specification and the associated static and dynamic checking routines to inform the process. To enable GIPO to be used as a general domain modelling tool we have developed translators between our internal language OCL_h and PDDL [9]. We also provide an API to enable external planning systems to interface to the tools to provide scope for testing and fielding alternative planning algorithms to those internal to GIPO. Currently the interface allows planners which can input OCL version 2.1 [4] or typed/conditional PDDL. As an example, we have successfully tested the integration of FF version 2.3 [3] with GIPO using our open interface without the requirement to amend any of the FF code. We hope to extend the open nature of GIPO in the future and allow the utilisation of other external tools such the domain analysis provided by TIM [2].

5   Conclusions and Future Work

In this paper we have illustrated a methodological approach to knowledge acquisition for planning domain knowledge resulting in a conceptualisation at the object level. We have demonstrated a tool support framework using snapshots from GIPO, a prototype GUI which supports this process for domains where classical planning assumptions are valid. This approach has the following advantages:

- The process of domain model validation can proceed independently and in advance of final product validation. Hence, domain models are developed initially independently of operational matters (a point argued for as a result of experience in the Remote Agent Experiment [7]) allowing non-planning experts to input the structure and dynamics of a domain without the need to consider how plans will be constructed by a target planner.

 – Validation checks are integrated into the environment at each point of the acquisition process, with many being transparent to the user. This will reduce the emphasis on the current painstaking method of debugging via dynamic testing.
 – The tool can be used to develop a domain within any concrete domain language which is consistent with the object centred planning ontology. We have demonstrated this with translators to/from the PDDL language, which is based on the classical approach of encapsulating the dynamics of a domain with pre- and post condition operators.

We plan to widen the scope of the tool in several directions. Firstly, it can be extended to the non-classical domains by introducing new modalities in object transitions. For example, a probability value attached to a transition will produce operators with uncertainty of action, and transitions resulting in sets of object substates will produce non-deterministic operators and incomplete knowledge of an object's substate. Secondly, although the object centred method lifts domain acquisition to a conceptual level, the details of specifying substate definitions and transitions are still too theoretical for an unskilled user. We aim in the future to incorporate more inferencing mechanisms to aid the unskilled user in this task.

References

1. David E. Wilkins. Can AI Planners Solve Practical Problems. *Computational Intelligence Journal*, 1990.
2. M. Fox and D. Long. The Automatic Inference of State Invariants in TIM. *JAIR*, 9:367–421, 1997.
3. J. Hoffmann. A Heuristic for Domain Independent Planning and its Use in an Enforced Hill-climbing Algorithm. In *Proceedings of the 14th Workshop on Planning and Configuration - New Results in Planning, Scheduling and Design*, 2000.
4. D. Liu and T. L. McCluskey. The OCL Language Manual, Version 1.2. Technical report, Department of Computing and Mathematical Sciences, University of Huddersfield , 2000.
5. T. L. McCluskey, R. Aler, D. Borrajo, P. Haslum, P. Jarvis, and U. Scholz. Knowledge Engineering for Planning ROADMAP. *http://scom.hud.ac.uk/planet/*, 2000.
6. T. L. McCluskey and J. M. Porteous. Engineering and Compiling Planning Domain Models to Promote Validity and Efficiency. *Artificial Intelligence*, 95:1–65, 1997.
7. N. Muscettola, P. P. Nayak, B. Pell, and B. C. Williams. Remote Agent: To Boldly Go Where No AI System Has Gone Before. *Artificial Intelligence*, 103(1-2):5–48, 1998.
8. S.Chien, R.Hill, X.Wang, T.Estlin, K.Fayyad and H.Mortenson. Why Real-World Planning is Difficult: A Tale of Two Applications. In M. Ghallab and A. Milani, editors, *New Directions in AI Planning*, pages 287–298 . IOS Press, 1996.
9. R. M. Simpson, T. L. McCluskey, D. Liu, and D. E. Kitchin. Knowledge Representation in Planning: A PDDL to OCL_h Translation. In *Proceedings of the 12th International Symposium on Methodologies for Intelligent Systems*, 2000.
10. R. M. Simpson, T. L. McCluskey, W. Zhao, R. S. Aylett, and C. Doniat. GIPO: An Integrated Graphical Tool to support Knowledge Engineering in AI Planning. In *Proceedings of the 6th European Conference on Planning*, 2001.
11. A. Tate, B. Drabble, and J. Dalton. O-Plan: a Knowledged-Based Planner and its Application to Logistics. AIAI, University of Edinburgh, 1996.

Probabilistic Aggregates

Robert Ross[1], V.S. Subrahmanian[1], and John Grant[2]

[1] University of Maryland, College Park MD 20742, USA
[2] Towson University, Towson MD 21252, USA

Abstract. Though extensions of the relational model of data have been proposed to handle probabilistic information, there has been no work to date on handling aggregate operators in such databases. In this paper, we show how classical aggregation operators (like COUNT, SUM, etc.) as well as other statistical operators (like weighted average, variance, etc.) can be defined as well as implemented over probabilistic databases. We define these operations, develop a formal linear program model for computing answers to such queries, and then develop a generic algorithm to compute aggregates.

1 Introduction

Over the last few years, there has been a rapid increase in the number of applications that need to deal with uncertain information. For instance, image processing and video surveillance programs produce uncertain image identifications [10] that need to be stored and indexed. Likewise, prediction programs that use statistical prediction models [15] produce predictions parametrized by uncertainty. Dyreson and Snodgrass [6] have argued that uncertainty arises naturally in temporal databases in many applications. Fuhr and Rolleke [9] argue for the need for probabilistic databases to handle information retrieval problems. For instance, consider a commercial shipping company (e.g. UPS or Fedex). They have probability distributions over transportation times between various sites on their transportation network. These include probability distributions on when a package will reach an interim destination, when a package will be delivered to its final destination, etc.

Although models for probabilistic relational databases [1,2,5,12], probabilistic deductive databases [11,13,14], probabilistic object bases [7], probabilistic temporal databases [4,6], and probabilistic logics in general [8] have been well studied, there has been no work to date on handling aggregates in probabilistic databases. However, such operations are extremely important. For example, a commercial shipper may want to estimate how many packages are expected to be at a given distribution point by a given time, taking the schedules of these packages into account. Likewise, in a database containing stock predictions, there may be interest in determining the three predicted that are predicted to undergo the largest change in expected value.

This paper is organized in the following way: In Section 2, we define FP-relations as paradigms for storing data about events and their associated probabilities. Similar to ProbView [12], conjunctions and disjunctions over these events

M.-S. Hacid et al. (Eds.): ISMIS 2002, LNAI 2366, pp. 553–564, 2002.

can be computed under a number of different strategies; the independence assumption is not required. Thus within this section, we also review the concept of a probabilistic conjunction strategy (PCS) and a probabilistic disjunction strategy (PDS).

Next, in Section 3, we define aggregate operators over FP-relations. These definitions are rich enough to apply to a wide variety of traditional aggregates (e.g. SUM, COUNT, AVG, etc.) as well as other statistical aggregates (e.g. trimmed mean, median, mode, variance, etc.). Section 3 also provides a formal declarative semantics for such aggregates using linear programming methods that extend those of [8]. Section 4 provides a "generic" algorithm called **GPA** for performing aggregate operations. **GPA** is provably sound and complete with respect to the semantics in Section 3. Related work and conclusions follow in Section 5.

2   Preliminaries: FP-Relations, PCSs, and PDSs

We begin by reviewing the concept of a probabilistic relation. Probabilistic relations were proposed in [12] as a powerful device for expressing uncertainty. However, since they are not in first normal form, probabilistic relations are difficult to manipulate. Thus, we introduce the concept of a flat probabilistic (FP) relation. An FP-relation is a convenient representation for a probabilistic relation, and it is a simplification of the path-annotated relations described in [12].

We now present our definition for probabilistic relations. Here, we assume that readers are familiar with standard terms in relational database theory [16].

Definition 1 (Probabilistic tuples and probabilistic relations). Suppose $R = (A_1, \ldots, A_k)$ is a relation scheme that is in first normal form. Then a *probabilistic tuple* over R is a k-tuple of the form $(\langle V_1, f_1 \rangle, \ldots, \langle V_k, f_k \rangle)$ where for all $i \in [1, k]$, $V_i \subseteq dom(A_i)$ and f_i is a function that maps each value in V_i to a probability interval (i.e., a closed subinterval of $[0, 1]$).

A *probabilistic relation* over R is a finite set of probabilistic tuples over R.

The following example demonstrates one situation where probabilistic relations are beneficial. We will refer to this example throughout the paper.

Example 1 (Probabilistic relation). Consider a day-ahead energy market (such as those used to trade virtually all US energy). Energy producers in such a market try to estimate prices (today) for sales tomorrow. In such a case, they may need to represent the probabilistic information shown in Figure 1.

The first two rows in Figure 1 describe expectations on price for a unit of power in the NY market. The expectation is $5600 with 60% to 70% probability and $5700 with 30% to 40% probability. The next four rows apply to the Bos market where the expectation is $5500, $5600, $5700, and $5800 with 10%, 20%, 30%, and 40% probability respectively. This information is encoded by the probabilistic relation named priceEstimates that is shown in Figure 2.

It is often convenient to require each probabilistic tuple to have a unique identifier. This desideratum motivates the following definition for a P-relation.

Id	Market	Day	Price
1	NY	10	5600 [0.6, 0.7]
			5700 [0.3, 0.4]
2	Bos	10	5500 [0.1, 0.1]
			5600 [0.2, 0.2]
			5700 [0.3, 0.3]
			5800 [0.4, 0.4]

Fig. 1. Probabilistic data

Id	Market	Day	Price
$V_1 = \{1\}$	$V_2 = \{NY\}$	$V_3 = \{10\}$	$V_4 = \{5600, 5700\}$
$f_1(1) = [1,1]$	$f_2(NY) = [1,1]$	$f_3(10) = [1,1]$	$f_4(5600) = [0.6, 0.7]; f_4(5700) = [0.3, 0.4]$
$V_5 = \{2\}$	$V_6 = \{Bos\}$	$V_7 = \{10\}$	$V_8 = \{5500, 5600, 5700, 5800\}$
$f_5(2) = [1,1]$	$f_6(Bos) = [1,1]$	$f_7(10) = [1,1]$	$f_8(5500) = [0.1, 0.1]; f_8(5600) = [0.2, 0.2]$
			$f_8(5700) = [0.3, 0.3]; f_8(5800) = [0.4, 0.4]$

Fig. 2. P-relation priceEstimates

Definition 2 (P-relations). A probabilistic tuple $t_p = (\langle V_1, f_1 \rangle, \ldots, \langle V_k, f_k \rangle)$ over $R = (A_1, \ldots, A_k)$ is a *P-tuple* iff $A_1 = $ Id, $V_1 = \{id\}$, and $f_1(id) = [1,1]$ for some identifier $id \in dom(\mathsf{Id})$. A *P-relation* over R is a finite set r_p of P-tuples over R where $(\forall t_p, t'_p \in r_p) ((t_p.A_1 = t'_p.A_1) \rightarrow (t_p = t'_p))$.

Clearly, priceEstimates is a P-relation. Our goal is to represent P-relations as FP-relations. In order to do so, we use two special attributes, L and U, where $dom(L) \in [0,1]$ and $dom(U) \in [0,1]$. Given a relation scheme $R = (A_1, \ldots, A_k)$ where R is in first normal form and attribute $A_i \notin \{L, U\}$ for all $1 \leq i \leq k$, we say that $\hat{R} = (A_1, \ldots, A_k, L, U)$ is an *FP-schema* for R. Here, $A_1, \ldots, A_k$ are called the *data attributes* of $\hat{R}$.

Definition 3 (FP-relations). Suppose $\hat{R} = (A_1, \ldots, A_k, L, U)$ is an FP-schema for R. An *FP-tuple* over $\hat{R}$ is any $pt \in dom(A_1) \times \cdots \times dom(A_k) \times dom(L) \times dom(U)$ where $pt.L \leq pt.U$. We use the notation $data(pt)$ to denote the restriction of pt to its data attributes.

An *FP-relation* over $\hat{R}$ is a set pr of FP-tuples over $\hat{R}$ where R is a superkey for pr. We use $data(pr)$ to denote the classical relation $\{ data(pt) \mid pt \in pr \}$.

Lakshmanan et. al. [12] provide an algorithm for converting probabilistic relations into path-annotated relations. If we apply this algorithm to a P-relation r_p and then remove the nonessential PATH attribute, the result is an FP-relation pr. Here, we say that pr is the *flattening* of r_p.

Example 2 (FP-relations). The flattening of P-relation priceEstimates in Figure 2 is the FP-relation named prices that is shown in Figure 3(b). This FP-relation estimates the prices that an energy producer may expect to realize for its power in tomorrow's market.

d
d_1
d_2
d_3
d_4
d_5
d_6

Id	Market	Day	Price	L	U
1	NY	10	5600	0.6	0.7
1	NY	10	5700	0.3	0.4
2	Bos	10	5500	0.1	0.1
2	Bos	10	5600	0.2	0.2
2	Bos	10	5700	0.3	0.3
2	Bos	10	5800	0.4	0.4

Id	$\text{avg}_{\text{Price}}$	L	U
1	5500	0	.01
1	5550	.06	.07
1	5600	.15	.20
1	5650	.24	.29
1	5700	.33	.43
1	5750	.12	.16
1	5800	0	.04

(a)   (b)   (c)

w	$P(\text{prices}, \otimes_{\text{prices}}, w)$
$w_1 = \{d_1, d_3\}$	$(e_1, [.6, .7]) \otimes_{in} (e_3, [.1, .1]) = [.06, .07]$
$w_2 = \{d_1, d_4\}$	$(e_1, [.6, .7]) \otimes_{in} (e_4, [.2, .2]) = [.12, .14]$
$w_3 = \{d_1, d_5\}$	$(e_1, [.6, .7]) \otimes_{in} (e_5, [.3, .3]) = [.18, .21]$
$w_4 = \{d_1, d_6\}$	$(e_1, [.6, .7]) \otimes_{in} (e_6, [.4, .4]) = [.24, .28]$
$w_5 = \{d_2, d_3\}$	$(e_2, [.3, .4]) \otimes_{in} (e_3, [.1, .1]) = [.03, .04]$
$w_6 = \{d_2, d_4\}$	$(e_2, [.3, .4]) \otimes_{in} (e_4, [.2, .2]) = [.06, .08]$
$w_7 = \{d_2, d_5\}$	$(e_2, [.3, .4]) \otimes_{in} (e_5, [.3, .3]) = [.09, .12]$
$w_8 = \{d_2, d_6\}$	$(e_2, [.3, .4]) \otimes_{in} (e_6, [.4, .4]) = [.12, .16]$
$w_9 = \{d_3\}$	$(\neg e_1 \wedge \neg e_2, (\neg e_1, [.3, .4]) \otimes_{nc} (\neg e_2, [.6, .7])) \otimes_{in} (e_3, [.1, .1]) = [0, .01]$
$w_{10} = \{d_4\}$	$(\neg e_1 \wedge \neg e_2, (\neg e_1, [.3, .4]) \otimes_{nc} (\neg e_2, [.6, .7])) \otimes_{in} (e_4, [.2, .2]) = [0, .02]$
$w_{11} = \{d_5\}$	$(\neg e_1 \wedge \neg e_2, (\neg e_1, [.3, .4]) \otimes_{nc} (\neg e_2, [.6, .7])) \otimes_{in} (e_5, [.3, .3]) = [0, .03]$
$w_{12} = \{d_6\}$	$(\neg e_1 \wedge \neg e_2, (\neg e_1, [.3, .4]) \otimes_{nc} (\neg e_2, [.6, .7])) \otimes_{in} (e_6, [.4, .4]) = [0, .04]$

(d)

Fig. 3. FP-relation prices and related calculations

The interested reader can study [12] to see how the operators of the standard relational algebra may be extended to handle queries over these kinds of relations. In this paper, we are concerned with aggregate queries such as "What is the average estimated price for energy sales on day 10?" Instead of a single, definite value, the answer is the FP-relation shown in Figure 3(c).

For instance, the average price will be $5650 if NY sells at $5600 and Bos sells at $5700 or if NY sells at $5700 and Bos sells at $5600. Thus, the probability that tomorrow's average estimate will be $5650 must lie within the probability interval for the disjunction of two conjunctive events.

Lakshmanan et. al. [12] introduce the important concept of a probabilistic conjunction strategy (PCS) and a probabilistic disjunction strategy (PDS). In general, the probability of a conjunction (resp. disjunction) of two events depends on the relationship between these events. If nothing is known about their interdependence, then the probability of the compound event can be bounded by solving a pair of linear programs. Although linear programming generally requires polynomial time, the two linear programs that need to be solved for the case of complete ignorance have a closed form solution that can be computed in very low-order constant time [8] and yields a closed interval for the probability of the conjunction (or disjunction). We now present the definition for a PCS.

Definition 4 (PCS). Suppose $[L_1, U_1]$ and $[L_2, U_2]$ are the probability intervals associated with events e_1 and e_2 respectively. Then a *PCS* $\otimes$ is a function that takes $(e_1, [L_1, U_1])$ and $(e_2, [L_2, U_2])$ as input, and returns as output the probability interval that is associated with the event $e_1 \wedge e_2$. If e_1 and e_2 are mutually exclusive, then this probability interval must be $[0, 0]$. Otherwise, every PCS must conform to the following postulates of probabilistic conjunction:[1]

1. Bottomline: $(e_1, [L_1, U_1]) \otimes (e_2, [L_2, U_2]) \leq [\min(L_1, L_2), \min(U_1, U_2)]$.
2. Ignorance: $(e_1, [L_1, U_1]) \otimes (e_2, [L_2, U_2]) \subseteq [\max(0, L_1 + L_2 - 1), \min(U_1, U_2)]$.
3. Identity: $(e_1, [L_1, U_1]) \otimes (e_2, [1, 1]) = [L_1, U_1]$.
4. Annihilator: $(e_1, [L_1, U_1]) \otimes (e_2, [0, 0]) = [0, 0]$.
5. Commutativity: $(e_1, [L_1, U_1]) \otimes (e_2, [L_2, U_2]) = (e_2, [L_2, U_2]) \otimes (e_1, [L_1, U_1])$.
6. Associativity: $(e_1 \wedge e_2, (e_1, [L_1, U_1]) \otimes (e_2, [L_2, U_2])) \otimes (e_3, [L_3, U_3]) =$
   $(e_1, [L_1, U_1]) \otimes (e_2 \wedge e_3, (e_2, [L_2, U_2]) \otimes (e_3, [L_3, U_3]))$.
7. Monotonicity: $(e_1, [L_1, U_1]) \otimes (e_2, [L_2, U_2]) \leq (e_1, [L_1, U_1]) \otimes (e_3, [L_3, U_3])$
   if $[L_2, U_2] \leq [L_3, U_3]$.

We shall use the notation $\otimes(S)$ to denote the application of PCS $\otimes$ to a set of events. Specifically, $\otimes(\emptyset) = [0, 0]$, $\otimes(\{(e_1, [L_1, U_1])\}) = [L_1, U_1]$, and $\otimes(\{(e_1, [L_1, U_1]), \ldots, (e_n, [L_n, U_n])\}) = (e_1, [L_1, U_1]) \otimes \cdots \otimes (e_n, [L_n, U_n])$.

Example 3 (PCSs). The following table provides some common PCS examples.

Relationship	Strategy	Interval returned when $e_1 \wedge e_2$ is consistent
Ignorance	$\otimes_{ig}$	$[\max(0, L_1 + L_2 - 1), \min(U_1, U_2)]$
Positive correlation	$\otimes_{pc}$	$[\min(L_1, L_2), \min(U_1, U_2)]$
Negative correlation	$\otimes_{nc}$	$[\max(0, L_1 + L_2 - 1), \max(0, U_1 + U_2 - 1)]$
Independence	$\otimes_{in}$	$[L_1 \cdot L_2, U_1 \cdot U_2]$

Every FP-relation pr has an associated PCS $\otimes_{pr}$ that describes the relationship between the FP-tuples in pr. The following example shows how $\otimes_{\text{prices}}$ handles conjunctions over simple events.

Example 4 (PCS $\otimes_{pr}$). Suppose $e_1 = data(pt)$, $[L_1, U_1] = [pt.L, pt.U]$, $e_2 = data(pt')$, $[L_2, U_2] = [pt'.L, pt'.U]$, and $(e_1, [L_1, U_1]) \otimes_{\text{prices}} (e_2, [L_2, U_2]) = [L, U]$ for some pair of FP-tuples $pt, pt' \in \text{prices}$. Then $\otimes_{\text{prices}}$ defines the probability interval $[L, U]$ for the event $e_1 \wedge e_2$ in the following way:

- $[L, U] = (e_1, [L_1, U_1]) \otimes_{pc} (e_2, [L_2, U_2])$ if $e_1 = e_2$.
- $[L, U] = (e_1, [L_1, U_1]) \otimes_{nc} (e_2, [L_2, U_2])$ if $pt.\text{Id} = pt'.\text{Id}$ and $e_1 \neq e_2$.
- $[L, U] = (e_1, [L_1, U_1]) \otimes_{in} (e_2, [L_2, U_2])$ if $pt.\text{Id} \neq pt'.\text{Id}$.

---

[1] Note that $[L, U] \leq [L', U']$ iff $L \leq L'$ and $U \leq U'$.

Intuitively, $\otimes_{\text{prices}}$ uses $\otimes_{pc}$ for data-identical FP-tuples (since they represent the same event), $\otimes_{nc}$ for distinct FP-tuples that share the same Id (since their events are mutually exclusive), and $\otimes_{in}$ otherwise (although another reasonable choice could have been $\otimes_{ig}$). For example, the probability that NY will sell at \$5600 and \$5700 on day 10 is zero while the probability that NY and Bos will sell at \$5600 on day 10 is within the interval $[0.6 \times 0.2, 0.7 \times 0.2] = [0.12, 0.14]$.

The definition for a PDS can be found in [12]. In this paper, we will only use $\oplus_{nc}$ PDS. This PDS is defined as $(e_1, [L_1, U_1]) \oplus_{nc} (e_2, [L_2, U_2]) = [\min(1, L_1 + L_2), \min(1, U_1 + U_2)]$ and it is appropriate when e_1, e_2 are mutually exclusive. Since the result of this PDS does not depend on the input events, we simplify notation and write $[L_1, U_1] \oplus_{nc} [L_2, U_2]$ instead of $(e_1, [L_1, U_1]) \oplus_{nc} (e_2, [L_2, U_2])$.

3   Aggregate Operators: Declarative Semantics

In this section, we describe aggregate operations on FP-relations and use linear programming methods to provide a formal declarative semantics for them. We first define a little more notation.

Definition 5 $(P(pr, \otimes, r))$. Suppose pr is an FP-relation, $\otimes$ is a PCS, and r is a classical relation where $r \subseteq data(pr)$. Then the probability interval $P(pr, \otimes, r)$ is defined in the following way:

$$P(pr, \otimes, r) = \otimes(\{(data(pt), [pt.L, pt.U]) \mid data(pt) \in r\} \cup$$
$$\{(\neg data(pt), [1 - pt.U, 1 - pt.L]) \mid data(pt) \in data(pr) - r\})$$

Intuitively, if p is the probability that all of the events represented by r are true AND all of the events represented by $data(pr) - r$ are false, then $p \in P(pr, \otimes, r)$. This intuition is clear after one studies the following example.

Example 5 $(P(\text{prices}, \otimes_{\text{prices}}, r))$. Consider the FP-relation named prices that was given in Figure 3(b). Let pt_i denote the i-th FP-tuple in prices, let d_i denote $data(pt_i)$, let e_i denote the event represented by d_i, and suppose $r = \{d_1, d_3\} = \{(1, \text{NY}, 10, 5600), (2, \text{Bos}, 10, 5500)\}$. Then $P(\text{prices}, \otimes_{\text{prices}}, r)$ is the probability interval that $\otimes_{\text{prices}}$ assigns to the event $e_1 \wedge e_3 \wedge \neg e_2 \wedge \neg e_4 \wedge \neg e_5 \wedge \neg e_6$. Note that because the probability interval associated with e_2 is $[pt_2.L, pt_2.U] = [.3, .4]$, the probability interval associated with $\neg e_2$ must be $[1 - .4, 1 - .3] = [.6, .7]$.

Definition 6 (World). A *world* for FP-relation pr under the $\otimes$ PCS is a classical relation $w \subseteq data(pr)$ where $(\forall d, d' \in w)((d.\text{Id} = d'.\text{Id}) \to (d = d'))$ and $P(pr, \otimes, w) \neq [0, 0]$. We let $W_{pr, \otimes}$ denote the set of all worlds for pr under $\otimes$.

Example 6 (Worlds). Let pt_i denote the i-th FP-tuple in prices, let d_i denote $data(pt_i)$, and let e_i denote the event represented by d_i. Then the twelve worlds in $W_{\text{prices}, \otimes_{\text{prices}}}$ are shown in Figure 3(d).

$$\textbf{count}(pr, w) = |w|$$

$$\textbf{sum}_A(pr, w) = \sum\{pt.A \mid pt \in pr \wedge data(pt) \in w\}$$

$$\textbf{avg}_A(pr, w) = \textbf{sum}_A(pr, w) \, / \, \textbf{count}(pr, w) \text{ if } w \neq \emptyset$$

$$\textbf{min}_A(pr, w) = \min\{pt.A \mid pt \in pr \wedge data(pt) \in w\} \text{ if } w \neq \emptyset$$

$$\textbf{max}_A(pr, w) = \max\{pt.A \mid pt \in pr \wedge data(pt) \in w\} \text{ if } w \neq \emptyset$$

$$\textbf{wtavg}_{A, x_u}(pr, w) = (1/N) \sum\{(pt.A)(pt.P) \mid pt \in pr \wedge data(pt) \in w\}$$

$$\text{where } N = \sum\{pt.P \mid pt \in pr \wedge data(pt) \in w\}$$

$$\text{and } pt.P \text{ denotes } (1 - x_u)(pt.L) + (x_u)(pt.U)$$

$$\text{if } A \in R, \; x_u \in [0, 1], \text{ and } N \neq 0$$

$$\textbf{variance}_{A, x_{samp}}(pr, w) = (1/N)\left(\sum\{(pt.A)^2 \mid pt \in pr \wedge data(pt) \in w\} - E\right)$$

$$\text{where } E = \left(\textbf{sum}_A(pr, w)^2\right) / \textbf{count}(pr, w)$$

$$\text{and } N = |w| - x_{samp} \text{ if } x_{samp} \in \{0, 1\} \text{ and } N > 0$$

$$\textbf{stdev}_{A, x_{samp}}(pr, w) = \sqrt{\textbf{variance}_{A, x_{samp}}(pr, w)}$$

Fig. 4. Aggregate functions

Worlds w_1 through w_8 contain exactly one tuple for each distinct Id. Worlds w_9 through w_{12} arise since there is a small chance that the price for NY will be neither \$5600 nor \$5700. Intuitively, this can occur since $pt_1.L + pt_2.L < 1$. In contrast, $\sum_{i=3}^6 pt_i.L = 1$ so every possible price estimate for Bos is included in prices. Note that there is no $w \in W_{\text{prices}, \otimes_{\text{prices}}}$ where $d_i, d_j \in w$, $d_i \neq d_j$, and $d_i.\text{Id} = d_j.\text{Id}$. For example, $r = \{d_1, d_2\} \notin W_{\text{prices}, \otimes_{\text{prices}}}$ since $(e_1, [.6, .7]) \otimes_{\text{prices}}$ $(e_2, [.3, .4]) = (e_1, [.6, .7]) \otimes_{nc} (e_2, [.3, .4]) = [0, 0]$ so $P(\text{prices}, \otimes_{\text{prices}}, r) = [0, 0]$. In fact, Definition 6 ensures that r is not a world even if we selected an inappropriate PCS $\otimes$ where $P(\text{prices}, \otimes, r) \neq [0, 0]$. This is important since P-relation priceEstimates does not allow two different estimates for the same Id.

To compute $P(\text{prices}, \otimes_{\text{prices}}, w_1)$, we can consider the event $(e_1 \wedge \neg e_2 \wedge e_3 \wedge \neg e_4 \wedge \neg e_5 \wedge \neg e_6)$. However, since $e_1 \rightarrow \neg e_2$ and $e_3 \rightarrow (\neg e_4 \wedge \neg e_5 \wedge \neg e_6)$, the conjunct can be simplified to $(e_1 \wedge e_3)$. Similarly, when we compute $P(\text{prices}, \otimes_{\text{prices}}, w_{10})$, the conjunct $(\neg e_1 \wedge \neg e_2 \wedge \neg e_3 \wedge e_4 \wedge \neg e_5 \wedge \neg e_6)$ can be simplified to $(\neg e_1 \wedge \neg e_2 \wedge e_4)$ since $e_4 \rightarrow (\neg e_3 \wedge \neg e_5 \wedge \neg e_6)$.

Definition 7 (Aggregate function). An *aggregate function* is any mapping that takes an FP-relation pr and a world w for pr as input, and returns a real number as output.

Suppose $\hat{R}$ is the FP-schema for pr, R is the set of all data attributes in $\hat{R}$, and A is a numerical attribute in $\hat{R}$. Then Figure 4 defines the aggregate functions for count, sum, average, minimum, maximum, weighted average, variance, and standard deviation.

Example 7 (Aggregate functions). If $pr = $ prices and $A = $ Price, then it is easy to verify that $\mathbf{count}(pr, w_1) = 2$, $\mathbf{sum}_A(pr, w_1) = 11100$, $\mathbf{avg}_A(pr, w_1) = 5550$, $\mathbf{min}_A(pr, w_1) = 5500$, $\mathbf{max}_A(pr, w_1) = 5600$, and $\mathbf{wtavg}_{A,.5}(pr, w_1) = ((5600)(\frac{.6+.7}{2}) + (5500)(\frac{.1+.1}{2})) / (\frac{.6+.7}{2} + \frac{.1+.1}{2}) = 5586.\overline{6}$.

Given an FP-relation pr, a PCS $\otimes$, and an aggregate function agg, we want to define an aggregate operator that applies agg to worlds for pr under $\otimes$, and produces an FP-relation as output. To accomplish this goal, we introduce the concept of a linear program associated with $pr, \otimes$. In the following, $\mathsf{LP}(pr, \otimes)$ encodes constraints on probabilities of worlds based on the event probabilities in pr and the event dependencies specified by $\otimes$.

Definition 8 (LP). For any FP-relation pr and PCS $\otimes$, $\mathsf{LP}(pr, \otimes)$ is defined as the following set of linear constraints:

1. For each $pt \in pr$, $(pt.L \leq \sum_{w \in W_{pt}} p(w) \leq pt.U)$ is in $\mathsf{LP}(pr, \otimes)$ where $W_{pt} = \{w \in W_{pr, \otimes} \mid data(pt) \in w\}$.
2. For each $w \in W_{pr, \otimes}$, $(L_w \leq p(w) \leq U_w)$ is in $\mathsf{LP}(pr, \otimes)$ where $[L_w, U_w] = P(pr, \otimes, w)$.[2]
3. $(\sum_{w \in W_{pr, \otimes}} p(w) = 1)$ is in $\mathsf{LP}(pr, \otimes)$.

Example 8 (LP). Recall from Example 6 that $W_{\text{prices}, \otimes_{\text{prices}}} = \{w_1, \ldots, w_{12}\}$. Thus

$$\mathsf{LP}(\text{prices}, \otimes_{\text{prices}}) = \{(.6 \leq p(w_1) + p(w_2) + p(w_3) + p(w_4) \leq .7),$$
$$(.3 \leq p(w_5) + p(w_6) + p(w_7) + p(w_8) \leq .4),$$
$$(.1 \leq p(w_1) + p(w_5) + p(w_9) \leq .1),$$
$$(.2 \leq p(w_2) + p(w_6) + p(w_{10}) \leq .2),$$
$$(.3 \leq p(w_3) + p(w_7) + p(w_{11}) \leq .3),$$
$$(.4 \leq p(w_4) + p(w_8) + p(w_{12}) \leq .4)\} \cup$$
$$\{(.06 \leq p(w_1) \leq .07), (.12 \leq p(w_2) \leq .14), \ldots,$$
$$(0 \leq p(w_{11}) \leq .03), (0 \leq p(w_{12}) \leq .04)\} \cup$$
$$\{(\textstyle\sum_{i=1}^{12} p(w_i) = 1)\}$$

For example, $(.1 \leq p(w_1) + p(w_5) + p(w_9) \leq .1) \in \mathsf{LP}(\text{prices}, \otimes_{\text{prices}})$ because $[pt_3.L, pt_3.U] = [.1, .1]$ and $W_{pt_3} = \{w \in W_{\text{prices}, \otimes_{\text{prices}}} \mid d_3 \in w\} = \{w_1, w_5, w_9\}$. Furthermore, $(.12 \leq p(w_2) \leq .14) \in \mathsf{LP}(\text{prices}, \otimes_{\text{prices}})$ because $P(\text{prices}, \otimes_{\text{prices}}, w_2) = [.12, .14]$.

In the following, we define the concept of an aggregate operator. Note that since aggregate operators map FP-relations to FP-relations, it is easy to nest aggregates or to compose them with operators in the FP-algebra (the FP-algebra extends the relational algebra to handle FP-relations).

---

[2] If $\otimes = \otimes_{ig}$, then this can be simplified to $(p(w) \geq 0) \in \mathsf{LP}(pr, \otimes)$ for each $w \in W_{pr, \otimes}$.

Definition 9 (Aggregate operator). Suppose agg is an aggregate function. Then an *aggregate operator* associated with agg is a mapping that takes an FP-relation pr and a PCS $\otimes$ as input, and returns as output an FP-relation pr'' over FP-schema (Id, A, L, U) where $dom(A) = \mathbf{R}$ and

$$pr'' = \{pt'' \mid (\exists W) \, (\, W = \{w \in W_{pr,\otimes} \mid agg(pr, w) = pt''.A\} \neq \emptyset \wedge pt''.\mathsf{Id} = 1 \wedge$$
$$pt''.L = \text{minimize } \textstyle\sum_{w \in W} p(w) \text{ subject to } \mathsf{LP}(pr, \otimes) \wedge$$
$$pt''.U = \text{maximize } \textstyle\sum_{w \in W} p(w) \text{ subject to } \mathsf{LP}(pr, \otimes) \,)\}$$

Example 9 (Average). The answer that is returned by the aggregate operator[3] $\mathbf{avg}_{\mathsf{Price}}(\mathsf{prices}, \otimes_{\mathsf{prices}})$ is the FP-relation shown in Figure 3(c). Consider for instance the FP-tuple $(1, 5650, .24, .29)$ in this answer. The probability $.24$ (resp. $.29$) was generated by minimizing (resp. maximizing) $p(w_3) + p(w_6)$ subject to $\mathsf{LP}(\mathsf{prices}, \otimes_{\mathsf{prices}})$ because $\mathbf{avg}_{\mathsf{Price}}(\mathsf{prices}, w_3) = \mathbf{avg}_{\mathsf{Price}}(\mathsf{prices}, w_6) = 5650$ and since there are no other worlds $w \in W_{\mathsf{prices}, \otimes_{\mathsf{prices}}}$ where $\mathbf{avg}_{\mathsf{Price}}(\mathsf{prices}, w) = 5650$.

4 Aggregate Operators: Algorithm GPA

In this section, we present a generic algorithm named **GPA** to determine the answer for a probabilistic aggregate query. This algorithm takes an FP-relation pr, a PCS $\otimes$, and any aggregate function[4] agg as input, and returns as output an FP-relation pr''. We say that **GPA** is generic since its implementation does not depend on the specific properties of aggregate function agg. In the following, we assume that h is any data structure that can store a set of $(v, [L, U])$ pairs.

Algorithm 1. GPA$(pr, \otimes, agg)$:

1. $pr'' \leftarrow \emptyset; h \leftarrow \emptyset;$
2. **for** each $w \in W_{pr,\otimes}$ **do** $\{$
3. $P(w) \leftarrow P(pr, \otimes, w);$
4.   **if** $v \leftarrow agg(pr, w)$ is not defined **then continue**;
5.   **if** there exists $[L, U]$ such that $(v, [L, U]) \in h$
6.   **then** $h \leftarrow h - \{(v, [L, U])\} \cup \{(v, [L, U] \oplus_{nc} P(w))\};$
7.   **else** $h \leftarrow h \cup \{(v, P(w))\}; \}$
8. **for** each $(v, [L, U]) \in h$ **do** $\{$
9. $pr'' \leftarrow pr'' \cup \{(1, v, L, U)\}; \}$
10. **return** $pr'';$

---

[3] Although we use the same notation for an aggregate operator and its associated aggregate function, the reader may easily distinguish between these uses by checking the second argument – if this argument is a world (resp. PCS), then the mapping is an aggregate function (resp. aggregate operator).

[4] This aggregate function does not have to be one of the examples listed in Figure 4.

Example 10 (GPA). Consider the computation of $\mathbf{GPA}(\text{prices}, \otimes_{\text{prices}}, \mathbf{avg}_{\text{Price}})$. Here, for every $w \in W_{\text{prices}, \otimes_{\text{prices}}}$ where $v = \mathbf{avg}_{\text{Price}}(\text{prices}, w)$ is defined, $\mathbf{GPA}$ uses $P(w) = P(\text{prices}, \otimes_{\text{prices}}, w)$ to update the probability interval that h associates with v. Since $\mathbf{avg}_{\text{Price}}(\text{prices}, w)$ is only undefined when $w = \emptyset$, our call to $\mathbf{GPA}$ will iterate over every world $w \in W_{\text{prices}, \otimes_{\text{prices}}}$. Figure 5 shows how h is transformed during the execution of $\mathbf{GPA}(\text{prices}, \otimes_{\text{prices}}, \mathbf{avg}_{\text{Price}})$.

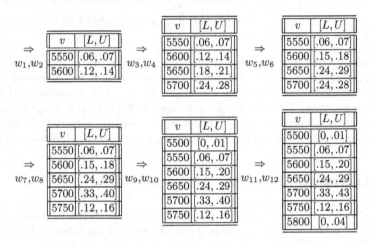

Fig. 5. Computation of $\mathbf{GPA}(\text{prices}, \otimes_{\text{prices}}, \mathbf{avg}_{\text{Price}})$

For example, after processing world w_4, h will contain a pair of the form $(agg(\text{prices}, w), P(w))$ for each $w \in \{w_1, w_2, w_3, w_4\}$. Since $\mathbf{avg}_{\text{Price}}(\text{prices}, w_5) = \mathbf{avg}_{\text{Price}}(\text{prices}, w_2) = 5600$, we replace the pair $(5600, P(w_2))$ in h with the pair $(5600, P(w_2) \oplus_{nc} P(w_5))$ in order to associate 5600 with the probability interval for $w_2 \vee w_5$. Similarly, $\mathbf{GPA}$ replaces the pair $(5650, P(w_3))$ in h with $(5650, P(w_3) \oplus_{nc} P(w_6))$. Finally, after processing world w_{12}, $\mathbf{GPA}$ copies the data in h to pr''.

The following theorem asserts that $\mathbf{GPA}$ satisfies the declarative semantics.

Theorem 1 (Correctness of GPA). $\mathbf{GPA}(pr, \otimes, agg) = agg(pr, \otimes)$.

5   Conclusions

Though there has been a substantial amount of work on probabilistic databases, there has been no work that we are aware of on defining and computing aggregate operators on such databases. In this paper, we have shown how the ProbView framework for probabilistic databases [12] can be extended to handle aggregate computations. We have described a linear programming based declarative semantics for aggregate queries, and developed a correct generic algorithm named $\mathbf{GPA}$ to handle such queries.

Our work builds on extensive work by other researchers in probabilistic databases. Cavallo and Pittarelli [2] pioneered probabilistic database research by proposing projection and join operators. The next major advance was due to Barbara et. al. [1] who proposed an algebra where probabilities of compound events can be precisely determined in terms of the probabilities of simpler events (an assumption that does not hold in many cases). They also made a set of conditional independence assumptions. Dey and Sarkar [5] proposed an elegant 1NF approach to handling probabilistic databases, introduced operators like conditionalization, and removed various assumptions in the works of previous authors. Later, Lakshmanan et. al. [12] proposed an algebra where users can specify in their query what probabilistic strategy (or strategies) should be used to parametrize the query. ProbView removed the independence assumption from previous works.

Acknowledgements. The authors were supported in part by ARL contract DAAL-0197K0135 and the CTA on Advanced Decision Architectures, by ARO contract DAAL-0197K0135, and by DARPA/RL contract F306029910552.

References

1. D. Barbara, H. Garcia-Molina, and D. Porter. (1992) The Management of Probabilistic Data, *IEEE Trans. on Knowledge and Data Engineering*, Vol. 4, pps 487–502.
2. R. Cavallo and M. Pittarelli. (1987) The Theory of Probabilistic Databases, in *Proc. VLDB'87*.
3. T.H. Cormen, C.E. Leiserson, and R.L. Rivest. (1992) *Introduction to Algorithms*, MIT Press, Cambridge.
4. A. Dekhtyar, R. Ross, and V.S. Subrahmanian, Probabilistic Temporal Databases, Part I: Algebra, *ACM Transactions on Database Systems*, Vol. 26, 1.
5. D. Dey and S. Sarkar. (1996) A Probabilistic Relational Model and Algebra, *ACM Transactions on Database Systems*, Vol. 21, 3, pps 339–369.
6. C. Dyreson and R. Snodgrass. (1998) Supporting Valid-Time Indeterminacy, *ACM Transactions on Database Systems*, Vol. 23, Nr. 1, pps 1–57.
7. T. Eiter, T. Lukasiewicz, and M. Walter. Extension of the relational algebra to probabilistic complex values. In *Proceedings of the International Symposium on Foundations of Information and Knowledge Systems (FoIKS 2000)*, Volume 1762 of *LNCS* (2000), pp. 94–115. Springer.
8. R. Fagin, J. Halpern, and N. Megiddo. (1990) A logic for reasoning about probabilities. *Information and Computation 87*, 78–128.
9. N.Fuhr and T. Rolleke. (1996) A probabilistic NF2 relational algebra for integrated information retrieval and database systems. *ACM Transactions on Information Systems*, *15*, 1, 32–66.
10. G. Kamberova and R. Bajcsy. (1998) Stereo Depth Estimation: the Confidence Interval Approach, *Proc. Intl. Conf. Computer Vision ICCV98*, Bombay, India, Jan. 1998
11. W. Kiessling, H. Thone, and U. Guntzer. (1992) Database Support for Problematic Knowledge, in *Proc. EDBT-92*, pp. 421–436, Springer LNCS Vol. 580.

12. V.S. Lakshmanan, N. Leone, R. Ross, and V.S. Subrahmanian. (1996) ProbView: A Flexible Probabilistic Database System. *ACM Transactions on Database Systems*, Vol. 22, Nr. 3, pp. 419–469.
13. V.S. Lakshmanan and F. Sadri. (1994) Modeling Uncertainty in Deductive Databases, in *Proc. Int. Conf. on Database Expert Systems and Applications, (DEXA'94)*, Lecture Notes in Computer Science, Vol. 856, Springer (1994), pp. 724-733.
14. V.S. Lakshmanan and F. Sadri. (1994) Probabilistic Deductive Databases, in *Proc. Int. Logic Programming Symp., (ILPS'94)*, MIT Press.
15. W. N. Street, O. L. Mangasarian, and W.H. Wolberg. (1995) An inductive learning approach to prognostic prediction. *Proceedings of the Twelfth International Conference on Machine Learning*, A. Prieditis and S. Russell, eds., pages 522-530, Morgan Kaufmann, 1995.
16. J.D. Ullman. (1989) *Principles of Database and Knowledge Base Systems*, Computer Science Press, 1989.

Samples for Understanding Data-Semantics in Relations[*]

Fabien De Marchi[1], Stéphane Lopes[2], and Jean-Marc Petit[1]

[1] Laboratoire LIMOS, CNRS UMR 2239
Université Blaise Pascal - Clermont-Ferrand II,
24 avenue des Landais 63 177 Aubière cedex, France
{demarchi,jmpetit}@math.univ-bpclermont.fr
[2] Laboratoire PRISM, CNRS FRE 8636
45, avenue des Etats-Unis, 78035 Versailles Cedex, France
stephane.lopes@prism.uvsq.fr

Abstract. From statistics, sampling technics were proposed and some of them were proved to be very useful in many database applications. Rather surprisingly, it seems these works never consider the preservation of data semantics. Since functional dependencies (FDs) are known to convey most of data semantics, an interesting issue would be to construct samples preserving FDs satisfied in existing relations.

To cope with this issue, we propose in this paper to define Informative Armstrong Relations (IARs); a relation s is an IAR for a relation r if s is a subset of r and if FDs satisfied in s are exactly the same as FDs satisfied in r. Such a relation always exists since r is obviously an IAR for itself; moreover we shall point out that small IARs with interesting bounded sizes exist. Experiments on relations available in the KDD archive were conducted and highlight the interest of IARs to sample existing relations.

1 Introduction

Armstrong relations, introduced (and studied) in [Arm74,Fag82b], are example relations satisfying exactly a given set of functional dependencies (FDs). They are an alternative representation of a set of FDs and can reveal both the existence and the nonexistence of FDs for a given relation [Fag82a,MR86]. Up to now, they are mainly proven to be useful in database design to provide feedbacks to the designer [SM79,MR86].

Starting from a set of FDs, algorithms for computing Armstrong relations are given in [MR86,DT95]. These algorithms first compute either closed sets (or generators of closed set) from a set of FDs, and then Armstrong relations are built.

Instead of starting from a set of FDs, Armstrong relations can also be inferred from an existing relation [MR86,MR94,DT95,LPL00], w.r.t. the set of FDs satisfied in this relation. In this case, experimental results show that the size of these

---

[*] This work is partially supported by the AS CNRS-STIC "Data Mining"

M.-S. Hacid et al. (Eds.): ISMIS 2002, LNAI 2366, pp. 565–573, 2002.

Armstrong relations can be smaller of several orders of magnitude with respect to the size of the initial relation. For instance, from a relation with 20 attributes and 100,000 tuples, an Armstrong relation with 116 tuples can be constructed [LPL00]. Nevertheless, even if values of Armstrong relations are taken in the initial relation, tuples can be completely fictitious: they may not represent "real word entities" (cf. example 1 in Section 3.1). Moreover, the existence of such relations depends on the number of distinct values of each column in the initial relation. In some cases, such Armstrong relations can not be computed [LPL00].

The main contribution of this paper is to define and investigate a new form of Armstrong relation, called Informative Armstrong Relation (IAR). Given a relation r, an Informative Armstrong Relation for r is an Armstrong relation for the set of FDs holding in r, that is also a subset of r. Obviously, such a relation always exists since any relation r is an Informative Armstrong Relation for itself. We show that we can always compute IARs with an interesting bounded size. Then, we give a heuristic to construct "small" IAR $\bar{r}$ for a given relation r.

Experiments on real-life relations from the KDD Archive [Bay99] have been performed. They point out that IARs are easily obtained from existing relations and that their sizes are very small.

Paper outline. In Section 2 we give some definitions and results in relational database theory. Section 3 deals with Armstrong relations from relations; We define the notion of Informative Armstrong Relation, and present our approach for constructing small Informative Armstrong Relations. Section 4 shows experimental results on real-life relations, and we conclude in Section 5.

2   Preliminaries

We assume the reader is familiar with basic concepts from relational database theory, such as relational schema, domains, tuples and relations (see e.g. [LL99]). We just recall here concepts related to functional dependencies theory, which are useful for the understanding of the paper.

A *functional dependency* over R is an expression $X \rightarrow A$ where $X \subseteq R$ and $A \in R$. A functional dependency $X \rightarrow A$ *holds* in a relation r (denoted by $r \models X \rightarrow A$) if and only if $\forall t_i, t_j \in r, t_i[X] = t_j[X] \Rightarrow t_i[A] = t_j[A]$. We denote by F_r the set of all functional dependencies that hold in r.

Let F be a set of functional dependencies over R. A functional dependency $X \rightarrow A$ is said to be logically implied by F, denoted $F \models X \rightarrow A$, iff $\forall r$ over R, if $r \models F$ then $r \models X \rightarrow A$.

The closure of X with respect to F, denoted by X_F^+, is the set of attributes $A \in R$ such that $X \rightarrow A$ is logically implied by F: $X_F^+ = \{A \in R \mid F \models X \rightarrow A\}$. A set $X \subseteq R$ is *closed* if and only if $X_F^+ = X$. We note $CL(F)$ the family of closed sets induced by F and by $GEN(F)$ the unique minimal subfamily of generators in $CL(F)$ such that each member of $CL(F)$ can be expressed as an intersection of sets in $GEN(F)$ [AD80].

Let t_i and t_j be tuples and X an attribute set. The tuples t_i and t_j *agree* on X if $t_i[X] = t_j[X]$ and, for any attribute $A \in R \setminus X$, $t_i[A] \neq t_j[A]$. The *agree set* of t_i and t_j is defined as follows: $ag(t_i, t_j) = \{A \in R \mid t_i[A] = t_j[A]\}$. If r is a relation, $ag(r) = \{ag(t_i, t_j) \mid t_i, t_j \in r, t_i \neq t_j\}$.

Given a set F of FDs over a schema R, a maximal set is an attribute set $X \subseteq R$ which, for some attribute A, is the largest possible set not determining A w.r.t. F. We denote by $max(F, A)$ the set of maximal sets for A w.r.t. F: $max(F, A) = \{X \subseteq R \mid F \not\models X \to A \text{ and } \forall Y \subseteq R, X \subset Y, F \models Y \to A\}$; and $MAX(F) = \bigcup_{A \in R} max(F, A)$.

In fact, maximal sets and generators denote the same sets [MR86]: $MAX(F) = GEN(F)$.

From agree sets, a characterization of maximal sets for a given attribute A is given in [LPL00]: $max(F_r, A) = Max_{\subseteq}\{X \in ag(r) \mid A \notin X\}$

Given a set F of functional dependencies, a relation r is an Armstrong relation for F iff F_r and F are equal. A necessary and sufficient condition for that is $MAX(F) \subseteq ag(r) \subseteq CL(F)$ [BDFS84]. Lower bound for the size of r is $\lceil \frac{1+\sqrt{1+8|MAX(F)|}}{2} \rceil$ [BDFS84].

3   Armstrong Relations from Relations

Instead of starting from a set of FDs, Armstrong relations can be constructed from FDs holding in an existing relation. In the sequel, in order to alleviate notations, we will speak about *Armstrong relation for a relation r* being understood that we mean *Armstrong relation for the FDs that hold in r*.

Before introducing Informative Armstrong Relations, we shall motivate their interest w.r.t. related contributions [MR86,DT95,LPL00].

3.1   Related Contributions

Given a relation r, one approach consists in discovering FDs that hold in r, i.e. F_r, apply existing algorithms to obtain maximal sets and hence build an Armstrong relation [MR86,DT95]. To avoid the cost of computing FDs, a better approach consists in directly computing maximal sets from r, and then computing Armstrong relations for r. Such an algorithm is quadratic in the size of the input relation. This complexity leads from the computation of $MAX(F_r)$, which can be done via agree sets computation (see section 2). Agree sets are known to be a data centric step of many algorithms: they can be calculated either from *stripped partitions* [LPL00] or from SQL queries [LPL01].

One of the drawbacks with these Armstrong relations is that they do not always exist since one needs to have enough values in each column. An existence condition is given in [LPL00]: $\forall A \in R, |\pi_A(r)| \geq |\{X \in MAX(F_r) \mid A \notin X\}| + 1$.

Example 1. Let $EMPLOYEE$ be the following relation:

Table 1. $EMPLOYEE$ relation

No	empnum (A)	name (B)	age (C)	role (D)	salary (E)
t_1	17	Wilson	18	clerk	2000
t_2	29	King	45	boss	10000
t_3	28	Smith	30	workman	2200
t_4	15	Smith	30	salesman	3000
t_5	21	James	40	technician	2500
t_6	25	James	34	secretary	2500
t_7	40	Smith	32	salesman	2200
t_8	12	King	45	manager	6000
t_9	19	Wilson	48	clerk	4000

From this relation, agree sets are $\{BE, BC, BD, \emptyset\}$. Maximal sets can then be extracted, according to their characterization from agree sets (cf. Section 2): $MAX(F_{EMPLOYEE}) = \{BE, BC, BD, \emptyset\}$. Existing algorithms could produce the following Armstrong relation:

Table 2. $\overline{EMPLOYEE}$ relation

empnum (A)	name (B)	age (C)	role (D)	salary (E)
17	Wilson	18	clerk	2000
29	Wilson	45	boss	2000
28	Wilson	18	workman	10000
15	Wilson	30	clerk	2200
21	King	40	salesman	3000

It is worth noting that several tuples in $\overline{EMPLOYEE}$ do not make sense in "real world". For example, no boss named Wilson exists in $EMPLOYEE$ (second tuple). Moreover, this boss earns five times less money than a 18 years old workman (third tuple). This kind of situation arises frequently in practice, since values are inserted randomly into a given tuple when such Armstrong relations are built.

As a consequence, the overall interest of these Armstrong relations is limited. We now define a new form of Armstrong relations which copes with these limitations.

3.2   Informative Armstrong Relations

Informative Armstrong Relations are defined as follows:

Definition 1. *Let R be a relational schema, and r a relation over R. An Informative Armstrong Relation (IAR) $\overline{r}$ for r is defined by:*
- $\overline{r}$ is an Armstrong relation for r;
- $\overline{r} \subseteq r$.

The intuition underlying this definition is to keep a subset of a relation, with an equivalent set of FDs. Thus, this kind of Armstrong Relations will be really informative since their tuples will exist in the initial relation. Such a relation always exists, since any relation is an Informative Armstrong Relation for itself; an interesting challenge is now to investigate IARs with few tuples.

The next theorem gives a simple necessary and sufficient condition for a relation to be an Informative Armstrong Relation:

Theorem 1. *Let R be a relation schema, and r a relation over R. A subset $\bar{r}$ of r is an IAR for r if and only if:*
$$\forall X \in MAX(F_r), \exists(t_1, t_2) \in \bar{r} \text{ such that } ag(t_1, t_2) = X.$$

Proof. ($\Leftarrow$) Since $\bar{r} \subseteq r$, it is just enough to show that $\bar{r}$ is an Armstrong relation for F_r, i.e.: $MAX(F_r) \subseteq ag(\bar{r}) \subseteq CL(F_r)$.
This result can be reached in the following way:
 1) $MAX(F_r) \subseteq ag(\bar{r})$:
 Let $X \in MAX(F_r)$. Then $\exists t_i, t_j \in \bar{r}$ such that $ag(t_i, t_j) = X$. Thus $X \in ag(\bar{r})$.
 2) $ag(\bar{r}) \subseteq CL(F_r)$:
 By construction, $\bar{r} \subseteq r$. Then, obviously, $ag(\bar{r}) \subseteq ag(r)$. As $ag(r) \subseteq CL(F_r)$, the result follows.

($\Rightarrow$) $\bar{r}$ is an Armstrong relation for F_r, so F_r and $F_{\bar{r}}$ are equivalent, and thus $MAX(F_r) = MAX(F_{\bar{r}})$. Since $MAX(F_{\bar{r}}) \subseteq ag(\bar{r})$, we have the wondering property which concludes the proof.

Informally, $\bar{r}$ must have at least one couple of tuple that agree on each maximal set of F_r. This property leads to the existence of IARs with a size (number of tuples) bounded as follows:

Corollary 1. *Let R be a relation schema, and r a relation over R. At least one Informative Armstrong Relation $\bar{r}$ for r exists such that:*

 - $|\bar{r}| \geq \lceil \frac{1+\sqrt{1+8\times M}}{2} \rceil$ *and*
 - $|\bar{r}| \leq Min(2 \times M, |r|)$ *where* $M = |MAX(F_r)|$.

The upper bound follows since by construction there is in $\bar{r}$ exactly two tuples in agreement on each element of $MAX(F_r)$. The lower bound given in [BDFS84] remains obviously true in that case.

It is worth noting that $2 \times M$ is less than $|r|$ of several orders of magnitude in practice, which can be of great importance for the understandability of such relations.

In the sequel, we call "small" IAR an IAR having a size bounded by corollary 1. Although our problem is more constrained, the size of small IARs is of the same order as the size of other Armstrong relations presented so far [BDFS84, MR86,DT95,LPL00], i.e. $2 \times |MAX(F_r)|$ instead of $|MAX(F_r)| + 1$.

A naive algorithm (algorithm 1) can be devised from theorem 1 and corollary 1, for computing a small IAR given an input relation r. This algorithm is polynomial in the size of r (being understood that the number of maximal sets can be exponential in the number of attributes of R [BDFS84]). This complexity comes from maximal sets and hence agree sets computation (line 1).

Algorithm 1 Informative Armstrong relation

Input: a relation r
Output: an informative Armstrong relation $\bar{r}$ for r;
1: $C = MAX(F_r)$;
2: $\bar{r} = \emptyset$
3: **for all** $X \in C$ **do**
4:     let $t_1, t_2 \in r$ s.t. $ag(t_1, t_2) = X$;
5:     $\bar{r} = \bar{r} \cup \{t_1\} \cup \{t_2\}$
6: **end for**
7: return $\bar{r}$.

Example 2. From relation *EMPLOYEE* of example 1, Algorithm 1 could give the following IAR:

Table 3. $\overline{EMPLOYEE}$ relation

empnum (A)	name (B)	age (C)	role (D)	salary (E)
17	Wilson	18	clerk	2000
28	Smith	30	workman	2200
15	Smith	30	salesman	3000
40	Smith	32	salesman	2200

Note that drawbacks mentioned in example 1 no longer exist.

For a maximal set, Algorithm 1 chooses a couple of tuples "randomly" among possible candidates. In general, many possible couples of tuples can be taken for each maximal set, and then many small Informative Armstrong Relations can be computed for a given relation, as mentioned in the next corollary:

Corollary 2. *Given a relation r, the number n of small IARs $\bar{r}$ for r is bounded by:*

$$0 < n \le \prod_{X \in MAX(F_r)} |\{(t_1, t_2) \mid t_1, t_2 \in r, ag(t_1, t_2) = X\}|$$

Note that the upper bound given in this corollary may be very high in practice. Consider for instance a relation with 100 maximal sets. Suppose there is on each maximal set two couples of tuples in agreement, then we would have 2^{100} possibilities to compute an IAR for this relation! Since all these solutions do not have the same size, an interesting challenge would be to compute the smallest one. We show in [DLP01] that this problem is NP-complete.

3.3   Generating Small Informative Armstrong Relations

The problem of computing minimal IARs could be designed and studied, for example, using technics for Linear Programming or Constraint Satisfaction Problem (CSP). Obviously, their study goes beyond the scope of this paper. Nevertheless, we just sketch here an "home-made" heuristic from which we have obtained preliminary results (cf. next section).

Basically, we need to assign a couple of tuples for each maximal set and insert it in the IAR being built. Our heuristic can be formulated as follows: "give the priority to maximal sets whose number of candidate couples is small".

Therefore, we start with mandatory couples, i.e. maximal sets which have only one couple. Then, we continue with maximal sets which have two possible couples, and so on. For each maximal set, we try to choose one couple of tuples which is already in the IAR in construction. If no such couple exists, we try to choose one couple with one tuple in the IAR being built, or finally both the two tuples are taken in the initial relation. When several couples are eligible, one is chosen randomly.

In fact, at each step we take the best solution regarding what is already done. Clearly, this method is not exact, since we do not consider consequences of each choice for future steps. In other words, no backtracking is performed.

4   Experiments

The Movies database. The relations we consider are part of the *UCI KDD Archive*, from the *Movies* database [Bay99]. This data set contains a list of over 10000 films. There is information on actors, casts, directors, producers, studios, etc.

The central relation MOVIES (12 attributes, 11405 tuples) is a list of movies. The actors for those movies are listed with their roles in the relation CASTS (7 attributes, 45442 tuples). More information about individual actors is in ACTORS (12 attributes, 6728 tuples). All directors in MOVIES are listed in the relation PEOPLE (11 attributes, 3304 tuples). REMAKES (7 attributes, 1188 tuples) links movies that were copied to a substantial extent from each other. STUDIOS (9 attributes, 195 tuples) provides some information about studios shown in MOVIES. Note that NULL values are common.

This database has been imported in Oracle 8 using SQL*Loader.

Experimental results. Experimental results are reported in table 4. The second column shows the number of maximal sets for each relation. In the third column, the number of possibilities for building small IARs (according to corollary 2) is given. These results make impossible, in general, an exhaustive search of a minimal IAR.

From the number of maximal sets, we can also compute lower and upper bounds for small IAR sizes, as given in theorem 1. These bounds are reported in columns 4 and 5 of table 4. It is very interesting to observe that upper bounds are very small w.r.t. sizes of initial relations; for instance, the relation CASTS has 45442 tuples, and any small IAR for this relation have a size less or equal to 14 tuples.

An other important remark is the gap between lower bounds and upper bounds: for example, small IARs for ACTORS have a size between 16 and 164.

We think these lower bounds are not really appropriated, because they only depend on the number of maximal sets in a relation; the formula corresponds to very specific cases. Better lower bounds should also depend on the *structure* of maximal sets. To the best of our knowledge, there is no more precise result about this subject.

Finally, the heuristic sketched in section 3.3 was implemented and ran against these relations; results are reported in column 6 of table 4. Sizes of obtained IARs are always smaller than upper bounds while being always very far from lower bounds. We have already mentioned the size of minimal IARs is unknown: these results corroborate the intuition that the existing lower bound is not appropriated in practice.

Table 4. Experimental results

Name	$|MAX(F_r)|$	nb of 'small' IARs	l. bound	u. bound	heuristic
Actors	82	$\simeq 2.8 \times 10^{27}$	16	164	145
Casts	7	$\simeq 20 \times 10^9$	7	14	13
Movies	44	$\simeq 5.6 \times 10^{10}$	13	88	84
People	44	$\simeq 6.7 \times 10^{15}$	11	88	79
Remakes	9	$\simeq 71 \times 10^6$	7	18	17
Studios	19	27 648	8	38	33

5   Conclusion

Given a relation, we have introduced the concept of *Informative Armstrong Relations* whose main interest w.r.t. existing contributions is to be a "subset" of the initial relation. We have shown that, whatever the starting relation is, we can always build an Informative Armstrong Relation of size bounded by two times the number of maximal sets. In practice, our experiments show that this upper bound is very small w.r.t. initial relation size. Due to the NP-completeness of computing IARs with minimal sizes, an "home made" heuristic is proposed to try to compute small IARs.

This work takes place in an ongoing project devoted to the logical tuning of existing databases (see e.g. [LPL00,DLP02,LPT02]). We use data mining techniques to discover functional and inclusion dependencies, Armstrong relations and some other related concepts in relational database.

A natural extension of the work presented in this paper is to consider a database from which *minimal informative Armstrong databases* could be inferred w.r.t. both functional and inclusion dependencies satisfied in the database.

References

[AD80]   William Ward Armstrong and Claude Delobel. Decomposition and functional dependencies in relations. *ACM Transactions on Database Systems*, 5(4):404–430, 1980.

[Arm74]   W. W. Armstrong. Dependency structures of database relationships. In Jack L. Rosenfeld, editor, *International Federation for Information Processing, Amsterdam*, pages 580–583, 1974.

[Bay99]   S. D. Bay. The UCI KDD Archive [http://kdd.ics.uci.edu]. Technical report, Irvine, CA: University of California, Department of Information and Computer Science, 1999.

[BDFS84] C. Beeri, M. Dowd, R. Fagin, and R. Statman. On the structure of Armstrong relations for functional dependencies. *Journal of the ACM*, 31(1):30–56, January 1984.

[DLP01]   F. De Marchi, S. Lopes, and J-M. Petit. Informative armstrong relations: Application to database analysis. In *Bases de Données Avancées, Agadir, Maroc*, October 2001.

[DLP02]   F. De Marchi, S. Lopes, and J.-M. Petit. Efficient algorithms for mining inclusion dependenciess. In *International Conference on Extending Database Technology, Prague, Czech Republic*. To appear, 2002.

[DT95]   J. Demetrovics and V.D. Thi. Some remarks on generating armstrong and inferring functional dependencies relation. *Acta Cybernetica*, 12(2):167–180, 1995.

[Fag82a] R. Fagin. Armstrong databases. In *IBM Symposium on Mathematical Foundations of Computer Science, Kanagawa, Japan*, 1982.

[Fag82b] R. Fagin. Horn clauses and database dependencies. *Journal of the ACM*, 99(4):952–985, 1982.

[LL99]   M. Levene and G. Loizou. *A Guided Tour of Relational Databases and Beyond*. Springer, 1999.

[LPL00]   S. Lopes, J.-M. Petit, and L. Lakhal. Efficient discovery of functional dependencies and armstrong relations. In Carlo Zaniolo, Peter C. Lockemann, Marc H. Scholl, and Torsten Grust, editors, *International Conference on Extending Database Technology, Konstanz, Germany*, volume 1777 of *Lecture Notes in Computer Science*, pages 350–364. Springer, 2000.

[LPL01]   S. Lopes, J-M. Petit, and L. Lakhal. A framework for understanding existing databases. In Michel E. Adiba, Christine Collet, and Bipin C. Desai, editors, *International Database Engineering and Applications Symposium, Grenoble, France*, pages 330–338, July 2001.

[LPT02]   S. Lopes, J-M. Petit, and F. Toumani. Discovering interesting inclusion dependencies: Application to logical database tuning. *Information System*, 17(1):1–19, 2002.

[MR86]   H. Mannila and K.-J. Räihä. Design by example: An application of armstrong relations. *Journal of Computer and System Sciences*, 63(2):126–141, October 1986.

[MR94]   H. Mannila and K. J. Räihä. Algorithms for inferring functional-dependencies from relations. *Data and Knowledge Engineering*, 12(1):83–99, 1994.

[SM79]   A. M. Silva and M. A. Melkanoff. A method for helping discover the dependencies of a relation. In Hervé Gallaire, Jean-Marie Nicolas, and Jack Minker, editors, *Advances in Data Base Theory*, pages 115–133, Toulouse, France, 1979.

Cooperation of Multiple Strategies for Automated Learning in Complex Environments

Floriana Esposito, Stefano Ferilli, Nicola Fanizzi,
Teresa Maria Altomare Basile, and Nicola Di Mauro

Dipartimento di Informatica
Università di Bari
via E. Orabona, 4 - 70125 Bari - Italia
{esposito, ferilli, fanizzi, basile, nicodimauro}@di.uniba.it

Abstract. This work presents a new version of the incremental learning system INTHELEX, whose multistrategy learning capabilities have been further enhanced. To improve effectiveness and efficiency of the learning process, pure induction and abduction have been augmented with abstraction and deduction. Some results proving the benefits that the addition of each strategy can bring are also reported. INTHELEX will be the learning component in the architecture of the EU project COLLATE, dealing with cultural heritage documents.

1 Introduction

Automatic revision of logic theories, that empirical results have shown to yield more accurate definitions from fewer examples than pure induction, is a complex and computationally expensive task. In fact, most systems for theory revision deal with propositional logic and try to modify an existing incorrect theory to fit a set of pre-classified training examples. Other systems revise first-order theories, to overcome the expressive and representational limits showed by the propositional ones. Most of them try to limit the search space by exploiting information and, generally, require a wide, although incomplete, domain theory or a deep knowledge acquired from the user. Some others strongly rely on the interaction with the user, or adopt sophisticated search strategies or more informative search structures. Others do not allow negative information items to be expressed in the theories because of computational complexity considerations. Many of such systems adopt multi-strategy approaches integrating several types of inferential mechanisms. Such considerations, plus the need of testing theoretical results on the Object Identity paradigm [6] in practice, led to the design and implementation of INTHELEX. Its most characterizing features (compared in [5] with similar systems) are in its incremental nature, in the reduced need of a deep background knowledge, in the exploitation of negative information and in the peculiar bias on the generalization model, which reduces the search space and does not limit the expressive power of the adopted representation language.

The following Section presents the inductive core of INTHELEX; Section 3 shows how other reasoning strategies were added and provides some results; Section 4 introduces the EU project COLLATE; Section 5 draws some conclusions.

M.-S. Hacid et al. (Eds.): ISMIS 2002, LNAI 2366, pp. 574–582, 2002.

2 INTHELEX: The Inductive Core

INTHELEX (INcremental THEory Learner from EXamples) is a learning system for the induction of *hierarchical* logic theories from examples [5]: it is *fully incremental* (in addition to the possibility of refining a previously generated version of the theory, learning can also start from an empty theory); it is based on the *Object Identity assumption* (terms, even variables, denoted by different names within a formula must refer to different objects)[1]; it learns theories expressed as sets of Datalog^{OI} clauses [12] from positive and negative examples; it can learn simultaneously *multiple concepts*, possibly related to each other according to a given hierarchy (recursion is not allowed); it retains all the processed examples, so to guarantee validity of the learned theories on all of them; it is a *closed loop* learning system (i.e. a system in which feedback on performance is used to activate the theory revision phase [1]).

Incremental learning is necessary when either incomplete information is available at the time of initial theory generation, or the nature of the concepts evolves dynamically. Both cases are very frequent in real-world situations, hence the need for incremental models to complete and support the classical batch ones, that perform learning in one step and thus require the whole set of observations to be available since the beginning. INTHELEX incorporates two refinement operators, one for generalizing hypotheses that reject positive examples, and the other for specializing hypotheses that explain negative examples. It exploits a (possibly empty) previous theory, a graph describing the dependence relationships among concepts, and a historical memory of all the past examples that led to the current theory. Whenever a new example is taken into account, it is stored in such a repository and the current theory is checked against it.

If it is positive and not covered, generalization must be performed. One of the clauses defining the concept the example refers to is chosen by the system for generalization. The lgg$_{OI}$ of this clause and the example is computed [12], by taking into account a number of parameters that restrict the search space according to the degree of generalization to be obtained and the computational budget allowed. If one of the lgg$_{OI}$'s is consistent with all the past negative examples, then it replaces the chosen clause in the theory, or else a new clause is chosen to compute the lgg$_{OI}$. If no clause can be generalized in a consistent way, the system checks if the example itself, with the constants properly turned into variables, is consistent with the past negative examples. If so, such a clause is added to the theory, or else the example itself is added as an exception.

If the example is negative and covered, specialization is needed. Among the theory clauses occurring in the SLD-derivation of the example, INTHELEX tries to specialize one at the lowest possible level in the dependency graph by adding to it one (or more) positive literal(s), which characterize all the past positive examples and can discriminate them from the current negative one. Again, parameters that bound the search for the set of literals to be added are considered.

---

[1] This often corresponds to human intuition, while allowing the search space to fulfill nice properties affecting efficiency and effectiveness of the learning process [12].

In case of failure on all of the clauses in the derivation, the system tries to add the negation of a literal, that is able to discriminate the negative example from all the past positive ones, to the clause related to the concept the example is an instance of. If this fails too, the negative example is added to the theory as an exception. New incoming observations are always checked against the exceptions before applying the rules that define the concept they refer to.

3   Multistrategy Learning

While at the beginning ML research focused on single-strategy methods that apply a primary type of inference and/or computational mechanism, more recently the limitations of these methods led to exploit/combine various, different and complementary learning strategies together. This mimes the typical ability of humans to apply a great variety of learning strategies depending on the particular situation and problem faced. A theoretical framework for integrating different learning strategies is the Inferential Learning Theory [10].

Another peculiarity in INTHELEX is the integration of multistrategy operators that may help in the solution of the theory revision problem by preprocessing the incoming information [6]. Namely, deduction is exploited to fill observations with information that is not explicitly stated, but is implicit in their description, and hence refers to the possibility of better representing the examples and, consequently, the inferred theories. Conversely, abduction aims at completing possibly partial information in the examples (adding more details), whereas abstraction removes superfluous details from the description of both the examples and the theory. Thus, even if with opposite perspectives, both aim at reducing the computational effort required to learn a correct theory with respect to the incoming examples. More details on the theoretical foundations of the cooperation of these strategies in our environment are given in [3], whereas this paper focuses on their implementation and cooperation into a single system.

3.1   Deduction

INTHELEX requires the observations to be expressed only in terms of the set of predicates that make up the description language for the given learning problem. To ensure uniformity of the example descriptions, such predicates have no definition. Nevertheless, since the system is able to handle a hierarchy of concepts, combinations of these predicates might identify higher level concepts that is worth adding to the descriptions in order to raise their semantic level. For this reason, INTHELEX implements a saturation operator that exploits deduction to recognize such concepts and explicitly add them to the examples description.

The system can be provided with a Background Knowledge, supposed to be correct and hence not modifiable, containing (complete or partial) definitions in the same format as the theory rules. This way, any time a new example is considered, a preliminary saturation phase can be performed, that adds the higher level concepts whose presence can be deduced from such rules by subsumption and/or resolution. In particular, the generalization model of implication under Object Identity is exploited [4]. Given a set of terms T, a substitution σ is an *OI-substitution w.r.t.* T iff $\forall t_1, t_2 \in T : t_1 \neq t_2$ implies $t_1\sigma \neq t_2\sigma$. In this setting, an interpretation I is an *OI-model* for the clause C iff for all ground OI-substitutions γ it holds that $I \cap C\gamma \neq \emptyset$. A set of clauses Σ *OI-implies* a clause C ($\Sigma \models_{OI} C$) iff all OI-models I for Σ are also OI-models for C. A sound and refutation-complete proof-theory has been built upon this semantics, by defining notions of OI-unifiers, OI-resolution and OI-derivation ($\vdash_{OI}$). It holds that:

Theorem 1 (Subsumption Theorem). *Let Σ be a finite set of clauses and C be a clause. Then $\Sigma \models_{OI} C$ iff there exists a clause D such that $\Sigma \vdash_{OI} D$ and D θ_{OI}-subsumes C.*

Differently from abstraction (see next), all the specific information used by saturation is left in the example description. Hence, it is preserved in the learning process until other evidence reveals it is not significant for the concept definition, which is a more cautious behaviour. This is fundamental if some concept to be learnt are related, since their definition could not be stable yet, and hence one cannot afford to drop the source from which deductions were made in order to be able to recover from deductions made because of wrong rules.

3.2 Abduction

Induction and abduction are, both, important strategies to perform hypothetical reasoning (i.e., inferences from incomplete information). Induction means inferring from a certain number of significant observations regularities and laws valid for the whole population. Abduction was defined by Peirce as hypothesizing some facts that, together with a given theory, could explain a given observation.

According to the framework proposed in [8], an *abductive logic theory* is made up by a normal logic program [9], a set of *abducibles* and a set of *integrity constraints* (each corresponding to a combination of literals that is not allowed to occur). Abducibles are the predicates about which assumptions (*abductions*) can be made: They carry all the incompleteness of the domain (if it were possible to complete these predicates then the theory would be correctly described). Integrity constraints provide indirect information about them and, since several explanations may hold for this problem setting, are also exploited to encode preference criteria for selecting the best ones. The proof procedure implemented in INTHELEX starts from a goal and a set of initial assumptions and results in a set of consistent hypotheses (abduced literals) by intertwining *abductive* and *consistency derivations*. Intuitively, an abductive derivation is the standard Logic Programming derivation suitably extended in order to consider abducibles. As soon as an abducible atom δ is encountered, it is added to the current set of hypotheses, provided that any integrity constraint containing δ is satisfied. This is checked by starting a consistency derivation. Every integrity constraint containing δ is considered satisfied if the goal obtained by removing δ from it fails. In the consistency derivation, when an abducible is encountered, an abductive derivation for its complement is started in order to prove its falsity.

An experiment was run to test if and how much the addition of abduction could improve the learning process. It aimed at learning definitions for a class of paper documents starting from the empty theory. The learning set consisted of 11 positive and 11 negative examples; the test set for performance evaluation was composed of 6 positive and 9 negative examples. Incomplete documents were described by about 30 literals, complete ones by about 100 literals. The description language included predicates concerning the size, type and relative position of the layout blocks. Running the system with abduction not enabled, the resulting theory was made up of 2 clauses (including 10 and 14 literals, respectively), obtained through 6 successive generalizations. The predictive accuracy of such a theory on the test set was 86%. In order to exploit abduction, all the basic predicates in the description language were considered as abducibles, while integrity constraints expressed the mutual exclusion among layout block sizes, types and positions, and the non-reflexivity of the relative positions among blocks. Abduction makes sense in this environment since the absence of a layout block in a document could be due to the writer not fulfilling the style requirements, and not to the insignificance of that block to a correct definition. In other words, a block should not be drop from the definition just because a few examples miss it; conversely, integrity constraints are in charge of avoiding that superfluous blocks that are found in the first few examples introduce unnecessary blocks that can be always abduced in the future. The resulting theory was now made up of just 1 clause of 18 literals, obtained through only 2 generalizations and 7 abductions. This means that in some cases abduction succeeded in covering the examples without firing the refinement operators, and hence the system was able to characterize the target concept by means of less clauses. Again, an 86% accuracy was reached, that grew up to 100% if allowing INTHELEX to exploit abduction also when evaluating the documents in the test set.

3.3 Abstraction

Abstraction is a pervasive activity in human perception and reasoning. When we are interested in the role it plays in ML, inductive inference must be taken into account as well. The exploitation of abstraction concerns the shift from the language in which the theory is described to a higher level one.

According to the framework proposed in ([14]), concept representation deals with entities belonging to three different levels. Concrete objects reside in the *world* W, but any observer's access to it is mediated by his *perception* of it $P(W)$. To be available over time, these stimuli must be memorized in an organized *structure* S, i.e. an *extensional* representation of the perceived world. Finally, to reason about the perceived world and communicate with other agents, a *language* L is needed, that describes it *intensionally*. If we assume that $P(W)$ is the source of information, that is recorded into S and then described by L, modifications to the structure and language are just a consequence of differences in the perception of the world (due, e.g., to the medium used and the focus-of-attention). Thus, abstraction takes place at the world-perception level by means of a set of operators, and then propagates to higher levels, where it is possible to identify operators corresponding to the previous ones. An abstraction theory contains information for performing the shift specified by the abstraction operators. In INTHELEX, it is assumed that the abstraction theory is already given (i.e. it has not to be learned by the system), and that the system automatically applies it to the learning problem at hand before processing the examples. The implemented abstraction operators allow the system to replace a number of components by a compound object, to decrease the granularity of a set of values, to ignore whole objects or just part of their features, and to neglect the number of occurrences of some kind of object.

The effectiveness of the abstraction operator introduced in INTHELEX was tested on the problem of Text Categorization [11], in order to infer rules for recognizing the subject of a document. Natural language is particularly suitable for abstraction, owing to the presence of many terms that are synonyms or whose meaning differs just slightly, since without binding them onto a common concept it would be impossible for an automatic learning system to grasp the similarities between two lexically different sentences. In order to obtain, from raw text, the structured representations of sentences that can be expressed in the input language required by the symbolic learner, a parser was used as a pre-processor. In the formal representation of texts, we used descriptors expressing the logical/grammatical role and the stem of the words in a sentence.

Experiments were run on the documents used for abduction, concerning foreign commerce. One aimed at learning the concept of "import". Starting from the empty theory, INTHELEX was fed with a total of 67 examples, 39 positive (not all explicitly using verb 'to import') and 28 negative, and yielded a theory composed by 9 clauses. Some of them were only slightly different, considering that: 'enterprise', 'society', 'firm' and 'agency' all can be seen as instances of the concept '*company*'; 'provider' and 'distributor' play the same role (let us call it '*providing_role*'); 'to look for' and 'to be interested in' are almost synonyms (and hence may be grouped in one category, say '*interest_cat*'); 'to buy' and 'to import' bear more or less the same meaning of acquiring something ('*acquisition_cat*'). Exploiting such an ontological information as an abstraction theory results in a theory made up of just 3 rules (67% savings), thus confirming that the use of abstraction improves compactness and readability. Another experiment, aimed at learning the concept of "specialization" (of someone in some field), confirmed the above findings. The system was run on 40 examples, 24 positive and 16 negative. The resulting theory, originally made up of 5 clauses, by exploiting abstraction was reduced to 2 rules (60% savings).

4   The COLLATE Project

Many important historic and cultural sources, which constitute a major part of our cultural heritage, are fragile and distributed in various archives, which causes severe problems to full access, knowledge and usage. Moreover, many informal and non-institutional contacts between archives constitute specific professional communities, which today still lack effective and efficient technological

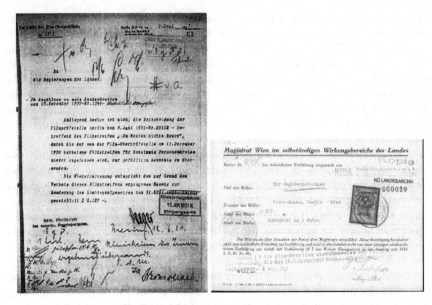

Fig. 1. Sample COLLATE documents

support for cooperative and collaborative knowledge working. The IST-1999-20882 project COLLATE (Collaboratory for Annotation, Indexing and Retrieval of Digitized Historical Archive Material) aims at developing a WWW-based *collaboratory* [7] for archives, researchers and end-users working with digitized historic/cultural material (URL: http://www.collate.de).

Though the developed tools and interfaces are generic, the chosen sample domain concerns historic film documentation. Multi-format documents on European early 20th century films, provided by three major European film archives, include a large corpus of rare historic film censorship documents from the 20ies and 30ies, but also newspaper articles, photos, stills, posters and film fragments. In-depth analysis and comparison of such documents can give evidence about different film versions and cuts, and allow to restore lost/damaged films or identify actors and film fragments of unknown origin. All material is analyzed, indexed, annotated and interlinked by film experts, to which the COLLATE system will provide suitable task-based interfaces and knowledge management tools to support individual work and collaboration. Continuously integrating the hereby-derived user knowledge into its digital data and metadata repositories, it can offer improved content-based retrieval functionality. Thus, enabling users to create and share valuable knowledge about the cultural, political and social contexts in turn allows other end-users to better retrieve and interpret the historic material.

Supported by previous successful experience in the application of symbolic learning techniques to paper documents [6,13], our aim is applying INTHELEX to these documents. The objective is learning to automatically identify and label document classes and significant components, to be used for indexing/retrieval purposes and to be submitted to the COLLATE users for annotation. Combining results from the manual and automatic indexing procedures, elaborate content-based retrieval mechanisms can be applied [2]. The challenge comes from the low layout quality and standard of such a material, which introduces a considerable amount of noise in its description (see Fig.1). As regards the layout quality, it is often affected by manual annotations, stamps that overlap to sensible components, ink specks, etc.. As to the layout standard, many documents are typewritten sheets, that consist of all equally spaced lines in Gothic type. Such a situation should account for a profitable use of the abduction and abstraction features of INTHELEX: While the former could make the system more flexible in the absence of particular layout components due to the typist's style, the latter could help in ignoring layout details that are meaningless or superfluous to the identification of the interesting ones.

Preliminary experiments showed that INTHELEX is able to distinguish at least 3 classes of COLLATE censorship documents, and to single out a number of logical components inside them. For instance, it learns rules that can separate the censorship authority, applicant and decision in documents like the one on the right in Fig. 1.

5 Conclusions and Future Work

Incremental approaches to machine learning can help in obtaining more efficiency, and are necessary in a number of real-world situations. The incremental system INTHELEX works on first-order logic representations. Its multistrategy learning capabilities have been further enhanced in order to improve effectiveness and efficiency of the learning process, by augmenting pure induction and abduction with abstraction and deduction. This paper presents some sample results proving the benefits that the addition of each strategy can bring. INTHELEX is included in the architecture of the EU project COLLATE, in order to learn rules for automatic classification and interpretation of cultural heritage documents dating back to the 20s and 30s. Future work will concern a more extensive experimentation, aimed at finding tighter ways of cooperation among the learning strategies, and an analysis of the complexity of the presented techniques. Moreover, the addition of numeric capabilities can be considered fundamental for effective learning in some contexts, and hence deserves further study

Acknowledgements. This work was partially funded by the EU project IST-1999-20882 COLLATE "Collaboratory for Annotation, Indexing and Retrieval of Digitized Historical Archive Material".

References

[1] J. M. Becker. Inductive learning of decision rules with exceptions: Methodology and experimentation. B.s. diss., Dept. of Computer Science, University of Illinois at Urbana-Champaign, Urbana, Illinois, USA, 1985. UIUCDCS-F-85-945.

[2] H. Brocks, U. Thiel, A. Stein, and A. Dirsch-Weigand. Customizable retrieval functions based on user tasks in the cultural heritage domain. In *Research and Advanced Technology for Digital Libraries. Proceedings of ECDL2001*, Lecture Notes in Computer Science. Springer, 2001.

[3] F. Esposito, N. Fanizzi, S. Ferilli, and G. Semeraro. Abduction and abstraction in inductive learning. In *Proceedings of the 5th International Workshop on Multistrategy Learning*, Guimarães, Portugal, 2000.

[4] F. Esposito, N. Fanizzi, S. Ferilli, and G. Semeraro. Oi-implication: Soundness and refutation completeness. In *Proceedings of the 17th International Joint Conference on Artificial Intelligence*, pages 847–852, San Francisco, CA, USA, 2001. Morgan Kaufmann Publishers.

[5] F. Esposito, G. Semeraro, N. Fanizzi, and S. Ferilli. Multistrategy Theory Revision: Induction and abduction in INTHELEX. *Machine Learning Journal*, 38(1/2):133–156, 2000.

[6] S. Ferilli. *A Framework for Incremental Synthesis of Logic Theories: An Application to Document Processing.* Ph.D. thesis, Dipartimento di Informatica, Università di Bari, Bari, Italy, November 2000.

[7] R.T. Kouzes, J.D. Myers, and W.A. Wulf. Collaboratories: Doing science on the internet. *IEEE Computer*, 29(8), 1996.

[8] E. Lamma, P. Mello, F. Riguzzi, F. Esposito, S. Ferilli, and G. Semeraro. Cooperation of abduction and induction in logic programming. In A. C. Kakas and P. Flach, editors, *Abductive and Inductive Reasoning: Essays on their Relation and Integration.* Kluwer, 2000.

[9] J. W. Lloyd. *Foundations of Logic Programming.* Springer-Verlag, Berlin, second edition, 1987.

[10] R.S. Michalski. Inferential theory of learning. developing foundations for multistrategy learning. In R.S. Michalski and G. Tecuci, editors, *Machine Learning. A Multistrategy Approach*, volume IV, pages 3–61. Morgan Kaufmann, San Mateo, CA, 1994.

[11] F. Sebastiani. Machine learning in automated text categorization. Technical Report Technical Report IEI:B4-31-12-99, CNR - IEI, Pisa, Italy, December 1999. Rev. 2001.

[12] G. Semeraro, F. Esposito, D. Malerba, N. Fanizzi, and S. Ferilli. A logic framework for the incremental inductive synthesis of Datalog theories. In N.E. Fuchs, editor, *Proceedings of 7th International Workshop on Logic Program Synthesis and Transformation - LOPSTR97*, volume 1463 of *LNCS*, pages 300–321. Springer, 1998.

[13] G. Semeraro, N. Fanizzi, S. Ferilli, and F. Esposito. Document classification and interpretation through the inference of logic-based models. In P. Constantopoulos and I.T. Sølvberg, editors, *Research and Advanced Technology for Digital Libraries*, number 2163 in Lecture Notes in Computer Science, pages 59–70. Springer-Verlag, 2001.

[14] J.-D. Zucker. Semantic abstraction for concept representation and learning. In R. S. Michalski and L. Saitta, editors, *Proceedings of the 4th International Workshop on Multistrategy Learning*, Desenzano del Garda, Italy, 1998.

Classifier Fusion Using Local Confidence

Eunju Kim[1], Wooju Kim[2], and Yillbyung Lee[1]

[1] Dept of Computer Science, Yonsei University,
134 Shinchon-Dong, Seodaemoon-gu, Seoul, 12—749, Korea
{outframe, yblee}@csai.yonsei.ac.kr
[2] Dept. of Industrial Engineering, Chonbuk National University,
66-14 Deokjin-Dong, Deokjin-Gu, Chonju, Chonbuk, Korea
wjkim@moak.chonbuk.ac.kr

Abstract. Combined classifiers can show better performance than the best single classifier used in isolation, while involving little additional computational effort. This is because different classifier can potentially offer complementary information about the pattern and group decisions can take the advantage of the benefit of combining multiple classifiers in making final decision. In this paper we propose a new combining method, which harness the local confidence of each classifier in the combining process. This method learns the local confidence of each classifier using training data and if an unknown data is given, the learned knowledge is used to evaluate the outputs of individual classifiers. An empirical evaluation using five real data sets has shown that this method achieves a promising performance and outperforms the best single classifiers and other known combining methods we tried.

1 Introduction

Combined classifiers can show better performance than the best single classifier used in isolation, while involving little additional computational effort. This is because different classifier can potentially offer complementary information about the pattern and group decisions can take the advantage of the benefit of combining multiple classifiers in making final decision. Many experimental evidences gathered in several application domains demonstrate that classifier combination offers an effective way to improve the performance of the pattern recognition system [8, 9, 10, 11].

From the point of view of their analysis, there are three basic classifier combination approaches: Serial Combination, Classifier Fusion (or parallel combination), and Dynamic Classifier Selection. In serial combination, classifiers with a reject option are arranged sequentially and the result from the prior classifier is fed to the next classifier [2, 6]. A simple classifier using a small set of cheap features classifies input patterns first. For the more difficult inputs rejected by the prior classifier, more complex classifier based on different features are used. In serial combination, the order of arrangement is crucial for the classification performance of the system. In classifier fusion, all classifiers are trained over the whole feature space. If an input is given, individual

M.-S. Hacid et al. (Eds.): ISMIS 2002, LNAI 2366, pp. 583–591, 2002.

classifiers are applied in parallel and the classification results from them are fed to the combining module to be integrated in some manner to achieve a "group consensus"[1, 5, 7]. This category includes majority voting, Bayesian, BKS, Borda Count, fuzzy integral and neural network [1, 6, 13]. Finally, Dynamic Classifier Selection each classifier is trained as a local expert in some area of feature space. When an input is submitted for classification, it attempts to predict which local expert is most likely to be correct for a given sample. The outputs of the one classifier or more than one are considered in the final decision [15, 16].

Previous approaches to multiple classifier fusion can also be divided into two categories. The first group treats all classifier equally and does not consider their difference in performance. In the other group assumes that the outputs of each classifier have the different influence on the final decision and the outputs of each classifier have non-uniform weights. Generally, it is known that a non-uniform weighting of classifier outputs outperforms a uniform one. The most fusion methods don't take into account local expertise of each classifier whether they use non-uniform weights or not. This can mislead the consensus of multiple classifiers by overlooking the opinion of some better skilled classifiers in a specific region the given input belongs to.

In this paper, we present a new classifier fusion method, which harness the local confidence of each classifier in multiple classifier combination. Confidence of individual classifier in some local region is evaluated during the training time. When the unknown input is given, the learned knowledge is used for combining each classifier. This method can be categorized into the classifier fusion method and belongs to the measurement level combination method [12].

The remainder of this paper is organized as follows. Section 2 defines the problem and introduces the notation. In section 3, we describe the concept of local confidence of individual classifier. Multiple classifier combination method based on local confidence is presented in section 4. Experimental results on five real data sets are provided in Section 5. Finally, Section 6 summarizes the main results of this paper and draws our conclusions.

2 Problem Formulation

Let $\Lambda = \{C_1, C_2, ..., C_M\}$ be a set of M possible class labels. Let $x \in R^n$ be an n-dimensional observation vector when the task is to assign x to one of M classes. Assume that we have K classifier. Then, A classifier is any mapping

$$E_k : R^n \rightarrow [0, 1]^M \qquad (7)$$

where $k=1, ..., K$ and K is the total number of classifiers. $E_k(x) = \{m_{1k}, m_{2k}, ..., m_{Mk}\}$ is the M-dimensional vector whose ith value means that kth classifier assigns input x to class i with a measurement m_{ik}.

The measurement measurement m_{ik} can be viewed as a approximation to a posterior probability $p(C_i|x)$ as follows:

$$m_{ik} = p(C_i|x) + \varepsilon_{ik}(x) \qquad (8)$$

where ε is a error that classifier k introduce, when approximating the posterior probability.

In classifier fusion, the output values produced from each classifier are fed to the combining module and integrated to make a final decision. The General classifier fusion rule can be expressed as follows:

$$Y_{comb}(x) = f(E_1(x), \ldots, E_K(x)) \tag{9}$$

where f is the chosen fusion method.

From the viewpoint of probability, this combining is calculating a new approximation to a posterior probability $p(C_i|x)$ based on a underlying information produced by multiple classifiers.

The focus of this paper is to harness the local confidence of each classifier in some local area of feature space. Then, the combining rule considering locality can be expressed as

$$Y_{comb}(x) = f(E_1(x), \ldots, E_K(x), g(x)) \tag{10}$$

where g is the feature transformation function.

3 Local Confidence

Let's consider Bayesian decision theory as a combining rule $Y_{comb}(x)$ in (10). According to the Bayesian theory, given measurements $E_1(x), \ldots, E_K(x)$ the input pattern x will be assigned to the class C_j, whose posterior probability of that interpretation is maximum, i.e.

$$assign\ x \rightarrow C_j \quad if\ P(C_j \mid E_1(x),\ldots,E_K(x)) = \max_{i=1}^{M} P(C_i \mid E_1(x),\ldots,E_K(x)) \tag{11}$$

If we assume that a posteriori probabilities computed by the respective classifiers will not deviate dramatically from the prior probabilities, we obtain a sum decision rule [14]:

$$assign\ x \rightarrow C_j \quad if\ (1\text{-}M)P(C_j) + \sum_{k=1}^{K} P(C_j \mid E_k(x)) = \max_{i=1}^{M} (1\text{-}M)P(C_i) + \sum_{k=1}^{K} P(C_i \mid E_k(x))$$
$$\tag{12}$$

Under the equal prior assumption, this can be rewrite as follows:

$$assign\ x \rightarrow C_j \quad if\ \sum_{k=1}^{K} P(C_j \mid E_k(x)) = \max_{i=1}^{M} \sum_{k=1}^{K} P(C_i \mid E_k(x)) \tag{13}$$

In this paper, we take the influence of each classifier's decision on a given input into account. Considering the locality, a posteriori probability $P(C_i|E_1(x), \ldots, E_K(x))$ and $P(C_i|E_k(x))$ can be viewed as a computed average of local posteriori probabilities for each class over all input data as follows:

$$P(C_i \mid E_1(x),\ldots,E_K(x)) = \sum_{p=1}^{Y} P(C_i \mid E_1(x),\ldots,E_K(x),x_p)P(x_p) \tag{14}$$

$$P(C_i \mid E_k(x)) = \sum_{p=1}^{Y} P(C_i \mid E_k(x), x_p) P(x_p) \tag{15}$$

where x_p is a local region where x belongs to and Y is the number of local regions forming total feature space.

Under the equal prior assumption, we can rewrite (11) by hardening the probability according to (14).

$$assign \; x \to C_j \;\; if \; P(C_j \mid E_1(x),...,E_K(x),x_p) = \max_{i=1}^{M} P(C_j \mid E_1(x),...,E_K(x),x_p) P(x_p)$$
$$\tag{16}$$

In a similar vein, we obtain a new decision rule called *local sum rule* on a given input pattern by substituting (15) into (13).

$$assign \; x \to C_j \;\; if \; \sum_{k=1}^{K} P(C_j \mid E_k(x), x_p) = \max_{i=1}^{M} \sum_{k=1}^{K} P(C_i \mid E_k(x), x_p) \tag{17}$$

According to this local sum rule, given measurements $E_1(x)$, ..., $E_K(x)$ the input pattern x will be assigned to the class C_j, whose local posterior probability of that interpretation on a local region x_p is maximum.

A typical estimator of probability $P(C_i \mid E_1(x), ..., E_K(x))$ is based on weighted summation of approximated probability from each classifier.

$$P(C_j \mid E_1(x),...,E_K(x)) = \sum_{k=1}^{K} P_k(C_j \mid E_k) = \sum_{k=1}^{K} w_{jk} P_k(C_j \mid x) \tag{18}$$

where w_{jk} means how reliable the opinion of classifier k on the class C_j is and $P_k(C_j \mid x)$ is the estimated posterior probability provided by classifier k.

If $w_{jk} = (1/K)$, this estimator is the simple averaging estimator. These conventional approaches to combining multiple classifiers with weight calculate the weight of each classifier by estimating average error of it on the whole training data. Different classifiers will tend to make errors in different ways because of their varying architecture or their different measurement extracted from the pattern. Due to the same reasons, the skilled regions of one classifier can also be distinct from those of other classifiers. Because of the diversity of the ways in which individual classifiers make a mistake as described above, a more elaborate weighting scheme is needed. In this paper, we propose a more elaborate weighting scheme considering local expertise.

To exploit the local expertise of each classifier, we can modify (18) as follows:

$$P(C_j \mid E_1(x),...,E_K(x),x_p) = \sum_{k=1}^{K} P(C_j \mid E_k(x), x_p) = \sum_{k=1}^{K} w_{jk}(x) P_k(C_j \mid x) \tag{19}$$

where $w_{jk}(x)$ is the weight denoting the relative importance of classifier k on class C_j in a local region x_p where x belongs to.

Local Confidence (LC) is a relative degree of expertness of each classifier in a specific area. The degree of local importance $w_{jk}(x)$ in (19) is the Local Confidence of classifier k on class C_j in the local region x_p. The main focus of our method is to estimate the local posterior probability $P(C_j \mid E_k(x), x_p)$ by approximating the Local Confidence of each classifier and using it as a weight of the opinion from the corresponding classifier. We employs a *weight-gating network* to learn the local confidence $w_{jk}(x)$. After learning process, the *weight-gating network* can changes the influences of individual classifiers on the final decision dynamically according to the given pattern. The framework of the process will be described in more detail in the next section

4 Classifier Fusion Based on Local Confidence

Here, we propose a framework of classifier fusion method based on Local Confidence. Our system consists of three parts: multiple classifiers, aggregation network and a *weight-gating network* as shown in Figure 1. The aggregation network and *weight-gating network* can be single- or multi-layered perceptrons.

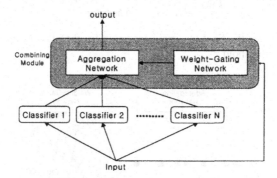

Fig. 1. A Combination Framework based on Local Confidence.

The aggregation network takes $E_1, ..., E_K$, as input, where $E_k = \{ m_{1k}, m_{2k}, ..., m_{Mk} \}$ is a M-dimensional vector containing the measurement values kth classifier produces for the given pattern and outputs the final decision. The equation that describe the inner operation of the aggregation network are

$$o^{m+1} = f^{m+1}(w^{m+1}a^m + b^{m+1}) \text{ for m} = 0, ..., L\text{-}1, \tag{20}$$

where o^i is the outputs of the neurons in the ith layer, L is the number of layers in the network and f^{m+1} is the activation function.

Let $O = (o_1, ..., o_M)$ be the final decision vector. If we consider a single-layered perceptron as a aggregation network and the linear transfer function as activation function, the output o_i for class i is the summation of the weighted measurement values. This can be shown as:

$$o_i = \sum_{k=1}^{K} w_{ik} m_{ik} \tag{21}$$

The weight w_{ik} is the degree of importance of kth classifier for class i and implies the estimation of how important kth classifier is in the classification of the class i

compared to the other classifiers. This weight is the approximated Local Confidence of classifier k in (19). This expression can be written in matrix form:

$$
\begin{bmatrix} o_1 \\ o_2 \\ \vdots \\ o_M \end{bmatrix} = \begin{bmatrix} m_{11} & m_{12} & \cdots & m_{1K} \\ m_{21} & m_{22} & \cdots & m_{2K} \\ \vdots & \vdots & & \vdots \\ m_{M1} & m_{M2} & \cdots & m_{MK} \end{bmatrix} \begin{bmatrix} w_{11} & w_{21} & \cdots & w_{M1} \\ w_{12} & w_{22} & \cdots & w_{M2} \\ \vdots & \vdots & & \vdots \\ w_{1K} & w_{2K} & \cdots & w_{MK} \end{bmatrix} \tag{22}
$$

The neurons in the first layer receive the measurement values from individual classifier for the given input. The final decision is given by selecting the class label whose output value o_i is the highest as follows:

$$
E(x) = \begin{cases} j & if \ o_j = \max_{i \in \Lambda} o_i \ and \ o_j \geq \alpha \\ reject & otherwise \end{cases} \tag{23}
$$

where o_j denotes the final measurement value for the class C_j by aggregation network and α is a threshold.

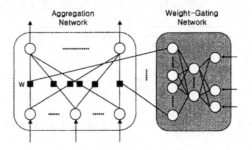

Fig. 2. Inner architecture of combining module.

The weight-gating network takes the input pattern as input like individual classifiers but it output the weights of the aggregation network. This is the sharp contrast to the conventional gating network in dynamic classifier selection. Fig. 2 shows the relation between aggregation network and *weight-gating network*. The number of nodes in output layer equals that of the total number of weight in aggregation network. The main difference between the presented method and most classifier fusion methods is that the proposed method recalculates the relative importance of individual classifier dynamically according to the given input, while the most method adhere to the trained weight.

In learning phase, starting from randomized weight values, the weights of *weight-gating network* gradually reflect the relative importance of each classifier on input pattern. In next section, we will treat the learning algorithm in more details.

4.1 Learning Algorithm

Our method employs neural network architectures for aggregation network and *weight-gating network*. The feed-forward step is computed in the usual way, but the step is first performed in the weight-gating network and after setting outputs of the network as weights of aggregation network, feed-forward step is also performed in aggregation network. Once feed-forward step is completed in aggregation network, backpropagation step for learning is started. Learning occurs only in *weight-gating network*. Weight-gating network is trained by a kind of backpropagation algorithm. As mentioned already, the outputs of the network are the weights of aggregation network. So the error of output node in weight-gating network is calculated from the error of the weight in aggregation as follows:

$$\Delta w_{jk}^{aggr} = (t_j - o_j^{aggr}) o_j^{aggr} (1 - o_j^{aggr}) m_{jk} \tag{24}$$

where t_j is the target value of output node j in aggregation network, m_{jk} is the measurement value of classifier k for class j and o_j is the output value of output node j for the given input x.

Here Δw_{jk}^{aggr} is considered as the output error of the corresponding output node in the *weight-gating network*. With this error, the weight-gating network performs backprapagation learning step to minimize the error.

5 Experimental Results

Five data sets from UCI data repository are used in the experiment for our combining approach. The properties of the data set are shown in Table 2. We use three neural networks NN1, NN2, and NN3 with different number of hidden units as individual classifier. For the aggregation network, single-layered perceptron is used and the weight-gating network multi-layered perceptron is used. The weight-gating network is trained using the gradient method with a momentum. Table 3 presents the results of each classifier, neural network based combining and the Local Confidence based combining method (LC_COMB). The table shows that the proposed method has better performance than any individual classifiers on all the data set we tried.

Table 2. Data set properties

Data Set	Data set Properties			
	# Cls.	# Attr.	# Train	# Test
Australian Credit	2	14	690	10-fold CV
Image Segment	7	19	2310	10-fold CV
Satellite image	7	36	4,435	2,000
Vehicle	4	18	846	9-fold CV
Pima Indian	2	8	768	10-fold CV

Table 3. Results of the individual classifiers

Data Set	Error Rate (%)		
	NN1	NN2	NN3
Australian Credit	14.78	14.49*	14.78
Image Segment	5.15*	5.24	5.15
Satellite image	17.75	18.30	17.65*
Vehicle	19.51	19.27*	19.27
Pima Indian	24.48*	24.48	24.48

Table 4 compares the error rate of our proposed method with those of other combining algorithms. Four fusion methods: majority vote, summation, product, max rule method are used in this experiment.

Table 4. Comparison of the best-performed individual classifier, other combining approaches, and the proposed method

	Error Rate (%)					
	bestNN	majvote	sum	product	maxrule	lc_comb
Australian Credit	14.49	14.05	14.05	14.20	14.35	13.91
Image Segment	5.15	5.16	4.98	5.03	4.85	3.89
Satellite image	17.65	17.95	17.4	17.4	18	11.8
Vehicle	19.51	18.68	18.68	18.68	18.45	16.79
Pima Indian	24.48	24.08	24.61	24.61	24.48	22.5

6 Discussion and Future Work

We have proposed a multiple classifier combining method based on Local Confidence. Our main idea in the proposed method is based on the fact that different classifiers potentially offer complementary information about the patterns to be classified. Especially, if we can consider the local expertness of each classifier into the combining process, the performance will be improved. The proposed method combines the advantages of classifier fusion and dynamic selection, which are the two main categories of traditional combining algorithms. This method reflects relative opinions of all classifiers like in classifier fusion approach and the weight of each classifier's opinion (the relative importance of individual classifier) is recalculated dynamically according to the given input like in dynamic selection approach.

Our experiment for the five real data sets shows that the proposed combining method outperforms other combining methods we tried as well as any individual classifiers. Due to the encouraging results obtained from these experiments, we can expect that the proposed combining method can be successfully applied to the classification task in the real world case with more accuracy than the traditional data mining approaches.

In our future research, we will apply the method proposed here to additional classification problem domains and we also consider further extension of our approach to integrate different level classifiers such as rank level or abstract level.

References

1. S.B. Cho and J.H. Kim, Multiple network fusion using fuzzy logic, IEEE Trans. on Neural Networks, 6 (2) (1995) 497-501.
2. P.D. Gader, D. Hepp, B. Forester, T. Peurach, and B.T. Mitchell, Pipelined systems for recognition of handwritten digits in USPS ZIP codes, Proc. of U.S. Postal Service Advanced Technology Conference, 1990, pp. 539-548.
3. T.K. Ho, J.J. Hull, and S.N. Srihari, Decision Combination in Multiple Classifier Systems, IEEE Trans. on Pattern Analysis and Machine Intelligence 16 (1) (1994) 66-75.
4. Y.S. Huang and C. Y. Suen, The Behavior-Knowledge Space Method for Combination of Multiple Classifiers, Proc. of the IEEE Conf. on CVPR, 1993, pp. 347-352.
5. Y.S. Huang, K. Liu, and C.Y. Suen, A Neural Network Approach for Multi-Classifier Recognition Systems, Proc. of 4th IWFHR, 1994, pp. 235-244.
6. F. Kimura, and M. Shridhar, Handwritten Numeral Recognition Based on Multiple Algorithms, Pattern Recognition, 24 (10) (1991) 969-983.
7. J. Kittler, M. Hatef, and R.P.W. Duin, Combining Classifiers, Proc. of IEEE Conf. on ICPR, 1996, pp. 897-901.
8. T. Matsui, T. Noumi, I. Yamashita, T. Wakahara, and M. Yoshimuro, State of the Art of Handwritten Numeral Recognition in japan - The results of the First IPTP Character Recognition Competition, Proc. of the Second ICDAR, 1993, pp. 391-396.
9. T. Noumi et al, Result of Second IPTP Character Recognition Competition and Studies on Multi-Expert Handwritten Numeral Recognition, Proc. of 4th IWFHR, 1994, pp. 338-346.
10. J. Paik, S. Jung, and Y. Lee, Multiple Combined Recognition System for Automatic Processing of Credit Card Slip Applications, Proc. of the Second ICDAR, 1993, pp. 520-523.
11. H. Takahashi and T.D. Griffin, Recognition Enhancement by linear Tournament Verification, Proc. of the Second ICDAR, 1993, pp. 585-588.
12. L. Xu, A. Krzyzak, and C.Y. Suen, Method of Combining Multiple Classifiers and Their Application to Handwritten Numeral Recognition, IEEE Trans. on Systems, Man and Cybernetics, 22 (3) (1992) 418-435.
13. F. Yamaoka, Y. Lu, A. Shaout, and M. Shridhar, Fuzzy Integration of Classification Results in Handwritten Digit Recognition System, Proc. of 4th IWFHR, 1994, pp. 255-264.
14. J. Kittler, M. Hatef and R.P.W Duin, Combining Classifiers, Proc. of ICPR, 1996, pp. 897-901.
15. R.A. Jacobs, M.I. Jordan, S.J. Nowlan, and G.E. Hinton, Adaptive mixtures of local experts, Neural Computation, 3 (1991), 79-87.
16. E. Alpaydin and M.I.Jordan, Local linear perception for classification, IEEE Trans. on Neural Networks, 7 (3) (1996) 788-792.

Feature Selection for Ensembles of Simple Bayesian Classifiers

Alexey Tsymbal[1], Seppo Puuronen[1], and David Patterson[2]

[1]University of Jyväskylä, P.O.Box 35, FIN-40351 Jyväskylä, Finland
{Alexey, Sepi}@jytko.jyu.fi
[2]Northern Ireland Knowledge Engineering Laboratory, University of Ulster, U.K.
WD.Patterson@ulst.ac.uk

Abstract. A popular method for creating an accurate classifier from a set of training data is to train several classifiers, and then to combine their predictions. The ensembles of simple Bayesian classifiers have traditionally not been a focus of research. However, the simple Bayesian classifier has much broader applicability than previously thought. Besides its high classification accuracy, it also has advantages in terms of simplicity, learning speed, classification speed, storage space, and incrementality. One way to generate an ensemble of simple Bayesian classifiers is to use different feature subsets as in the random subspace method. In this paper we present a technique for building ensembles of simple Bayesian classifiers in random subspaces. We consider also a hill-climbing-based refinement cycle, which improves accuracy and diversity of the base classifiers. We conduct a number of experiments on a collection of real-world and synthetic data sets. In many cases the ensembles of simple Bayesian classifiers have significantly higher accuracy than the single "global" simple Bayesian classifier. We consider several methods for integration of simple Bayesian classifiers. The dynamic integration better utilizes ensemble diversity than the static integration.

1   Introduction

A popular method for creating an accurate classifier from a set of training data is to train several classifiers, and then to combine their predictions [5]. Previous theoretical and empirical research has shown that an ensemble is often more accurate than any of the single classifiers in the ensemble [1,5,8,11].

The ensembles of simple Bayesian classifiers have traditionally not been a focus of research. One reason for that is that simple Bayes relies on an assumption that is rarely valid in practical learning problems: that the features are independent of each other, given the predicted value. Another reason is that simple Bayes is an extremely stable learning algorithm, and many ensemble techniques are mostly variance reduction techniques, thus not being able to benefit from its integration [1].

However, it has been recently shown that simple Bayes can be optimal even when the independence assumption is violated by a wide margin [6]. Besides, simple Bayes can be effectively used in ensemble techniques, which perform also bias reduction, such as boosting. For example, Elkan's application of boosted simple Bayes won first place out of 45 entries in the data mining competition KDD'97 [7]. Besides, when

M.-S. Hacid et al. (Eds.): ISMIS 2002, LNAI 2366, pp. 592–600, 2002.
© Springer-Verlag Berlin Heidelberg 2002

simple Bayes is applied to sub-problems of lower dimensionalities as in the random subspace method [9], the error bias of the Bayesian probability estimates caused by the independence assumption becomes less. One successful application of ensembles of simple Bayesian classifiers built on different feature subsets to word sense disambiguation was presented in [13].

In this paper we present a technique for building ensembles of simple Bayesian classifiers in random subspaces. We consider also a hill-climbing-based refinement cycle, which improves accuracy and diversity of the base classifiers. We conduct a number of experiments on a collection of real-world and synthetic data sets. We compare two commonly used static integration techniques such as static selection and weighted voting [5] with three recently proposed techniques for dynamic integration of classifiers such as dynamic selection, dynamic voting, and dynamic voting with selection [14,17]. The dynamic integration is based on estimation of local accuracies of the base classifiers. We show that the dynamic integration better utilizes ensemble diversity.

The paper is organized as follows. In Section 2 the general problem of construction of an ensemble of classifiers is considered. In Section 3 we review the random subspace method. In Section 4 we present our algorithm for feature selection in ensembles of simple Bayesian classifiers. In Section 5 experiments with this algorithm are considered. We conclude briefly in Section 6 with a summary and further research topics.

2 An Ensemble of Classifiers

Both theoretical and empirical research has shown that an effective ensemble should consist of a set of models that do not only have high classification accuracy, but also make their errors on different parts of the input space [1,3,8,11]. Obviously, combining several identical classifiers produces no gain. Brodley and Lane [3] show that main objective when generating the base classifiers is to maximize the *coverage* of the data, which is the percentage of the data that at least one base classifier can classify correctly. Achieving coverage greater than the accuracy of the best base classifier requires diversity among the base classifiers. Several researchers have presented theoretical evidences supporting this claim [8,11].

In this paper, to measure the disagreement of a base classifier i and the whole ensemble, we calculate its diversity Div_i on test instances as the average difference in predictions in all the pairs of classifiers containing i:

$$Div_i = \frac{\sum_{j=1}^{M} \sum_{k=1,k\neq i}^{S} Dif\left(h_i\left(x_j\right), h_k\left(x_j\right)\right)}{M \cdot (S-1)}, \tag{1}$$

where S is the number of the base classifiers, $h_i(\mathbf{x}_j)$ is the classification of the instance $\mathbf{x}_j$ by the classifier h_i, and $Dif(a,b)$ is zero if the classifications a and b are the same and one if they are different, and M is the number of instances in the test set. The total diversity of the ensemble can be defined as the average diversity of its members.

The second important aspect of creating an effective ensemble is the choice of the method for integration of the predictions of the base classifiers [3,5]. Brodley and Lane [3] have shown that only increasing coverage of an ensemble through diversity is not enough to insure increased prediction accuracy – if the integration method does not utilize the coverage, then no benefit arises from integrating multiple models. Thus, diversity and coverage of an ensemble is not a sufficient condition for the ensemble accuracy. It is also important for the ensemble accuracy to have a good integration procedure that will utilize diversity of the base classifiers.

The most commonly used integration techniques are voting-based schemas for discrete predictors [1] and simple and weighted averaging for numeric and a posteriori probability predictors [11]. These techniques are simple and well studied both in theory [8,11] and experimentally [1]. However, the voting and averaging ensembles do not take into account local expertise of the base classifiers. Classification accuracy can be significantly improved with an integration technique that is capable of identifying the regions of expertise of the base classifiers (e.g. with the dynamic integration) [14,17].

3   The Random Subspace Method

One effective approach for generation of a set of base classifiers is *ensemble feature selection* [12]. Ensemble feature selection is finding a set of feature subsets for generation of the base classifiers for an ensemble with one learning algorithm.

Ho [9] has shown that simple random selection of feature subsets may be an effective technique for ensemble feature selection. This technique is called the *random subspace method* (*RSM*) [9]. In the RSM, one randomly selects $N^*<N$ features from the N-dimensional data set. By this, one obtains the N^*-dimensional random subspace of the original N-dimensional feature space. This is repeated S times so that to get S feature subsets for constructing the base classifiers. Then one constructs classifiers in the random subspaces and aggregates them in the final integration procedure.

The RSM has much in common with bagging. Instead of instances, one samples the features [16]. Like bagging, the RSM is a parallel learning algorithm, that is, the generation of each base classifier is independent [9]. This makes it suitable for parallel implementation for fast learning that is desirable in some practical applications. Like in bagging, the ensemble accuracy can be only increased with the addition of new members, even when the ensemble complexity grows [9]. However, the RSM has some important distinctive features. In the case when the number of training objects is relatively small as compared with the data dimensionality, by constructing classifiers in random subspaces one may solve the small sample size problem, because the training sample size relatively increases in random subspaces [16]. Ho [9] shows that while most other classification methods suffer from the curse of dimensionality, this method can take advantage of high dimensionality. Skurichina & Duin [16] have found that the RSM performs relatively better when the classification ability (discrimination power and also the redundancy) is spread over many features (i.e., for the data sets having many informative features) than when the classification ability is condensed in few features (i.e., for the data sets with many completely redundant noisy features).

The RSM is implicitly applied in many feature selection techniques. For example, Opitz [12] uses this method for generating an initial population of feature subsets in his genetic-algorithm-based ensemble feature selection. He also mentioned that the initial population was surprisingly good and produced better ensembles on average than the popular and powerful ensemble approaches of bagging and boosting [1].

Ho [9] has shown experimentally that the RSM ensembles can produce very good results – presumably because the lack of accuracy in the ensemble members is compensated for by the diversity. Cunningham [4] has made an attempt to improve the accuracy of the RSM base classifiers using a hill-climbing procedure, including or deleting one feature at a time from a given feature subset if this raised the classification accuracy. However, the results were mainly negative, as this kind of hill-climbing often led to overly small diversity of the base classifiers (in some cases the feature subsets had become even identical), and hence, to bad ensemble accuracy.

4   An Algorithm of Feature Selection for Ensembles of Simple Bayesian Classifiers

In this section we present the outline of our algorithm called EFS_SBC (Ensemble Feature Selection for the Simple Bayesian Classifier). Our algorithm presented in Figure 1 is composed of two main phases: (1) construction of the initial ensemble in random subspaces; and (2) iterative refinement of the ensemble members.

First, the data set is divided into the training set, the validation set, and the test set using stratified random sampling. The training set is used for calculating the Bayesian probabilities and building the base classifiers, the validation set is used in the refinement cycle, and the test set is used for evaluation of the final refined ensemble. Then, the Bayesian probabilities' table is calculated for all the N features on the training set. An advantage of this algorithm in comparison with the boosted simple Bayes [7] is that the Bayesian table needs to be calculated only once, as there is no change in instance weights as in boosting. Each base classifier, instead, selects appropriate probabilities from this "global" table corresponding to features selected in this classifier. This makes EFS_SBC much less computationally expensive than the boosted simple Bayes. After, the initial feature subsets are constructed using the random subspace method. Instead of selecting a fixed number of features as in [9] we consider all the features as having equal probability 0.5 of being selected to each feature subset.

Then, the iterative refinement of the ensemble members is used to improve the accuracy and diversity of the base classifiers. The iterative refinement is based on hill-climbing search. For all the feature subsets, each feature is tried to be switched (included or deleted). If the resulting feature subset produces better performance on the validation set, that change is kept. This process is continued until no further improvements are possible. The process usually terminates after no more than four passes through the feature set.

As the feature subset's performance measure we use the fitness function proposed by Opitz [12] in a genetic algorithm, in which the fitness of a feature subset *i* was selected to be proportional to the classification accuracy and diversity of the corresponding classifier:

$$Fitness_i = acc_i + \alpha \cdot div_i, \tag{2}$$

where acc_i and div_i are accuracy and diversity calculated over the validation set, and α is the coefficient determining the degree with which the diversity influences on the fitness of the current feature subset.

```
Algorithm EFS_SBC(DS,S, α )
DS           the whole data set
S            size of the ensemble
α            diversity coefficient
N            number of features
TrS          training set
VS           validation set used during the refinement cycle
TS           test set for final evaluation
acc          accuracy of current base classifier
div          diversity of current base classifier
FS           set of feature subsets for the base classifiers
BT           table of Bayesian probabilities for N features
begin
    divide_instances(DS,TrS,VS,TS)
    {divides DS into TrS, VS, and TS with stratified
    random sampling}
    BT=Bayesian_table(TrS)
    FS=RSM(S,N) {the random subspace method}
    for i=1 to S {refinement of each random feature set}
        accu=acc(VS,FS[i],BT); div=div(VS,FS[i],BT)
        {SBC accuracy and diversity for FS[i] on VS}
        loop
            for j=1 to N {for each feature}
                switch f_j in FS[i]
                accu*=acc(VS,FS[i],BT); div*=div(VS,FS[i],BT)
                if (acc*+α div*)>(acc+α div) then accept FS[i]
                and update FS, acc, and div
                else restore previous feature subset FS[i]
            end for N
        until no_changes
    end for S
end algorithm EFS_SBC
```

Fig. 1. Outline of the EFS_SBC algorithm for ensemble feature selection with simple Bayes

In the next section we present experiments with EFS_SBC. The diversity is calculated using (1), but only for already refined base classifiers. Thus, diversity for the first refined feature subset is always zero, and the fitness in this case represents only accuracy.

5   Experiments

In this section experiments with our algorithm EFS_SBC are presented. First, the experimental setting is described, and then, results of the experiments are presented. The experiments are conducted on 21 data sets taken from the UCI machine learning repository [2]. These data sets include real-world and synthetic problems, vary in characteristics, and have been investigated by previous researchers.

For each data set 30 test runs of EFS_SBC are made. In each run the data set is first split into the training set, the validation set, and the test set by random sampling. The sampling is stratified so that the class distributions of instances in each set are approximately the same as in the initial data set. Each time 60 percent instances are picked up to the training set. The rest 40 percent instances of the data set are divided into two approximately equal test sets (VS and TS).

We experimented with six different values of the diversity coefficient α: 0, 0.25, 0.5, 1, 2, and 4. The size of ensemble S was selected to be equal to 25. It was shown that for many ensemble types, the biggest gain in accuracy is achieved already with this number of base classifiers [1].

At each run of the algorithm, we collect accuracies for the five types of integration of classifiers [14,17]: Static Selection (SS), Weighted Voting (WV), Dynamic Selection (DS), Dynamic Voting (DV), and Dynamic Voting with Selection (DVS). In the dynamic integration strategies DS, DV, and DVS [14,17], the number of nearest neighbors for the local accuracy estimates was pre-selected from the set of six values: 1, 3, 7, 15, 31, 63, for each data set.

The test environment was implemented within the MLC++ framework (the machine learning library in C++) [10]. For the simple Bayesian classifier, the numeric features were discretized into ten equal-length intervals (or one per observed value, whichever was less), as it was done in [6]. Although this approach was found to be slightly less accurate than more sophisticates ones, it has the advantage of simplicity, and is sufficient for comparing different ensembles of simple Bayesian classifiers. A multiplicative factor of 1 was used for the Laplace correction in simple Bayes [6].

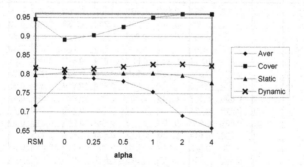

Fig. 2. Main average ensemble characteristics for the random RSM ensembles and different α

In Figure 2, the average accuracies of the base classifiers (*Aver*), the average ensemble coverages (*Cover*), and the average accuracies of static (SS and WV, *Static*) and dynamic (DS, DV, and DVS, *Dynamic*) integration techniques are presented for the initial RSM ensembles and for the refined ensembles with different α. One can see that the initial RSM ensembles show very good results, because the lack of accuracy in the ensemble members (0.716) is compensated for by the ensemble coverage

(0.945). This supports the results presented in [9, 16]. As could be expected, the ensemble coverage grows (0.891-0.959) and the average base classifiers' accuracy drops (0.791-0.659) with the growth of alpha. One important conclusion that can be done is that the dynamic integration better utilizes the ensemble coverage. As it was shown in [15], the dynamic integration of base classifiers built on different feature subsets implicitly performs local feature selection (DS) or local feature weighting (DV and DVS). When the average base accuracy drops, the accuracy of static integration drops significantly as well, but the accuracy of dynamic integration even grows in many cases, and the difference between the static and dynamic approaches grows from 0.008 for $\alpha = 0$ to 0.045 for $\alpha = 4$.

The best accuracy on average is achieved with the dynamic integration when $\alpha = 2$, 0.827. However, the optimal α is different for different data sets. In Table 1 the experimental results for iterative refinement on the 21 data sets are presented. The table includes the names of the data sets, the best α (alpha), average accuracies of the base classifiers (Aver), accuracies for the five integration techniques (SS, WV, DS, DV, DVS), accuracies of simple Bayes on the whole feature sets (Bayes), the average relative numbers of features selected (feat), and improvements of the refinement cycle in comparison with the initial random ensembles (impr). The best accuracies of integration techniques are given in italic, and significantly better results than those of single simple Bayes are given also in bold (the statistical significance is checked with the 1-tailed Student t-test with 0.95 level of significance). Statistically significant improvements over the initial random ensembles are given in bold (the last column).

Table 1. Results of the iterative refinement of feature subsets

Data set	alpha	Aver	SS	WV	DS	DV	DVS	Bayes	feat	impr
Balance	2	0.719	0.893	0.899	0.901	0.901	*0.903*	0.900	0.50	0.002
Breast	1	0.725	0.729	0.744	0.739	*0.752*	*0.752*	0.742	0.50	0.001
Car	2	0.779	0.836	0.819	*0.903*	0.855	0.893	0.846	0.60	**0.016**
Diabetes	1	0.723	0.761	0.755	*0.757*	0.755	0.756	0.756	0.48	0.000
Glass	4	0.475	0.574	0.608	0.609	*0.679*	*0.679*	0.586	0.33	**0.055**
Heart	1	0.777	0.815	0.832	0.810	0.830	*0.833*	0.832	0.52	0.002
Ionosphere	1	0.894	0.895	0.909	0.899	*0.914*	*0.914*	0.901	0.55	0.004
Iris	2	0.800	0.913	0.889	*0.931*	0.920	0.922	0.891	0.47	**0.014**
Led	1	0.618	0.734	0.746	*0.757*	0.748	0.748	0.757	0.72	0.004
Led17	0.25	0.662	0.670	0.700	0.670	*0.702*	0.693	0.648	0.60	**0.052**
Liver	1	0.588	0.614	0.620	0.613	*0.633*	0.622	0.623	0.45	0.004
Lymph	2	0.732	0.822	0.844	0.818	0.852	*0.859*	0.846	0.46	**0.012**
Monk1	4	0.569	0.756	0.663	*0.925*	0.811	0.879	0.756	0.43	**0.008**
Monk2	0.25	0.664	0.662	*0.667*	0.664	*0.667*	0.664	0.625	0.51	0.001
Monk3	2	0.797	0.973	0.973	*0.985*	*0.985*	*0.985*	0.973	0.58	-0.002
Soybean	1	0.949	0.993	*1.000*	0.993	*1.000*	*1.000*	1.000	0.52	0.000
Thyroid	2	0.878	0.955	0.940	*0.967*	0.961	0.961	0.960	0.54	-0.006
Tic	4	0.676	0.690	0.718	*0.947*	0.820	0.935	0.707	0.40	**0.056**
Vehicle	4	0.423	0.569	0.594	0.657	*0.679*	0.688	0.592	0.19	**0.057**
Vote	0.5	0.923	0.941	0.935	*0.951*	0.935	0.946	0.898	0.49	**0.009**
Zoo	2	0.773	0.927	0.948	0.935	*0.953*	0.950	0.925	0.49	**0.011**
Average	1.810	0.721	0.796	0.800	0.830	0.826	*0.837*	0.798	0.49	**0.014**

From Table 1 one can see that on 14 out of 21 data sets the ensembles are better with statistical significance than single Bayes. In all these cases, dynamic approaches are the best. For example, on MONK-1, DS improves the single simple Bayes by 17%. Bad performance of simple and boosted Bayes over the first two Monk's problems is discussed in [7]. The initial random ensembles are improved with statistical significance on only 10 data sets. The best improvement is 0.057 on the Vehicle data set. This again shows good performance of the random subspace method. The best integration technique on average is DVS. It is quite stable, as it combines the power of dynamic selection and dynamic voting.

6 Conclusion

One way to construct an ensemble of diverse classifiers is to use feature subsets generated by the random subspace method. Ensembles of this type can produce very good results, because the lack of accuracy in the ensemble members is compensated for by the diversity. However, generating a set of diverse base classifiers with good coverage is not enough to insure increased prediction accuracy. If the integration method does not utilize the coverage, then no benefit arises from integrating multiple models.

In this paper we presented an algorithm for ensemble feature selection with simple Bayesian classifiers. We considered a hill-climbing-based refinement cycle, which improved accuracy and diversity of the base classifiers built with the random subspace method. We conducted a number of experiments on a collection of data sets. In many cases the ensembles of simple Bayesian classifiers had higher accuracy than the single "global" simple Bayesian classifier. We compared two commonly used static integration techniques with three recently proposed techniques for dynamic integration of classifiers. We have shown that the dynamic integration better utilizes the diversity of the base classifiers.

In future research it would be interesting to compare the performance of the presented algorithm with the genetic-algorithm-based approach of Opitz [12]. Presumably, the power of genetic algorithms won't give much gain in this case, as the random ensembles have already quite good performance. Besides, the genetic algorithm is more computationally expensive. Another interesting future research direction is the comparison of the presented algorithm with the boosted simple Bayes.

Acknowledgments. This research is supported by the COMAS Graduate School of the University of Jyväskylä. We would like to thank the UCI machine learning repository of databases, domain theories and data generators for the data sets, and the machine learning library in C++ for the source code used in this study. We are thankful to the anonymous referees for their valuable comments and constructive criticism.

References

1.   Bauer, E., Kohavi, R.: An empirical comparison of voting classification algorithms: bagging, boosting, and variants. Machine Learning, Vol. 36, Nos. 1,2 (1999) 105-139.

2.   Blake, C.L., Merz, C.J.: UCI repository of machine learning databases [http://www.ics.uci.edu/ ~mlearn/ MLRepository.html]. Dep-t of Information and CS, Un-ty of California, Irvine CA (1998).
3.   Brodley, C., Lane, T.: Creating and exploiting coverage and diversity. In: Proc. AAAI-96 Workshop on Integrating Multiple Learned Models (1996) 8-14.
4.   Cunningham, P.: Diversity versus quality in classification ensembles based on feature selection. Tech. Report TCD-CS-2000-02, Dept. of Computer Science, Trinity College Dublin, Ireland (2000).
5.   Dietterich, T. G.: Ensemble Learning Methods. In: M.A. Arbib (ed.), Handbook of Brain Theory and Neural Networks, 2nd ed., MIT Press (2001).
6.   Domingos, P., Pazzani, M.: On the optimality of the simple Bayesian classifier under zero-one loss. Machine Learning, Vol. 29, Nos. 2,3 (1997) 103-130.
7.   Elkan C.: Boosting and naïve Bayesian learning. Tech. Report CS97-557, Dept. of CS and Engineering, Un-ty of California, San Diego, USA (1997).
8.   Hansen, L., Salamon, P.: Neural network ensembles. IEEE Transactions on Pattern Analysis and Machine Intelligence, Vol.12 (1990) 993-1001.
9.   Ho, T. K.: The random subspace method for constructing decision forests. IEEE Transactions on Pattern Analysis and Machine Intelligence, Vol. 20, No. 8 (1998) 832-844.
10.   Kohavi, R., Sommerfield, D., Dougherty, J.: Data mining using MLC++: a machine learning library in C++. Tools with Artificial Intelligence, IEEE CS Press (1996) 234-245.
11.   Krogh, A., Vedelsby, J.: Neural network ensembles, cross validation, and active learning. In D. Touretzky, T. Leen (eds.), Advances in Neural Information Processing Systems, Vol. 7, Cambridge, MA, MIT Press (1995) 231-238.
12.   Opitz, D.: Feature selection for ensembles. In: Proc. 16th National Conf. on Artificial Intelligence, AAAI (1999) 379-384.
13.   Pedersen, T.: A simple approach to building ensembles of naive Bayesian classifiers for word sense disambiguation. In: Proc. 1st Annual Meeting of the North American Chapter of the Association for Computational Linguistics, Seattle, WA (2000) 63-69.
14.   Puuronen, S., Terziyan, V., Tsymbal, A.: A dynamic integration algorithm for an ensemble of classifiers. In: Z.W. Ras, A. Skowron (eds.), Foundations of Intelligent Systems: ISMIS'99, Lecture Notes in AI, Vol. 1609, Springer-Verlag, Warsaw (1999) 592-600.
15.   Puuronen, S., Tsymbal, A.: Local feature selection with dynamic integration of classifiers, In: Fundamenta Informaticae, Special Issue "Intelligent Information Systems", Vol. 47, Nos. 1-2, IOS Press (2001) 91-117.
16.   Skurichina, M., Duin, R.P.W.: Bagging and the random subspace method for redundant feature spaces. In: J. Kittler, F. Roli (eds.), Proc. 2nd Int. Workshop on Multiple Classifier Systems MCS 2001, Cambridge, UK (2001) 1-10.
17.   Tsymbal, A., Puuronen, S., Skrypnyk, I.: Ensemble feature selection with dynamic integration of classifiers, In: Proc. Int. ICSC Congress on Computational Intelligence Methods and Applications CIMA'2001, Bangor, Wales, U.K. (2001).

Data Squashing for Speeding Up Boosting-Based Outlier Detection

Shutaro Inatani and Einoshin Suzuki

Electrical and Computer Engineering, Yokohama National University,
79-5 Tokiwadai, Hodogaya, Yokohama 240-8501, Japan
{shuta, suzuki}@slab.dnj.ynu.ac.jp

Abstract. In this paper, we apply data squashing to speed up outlier detection based on boosting. One person's noise is another person's signal. Outlier detection is gaining increasing attention in data mining. In order to improve computational time for AdaBoost-based outlier detection, we beforehand compress a given data set based on a simplified method of BIRCH. Effectiveness of our approach in terms of detection accuracy and computational time is investigated by experiments with two real-world data sets of drug stores in Japan and an artificial data set of unlawful access to a computer network.

1   Introduction

Data mining [4] can be defined as extraction of useful knowledge from massive data, and is gaining increasing attention due to advancement of various information technologies. In addition to predictions, decision optimization is important in data mining [14]. Exceptions and/or deviations, which focus on a very small portion of a data set, have long been ignored or mistaken as noise in machine learning. We strongly believe that exception and/or deviation can improve the quality of decisions, and their detection deserves more attention. Recently exception and/or deviation detection has attracted attention in various domains including crisis management and marketing. Examples of the applications include detection of fraudulent behavior from telephone call records [15] and unlawful access to computer networks [11].

An outlier can be considered as representing one of the important classes of exceptions and/or deviations. An intuitive definition of an outlier can be stated as an interesting example which differs from the rest. In data mining, various approaches have been proposed for outlier detection. Examples include Knorr's distance-based outliers [7,8,9,10], Sugaya's instance discovery based on support vector machines [18,19], and Freund's outlier detection based on his AdaBoost algorithm [5].

A boosting algorithm can improve classification accuracy of a classifier by committee learning [5,16,17], and is reputed as one of the most important achievements in machine learning in these ten years. An outlier based on a boosting algorithm can be considered as interesting because the outlier is hard to be classified even by the sophisticated algorithm. In this paper, we focus on Freund's outlier detection based on AdaBoost.

M.-S. Hacid et al. (Eds.): ISMIS 2002, LNAI 2366, pp. 601–611, 2002.
© Springer-Verlag Berlin Heidelberg 2002

One of the major drawbacks of a boosting algorithm is its computational time. Its iterative application of a classification algorithm can be problematic in practice when the number of examples becomes huge. This situation is typical in data mining, and for an effective decision making, we should shorten turn around time. We apply a simple version of data squashing [3,21] to outlier detection based on boosting, and empirically evaluate its effectiveness with two large-scale data sets from Japanese drug stores and a data set of unlawful access to a computer network used in KDD Cup 1999[1].

2   Outlier Detection Based on Boosting

2.1   AdaBoost

We introduce AdaBoost [5,16,17], which is proved to exhibit high accuracy. AdaBoost is a method of choice for a noise-free data set when high accuracy is demanded even at the sacrifice of readability of the obtained classifier.

Let a training data set be (x_1, y_1) (x_2, y_2) $\cdots$ (x_l, y_l), where x_i is a vector in the example space and y_i represents a class value (i.e. -1 or 1). AdaBoost applies a classification algorithm T rounds each time by modifying the training data set to obtain T classifiers, and outputs a final classifier by combining them. Each classifier obtained in a round is also called a weak hypothesis. Here, T is the only parameter specified by the user. AdaBoost assumes a weight for each training example, and updates it in each round. Let a weight of a training example (x_i, y_i) in round t be $D_t(i)$.

The algorithm of AdaBoost is shown below, where the misclassification rate of a weak hypothesis $h_t : X \to \{-1, +1\}$ in round t is represented by $\epsilon_t = \Pr_{i \sim D_t}[h_t(x_i) \neq y_i]$, and Z_t represents a normalization factor for D_{t+1} to form a distribution.

Procedure: *AdaBoost*
Input: (x_1, y_1) (x_2, y_2) $\cdots$ (x_l, y_l), where $x_i \in X$ $y_i \in \{-1, +1\}$
Return value: a classifier $H(x)$
begin
foreach(i)
   $D_1(i) = 1/m$
for$(i = 1, 2, \cdots, T)$
  begin
  Apply a classification algorithm under a distribution D_t
  $\alpha_t = \frac{1}{2} \ln \left(\frac{1 - \epsilon_t}{\epsilon_t} \right)$
  $D_{t+1}(i) = \frac{D_t(i) \exp(-\alpha_t y_i h_t(x_i))}{Z_t}$
  end
  return $H(x) = \text{sign} \left(\sum_{t=1}^{T} \alpha_t h_t(x) \right)$
end

Note that the followings hold in the algorithm.

$$\epsilon_t = \sum_{i:h_t(\mathbf{x}_i)\neq y_i} D_t(i) \tag{1}$$

$$D_{t+1}(i) = \frac{D_t(i)}{Z_t} * \begin{cases} \exp(-\alpha_t) \text{ if } h_t(\mathbf{x}_i) = y_i \\ \exp(\alpha_t) \quad \text{ if } h_t(\mathbf{x}_i) \neq y_i \end{cases} \tag{2}$$

Intuitively, α_t represents the degree of importance of h_t. α_t decreases monotonously for ϵ_t, and $\alpha_t \geq 0$ when $\epsilon_t \leq 1/2$.

Figure 1 shows an example of an execution of AdaBoost, where a weak hypothesis is a decision stump. In round 1, a weak hypothesis h_1 is learnt, and three circled examples are misclassified. Since the misclassification rate is $\epsilon_1 = 0.30$, $\alpha_1 = 0.42$. Each weight for an example is updated, and a misclassified example is regarded as more important in the next round. This is why the weak hypothesis h_2 is different from h_1. In this example, $T = 3$ and the final classifier is $\text{sign}(0.42h_1 + 0.65h_2 + 0.92h_3)$. Note that this classifier correctly predicts all training examples.

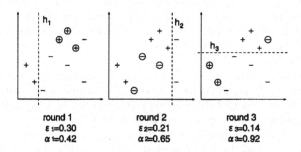

Fig. 1. Example of execution of AdaBoost

2.2   Outlier Detection Based on Boosting

A margin $\text{margin}(\mathbf{x}, y)$ for a training example $(\mathbf{x}, y)$ is defined as follows.

$$\text{margin}(\mathbf{x}, y) \equiv \frac{y\sum_{t=1}^{T}\alpha_t h_t(\mathbf{x})}{\sum_{t=1}^{T}\alpha_t} \tag{3}$$

A margin takes a value among $[-1, +1]$, and takes a positive value if and only if H correctly classifies the example. It has been proved that the obtained classifier exhibits high accuracy to the test data set when the distribution of the margins for the training data set is large [16]. A straightforward method for outlier detection would be to regard an example with a small margin after the final round as an outlier.

In Freund's outlier detection, however, an example with a large weight after the final round is considered as an outlier [5]. This method can be justified since a misclassified example gains weight in AdaBoost. We empirically compared this approach with the former approach with a data set in section 4.1, and found that the results are almost identical. Therefore, we adopt Freund's outlier detection in this paper.

3   Application of Data Squashing

The main stream of conventional data mining research concerned how to scale up a learning/mining algorithm to cope with a huge amount of data. Contrary to this approach, data squashing [3] concerns how to scale down such data so that they can be dealt by a conventional algorithm. Our approach is a simplification of data squashing employed in BIRCH [21]. BIRCH, which represents a fast clustering algorithm [6] for a huge amount of data, is a pioneering work of data squashing.

Data reduction methods can be classified into feature selection [12] and instance selection [13]. In machine learning, feature selection has gained greater attention since it is more effective in improving time-efficiency. We, however, have adopted instance selection since it can deal with massive data which do not fit in memory, and crucial information for outlier detection would be lost with feature selection.

BIRCH takes a training data set $x_1, x_2, \cdots, x_l$ as input, and outputs its partition $\gamma_1, \gamma_2, \cdots, \gamma_{n+1}$, where each of $\gamma_1, \gamma_2, \cdots, \gamma_n$ represents a cluster, and γ_{n+1} is a set of noise. Any global clustering algorithm can be used in BIRCH. In this paper we employ the k-means clustering algorithm.

A training data set is assumed to be so huge that it is stored in a hard disk, and cannot be dealt by a global clustering algorithm since it does not fit in memory. Data squashing, which transforms a given data set to a much smaller data set by abstraction, can be considered to speed up learning in this situation.

BIRCH compresses the training data set stored on a hard disk to obtain a CF (clustering feature) tree, and applies a global clustering algorithm to sub-clusters each of which is represented by a leaf of the tree.

A CF tree represents a height-balanced tree which is similar to a B+ tree [2]. A node of a CF tree represents a CF vector, which corresponds to an abstracted expression of a set of examples. For a set of compressed examples, a CF vector consists of the number N_0 of examples, the add-sum vector LS_0 of examples, and the squared-sum SS_0 of attribute values of examples.

$$\text{CF} = (N_0, \text{LS}_0, SS_0) \tag{4}$$

$$\text{LS}_0 = \sum_{i=1}^{N_0} x_i \tag{5}$$

$$SS_0 = \sum_{i=1}^{N_0} \|x_i\|^2 \tag{6}$$

The CF vector can be updated incrementally, and various inter-cluster distances can be calculated with the corresponding two CF vectors only. This signifies that the original data set need not be stored, and clustering can be performed with their CF vectors only.

A CF tree is constructed with a similar procedure for a B+ tree. When a new example is read, it follows a path from the root node to a leaf, then nodes along this path are updated. Selection of an appropriate node in this procedure is based on a distance function which is specified by a user. The example is assigned to its closest leaf if the distance between the new example and the examples of the leaf is below a given threshold Θ. Otherwise the new example becomes a novel leaf. Note that a large CF tree is obtained with a small Θ, and vice versa. For more details, please refer to [21].

The data squashing employed here for speeding up the outlier detection is a simplification of this method. Since we apply AdaBoost for the weighted gravities of the leaves, we don't store squared-sums in our approach. A weight of a gravity corresponds to the number of examples of the leaf. Since detection of a correct sub-cluster for an example when a CF tree is constructed is relatively difficult, we have developed a method based on a simultaneous equation system. Currently, the method is effective for a sub-cluster with a small number of examples.

4   Experimental Evaluation

4.1   Data Sets

The first series of experiments employ POS data of 99 drug stores in Japan. We have chosen 10 stores among them due to ease of pre-processing, and have generated two data sets. The first data set consists of 5417 transactions stored during a month at a drug store. The second data set consists of 182246 transactions stored during three months at 10 drug stores. The latter data set has been transformed to a data set which consists of 19582 customers for comparison.

Each example in these data sets is represented by 70 attributes. Among these attributes, 10 attributes are missing due to confidential reasons. The use of a (simplified) CF tree restricted us to use continuous attributes. We have chosen 9 attributes which seemed important in the domain among 17 continuous attributes. The 9 attributes together with their respective transformation method are shown in table 1. We have transformed the gross margin (attribute 8) in table 1 into a binary attribute, and have chosen it as the class in the first series of experiments. An example with a gross margin below average is considered to belong to the negative class, and other examples are considered to belong to the positive class.

The second series of experiments employ a data set of unlawful access to a computer network used in KDD Cup 1999[1]. It consists of 100000 examples each of which is represented by 10 attributes. The 10 attributes are shown in table 2.

Table 1. Used attributes in the first series of experiments (drug store data)

No.	Attribute name	mean1	mean2	standard deviation1	standard deviation2	transformation method
1	sell price per item	703	822	851	933	mean value
2	normal sell price	742	848	854	965	mean value
3	sell price	757	7079	972	11688	add-sum
4	sold number of items	1.14	10.7	0.7	16	add-sum
5	stock price per item	507	601	627	618	mean value
6	stock price	589	5656	705	9160	add-sum
7	gross margin per item	160	190	313	366	mean value
8	gross margin	168	1422	391	3727	add-sum
9	sell price before bargaining	799	8207	998	12348	add-sum

Table 2. Used attributes in the second series of experiments (unlawful access data)

No.	Attribute name	mean	standard deviation
1	time of connection (sec.)	28	653
2	number of data bytes received	9779	2194364
3	number of data bytes transmitted	1887	50918
4	number of wrong flags	0.0064	0.13
5	number of urgent packets	0.00001	0.0032
6	number of hot states	0.079	1.19
7	number of times tried for unjust login	0.00045	0.029
8	number of doubtful states	0.011	0.15
9	number of root access	0.00016	0.013
10	number of file generation operations	0.00006	0.0089

4.2   Experiments with the Drug Store Data Sets

We applied AdaBoost to the original data sets and their respective compressed data sets, where the number T of rounds is settled to 100. We varied the threshold Θ, and the top 5 sub-clusters are shown in table 3 and 4.

A rank in the tables represents the rank of a margin in a compressed data set, and an original rank corresponds to a rank before compression. A "?" in the tables represents that the exact original rank is not identified by our sub-cluster detection method. Pursuing correctness can be considered as a double-edged sword. We are currently developing an approximate method to handle this situation. It can happen that different examples have an identical value for their margins, therefore several thresholds have identical ranks in table 4. Correctness of our method has been defined as follows. We first defined outliers as the top 0.1 % examples with the smallest margins, and considered that a user would likely to check 100 examples easily. In this paper, accuracy is defined as the ratio of outliers in the top 100 examples detected by our method. For the first and second drug store data sets, the numbers of outliers are 5 and 20 respectively.

Table 3. Comparison of original ranks, the number of leaves, execution time, and accuracies in terms of threshold value Θ at the experiments with the first drug store data set, where n.c. represents no compression

threshold Θ	Rank 1	Rank 2	Rank 3	Rank 4	Rank 5	# of leaves	execution time (sec.)	accuracy
n.c	-	-	-	-	-	5417	2413	1
0.001	1	2	3	?	17	1807	465	1
0.01	1	3	4	17	?	1735	463	1
0.05	1	2	4	10	3	1384	398	1
0.1	1	10	?	683	3	1029	279	1
0.2	1	2	?	683	10	766	176	1
0.3	1	10	683	?	?	514	96	0.8
0.4	1	10	683	?	2	451	79	0.8
0.5	1	?	?	683	10	352	48	0.4

Table 4. Comparison of original ranks, the number of leaves, execution time, and accuracies in terms of threshold value Θ at the experiments with the second drug store data set, where n.c. represents no compression

threshold Θ	Rank 1	Rank 2	Rank 3	Rank 4	Rank 5	# of leaves	execution time (sec.)	accuracy
n.c	-	-	-	-	-	19582	206000	1
0.001	13	135	135	218	52	18897	186993	0.3
0.01	13	135	218	135	52	18825	204073	0.45
0.05	13	135	52	218	156	17181	193681	0.4
0.1	13	218	52	218	135	13177	125583	0.2
0.2	13	218	52	266	93	7900	54718	0.1
0.3	19576	13	52	6101	266	4906	20999	0.05
0.4	8243	18809	9577	3168	218	3492	8973	0.05
0.5	8243	4382	9577	218	3168	2680	4609	0.05

We have analyzed these examples in terms of the original data set, and found that each of them can be recognized as an interesting outlier. We show such examples for the first experiment in table 5. We consider that these examples, in which the second transaction is subsequent to the first, jointly represents a mistake of a sales clerk. The fourth attribute represents that -20 items and 22 items were sold in the first and second transactions respectively, and these numbers are rare in this data set. The sales clerk might have typed 22 items to the register although the actual number of purchased items would have been 2. The subsequent transaction might represent that the sales clerk corrected the mistake by typing -20. In analyzing the drug store data set, we were not aware of such mistakes. We can argue that our outlier detection method has "discovered" such a mistake.

Table 6 shows another interesting example from the second experiment. The sell price of this customer is high, but to our surprise, its gross margin is below

Table 5. Interesting outliers detected from the first data set

Rank	1	2	3	4	5	6	7	8	9
16	198	398	4356	22	70	7700	-30	-3344	8756
1	198	398	-3960	-20	70	-7000	-30	3040	-7960

average. We examined this customer, and found that most of its transactions exhibit small or even minus gross margins though their sell prices were high. We would have missed the customer with a conventional method since values of the other attributes are normal. Our outlier detection was useful in automatically detecting the customer without investigating on possible combinations of attributes.

Table 6. Interesting outlier detected from the second data set

Rank	1	2	3	4	5	6	7	8	9
13	754	1047	44560	68	563	43384	107	1176	59030

4.3   Experiments with the Unlawful Access Data Set

We applied AdaBoost to the original data set and its compressed data set. The number of outliers for this data set is 100.

Table 7. Comparison of original ranks, the number of leaves, execution time, and accuracies in terms of threshold value Θ at the experiments with the unlawful access data set, where n.c. represents no compression

threshold Θ	Rank 1	Rank 2	Rank 3	Rank 4	Rank 5	# of leaves	execution time (sec.)	accuracy
n.c	-	-	-	-	-	100000	32184	1
0.001	?	454	454	657	?	4014	286	0.03
0.01	?	4348	454	?	?	1015	14	0.02
0.05	1029	15	454	?	?	551	5	0.03
0.1	?	?	4348	18	2309	444	3	0.06
0.2	?	?	454	4348	?	337	2	0.06
0.3	2309	?	2309	22805	?	305	1	0.03
0.4	76863	?	12	4348	2309	256	1	0.03
0.5	74863	1029	454	76856	?	237	1	0.02

From the table, we see that our method shows low accuracies for this data set. We will analyze this reason in the next section.

4.4   Analysis of Accuracies

From table 3, we see that the detected outliers are often accurate. Accuracies in table 4 are moderate, i.e. we see a degradation of accuracies compared with table 3. On the contrary, accuracies in table 7 are obviously low.

The results in table 4 can be explained as follows. From the table, we see that the data set is less compressed than the first data set. Degradation of accuracies signifies that the model learnt from the compressed data set is different from the model learnt from the original data set. We attribute this to inadequate compression of examples near the class boundaries.

The results in table 7 can be explained as follows. From the table, we see that the data set is much more compressed than the first data set. In this case, degradation of accuracies would signify that outliers are merged with normal examples in the excessive compression procedure. We analyzed the compressed data set, and frequently observed this phenomenon. The unlawful access data set has two attributes of which values vary to a large extent, and most of the other attributes are binary. This might be the reason for the excessive compression.

The second and the third data sets pose two challenges for our boosting-based outlier detection with data squashing. We can conclude that our method is accurate for data sets which allows adequate compression in class discrimination such as the first data set.

5   Conclusions

The main contribution of this paper is threefold. 1) We have discussed the importance of outlier detection in data mining, especially in the context of a decision making. 2) We have proposed a method to speed up outlier detection based on data squashing. 3) We have conducted experiments with two real-world data sets of drug stores and the KDD Cup 1999 data set, and investigated the effectiveness of the proposed method.

Since our proposed method detects outliers by reducing the number of examples, it can be promising for outlier detection from multimedia database with a huge number of examples. Recently, such application has gained increasing attention, and has produced promising results such as a pedestrian surveillance system [10].

Future work includes a more sophisticated method of data squashing devoted for outlier detection as well as further experiments with other 89 drug stores. Our method can deal with only metric data since it employs a simplified method of BIRCH, and we plan to develop methods to handle nominal attributes such as [3].

Acknowledgement. This work was partially supported by the grant-in-aid for scientific research on priority area (B) "Active Mining" and (C) 13680436 from the Japanese Ministry of Education, Culture, Sports, Science and Technology.

References

1. S. Bay: UCI Repository of KDD databases, http://kdd.ics.uci.edu/, University of California, Department of Information and Computer Science (1999)
2. D. Comer: "The Ubiquitous B-Tree", *ACM Computing Surveys*, Vol. 11, No. 2, pp. 121–137 (1979)
3. W. DuMouchel, C. Volinsky, T. Johnson, C. Cortes, and D. Pregibon: "Squashing Flat Files Flatter", *Proc. Fifth ACM SIGKDD Int'l Conf. on Knowledge Discovery and Data Mining (KDD)*, pp. 6–15 (1999)
4. U. M. Fayyad, G. Piatetsky-Shapiro, and P. Smyth: "From Data Mining to Knowledge Discovery: An Overview", *Advances in Knowledge Discovery and Data Mining*, AAAI/MIT Press, pp. 1–34, Menlo Park, Calif. (1996).
5. Y. Freund and R. E. Schapire: "Experiments with a New Boosting Algorithm", *Proc. Thirteenth Int'l Conf. on Machine Learning (ICML)*, pp .148–156 (1996)
6. L. Kaufman and P. J. Rousseeuw: *Finding Groups in Data*, Wiley, New York (1990)
7. E. M. Knorr and R. T. Ng: "A Unified Notion of Outliers: Properties and Computation", *Proc. Third Int'l Conf. on Knowledge Discovery and Data Mining (KDD)*, pp. 219–222 (1997).
8. E. M. Knorr and R. T. Ng: "Algorithms for Mining Distance-Based Outliers in Large Datasets", *Proc. 24th Ann. Int'l Conf. Very Large Data Bases (VLDB)*, pp. 392–403 (1998).
9. E. M. Knorr and R. T. Ng: "Finding Intensional Knowledge of Distance-Based Outliers", *Proc. 25th Ann. Int'l Conf. Very Large Data Bases (VLDB)*, pp. 211–222 (1999).
10. E. M. Knorr, R. T. Ng, and V. Tucakov: "Distance-Based Outliers: Algorithms and Applications", *VLDB Journal*, Vol. 8, No. 3/4, pp. 237–253 (2000).
11. W. Lee, S. J. Stolfo, and K. W. Mok: "Mining Audit Data to Build Intrusion Detection Models", *Proc. Fourth Int'l Conf. on Knowledge Discovery and Data Mining (KDD)*, pp. 66–72 (1998)
12. H. Liu and H. Motoda: *Feature Selection for Knowledge Discovery and Data Mining*, Kluwer, Norwell, Mass. (1998)
13. H. Liu and Hiroshi Motoda (eds.): *Instance Selection and Construction for Data Mining*, Kluwer, Norwell, Mass. (2001)
14. T. M. Mitchell: "Machine Learning and Data Mining", *CACM*, Vol. 42, No. 11, pp. 31–36 (1999).
15. S. Rosset, U. Murad, E. Neumann, Y. Idan, and G. Pinkas: "Discovery of Fraud Rules for Telecommunications - Challenges and Solutions", *Proc. Fifth ACM SIGKDD Int'l Conf. on Knowledge Discovery and Data Mining (KDD)*, pp. 409–413 (1999)
16. R. E. Schapire, Y. Freund, P. Bartlett, and W. S. Lee: "Boosting the Margin: A New Explanation for the Effectiveness of Voting Methods", *The Annals of Statistics*, Vol. 26, No. 5, pp. 1651–1686 (1998)
17. R. E. Schapire: "A Brief Introduction to Boosting", *Proc. Sixteenth Int'l Joint Conf. on Artificial Intelligence (IJCAI)*, pp .1401–1406 (1999)
18. S. Sugaya, E. Suzuki, and S. Tsumoto: "Support Vector Machines for Knowledge Discovery", *Principles of Data Mining and Knowledge Discovery, LNAI 1704 (PKDD)*, pp. 561-567 (1999)
19. S. Sugaya, E. Suzuki, and S. Tsumoto: "Instance Selection Based on Support Vector Machine for Knowledge Discovery in Medical Database", *Instance Selection and Construction for Data Mining*, H. Liu and H. Motoda (eds.), pp. 395-412, Kluwer, Norwell, Mass. (2001)

20. E. Suzuki: "Autonomous Discovery of Reliable Exception Rules", *Proc. Third Int'l Conf. on Knowledge Discovery and Data Mining (KDD)*, pp. 259–262 (1997).
21. T. Zhang, R. Ramakrishnan, and M. Livny: "BIRCH: An Efficient Data Clustering Method for Very Large Databases", *Proc. 1996 ACM SIGMOD Int'l Conf. on Management of Data*, pp. 103–114 (1996)

Author Index